The Ancient Church

Its History, Doctrine, Worship, and Constitution

W.D. Killen

The Ancient Church: Its History, Doctrine, Worship, and Constitution

Copyright © 2022 Indo-European Publishing

The present edition is a reproduction of previous publication of this classic work. Minor typographical errors may have been corrected without note; however, for an authentic reading experience the spelling, punctuation, and capitalization have been retained from the original text.

ISBN: 978-1-64439-585-1

CONTENTS

PREFACE vi

PERIOD I
FROM THE BIRTH OF CHRIST TO THE DEATH OF THE APOSTLE JOHN, A.D. 100

SECTION I
HISTORY OF THE PLANTING AND GROWTH OF THE APOSTOLIC CHURCH

CHAP. I   THE ROMAN EMPIRE AT THE TIME OF THE BIRTH OF CHRIST 1

CHAP. II   THE LIFE OF CHRIST 6

CHAP. III   THE TWELVE AND THE SEVENTY 17

CHAP. IV   THE PROGRESS OF THE GOSPEL FROM THE DEATH OF CHRIST TO THE DEATH OF THE APOSTLE JAMES, THE BROTHER OF JOHN.—A.D. 31 TO A.D. 44 24

CHAP. V   THE ORDINATION OF PAUL AND BARNABAS; THEIR MISSIONARY TOUR IN ASIA MINOR; AND THE COUNCIL OF JERUSALEM.—A.D. 44 TO A.D. 51 32

CHAP. VI   THE INTRODUCTION OF THE GOSPEL INTO EUROPE, AND THE MINISTRY OF PAUL AT PHILIPPI.-A.D. 52 41

CHAP. VII   THE MINISTRY OF PAUL IN THESSALONICA, BEREA, ATHENS, AND CORINTH. —A.D. 52 TO A.D. 54 46

CHAP. VIII   THE CONVERSION OF APOLLOS; HIS CHARACTER; AND THE MINISTRY OF PAUL IN EPHESUS.—A.D. 54 TO A.D. 57 53

CHAP. IX   PAUL'S EPISTLES; HIS COLLECTION FOR THE POOR SAINTS AT JERUSALEM; HIS IMPRISONMENT THERE, AND AT CAESAREA AND ROME.—A.D. 57 TO A.D. 63 59

CHAP. X   PAUL'S SECOND IMPRISONMENT, AND MARTYRDOM; PETER, HIS EPISTLES, HIS MARTYRDOM, AND THE ROMAN CHURCH 69

CHAP. XI   THE PERSECUTIONS OF THE APOSTOLIC CHURCH, AND ITS CONDITION AT THE TERMINATION OF THE FIRST CENTURY 74

SECTION II
THE LITERATURE AND THEOLOGY OF THE APOSTOLIC CHURCH

CHAP. I   THE NEW TESTAMENT, ITS HISTORY, AND THE AUTHORITY OF ITS VARIOUS PARTS.— THE EPISTLE OF CLEMENT OF ROME 81

CHAP. II   THE DOCTRINE OF THE APOSTOLIC CHURCH 86

CHAP. III   THE HERESIES OF THE APOSTOLIC AGE 92

SECTION III
THE WORSHIP AND CONSTITUTION OF THE APOSTOLIC CHURCH

CHAP. I   THE LORD'S DAY; THE WORSHIP OF THE APOSTOLIC CHURCH; ITS SYMBOLIC ORDINANCES, AND ITS DISCIPLINE 97

CHAP. II   THE EXTRAORDINARY TEACHERS OF THE APOSTOLIC CHURCH; AND ITS ORDINARY OFFICE-BEARERS, THEIR APPOINTMENT, AND ORDINATION 106

CHAP. III   THE ORGANIZATION OF THE APOSTOLIC CHURCH 113

CHAP. IV   THE ANGELS OF THE SEVEN CHURCHES 120

PERIOD II
FROM THE DEATH OF THE APOSTLE JOHN TO THE CONVERSION OF CONSTANTINE.— A.D. 100 TO AD. 312

SECTION I
THE HISTORY OF THE CHURCH

CHAP. I   THE GROWTH OF THE CHURCH 126

CHAP. II   THE PERSECUTIONS OF THE CHURCH 130

CHAP. III   FALSE BRETHREN AND FALSE PRINCIPLES IN THE CHURCH; SPIRIT AND CHARACTER OF THE CHRISTIANS 143

CHAP. IV   THE CHURCH OF ROME IN THE SECOND CENTURY ... 151

CHAP. V   THE CHURCH OF ROME IN THE THIRD CENTURY 157

SECTION II
THE LITERATURE AND THEOLOGY OF THE CHURCH

CHAP. I   THE ECCLESIASTICAL WRITERS 167

CHAP. II   THE IGNATIAN EPISTLES AND THEIR CLAIMS—THE EXTERNAL EVIDENCE 178

CHAP. III   THE IGNATIAN EPISTLES AND THEIR CLAIMS—THE INTERNAL EVIDENCE 188

CHAP. IV   THE GNOSTICS, THE MONTANISTS, AND THE MANICHAEANS 195

CHAP. V   THE DOCTRINE OF THE CHURCH 202

SECTION III
THE WORSHIP AND CONSTITUTION OF THE CHURCH

CHAP. I   THE WORSHIP OF THE CHURCH 210

CHAP. II   BAPTISM 214

CHAP. III   THE LORD'S SUPPER 219

CHAP. IV   CONFESSION AND PENANCE 222

CHAP. V   THE CONSTITUTION OF THE CHURCH IN THE SECOND CENTURY 226

CHAP. VI   THE RISE OF THE HIERARCHY CONNECTED WITH THE SPREAD OF HERESIES 236

CHAP. VII   PRELACY BEGINS IN ROME 242

CHAP. VIII THE CATHOLIC SYSTEM 252

CHAP. IX   PRIMITIVE EPISCOPACY AND PRESBYTERIAN ORDINATION 258

CHAP. X   THE PROGRESS OF PRELACY 265

CHAP. XI   SYNODS—THEIR HISTORY AND CONSTITUTION 272

CHAP. XII   THE CEREMONIES AND DISCIPLINE OF THE CHURCH, AS ILLUSTRATED BY CURRENT CONTROVERSIES AND DIVISIONS 281

CHAP. XIII THE THEORY OF THE CHURCH, AND THE HISTORY OF ITS PERVERSION— CONCLUDING OBSERVATIONS 287

           ENDNOTES 297

PREFACE

The appearance of another history of the early Church requires some explanation. As the progress of the Christian commonwealth for the first three hundred years has been recently described by British, German, and American writers of eminent ability, it may, perhaps, be thought that the subject is now exhausted. No competent judge will pronounce such an opinion. During the last quarter of a century, various questions relating to the ancient Church, which are almost, if not altogether, ignored in existing histories, have been earnestly discussed; whilst several documents, lately discovered, have thrown fresh light on its transactions. There are, besides, points of view, disclosing unexplored fields for thought, from which the ecclesiastical landscape has never yet been contemplated. The following work is an attempt to exhibit some of its features as seen from a new position.

The importance of this portion of the history of the Church can scarcely be over-estimated. Our attention is here directed to the life of Christ, to the labours of the apostles and evangelists, to the doctrines which they taught, to the form of worship which they sanctioned, to the organization of the community which they founded, and to the indomitable constancy with which its members suffered persecution. The practical bearing of the topics thus brought under review must be sufficiently obvious.

In the interval between the days of the apostles and the conversion of Constantine, the Christian commonwealth changed its aspect. The Bishop of Rome—a personage unknown to the writers of the New Testament— meanwhile rose into prominence, and at length took precedence of all other churchmen. Rites and ceremonies, of which neither Paul nor Peter ever heard, crept silently into use, and then claimed the rank of divine institutions. Officers, for whom the primitive disciples could have found no place, and titles, which to them would have been altogether unintelligible, began to challenge attention, and to be named apostolic. It is the duty of the historian to endeavour to point out the origin, and to trace the progress of these innovations. A satisfactory account of them must go far to settle more than one of our present controversies. An attempt is here made to lay bare the causes which produced these changes, and to mark the stages of the ecclesiastical revolution. When treating of the rise and growth of the hierarchy, several remarkable facts and testimonies which have escaped the notice of preceding historians are particularly noticed.

Some may, perhaps, consider that, in a work such as this, undue prominence has been given to the discussion of the question of the Ignatian epistles. Those who have carefully examined the subject will scarcely think so. If we accredit these documents, the history of the early Church is thrown into a state of hopeless confusion; and men, taught and honoured by the apostles themselves, must have inculcated the most dangerous errors. But if their claims vanish, when touched by the wand of truthful criticism, many clouds which have hitherto darkened the ecclesiastical atmosphere disappear; and the progress of corruption can be traced on scientific principles. The special attention of all interested in the Ignatian controversy is invited to the two chapters of this work in which the subject is investigated. Evidence is there produced to prove that these Ignatian letters, even as edited by the very learned and laborious Doctor Cureton, are utterly spurious, and that they should be swept away from among the genuine remains of early Church literature with the besom of scorn.

Throughout the work very decided views are expressed on a variety of topics; but it must surely be unnecessary to tender an apology for the free utterance of these sentiments; for, when recording the progress of a revolution affecting the highest interests of man, the narrator cannot be expected to divest himself of his cherished convictions; and very few will venture to maintain that a writer, who feels no personal interest in the great principles brought to light by the gospel, is, on that account, more competent to describe the faith, the struggles, and the triumphs of the primitive Christians. I am not aware that mere prejudice has ever been permitted to influence my narrative, or that any statement has been made which does not rest upon solid evidence. Some of the views here presented may not have been suggested by any previous investigator, and they may be exceedingly damaging to certain popular theories; but they should not, therefore, be summarily condemned. Surely every honest effort to explain and reconcile the memorials of antiquity is entitled to a candid criticism. Nor, from those whose opinion is really worthy of respect, do I despair of a kindly reception for this volume. One of the most hopeful signs of the times is the increasing charity of evangelical Christians. There is a growing disposition to discountenance the spirit of religious partisanship, and to bow to the supremacy of TRUTH. I trust that those who are in quest of the old paths trodden by the apostles and the martyrs will find some light to guide them in the following pages.

PERIOD I

FROM THE BIRTH OF CHRIST TO THE DEATH OF THE APOSTLE JOHN, A.D. 100

SECTION I

HISTORY OF THE PLANTING AND GROWTH OF THE APOSTOLIC CHURCH

CHAPTER I

THE ROMAN EMPIRE AT THE TIME OF THE BIRTH OF CHRIST

Upwards of a quarter of a century before the Birth of Christ, the grandnephew of Julius Caesar had become sole master of the Roman world. Never, perhaps, at any former period, had so many human beings acknowledged the authority of a single potentate. Some of the most powerful monarchies at present in Europe extend over only a fraction of the territory which Augustus governed: the Atlantic on the west, the Euphrates on the east, the Danube and the Rhine on the north, and the deserts of Africa on the south, were the boundaries of his empire.

We do not adequately estimate the rank of Augustus among contemporary sovereigns, when we consider merely the superficial extent of the countries placed within the range of his jurisdiction. His subjects probably formed more than one-third of the entire population of the globe, and amounted to about one hundred millions of souls.[Endnote 3:1] His empire embraced within its immense circumference the best cultivated and the most civilised portions of the earth. The remains of its populous cities, its great fortresses, its extensive aqueducts, and its stately temples, may still be pointed out as the memorials of its grandeur. The capital was connected with the most distant provinces by carefully constructed roads, along which the legions could march with ease and promptitude, either to quell an internal insurrection, or to encounter an invading enemy. And the military resources at the command of Augustus were abundantly sufficient to maintain obedience among the myriads whom he governed. After the victory of Actium he was at the head of upwards of forty veteran legions; and though some of these had been decimated by war, yet, when recruited, and furnished with their full complement of auxiliaries, they constituted a force of little less than half a million of soldiers.

1

The arts of peace now nourished under the sunshine of imperial patronage. Augustus could boast, towards the end of his reign, that he had converted Rome from a city of brick huts into a city of marble palaces. The wealth of the nobility was enormous; and, excited by the example of the Emperor and his friend Agrippa, they erected and decorated mansions in a style of regal magnificence. The taste cherished in the capital was soon widely diffused; and, in a comparatively short period, many new and gorgeous temples and cities appeared throughout the empire. Herod the Great expended vast sums on architectural improvements. The Temple of Jerusalem, rebuilt under his administration, was one of the wonders of the world.

The century terminating with the death of Augustus claims an undisputed pre-eminence in the history of Roman eloquence and literature. Cicero, the prince of Latin orators, now delivered those addresses which perpetuate his fame; Sallust and Livy produced works which are still regarded as models of historic composition; Horace, Virgil, and others, acquired celebrity as gifted and accomplished poets. Among the subjects fitted to exercise and expand the intellect, religion was not overlooked. In the great cities of the empire many were to be found who devoted themselves to metaphysical and ethical studies; and questions, bearing upon the highest interests of man, were discussed in the schools of the philosophers.

The barbarous nations under the dominion of Augustus derived many advantages from their connexion with the Roman empire. They had, no doubt, often reason to complain of the injustice and rapacity of provincial governors; but, on the whole, they had a larger share of social comfort than they could have enjoyed had they preserved their independence; for their domestic feuds were repressed by the presence of their powerful rulers, and the imperial armies were at hand to protect them against foreign aggression. By means of the constant intercourse kept up with all its dependencies, the skill and information of the metropolis of Italy were gradually imparted to the rude tribes under its sway, and thus the conquest of a savage country by the Romans was an important step towards its civilisation. The union of so many nations in a great state was otherwise beneficial to society. A Roman citizen might travel without hindrance from Armenia to the British Channel; and as all the countries washed by the Mediterranean were subject to the empire, their inhabitants could carry on a regular and prosperous traffic by availing themselves of the facilities of navigation.

The conquests of Rome modified the vernacular dialects of not a few of its subjugated provinces, and greatly promoted the diffusion of Latin. That language, which had gradually spread throughout Italy and the west of Europe, was at length understood by persons of rank and education in most parts of the empire. But in the time of Augustus, Greek was spoken still more extensively. Several centuries before, it had been planted in all the countries conquered by Alexander the Great, and it was now, not only the most general, but also the most fashionable medium of communication. Even Rome swarmed with learned Greeks, who employed their native tongue when giving instruction in the higher branches of education. Greece itself, however, was considered the head-quarters of intellectual cultivation, and the wealthier Romans were wont to send their sons to its celebrated seats of learning, to improve their acquaintance with philosophy and literature.

The Roman Empire in the time of Augustus presents to the eye of contemplation a most interesting spectacle, whether we survey its territorial magnitude, its political power, or its intellectual activity. But when we look more minutely at its condition, we may discover many other strongly marked and less inviting features. That stern patriotism, which imparted so much dignity to the old Roman character, had now disappeared, and its place was occupied by ambition or covetousness. Venality reigned throughout every department of the public administration. Those domestic virtues, which are at once the ornaments and the strength of the community, were comparatively rare; and the prevalence of luxury and licentiousness proclaimed the unsafe state of the social fabric. There was a growing disposition to evade the responsibilities of marriage, and a large portion of the citizens of Rome deliberately preferred the system of concubinage to the state of wedlock. The civil wars, which had created such confusion and involved such bloodshed, had passed away; but the peace which followed was, rather the quietude of exhaustion, than the repose of contentment.

The state of the Roman Empire about the time of the birth of Christ abundantly proves that there is no necessary connexion between intellectual refinement and social regeneration. The cultivation of the arts and sciences in the reign of Augustus may have been beneficial to a few, by diverting them from the pursuit of vulgar pleasures, and opening up to them sources of more rational enjoyment; but it is a most humiliating fact that, during the brightest period in the history of Roman literature, vice in every form was fast gaining ground among almost all classes of the population. The Greeks, though occupying a higher position as to mental accomplishments, were still more dissolute than the Latins. Among them literature and sensuality appeared in revolting combination, for their courtesans were their only females who attended to the culture of the intellect. [7:1]

Nor is it strange that the Roman Empire at this period exhibited such a scene of moral pollution. There was nothing in either the philosophy or the religion of heathenism sufficient to counteract the influence of man's native depravity. In many instances the speculations of the pagan sages had a tendency, rather to weaken, than to sustain, the authority of conscience. After unsettling the foundations of the ancient superstition, the mind was left in doubt and bewilderment; for the votaries of what was called wisdom entertained widely different views even of its elementary principles. The Epicureans, who formed a large section of the intellectual aristocracy, denied the doctrine of Providence, and pronounced pleasure to be the ultimate end of man. The Academics encouraged a spirit of disputatious scepticism; and the Stoics, who taught that the practice of, what they rather vaguely designated, virtue, involves its own reward, discarded the idea of a future retribution. Plato had still a goodly number of disciples; and though his doctrines, containing not a few elements of sublimity and beauty, exercised a better influence, it must be admitted, after all, that they constituted a most unsatisfactory system of cold and barren mysticism. The ancient philosophers delivered many excellent moral precepts; but, as they wanted the light of revelation, their arguments in support of duty were essentially defective, and the lessons which they taught had often very little influence either on themselves or others. [8:1] Their own conduct seldom marked them out as greatly superior to those around them, so that neither their instructions nor their example contributed efficiently to elevate the character of their generation.

3

Though the philosophers fostered a spirit of inquiry, yet, as they made little progress in the discovery of truth, they were not qualified to act with the skill and energy of enlightened reformers; and, whatever may have been the amount of their convictions, they made no open and resolute attack on the popular mythology. A very superficial examination was, indeed, enough to shake the credit of the heathen worship. The reflecting subjects of the Roman Empire might have remarked the very awkward contrast between the multiplicity of their deities, and the unity of their political government. It was the common belief that every nation had its own divine guardians, and that the religious rites of one country might be fully acknowledged without impugning the claims of those of another; but still a thinking pagan might have been staggered by the consideration that a human being had apparently more extensive authority than some of his celestial overseers, and that the jurisdiction of the Roman emperor was established over a more ample territory than that which was assigned to many of the immortal gods.

But the multitude of its divinities was by no means the most offensive feature of heathenism. The gods of antiquity, more particularly those of Greece, were of an infamous character. Whilst they were represented by their votaries as excelling in beauty and activity, strength and intelligence, they were at the same time described as envious and gluttonous, base, lustful, and revengeful. Jupiter, the king of the gods, was deceitful and licentious; Juno, the queen of heaven, was cruel and tyrannical. What could be expected from those who honoured such deities? Some of the wiser heathens, such as Plato, [9:1] condemned their mythology as immoral, for the conduct of one or other of the gods might have been quoted in vindication of every species of transgression; and had the Gentiles but followed the example of their own heavenly hierarchy, they might have felt themselves warranted in pursuing a course either of the most diabolical oppression, or of the most abominable profligacy. [9:2]

At the time of the birth of our Lord even the Jews had sunk into a state of the grossest degeneracy. They were now divided into sects, two of which, the Pharisees and the Sadducees, are frequently mentioned in the New Testament. The Pharisees were the leading denomination, being by far the most numerous and powerful. By adding to the written law a mass of absurd or frivolous traditions, which, as they foolishly alleged, were handed down from Moses, they completely subverted the authority of the sacred record, and changed the religion of the patriarchs and prophets into a wearisome parade of superstitious observances. The Sadducees were comparatively few, but as a large proportion of them were persons of rank and wealth, they possessed a much greater amount of influence than their mere numbers would have enabled them to command. It has been said that they admitted the divine authority only of the Pentateuch, [10:1] and though it may be doubted whether they openly ventured to deny the claims of all the other books of the Old Testament, it is certain that they discarded the doctrine of the immortality of the soul, [10:2] and that they were disposed to self-indulgence and to scepticism. There was another still smaller Jewish sect, that of the Essenes, of which there is no direct mention in the New Testament. The members of this community resided chiefly in the neighbourhood of the Dead Sea, and as our Lord seldom visited that quarter of the country, it would appear that, during the course of His public ministry, He rarely or never came in contact with these religionists. Some of them were married, but the greater number lived

4

in celibacy, and spent much of their time in contemplation. They are said to have had a common-stock purse, and their course of life closely resembled that of the monks of after-times.

Though the Jews, as a nation, were now sunk in sensuality or superstition, there were still some among them, such as Simeon and Anna, noticed in the Gospel of Luke, [10:3] who were taught of God, and who exhibited a spirit of vital piety. "The law of the Lord is perfect converting the soul," and as the books of the Old Testament were committed to the keeping of the posterity of Abraham, there were "hidden ones" here and there who discovered the way to heaven by the perusal of these "lively oracles." We have reason to believe that the Jews were faithful conservators of the inspired volume, as Christ uniformly takes for granted the accuracy of their "Scriptures." [11:1] It is an important fact that they did not admit into their canon the writings now known under the designation of the Apocrypha. [11:2] Nearly three hundred years before the appearance of our Lord, the Old Testament had been translated into the Greek language, and thus, at this period, the educated portion of the population of the Roman Empire had all an opportunity of becoming acquainted with the religion of the chosen people. The Jews were now scattered over the earth, and as they erected synagogues in the cities where they settled, the Gentile world had ample means of information in reference to their faith and worship.

Whilst the dispersion of the Jews disseminated a knowledge of their religion, it likewise suggested the approaching dissolution of the Mosaic economy, as it was apparent that their present circumstances absolutely required another ritual. It could not be expected that individuals dwelling in distant countries could meet three times in the year at Jerusalem to celebrate the great festivals. The Israelites themselves had a presentiment of coming changes, and anxiously awaited the appearance of a Messiah. They were actuated by an extraordinary zeal for proselytism, [11:3] and though their scrupulous adherence to a stern code of ceremonies often exposed them to much obloquy, they succeeded, notwithstanding, in making many converts in most of the places where they resided. [12:1] A prominent article of their creed was adopted in a quarter where their theology otherwise found no favour, for the Unity of the Great First Cause was now distinctly acknowledged in the schools of the philosophers. [12:2]

From the preceding statements we may see the peculiar significance of the announcement that God sent forth His Son into the world "when the fulness of the time was come." [12:3] Various predictions [12:4] pointed out this age as the period of the Messiah's Advent, and Gentiles, as well as Jews, seem by some means to have caught up the expectation that an extraordinary personage was now about to appear on the theatre of human existence. [12:5] Providence had obviously prepared the way for the labours of a religious reformer. The civil wars which had convulsed the state were now almost forgotten, and though the hostile movements of the Germans, and other barbarous tribes on the confines of the empire, occasionally created uneasiness or alarm, the public mind was generally unoccupied by any great topic of absorbing interest. In the populous cities the multitude languished for excitement, and sought to dissipate the time in the forum, the circus, or the amphitheatre. At such a crisis the heralds of the most gracious message that ever greeted the ears of men might hope for a patient hearing. Even the consolidation of so many nations under one government tended to "the furtherance of the gospel," for the gigantic roads, which radiated from Rome to the distant regions of the east and of the west, facilitated intercourse; and the messengers of the Prince of Peace could travel from country to country without suspicion and without passports. And well might the Son of God be called "The desire of all nations." [13:1] Though the wisest of the pagan sages could not have described the renovation which the human family required, and though, when the Redeemer actually appeared, He was despised and rejected of men, there was, withal, a wide spread conviction that a Saviour was required, and there was a longing for deliverance from the evils which oppressed society. The ancient superstitions were rapidly losing their hold on the affection and confidence of the people, and whilst the light of philosophy was sufficient to discover the absurdities of the prevailing polytheism, it failed to reveal any more excellent way of purity and comfort. The ordinances of Judaism, which were "waxing old" and "ready to vanish away," were types which were still unfulfilled; and though they pointed out the path to glory, they required an interpreter to expound their import. This Great Teacher now appeared. He was born in very humble circumstances, and yet He was the heir of an empire beyond comparison more illustrious than that of the Caesars. "There was given him dominion, and glory, and a kingdom, that all people, nations, and languages, should serve him; his dominion is an everlasting dominion, which shall not pass away, and his kingdom that which shall not be destroyed." [13:2]

CHAPTER II

THE LIFE OF CHRIST

Nearly three years before the commencement of our era, [14:1] Jesus Christ was born. The Holy Child was introduced into the world under circumstances extremely humiliating. A decree had gone forth from Caesar Augustus that all the Roman Empire should be taxed, and the Jews, as a conquered people, were obliged to submit to an arrangement which proclaimed their national degradation. The reputed parents of Jesus resided at Nazareth, a town of Galilee; but, as they were "of the house and lineage of David," they were obliged to repair to Bethlehem, a village about six miles south of Jerusalem, to be entered in their proper place in the imperial registry. "And so it was, that, while they were there, the days were accomplished that Mary should be delivered, and she brought forth her first-born son, and wrapped him in swaddling clothes, and laid him in a manger; because there was no room for them in the inn." [14:2]

This child of poverty and of a despised race, born in the stable of the lodging-house of an insignificant town belonging to a conquered province, did not enter upon life surrounded by associations which betokened a career of earthly prosperity. But intimations were not wanting that the Son of Mary was regarded with the deepest interest by the inhabitants of heaven. An angel had appeared to announce the conception of the individual who was to be the herald of his ministry; [15:1] and another angel had been sent to give notice of the incarnation of this Great Deliverer. [15:2] When He was born, the angel of the Lord communicated the tidings to shepherds in the plains of Bethlehem; "and suddenly there was with the angel a multitude of the heavenly host praising God and saying—Glory to God in the highest, and on earth peace, good will toward men." [15:3] Inanimate nature called attention to the advent of the illustrious babe, for a wonderful star made known to wise men from the east the incarnation of the King of Israel; and when they came to Jerusalem "the star, which they saw in the east, went before them, till it came and stood over where the young child was." [15:4] The history of these eastern sages cannot now be explored, and we know not on what grounds they regarded the star as the sign of the Messiah; but they rightly interpreted the appearance, and the narrative warrants us to infer that they acted under the guidance of divine illumination. As they were "warned of God in a dream" [15:5] to return to their own country another way, we may presume that they were originally directed by some similar communication to undertake the journey. It is probable that they did not belong to the stock of Abraham; and if so, their visit to the babe at Bethlehem may be recognised as the harbinger of the union of Jews and Gentiles under the new economy. The presence of these Orientals in Jerusalem attracted the notice of the watchful and jealous tyrant who then occupied the throne of Judea. Their story filled him with alarm; and his subjects anticipated some tremendous outbreak of his suspicions and savage temper. "When the king had heard these things he was troubled, and all Jerusalem with him." [15:6] His rage soon vented itself in a terrible explosion. Having ascertained from the chief priests and scribes of the people where Christ was to be born, he "sent forth and slew all the children that were in Bethlehem, and in all the coasts thereof, from two years old and under." [16:1]

Joseph and Mary, in accordance with a message from heaven, had meanwhile fled towards the border of Egypt, and thus the holy infant escaped this carnage. The wise men, on the occasion of their visit, had "opened their treasures," and had "presented unto him gifts, gold, and frankincense, and myrrh," [16:2] so that the poor travellers had providentially obtained means for defraying the expenses of their journey. The slaughter of the babes of Bethlehem was one of the last acts of the bloody reign of Herod; and, on his demise, the exiles were divinely instructed to return, and the child was presented in the temple. This ceremony evoked new testimonies to His high mission. On His appearance in His Father's house, the aged Simeon, moved by the Spirit from on high, embraced Him as the promised Shiloh; and Anna, the prophetess, likewise gave thanks to God, and "spake of him to all them that looked for redemption in Jerusalem." [16:3] Thus, whilst the Old Testament predictions pointed to Jesus as the Christ, living prophets appeared to interpret these sacred oracles, and to bear witness to the claims of the new-born Saviour.

Though the Son of Mary was beyond all comparison the most extraordinary personage that ever appeared on earth, it is remarkable that the sacred writers enter into scarcely any details respecting the history of His infancy, His youth, or His early manhood. They tell us that "the child grew and waxed strong in spirit," [17:1] and that He "increased in wisdom and stature, and in favour with God and man;" [17:2] but they do not minutely trace the progress of His mental development, neither do they gratify any feeling of mere curiosity by giving us His infantile biography. In what is omitted by the penmen of the New Testament, as well as in what is written we must acknowledge the guidance of inspiration; and though we might have perused with avidity a description of the pursuits of Jesus when a child, such a record has not been deemed necessary for the illustration of the work of redemption. It would appear that He spent about thirty years on earth almost unnoticed and unknown; and He seems to have been meanwhile trained to the occupation of a carpenter. [17:3] The obscurity of His early career must doubtless be regarded as one part of His humiliation. But the circumstances in which He was placed enabled Him to exhibit more clearly the divinity of His origin. He did not receive a liberal education, so that when He came forward as a public teacher "the Jews marvelled, saying—How knoweth this man letters having never learned?" [17:4] When He was only twelve years old, He was "found in the temple sitting in the midst of the doctors, both hearing them, and asking them questions; and all that heard Him were astonished at His understanding and answers." [18:1] As He grew up, He was distinguished by His diligent attendance in the house of God; and it seems not improbable that He was in the habit of officiating at public worship by assisting in the reading of the law and the prophets; for we are told that, shortly after the commencement of His ministry, "He came to Nazareth, where he had been brought up, and, as his custom was, he went into the synagogue on the Sabbath-day, and stood up for to read." [18:2]

When He was about thirty years of age, and immediately before His public appearance as a prophet, our Lord was baptized of John in Jordan. [18:3] The Baptist did not, perhaps, preach longer than six months, [18:4] but it is probable that during his imprisonment of considerably upwards of a year, he still contributed to prepare the way of Christ; for, in the fortress of Machaerus in which he was incarcerated, [18:5] he was not kept in utter ignorance of passing occurrences, and when permitted to hold intercourse with his friends, he would doubtless direct their special attention to the proceedings of the Great Prophet. The claims of John, as a teacher sent from God, were extensively acknowledged; and therefore his recognition of our Lord as the promised Messiah, must have made a deep impression upon the minds of the Israelites. The miracles of our Saviour corroborated the testimony of His forerunner, and created a deep sensation. He healed "all manner of sickness, and all manner of disease." [19:1] It was, consequently, not strange that "His fame went throughout all Syria," and that "there followed him great multitudes of people, from Galilee, and from Decapolis, and from Jerusalem, and from Judea, and from beyond Jordan." [19:2]

Even when the Most High reveals himself there is something mysterious in the manifestation, so that, whilst we acknowledge the tokens of His presence, we may well exclaim—"Verily thou art a God that hidest thyself, O God of Israel, the Saviour." [19:3] When He displayed His glory in the temple of old, He filled it with thick darkness; [19:4] when He delivered the sure word of prophecy, He employed strange and misty language; when He announced the Gospel itself, He uttered some things hard to be understood. It might have been said, too, of the Son of God, when He appeared on earth, that His "footsteps were not known." In early life He does not seem to have arrested the attention of His own townsmen; and when He came forward to assert His claims as the Messiah, He did not overawe or dazzle his countrymen by any sustained demonstration of tremendous power or of overwhelming splendour. To-day the multitude beheld His miracles

8

with wonder, but to-morrow they could not tell where to meet with Him; [19:5] ever and anon He appeared and disappeared; and occasionally His own disciples found it difficult to discover the place of His retirement. When He arrived in a district, thousands often hastily gathered around Him; [19:6] but He never encouraged the attendance of vast assemblages by giving general notice that, in a specified place and on an appointed day, He would deliver a public address, or perform a new and unprecedented miracle. We may here see the wisdom of Him who "doeth all things well." Whilst the secresy with which He conducted His movements baffled any premature attempts on the part of His enemies, to effect His capture or condemnation, it also checked that intense popular excitement which a ministry so extraordinary might have been expected to awaken.

Four inspired writers have given separate accounts of the life of Christ—all repeat many of His wonderful sayings—all dwell with marked minuteness on the circumstances of His death—and all attest the fact of His resurrection. Each mentions some things which the others have omitted; and each apparently observes the order of time in the details of his narrative. But when we combine and arrange their various statements, so as to form the whole into one regular and comprehensive testimony, we discover that there are not a few periods of His life still left utterly blank in point of incidents; and that there is no reference whatever to topics which we might have expected to find particularly noticed in the biography of so eminent a personage. After His appearance as a public teacher, He seems, not only to have made sudden transitions from place to place, but otherwise to have often courted the shade; and, instead of unfolding the circumstances of His private history, the evangelists dwell chiefly on His Discourses and His Miracles. During His ministry, Capernaum was His headquarters; [20:1] but we cannot positively tell with whom He lodged in that place; nor whether the twelve sojourned there under the same roof with Him; nor how much time He spent in it at any particular period. We cannot point out the precise route which He pursued on any occasion when itinerating throughout Galilee or Judea; neither are we sure that He always journeyed on foot, or that He adhered to a uniform mode of travelling. It is most singular that the inspired writers throw out no hint on which an artist might seize as the groundwork of a painting of Jesus. As if to teach us more emphatically that we should beware of a sensuous superstition, and that we should direct our thoughts to the spiritual features of His character, the New Testament never mentions either the colour of His hair, or the height of His stature, or the cast of His countenance. How wonderful that even "the beloved disciple," who was permitted to lean on the bosom of the Son of man, and who had seen him in the most trying circumstances of His earthly history, never speaks of the tones of His voice, or of the expression of His eye, or of any striking peculiarity pertaining to His personal appearance! The silence of all the evangelists respecting matters of which at least some of them must have retained a very vivid remembrance, and of which ordinary biographers would not have failed to preserve a record, supplies an indirect and yet a most powerful proof of the Divine origin of the Gospels.

But whilst the sacred writers enter so sparingly into personal details, they leave no doubt as to the perfect integrity which marked every part of our Lord's proceedings. He was born in a degenerate age, and brought up in a city of Galilee which had a character so infamous that no good thing was expected to proceed from it; [21:1] and yet, like a ray of purest light shining into some den of

9

uncleanness, He contracted no defilement from the scenes of pollution which He was obliged to witness. Even in boyhood, He must have uniformly acted with supreme discretion; for though His enemies from time to time gave vent to their malignity in various accusations, we do not read that they ever sought to cast so much as a solitary stain upon His youthful reputation. The most malicious of the Jews failed to fasten upon Him in after life any charge of immorality. Among those constantly admitted to His familiar intercourse, a traitor was to be found; and had Judas been able to detect anything in His private deportment inconsistent with His public profession, he would doubtless have proclaimed it as an apology for his perfidy; but the keen eye of that close observer could not discover a single blemish in the character of his Master; and, when prompted by covetousness, he betrayed Him to the chief priests, the thought of having been accessory to the death of one so kind and so holy, continued to torment him, until it drove him to despair and to self-destruction.

The doctrine inculcated by our Lord commended itself by the light of its own evidence. It was nothing more than a lucid and comprehensive exposition of the theology of the Old Testament; and yet it, presented such a new view of the faith of patriarchs and of prophets, that it had all the freshness and interest of an original revelation. It discovered a most intimate acquaintance with the mental constitution of man—it appealed with mighty power to the conscience—and it was felt to be exactly adapted to the moral state and to the spiritual wants of the human family. The disciples of Jesus did not require to be told that He had "the key of knowledge," for they were delighted and edified as "He opened" to them the Scriptures. [22:1] He taught the multitude "as one having authority;" [22:2] and they were "astonished at His doctrine." The discourses of the Scribes, their most learned instructors, were meagre and vapid—they were not calculated to enlarge the mind or to move the affections—they consisted frequently of doubtful disputations relating to the ceremonials of their worship—and the very air with which they were delivered betrayed the insignificance of the topics of discussion. But Jesus spake with a dignity which commanded respect, and with the deep seriousness of a great Teacher delivering to perishing sinners tidings of unutterable consequence.

There was something singularly beautiful and attractive, as well as majestic and impressive, in the teaching of our Lord. The Sermon on the Mount is a most pleasing specimen of His method of conveying instruction. Whilst He gives utterance to sentiments of exalted wisdom, He employs language so simple, and imagery so chaste and natural, that even a child takes a pleasure in perusing His address. There is reason to think that He did not begin to speak in parables until a considerable time after He had entered upon His ministry. [23:1] By these symbolical discourses He at once blinded the eyes of His enemies, and furnished materials for profitable meditation to His genuine disciples. The parables, like the light of prophecy, are, to this very day, a beacon to the Church, and a stumbling-block to unbelievers.

The claims of Jesus as the Christ were decisively established by the Divine power which He manifested. It had been foretold that certain extraordinary recoveries from disease and infirmity would be witnessed in the days of the Messiah; and these predictions were now literally fulfilled. The eyes of the blind were opened, and the ears of the deaf were unstopped; the lame man leaped as an hart, and the tongue of the dumb sang. [23:2] Not a few of the cures of our

Saviour were wrought on individuals to whom He was personally unknown; [23:3] and many of His works of wonder were performed in the presence of friends and foes. [23:4] Whilst His miracles exceeded in number all those recorded in the Old Testament, they were still more remarkable for their variety and their excellence. By His touch, or His word, he healed the most inveterate maladies; He fed the multitude by thousands out of a store of provisions which a little boy could carry; [24:1] He walked upon the waves of the sea, when it was agitated by a tempest; [24:2] He made the storm a calm, so that the wind at once ceased to blow, and the surface of the deep reposed, at the same moment, in glassy smoothness; [24:3] He cast out devils; and He restored life to the dead. Well might the Pharisees be perplexed by the inquiry—"How can a man that is a sinner do such miracles?" [23:4] It is quite possible that false prophets, by the help of Satan, may accomplish feats fitted to excite astonishment; and yet, in such cases, the agents of the Wicked One may be expected to exhibit some symptoms of his spirit and character. But nothing diabolical, or of an evil tendency, appeared in the miracles of our Lord. With the one exception of the cursing of the barren fig-tree [24:5]—a malediction which created no pain, and involved no substantial loss—all his displays of power were indicative of His goodness and His mercy. No other than a true prophet would have been enabled so often to control the course of nature, in the production of results of such utility, such benignity, and such grandeur.

The miracles of Christ illustrated, as well as confirmed, His doctrines. When, for instance, He converted the water into wine at the marriage in Cana of Galilee. [24:6] He taught, not only that he approved of wedlock, but also that, within proper limits, He was disposed to patronise the exercise of a generous hospitality, in some cases He required faith in the individuals whom He vouchsafed to cure, [24:7] thus distinctly suggesting the way of a sinner's salvation. Many of His miracles were obviously of a typical character. When He acted as the physician of the body, He indirectly gave evidence of His efficiency as the physician of the soul; when He restored sight to the blind, He indicated that He could turn men from darkness to light; when He raised the dead, He virtually demonstrated His ability to quicken such as are dead in trespasses and sins. Those who witnessed the visible exhibitions of His power were prepared to listen with the deepest interest to His words when He declared—"I am the light of the world; he that followeth me shall not walk in darkness, but shall have the light of life." [25:1]

Though our Lord's conduct, as a public teacher, fully sustained His claims as the Messiah, it must have been a complete enigma to all classes of politicians. He did not seek to obtain power by courting the favour of the great, neither did He attempt to gain popularity by flattering the prejudices of the multitude. He wounded the national pride by hinting at the destruction of the temple; He gave much offence by holding intercourse with the odious publicans; and with many, He forfeited all credit, as a patriot, by refusing to affirm the unlawfulness of paying tribute to the Roman emperor. The greatest human characters have been occasionally swayed by personal predilections or antipathies, but, in the life of Christ, we can discover no memorial of any such infirmity. Like a sage among children, He did not permit Himself to be influenced by the petty partialities, whims, or superstitions of His countrymen. He inculcated a theological system for which He could not expect the support of any of the existing classes of religionists. He differed from the Essenes, as He did not adopt their ascetic

11

habits; He displeased the Sadducees, by asserting the doctrine of the resurrection; He provoked the Pharisees, by declaring that they worshipped God in vain, teaching for doctrines the commandments of men; and He incurred the hostility of the whole tribe of Jewish zealots, by maintaining His right to supersede the arrangements of the Mosaic economy. By pursuing this independent course He vindicated His title to the character of a Divine lawgiver, but at the same time He forfeited a vast amount of sympathy and aid upon which He might otherwise have calculated.

There has been considerable diversity of opinion regarding the length of our Saviour's ministry. [26:1] We could approximate very closely to a correct estimate could we tell the number of passovers from its commencement to its close, but this point cannot be determined with absolute certainty. Four are apparently mentioned [26:2] by the evangelist John; and if, as is probable, they amounted to no more, it would seem that our Lord's career, as a public teacher, was of about three years' duration. [26:3] The greater part of this period was spent in Galilee; and the sacred writers intimate that He made several circuits, as a missionary, among the cities and villages of that populous district. [26:4] Matthew, Mark, and Luke dwell chiefly upon this portion of His history. Towards the termination of His course, Judea was the principal scene of His ministrations. Jerusalem was the centre of Jewish power and prejudice, and He had hitherto chiefly laboured in remote districts of the land, that He might escape the malignity of the scribes and Pharisees; but, as His end approached, He acted with greater publicity, and often taught openly in the very courts of the temple. John supplements the narratives of the other evangelists by recording our Lord's proceedings in Judea.

A few members of the Sanhedrim, such as Nicodemus, [27:1] believed Jesus to be "a teacher come from God," but by far the majority regarded Him with extreme aversion. They could not imagine that the son of a carpenter was to be the Saviour of their country, for they expected the Messiah to appear surrounded with all the splendour of secular magnificence. They were hypocritical and selfish; they had been repeatedly rebuked by Christ for their impiety; and, as they marked His increasing favour with the multitude, their envy and indignation became ungovernable. They accordingly seized Him at the time of the Passover, and, on the charge that He said He was the Son of God, He was condemned as a blasphemer. [27:2] He suffered crucifixion—an ignominious form of capital punishment from which the laws of the empire exempted every Roman citizen— and, to add to His disgrace, He was put to death between two thieves. [27:3] But even Pontius Pilate, who was then Procurator of Judea, and who, in that capacity, endorsed the sentence, was constrained to acknowledge that He was a "just person" in whom He could find "no fault." [27:4] Pilate was a truckling time-server, and he acquiesced in the decision, simply because he was afraid to exasperate the Jews by rescuing from their grasp an innocent man whom they persecuted with unrelenting hatred. [27:5]

The death of Christ, of which all the evangelists treat so particularly, is the most awful and the most momentous event in the history of the world. He, no doubt, fell a victim to the malice of the rulers of the Jews; but He was delivered into their hands "by the determinate counsel and foreknowledge of God;" [28:1] and if we discard the idea that He was offered up as a vicarious sacrifice, we must find it impossible to give anything like a satisfactory account of what occurred in Gethsemane and at Calvary. The amount of physical suffering He sustained from

12

man did not exceed that endured by either of the malefactors with whom He was associated; and such was His magnanimity and fortitude, that, had He been an ordinary martyr, the prospect of crucifixion would not have been sufficient to make Him "exceeding sorrowful" and "sore amazed." [28:2] His holy soul must have been wrung with no common agony, when "His sweat was as it were great drops of blood falling down to the ground," [28:3] and when He was forced to cry out—"My God, my God, why hast thou forsaken me?" [28:4] In that hour of "the power of darkness" He was "smitten of God and afflicted," and there was never sorrow like unto His sorrow, for upon Him were laid "the iniquities of us all."

The incidents which accompanied the death of Jesus were even more impressive than those which signalised His birth. When He was in the garden of Gethsemane there appeared unto Him an angel from Heaven strengthening Him. [28:5] During the three concluding hours of His intense anguish on the cross, there was darkness overall the land, [28:6] as if nature mourned along with the illustrious sufferer. When He bowed His head on Calvary and gave up the ghost, the event was marked by notifications such as never announced the demise of any of this world's great potentates, for "the veil of the temple was rent in twain," and the rocks were cleft asunder, and the graves were opened, and the earth trembled. [29:1] "The centurion and they that were with him," in attendance at the execution, seem to have been Gentiles; and though, doubtless, they had heard that Jesus claimed to be the Messiah of the Jews, they perhaps very imperfectly comprehended the import of the designation; but they were forthwith overwhelmed with the conviction, that He, whose death they had just witnessed, must have given a true account of His mission and His dignity, for "when they saw the earthquake, and those things that were done, they feared greatly, saying—Truly this was the Son of God" [29:2]

The body of our Lord was committed to the grave on the evening of Friday, and, early on the morning of the following Sunday, He issued from the tomb. An ordinary individual has no control over the duration of his existence, but Jesus demonstrated that He had power to lay down His life, and that He had power to take it again. [29:3] Had He been a deceiver His delusions must have terminated with His death, so that His resurrection must be regarded as His crowning miracle, or rather, as the affixing of the broad seal of heaven to the truth of His mission as the Messiah. It was, besides, the fulfilment of an ancient prophecy; [29:4] a proof of His fore-knowledge; [29:5] and a pledge of the resurrection of His disciples. [29:6] Hence, in the New Testament, [29:7] it is so often mentioned with marked emphasis.

There is no fact connected with the life of Christ better attested than that of His resurrection. He was put to death by His enemies; and His body was not removed from the cross until they were fully satisfied that the vital spark had fled. [29:8] His tomb was scooped out of a solid rock; [29:9] the stone which blocked up the entrance was sealed with all care; and a military guard kept constant watch to prevent its violation. [30:1] But in due time an earthquake shook the cemetery—"The angel of the Lord descended from heaven, and came and rolled back the stone from the door and sat upon it ... and for fear of him the keepers did shake, and became as dead men." [30:2] Our Lord meanwhile came forth from the grave, and the sentinels, in consternation, hastened to the chief priests and communicated the astounding intelligence. [30:3] But these infatuated men, instead of yielding to the force of this overwhelming evidence, endeavoured to conceal their infamy by the base arts of bribery and falsehood. "They gave large money unto the soldiers, saying—Say ye—His disciples came by night and stole him away while we slept...so they took the money, and did as they were taught." [30:4]

Jesus, as the first-born of Mary, was presented in the temple forty days after His birth; and, as "the first-begotten of the dead," [30:5] He presented Himself before His Father, in the temple above, forty days after He had opened the womb of the grave. During the interval he appeared only to His own followers. [30:6] Those who had so long and so wilfully rejected the testimony of His teaching and His miracles, had certainly no reason to expect any additional proofs of His Divine mission. But the Lord manifests Himself to His Church, "and not unto the world," [30:7] and to such as fear His name He is continually supplying new and interesting illustrations of His presence, His power, His wisdom, and His mercy. Whilst He is a pillar of darkness to His foes, He is a pillar of light to His people. Though Jesus was now invisible to the Scribes and Pharisees, He admitted His disciples to high and holy fellowship. Now their hearts burned within them as He spake to them "of the things pertaining to the kingdom of God," [31:1] and as "He expounded unto them in all the Scriptures the things concerning Himself." [31:2] Now He doubtless pointed out to them how He was symbolised in the types, how He was exhibited in the promises, and how He was described in the prophecies. Now He explained to them more fully the arrangements of His Church, and now He commanded His apostles to go and "teach all nations, baptizing them in the name of the Father, and of the Son, and of the Holy Ghost." [31:3] Having assured the twelve of His presence with His true servants even unto the end of the world, and having led them out as far as Bethany, a village a few furlongs from Jerusalem, "he lifted up his hands and blessed them. And it came to pass, while he blessed them, he was parted from them, and carried up into heaven." [31:4]

Thus closed the earthly career of Him who is both the Son of man and the Son of God. Though He was sorely tried by the privations of poverty, though He was exposed to the most brutal and degrading insults, and though at last He was forsaken by His friends and consigned to a death of lingering agony, He never performed a single act or uttered a single word unworthy of His exalted and blessed mission. The narratives of the evangelists supply clear internal evidence that, when they described the history of Jesus, they must have copied from a living original; for otherwise, no four individuals, certainly no four Jews, could have each furnished such a portrait of so great and so singular a personage. Combining the highest respect for the institutions of Moses with a spirit eminently catholic, He was at once a devout Israelite and a large-hearted citizen of the world. Rising far superior to the prejudices of His countrymen, He visited Samaria, and conversed freely with its population; and, whilst declaring that He was sent specially to the seed of Abraham, He was ready to extend His sympathy to their bitterest enemies. Though He took upon Him the form of a servant, there was nothing mean or servile in His behaviour; for, when He humbled Himself, there was ever about Him an air of condescending majesty. Whether He administers comfort to the mourner, or walks upon the waves of the sea, or replies to the cavils of the Pharisees, He is still the same calm, holy, and gracious Saviour. When His passion was immediately in view, He was as kind and as considerate as ever, for, on the very night in which He was betrayed, He was

14

employed in the institution of an ordinance which was to serve as a sign and a seal of His grace throughout all generations. His character is as sublime as it is original. It has no parallel in the history of the human family. The impostor is cunning, the demagogue is turbulent, and the fanatic is absurd; but the conduct of Jesus Christ is uniformly gentle and serene, candid, courteous, and consistent. Well, indeed, may His name be called Wonderful. "He was in the world, and the world was made by him, and the world know him not. He came unto his own, and his own received him not. But an many as received him, to them gave he power to become the sons of God, even to them that believe on his name." [32:1]

SUPPLEMENTARY NOTE TO CHAPTER II

THE YEAR OF CHRIST'S BIRTH

The Christian era commences on the 1st of January of the year 754 of the city of Rome. That our Lord was born about the time stated in the text may appear from the following considerations—

The visit of the wise men to Bethlehem must have taken place a very few days after the birth of Jesus, and before His presentation in the temple. Bethlehem was not the stated residence of Joseph and Mary, either before or after the birth of the child (Luke i. 26, ii. 4, 39; Matt. ii. 2). They were obliged to repair to the place on account of the taxing, and immediately after the presentation in the temple, they returned to Nazareth and dwelt there (Luke ii. 39). Had the visit of the wise men occurred, as some think, six, or twelve, or eighteen months after the birth, the question of Herod to "the chief priests and scribes of the people" where "Christ should be born"—would have been quite vain, as the infant might have been removed long before to another part of the country. The wise men manifestly expected to see a newly born infant, and hence they asked—"where is he that is born King of the Jews?" (Matt. ii. 2.) The evangelist also states expressly that they came to Jerusalem "when Jesus was born" (Matt. ii. 1). At a subsequent period they would have found the Holy Child, not at Bethlehem, but at Nazareth.

The only plausible objection to this view of the matter is derived from the statement that Herod "sent forth and slew all the children that were in Bethlehem and in all the coasts thereof, from two years old and under, according to the time which he had diligently enquired of the wise men" (Matt. ii. 16). The king had ascertained from these sages "what time the star appeared" (Matt. ii. 7), and they seem to have informed him that it had been visible a year before. A Jewish child was said to be two years old when it had entered on its second year (see Greswell's "Dissertations," vol. ii. 136); and, to make sure of his prey, Herod murdered all the infants in Bethlehem and the neighbourhood under the age of thirteen months. The wise men had not told him that the child was a year old—it was obvious that they thought very differently—but the tyrant butchered all who

15

came, within the range of suspicion. It is highly probable that the star announced the appearance of the Messiah twelve months before he was born. Such an intimation was given of the birth of Isaac, who was a remarkable type of Christ (Gen. xvii. 21). See also 2 Kings iv. 16, and Dan. iv. 29, 33.

The presentation of the infant in the temple occurred after the death of Herod. This follows as a corollary from what has been already advanced, for if the wise men visited Bethlehem immediately after the birth, and if the child was then hurried away to Egypt, the presentation could not have taken place earlier. The ceremony was performed forty days after the birth (Luke ii. 22, and Lev. xii. 2, 3, 4), and as the flight and the return might both have been accomplished in eight or ten days, there was ample time for a sojourn of at least two or three weeks in that part of Egypt which was nearest to Palestine. Herod died during this brief exile, and yet his demise happened so soon before the departure of the holy family on their way home, that the intelligence had not meanwhile reached Joseph by the voice of ordinary fame; and until his arrival in the land of Israel, he did not even know that Archelaus reigned in Judea (Matt. ii. 22). He seems to have inferred from the dream that the dynasty of the Herodian family had been completely subverted, so that when he heard of the succession of Archelaus "he was afraid" to enter his territory; but, at this juncture, being "counselled of God" in another dream, he took courage, proceeded on his journey, and, after the presentation in the temple, "returned into the parts of Galilee."

That the presentation in the temple took place after the death of Herod is further manifest from the fact that the babe remained uninjured, though his appearance in the sacred courts awakened uncommon interest, and though Anna "spake of him to all them that looked for redemption in Jerusalem" (Luke ii. 38). Herod had his spies in all quarters, and had he been yet living, the intelligence of the presentation and of its extraordinary accompaniments, would have soon reached his ears, and he would have made some fresh attempt upon the life of the infant. But when the babe was actually brought to the temple, the tyrant was no more. Jerusalem was in a state of great political excitement, and Archelaus had, perhaps, already set sail for Rome to secure from the emperor the confirmation of his title to the kingdom (see Josephus' Antiq. xvii. c. 9), so that it is not strange if the declarations of Simeon and Anna did not attract any notice on the part of the existing rulers.

Assuming, then, that Christ was born a very short time before the death of Herod, we have now to ascertain the date of the demise of that monarch. Josephus states (Antiq. xiv. 14, § 5) that Herod was made king by the Roman Senate in the 184th Olympiad, when Calvinus and Pollio were consuls, that is, in the year of Rome 714; and that he reigned thirty-seven years (Antiq. xvii. 8, § 1). We may infer, therefore, that his reign terminated in the year 751 of the city of Rome. He died shortly before the passover; his disease seems to have been of a very lingering character; and he appears to have languished under it upwards of a year (Josephus' Antiq. xvii. 6, § 4, 5, and xvii. 9, § 2, 3). The passover of 751 fell on the 31st of March (see Greswell's "Dissertations," vol. i. p. 331), and as our Lord was in all likelihood born early in the month, the Jewish king probably ended his days a week or two afterwards, or about the time of the vernal equinox. According to this computation the conception took place exactly at the feast of Pentecost, which fell, in 750, on the 31st of May.

This view is corroborated by Luke iii. 1, where it is said that the word of God came to John the Baptist "in the fifteenth year of the reign of Tiberius Caesar." John's ministry had continued only a short time when he was imprisoned, and then Jesus "began to be about thirty years of age" (Luke iii. 23). Augustus died in August 767, and this year 767, according to a mode of reckoning then in use (see Hales' "Chronology," i. 49, 171, and Luke xxiv. 21), was the first year of his successor Tiberius. The fifteenth year of Tiberius, according to the same mode of calculation, commenced on the 1st of January 781 of the city of Rome, and terminated on the 1st of January 782. If then our Lord was born about the 1st of March 751 of Rome, and if the Baptist was imprisoned early in 781, it could be said with perfect propriety that Jesus then "began to be about thirty years of age." This view is further confirmed by the fact that Quirinius, or Cyrenius, mentioned Luke ii. 2, was first governor of Syria from the close of the year 750 of Rome to 753. (See Merivale, iv. p. 457, note.) Our Lord was born under his administration, and according to the date we have assigned to the nativity, the "taxing" at Bethlehem must have taken place a few months after Cyrenius entered into office.

This view of the date of the birth of Christ, which differs somewhat from that of any writer with whom I am acquainted, appears to meet all the difficulties connected with this much-disputed question. It is based partly upon the principle, so ingeniously advocated by Whiston in his "Chronology," that the flight into Egypt took place before the presentation in the temple. I have never yet met with any antagonist of that hypothesis who was able to give a satisfactory explanation of the text on which it rests. Some other dates assigned for the birth of Christ are quite inadmissible. In Judea shepherds could not have been found "abiding in the field, keeping watch over their flock by night" (Luke ii. 8) in November, December, January, or, perhaps, February; but in March, and especially in a mild season, such a thing appears to have been quite common. (See Greswell's "Dissertations," vol. i. p. 391, and Robinson's "Biblical Researches," vol ii. p. 97, 98.) Hippolytus, one of the earliest Christian writers who touches on the subject, indicates that our Lord was born about the time of the passover. (See Greswell, i. 461, 462.)

CHAPTER III

THE TWELVE AND THE SEVENTY

It has often been remarked that the personal preaching of our Lord was comparatively barren. There can be no doubt that the effects produced did not at all correspond to what might have been expected from so wonderful a ministry; but it had been predicted that the Messiah would be "despised and rejected of men," [36:1] and the unbelief of the Jews was one of the humiliating trials He was ordained to suffer during His abode on earth. "The Holy Ghost was not yet given, because that Jesus was not yet glorified." [36:2] We have, certainly, no evidence that any of His discourses made such an impression as that which accompanied

17

the address of Peter on the day of Pentecost. Immediately after the outpouring of the Spirit at that period an abundant blessing followed the proclamation of the gospel. But though Jesus often mourned over the obduracy of His countrymen, and though the truth, preached by His disciples, was often more effective than when uttered by Himself, it cannot with propriety be said that His own evangelical labours were unfruitful. The one hundred and twenty, who met in an upper room during the interval between His Ascension and the day of Pentecost [36:3] were but a portion of His followers. The fierce and watchful opposition of the Sanhedrim had kept Him generally at a distance from Jerusalem; it was there specially dangerous to profess an attachment to His cause; and we may thus, perhaps, partially account for the paucity of His adherents in the Jewish metropolis. His converts were more numerous in Galilee; and it was, probably, in that district He appeared to the company of upwards of five hundred brethren who saw Him after His resurrection. [37:1] He had itinerated extensively as a missionary; and, from some statements incidentally occurring in the gospels, we may infer, that there were individuals who had imbibed His doctrines in the cities and villages of almost all parts of Palestine. [37:2] But the most signal and decisive proof of the power of His ministry is presented in the fact that, during the three years of its duration, He enlisted and sent forth no less than eighty-two preachers. Part of these have since been known as "The Twelve," and the rest as "The Seventy."

The Twelve are frequently mentioned in the New Testament, and yet the information we possess respecting them is exceedingly scanty. Of some we know little more than their names. It has been supposed that a town called Kerioth, [37:3] or Karioth, belonging to the tribe of Judah, was the birthplace of Judas, the traitor; [37:4] but it is probable that all his colleagues were natives of Galilee. [37:5] Some of them had various names; and the consequent diversity which the sacred catalogues present has frequently perplexed the reader of the evangelical narratives. Matthew was also called Levi; [37:6] Nathanael was designated Bartholomew; [36:7] and Jude had the two other names of Lebbaeus and Thaddaeus. [38:1] Thomas was called Didymus, [38:2] or the twin, in reference, we may presume, to the circumstances of his birth; James the son of Alphaeus was styled, perhaps by way of distinction, James "the Less" [38:3]—in allusion, it would seem, to the inferiority of his stature; the other James and John were surnamed Boanerges, [38:4] or the sons of thunder—a title probably indicative of the peculiar solemnity and power of their ministrations; and Simon stands at the head of all the lists, and is expressly said to be "first" of the Twelve, [38:5] because, as we have reason to believe, whilst his advanced age might have warranted him to claim precedence, his superior energy and promptitude enabled him to occupy the most prominent position. The same individual was called Cephas, or Peter, or Stone, [38:6] apparently on account of the firmness of his character. His namesake, the other Simon, was termed the Canaanite, and also Zelotes, [38:7] or the zealot—a title expressive, in all likelihood, of the zeal and earnestness with which he was wont to carry out his principles. We are informed that our Lord sent forth the Twelve "by two and two," [38:8] but we cannot tell whether He observed any general rule in the arrangement of those who were to travel in company. The relationship of the parties to each other might, at least in three instances, have suggested a classification; as Peter and Andrew, James and John, James the Less and Jude, were, respectively, brothers.

18

James the Less is described as "the Lord's brother," [39:1] and Jude is called "the brother of James," [39:2] so that these two disciples must have been in some way related to our Saviour; but the exact degree of affinity or consanguinity cannot now, perhaps, be positively ascertained. [39:3] Some of the disciples, such as Andrew, [39:4] and probably John, [39:5] had previously been disciples of the Baptist, but their separation from their former master and adherence to Jesus did not lead to any estrangement between our Lord and His pious forerunner. As the Baptist contemplated the more permanent and important character of the Messiah's mission, he could cheerfully say—"He must increase, but I must decrease." [39:6]

All the Twelve, when enlisted as disciples of Christ, appear to have moved in the humbler walks of life; and yet we are scarcely warranted in asserting that they were extremely indigent. Peter, the fisherman, pretty plainly indicates that, in regard to worldly circumstances, he had been, to some extent, a loser by obeying the call of Jesus. [39:7] Though James and John were likewise fishermen, the family had at least one little vessel of their own, and they could afford to pay "hired servants" to assist them in their business. [40:1] Matthew acted, in a subordinate capacity, as a collector of imperial tribute; but though the Jews cordially hated a functionary who brought so painfully to their recollection their condition as a conquered people, it is pretty clear that the publican was engaged in a lucrative employment. Zacchaeus, said to have been a "chief among the publicans," [40:2] is represented as a rich man; [40:3] and Matthew, though probably in an inferior station, was able to give an entertainment in his own house to a numerous company. [40:4] Still, however, the Twelve, as a body, were qualified, neither by their education nor their habits, for acting as popular instructors; and had the gospel been a device of human wisdom, it could not have been promoted by their advocacy. Individuals who had hitherto been occupied in tilling the land, in fishing, and in mending nets, or in sitting at the receipt of custom, could not have been expected to make any great impression as ecclesiastical reformers. Their position in society gave them no influence; their natural talents were not particularly brilliant; and even their dialect betokened their connexion with a district from which nothing good or great was anticipated. [40:5] But God exalted these men of low degree, and made them the spiritual illuminators of the world.

Though the New Testament enters very sparingly into the details of their personal history, it is plain that the Twelve presented a considerable variety of character. Thomas, though obstinate, was warm-hearted and manly. Once when, as he imagined, his Master was going forward to certain death, he chivalrously proposed to his brethren that they should all perish along with Him; [40:6] and though at first he doggedly refused to credit the account of the resurrection, [41:6] yet, when his doubts were removed, he gave vent to his feelings in one of the most impressive testimonies [41:2] to the power and godhead of the Messiah to be found in the whole book of revelation. James, the son of Alphaeus, was noted for his prudence and practical wisdom; [41:3] and Nathanael was frank and candid—"an Israelite indeed, in whom was no guile." [41:4] Our Lord bestowed on Peter and the two sons of Zebedee peculiar proofs of confidence and favour, for they alone were permitted to witness some of the most remarkable scenes in the history of the Man of Sorrows. [41:5] Though these three brethren displayed such a congeniality of disposition, it does not appear that they possessed minds of the same mould, but each had excellencies of his own which threw a charm around his character. Peter yielded to the impulse of the moment and acted with promptitude and vigour; James became the first of the apostolic martyrs, probably because by his ability and boldness, as a preacher, he had provoked the special enmity of Herod and the Jews; [41:6] whilst the benevolent John delighted to meditate on the "deep things of God," and listened with profound emotion to his Master as He discoursed of the mystery of His Person, and of the peace of believers abiding in His love. It has been conjectured that there was some family relationship between the sons of Zebedee and Jesus; but of this there is no satisfactory evidence. [41:7] It was simply, perhaps, the marked attention of our Saviour to James and John which awakened the ambition of their mother, and induced her to bespeak their promotion in the kingdom of the Son of Man. [42:1]

Though none of the Twelve had received a liberal education, [42:2] it cannot be said that they were literally "novices" when invested with the ministerial commission. It is probable that, before they were invited to follow Jesus, they had all seriously turned their attention to the subject of religion; some of them had been previously instructed by the Baptist; and all, prior to their selection, appear to have been about a year under the tuition of our Lord himself. From that time until the end of His ministry they lived with Him on terms of the most intimate familiarity. From earlier acquaintance, as well as from closer and more confidential companionship, they had a better opportunity of knowing His character and doctrines than any of the rest of His disciples. When, perhaps about six or eight months [42:3] after their appointment, they were sent forth as missionaries, they were commanded neither to walk in "the way of the Gentiles," nor to enter "into any city of the Samaritans," but rather to go "to the lost sheep of the house of Israel." [42:4] Their number Twelve corresponded to the number of the tribes, and they were called apostles probably in allusion to a class of Jewish functionaries who were so designated. It is said that the High Priest was wont to send forth from Jerusalem into foreign countries certain accredited agents, or messengers, styled apostles, on ecclesiastical errands. [42:5]

During the personal ministry of our Lord the Twelve seem to have been employed by Him on only one missionary excursion. About twelve months after that event [43:1] He "appointed other seventy also" to preach His Gospel. Luke is the only evangelist who mentions the designation of these additional missionaries; and though we have no reason to believe that their duties terminated with the first tour in which they were engaged, [43:2] they are never subsequently noticed in the New Testament. Many of the actions of our Lord had a typical meaning, and it is highly probable that He designed to inculcate an important truth by the appointment of these Seventy new apostles. According to the ideas of the Jews of that age there were seventy heathen nations; [43:3] and it is rather singular that, omitting Peleg the progenitor of the Israelites, the names of the posterity of Shem, Ham, and Japheth, recorded in the 10th chapter of Genesis, amount exactly to seventy. "These," says the historian, "are the families of the sons of Noah, after their generations, in their nations; and by these were the nations divided in the earth after the flood." [43:4] Every one who looks into the narrative will perceive that the sacred writer does not propose to furnish a complete catalogue of the descendants of Noah, for he passes over in entire silence the posterity of the greater number of the patriarch's grandchildren; he apparently intends to name only those who were the founders of nations; and thus it happens that whilst, in a variety of instances, he does not trace the line of succession, he takes care, in others, to mention the father and many of his sons. [44:1] The Jewish notion current in the time of our Lord as to the existence of seventy heathen nations, seems, therefore, to have rested on a sound historical basis, inasmuch as, according to the Mosaic statement, there were, beside Peleg, precisely seventy individuals by whom "the nations were divided in the earth after the flood." We may thus infer that our Lord meant to convey a great moral lesson by the appointment alike of the Twelve and of the Seventy. In the ordination of the Twelve He evinced His regard for all the tribes of Israel; in the ordination of the Seventy He intimated that His Gospel was designed for all the nations of the earth. When the Twelve were about to enter on their first mission He required them to go only to the Jews, but He sent forth the Seventy "two and two before His face into every city and place whither He himself would come." [45:1] Towards the commencement of His public career, He had induced many of the Samaritans to believe on Him, [45:2] whilst at a subsequent period His ministry had been blessed to Gentiles in the coasts of Tyre and Sidon; [45:3] and there is no evidence that in the missionary journey which He contemplated when He appointed the Seventy as His pioneers, He intended to confine His labours to His kinsmen of the seed of Abraham. It is highly probable that the Seventy were actually sent forth from Samaria, [45:4] and the instructions given them apparently suggest that, in the circuit now assigned to them, they were to visit certain districts lying north of Galilee of the Gentiles. [45:5] The personal ministry of our Lord had respect primarily and specially to the lost sheep of the house of Israel, [45:6] but His conduct in this case symbolically indicated the catholic character of His religion. He evinced His regard for the Jews by sending no less than twelve apostles to that one nation, but He did not Himself refuse to minister either to Samaritans or Gentiles; and to shew that He was disposed to make provision for the general diffusion of His word, He "appointed other seventy also, and sent them two and two before His face into every city and place whither He himself would come."

It is very clear that our Lord committed, in the first instance, to the Twelve the organisation of the ecclesiastical commonwealth. The most ancient Christian Church, that of the metropolis of Palestine, was modelled under their superintendence; and the earliest converts gathered into it, after His ascension, were the fruits of their ministry. Hence, in the Apocalypse, the wall of the "holy Jerusalem" is said to have "twelve foundations, and in them the names of the twelve apostles of the Lamb." [46:1] But it does not follow that others had no share in founding the spiritual structure. The Seventy also received a commission from Christ, and we have every reason to believe that, after the death of their Master, they pursued their missionary labours with renovated ardour. That they were called apostles as well as the Twelve, cannot, perhaps, be established by distinct testimony; [46:2] but it is certain, that they were furnished with supernatural endowments; [46:3] and it is scarcely probable that they are overlooked in the description of the sacred writer when He represents the New Testament Church as "built upon the foundation of the apostles and prophets, Jesus Christ himself being the chief corner stone." [46:4]

The appointment of the Seventy, like that of the Twelve, was a typical act; and it is not, therefore, extraordinary that they are only once noticed in the sacred volume. Our Lord never intended to constitute two permanent corporations, limited, respectively, to twelve and seventy members, and empowered to transmit their authority to successors from generation to generation. In a short time after His death the symbolical meaning of the mission of the Seventy was explained, as it very soon appeared that the gospel was to be transmitted to all the ends of the earth; and thus it was no longer necessary to refer to these representatives of the ministry of the universal Church. When the Twelve turned to the Gentiles, their number lost its significance, and from that date they accordingly ceased to fill up vacancies occurring in their society; and, as the Church assumed a settled form, the apostles were disposed to insist less and less on any special powers with which they had been originally furnished, and rather to place themselves on a level with the ordinary rulers of the ecclesiastical community. Hence we find them sitting in church courts with these brethren, [47:1] and desirous to be known not as apostles, but as elders. [47:2] We possess little information respecting either their official or their personal history. A very equivocal, and sometimes contradictory, tradition [47:3] is the only guide which even professes to point out to us where the greater number of them laboured; and the same witness is the only voucher for the statements which describe how most of them finished their career. It is an instructive fact that no proof can be given, from the sacred record, of the ordination either by the Twelve or by the Seventy, of even one presbyter or pastor. With the exception of the laying on of hands upon the seven deacons, [47:4] no inspired writer mentions any act of the kind in which the Twelve ever engaged. The deacons were not rulers in the Church, and therefore could not by ordination confer ecclesiastical power on others.

There is much meaning in the silence of the sacred writers respecting the official proceedings and the personal career of the Twelve and the Seventy. It thus becomes impossible for any one to make out a title to the ministry by tracing his ecclesiastical descent; for no contemporary records enable us to prove a connexion between the inspired founders of our religion, and those who were subsequently entrusted with the government of the Church. At the critical point where, had it been deemed necessary, we might have had the light of inspiration, we are left to wander in total darkness. We are thus shut up to the conclusion that the claims of those who profess to be heralds of the gospel are to be tested by some other criterion than their ecclesiastical lineage. It is written—"By their fruits ye shall know them." [48:1] God alone can make a true minister; [48:2] and he who attempts to establish his right to feed the flock of Christ by appealing to his official genealogy miserably mistakes the source of the pastoral commission. It would, indeed, avail nothing though a minister could prove his relationship to the Twelve or the Seventy by an unbroken line of ordinations, for some who at the time may have been able to deduce their descent from the apostles were amongst the most dangerous of the early heretics. [48:3] True religion is sustained, not by any human agency, but by that Eternal Spirit who quickens all the children of God, and who has preserved for them a pure gospel in the writings of the apostles and evangelists. The perpetuity of the Church no more depends on the uninterrupted succession of its ministers than does the perpetuity of a nation depend on the continuance of the dynasty which may happen at a particular date to occupy the throne. As plants possess powers of reproduction enabling them, when a part decays, to throw it off, and to supply its place by a new and vigorous vegetation, so it is with the Church—the spiritual vine which the Lord has planted. Its government may degenerate into a corrupt tyranny by which its most precious liberties may be invaded or destroyed, but the freemen of the Lord are not bound to submit to any such domination. Were even all the ecclesiastical rulers to become traitors to the King of Zion, the Church would not therefore perish. The living members of the body of Christ would be then required to repudiate the authority of overseers by whom they were betrayed, and to choose amongst themselves such faithful men as were found most competent to teach and to guide the spiritual community. The Divine Statute-book clearly warrants the adoption of such an alternative. "Beloved," says the Apostle John, "believe not every spirit, but try the spirits whether they are of God. .... We are of God, he that knoweth God heareth us, he that is not of God heareth not us. Hereby know we the spirit of truth and the spirit of error." [49:1] "If there come any unto you, and bring not this doctrine, receive him not into your house, neither bid him God-speed; for he that biddeth him God-speed is partaker of his evil deeds." [49:2] Paul declares, still more emphatically—"Though WE, or AN ANGEL FROM HEAVEN, preach any other gospel unto you than that which we have preached unto you, let him be accursed. As we said before, so say I now again, If any man preach any other gospel unto you than that ye have received, let him be accursed." [49:3]

In one sense neither the Twelve nor the Seventy had successors. All of them were called to preach the gospel by the living voice of Christ himself; all had "companied" with Him during the period of His ministry; all had listened to His sermons; all had been spectators of His works of wonder; all were empowered to perform miracles; all seem to have conversed with Him after His resurrection; and all appear to have possessed the gift of inspired utterance. [50:1] But in another sense every "good minister of Jesus Christ" is a successor of these primitive preachers; for every true pastor is taught of God, and is moved by the Spirit to undertake the service in which he is engaged, and is warranted to expect a blessing on the truth which he disseminates. As of old the descent from heaven of fire upon the altar testified the Divine acceptance of the sacrifices, so now the descent of the Spirit, as manifested in the conversion of souls to God, is a sure token that the labours of the minister have the seal of the Divine approbation. The great Apostle of the Gentiles did not hesitate to rely on such a proof of his commission from heaven. "Need we," says he to the Corinthians, "epistles of commendation to you, or letters of commendation from you? Ye are our epistle written in our hearts, known and read of all men; forasmuch as ye are manifestly declared to be the epistle of Christ ministered by us, written, not with ink, but with the Spirit of the living God, not in tables of stone, but in the fleshy tables of the heart." [50:2] No true pastor will be left entirely destitute of such encouragement, and neither the Twelve nor the Seventy could produce credentials more trustworthy or more intelligible.

CHAPTER IV

THE PROGRESS OF THE GOSPEL FROM THE DEATH OF CHRIST TO THE DEATH OF THE APOSTLE JAMES, THE BROTHER OF JOHN
A.D. 31 TO A.D. 44

When our Lord bowed His head on the cross and "gave up the ghost," the work of atonement was completed. The ceremonial law virtually expired when He explained, by His death, its awful significance; and the crisis of His passion was the birthday of the Christian economy. At this date the history of the New Testament Church properly commences.

After His resurrection Jesus remained forty days on earth, [51:1] and, during this interval, He often took occasion to point out to His disciples the meaning of His wonderful career. He is represented as saying to them—"Thus it is written, and thus it behoved Christ to suffer, and to rise from the dead the third day, and that repentance and remission of sins should be preached in His name among all nations, beginning at Jerusalem." [51:2] The inspired narratives of the teaching and miracles of our Lord are emphatically corroborated by the fact, that a large Christian Church was established, almost immediately after His decease, in the metropolis of Palestine. The Sanhedrim and the Roman governor had concurred in His condemnation; and, on the night of His trial, even the intrepid Peter had been so intimidated that he had been tempted to curse and to swear as he averred that he knew not "The Man." It might have been expected that the death of Jesus would have been followed by a reign of terror, and that no attempt would have been made, at least in the place where the civil and ecclesiastical authorities resided, to assert the Divine mission of Him whom they had crucified as a malefactor. But perfect love casteth out fear. In the very city where He had suffered, and a few days after His passion, His disciples ventured in the most public manner to declare His innocence and to proclaim Him as the Messiah. The result of their appeal is as wonderful as its boldness. Though the imminent peril of confessing Christ was well known, such was the strength of their convictions that multitudes resolved, at all hazards, to enrol themselves among His followers. The success which accompanied the preaching of the apostolic missionaries at the feast of Pentecost was a sign and a pledge of their future triumphs, for "the same day there were added unto them about three thousand souls." [52:1]

The disinterested behaviour of the converts betokened their intense earnestness. "All that believed were together and had all things common, and sold their possessions and goods and parted them to all men, as every man had need." [52:2] These early disciples were not, indeed, required, as a term of communion, to deposit their property in a common stock-purse; but, in the overflowings of their first love, they spontaneously adopted the arrangement. On the part of the more opulent members of the community residing in a place which was the stronghold of Jewish prejudice and influence, this course was, perhaps, as prudent as it was generous. By joining a proscribed sect they put their lives, as well as their wealth, into jeopardy; but, by the sale of their effects, they displayed a spirit of self-sacrifice which must have astonished and confounded their adversaries. They thus anticipated all attempts at spoliation, and gave a proof of their readiness to submit to any suffering for the cause which they had espoused. An inheritance, when turned into money, could not be easily sequestered; and those who were in want could obtain assistance out of the secreted treasure. Still, even at this period, the principle of a community of goods was not carried out into universal operation; for the foreign Jews who were now converted to the faith, and who were "possessors of lands or houses" [53:1] in distant countries, could neither have found purchasers, nor negotiated transfers, in the holy city. The first sales must obviously have been confined to those members of the Church who were owners of property in Jerusalem and its neighbourhood.

The system of having all things common was suggested in a crisis of apparently extreme peril, so that it was only a temporary expedient; and it is evident that it was soon given up altogether, as unsuited to the ordinary circumstances of the Christian Church. But though, in a short time, the disciples in general were left to depend on their own resources, the community continued to provide a fund for the help of the infirm and the destitute. At an early period complaints were made respecting the distribution of this charity, and we are told that "there arose a murmuring of the Grecians against the Hebrews because their widows were neglected in the daily ministration." [53:2] The Grecians, or those converts from Judaism who used the Greek language, were generally of foreign birth; and as the Hebrews, or the brethren who spoke the vernacular tongue of Palestine, were natives of the country, there were, perhaps, suspicions that local influence secured for their poor an undue share of the public bounty. The expedient employed for the removal of this "root of bitterness" seems to have been completely successful. "The twelve called the multitude of the disciples unto them and said, It is not reason that we should leave the word of God and serve tables. Wherefore, brethren, look ye out among you seven men of honest report, full of the Holy Ghost and wisdom, whom we may appoint over this business." [54:1]

Had the apostles been anxious for power they would themselves have nominated the deacons. They might have urged, too, a very plausible apology for here venturing upon an exercise of patronage. They might have pleaded that the disciples were dissatisfied with each other—that the excitement of a popular election was fitted to increase this feeling of alienation—and that, under such circumstances, prudence required them to take upon themselves the responsibility of the appointment. But they were guided by a higher wisdom; and their conduct is a model for the imitation of ecclesiastical rulers in all succeeding generations. It was the will of the Great Lawgiver that His Church should possess a free constitution; and accordingly, at the very outset, its members were intrusted with the privilege of self-government. The community had already been invited to choose an apostle in the room of Judas, [54:2] and they were now required to name office-bearers for the management of their money transactions. But, whilst the Twelve, on this occasion, appealed to the suffrages of the Brotherhood, they reserved to themselves the right of confirming the election; and they might, by withholding ordination, have refused to fiat an improper appointment. Happily no such difficulty occurred. In compliance with the instructions addressed to them, the multitude chose seven of their number "whom they set before the apostles, and, when they had prayed, they laid their hands on them." [54:3]

Prior to the election of the deacons, Peter and John had been incarcerated.

The Sanhedrim wished to extort from them a pledge that they would "not speak at all nor teach in the name of Jesus," [55:1] but the prisoners nobly refused to consent to any such compromise. They "answered and said unto them—Whether it be right in the sight of God to hearken unto you more than unto God, judge ye." [55:2] The apostles here disclaimed the doctrine of passive obedience, and asserted principles which lie at the foundation of the true theory of religious freedom. They maintained that "God alone is Lord of the conscience"—that His command overrides all human regulations—and that, no matter what may be the penalties which earthly rulers may annex to the breach of the enactments of their statute-book, the Christian is not bound to obey, when the civil law would compel him to violate his enlightened convictions. But the Sanhedrim obviously despised such considerations. For a time they were obliged to remain quiescent, as public feeling ran strongly in favour of the new preachers; but, soon after the election of the deacons, they resumed the work of persecution. The tide of popularity now began to turn; and Stephen, one of the Seven, particularly distinguished by his zeal, fell a victim to their intolerance.

The martyrdom of Stephen appears to have occurred about three years and a half after the death of our Lord. [55:3] Daniel had foretold that the Messiah would "confirm the covenant with many for one week" [55:4]—an announcement which has been understood to indicate that, at the time of his manifestation, the gospel would be preached with much success among his countrymen for seven years—and if the prophetic week commenced with the ministry of John the Baptist, it probably terminated with this bloody tragedy. [56:1] The Christian cause had hitherto prospered in Jerusalem, and there are good grounds for believing that, mean while, it had also made considerable progress throughout all Palestine; but, at this date, it is suddenly arrested in its career of advancement. The Jewish multitude begin to regard it with aversion; and the Roman governor discovers that he may, at any time, obtain the tribute of their applause by oppressing its ablest and most fearless advocates.

After His resurrection our Lord commanded the apostles to go and "teach all nations" [56:2] and yet years rolled away before they turned their thoughts towards the evangelisation of the Gentiles. The Jewish mind was slow to apprehend such an idea, for the posterity of Abraham had been long accustomed to regard themselves as the exclusive heirs of divine privileges; but the remarkable development of the kingdom of God gradually led them to entertain more enlarged and more liberal sentiments. The progress of the gospel in Samaria, immediately after the death of Stephen, demonstrated that the blessings of the new dispensation were not to be confined to God's ancient people. Though many of the Samaritans acknowledged the divine authority of the writings of Moses, they did not belong to the Church of Israel; and between them and the Jews a bitter antipathy had hitherto existed. When Philip appeared among them, and preached Jesus as the promised Messiah, they listened most attentively to his appeals, and not a few of them gladly received Christian baptism. [57:1] It could now no longer be said that the Jews had "no dealings with the Samaritans," [57:2] for the gospel gathered both into the fold of a common Saviour, and taught them to keep "the unity of the Spirit in the bond of peace."

When the disciples were scattered abroad by the persecution which arose after the martyrdom of Stephen, the apostles still kept their post in the Jewish capital; [57:3] for Christ had instructed them to begin their ministry in that place:

26

[57:4] and they perhaps conceived that, until authorised by some further intimation, they were bound to remain at Jerusalem. But the conversion of the Samaritans must have reminded them that the sphere of their labours was more extensive. Our Lord had said to them—"Ye shall be witnesses unto me both in Jerusalem, and in all Judea, and in Samaria, and unto the uttermost part of the earth," [57:5] and events, which were now passing before their view, were continually throwing additional light upon the meaning of this announcement. The baptism of the Ethiopian eunuch, [57:6] about this period, was calculated to enlarge their ideas; and the baptism of Cornelius pointed out, still more distinctly, the wide range of their evangelical commission. The minuteness with which the case of the devout centurion is described is a proof of its importance as connected with this transition-stage in the history of the Church. He had before known nothing of Peter; and, when they met at Caesarea, each could testify that he had been prepared for the interview by a special revelation from heaven. [57:7] Cornelius was "a centurion of the band called the Italian band" [57:8]—he was a representative of that military power which then ruled the world—and, in his baptism, we see the Roman Empire presenting, on the altar of Christianity, the first-fruits of the Gentiles.

It was not, however, very obvious, from any of the cases already enumerated, that the salvation of Christ was designed for all classes and conditions of the human family. The Samaritans did not, indeed, worship at Jerusalem, but they claimed some interest in "the promises made unto the fathers;" and they conformed to many of the rites of Judaism. It does not appear that the Ethiopian eunuch was of the seed of Abraham; but he acknowledged the inspiration of the Old Testament, and he was disposed, at least to a certain extent, to observe its institutions. Even the Roman centurion was what has been called a proselyte of the gate, that is, he professed the Jewish theology—"he feared God with all his house" [58:1]—though he had not received circumcision, and had not been admitted into the congregation of Israel. But the time was approaching when the Church was to burst forth beyond the barriers within which it had been hitherto inclosed, and an individual now appeared upon the scene who was to be the leader of this new movement. He is "a citizen of no mean city" [58:2]—a native of Tarsus in Cilicia, a place famous for its educational institutes [58:3]—and he is known, by way of distinction, as "an apostle of the nations." [58:4]

The apostles were at first sent only to their own countrymen; [58:5] and we have seen that, for some time after our Lord's death, they do not appear to have contemplated any more comprehensive mission. When Peter called on the disciples to appoint a successor to Judas, he seems to have acted under the conviction that the company of the Twelve must still be maintained in its integrity, and that its numbers must still exactly correspond to the number of the tribes of Israel. But the Jews, after the death of Stephen, evinced an increasing aversion to the gospel; and as the apostles were eventually induced to direct their views elsewhere, they were, of course, also led to abandon an arrangement which had a special reference to the sectional divisions of the chosen people. Meanwhile, too, the management of ecclesiastical affairs had partially fallen into other hands; new missions, in which the Twelve had no share, had been undertaken; and Paul henceforth becomes most conspicuous and successful in extending and organising the Church.

Paul describes himself as "one born out of due time." [59:1] He was converted to Christianity when his countrymen seemed about to be consigned to judicial blindness; and he was "called to be an apostle" [59:2] when others had been labouring for years in the same vocation. But he possessed peculiar qualifications for the office. He was ardent, energetic, and conscientious, as well as acute and eloquent. In his native city Tarsus he had probably received a good elementary education, and afterwards, "at the feet of Gamaliel," [59:3] in Jerusalem, he enjoyed the tuition of a Rabbi of unrivalled celebrity. The apostle of the Gentiles had much the same religious experience as the father of the German Reformation; for as Luther, before he understood the doctrine of a free salvation, attempted to earn a title to heaven by the austerities of monastic discipline, so Paul in early life was "taught according to the perfect manner of the law of the fathers," [59:4] and "after the strictest sect of his religion lived a Pharisee." [59:5] His zeal led him to become a persecutor; and when Stephen was stoned, the witnesses, who were required to take part in the execution, prepared themselves for the work of death, by laying down their upper garments at the feet of the "young man" Saul. [59:6] He had established himself in the confidence of the Sanhedrim, and he appears to have been a member of that influential judicatory, for he tells us that he "shut up many of the saints in prison," and that, when they were put to death, "he gave his voice, or his vote, [60:1] against them"—a statement implying that he belonged to the court which pronounced the sentence of condemnation. As he was travelling to Damascus armed with authority to seize any of the disciples whom he discovered in that city, and to convey them bound to Jerusalem, [60:2] the Lord appeared to him in the way, and he was suddenly converted. [60:3] After reaching the end of his journey, and boldly proclaiming his attachment to the party he had been so recently endeavouring to exterminate, he retired into Arabia, [60:4] where he appears to have spent three years in the devout study of the Christian theology. He then returned to Damascus, and entered, about A.D. 37, [60:5] on those missionary labours which he prosecuted with so much efficiency and perseverance for upwards of a quarter of a century.

Paul declares that he derived a knowledge of the gospel immediately from Christ; [60:6] and though, for many years, he had very little intercourse with the Twelve, he avers that he was "not a whit behind the very chiefest apostles." [60:7] Throughout life he was associated, not with them, but with others as his fellow-labourers; and he obviously occupied a distinct and independent position. When he was baptized, the ordinance was administered by an individual who is not previously mentioned in the New Testament, [61:1] and when he was separated to the work to which the Lord had called him, [61:2] the ordainers were "prophets and teachers," respecting whose own call to the ministry the inspired historian supplies us with no information. But it may fairly be presumed that they were regularly introduced into the places which they are represented as occupying; they are all described by the evangelist as receiving the same special instructions from heaven; and the tradition that, at least some of them, were of the number of the Seventy, [61:3] is exceedingly probable. And if, as has already been suggested, the mission of the Seventy indicated the design of our Saviour to diffuse the gospel all over the world, we can see a peculiar propriety in the arrangement that Paul was ushered into the Church under the auspices of these ministers. [61:4] It was most fitting that he who was to be, by way of eminence, the apostle of the

Gentiles, was baptized and ordained by men whose own appointment was intended to symbolise the catholic spirit of Christianity.

In the treatment of Paul by his unbelieving countrymen we have a most melancholy illustration of the recklessness of religious bigotry. These Jews must have known that, in as far as secular considerations were concerned, he had everything to lose by turning into "the way which they called heresy;" they were bound to acknowledge that, by connecting himself with an odious sect, he at least demonstrated his sincerity and self-denial; but they were so exasperated by his zeal that they "took counsel to kill him." [62:1] When, after his sojourn in Arabia, he returned to Damascus that city was in the hands of Aretas, the king of Arabia Petraea; [62:2] who seems to have contrived to gain possession of it during the confusion which immediately followed the death of the Emperor Tiberius. This petty sovereign courted the favour of the Jewish portion of the population by permitting them to persecute the disciples; [62:3] and the apostle, at this crisis, would have fallen a victim to their malignity had not his friends let him down "through a window, in a basket, by the wall," [62:4] and thus enabled him to escape a premature martyrdom. He now repaired to Jerusalem, where the brethren do not appear to have heard of his conversion, and where they at first refused to acknowledge him as a member of their society; [62:5] for he had been obliged to leave Damascus with so much precipitation that he had brought with him no commendatory letters; but Barnabas, who is said to have been his school-fellow, [62:6] and who had in some way obtained information respecting his subsequent career, made the leaders of the Mother Church acquainted with the wonderful change which had taken place in his sentiments and character, and induced them to admit him to fellowship. During this visit to the holy city, while he prayed in the temple, he was more fully instructed respecting his future destination. In a trance, he saw Jesus, who said to him—"Depart, for I will send thee far hence unto the Gentiles." [62:7] Even had he not received this intimation, the murderous hostility of the Jews would have obliged him to retire. "When he spake boldly in the name of the Lord Jesus, and disputed against the Grecians, they went about to slay him—which, when the brethren knew, they brought him down to Caesarea, and sent him forth to Tarsus." [63:1]

The apostle now laboured for some years as a missionary in "the regions of Syria and Cilicia." [63:2] His native city and its neighbourhood probably enjoyed a large share of his ministrations, and his exertions seem to have been attended with much success, for, soon afterwards, the converts in these districts attract particular notice. [63:3] Meanwhile the gospel was making rapid progress in the Syrian capital, and as Saul was considered eminently qualified for conducting the mission in that place, he was induced to proceed thither. "Then," says the sacred historian, "Barnabas departed to Tarsus to seek Saul, and when he had found him he brought him unto Antioch. And it came to pass that a whole year they assembled themselves with the Church, and taught much people; and the disciples were called Christians first in Antioch." [63:4]

The establishment of a Church in this city formed a new era in the development of Christianity. Antioch was a great commercial mart with a large Jewish, as well as Gentile, population; it was virtually the capital of the Roman Empire in the East—being the residence of the president, or governor, of Syria; its climate was delightful; and its citizens, enriched by trade, were noted for their gaiety and voluptuousness. In this flourishing metropolis many proselytes from heathenism were to be found in the synagogues of the Greek-speaking Jews, and the gospel soon made rapid progress among these Hellenists. "Some of them (which were scattered abroad upon the persecution that arose about Stephen) were men of Cyprus and Cyrene, which when they were come to Antioch, spake unto the Grecians, [64:1] preaching the Lord Jesus. And the hand of the Lord was with them, and a great number believed and turned unto the Lord." [64:2] The followers of Jesus at this time received a new designation. They had hitherto called themselves "brethren" or "disciples" or "believers," but now they "were called Christians" by some of the inhabitants of the Syrian capital. As the unconverted Jews did not admit that Jesus was the Christ they were obviously not the authors of this appellation, and, in contempt, they probably styled the party Nazarenes or Galileans; but it is easy to understand how the name was suggested to the Pagans as most descriptive and appropriate. No one could be long in company with the new religionists without perceiving that Christ was "the end of their conversation." They delighted to tell of His mighty miracles, of His holy life, of the extraordinary circumstances which accompanied His death, of His resurrection and ascension. Out of the fulness of their hearts they discoursed of His condescension and His meekness, of His wonderful wisdom, of His sublime theology, and of His unutterable love to a world lying in wickedness. When they prayed, they prayed to Christ; when they sang, they sang praise to Christ; when they preached, they preached Christ. Well then might the heathen multitude agree with one voice to call them Christians. The inventor of the title may have meant it as a nickname, but if so, He who overruled the waywardness of Pilate so that he wrote on the cross a faithful inscription, [65:1] also caused this mocker of His servants to stumble on a most truthful and complimentary designation.

From his first appearance in Antioch Paul seems to have occupied a very influential position among his brethren. In that refined and opulent city his learning, his dialectic skill, his prudence, and his pious ardour were all calculated to make his ministry most effective. About a year after his arrival there, he was deputed, in company with a friend, to visit Palestine on an errand of love. "In those days came prophets from Jerusalem unto Antioch. And there stood up one of them, named Agabus, and signified by the Spirit that there should be great dearth throughout all the world; which came to pass in the days of Claudius Caesar. Then the disciples, every man according to his ability, determined to send relief to the brethren which dwelt in Judea. Which also they did, and sent it to the elders by the hands of Barnabas and Saul." [65:2]

This narrative attests that the principle of a community of goods was not recognised in the Church of Antioch, for the aid administered was supplied, not out of a general fund, but by "every man according to his ability." There was here no "murmuring of the Grecians against the Hebrews," as, in the spirit of true brotherhood, the wealthy Hellenists of Antioch cheerfully contributed to the relief of the poor Hebrews of their fatherland. It does not appear that "the elders" in whose hands the money was deposited, were all office-bearers connected with the Church of Jerusalem. These would, of course, receive no small share of the donations, but as the assistance was designed for the "brethren which dwelt in Judea," and not merely for the disciples in the holy city, we may infer that it was distributed among the elders of all the Churches now scattered over the southern part of Palestine. [66:1] Neither would Barnabas and Paul require to make a tour

30

throughout the district to visit these various communities. All the elders of Judea still continued to observe the Mosaic law, and as the deputies from Antioch were in Jerusalem at the time of the Passover, [66:2] they would find their brethren in attendance upon the festival.

It is reported by several ancient writers that the apostles were instructed to remain at Jerusalem for twelve years after the crucifixion of our Lord, [66:3] and if the tradition is correct, the holy city continued to be their stated residence until shortly before the period of the arrival of these deputies from the Syrian capital. The time of this visit can be pretty accurately ascertained, and there is perhaps no point connected with the history of the book of the Acts respecting which there is such a close approximation to unanimity amongst chronologists; for, as Josephus notices [66:4] both the sudden death of Herod Agrippa, grandson of Herod the Great, which now occurred, [66:5] and the famine against which this contribution was intended to provide, it is apparent from the date which he assigns to them, that Barnabas and Saul must have reached Jerusalem about A.D. 44. [66:6] At this juncture at least two of the apostles, James the brother of John, and Peter, were in the Jewish capital; and it is probable that all the rest had not yet finally taken their departure. The Twelve, it would seem, did not set out on distant missions until they were thoroughly convinced that they had ceased to make progress in the conversion of their countrymen in the land of their fathers. And it is no trivial evidence, at once of the strength of their convictions, and of the truth of the evangelical history, that they continued so long and so efficiently to proclaim the gospel in the chief city of Palestine. Had they not acted under an overwhelming sense of duty, they would not have remained in a place where their lives were in perpetual jeopardy; and had they not been faithful witnesses, they could not have induced so many, of all classes of society, to believe statements which, if unfounded, could have been easily contradicted on the spot. The apostles must have been known to many in Jerusalem as the companions of our Lord; for, during His public ministry, they had often been seen with Him in the city and the temple; and it was to be, therefore, expected, that peculiar importance would be attached to their testimony respecting His doctrines and His miracles. Their preaching in the head-quarters of Judaism was fitted to exert an immense influence, as that metropolis itself contained a vast population, and as it was, besides, the resort of strangers from all parts of the world. And so long as the apostles ministered in Jerusalem or in Palestine only to the house of Israel, it was expedient that their number, which was an index of the Divine regard for the whole of the twelve tribes, should be maintained in its integrity. But when, after preaching twelve years among their countrymen at home, they found their labours becoming comparatively barren; and when, driven by persecution from Judea, they proceeded on distant missions, their position was quite altered. Their number had now at least partially [67:1] lost its original significance; and hence, when an apostle died, the survivors no longer deemed it necessary to take steps for the appointment of a successor. We find accordingly that when Herod "killed James, the brother of John, with the sword," [68:1] no other individual was selected to occupy the vacant apostleship.

It has been already stated that when Paul appeared in Jerusalem for the first time after his conversion, he received, when praying in the temple, a divine communication informing him of his mission to the heathen. [68:2] It would seem that, during his present visit, as the bearer of the contributions from

31

Antioch, he was favoured with another revelation. In his Second Epistle to the Corinthians he apparently refers to this most comfortable, yet mysterious, manifestation. "I know," [68:3] says he, "a man in Christ fourteen years ago [68:4] (whether in the body, I cannot tell, or whether out of the body, I cannot tell; God knoweth) such an one caught up to the third heaven. And I know such a man (whether in the body, or out of the body, I cannot tell; God knoweth) that he was caught up into paradise, and heard unspeakable words which it is not lawful for man to utter." [68:5] The present position of the apostle explains the design of this sublime and delightful vision. As Moses was encouraged to undertake the deliverance of his countrymen when God appeared to him in the burning bush, [68:6] and as Isaiah was emboldened to go forth, as the messenger of the Lord of hosts, when he saw Jehovah sitting upon His throne attended by the seraphim, [68:7] so Paul was stirred up by an equally impressive revelation to gird himself for the labours of a new appointment. He was about to commence a more extensive missionary career, and before entering upon so great and so perilous an undertaking, the King of kings condescended to encourage him by admitting him to a gracious audience, and by permitting him to enjoy some glimpses of the glory of those realms of light where "they that be wise shall shine as the brightness of the firmament, and they that turn many to righteousness as the stars for ever and ever."

CHAPTER V

THE ORDINATION OF PAUL AND BARNABAS; THEIR MISSIONARY TOUR IN ASIA MINOR; AND THE COUNCIL OF JERUSALEM
A.D. 44 TO A.D. 51

Soon after returning from Jerusalem to Antioch, Paul was formally invested with his new commission. His fellow-deputy, Barnabas, was appointed, as his coadjutor, in this important service. "Now," says the evangelist, "there were in the church that was at Antioch certain prophets and teachers, as Barnabas, and Simeon that was called Niger, and Lucius of Cyrene, and Manaen, which had been brought up with Herod the tetrarch, and Saul. As they ministered to the Lord and fasted, the Holy Ghost said—Separate me Barnabas and Saul for the work whereunto I have called them. And when they had fasted, and prayed, and laid their hands on them, they sent them away." [70:1]

Ten years had now elapsed since the conversion of Paul; and during the greater part of this period, he had been busily engaged in the dissemination of the gospel. In the days of his Judaism the learned Pharisee had, no doubt, been accustomed to act as a teacher in the synagogues, and, when he became obedient to the faith, he was permitted, as a matter of course, to expound his new theology in the Christian assemblies. Barnabas, his companion, was a Levite; [70:2] and as his tribe was specially charged with the duty of public instruction, [71:1] he too had probably been a preacher before his conversion. Both these men had been called of God to labour as evangelists, and the Head of the Church had already abundantly honoured their ministrations; but hitherto neither of them seems to have been clothed with pastoral authority by any regular ordination. Their constant presence in Antioch was now no longer necessary, so that they were thus left at liberty to prosecute their missionary operations in the great field of heathendom; and at this juncture it was deemed necessary to designate them, in due form, to their "ministry and apostleship." "The Holy Ghost said—Separate me Barnabas and Saul for the work whereunto I have called them." When we consider the present circumstances of these two brethren, we may see, not only why these instructions were given, but also why their observance has been so distinctly registered.

It is apparent that Barnabas and Saul were now called to a position of higher responsibility than that which they had previously occupied. They had heretofore acted simply as preachers of the Christian doctrine. Prompted by love to their common Master, and by a sense of individual obligation, they had endeavoured to diffuse all around them a knowledge of the Redeemer. They taught in the name of Jesus, just because they possessed the gifts and the graces required for such a service; and, as their labours were acknowledged of God, they were encouraged to persevere. But they were now to go forth as a solemn deputation, under the sanction of the Church, and not only to proclaim the truth, but also to baptize converts, to organise Christian congregations, and to ordain Christian ministers. It was, therefore, proper, that, on this occasion, they should be regularly invested with the ecclesiastical commission.

On other grounds it was desirable that the mission of Barnabas and Paul should be thus inaugurated. Though the apostles had been lately driven from Jerusalem, and though the Jews were exhibiting increasing aversion to the gospel, the Church was, notwithstanding, about to expand with extraordinary vigour by the ingathering of the Gentiles. In reference to these new members Paul and Barnabas pursued a bold and independent course, advocating views which many regarded as dangerous, latitudinarian, and profane; for they maintained that the ceremonial law was not binding on the converts from heathenism. Their adoption of this principle exposed them to much suspicion and obloquy; and because of the tenacity with which they persisted in its vindication, not a few were disposed to question their credentials as expositors of the Christian faith. It was, therefore, expedient that their right to perform all the apostolic functions should be placed above challenge. In some way, which is not particularly described, their appointment by the Spirit of God was accordingly made known to the Church at Antioch, and thus all the remaining prophets and teachers, who officiated there, were warranted to testify that these two brethren had received a call from heaven to engage in the work to which they were now designated. Their ordination, in obedience to this divine communication, was a decisive recognition of their spiritual authority. The Holy Ghost had attested their commission, and the ministers of Antioch, by the laying on of hands, set their seal to the truth of the oracle. Their title to act as founders of the Church was thus authenticated by evidence which could not be legitimately disputed. Paul himself obviously attached considerable importance to this transaction, and he afterwards refers to it in language of marked emphasis, when, in the beginning of the Epistle to the

Romans, he introduces himself as "a servant of Jesus Christ, called to be an apostle, separated unto the gospel of God." [71:1]

In the circumstantial record of this proceeding, to be found in the Acts of the Apostles, we have a proof of the wisdom of the Author of Revelation. He foresaw that the rite of "the laying on of hands" would be sadly abused; that it would be represented as possessing something like a magic potency; and that it would be at length converted, by a small class of ministers, into an ecclesiastical monopoly. He has, therefore, supplied us with an antidote against delusion by permitting us, in this simple narrative, to scan its exact import. And what was the virtue of the ordination here described? Did it furnish Paul and Barnabas with a title to the ministry? Not at all. God himself had already called them to the work, and they could receive no higher authorisation. Did it necessarily add anything to the eloquence, or the prudence, or the knowledge, or the piety, of the missionaries? No results of the kind could be produced by any such ceremony. What then was its meaning? The evangelist himself furnishes an answer. The Holy Ghost required that Barnabas and Saul should be separated to the work to which the Lord had called them, and the laying on of hands was the mode, or form, in which they were set apart, or designated, to the office. This rite, to an Israelite, suggested grave and hallowed associations. When a Jewish father invoked a benediction on any of his family, he laid his hand upon the head of the child; [73:1] when a Jewish priest devoted an animal in sacrifice, he laid his hand upon the head of the victim; [73:2] and when a Jewish ruler invested another with office, he laid his hand upon the head of the new functionary. [73:3] The ordination of these brethren possessed all this significance. By the laying on of hands the ministers of Antioch implored a blessing on Barnabas and Saul, and announced their separation, or dedication, to the work of the gospel, and intimated their investiture with ecclesiastical authority.

It is worthy of note that the parties who acted as ordainers were not dignitaries, planted here and there throughout the Church, and selected for this service on account of their official pre-eminence. They were all, at the time, connected with the Christian community assembling in the city which was the scene of the inauguration. It does not appear that any individual amongst them claimed the precedence; all engaged on equal terms in the performance of this interesting ceremony. We cannot mistake the official standing of these brethren if we only mark the nature of the duties in which they were ordinarily occupied. They were "prophets and teachers;" they were sound scriptural expositors; some of them, perhaps, were endowed with the gift of prophetic interpretation; and they were all employed in imparting theological instruction. Though the name is not here expressly given to them, they were, at least virtually, "the elders who laboured in the word and doctrine." [74:1] Paul, therefore, was ordained by the laying on of the hands of the Presbytery of Antioch. [74:2]

If the narrative of Luke was designed to illustrate the question of ministerial ordination, it plainly suggests that the power of Church rulers is very circumscribed. They have no right to refuse the laying on of hands to those whom God has called to the work of the gospel, and who, by their gifts and graces, give credible evidences of their holy vocation; and they are not at liberty to admit the irreligious or incompetent to ecclesiastical offices. In the sight of the Most High the ordination to the pastorate of an individual morally and mentally disqualified is invalid and impious.

Immediately after their ordination Paul and Barnabas entered on their

34

apostolic mission. Leaving Antioch they quickly reached Seleucia [75:1]—a city distant about twelve miles—and from thence passed on to Cyprus, [75:2] the native country of Barnabas. [75:3] They probably spent a considerable time in that large island. It contained several towns of note; it was the residence of great numbers of Jews; and the degraded state of its heathen inhabitants may be inferred from the fact that Venus was their tutelary goddess. The preaching of the apostles in this place appears to have created an immense sensation; their fame at length attracted the attention of persons of the highest distinction; and the heart of Paul was cheered by the accession of no less illustrious a convert than Sergius Paulus, [75:4] the Roman proconsul. Departing from Cyprus, Paul and Barnabas now set sail for Asia Minor, where they landed at Perga in Pamphylia. Here John Mark, the nephew of Barnabas, by whom they had been hitherto accompanied, refused to proceed further. He seems to have been intimidated by the prospect of accumulating difficulties. From many, on religious grounds, they had reason to anticipate a most discouraging reception; and the land journey now before them was otherwise beset with dangers. Whilst engaged in it, Paul seems to have experienced those "perils of waters," or of "rivers," [75:5] and "perils of robbers," which he afterwards mentions; for the highlands of Asia Minor were infested with banditti, and the mountain streams often rose with frightful rapidity, and swept away the unwary stranger. John Mark now returned to Jerusalem, and, at a subsequent period, we find Paul refusing, in consequence, to receive him as a travelling companion. [76:1] But though Barnabas was then dissatisfied because the apostle continued to be distrustful of his relative, and though "the contention was so sharp" between these two eminent heralds of the cross that "they departed asunder one from the other," [76:2] the return of this young minister from Perga appears to have led to no change in their present arrangements. Continuing their journey into the interior of the country, they now preached in Antioch of Pisidia, in Iconium, in "Lystra and Derbe, cities of Lycaonia," and in "the region that lieth round about." [76:3] When they had proceeded thus far, they began to retrace their steps, and again visited the places where they had previously succeeded in collecting congregations. They now supplied their converts with a settled ministry. When they had presided in every church at an appointment of elders, [76:4] in which the choice was determined by popular suffrage, [76:5] and when they had prayed with fasting, they laid their hands on the elected office-bearers, and in this form "commended them to the Lord on whom they believed." Having thus planted the gospel in many districts which had never before been trodden by the feet of a Christian missionary, they returned to Antioch in Syria to rehearse "all that God had done with them, and how he had opened the door of faith unto the Gentiles." [76:6]

Paul and Barnabas spent about six years in this first tour; [76:7] and, occasionally, when their ministrations were likely to exert a wide and permanent influence, remained long in particular localities. The account of their designation, and of their labours in Cyprus, Pamphylia, Lycaonia, and the surrounding regions, occupies two whole chapters of the Acts of the Apostles. The importance of their mission may be estimated from this lengthened notice. Christianity now greatly extended its base of operations, and shook paganism in some of its strongholds. In every place which they visited, the apostles observed a uniform plan of procedure. In the first instance, they made their appeal to the seed of Abraham; as they were themselves learned Israelites, they were generally permitted, on their arrival in a town, to set forth the claims of Jesus of Nazareth in the synagogue; and it was not until the Jews had exhibited a spirit of unbelief, that they turned to the heathen population. In the end, by far the majority of their converts were reclaimed idolaters. "The Gentiles were glad, and glorified the word of the Lord, and as many as were ordained to eternal life, believed." [77:1] Astonished at the mighty miracles exhibited by the two missionaries, the pagans imagined that "the gods" had come down to them "in the likeness of men;" and at Lystra the priest of Jupiter "brought oxen and garlands unto the gates, and would have done sacrifice with the people;" [77:2] but the Jews looked on in sullen incredulity, and kept alive an active and implacable opposition. At Cyprus, the apostles had to contend against the craft of a Jewish conjuror; [77:3] at Antioch, "the Jews stirred up the devout and honourable women, and the chief men of the city, and raised persecution" against them, "and expelled them out of their coasts;" [77:4] at Iconium, the Jews again "stirred up the Gentiles, and made their minds evil affected against the brethren;" [77:5] and at Lystra, the same parties "persuaded the people, and having stoned Paul, drew him out of the city, supposing he had been dead" [78:1] The trials through which he now passed seem to have made an indelible impression on the mind of the great apostle, and in the last of his epistles, written many years afterwards, he refers to them as among the most formidable he encountered in his perilous career. Timothy, who at this time must have been a mere boy, appears to have witnessed some of these ebullitions of Jewish malignity, and to have marked with admiration the heroic spirit of the heralds of the Cross. Paul, when about to be decapitated by the sword of Nero, could, therefore, appeal to the evangelist, and could fearlessly declare that, twenty years before, when his life was often at stake, he had not quailed before the terrors of martyrdom. "Thou," says he, "hast fully known my long-suffering, charity, patience, persecutions, afflictions, which came unto me at Antioch, at Iconium, at Lystra, what persecutions I endured, but, out of them all, the Lord delivered me." [78:2]

The hostile efforts of the Jews did not arrest the gospel in its triumphant career. The truth prevailed mightily among the Gentiles, and the great influx of converts began to impart an entirely new aspect to the Christian community. At first the Church consisted exclusively of Israelites by birth, and all who entered it still continued to observe the institutions of Moses. But it was now evident that the number of its Gentile adherents would soon very much preponderate, and that, ere long, the keeping of the typical law would become the peculiarity of a small minority of its members. Many of the converted Jews were by no means prepared for such an alternative. They prided themselves upon their divinely-instituted worship; and, misled by the fallacy that whatever is appointed by God can never become obsolete, they conceived that the spread of Christianity must be connected with the extension of their national ceremonies. They accordingly asserted that the commandment relative to the initiatory ordinance of Judaism was binding upon all admitted to Christian fellowship. "Certain men which came down from Judea" to Antioch, "taught the brethren, and said, Except ye be circumcised after the manner of Moses, ye cannot be saved." [79:1]

Paul was eminently qualified to deal with such errorists. There was a time when he had valued himself upon his Pharisaic strictness, but when God revealed to him His glory in the face of Jesus Christ, he was taught to distinguish between a living faith, and a dead formalism. He still maintained his social status, as one

36

of the "chosen people," by the keeping of the law; but he knew that it merely prefigured the great redemption, and that its types and shadows must quickly disappear before the light of the gospel. He saw, too, that the arguments urged for circumcision could also be employed in behalf of all the Levitical arrangements, [79:2] and that the tendency of the teaching of these "men which came down from Judea" was to encumber the disciples with the weight of a superannuated ritual. Nor was this all. The apostle was well aware that the spirit which animated those Judaising zealots was a spirit of self-righteousness. When they "taught the brethren and said, Except ye be circumcised after the manner of Moses, ye cannot be saved" they subverted the doctrine of justification by faith alone. [79:3] A sinner is saved as soon as he believes on the Lord Jesus Christ, [79:4] and he requires neither circumcision, nor any other ordinance, to complete his pardon. Baptism is, indeed, the sign by which believers solemnly declare their acceptance of the gospel, and the seal by which God is graciously pleased to recognise them as heirs of the righteousness of faith; and yet even baptism is not essential to salvation, for the penitent thief, though unbaptized, was admitted into paradise. [80:1] But circumcision is no part of Christianity at all; it does not so much as indicate that the individual who submits to it is a believer in Jesus. Faith in the Saviour is the only and the perfect way of justification. "Blessed are all they that put their trust in him," [80:2] for Christ will, without fail, conduct to glory all who commit themselves to His guidance and protection. Those who trust in Him cannot but love Him, and those who love Him cannot but delight to do His will; and as faith is the root of holiness and happiness, so unbelief is the fountain of sin and misery. But though the way of salvation by faith can only be spiritually discerned, many seek to make it palpable by connecting it with certain visible institutions. Faith looks to Jesus as the only way to heaven; superstition looks to some outward observance, such as baptism or circumcision, (which is only a finger-post on the way,) and confounds it with the way itself. Faith is satisfied with a very simple ritual; superstition wearies itself with the multiplicity of its minute observances. Faith holds communion with the Saviour in all His appointments, and rejoices in Him with joy unspeakable; superstition leans on forms and ceremonies, and is in bondage to these beggarly elements. No wonder then that the attempt to impose on the converted Gentiles the rites of both Christianity and Judaism encountered such resolute opposition. Paul and Barnabas at once withstood its abettors, and had "no small dissension and disputation with them." [80:3] It was felt, however, that a matter of such grave importance merited the consideration of the collective wisdom of the Church, and it was accordingly agreed to send these two brethren, "and certain other of them" "to Jerusalem unto the apostles and elders about this question." [81:1]

It is not stated that the Judaising teachers confined their interference to Antioch, and the subsequent narrative apparently indicates that the deputation to Jerusalem acted on behalf of all the Churches in Syria and Cilicia. [81:2] The Christian societies scattered throughout Pamphylia, Lycaonia, and some other districts of Asia Minor, do not seem to have been directly concerned in sending forward the commissioners; but as these communities had been collected and organised by Paul and Barnabas, they doubtless considered that they were represented by their founders, and they at once acceded to the decision of the assembly which met in the Jewish metropolis. [81:3] That assembly approached, perhaps, more closely than any ecclesiastical convention that has ever since been held, to the character of a general council. It is pretty clear that its deliberations must have taken place at the time of one of the great annual festivals, for, seven or eight years before, the apostles had commenced their travels as missionaries, and except about the season of the Passover or of Pentecost, the Syrian deputation could have scarcely reckoned on finding them in the holy city. It is not said that the officials who were to be consulted belonged exclusively to Jerusalem. [81:4] They, not improbably, included the elders throughout Palestine who usually repaired to the capital to celebrate the national solemnities. This meeting, therefore, seems to have been constructed on a broader basis than what a superficial reading of the narrative might suggest. Amongst its members were the older apostles, as well as Barnabas and Paul, so that it contained the principal founders of the Jewish and Gentile Churches: there were also present the elders of Jerusalem, and deputies from Antioch, that is, the representatives of the two most extensive and influential Christian societies in existence: whilst commissioners from the Churches of Syria and Cilicia, and elders from various districts of the holy land, were, perhaps, likewise in attendance. The Universal Church was thus fairly represented in this memorable Synod.

The meeting was held A.D. 51, and Paul, exactly fourteen years before, [82:1] had visited Jerusalem for the first time after his conversion. [82:2] So little was then known of his remarkable history, even in the chief city of Judea, that when he "assayed to join himself to the disciples, they were all afraid of him, and believed not that he was a disciple;" [82:3] but now his position was completely changed, and he was felt to be one of the most influential personages who took part in the proceedings of this important convention. Some have maintained that the whole multitude of believers in the Jewish capital deliberated and voted on the question in dispute, but there is certainly nothing in the statement of the evangelist to warrant such an inference. It is very evident that the disciples in the holy city were not prepared to approve unanimously of the decision which was actually adopted, for we are told that, long afterwards, they were "all zealous of the law," [83:1] and that they looked with extreme suspicion on Paul himself, because of the lax principles, in reference to its obligation, which he was understood to patronise. [83:2] When he arrived in Jerusalem on this mission he found there a party determined to insist on the circumcision of the converts from heathenism; [83:3] he complains of the opposition he now encountered from these "false brethren unawares brought in;" [83:4] and, when he returned to Antioch, he was followed by emissaries from the same bigoted and persevering faction. [83:5] It is quite clear, then, that the finding of the meeting, mentioned in the fifteenth chapter of the Acts, did not please all the members of the church of the metropolis. The apostle says expressly that he communicated "privately" on the subject with "them which were of reputation," [83:6] and in the present state of feeling, especially in the head-quarters of Judaism, Paul would have recoiled from the discussion of a question of such delicacy before a promiscuous congregation. The resolution now agreed upon, when subsequently mentioned, is set forth as the act, not of the whole body of the disciples, but of "the apostles and elders," [83:7] and as they were the arbiters to whom the appeal was made, they were obviously the only parties competent to pronounce a deliverance.

Two or three expressions of doubtful import, which occur in connexion with the history of the meeting, have induced some to infer that all the members of the Church of Jerusalem were consulted on this occasion. It is said that "all the multitude kept silence and gave audience to Barnabas and Paul"; [84:1] that it "pleased the apostles and elders with the whole church to send chosen men of their own company to Antioch:" [84:2] and, according to our current text, that the epistle, intrusted to the care of these commissioners, proceeded from "the apostles and elders and brethren." [84:3] But "the whole church," and "all the multitude," merely signify the whole assembly present, and do not necessarily imply even a very numerous congregation. [84:4] Some, at least, of the "certain other" deputies [84:5] sent with Paul and Barnabas to Jerusalem, were, in all likelihood, disposed to doubt or dispute their views; as it is not probable that a distracted constituency would have consented to the appointment of commissioners, all of whom were already committed to the same sentiments. When, therefore, the evangelist reports that the proposal made by James "pleased the apostles and elders with the whole Church," he thus designs to intimate that it met the universal approval of the meeting, including the deputies on both sides. There were prophets, and others possessed of extraordinary endowments, in the early Church, [84:6] and, as some of these were, no doubt, at this time in Jerusalem, [84:7] we can scarcely suppose that they were not permitted to be present in this deliberative assembly. If we adopt the received reading of the superscription of the circular letter, [84:8] the "brethren," who are there distinguished from "the apostles and elders," were, in all likelihood, these gifted members. [84:9] But, according to the testimony of the best and most ancient manuscripts, the true reading of the commencement of this encyclical epistle is, "The apostles and elders brethren." [85:1] As the Syrian deputies were commissioned to consult, not the general body of Christians at Jerusalem, but the apostles and elders, this reading, now recognised as genuine by the highest critical authorities, is sustained by the whole tenor of the narrative. The same parties who "came together to consider of this matter" also framed the decree. The apostles and elders brethren were the only individuals officially concerned in this important transaction. [85:2]

In this council the apostles acted, not as men oracularly pronouncing the will of the Eternal, but, as ordinary church rulers, proceeding, after careful inquiry, to adopt the suggestions of an enlightened judgment. One passage of the Synodical epistle has been supposed to countenance a different conclusion, for those assembled "to consider of this matter" are represented as saying to the Syrian and Cilician Churches—"It seemed good to the Holy Ghost and to us to lay upon you no greater burden" [85:3] than the restrictions which are presently enumerated. But it is to be observed that this is the language of "the elders brethren," as well as of the apostles, so that it must have been used by many who made no pretensions to inspiration; and it is apparent from the context that the council here merely reproduces an argument against the Judaizers which had been always felt to be irresistible. The Gentiles had received the Spirit "by the hearing of faith," [86:1] and not by the ordinance of circumcision; and hence it was contended that the Holy Ghost himself had decided the question. Peter, therefore, says to the meeting held at Jerusalem—"God, which knoweth the hearts, bare them witness, giving them the Holy Ghost, even as he did unto us; and put no difference between us and them, purifying their hearts by faith. Now, therefore, why tempt ye God, to put a yoke upon the neck of the disciples, which neither our fathers, nor we, were able to bear?" [86:2] He had employed the same reasoning long before, in defence of the baptism of Cornelius and his friends.

"The Holy Ghost," said he, "fell on them.... Forasmuch, then, as God gave them the like gift as he did unto us, who believed on the Lord Jesus Christ,—what was I that I could withstand God?" [86:3] When, then, the members of the council here declared, "It seemed good to the Holy Ghost and to us," [86:4] they thus simply intimated that they were shut up to the arrangement which they now announced—that God himself, by imparting His Spirit to those who had not received the rite of circumcision, had already settled the controversy—and that, as it had seemed good to the Holy Ghost not to impose the ceremonial law upon the Gentiles, so it also seemed good to "the apostles and elders brethren."

But whilst the abundant outpouring of the Spirit on the Gentiles demonstrated that they could be sanctified and saved without circumcision, and whilst the Most High had thus proclaimed their freedom from the yoke of the Jewish ritual, it is plain that, in regard to this point, as well as other matters noticed in the letter, the writers speak as the accredited interpreters of the will of Jehovah. They state that it seemed good to the Holy Ghost and to them to require the converts from paganism "to abstain from meats offered to idols, and from blood, and from things strangled, and from fornication." [87:1] And yet, without any special revelation, they might have felt themselves warranted to give such instructions in such language, for surely they were at liberty to say that the Holy Ghost had interdicted fornication; and, as the expounders of the doctrine of Christian expediency, [87:2] their views may have been so clear that they could speak with equal confidence as to the duty of the disciples under present circumstances to abstain from blood, and from things strangled, and from meats offered to idols. If they possessed "the full assurance of understanding" as to the course to be pursued, they doubtless deemed it right to signify to their correspondents that the decision which they now promulgated was, not any arbitrary or hasty deliverance, but the very "mind of the Spirit" either expressly communicated in the Word, or deduced from it by good and necessary inference. In this way they aimed to reach the conscience, and they knew that they thus furnished the most potential argument for submission.

It may at first sight appear strange that whilst the apostles, and those who acted with them at this meeting, condemned the doctrine of the Judaizers, and affirmed that circumcision was not obligatory on the Gentiles, they, at the same time, required the converts from paganism to observe a part of the Hebrew ritual; and it may seem quite as extraordinary that, in a letter which was the fruit of so much deliberation, they placed an immoral act, and a number of merely ceremonial usages, in the same catalogue. But, on mature reflection, we may recognise their tact and Christian prudence in these features of their communication. Fornication was one of the crying sins of Gentilism, and, except when it interfered with social arrangements, the heathen did not even acknowledge its criminality. When, therefore, the new converts were furnished with the welcome intelligence that they were not obliged to submit to the painful rite of circumcision, it was well, at the same time, to remind them that there were lusts of the flesh which they were bound to mortify; and it was expedient that, whilst a vice so prevalent as fornication should be specified, they should be distinctly warned to beware of its pollutions. For another reason they were directed to abstain from "meats offered to idols." It often happened that what had been presented at the shrine of a false god was afterwards exposed for sale, and the council cautioned the disciples against partaking of such food, as they might

40

thus appear to give a species of sanction to idolatry, as well as tempt weak brethren to go a step further, and directly countenance the superstitions of the heathen worship. [88:1] The meeting also instructed the faithful in Syria and Cilicia to abstain from "blood and from things strangled," because the Jewish converts had been accustomed from infancy to regard aliment of this description with abhorrence, and they could scarcely be expected to sit at meat with parties who partook of such dishes. Though the use of them was lawful, it was, at least for the present, not expedient; and on the same principle that, whether we eat, or drink, or whatever we do, we should do all to the glory of God, the Gentile converts were admonished to remove them from their tables, that no barrier might be raised up in the way of social or ecclesiastical communion with their brethren of the seed of Abraham.

It was high time for the authoritative settlement of a question at once so perplexing and so delicate. It already threatened to create a schism in the Church; and the agitation, which had commenced before the meeting of the council, was not immediately quieted. When Peter visited Antioch shortly afterwards, he at first triumphed so far over his prejudices as to sit at meat with the converts from paganism; but when certain sticklers for the law arrived from Jerusalem, "he withdrew, and separated himself, fearing them which were of the circumcision." [89:1] The "decree" of the apostles and elders undoubtedly implied the lawfulness of eating with the Gentiles, but it contained no express injunction on the subject, and Peter, who was now about to "go unto the circumcision," [89:2] and who was, therefore, most anxious to conciliate the Jews, may have pleaded this technical objection in defence of his inconsistency. It is said that others, from whom better things might have been expected, followed his example, "insomuch that Barnabas also was carried away with their dissimulation." [89:3] But, on this critical occasion, Paul stood firm; and his bold and energetic remonstrances appear to have had the effect of preventing a division which must have been most detrimental to the interests of infant Christianity.

CHAPTER VI

THE INTRODUCTION OF THE GOSPEL INTO EUROPE, AND THE MINISTRY OF PAUL AT PHILIPPI A.D. 52

After the Council of Jerusalem, the gospel continued its prosperous career. When Paul had remained for some time at Antioch, where he returned with the deputation, he set out to visit the Churches of Syria and Cilicia; and then travelled through Lycaonia, Galatia, and some other portions of Asia Minor. He was now directed, by a vision, [90:1] to pass over into Greece; and about the spring of A.D. 52, or twenty-one years after the crucifixion, Europe was entered, for the first time, by the Apostle of the Gentiles. Paul commenced his ministry in this new sphere of labour by announcing the great salvation to the inhabitants of Philippi, a city of Macedonia, and a Roman colony. [90:2]

Nearly a century before, two powerful factions, contending for the government of the Roman world, had converted the district now visited into a theatre of war; immense armies had been here drawn out in hostile array; and two famous battles, which issued in the overthrow of the Republic, had been fought in this very neighbourhood. The victor had rewarded some of his veterans by giving them possessions at Philippi. The Christian missionary entered, as it were, the suburbs of the great metropolis of the West, when he made his appearance in this military colony; for, it had the same privileges as the towns of Italy, [91:1] and its inhabitants enjoyed the status of Roman citizens. Here he now originated a spiritual revolution which eventually changed the face of Europe. The Jews had no synagogue in Philippi; but, in places such as this, where their numbers were few, they were wont, on the Sabbath, to meet for worship by the side of some river in which they could conveniently perform their ablutions; and Paul accordingly repaired to the banks of the Gangitas, [91:2] where he expected to find them assembled for devotional exercises. A small oratory, or house of prayer, seems to have been erected on the spot; but the little society connected with it must have been particularly apathetic, as the apostle found only a few females in attendance. One of these was, however, the first-fruits of his mission to the Western continent. Lydia, a native of Thyatira, and a seller of purple,—a species of dye for which her birthplace had acquired celebrity,—was the name of the convert; and though the gospel may already have made some progress in Rome, it must be admitted that, in as far as direct historical testimony is concerned, this woman has the best claim to be recognised as the mother of European Christianity. It is said that she "worshipped God," [91:3] that is, though a Gentile, she had been proselyted to the Jewish faith; and the history of her conversion is given by the evangelist with remarkable clearness and simplicity. "The Lord opened her heart that she attended unto the things that were spoken of Paul." [91:4] When she and her family were baptized, she entreated the missionaries to "come into her house and abide there" during their sojourn in the place; and, after some hesitation, they accepted the proffered hospitality.

Another female acts a conspicuous part in connexion with this apostolic visit. "It came to pass," says Luke, "as we went to prayer, a certain damsel possessed with a spirit of divination met us, which brought her masters much gain by soothsaying: the same followed Paul and us, and cried, saying, These men are the servants of the Most High God, which shew unto us the way of salvation. And this did she many days." [92:1] It is quite possible that even daemons have the power of discerning certain classes of future events with the quickness of intuition; [92:2] and if, as the Scriptures testify, they have sometimes entered into human bodies, we can well understand how the individuals thus possessed have obtained credit for divination. In this way the damsel mentioned by the evangelist may have acquired her celebrity. We cannot explain how disembodied spirits maintain intercourse; but it is certain that they possess means of mutual recognition, and that they can be impressed by the presence of higher and holier intelligences. And as the approach of a mighty conqueror spreads dismay throughout the territory he invades, so when the Son of God appeared on earth, the devils were troubled at His presence, and, in the agony of their terror, proclaimed His dignity. [92:3] It would appear that some influence of an analogous character operated on this Pythoness. The arrival of the missionaries in Philippi alarmed the powers of darkness, and the damsel, under the pressure

42

of an impulse which she found it impossible to resist, told their commission. But neither the apostles, nor our Lord, cared for credentials of such equivocal value. As this female followed the strangers through the streets, and in a loud voice announced their errand to the city, "Paul, being grieved, turned and said to the spirit, I command thee, in the name of Jesus Christ, to come out of her, and he came out the same hour." [93:1]

The unbelieving Jews had hitherto been the great persecutors of the Church; but now, for the first time, the apostles encountered opposition from another quarter; and the expulsion of the spirit from the damsel evoked the hostility of this new adversary. When the masters of the Pythoness "saw that the hope of their gains was gone, they caught Paul and Silas, and drew them into the marketplace unto the rulers." [93:2] We here discover one great cause of our Lord under the government of the pagan emperors. The Jews were prompted by mere bigotry to display hatred to the gospel—but the Gentiles were generally guided by the still more ignoble principle of selfishness. Many of the heathen multitude cared little for their idolatrous worship; but all who depended for subsistence on the prevalence of superstition, such as the image-makers, the jugglers, the fortune-tellers, and a considerable number of the priests, [93:3] were dismayed and driven to desperation by the progress of Christianity. They saw that, with its success, "the hope of their gains was gone;" and, under pretence of zeal for the public interest, and for the maintenance of the "lawful" ceremonies, they laboured to intimidate and oppress the adherents of the new doctrine.

The appearance of the missionaries at Philippi must have created a profound sensation, as otherwise it is impossible to account for the tumult which now occurred. The "masters" of the damsel possessed of the "spirit of divination," no doubt, took the initiatory step in the movement; but had not the public mind been in some degree prepared for their appeals, they could not have induced all classes of their fellow-citizens so soon to join in the persecution. "The multitude rose up together" at their call; the duumviri, or magistrates, rent off the clothes of the apostles with their own hands, and commanded them to be scourged; the lictors "laid many stripes upon them;" they wore ordered to be kept in close confinement; and the jailer exceeded the exact letter of his instructions by thrusting them "into the inner prison," and by making "their feet fast in the stocks." [94:1] The power of Imperial Rome arrayed itself against the preachers of the gospel, and now distinctly gave note of warning of the approach of that long night of affliction throughout which the church was yet to struggle.

If the proceedings of the missionaries, before their committal to prison, produced such a ferment, it is clear that the circumstances attending their incarceration were not calculated to abate the excitement. It soon appeared that they had sources of enjoyment which no human authority could either destroy or disturb; for as they lay in the pitchy darkness of their dungeon with their feet compressed in the stocks, their hearts overflowed with divine comfort. "At midnight Paul and Silas prayed, and sang praises unto God: and the prisoners heard them." [94:2] What must have been the wonder of the other inmates of the jail, as these sounds fell upon their ears! Instead of a cry of distress issuing from "the inner prison," there was the cheerful voice of thanksgiving! The apostles rejoiced that they were counted worthy to suffer in the service of Christ. The King of the Church sympathised with His oppressed saints, and speedily vouchsafed to them most wonderful tokens of encouragement. Scarcely had they finished their song of praise when it was answered by a very significant response, proclaiming that they were supported by a power which could crush the might of Rome. "Suddenly there was a great earthquake, so that the foundations of the prison were shaken, and immediately all the doors were opened, and every one's bands were loosed." [95:1]

It is not improbable that the mind of the jailer had already been ill at ease. He must have heard of the extraordinary history of the damsel with the spirit of divination who announced that his prisoners were the servants of the Most High God, and that they shewed unto men the way of salvation. Rumour had, perhaps, supplied him with some information in reference to their doctrines; and during even his short intercourse with Paul and Silas in the jail, he may have been impressed by much that he noticed in their spirit and deportment. But he had meanwhile gone to rest, and he remained asleep until roused by the noise and tremor of the earthquake. When he awoke and saw "the prison doors open," he was in a paroxysm of alarm; and concluding that the prisoners had escaped, and that he might expect to be punished, perhaps capitally, for neglect of duty, he resolved to anticipate such a fate, and snatched his sword to commit suicide. At this moment, a voice issuing from the dungeon where the missionaries were confined, at once dispelled his fears as to the prisoners, and arrested him almost in the very act of self-murder. "Paul cried with a loud voice, saying—Do thyself no harm, for we are all here." [95:2] These words operated on the unhappy man like a shock of electricity. They instantaneously directed his thoughts into another channel, and imparted intensity to feelings which, had hitherto been comparatively dormant. The conviction flashed upon his conscience that the men whom he had so recently thrust into the inner prison were no impostors; that they had, as they alleged, authority to treat of matters infinitely more important than any of the passing interests of time; that they had, verily, a commission from heaven to teach the way of eternal salvation; and that he and others, who had taken part in their imprisonment, had acted most iniquitously. For what now could be more evident than that the apostles were the servants of the Most High God? When everything around them was enveloped in the gloom of midnight, they seemed able to tell what was passing all over the prison. How strange that, when the jailer was about to kill himself, a voice should issue from a different apartment saying—Do thyself no harm! How strange that the very man whose feet, a few hours before, had boon made fast in the stocks, should now be the giver of this friendly counsel! How remarkable that, when all the doors were opened, no one attempted to escape! And how extraordinary that, during the very night on which the apostles were imprisoned, the bands of all the inmates were loosed, and that the building was made to rock to its foundations! Did not the earthquake indicate that He, whom the apostles served, was able to save and to destroy? Did it not proclaim, trumpet-tongued, that He would surely punish their persecutors? When the jailer thought on these things, well might he be paralysed with fear, and believing that the apostles alone could tell him how he was Lo obtain relief from the anxiety which oppressed his spirit, it is not strange that "he called for a light, and sprang in, and came trembling, and fell down before Paul and Silas, and brought them out, and said—Sirs, what must I do to be saved?" [96:1]

The missionaries were prepared with a decisive reply to this earnest inquiry, and it is probable that their answer took the jailer by surprise. He expected, perhaps, to be called upon to do something, either to propitiate the apostles .

44

themselves, or to turn away the wrath of the God of the apostles. It is obvious, from the spirit which he manifested, that, to obtain peace of conscience, he was ready to go very far in the way of self-sacrifice. He may have been willing to part with his property, or to imperil his life, or to give "the fruit of his body for the sin of his soul." What, then, must have been his astonishment when he found that the divine mercy so far transcended anything he could have possibly anticipated! With what satisfaction must he have listened to the assurance that an atonement had already been made, and that the sinner is safe as soon as he lays the hand of faith on the head of the great Sacrifice! What delight must he have experienced when informed that unbelief alone could shut him out from heaven; that the Son of God had died the just for the unjust; and that this almighty Saviour now waited to be gracious to-himself! How must the words of the apostles have thrilled through his soul, as he heard them repeating the invitation-"Believe on the Lord Jesus Christ, and thou shalt be saved, and thy house." [97:1]

The jailer joyfully accepted the proffered Deliverer; and felt that, resting on this Rock of Salvation, he was at peace. Though well aware that, by openly embracing the gospel, he exposed himself to considerable danger, he did not shrink from the position of a confessor. The love of Christ had obtained full possession of his soul, and he was quite prepared to suffer in the service of his Divine Master. He took Paul and Silas "the same hour of the night, and washed their stripes, and was baptized, he and all his, straightway; and when he had brought them into his house, he set meat before them, and rejoiced, believing in God with all his house." [98:1]

It is highly probable that the shock of the earthquake was felt beyond the precincts of the jail, and that the events which had occurred there had soon been communicated to the city authorities. We can thus best account for the fact that "when it was day, the magistrates sent the serjeants saying, Let those men go." [98:2] As it is not stated that the apostles had previously entered into any vindication of their conduct, it has been thought singular that they now declined to leave the prison without receiving an apology for the violation of their privileges as Roman citizens. But this matter presents no real difficulty. The magistrates had yielded to the clamour of an infuriated mob; and, instead of giving Paul and Silas a fair opportunity of defence or explanation, had summarily consigned them to the custody of the jailer. These functionaries now seemed prepared to listen to remonstrance; and Paid deemed it due to himself, and to the interests of the Christian Church, to complain of the illegal character of the proceedings from which he had suffered. He had been punished, without a trial, and scourged, though a Roman citizen. [98:3] Hence, when informed that the duumviri had given orders for the liberation of himself and his companion, the apostle exclaimed—"They have beaten us openly uncondemned, being Romans, and have cast us into prison, and now do they thrust us out privily? Nay, verily, but let them come themselves, and fetch us out." [98:4] These words, which were immediately reported by the serjeants, or lictors, inspired the magistrates with apprehension, and suggested to them the expediency of conciliation. "And they came" to the prison to the apostles, "and besought them, and brought them out, and desired them to depart out of the city." [99:1] The missionaries did not, however, leave Philippi until they had another opportunity of meeting with their converts. "They went out of the prison, and entered into the house of Lydia, and when they had seen the brethren, they comforted them and departed." [99:2]

45

On the whole Paul and Silas had reason to thank God and take courage, when they reviewed their progress in the first European city which they visited. Though they had met with much opposition, their ministry had been greatly blessed; and, in the end, the magistrates, who had treated them with much severity, had felt it necessary to apologise. The extraordinary circumstances accompanying their imprisonment must have made their case known to the whole body of the citizens, and thus secured a degree of attention to their preaching which could not have been otherwise expected. The Church, now established at Philippi, contained a number of most generous members, and Paul afterwards gratefully acknowledged the assistance he received from them. "Ye have well done," said he, "that ye did communicate with my affliction. Now, ye Philippians, know also, that in the beginning of the gospel, when I departed from Macedonia, no church communicated with me, as concerning giving and receiving, but ye only. For, even in Thessalonica, ye sent once and again unto my necessity." [99:3]

CHAPTER VII

THE MINISTRY OF PAUL IN THESSALONICA, BEREA, ATHENS, AND CORINTH
A.D. 52 TO A.D. 54

After leaving Philippi, and passing through Amphipolis and Apollonia, Paul made his way to Thessalonica. In this city there was a Jewish synagogue where he was permitted, for three successive Sabbaths, to address the congregation. His discourses produced a powerful impression; as some of the seed of Abraham believed, "and, of the devout Greeks, a great multitude, and of the chief women, not a few." [100:1] The unbelieving Jews attempted to create annoyance by representing the missionaries as acting "contrary to the decrees of Caesar, saying—that there is another king, one Jesus;" [100:2] but though they contrived to trouble "the rulers" [100:3] and to "set all the city in an uproar," they could not succeed in preventing the formation of a flourishing Christian community. Paul appeared next in Berea, and, when reporting his success here, the sacred historian bears a remarkable testimony to the right of the laity to judge for themselves as to the meaning of the Book of Inspiration; for he states that the Jews of this place "were more noble than those in Thessalonica, in that they received the word with all readiness of mind, and searched the scriptures daily" [101:1] to ascertain the truth of the apostolic doctrine. Paul now proceeded "to go as it were to the sea," and soon afterwards arrived at Athens.

The ancient capital of Attica had long been the literary metropolis of heathendom. Its citizens could boast that they were sprung from a race of heroes, as their forefathers had nobly struggled for freedom on many a bloody battlefield, and, by prodigies of valour, had maintained their independence against all the might of Persia. Minerva, the goddess of wisdom, was their tutelary deity. The Athenians, from time immemorial, had been noted for their intellectual elevation; and a brilliant array of poets, legislators, historians, philosophers, and orators, had crowned their community with immortal fame. Every spot connected with their city was classic ground. Here it was that Socrates had discoursed so sagely; and that Plato had illustrated, with so much felicity and genius, the precepts of his great master; and that Demosthenes, by addresses of unrivalled eloquence, had roused and agitated the assemblies of his countrymen. As the stranger passed through Athens, artistic productions of superior excellence everywhere met his eye. Its statues, its public monuments, and its temples, were models alike of tasteful design and of beautiful workmanship. But there may be much intellectual culture where there is no spiritual enlightenment, and Athens, though so far advanced in civilisation and refinement, was one of the high places of pagan superstition. Amidst the splendour of its architectural decorations, as well as surrounded with proofs of its scientific and literary eminence, the apostle mourned over its religious destitution, and "his spirit was stirred in him, when he saw the city wholly given to idolatry." [102:1]

On this new scene Paul exhibited his usual activity and earnestness. "He disputed in the synagogue with the Jews, and with the devout persons, and in the market daily with them that met with him." [102:2] The Christian preacher, doubtless, soon became an object of no little curiosity. He was of diminutive stature; [102:3] he seems to have laboured under the disadvantages of imperfect vision; [102:4] and his Palestinian Greek must have sounded harshly in the ears of those who were accustomed to speak their mother tongue in its Attic purity. But, though his "bodily presence was weak," [102:5] he speedily convinced those who came in contact with him, that the frail earthly tabernacle was the habitation of a master mind; and though mere connoisseurs in idioms and pronunciation might designate "his speech contemptible," [102:6] he riveted the attention of his hearers by the force and impressiveness of his oratory. The presence of this extraordinary stranger could not remain long unknown to the Athenian literati; but, when they entered into conversation with him, some of them were disposed to ridicule him as an idle talker, whilst others seemed inclined to denounce him as a dangerous innovator. "Certain philosophers of the Epicureans and of the Stoics encountered him; and some said—What will this babbler say? other some—He seemeth to be a setter forth of strange gods, because he preached unto them Jesus and the resurrection." [102:7] Upwards of four hundred years before, Socrates had been condemned to death by the Athenians as "a setter forth of strange gods," [103:1] and it may be that some of these philosophers hoped to intimidate the apostle by hinting that he was now open to the same indictment. But it is very improbable that they seriously contemplated a prosecution; as they had themselves no faith in the pagan mythology. They were quite ready to employ their wit to turn the heathen worship into scorn; and yet they could point out no "more excellent way" of religious service. In Athens, philosophy had demonstrated its utter impotence to do anything effective for the reformation of the popular theology; and its professors had settled down into the conviction that, as the current superstition exercised an immense influence over the minds of the multitude it was inexpedient for wise men to withhold from it the tribute of outward reverence. The discourses of Paul were very far from complimentary to parties who valued themselves so highly on their intellectual advancement; for he

47

quietly ignored all their speculations as so much folly; and, whilst he propounded his own system with the utmost confidence, he, at the same time, supported it by arguments which they were determined to reject, but unable to overturn. It is pretty clear that they were to some extent under the influence of pique and irritation when they noticed his deviations from the established faith, and applied to him the epithet of "babbler;" but Paul was not the man to be put down either by irony or insult; and at length it was found necessary to allow him a fair opportunity of explaining his principles. It is accordingly stated that "they took him and brought him unto Mars Hill saying—May we know what this new doctrine, whereof thou speakest, is, for thou bringest certain strange things to our ears—we would know, therefore, what these things mean." [103:2]

The speech delivered by Paul on this memorable occasion has been often admired for its tact, vigour, depth, and fidelity. Whilst giving the Athenians full credit for their devotional feeling, and avoiding any pointed and sarcastic attack on the absurdities of their religious ritual, he contrives to present such an outline of the prominent features of the Christian revelation, as might have convinced any candid and intelligent auditor of its incomparable superiority, as well to the doctrines of the philosophers, as to the fables of heathenism. In the very commencement of his observations he displays no little address. "Ye men of Athens," said he, "I perceive that, in every point of view, ye are carrying your religious reverence very far; for, as I passed by, and observed the objects of your worship, I found an altar with this inscription—To the unknown God—whom, therefore, ye worship, though ye know him not, him declare I unto you." [104:1] The existence in this city of inscriptions, such as that here given, is attested by several other ancient witnesses [104:2] as well as Paul, and the altars thus distinguished appear to have been erected when the place was afflicted by certain strange and unprecedented calamities which the deities, already recognised, were supposed to be unable to remove. The auditors of the apostle could not well be dissatisfied with the statement that they carried their "religious reverence very far;" and yet, perhaps, they were scarcely prepared for the reference to this altar by which the observation was illustrated; for the inscription which he quoted contained a most humiliating confession of their ignorance, and furnished him with an excellent apology for proposing to act as their theological instructor.

His discourse, which treats of the Being and Attributes of God, must have been heard with no ordinary interest by the polite and intelligent Athenians. Its reasoning is plain, pertinent, and powerful; and whilst adopting a didactic tone, and avoiding the language and spirit of controversy, the apostle, in every sentence, comes into direct collision, either with the errors of polytheism, or the dogmas of the Grecian philosophy. The Stoics were Pantheists, and held the doctrine of the eternity of matter; [105:1] whilst the Epicureans maintained that the universe arose out of a fortuitous concurrence of atoms; [105:2] and therefore Paul announced his opposition to both these sects when he declared that "God made the world and all things therein." [105:3] The Athenians boasted that they were of nobler descent than the rest of their countrymen; [105:4] and the heathen generally believed that each nation belonged to a distinct stock and was under the guardianship of its own peculiar deities; but the apostle affirmed that "God hath made of one blood all nations of men to dwell on all the face of the earth." [105:5] The Epicureans asserted that the gods did not interfere in the concerns of the human family, and that they were destitute of foreknowledge; but Paul here assured them that the great Creator "giveth to all life and breath and all things," and "hath determined the times before appointed, and the bounds of their habitation." [105:6] The heathen imagined that the gods inhabited their images; but whilst Paul was ready to acknowledge the excellence, as works of art, of the statues which he saw all around him, he at the same time distinctly intimated that these dead pieces of material mechanism could never even faintly represent the glory of the invisible First Cause, and that they were unworthy the homage of living and intellectual beings. "As we are the offspring of God," said he, "we ought not to think that the Godhead is like unto gold, or silver, or stone, graven by art and man's device." [106:1] After having thus borne testimony to the spirituality of the I am that I am, and asserted His authority as the Maker and Preserver of the world, Paul proceeded to point out his claims as its righteous Governor. "He hath appointed a day, in the which he will judge the world in righteousness by that man whom he hath ordained, whereof he hath given assurance unto all men in that he hath raised him from the dead." [106:2] The pleasure-loving Epicureans refused to believe in a future state of rewards and punishments; and concurred with the Stoics in denying the immortality of the soul. [106:3] Both these parties were, of course, prepared to reject the doctrine of a general judgment. The idea of the resurrection of the body was quite novel to almost all classes of the Gentiles; and, when at first propounded to the Athenians, was received, by many, with doubt, and by some, with ridicule. "When they heard of the resurrection of the dead, some mocked, and others said, We will hear thee again of this matter. So Paul departed from among them." [106:4]

The frivolous spirit cherished by the citizens of the ancient capital of Attica was exceedingly unfavourable to the progress of the earnest faith of Christianity. "All the Athenians, and strangers which were there, spent their time in nothing else but either to tell or to hear some new thing." [106:5] Though they had acquired a world-wide reputation for literary culture, it is an instructive fact that their city continued for several centuries afterwards to be one of the strongholds of Gentile superstition. But the labours of Paul at this time were not entirely unproductive. "Certain men clave unto him and believed, among the which was Dionysius, the Areopagite, and a woman, named Damaris, and others with them." [107:1] The court of Areopagus, long the highest judicial tribunal in the place, had not even yet entirely lost its celebrity; and the circumstance that Dionysius was connected with it, is a proof that this Christian convert must have been a respectable and influential citizen. He appears to have occupied a very high place among the primitive disciples; and the number of spurious writings ascribed to him [107:2] shew that his name was deemed a tower of strength to the cause with which it was associated. He seems to have been long at the head of the Athenian presbytery; and to have survived his conversion about forty years, or until the time of the Domitian persecution. [107:3]

From Athens Paul directed his steps to Corinth, where he appears to have arrived in the autumn of A.D. 52. Nearly two hundred years before, this city had been completely destroyed; but, after a century of desolation, it had been rebuilt; and having since rapidly increased, it was now flourishing and populous. As a place of trade, its position, near an isthmus of the same name, gave it immense advantages; for it had a harbour on each side, so that it was the central depôt of the commerce of the East and West. Its inhabitants valued themselves much upon their attainments in philosophy and general literature; but, whilst, by

49

traffic, they had succeeded in acquiring wealth, they had given way to the temptations of luxury and licentiousness. Corinth was, in fact, at this time one of the most dissolute cities of the Empire. It was the capital of the large province of Achaia, and the residence of the Roman proconsul.

When Paul was at Athens he was led to adapt his style of instruction to the character of his auditors, and he was thus obliged to occupy much of his time in discussing the principles of natural religion. He endeavoured to gain over the citizens by shewing them that their views of the Godhead could not stand the test of a vigorous and discriminating logic, and that Christianity alone rested on a sound philosophical foundation. But the exposition of a pure system of theism had comparatively little influence on the hearts and consciences of these system-builders. Considering the time and skill devoted to its culture, Athens had yielded perhaps less spiritual fruit than any field of labour on which he had yet operated. When he arrived in Corinth he resolved, therefore, to avoid, as much as possible, mere metaphysical argumentation, and he sought rather to stir up sinners to flee from the wrath to come by pressing home upon them earnestly the peculiar doctrines of revelation. In the first epistle, addressed subsequently to the Church now established in this place, he thus describes the spirit in which he conducted his apostolical ministrations. "And I, brethren," says he, "when I came to you, came not with excellency of speech or of wisdom, declaring unto you the testimony of God—for I determined not to know anything among you save Jesus Christ and Him crucified; and my speech and my preaching was, not with enticing words of man's wisdom, but in demonstration of the Spirit and of power—that your faith should not stand in the wisdom of men, but in the power of God." [108:1]

The result demonstrated that the apostle thus pursued the most effective mode of advancing the Christian cause. It might, indeed, have been thought that Corinth was a very ungenial soil for the gospel, as Venus was the favourite deity of the place; and a thousand priestesses, or, in other words, a thousand prostitutes, were employed in the celebration of her orgies. [109:1] The inhabitants generally were sunk in the very depths of moral pollution. But the preaching of the Cross produced a powerful impression even in this hotbed of iniquity. Notwithstanding the enmity of the Jews, who "opposed themselves and blasphemed," [109:2] Paul succeeded in collecting here a large and prosperous congregation. "Many of the Corinthians hearing, believed, and were baptized." [109:3] Most of the converts were in very humble circumstances, and hence the apostle says to them in his first epistle—"Ye see your calling, brethren, how that not many wise men after the flesh, not many mighty, not many noble are called;" [109:4] but still a few persons of distinction united themselves to the despised community. Thus, it appears [109:5] that Erastus, the chamberlain, or treasurer, of the city, was among the disciples. It may be that this civic functionary joined the Church at a somewhat later date; but, even now, Paul was encouraged by the accession of some remarkable converts. Of these, perhaps, the most conspicuous was Crispus, "the chief ruler of the synagogue," who, "with all his house," submitted to baptism. [109:6] About the same time Gaius, who seems to have been an opulent citizen, and who rendered good service to the common cause by his Christian hospitality, [109:7] openly embraced the gospel. Two other converts, who are often honourably mentioned in the New Testament, were now likewise added to the infant Church. These were Aquila and Priscilla. [109:8]

50

Some have, indeed, supposed that this couple had been already baptized; but, on the arrival of Paul in Corinth, Aquila is represented as a Jew [110:1]—a designation which would not have been descriptive of his position had he been previously a believer—and we must therefore infer that the conversion of himself and his excellent partner occurred at this period.

In this city, as well as in many other places, the apostle supported himself by the labour of his own hands. It was now customary, even for Israelites in easy circumstances, to train up their children to some mechanical employment, so that should they sink into penury, they could still, by manual industry, procure a livelihood. [110:2] Paul had been taught the trade of a tent-maker, or manufacturer of awnings of hair-cloth—articles much used in the East as a protection against the rays of the sun, by travellers and mariners; It was in connexion with this occupation that lie became acquainted with Aquila and Priscilla. "Because he was of the same craft, he abode with them, and wrought." [110:3] The Jew and his wife had probably a large manufactory, and thus they could furnish the apostle with remunerative employment. Whilst under their roof, he did not neglect the opportunities he enjoyed of presenting the gospel to their attention, and both soon became his ardent and energetic coadjutors in missionary service.

The conduct of Paul in working with his own hands, whilst engaged in the dissemination of the gospel, is a noble example of Christian self-denial. He could, it appears, expect little assistance from the mother church of Antioch; and had he, in the first instance, demanded support from those to whom he now ministered, he would have exposed himself and his cause to the utmost suspicion. In a commercial city, such as Corinth, he would have been regarded by many as a mere adventurer who had resorted to a new species of speculation in the hope of obtaining a maintenance. His disinterested behaviour placed him at once beyond the reach of this imputation; and his intense love to Christ prepared him to make the sacrifice, which the course he thus adopted, required. And what a proof of the humility of Paul that he cheerfully laboured for his daily bread at the trade of a tent-maker! The Rabbi who was once admired for his genius and his learning by the most distinguished of his countrymen—who had once sat among the members of the great Sanhedrim—and who might have legitimately aspired to be the son-in-law of the High Priest of Israel [111:1]—was now content to toil "night and day" at a menial occupation sitting among the workmen of Aquila and Priscilla! How like to Him, who, though He was rich, yet, for our sakes, became poor, that we, through His poverty, might be rich!

Paul was well aware of the importance of Corinth as a centre of missionary influence. Strangers from the East passed through it on their way to Rome, and travellers from the Western metropolis stopped here on their way to Asia Minor, Palestine, or Syria, so that it was one of the greatest thoroughfares in the Empire; and, as a commercial mart, it was second to very few cities in the world. The apostle therefore saw that if a Church could be firmly planted in this busy capital, it could scatter the seeds of truth to all the ends of the earth. We may thus understand why he remained in Corinth so much longer than in any other place he had yet visited since his departure from Antioch. "He continued there a year and six months teaching the Word of God among them." [111:2] He was, too, encouraged by a special communication from Heaven to prosecute his labours with zeal and diligence. "The Lord spake to Paul in the night by a vision—Be not

51

afraid, but speak, and hold not thy peace—for I am with thee, and no man shall set on thee to hurt thee, for I have much people in this city." [112:1] Though the ministry of the apostle was now attended with such remarkable success, his converts did not all continue to walk worthy of their profession. But if in the Church of this flourishing mercantile metropolis there were greater disorders than in perhaps any other of the early Christian communities, [112:2] the explanation is obvious. Even in a degenerate age Corinth was notorious for its profligacy; and it would have been indeed marvellous if excesses had not been occasionally committed by some of the members of a religious society composed, to a considerable extent, of reclaimed libertines. [112:3]

The success of the gospel in Corinth roused the unbelieving Jews to opposition; and here, as elsewhere, they endeavoured to avail themselves of the aid of the civil power; but, in this instance, their appeal to the Roman magistrate was signally unsuccessful. Gallio, brother of the celebrated Seneca the philosopher, was now "the deputy of Achaia;" [112:4] and when the bigoted and incensed Israelites "made insurrection with one accord against Paul, and brought him to the judgment-seat, saying—This fellow persuaded men to worship God contrary to the law," [112:5] the proconsul turned a deaf ear to the accusation. When the apostle was about to enter on his defence, Gallio intimated that such a proceeding was quite unnecessary, as the affair did not come within the range of his jurisdiction. "If," said he, "it were a matter of wrong, or wicked lewdness, O ye Jews, reason would that I should bear with you; but if it be a question of words and names and of your law, look ye to it, for I will be no judge of such matters. And he drive them from the judgment-seat." [113:1] On this occasion, for the first time since the arrival of Paul and his brethren in Europe, the mob was on the side of the missionaries, and under the very eye of the proconsul, and without any effort on his part to interfere and arrest their violence, the most prominent of the plaintiffs was somewhat roughly handled. "Then all the Greeks took Smoothens, the chief ruler of the synagogue, and beat him before the judgment-seat. And Gallio cared for none of these things." [113:2]

When Paul was at Corinth, and probably in A.D. 53, he wrote his two earliest letters, that is, the First and Second Epistles to the Thessalonians. These communications must, therefore, have been drawn up about twelve months after the original formation of the religious community to which they are addressed. The Thessalonian Church was already fully organised, as the apostle here points out to the disciples their duties to those who laboured among them and who were over them in the Lord. [113:3] In the meantime several errors had gained currency; and a letter, announcing that the day of Christ was at hand, and purporting to have been penned by Paul himself, had thrown the brethren into great consternation. [113:4] The apostle accordingly deemed it necessary to interpose, and to point out the dangerous character of the doctrines which had been so industriously promulgated. He now, too, delivered his famous prophecy announcing the revelation of the "Man of Sin" before the second coming of the Redeemer. [113:5] Almost all the members of the Thessalonian Church were probably converted Gentiles, [113:6] who must still have been but little acquainted with the Jewish Scriptures; and this is perhaps the reason why there is no quotation from the Old Testament in either of these letters. Even the Gospels do not seem to have been yet written, and hence Paul exhorts the brethren "to hold fast the traditions," or rather "ordinances," [114:1] which they had been taught, "whether by word or his epistle." [114:2]

CHAPTER VIII

THE CONVERSION OF APOLLOS, HIS CHARACTER, AND THE MINISTRY OF PAUL IN EPHESUS
A.D. 54 TO A.D. 57

The Apostle "took his leave" [115:1] of the Corinthian brethren in the spring of A.D. 54, and embarking at the port of Cenchrea, about eight or nine miles distant, set sail for Ephesus. The navigation among the islands of the Greek Archipelago was somewhat intricate; and the voyage appears to have not unfrequently occupied from ten to fifteen days. [115:2] At Ephesus Paul "entered into the synagogue, and reasoned with the Jews." [115:3] His statements produced a favourable impression, and he was solicited to prolong his visit; but as he was on his way to Jerusalem, where he was anxious to be present at the approaching feast of Pentecost, he could only assure them of his intention to return, and then bid them farewell. He left behind him, however, in this great city his two Corinthian converts, Aquila and Priscilla, who carried on with industry and success the work which he had commenced so auspiciously. Among the first fruits of their pious care for the spread of Christianity was the famous Apollos, an Alexandrian Jew, who now arrived in the metropolis of the Proconsular Asia.

The seed of Abraham in the birthplace of Apollos spoke the Greek language, and were in somewhat peculiar circumstances. They were free from some of the prejudices of the Jews in Palestine; and, though living in the midst of a heathen population, had advantages which were enjoyed by very few of their brethren scattered elsewhere among the Gentiles. At Alexandria their sumptuous synagogues were unequivocal evidences of their wealth; they constituted a large and influential section of the inhabitants; they had much political power; and, whilst their study of the Greek philosophy had modified their habits of thought, they had acquired a taste for the cultivation of eloquence and literature. Apollos, the Jew "born at Alexandria," [116:1] who now became acquainted with Aquila and Priscilla, was an educated and accomplished man. It is said that "he was instructed in the way of the Lord, and being fervent in the spirit, he spake and taught diligently the things of the Lord, knowing only the baptism of John." [116:2] The influence of the preaching of the Baptist may be estimated from this incidental notice; for though the forerunner of our Saviour had now finished his career about a quarter of a century, the Alexandrian Jew was only one of many still living witnesses to testify that he had not ministered in vain. In this case John had indeed "prepared the way" of his Master, as, under the tuition of Aquila and Priscilla, Apollos was led without difficulty to embrace the Christian doctrine. It is said of this pious couple that "they took him unto them, and expounded unto him the way of God more perfectly." [116:3] Priscilla was no less distinguished than her husband [116:4] for intelligence and zeal; and though she was prevented, as much, perhaps, by her native modesty, as by the constitution of the Church, [116:5] from officiating as a public instructor, she was, no doubt, "apt to teach;" and there must have been something most interesting and impressive in her private conversation. It is a remarkable fact that one of the ablest preachers of the apostolic age was largely indebted to a female for his acquaintance with Christian theology.

53

The accession, at this juncture, of such a convert as Apollos was of great importance to the evangelical cause. The Church of Corinth, in the absence of Paul, much required the services of a minister of superior ability; and the learned Alexandrian was eminently qualified to promote its edification. He was "an eloquent man, and mighty in the Scriptures." [117:1] After sojourning some time at Ephesus, it seems to have occurred to him that he would have a more extensive sphere of usefulness at Corinth; and "when he was disposed to pass into Achaia, the brethren wrote exhorting the disciples to receive him." [117:2] It soon appeared that his friends in Asia had formed no exaggerated idea of his gifts and acquirements. When he reached the Greek capital, he "helped them much which had believed through grace; for he mightily convinced the Jews, and that publicly, shewing by the Scriptures that Jesus was Christ." [117:3] His surpassing rhetorical ability soon proved a snare to some of the hypercritical Corinthians, and tempted them to institute invidious comparisons between him and their great apostle. Hence in the first epistle addressed to them, the writer finds it necessary to rebuke them for their folly and fastidiousness. "While one saith, I am of Paul, and another, I am of Apollos, are ye," says he, "not carnal? Who then is Paul, and who is Apollos, but ministers by whom ye believed, even as the Lord gave to every man? I have planted, Apollos watered, but God gave the increase." [117:4]

When Aquila and Priscilla were at Ephesus expounding "the way of God more perfectly" to the Jew of Alexandria, Paul was travelling to Jerusalem. Three years before, he had been there to confer with the apostles and elders concerning the circumcision of the Gentiles; and he had not since visited the holy city. His present stay seems to have been short—apparently not extending beyond a few days at the time of the feast of Pentecost,—and giving him a very brief opportunity of intercourse with his brethren of the Jewish capital. He then "went down to Antioch" [118:1]—a place with which from the commencement of his missionary career he had been more intimately associated. "After he had spent some time there, he departed and went over all the country of Galatia and Phrygia in order, strengthening all the disciples." [118:2] On a former occasion, after he had passed through the same districts, he had been "forbidden of the Holy Ghost to preach the word in (the Proconsular) Asia;" [118:3] but, at this time, the restriction was removed, and in accordance with the promise made to the Jews at Ephesus in the preceding spring, he now resumed his evangelical labours in that far-famed metropolis. There must have been a strong disposition on the part of many of the seed of Abraham in the place to attend to his instructions, as he was permitted "for the space of three months" to occupy the synagogue, "disputing and persuading the things concerning the kingdom of God." [118:4] At length, however, he began to meet with so much opposition that he found it expedient to discontinue his addresses in the Jewish meeting-house. "When divers were hardened and believed not, but spake evil of that way before the multitude, he departed from them, and separated the disciples, disputing daily in the school of one Tyrannus." [118:5] This Tyrannus was, in all probability, a Gentile convert, and a teacher of rhetoric—a department of education very much cultivated at that period by all youths anxious to attain social distinction. What is here called his "school," appears to have been a spacious lecture-room sufficient to accommodate a numerous auditory.

About this time the Epistle to the Galatians was, in all likelihood, written.

The Galatians, as their name indicated, were the descendants of a colony of Gaols settled in Asia Minor several centuries before; and, like the French of the present day, seem to have been distinguished by their lively and mercurial temperament. Paul had recently visited their country for the second time, [119:1] and had been received by them with the warmest demonstrations of regard; but meanwhile Humanizing zealots had appeared among them, and had been only too successful in their efforts to induce them to observe the Mosaic ceremonies. The apostle, at Antioch, and at the synod of Jerusalem, had already protested against these attempts; and subsequent reflection had only more thoroughly convinced him of their danger. Hence he here addresses the Galatians in terms of unusual severity. "I marvel," he exclaims, "that ye are so soon removed from him that called you into the grace of Christ unto another gospel"—"O foolish Galatians, who hath bewitched you that ye should not obey the truth, before whose eyes Jesus Christ hath been evidently set forth, crucified among you!" [119:2] At the same time he proves that the sinner is saved by faith alone; that the Mosaic institutions were designed merely for the childhood of the Church; and that the disciples of Jesus should refuse to be "entangled" with any such "yoke of bondage." [120:1] His epistle throughout is a most emphatic testimony to the doctrine of a free justification.

Some time after Paul reached Ephesus, on his return from Jerusalem, he appears to have made a short visit to Corinth. [120:2] There is no doubt that he encountered a variety of dangers of which no record is to be found in the Acts of the Apostles; [120:3] and it is most probable that many of these disasters were experienced about this period. Thus, not long after this date, he says—"Thrice I suffered shipwreck, a night and a day I have been in the deep." [120:4] There are good grounds for believing that he now visited Crete, as well as Corinth; and it would seem that these voyages exposed him to the "perils in the sea" which he enumerates among his trials. [120:5] On his departure from Crete he left Titus behind him to "set in order the things that were wanting, and to ordain elders in every city;" [120:6] and in the spring of A.D. 57 he wrote to the evangelist that brief epistle in which he points out, with so much fidelity and wisdom, the duties of the pastoral office. [120:7] The silence of Luke respecting this visit to Crete is the less remarkable, as the name of Titus does not once occur in the book of the Acts, though there is distinct evidence that he was deeply interested in some of the most important transactions which are there narrated. [120:8]

Paul, about two years before, had been prevented, as has been stated, by a divine intimation, from preaching in the district called Asia; but when he now commenced his ministrations in Ephesus, its capital, he continued in that city and its neighbourhood longer than in any other place he had yet visited. After withdrawing from the synagogue and resuming his labours in the school of Tyrannus, he remained there "by the space of two years; so that all they which dwelt in Asia heard the word of the Lord Jesus, both Jews and Greeks." [121:1] Meanwhile the churches of Laodicea, Colosse, and Hierapolis appear to have been founded. [121:2] The importance of Ephesus gave it a special claim to the attention which it now received. It was the metropolis of the district, and the greatest commercial city in the whole of Asia Minor. Whilst it was connected by convenient roads with all parts of the interior, it was visited by trading vessels from the various harbours of the Mediterranean. But, in another point of view, it was a peculiarly interesting field of missionary labour; for it was, perhaps, the most celebrated of all the high places of Eastern superstition. Its temple of Artemis, or Diana, was one of the wonders of the world. This gorgeous structure, covering an area of upwards of two acres, [121:3] was ornamented with columns one hundred and twenty-seven in number, each sixty feet high, and each the gift of a king. [121:4] It was nearly all open to the sky, but that part of it which was covered, was roofed with cedar. The image of the goddess occupied a comparatively small apartment within the magnificent enclosure. This image, which was said to have fallen down from Jupiter, [121:5] was not like one of those pieces of beautiful sculpture which adorned the Acropolis of Athens, but rather resembled an Indian idol, being an unsightly female form with many breasts, made of wood, and terminating below in a shapeless block. [122:1] On several parts of it were engraved mysterious symbols, called "Ephesian letters." [122:2] These letters, when pronounced, were believed to operate as charms, and, when written, were carried about as amulets. To those who sought an acquaintance with the Ephesian magic, they constituted an elaborate study, and many books were composed to expound their significance, and point out their application.

About this time the famous Apollonius of Tyana [122:3] was attracting uncommon attention by his tricks as a conjuror; and it has been thought not improbable that he now met Paul in Ephesus. If so, we can assign at least one reason why the apostle was prevented from making his appearance at an earlier date in the Asiatic metropolis. Men had thus an opportunity of comparing the wonders of the greatest of magicians with the miracles of the gospel; and of marking the contrast between the vainglory of an impostor, and the humility of a servant of Jesus. The attentive reader of Scripture may observe that some of the most extraordinary of the mighty works recorded in the New Testament were performed at this period; and it is not unreasonable to conclude that, in a city so much given to jugglery and superstition, these genuine displays of the power of Omnipotence were exhibited for the express purpose of demonstrating the incomparable superiority of the Author of Christianity. It is said that "God wrought special miracles by the hands of Paul, so that from his body were brought unto the sick handkerchiefs or aprons, and the diseases departed from them, and the evil spirits went out of them." [123:1] The disastrous consequences of an attempt, on the part of the sons of a Jewish priest, to heal the afflicted by using the name of the Lord Jesus as a charm, alarmed the entire tribe of exorcists and magicians. "The man, in whom the evil spirit was, leaped on them, and overcame them, and prevailed against them, so that they fled out of that house naked and wounded. And this was known to all the Jews and Greeks also dwelling at Ephesus, and fear fell on them all, and the name of the Lord Jesus was magnified." [123:2] The visit of Paul told upon the whole population, and tended greatly to discourage the study of the "Ephesian letters". "Many of them also which used curious arts brought their books together and burned them before all men; and they counted the price of them, and found it fifty thousand pieces of silver. [123:3] So mightily grew the word of God and prevailed." [123:4]

Some time before the departure of Paul from Ephesus, he wrote the First Epistle to the Corinthians. The letter contains internal evidence that it was dictated in the spring of A.D. 57. [123:5] The circumstances of the Corinthian disciples at this juncture imperatively required the interference of the apostle. Divisions had sprung up in their community; [123:6] the flagrant conduct of one member had brought dishonour on the whole Christian name; [123:7] and various forms of error had been making their appearance. [123:8] Paul therefore felt it right to address to them a lengthened and energetic remonstrance. This letter is more diversified in its contents than any of his other epistles; and presents us with a most interesting view of the daily life of the primitive Christians in a great commercial city. It furnishes conclusive evidence that the Apostolic Church of Corinth was not the paragon of excellence which the ardent and unreflecting have often pictured in their imaginations, but a community compassed with infirmities, and certainly not elevated, in point of spiritual worth, above some of the more healthy Christian congregations of the nineteenth century.

Shortly after this letter was transmitted to its destination, Ephesus was thrown into a ferment by the riotous proceedings of certain parties who had an interest in the maintenance of the pagan superstition. Among those who derived a subsistence from the idolatry of its celebrated temple were a class of workmen who "made silver shrines for Diana," [124:1] that is, who manufactured little models of the sanctuary and of the image which it contained. These models were carried about by the devotees of the goddess in processions, and set up, in private dwellings, as household deities. [124:2] The impression produced by the Christian missionaries in the Asiatic metropolis had affected the traffic in such articles, and those who were engaged in it began to apprehend that their trade would be ultimately ruined. An individual, named Demetrius, who appears to have been a master-manufacturer, did not find it difficult, under these circumstances, to collect a mob, and to disturb the peace of the city. Calling together the operatives of his own establishment, "with the workmen of like occupation," [124:3] he said to them—"Sirs, ye know, that by this craft we have our wealth. Moreover, ye see and know, that not alone at Ephesus, but almost throughout all Asia, this Paul hath persuaded and turned away much people, saying that they be no gods which are made with hands—so that not only this our craft is in danger to be set at nought, but also that the temple of the great goddess Diana should be despised, and her magnificence should be destroyed, whom all Asia and the world worshipped." [125:1] This address did not fail to produce the effect contemplated. A strong current of indignation was turned against the missionaries; and the craftsmen were convinced that they were bound to support the credit of their tutelary guardian. They were "full of wrath, and cried out saying—Great is Diana of the Ephesians." [125:2] This proceeding seems to have taken place in the month of May, and at a time when public games were celebrated in honour of the Ephesian goddess, [125:3] so that a large concourse of strangers now thronged the metropolis. An immense crowd rapidly collected; the whole city was filled with confusion; and it soon appeared that the lives of the Christian preachers were in danger; for the mob caught "Gaius and Aristech's, men of Macedonia, Paul's companions in travel," and "rushed with one accord into the theatre." [125:4] This edifice, the largest of the kind in Asia Minor, is said to have been capable of containing thirty thousand persons. [125:5] As it was sufficiently capacious to accommodate the multitudinous assemblage, and as it was also the building in which public meetings of the citizens were usually convened, it was now quickly occupied. Paul was at first prompted to enter it, and to plead his cause before the excited throng; but some of the magistrates, or, as they are called by the evangelist, "certain of the chief of Asia, which were his friends, sent unto him, desiring him that he would not adventure himself" into so perilous a position. [125:6] These Asiarchs were persons of exalted rank who presided at the celebration of the public spectacles. The apostle was now in very humble circumstances, for even in Ephesus he continued to work at the occupation of a tent-maker; [126:1] and it is no mean testimony to his worth that he had secured the esteem of such high functionaries. It was quickly manifest that any attempt to appease the crowd would have been utterly in vain. A Jew, named Alexander, who seems to have been one of the craftsmen, and who was, perhaps, the same who is elsewhere distinguished as "the coppersmith," [126:2] made an effort to address them, probably with the view of shewing that his co-religionists were not identified with Paul; but when the mob perceived that he was one of the seed of Abraham, they took it for granted that he was no friend to the manufacture of their silver shrines; and his appearance was the signal for increased uproar. "When they knew that he was a Jew, all with one voice, about the space of two hours, cried out—Great is Diana of the Ephesians." [126:3] At length the town-clerk, or recorder, of Ephesus, contrived to obtain a hearing; and, by his prudence and address, succeeded in putting an end to this scene of confusion. He told his fellow-townsmen that, if Paul and his companions had transgressed the law, they could be made amenable to punishment; but that, as their own attachment to the worship of Diana could not be disputed, their present tumultuary proceedings could only injure their reputation as orderly and loyal citizens. "We are in danger," said he, "to be called in question for this day's uproar, there being no cause whereby we may give an account of this concourse." [127:1] The authority of the speaker imparted additional weight to his suggestions, the multitude quietly dispersed, and the missionaries escaped unscathed.

Even this tumult supplies evidence that the Christian preachers had already produced an immense impression in this great metropolis. No more decisive test of their success could be adduced than that here furnished by Demetrius and his craftsmen; for a lucrative trade connected with the established superstition was beginning to languish. The silversmiths, and the other operatives whose interests were concerned, were obviously the instigators of all the uproar; and it does not appear that they could reckon upon the undivided sympathy even of the crowd they had congregated. "Some cried one thing, and some another, for the assembly was confused, and the more part knew not wherefore they were come together." [127:2] A number of the Asiarchs were decidedly favourable to the apostle and his brethren; and when the town-clerk referred to their proceedings his tone was apologetic and exculpatory. "Ye have," said he, "brought hither these men who are neither profaners of temples, [127:3] nor yet blasphemers of your goddess." [127:4] But here we see the real cause of much of that bitter persecution which the Christians endured for the greater part of three centuries. The craft of the imagemakers was in danger; the income of the pagan priests was at stake; the secular interests of many other parties were more or less affected; and hence the new religion encountered such a cruel and obstinate opposition.

CHAPTER IX

PAUL'S EPISTLES; HIS COLLECTION FOR THE POOR SAINTS AT JERUSALEM; HIS IMPRISONMENT THERE, AND AT CAESAREA AND ROME
A.D. 57 TO A.D. 63

Paul had already determined to leave Ephesus at Pentecost, [128:1] and as the secular games, at which the Asiarchs presided, took place during the month of May, the disorderly proceedings of Demetrius and the craftsmen, which occurred at the same period, do not seem to have greatly accelerated his removal. Soon afterwards, however, he "called unto him the disciples, and embraced them, and departed to go into Macedonia." [128:2] When he reached that district, he was induced to enter on new scenes of missionary enterprise; and now, "round about unto Illyricum," he "fully preached the gospel of Christ." [128:3] Shortly before, Timothy had returned from Greece to Ephesus, [128:4] and when the apostle took leave of his friends in that metropolis, he left the evangelist behind him to protect the infant Church against the seductions of false teachers. [128:5] He now addressed the first epistle to his "own son in the faith," [128:6] and thus also supplied to the ministers of all succeeding generations the most precious instructions on the subject of pastoral theology. [129:1] Soon afterwards he wrote the Second Epistle to the Corinthians. This letter throws much light on the private character of Paul, and enables us to understand how he contrived to maintain such a firm hold on the affections of those among whom he ministered. Though he uniformly acted with great decision, he was singularly amiable and gentle, as well as generous and warm-hearted. No one could doubt his sincerity; no one could question his disinterestedness; no one could fairly complain that he was harsh or unkind. In his First Epistle to the Corinthians he had been obliged to employ strong language when rebuking them for their irregularities; but now they exhibited evidences of repentance, and he is obviously most willing to forget and forgive. In his Second Epistle to them he enters into many details of his personal history unnoticed elsewhere in the New Testament, [130:1] and throughout displays a most loving and conciliatory spirit. He states that, when he dictated his former letter, it was far from his intention to wound their feelings, and that it was with the utmost pain he had sent them such a communication. "Out of much affliction, and anguish of heart," said he, "I wrote unto you with many tears, not that ye should be grieved, but that ye might know the love which I have more abundantly unto you." [130:2] The Corinthians could not have well resented an advice from such a correspondent.

When Paul had itinerated throughout Macedonia and Illyricum "he came into Greece, [130:3] and there abode three months." [130:4] He now visited Corinth for the third time; and, during his stay in that city, dictated the Epistle to the Romans. [130:5] At this date, a Church "spoken of throughout the whole world" [130:6] had been formed in the great metropolis; some of its members were the relatives of the apostle; [130:7] and others, such as Priscilla and Aquila, [130:8] had been converted under his ministry. As he himself contemplated an early visit to the far-famed city, [130:9] he sent this letter before him, to announce his intentions, and to supply the place of his personal instructions. The Epistle to the Romans is a precious epitome of Christian theology. It is more systematic in its structure than, perhaps, any other of the writings of Paul; and being a very lucid exposition of the leading truths taught by the inspired heralds of the gospel, it remains an emphatic testimony to the doctrinal defections of the religious community now bearing the name of the Church to which it was originally addressed.

The apostle had been recently making arrangements for another visit to Jerusalem; and he accordingly left Greece in the spring of A.D. 58; but the malignity of his enemies appears to have obliged him to change his plan of travelling. "When the Jews laid wait for him as he was about to sail" from Cenchrea, the port of Corinth, "into Syria," he found it expedient "to return through Macedonia." [131:1] Proceeding, therefore, to Philippi, [131:2] the city in which he had commenced his European ministry, he passed over to Troas; [131:3] and then continued his journey along the coast of Asia Minor. On his arrival at Miletus "he sent to Ephesus, and called the elders of the Church; and, when they were come to him," he delivered to them a very pathetic pastoral address, and bade them farewell. [131:4] At the conclusion, "he kneeled down and prayed with them all, and they all wept sore, and fell on Paul's neck, and kissed him, sorrowing most of all for the words which he spake that they should see his face no more: and they accompanied him unto the ship." [131:5] He now pursued his course to Jerusalem, and after various delays, arrived at Caesarea. There, says Luke, "we entered into the house of Philip, the evangelist, which was one of the seven, and abode with him." [131:6] In Caesarea, as in other cities through which he had already passed, he was told that bonds and afflictions awaited him in the place of his destination; [131:7] but he was not thus deterred from pursuing his journey. "When he would not be persuaded," says the sacred historian, "we ceased, saying, The will of the Lord be done, and after those days, having packed up, [131:8] we went up to Jerusalem." [131:9] The apostle and his companions reached the holy city about the time of the feast of Pentecost.

Paul was well aware that there were not a few, even among the Christians of Palestine, by whom he was regarded with jealousy or dislike; and he had reason to believe that the agitation for the observance of the ceremonial law, which had disturbed the Churches of Galatia, had been promoted by the zealots of the Hebrew metropolis. But he had a strong attachment to the land of his fathers; and he felt deeply interested in the well-being of his brethren in Judea. They were generally in indigent circumstances; for, after the crucifixion, when the Spirit was poured out on the day of Pentecost, those of them who had property "sold their possessions and goods, and parted them to all men, as every man had need;" [132:1] and, ever since, they had been harassed and persecuted by their unbelieving countrymen. "The poor saints" that were in Jerusalem [132:2] had, therefore, peculiar claims on the kind consideration of the disciples in other lands; and Paul had been making collections for their benefit among their richer co-religionists in Greece and Asia Minor. A considerable sum had been thus provided; and that there might be no misgivings as to its right appropriation, individuals chosen by the contributors had been appointed to travel with the apostle, and to convey it to Jerusalem. [132:3] The number of the deputies appears to have been seven, namely, "Sopater of Berea; and of the Thessalonians, Aristech's and Secundus; and Gaius of Derbe, and Timotheus; and of Asia,

Tychicus and Trophimus." [132:4] The apostle knew that he had enemies waiting for his halting; and as they would willingly have seized upon any apology for accusing him of tampering with this collection, he, no doubt, deemed it prudent to put it into other hands, and thus place himself above challenge. But he appears to have had a farther reason for suggesting the appointment of these commissioners. He was, in all likelihood, desirous that his brethren in Judea should have a favourable specimen of the men who constituted "the first fruits of the Gentiles;" and as all the deputies selected to accompany him to Jerusalem seem to have been persons of an excellent spirit, he probably reckoned that their wise and winning behaviour would do much to disarm the hostility of those who had hitherto contended so strenuously for the observance of the Mosaic ceremonies. Solomon has said that "a man's gift maketh room for him;" [133:1] and if Gentile converts could ever expect a welcome reception from those who were zealous for the law, it was surely when they appeared as the bearers of the liberality of the Gentile Churches.

When the apostle and his companions reached the Jewish capital, "the brethren received them gladly." [133:2] Paul was, however, given to understand that, as he was charged with encouraging the neglect of the Mosaic ceremonies, he must be prepared to meet a large amount of prejudice; and he was accordingly recommended to endeavour to pacify the multitude by giving some public proof that he himself "walked orderly and kept the law." [133:3] Acting on this advice, he joined with four men who had on them a Nazaritic vow; [133:4] and, "purifying himself with them, entered into the temple." [133:5] When there, he was observed by certain Jews from Asia Minor, who had probably become acquainted with his personal appearance during his residence in Ephesus; and as they had before seen him in the city with Trophimus, one of the seven deputies and a convert from paganism, whom they seem also to have known, [134:1] they immediately concluded that he had now some Gentile companions along with him, and that he was encouraging the uncircumcised to pollute with their presence the sacred court of the Israelites. A tumult forthwith ensued; the report of the defilement of the holy place quickly circulated through the crowd; "all the city was moved;" [134:2] the people ran together; and Paul was seized and dragged out of the temple. [134:3] The apostle would have fallen a victim to popular fury had it not been for the prompt interference of the officer who had the command of the Roman garrison in the tower of Antonia. This stronghold overlooked the courts of the sanctuary; and, no doubt, some of the sentinels on duty immediately gave notice of the commotion. The chief captain, whose name was Claudius Lysias, [134:4] at once "took soldiers and centurions," and running down to the rioters, arrived in time to prevent a fatal termination of the affray; for, as soon as the military made their appearance, the assailants "left beating of Paul." [134:5] "Then the chief captain came near, and took him, and commanded him to be bound with two chains, and demanded who he was, and what he had done. And some cried one thing, some another, among the multitude, and when he could not know the certainty for the tumult, he commanded him to be carried into the castle." [134:6] In proceeding thus, the commanding officer acted illegally; for, as Paul was a Roman citizen, he should not, without a trial, have been deprived of his liberty, and put in irons. But Lysias, in the hurry and confusion of the moment, had been deceived by false information; as he had been led to believe that his prisoner was an Egyptian, a notorious outlaw, who, "before

61

these days," had created much alarm by leading "out into the wilderness four thousand men that were murderers." [135:1] He was quite astonished to find that the individual whom he had rescued from such imminent danger was a citizen of Tarsus in Cilicia who could speak Greek; and as it was now evident that there existed much misapprehension, the apostle was permitted to stand on the stairs of the fortress, and address the multitude. When they saw him preparing to make some statement, the noise subsided; and, "when they heard that he spake to them in the Hebrew tongue," that is, in the Aramaic, the current language of the country, "they kept the more silence." [135:2] Paul accordingly proceeded to give an account of his early life, of the remarkable circumstances of his conversion, and of his subsequent career; but, when he mentioned his mission to the Gentiles, it was at once apparent that the topic was most unpopular, for his auditors lost all patience. "They gave him audience unto this word, and then lifted up their voices and said, Away with such a fellow from the earth, for it is not fit that he should live. And as they cried out, and cast off their clothes, and threw dust into the air, the chief captain commanded him to be brought into the castle." [135:3]

The confinement of Paul, which now commenced at the feast of Pentecost in A.D. 58, continued about five years. It may be enough to notice the mere outline of his history during this tedious bondage. In the first place, for the purpose of ascertaining the exact nature of the charge against him, he was confronted with the Sanhedrim; but when he informed them that "of the hope and resurrection of the dead" he was called in question, [136:1] there "arose a dissension between the Pharisees and the Sadducees" [136:2] constituting the council; and the chief captain, fearing lest his prisoner "should have been pulled in pieces of them, commanded the soldiers to go down, and to take him by force from among them, and to bring him into the castle." [136:3] Certain of the Jews, about forty in number, now entered into a conspiracy binding themselves "under a curse, saying, that they would neither eat nor drink till they had killed Paul;" [136:4] and it was arranged that the bloody vow should be executed when, under pretence of a new examination, he should be brought again before the Sanhedrim; but their proceedings meanwhile became known to the apostle's nephew; the chief captain received timely information; and the scheme thus miscarried. [136:5] Paul, protected by a strong military escort, was now sent away by night to Caesarea; and, when there, was repeatedly examined before Felix, the Roman magistrate who at this time, under the title of Procurator, had the government of Judea. The historian Tacitus says of this imperial functionary that "in the practice of all kinds of cruelty and lust, he exercised the power of a king with the mind of a slave;" [136:6] and it is a remarkable proof, as well of the intrepid faithfulness, as of the eloquence of the apostle, that he succeeded in arresting the attention, and in alarming the fears of this worthless profligate. Drusilla, his wife, a woman who had deserted her former husband, [136:7] was a Jewess; and, as she appears to have been desirous to see and hear the great Christian preacher who had been labouring with so much zeal to propagate his principles throughout the Empire, Paul, to satisfy her curiosity, was brought into her presence. But an interview, which seems to have been designed merely for the amusement of the Procurator and his partner, soon assumed an appearance of the deepest solemnity. As the grave and earnest orator went on to expound the faith of the gospel, and "as he reasoned of righteousness, temperance, and judgment to come, Felix trembled." [137:1] His apprehensions, however, soon passed away, and though he was fully convinced that Paul had not incurred any legal penalty, he continued to keep him in confinement, basely expecting to obtain a bribe for his liberation. When disappointed in this hope, he still perversely refused to set him at liberty. Thus, "after two years," when "Porcius Festus came into Felix' room," the ex-Procurator, "willing to shew the Jews a pleasure, left Paul bound." [137:2]

The apostle was soon required to appear before the new Governor. Festus has left behind him the reputation of an equitable judge; [137:3] and though he was obviously most desirous to secure the good opinion of the Jews, he could not be induced by them to act with palpable injustice. After he had brought them down to Caesarea, and listened to their complaints against the prisoner, he perceived that they could convict him of no violation of the law; but he proposed to gratify them so far as to have the case reheard in the holy city. Paul, however, well knew that they only sought such an opportunity to compass his assassination, and therefore peremptorily refused to consent to the arrangement. "I stand," said he, "at Caesar's judgment-seat, where I ought to be judged. To the Jews have I done no wrong, as thou very well knowest. For if I be an offender, or have committed anything worthy of death, I refuse not to die; but if there be none of these things whereof these accuse me, no man may deliver me unto them. I appeal unto Caesar." [138:1]

The right of appeal from the decision of an inferior tribunal to the Emperor himself was one of the great privileges of a Roman citizen; and no magistrate could refuse to recognise it without exposing himself to condign punishment. There were, indeed, a few exceptional cases of a flagrant character in which such an appeal could not be received; and Festus here consulted with his assessors to ascertain in what light the law contemplated that of the apostle. It appeared, however, that he was at perfect liberty to demand a hearing before the tribunal of Nero. "Then," says the evangelist, "when Festus had conferred with the council, he answered, Hast thou appealed unto Caesar? Unto Caesar shalt thou go." [138:2]

The Procurator was now placed in a somewhat awkward position; for, when sending Paul to Rome, he was required at the same time to report the crimes imputed to the prisoner; but the charges were so novel, and apparently so frivolous, that he did not well know how to embody them in an intelligible document. Meanwhile King Agrippa and his sister Bernice came to Caesarea "to salute Festus," [138:3] that is, to congratulate the new Governor on his arrival in the country; and the royal party expressed a desire to hear what the apostle had to say in his vindication. Agrippa was great-grandson of that Herod who reigned in Judea when Jesus was born in Bethlehem, and the son of the monarch of the same name whose sudden and awful death is recorded in the twelfth chapter of the Acts. On the demise of his father in A.D. 44, he was only seventeen years of age; and Judea, which was then reduced into the form a Roman province with Caesarea for its capital, had remained ever since under the government of Procurators. But though Agrippa had not been permitted to succeed to the dominions of his father, he had received various proofs of imperial favour; for he had obtained the government, first of the principality of Chalcis, and then of several other districts; and he had been honoured with the title of King. [139:1] The Gentile Procurators could not be expected to be very minutely acquainted with the ritual and polity of Israel; but as Agrippa was a Jew, and consequently familiar with the customs and sentiments of the native population, he had been entrusted with the care of the temple and its treasures, as well as with the appointment of the high priest. Festus, no doubt, felt that in a case such as that of Paul, the advice of this visitor should be solicited; and hoped that Agrippa would be able to supply some suggestion to relieve him out of his present perplexity. It was accordingly arranged that the apostle should be permitted to plead his cause in the hearing of the Jewish monarch. The affair seems to have created unusual interest; the public appear to have been partially admitted on the occasion; and seldom, or, perhaps, never before, had Paul enjoyed an opportunity of addressing such an influential and brilliant auditory. "Agrippa came, and Bernice, with great pomp, and entered into the place of hearing, with the chief captains, and principal men of the city." [139:2] Paul, still in bonds, made his appearance before this courtly throng; and though it might have been expected that a two years' confinement would have broken the spirit of the prisoner, he displayed powers of argument and eloquence which astonished and confounded his judges. The Procurator was quite bewildered by his reasoning, for he appealed to "the promise made unto the fathers," [139:3] and to things which "Moses and the prophets did say should come;" [140:1] and as Festus could not appreciate the lofty enthusiasm of the Christian orator (for he had never, when at Rome, been accustomed to hear the advocates of heathenism plead so earnestly in its defence), he "said with a loud voice—Paul, thou art beside thyself; much learning doth make thee mad." [140:2] But the apostle's self-possession was in nowise shaken by this blunt charge. "I am not mad, most noble Festus," he replied, "but speak forth the words of truth and soberness;" and then, turning to the royal stranger, vigorously pressed home his argument. "King Agrippa," he exclaimed, "believest thou the prophets? I know that thou believest." [140:3] The King, thus challenged, was a libertine; and at this very time was believed to be living in incestuous intercourse with his sister Bernice; and yet he seems to have been staggered by Paul's solemn and pointed interrogatory. "Almost," said he, "thou persuadest me to be a Christian." [140:4] It has been thought by some that these words were uttered with a sneer; but whatever may have been the frivolity of the Jewish King, they elicited from the apostle one of the noblest rejoinders that ever issued from human lips, "And Paul said, I would to God that not only thou, but also all that hear me this day, were both almost and altogether such as I am, except these bonds." [140:5]

The singularly able defence now made by the apostle convinced his judges of the futility of the charges preferred against him by the Sanhedrim. But at this stage of the proceedings it was no longer practicable to quash the prosecution. When Paul concluded his address "the king rose up, and the governor, and Bernice, and they that sat with them. And when they were gone aside, they talked between themselves, saying—This man doeth nothing worthy of death or of bonds. Then said Agrippa unto Festus—This man might have been set at liberty, if he had not appealed unto Caesar." [141:1]

At first sight it may appear extraordinary that so eminent a missionary in the meridian of his usefulness was subjected to so long an imprisonment. But "God's ways are not as our ways, nor His thoughts as our thoughts." When thus, to a great extent, laid aside from official duty, he had ample time to commune with his own heart, and to trace out, with adoring wonder, the glorious grace and the manifold wisdom of the work of redemption. Having himself partaken largely of affliction, and experienced the sustaining power of the gospel so abundantly, he was the better prepared to comfort the distressed; and hence his letters, written at this period, are so full of consolation. [141:2] And apart from other considerations, we may here recognise the fulfilment of a prophetic announcement. When Paul was converted, the Lord said to Ananias—"He is a chosen vessel unto me to bear my name before the Gentiles, and kings, and the children of Israel, for I will shew him how great things he must suffer for my name's sake." [141:3] During his protracted confinement he exhibited alike to Jew and Gentile an illustrious specimen of faith and constancy; and called attention to the truth in many quarters where otherwise it might have remained unknown. Though he was chained to a soldier, he was not kept in very rigorous custody, so that he had frequent opportunities of proclaiming the great salvation. He was peculiarly fitted by his education and his genius for expounding Christianity to persons moving in the upper circles of society; and had he remained at liberty he could have expected to gain access very rarely to such auditors. But already, as a prisoner, he had pleaded the claims of the gospel before no inconsiderable portion of the aristocracy of Palestine. He had been heard by the chief captain in command of the garrison in the castle of Antonia, by the Sanhedrim, by Felix and Drusilla, by Festus, by King Agrippa and his sister Bernice, and probably by "the principal men" of both Caesarea and Jerusalem. In criminal cases the appeals of Roman citizens were heard by the Emperor himself, so that the apostle was about to appear as an ambassador for Christ in the presence of the greatest of earth's potentates. Who can tell but that some of that splendid assembly of senators and nobles who surrounded Nero, when Paul was brought before his judgment-seat, will have reason throughout all eternity to remember the occasion as the birth-day of their blessedness!

The apostle and "certain other prisoners" embarked for Rome in the autumn of A.D. 60. The compass was then unknown; in weather, "when neither sun nor stars in many days appeared," [142:1] the mariner was without a guide; and, late in the season, navigation was peculiarly dangerous. The voyage proved disastrous; after passing into a second vessel at Myra, [142:2] a city of Lycia, Paul and his companions were wrecked on the coast of the island of Malta; [142:3] when they had remained there three months, they set sail once more in a corn ship of Alexandria, the Castor and Pollux; [142:4] and at length in the early part of A.D. 61, reached the harbour of Puteoli, [143:1] then the great shipping port of Italy.

The account of the voyage from Caesarea to Puteoli, as given in the Acts of the Apostles, is one of the most curious passages to be found in the whole of the sacred volume. Some may think it strange that the inspired historian enters so much into details, and the nautical terms which he employs may puzzle not a few readers; but these features of his narrative attest its authenticity and genuineness. No one, who had not himself shared the perils of the scene, could have been expected to describe with so much accuracy the circumstances of the shipwreck. It has been remarked that, after the lapse of eighteen hundred years, the references of the evangelist to prevailing winds and currents, to the indentations of the coast, to islands, bays, and harbours, may still be exactly verified. Recent investigators have demonstrated that the sailors, in the midst of danger, displayed no little ability, and that their conduct in "undergirding the ship," [143:2] and in casting "four anchors out of the stern," [143:3] evidenced their skilful seamanship. Luke states that, after a long period of anxiety and abstinence, "about midnight the shipmen deemed that they drew near to some country." [143:4] The headland they were approaching is very low, and in a stormy night is said to be invisible even at the distance of a quarter of a mile; [143:5] but the sailors could detect the shore by other indications. Even in a storm the roar of breakers can be distinguished from other sounds by the practised ear of a mariner; [144:1] and it can be shewn that, with such a gale as was then blowing, the sea still dashes with amazing violence against the very same point of land off which Paul and his companions were that night labouring. In the depth of the water at the place there is another most remarkable coincidence. We are told that the sailors "sounded and found it twenty fathoms, and when they had gone a little farther, they sounded, and found it fifteen fathoms." [144:2] "But what," observes a modern writer, "are the soundings at this point? They are now twenty fathoms. If we proceed a little farther we find fifteen fathoms. It may be said that this, in itself is nothing remarkable. But if we add that the fifteen-fathom depth is in the direction of the vessel's drift (W. by N.) from the twenty-fathom depth, the coincidence is startling." [144:3] It may be stated also that the "creek with a shore" [144:4] or sandy beach, and the "place where two seas met," [144:5] and where "they ran the ship aground" may still be recognised in what is now called St Paul's Bay at Malta. [144:6] Even in the nature of the submarine strata we have a most striking confirmation of the truth of the inspired history. It appears that the four anchors cast out of the stern retained their hold, and it is well known that the ground in St Paul's Bay is remarkably firm; for in our English sailing directions it is mentioned that "while the cables hold, there is no danger, as the anchors will never start." [144:7] Luke reports that when the ship ran aground, "the fore-part stuck fast and remained unmoveable" [144:8]—a statement which is corroborated by the fact that "the bottom is mud graduating into tenacious clay" [145:1]—exactly the species of deposit from which such a result might be anticipated.

When Paul landed at Puteoli, he must have contemplated with deep emotion the prospect of his arrival in Rome. The city to which he now approached contained, perhaps, upwards of a million of human beings. [145:2] But the amount of its inhabitants was one of the least remarkable of its extraordinary distinctions. It was the capital of the mightiest empire that had ever yet existed; one hundred races speaking one hundred languages were under its dominion; [145:3] and the sceptre which ruled so many subject provinces was wielded by an absolute potentate. This great autocrat was the high priest of heathenism—thus combining the grandeur of temporal majesty with the sacredness of religious elevation. Senators and generals, petty kings and provincial governors, were all obliged to bow obsequiously to his mandates. In this vast metropolis might be found natives of almost every clime; some engaged in its trade; some who had travelled to it from distant countries to solicit the imperial favour; some, like Paul, conveyed to it as prisoners; some stimulated to visit it by curiosity; and some attracted to it by the vague hope of bettering their condition. The city of the Caesars might well be described as "sitting upon many waters;" [145:4] for, though fourteen or fifteen miles from the mouth of the Tiber, the mistress of the world was placed on a peninsula stretching out into the middle of a great inland sea over which she reigned without a rival. In the summer months almost every port of every country along the shores of the Mediterranean sent forth vessels freighted with cargoes for the merchants of Rome. [146:1] The fleet from Alexandria laden with wheat for the supply of the city was treated with peculiar honour; for its ships alone were permitted to hoist their topsails as they approached the shore; a deputation of senators awaited its arrival; and, as soon as it appeared, the whole surrounding population streamed to the pier, and observed the day as a season of general jubilee. But an endless supply of other articles in which the poor were less interested found their way to Rome. The mines of Spain furnished the great capital with gold and silver, whilst its sheep yielded wool of superior excellence; and, in those times of Roman conquest, slaves were often transported from the shores of Britain. The horses and chariots and fine linen of Egypt, the gums and spices and silk and ivory and pearls of India, the Chian and the Lesbian wines, and the beautiful marble of Greece and Asia Minor, all met with purchasers in the mighty metropolis. [146:2] As John surveyed in vision the fall of Rome, and as he thought of the almost countless commodities which ministered to her insatiable luxury, well might he represent the world's traffic as destroyed by the catastrophe; and well might he speak of the merchants of the earth as weeping and mourning over her, because "no man buyeth their merchandise any more." [146:3]

Paul had often desired to prosecute his ministry in the imperial city; for he knew that if Christianity could obtain a firm footing in that great centre of civilisation and of power, its influence would soon be transmitted to the ends of the earth: but he now appeared there under circumstances equally painful and discouraging. And yet even in this embarrassing position he was not overwhelmed with despondency. At Puteoli he "found brethren," [146:4] and through the indulgence of Julius, the centurion to whose care he was committed, he was courteously allowed to spend a week [147:1] with the little Church of which they were members. He now set out on his way to the metropolis; but the intelligence of his arrival had travelled before him, and after crossing the Pomptine marshes, he was, no doubt, delighted to find a number of Christian friends from Rome assembled at Appii Forum to tender to him the assurances of their sympathy and affection. The place was twenty-seven miles from the capital; and yet, at a time when travelling was so tedious and so irksome, they had undertaken this lengthened journey to visit the poor, weather-beaten, and tempest-tossed prisoner. At the Three Taverns, ten miles nearer to the city, he met another party of disciples [147:2] anxious to testify their attachment to so distinguished a servant of their Divine Master. These tokens of respect and love made a deep impression upon the susceptible mind of the apostle; and it is accordingly stated that, when he saw the brethren, "he thanked God and took courage." [147:3]

The important services he had been able to render on the voyage gave him a claim to particular indulgence; and accordingly, when he reached Rome, and when the centurion delivered the prisoners to the Praetorian Prefect, or the commander-in-chief of the Praetorian guards, [147:4] "Paul was suffered to dwell by himself with a soldier that kept him." [147:5] But though he enjoyed this comparative liberty, he was chained to his military care-taker, so that his position must still have been very far from comfortable. And yet even thus he continued his ministry with as much ardour as if he had been without restraint, and as if he had been cheered on by the applause of his generation. Three days after his arrival in the city he "called the chief of the Jews together," [148:1] and gave them an account of the circumstances of his committal, and of his appeal to the imperial tribunal. They informed him that his case had not been reported to them by their brethren in Judea; and then expressed a desire to hear from him a statement of the claims of Christianity. "And when they had appointed him a day, there came many to him into his lodging; to whom he expounded and testified the kingdom of God, persuading them concerning Jesus, both out of the law of Moses and out of the prophets from morning till evening." [148:2] His appeals produced a favourable impression upon only a part of his audience. "Some believed the things which were spoken, and some believed not." [148:3]

Several years prior to this date a Christian Church existed in the Western metropolis, and at this time there were probably several ministers in the city; but the apostle, in all likelihood, now entered upon some field of labour which had not hitherto been occupied. He "dwelt two whole years in his own hired house, and received all that came in unto him—preaching the kingdom of God, and teaching those things which concern the Lord Jesus Christ with all confidence, no man forbidding him." [148:4] All this time Paul's right hand was chained to the left hand of a soldier, who was responsible for the safe keeping of his prisoner. The soldiers relieved each other in this duty. [148:5] It would appear that Paul's chain might be relaxed at meal-times, and perhaps he was occasionally granted some little additional indulgence; but day and night he and his care-taker must have remained in close proximity, as the life of the soldier was forfeited should his ward escape. We can well conceive that the very appearance of the preacher at this period invited special attention to his ministrations. He was now "Paul the aged;" [149:1] he had perhaps passed the verge of threescore years; and though his detractors had formerly objected that "his bodily presence was weak," [149:2] all would at this time have, probably, admitted, that his aspect was venerable. His life had been a career of unabated exertion; and now, though worn down by toils, and hardships, and imprisonments, his zeal burned with unquenched ardour. As the soldier who kept him belonged to the Praetorian guards, it has been thought that the apostle spent much of his time in the neighbourhood of their quarters on the Palatine hill, [149:3] and that as he was now so much conversant with military sights and sounds, we may in this way account for some of the allusions to be found in his epistles written during his present confinement. Thus, he speaks of Archippus and Epaphroditus as his "fellow-soldiers;" [149:4] and he exhorts his brethren to "put on the whole armour of God," including "the breastplate of righteousness, the shield of faith, the helmet of salvation, and the sword of the Spirit." [149:5] As the indefatigable old man, with the soldier who had charge of him, passed from house to house inviting attendance on his services, the very appearance of such "yoke-fellows" [149:6] must have created some interest; and, when the congregation assembled, who could remain unmoved as the apostle stretched forth his chained hand, [149:7] and proceeded to expound his message! He seems himself to have thought that the very position which he occupied, as "the prisoner of the Lord," [149:8] imparted somewhat to the power of his testimony. Hence we find him saying—"I would ye should understand, brethren, that the things which happened unto me have fallen out rather unto the furtherance of the gospel, so that my bonds in Christ are manifest in all the Praetorium, [150:1] and in all other places; and many of the brethren in

68

the Lord waxing confident by my bonds are much more bold to speak the word without fear." [150:2]

During this imprisonment at Rome, Paul dictated a number of his epistles. Of these, the letter to Philemon, a Christian of Colosse, seems to have been first written. The bearer of this communication was Onesimus, who had at one time been a slave in the service of the individual to whom it is addressed; and who, as it appears, after robbing his master, had left the country. The thief made his way to Rome, where he was converted under the ministry of the apostle; and where he had since greatly recommended himself as a zealous and trustworthy disciple. He was now sent back to Colosse with this Epistle to Philemon, in which the writer undertakes to be accountable for the property that had been pilfered, [150:3] and entreats his correspondent to give a kindly reception to the penitent fugitive. Onesimus, when conveying the letter to his old master, was accompanied by Tychicus, whom the apostle describes as "a beloved brother and a faithful minister and fellow-servant in the Lord" [150:4] who was entrusted with the Epistle to the Colossians. Error, in the form of false philosophy and Judaizing superstition, had been creeping into the Colossian Church, [150:5] and the apostle in this letter exhorts his brethren to beware of its encroachments. About the same time Paul wrote the Epistle to the Ephesians; and Tychicus was also the bearer of this communication. [150:6] Unlike most of the other epistles, it has no salutations at the close; it is addressed, not only "to the saints which are at Ephesus" in particular, but also "to the faithful in Christ Jesus" [151:1] in general; and as its very superscription thus bears evidence that it was originally intended to be a circular letter, it is probably "the epistle from Laodicea" mentioned in the Epistle to the Colossians. [151:2] The first division of it is eminently distinguished by the profound and comprehensive views of the Christian system it exhibits; whilst the latter portion is no less remarkable for the variety, pertinency, and wisdom, of its practical admonitions. The Epistle to the Philippians was likewise written about this period. Paul always took a deep interest in the well-being of his earliest European converts, and here he speaks in most hopeful terms of their spiritual condition. [151:3] They were less disturbed by divisions and heresies than perhaps any other of the Apostolic Churches.

CHAPTER X

PAUL'S SECOND IMPRISONMENT, AND MARTYRDOM; PETER, HIS EPISTLES, HIS MARTYRDOM, AND THE ROMAN CHURCH

The Book of the Acts terminates abruptly; and the subsequent history of Paul is involved in much obscurity. Some have contended that the apostle was never released from his first imprisonment at Rome, and accordingly consider that he was one of the earliest Christian martyrs who suffered under the Emperor Nero. But this theory is encumbered with insuperable difficulties. In his letters written after his first appearance in Rome, Paul evidently anticipates his liberation; [152:1] and in some of them he apparently speaks prophetically. Thus, he says to the Philippians—"I am in a strait betwixt two, having a desire to depart and to be with Christ, which is far better—nevertheless to abide in the flesh is more needful for you—and having this confidence I know that I shall abide and continue with you all for your furtherance and joy of faith." [152:2] The apostle had long cherished a desire to visit Spain; [152:3] and there is evidence that he actually preached the gospel in that country; for Clemens Romanus, who was his contemporary and fellow-labourer, positively affirms that he travelled "to the extremity of the west." [153:1] Clemens appears to have been himself a native of the great metropolis; [153:2] and as he makes the statement just quoted in a letter written from Rome, it cannot be supposed that, under such circumstances, he would have described Italy as the boundary of the earth. The Second Epistle to Timothy, which is generally admitted to have been written immediately before Paul's death, contains several passages which obviously indicate that the author had been very recently at liberty. Thus, he says—"The cloak [153:3] (or, as some render it, the case) [153:4] that I left at Troas, with Carpus, when thou comest bring with thee, and the books, but especially the parchments." [153:5] These words suggest that the apostle had lately visited Troas on the coast of Asia Minor. Again, he remarks—"Erastus abode at Corinth, but Trophimus have I left at Miletum sick." [153:6] Any ordinary reader would at once infer from this observation that the writer had just arrived from Miletum. [153:7] The language of the concluding verses of the Acts warrants the impression that Paul's confinement had ended some time before the book was completed; for had the apostle been still in bondage, it would scarcely have been said that, when a prisoner, he dwelt for two whole years in his own hired house—thereby implying that the period of his residence, at least in that abode, had terminated. And if Paul was released at the expiration of these two years, we can well understand why the sacred historian may have deemed it inexpedient to give an account of his liberation. The subjects of Rome at that time were literally living under a reign of terror; and it would perhaps have been most unwise to have proceeded farther with the narrative. Paul, as Peter once before, [154:1] may have been miraculously delivered; and prudence may have required the concealment of his subsequent movements. Or, the history of his release may have been so mixed up with the freaks of the tyrant who then oppressed the Roman world, that its publication might have brought down the imperial vengeance on the head of the evangelist.

We have seen that Paul arrived in Rome as a prisoner in the beginning of A.D. 61; and if at this time his confinement continued only two years, he must have been liberated in the early part of A.D. 63. Nero had not then commenced his memorable persecution of the Church; for the burning of the city took place in the summer of A.D. 64; and, until that date, the disciples do not appear to have been singled out as the special objects of his cruelty. It is probable that Paul, after his release, accomplished his intention of visiting the Spanish Peninsula; and, on his return to Italy, he appears to have written the Epistle to the Hebrews. [154:2] The destruction of Jerusalem was at this time approaching; and, as the apostle demonstrates in this letter that the law was fulfilled in Christ, he thus prepares the Jewish Christians for the extinction of the Mosaic ritual. In all likelihood he now once more visited Jerusalem, travelling by Corinth, [155:1] Philippi, [155:2] and Troas, [155:3] where he left for the use of Carpus the case with the books and parchments which he mentions in his Second Epistle to Timothy. Passing on then to Colosse, [155:4] he may have visited Antioch in Pisidia and other cities of Asia Minor, the scenes of his early ministrations; and reached Jerusalem [155:5] by way of Antioch in Syria. He perhaps returned from Palestine to Rome by sea, leaving Trophimus sick [155:6] at Miletum in Crete. The journey did not probably occupy much time; and, on his return to Italy, he seems to have been immediately incarcerated. His condition was now very different from what it had been during his former confinement; for he was deserted by his friends, and treated as a malefactor. [155:7] When he wrote to Timothy he had already been brought before the judgment-seat, and had narrowly escaped martyrdom. "At my first answer," says he, "no man stood with me, but all men forsook me. I pray God that it may not be laid to their charge. Notwithstanding the Lord stood with me and strengthened me, that by me the preaching might be fully known, and that all the Gentiles might hear; [155:8] and I was delivered out of the mouth of the lion." [155:9] The prospect, however, still continued gloomy; and he had no hope of ultimate escape. In the anticipation of his condemnation, he wrote those words so full of Christian faith and heroism, "I am now ready to be offered, and the time of my departure is at hand. I have fought a good fight—I have finished my course—I have kept the faith. Henceforth there is laid up for me a crown of righteousness, which the Lord, the righteous Judge, shall give me in that day, and not to me only, but unto all them also that love his appearing." [156:1]

Paul was martyred perhaps about A.D. 66. Tradition reports that he was beheaded; [156:2] and as he was a Roman citizen, it is not probable that he suffered any more ignominious fate. About the third or fourth century, a statement appeared to the effect that he and Peter were put to death at Rome on the same day; [156:3] but all the early documentary evidence we possess is quite opposed to such a representation. If Peter really finished his career in the Western metropolis, it would seem that he did not arrive there until very shortly before the decapitation of the Apostle of the Gentiles; for Paul makes no reference, in any of his writings, to the presence of such a fellow-labourer in the capital of the Empire. In the Epistle to the Romans, containing so many salutations to the brethren in the great city, the name of Peter is not found; and in none of the letters written from Rome is he ever mentioned. In the last of his Epistles—the Second to Timothy—the writer says—"only Luke is with me" [156:4]—and had Peter then been in the place, Paul would not have thus ignored the existence of the apostle of the circumcision.

But still there is a very ancient and apparently a well authenticated tradition that Peter suffered martyrdom at Rome; [156:5] and if, as is not improbable, Paul met him in Jerusalem, during his visit to that city after his release from his first imprisonment, it may be that he was then encouraged to undertake a journey to the West. [156:6] It is not improbable that he was recommended, at the same time, to visit the Churches of Asia Minor for the purpose of using his influence to defeat the efforts of the Judaizing zealots; and if, after passing through Galatia, Bithynia, and other districts, he continued his course to Home, we can well understand why, on reaching the seat of Empire, he addressed his first epistle to the Christians with whom he had so recently held intercourse. The tradition that the "Babylon" from which this letter was written, [157:1] is no other than Rome, or the mystical Babylon of the Apocalypse, [157:2] is unquestionably of great antiquity; [157:3] and some of the announcements it contains are certainly quite in unison with such an interpretation. Thus, Peter tells his brethren of "the fiery trial" which was "to try" them, [157:4] alluding, in all likelihood, to the extension of the Neronian persecution to the provinces; and it may be presumed that, in the capital, and in communication with some of "Caesar's household," he had means of information in reference to such matters, to which elsewhere he could have had no access, Mark, who probably arrived in Rome about the time of the death of Paul, [157:5] was with Peter when this letter was written; [157:6] and we have thus additional evidence that the apostle of the circumcision was now in the Western capital. It is also worthy of remark that this epistle was transmitted to its destination by Silas, or Silvanus, [157:7] apparently the same individual who had so frequently accompanied the Apostle Paul on his missionary journeys. [157:8] Silvanus had been for many years acquainted with the brethren to whom the letter is addressed, and therefore was well suited to be its bearer. But though he had long occupied a prominent position in the Church, he seems to have been very little known to Peter; and hence the somewhat singular manner in which he is noticed towards the close of this epistle—"By Silvanus, a faithful brother unto you, as I suppose, I have written briefly, exhorting, and testifying that this is the true grace of God wherein ye stand." [158:1]

If this letter was written from Rome about the time of the death of Paul, it is not strange that Peter deemed it prudent to conceal his place of residence under the designation of Babylon. Nero was then seeking the extermination of the Christians in the capital; and they had enemies in all quarters who would have rejoiced to point out to him such a distinguished victim as the aged apostle. And how could Peter more appropriately describe the seat of Empire than by naming it Babylon? Nebuchadnezzar, who reigned so gloriously in the great Eastern capital, had destroyed the temple of God; and now Nero, who ruled in the Western metropolis, was seeking to ruin the Church of God. Nebuchadnezzar had led the Jews into captivity; but Rome now enthralled both Jews and Gentiles. If Nebuchadnezzar had an antitype in Nero, assuredly Babylon had an antitype in Rome. [158:2]

The Second Epistle of Peter was written soon after the first, and was addressed to the same Churches. [158:3] The author now contemplated the near approach of death, so that the advices he here gives may be regarded as his dying instructions. "I think it meet," says he, "as long as I am in this tabernacle, [158:4] to stir you up by putting you in remembrance—knowing that shortly I must put off this my tabernacle, even as our Lord Jesus Christ hath shewed me." [159:1] If then Peter was martyred at Rome, we may infer that this letter must have been written somewhere in the same neighbourhood, and probably in the same city. We have thus a corroborative proof that the Babylon of the first letter is no other than the great metropolis.

It deserves notice that in this second epistle, Peter bears emphatic testimony to the character and inspiration of Paul. The Judaizing party, as there is reason to think, were in the habit of pleading that they were supported by the authority of the apostle of the circumcision; and as many of these zealots were to be found in the Churches of Asia Minor, [159:2] such a recognition of the claims of the Apostle of the Gentiles was calculated to exert a most salutary influence. "The strangers scattered throughout Pontus, Galatia, Cappadocia, Asia, and Bithynia," [159:3] were thus given to understand that all the true heralds of the gospel had but "one faith;" and that any attempt to create divisions in the Church, by representing the doctrine of one inspired teacher as opposed to the doctrine of another, was most unwarrantable. The reference to Paul, to be found in the Second Epistle of Peter, is favourable to the supposition that the Apostle of the Gentiles was now dead; as, had he been still living to correct such misinterpretations, it would scarcely have been said that in all his epistles were things "hard to be understood" which "the unlearned and unstable" wrested "unto their own destruction." [159:4] It would seem, too, that Peter here alludes particularly to the Epistle to the Hebrews—a letter, as we have seen, addressed to Jewish Christians, and written after Paul's liberation from his first Roman imprisonment. It must be admitted that this letter contains passages [159:5] which have often proved perplexing to interpreters; but, notwithstanding, it bears the impress of a divine original; and Peter, who maintains that all the writings of Paul were dictated by unerring wisdom, places them upon a level with "the other Scriptures" [160:1] either of the evangelists or of the Old Testament.

According to a current tradition, Peter suffered death at Rome by crucifixion. [160:2] He was not a Roman citizen; and was, therefore, like our Lord himself, consigned to a mode of punishment inflicted on slaves and the lowest class of malefactors. The story that, at his own request, he was crucified with his head downwards as more painful and ignominious than the doom of his Master, [160:3] is apparently the invention of an age when the pure light of evangelical religion was greatly obscured; for the apostle was too well acquainted with the truth to believe that he was at liberty to inflict upon himself any unnecessary suffering. The tradition that he died on the same day of the same month as Paul, but exactly a year afterwards, [160:4] is not destitute of probability. According to this statement he suffered A.D. 67; and he may have been about a year in Rome before his martyrdom.

In the New Testament it is impossible to find a trace of either the primacy of Peter or the supremacy of the Pope; but the facts already stated throw some light on the history of that great spiritual despotism whose seat of government has been so long established in the city of the Caesars. It is obvious that at a very early period various circumstances contributed to give prominence to the Church of Rome. The epistle addressed to it contains a more complete exhibition of Christian doctrine than any other of the apostolical letters; and, in that remarkable communication, Paul expresses an earnest desire to visit a community already celebrated all over the world. Five or six of his letters, now forming part of the inspired canon, were dictated in the capital of the Empire. The two epistles of the apostle of the circumcision appear to have emanated from the same metropolis. There is every reason to believe that the book of the Acts was written at Rome; and it is highly probable that the great city was also the birthplace of the Gospels of Mark and Luke. Thus, a large portion of the New Testament issued from the seat of Empire. Rome could also boast that it was for some time the residence of two of the most eminent of the apostles. Paul was there for at least two years as a prisoner; and Peter may have resided for twelve months within its walls. Some of the most illustrious of the early converts were members of the Church of Rome; for in the days of the Apostle of the Gentiles there were disciples in "Caesar's household." [161:1] And when Nero signalised himself as the first Imperial persecutor of the Christians, the Church of Rome suffered terribly from his insane and savage cruelty. Even the historian Tacitus acknowledges that the tortures to which its adherents were exposed excited the commiseration of the heathen multitude. Paul and Peter were cut off in his reign; and the soil of Rome absorbed the blood of these apostolic martyrs. [161:2] It was not strange, therefore, that the Roman Church was soon regarded with peculiar respect by all the disciples throughout the Empire. As time passed on, it increased rapidly in numbers and in affluence; and circumstances, which properly possessed nothing more than an historic interest, began to be urged as arguments in favour of its claims to pre-eminence. At first these claims assumed no very definite form; and, at the termination of a century after the days of Paul and Peter, they amounted simply to the recognition of something like an honorary precedence. At that period it was, perhaps, deemed equally imprudent and ungracious to quarrel with its pretensions, more especially as the community by which they were advanced was distributing its bounty all around, and was itself nobly sustaining the brunt of almost every persecution. In the course of time, the Church of Rome proceeded to challenge a substantial supremacy; and then the facts of its early history were mis-stated and exaggerated in accommodation to the demands of its growing ambition. It was said at first that "its faith was spoken of throughout the whole world;" it was at length alleged that its creed should be universally adopted. It was admitted at an early period that, as it had enjoyed the ministrations of Peter and Paul, it should be considered an apostolic church; it was at length asserted that, as an apostle was entitled to deference from ordinary pastors, a church instructed by two of the most eminent apostles had a claim to the obedience of other churches. In process of time it was discovered that Paul was rather an inconvenient companion for the apostle of the circumcision; and Peter alone then began to be spoken of as the founder and first bishop of the Church of Rome. Strange to say, a system founded on a fiction has since sustained the shocks of so many centuries. One of the greatest marvels of this "mystery of iniquity" is its tenacity of life; and did not the sure word of prophecy announce that the time would come when it would be able to boast of its antiquity, and did we not know that paganism can plead a more remote original, we might be perplexed by its longevity. But "the vision is yet for an appointed time—at the end it shall speak and not lie. Though it tarry, wait for it, because it will surely come, it will not tarry." [162:1]

CHAPTER XI

THE PERSECUTIONS OF THE APOSTOLIC CHURCH, AND ITS CONDITION AT THE TERMINATION OF THE FIRST CENTURY

Jesus Christ was a Jew, and it might have been expected that the advent of the most illustrious of His race, in the character of the Prophet announced by Moses, would have been hailed with enthusiasm by His countrymen. But the result was far otherwise. "He came unto his own, and his own received him not."

74

[163:1] The Jews cried "Away with him, away with him, crucify him;" [163:2] and He suffered the fate of the vilest criminal. The enmity of the posterity of Abraham to our Lord did not terminate with His death; they long maintained the bad pre-eminence of being the most inveterate of the persecutors of His early followers. Whilst the awful portents of the Passion, and the marvels of the day of Pentecost were still fresh in public recollection, their chief priests and elders threw the apostles into prison; [163:3] and soon afterwards the pious and intrepid Stephen fell a victim to their malignity. Their infatuation was extreme; and yet it was not unaccountable. They looked, not for a crucified, but for a conquering Messiah. They imagined that the Saviour would release them from the thraldom of the Roman yoke; that He would make Jerusalem the capital of a prosperous and powerful empire; and that all the ends of the earth would celebrate the glory of the chosen people. Their vexation, therefore, was intense when they discovered that so many of the seed of Jacob acknowledged the son of a carpenter as the Christ, and made light of the distinction between Jew and Gentile. In their case the natural aversion of the heart to a pure and spiritual religion was inflamed by national pride combined with mortified bigotry; and the fiendish spirit which they so frequently exhibited in their attempts to exterminate the infant Church may thus admit of the most satisfactory explanation.

Many instances of their antipathy to the new sect have already been noticed. In almost every town where the missionaries of the cross appeared, the Jews "opposed themselves and blasphemed;" and magistrates speedily discovered that in no way could they more easily gain the favour of the populace than by inflicting sufferings on the Christians. Hence, as we have seen, about the time of Paul's second visit to Jerusalem after his conversion, Herod, the grandson of Herod the Great, "killed James, the brother of John, with the sword; and because he saw it pleased the Jews, he proceeded further to take Peter also." [164:1] The apostle of the circumcision was delivered by a miracle from his grasp; but it is probable that other individuals of less note felt the effects of his severity. Even in countries far remote from their native land, the posterity of Abraham were the most bitter opponents of Christianity. [164:2] As there was much intercourse between Palestine and Italy, the gospel soon found its way to the seat of government; and it has been conjectured that some civic disturbance created in the great metropolis by the adherents of the synagogue, and intended to annoy and intimidate the new sect, prompted the Emperor Claudius, about A.D. 53, to interfere in the manner described by Luke, and to command "all Jews to depart from Rome." [165:1] But the hostility of the Israelites was most formidable in their own country; and for this, as well as other reasons, "the brethren which dwelt in Judea" specially required the sympathy of their fellow-believers throughout the Empire. When Paul appeared in the temple at the feast of Pentecost in A.D. 58, the Jews, as already related, made an attempt upon his life; and when the apostle was rescued by the Roman soldiers, a conspiracy was formed for his assassination. Four years afterwards, or about A.D. 62, [165:2] another apostle, James surnamed the Just, who seems to have resided chiefly in Jerusalem, finished his career by martyrdom. Having proclaimed Jesus to be the true Messiah on a great public occasion, his fellow-citizens were so indignant that they threw him from a pinnacle of the temple. As he was still alive when he reached the ground, he was forthwith assailed with a shower of stones, and beaten to pieces with the club of a fuller. [165:3]

As the Christians were at first confounded with the Jews, the administrators of the Roman law, for upwards of thirty years after our Lord's death, conceded to them the religious toleration enjoyed by the seed of Abraham. But, from the beginning, "the sect of the Nazarenes" enjoyed very little of the favour of the heathen multitude. Paganism had set its mark upon all the relations of life, and had erected an idol wherever the eye could turn. It had a god of War, and a god of Peace; a god of the Sea, and a god of the Wind; a god of the River, and a god of the Fountain; a god of the Field, and a god of the Barn Floor; a god of the Hearth, a god of the Threshold, a god of the Door, and a god of the Hinges. [166:1] When we consider its power and prevalence in the apostolic age, we need not wonder at the declaration of Paul—"All that will live godly in Christ Jesus shall suffer persecution." [166:2] Whether the believer entered into any social circle, or made his appearance in any place of public concourse, he was constrained in some way to protest against dominant errors; and almost exactly in proportion to his consistency and conscientiousness, he was sure to incur the dislike of the more zealous votaries of idolatry. Hence it was that the members of the Church were so soon regarded by the pagans as a morose generation instinct with hatred to the human race. In A.D. 64, when Nero, in a fit of recklessness, set fire to his capital, he soon discovered that he had, to a dangerous extent, provoked the wrath of the Roman citizens; and he attempted, in consequence, to divert the torrent of public indignation from himself, by imputing the mischief to the Christians. They were already odious as the propagators of what was considered "a pernicious superstition," and the tyrant, no doubt, reckoned that the mob of the metropolis were prepared to believe any report to the discredit of these sectaries. But even the pagan historian who records the commencement of this first imperial persecution, and who was deeply prejudiced against the disciples of our Lord, bears testimony to the falsehood of the accusation. Nero, says Tacitus, "found wretches who were induced to confess themselves guilty; and, on their evidence, a great multitude of Christians were convicted, not indeed on clear proof of their having set the city on fire, but rather on account of their hatred of the human race. [167:1] They were put to death amidst insults and derision. Some were covered with the skins of wild beasts, and left to be torn to pieces by dogs; others were nailed to the cross; and some, covered over with inflammable matter, were lighted up, when the day declined, to serve as torches during the night. The Emperor lent his own gardens for the exhibition. He added the sports of the circus, and assisted in person, sometimes driving a curricle, and occasionally mixing with the rubble in his coachman's dress. At length these proceedings excited a feeling of compassion, as it was evident that the Christians were destroyed, not for the public good, but as a sacrifice to the cruelty of a single individual." [167:2] Some writers have maintained that the persecution under Nero was confined to Rome; but various testimonies concur to prove that it extended to the provinces. Paul seems to contemplate its spread throughout the Empire when he tells the Hebrews that they had "not yet resisted unto blood striving against sin," [167:3] and when he exhorts them not to forsake the assembling of themselves together as they "see the day approaching." [167:4] Peter also, as has been stated in a preceding chapter, apparently refers to the same circumstance in his letter to the brethren "scattered throughout Pontus, Galatia, Cappadocia, Asia, and Bithynia," when he announces "the fiery trial" which was "to try" them, [168:1] and when he tells them of "judgment" beginning

76

"at the house of God." [168:2] If Nero enacted that the profession of Christianity was a capital offence, his law must have been in force throughout the Roman world; and an early ecclesiastical writer positively affirms that he was the author of such sanguinary legislation. [168:3] The horror with which his name was so long regarded by members of the Church in all parts of the Empire [168:4] strongly corroborates the statement that the attack on the disciples in the capital was only the signal for the commencement of a general persecution.

Nero died A.D. 68, and the war which involved the destruction of Jerusalem and of upwards of a million of the Jews, was already in progress. The holy city fell A.D. 70; and the Mosaic economy, which had been virtually abolished by the death of Christ, now reached its practical termination. At the same period the prophecy of Daniel was literally fulfilled; for "the sacrifice and the oblation" were made to cease, [168:5] as the demolition of the temple and the dispersion of the priests put an end to the celebration of the Levitical worship. The overthrow of the metropolis of Palestine contributed in various ways to the advancement of the Christian cause. Judaism, no longer able to provide for the maintenance of its ritual, was exhibited to the world as a defunct system; its institutions, now more narrowly examined by the spiritual eye, were discovered to be but types of the blessings of a more glorious dispensation; and many believers, who had hitherto adhered to the ceremonial law, discontinued its observances. Christ, forty years before, had predicted the siege and desolation of Jerusalem; [169:1] and the remarkable verification of a prophecy, delivered at a time when the catastrophe was exceedingly improbable, appears to have induced not a few to think more favourably of the credentials of the gospel. In another point of view the ruin of the ancient capital of Judea proved advantageous to the Church. In the subversion of their chief city the power of the Jews sustained a shock from which it has never since recovered; and the disciples were partially delivered from the attacks of their most restless and implacable persecutors.

Much obscurity rests upon the history of the period which immediately follows the destruction of Jerusalem. Though Philip and John, [169:2] and perhaps one or two more of the apostles, still survived, we know almost nothing of their proceedings. After the death of Nero the Church enjoyed a season of repose, but when Domitian, in A.D. 81, succeeded to the government, the work of persecution recommenced. The new sovereign, who was of a gloomy and suspicious temper, encouraged a system of espionage; and as he seems to have imagined that the Christians fostered dangerous political designs, he treated them with the greater harshness. The Jewish calumny, that they aimed at temporal dominion, and that they sought to set up "another king one Jesus," [169:3] had obviously produced an impression upon his mind; and he accordingly sought out the nearest kinsmen of the Messiah, that he might remove these heirs of the rival dynasty. But when the two grandchildren of Jude, [169:4] called the brother of our Lord, [169:5] were conducted to Rome, and brought to his tribunal, he discovered the groundlessness of his apprehensions. The individuals who had inspired the Emperor with such anxiety, were the joint-proprietors of a small farm in Palestine which they cultivated with their own hands; and the jealous monarch at once saw that, when his fears had been excited by reports of the treasonable designs of such simple and illiterate husbandmen, he had been miserably befooled. After a single interview, these poor peasants met with no farther molestation from Domitian.

Had all the disciples been in such circumstances as the grandchildren of Jude, the gospel might have been identified with poverty and ignorance; and it might have been said that it was fitted to make way only among the dregs of the population. But it was never fairly open to this objection. From the very first it reckoned amongst its adherents at least a sprinkling of the wealthy, the influential, and the educated. Joseph of Arimathea, one of the primitive followers of our Lord, was "a rich man" and an "honourable counsellor;" [170:1] Paul himself, as a scholar, stood high among his countrymen, for he had been brought up at the feet of Gamaliel; and Sergius Paulus, one of the first fruits of the mission to the Gentiles, was a Roman Proconsul. [170:2] In the reign of Nero the Church could boast of some illustrious converts; and the saints of "Caesar's household" are found addressing their Christian salutations to their brethren at Philippi. [170:3] In the reign of Domitian the gospel still continued to have friends among the Roman nobility. Flavius Clemens, a person of consular dignity, and the cousin of the Emperor, was now put to death for his attachment to the cause of Christ; [170:4] and his near relative Flavia Domitilla, for the same reason, was banished with many others to Pontia, [170:5] a small island off the coast of Italy used for the confinement of state prisoners.

Domitian governed the Empire fifteen years, but his persecution of the Christians appears to have been limited to the latter part of his reign. About this time the Apostle John, "for the word of God and for the testimony of Jesus Christ," [171:1] was sent as an exile into Patmos, a small rocky island in the Aegaean Sea not far from the coast of Asia Minor. It is said that he had previously issued unhurt from a cauldron of boiling oil into which he had been plunged in Rome by order of the Emperor; but this story, for which a writer who flourished about a century afterwards is the earliest voucher, [171:2] has been challenged as of doubtful authority. [171:3] We have no means of ascertaining the length of time during which he remained in banishment; [171:4] and all we know of this portion of his life is, that he had now those sublime and mysterious visions to be found in the Apocalypse. After the fall of Jerusalem, as well as after he was permitted to leave Patmos, he appears to have resided chiefly in the metropolis of the Proconsular Asia; and hence some ancient writers, who flourished after the establishment of the episcopal system, have designated him the "Bishop of Ephesus." [172:1] But the apostle, when advanced in life, chose to be known simply by the title of "the elder;" [172:2] and though he was certainly by far the most influential minister of the district where he sojourned, there is every reason to believe that he admitted his brethren to a share in the government of the Christian community. Like Peter and Paul before him, he acknowledged the other elders as his "fellow-presbyters," [172:3] and, as became his age and apostolic character, he doubtless exhorted them to take heed unto themselves and to all the flock over the which the Holy Ghost had made them overseers. [172:4]

John seems to have been the last survivor of the apostles. He is said to have reached the advanced age of one hundred years, and to have died about the close of the first century. He was a "Son of Thunder," [172:5] and he appears to have long maintained the reputation of a powerful and impressive preacher; but when his strength began to give way beneath the pressure of increasing infirmities, he ceased to deliver lengthened addresses. When he appeared before the congregation in extreme old age, he is reported to have simply repeated the exhortation "Children, love one another;" and when asked, why he always confined himself to the same brief admonition, he replied that "no more was necessary." [172:6] Such a narrative is certainly quite in harmony with the character of the beloved disciple, for he knew that love is the "bond of perfectness" and "the fulfilling of the law."

It has been thought that, towards the close of the first century, the Christian interest was in a somewhat languishing condition; [172:7] and the tone of the letters addressed to the Seven Churches in Asia is calculated to confirm this impression. The Church of Laodicea is said to be "neither cold nor hot;" [173:1] the Church of Sardis is admonished to "strengthen the things which remain that are ready to die;" [173:2] and the Church of Ephesus is exhorted to "remember from whence she has fallen, and repent, and do the first works." [173:3] When it was known that Christianity was under the ban of a legal proscription, it was not strange that "the love of many" waxed cold; and the persecutions of Nero and Domitian must have had a most discouraging influence. But though the Church had to encounter the withering blasts of popular odium and imperial intolerance, it struggled through an ungenial spring; and, in almost every part of the Roman Empire, it had taken root and was beginning to exhibit tokens of a steady and vigorous growth as early as the close of the first century. The Acts and the apostolical epistles speak of the preaching of the gospel in Palestine, Syria, Cyprus, Asia Minor, Greece, Illyricum, and Italy; and, according to traditions which we have no reason to discredit, the way of salvation was proclaimed, before the death of John, in various other countries. It is highly probable that Paul himself assisted in laying the foundations of the Church in Spain; at an early date there were disciples in Gaul; and there is good evidence that, before the close of the first century, the new faith had been planted even on the distant shores of Britain. [173:4] It is generally admitted that Mark laboured successfully as an evangelist in Alexandria, the metropolis of Egypt; [173:5] and it has been conjectured that Christians were soon to be found in "the parts of Libya about Cyrene," [173:6] for if Jews from that district were converted at Jerusalem by Peter's famous sermon on the day of Pentecost, they would not fail, on their return home, to disseminate the precious truths by which they had been quickened and comforted. On the same grounds it may be inferred that the gospel soon found its way into Parthia, Media, Persia, Arabia, and Mesopotamia. [174:1] Various traditions [174:2] attest that several of the apostles travelled eastwards, after their departure from the capital of Palestine.

Whilst Christianity, in the face of much obloquy, was gradually attracting more and more attention, it was at the same time nobly demonstrating its power as the great regenerator of society. The religion of pagan Rome could not satisfy the wants of the soul; it could neither improve the heart nor invigorate the intellect; and it was now rapidly losing its hold on the consciences of the multitude. The high places of idolatrous worship often exercised a most demoralising influence, as their rites were not unfrequently a wretched mixture of brutality, levity, imposture, and prostitution. Philosophy had completely failed to ameliorate the condition of man. The vices of some of its most distinguished professors were notorious; its votaries were pretty generally regarded as a class of scheming speculators; and they enjoyed neither the confidence nor the respect of the mass of the people. But, even under the most unpromising circumstances, it soon appeared that Christianity could accomplish social and spiritual changes of a very extraordinary character. The Church of Corinth was perhaps one of the least exemplary of the early Christian communities, and yet it stood upon a moral eminence far above the surrounding population; and, from the roll of its own membership, it could produce cases of conversion to which nothing parallel could, be found in the whole history of heathendom. Paul could say to it—"Neither fornicators, nor idolaters, nor adulterers, nor effeminate, nor abusers of themselves with mankind, nor thieves, nor covetous, nor drunkards, nor revilers, nor extortioners, shall inherit the kingdom of God, and such were some of you but ye are washed, but ye are sanctified, but ye are justified in the name of the Lord Jesus, and by the Spirit of our God." [175:1] Nor was this all. The gospel proved itself sufficient to meet the highest aspirations of man. It revealed to him a Friend in heaven who "sticketh closer than a brother;" [175:2] and, as it assured him of eternal happiness in the enjoyment of fellowship with God, it imparted to him a "peace that passeth all understanding." The Roman people witnessed a new spectacle when they saw the primitive followers of Christ expiring in the fires of martyrdom. The pagans did not so value their superstitions; but here was a religion which was accounted "better than life." Well then might the flames which illuminated the gardens of Nero supply some spiritual light to the crowds who were present at the sad scene; and, in the indomitable spirit of the first sufferers, well might the thoughtful citizen have recognised a system which was destined yet to subdue the world.

SECTION II

THE LITERATURE AND THEOLOGY OF THE APOSTOLIC CHURCH

CHAPTER I

THE NEW TESTAMENT, ITS HISTORY, AND THE AUTHORITY OF ITS VARIOUS PARTS.
THE EPISTLE OF CLEMENT OF ROME

The conduct of our Lord, as a religious teacher, betokened that He was something more than man. Mohammed dictated the Koran, and left it behind him as a sacred book for the guidance of his followers; many others, who have established sects, have also founded a literature for their disciples; but Jesus Christ wrote nothing. The Son of God was not obliged to condescend to become His own biographer, and thus to testify of Himself. He had at His disposal the hearts and the pens of others; and He knew that His words and actions would be accurately reported to the latest generations. During His personal ministry, even His apostles were only imperfectly acquainted with His theology; but, shortly before His death, He gave them an assurance that, in due time, He would disclose to them more fully the nature and extent of the great salvation. He said to them— "The Comforter, which is the Holy Ghost, whom the Father will send in my name, he shall teach you all things, and bring all things to your remembrance, whatsoever I have said unto you. [177:1].... He will guide you into all truth." [177:2]

The resurrection poured a flood of light into the minds of the apostles, and they forthwith commenced with unwonted boldness to proclaim the truth in all its purity and power; but, perhaps, no part of the evangelical history was written until upwards of twenty years after the death of our Saviour. [177:3] According to tradition, the Gospels of Matthew, Mark, and Luke, then appeared in the order in which they are now presented in our authorised version. [177:4] It is certain that all these narratives were published several years before the fall of Jerusalem in A.D. 70; and as each contains our Lord's announcement of its speedy catastrophe, there is much probability in the report, that the exact fulfilment of so remarkable a prophecy, led many to acknowledge the divine origin of the Christian religion. The Gospel of John is of a much later date, and seems to have been written towards the conclusion of the century.

Two of the evangelists, Matthew and John, were apostles; and the other two, Mark and Luke, appear to have been of the number of the Seventy. [177:5] All were, therefore, fully competent to bear testimony to the facts which they record, for the Seventy had "companied" with the Twelve "all the time that the Lord

Jesus went in and out among" them, [178:1] and all "were from the beginning eye-witnesses and ministers of the word." [178:2] These writers mention many miracles performed by Christ, and at least three of the Gospels were in general circulation whilst multitudes were still alive who are described in them as either the spectators or the subjects of His works of wonder; and yet, though the evangelists often enter most minutely into details, so that their statements, if capable of contradiction, might have been at once challenged and exposed, we do not find that any attempt was meanwhile made to impeach their accuracy. Their manner of recording the acts of the Great Teacher is characterised by remarkable simplicity, and the most acute reader in vain seeks to detect in it the slightest trace of concealment or exaggeration. Matthew artlessly confesses that he belonged to the odious class of publicans; [178:3] Mark tells how Peter, his friend and companion, "began to curse and to swear," and to declare that he knew not the Man; [178:4] Luke, who was probably one of the two brethren who journeyed to Emmaus, informs us how Jesus drew near to them on the way and upbraided them as "fools and slow of heart to believe all that the prophets had spoken;" [178:5] and John honestly repudiates the pretended prediction setting forth that he himself was not to die. [178:6] Each evangelist mentions incidents unnoticed by the others, and thus supplies proof that he is entitled to the credit of an original and independent witness. Matthew alone gives the formula of baptism "in the name of the Father, and of the Son, and of the Holy Ghost;" [178:7] Mark alone speaks of the great amazement of the people as they beheld the face of Christ on His descent from the Mount of Transfiguration; [179:1] Luke alone announces the appointment of the Seventy; [179:2] and John alone records some of those sublime discourses in which our Lord treats of the doctrine of His Sonship, of the mission of the Comforter, and of the mysterious union between Himself and His people. [179:3] All the evangelists direct our special attention to the scene of the crucifixion. As they proceed to describe it, they obviously feel that they are dealing with a transaction of awful import; and they accordingly become more impressive and circumstantial. Their statements, when combined, furnish a complete and consistent narrative of the sore travail, the deep humiliation, and the dying utterances of the illustrious sufferer.

If the appointment of the Seventy indicated our Lord's intention of sending the glad tidings of salvation to the ends of the earth, there was a peculiar propriety in the selection of an individual of their number as the historian of the earliest missionary triumphs. Whilst Luke records the wonderful success of Christianity amongst the Gentiles, he takes care to point out the peculiar features of the new economy; and thus it is that his narrative abounds with passages in which the doctrine, polity, and worship of the primitive disciples are illustrated or explained. It is well known that the titles of the several parts of the New Testament were prefixed to them, not by their authors, but at a subsequent period by parties who had no claim to inspiration; [179:4] and it is obvious that the book called—"The Acts of the Apostles" has not been very correctly designated. It is confined almost exclusively to the acts of Peter and Paul, and it sketches only a portion of their proceedings. As its narrative terminates at the end of Paul's second year's imprisonment at Rome, it was probably written about that period. Superficial readers may object to its information as curt and fragmentary; but the careful investigator will discover that it marks with great distinctness the most important stages in the early development of the Church.

[180:1] It shews how Christianity spread rapidly among the Jews from the day of Pentecost to the martyrdom of Stephen; it points out how it then took root among the Gentiles; and it continues to trace its dissemination from Judea westwards, until it was firmly planted by the apostle of the uncircumcision in the metropolis of the Empire.

It is highly probable that some of the fourteen epistles of Paul were written before any other portion of the New Testament, for we have already seen [180:2] that the greater number of them were transmitted to the parties to whom they are addressed during the time over which the Acts of the Apostles extend; but though Luke makes no mention of these letters, his account of the travels of their author throws considerable light on the question of their chronology. Guided by statements which he supplies, and by evidence contained in the documents themselves, we have endeavoured to point out the order of their composition. It thus appears that they are not placed chronologically in the New Testament. The present arrangement is, however, of great antiquity, as it can be traced up to the beginning of the fourth century; [180:3] and it is made upon the principle that the Churches addressed should be classed according to their relative importance. The Church of Rome at an early period was recognised as the most influential in existence, and hence the Epistle to the Romans stands at the head of the collection. The Church of Corinth seems to have ranked next, and accordingly the Epistles to the Corinthians occupy the second place. The letters to the Churches are followed by those to individuals, that is, to Timothy, Titus, and Philemon; and it has been conjectured that the Epistle to the Hebrews is put last, because it is anonymous. Some have contended that this letter was composed by Barnabas; others have ascribed it to Clement, or Luke, or Silas, or Apollos; but, though Paul has not announced his name, the external and internal evidences concur to prove that he was its author. [181:1]

"Every word of God is pure," [181:2] but the word of man is often deceitful; and nowhere do his fallibility and ignorance appear more conspicuously than in his appendages to Scripture. Even the titles prefixed to the writings of the apostles and evangelists are redolent of superstition, for no satisfactory reason can be given why the designation of saint, [181:3] has been bestowed on Matthew, Mark, Luke, and John, whilst it is withheld, not only from Moses and Isaiah, but also from such eminently holy ministers as Timothy and Titus. The postscripts to the epistles of Paul have been added by transcribers, and are also calculated to mislead. Thus, the Epistle to the Galatians is said to have been "written from Rome," though it is now generally acknowledged that Paul was not in the capital of the Empire until long after that letter was dictated. The first Epistle to Timothy is dated "from Laodicea, which is the chiefest city of Phrygia Pacatiana;" but it is well known that Phrygia was not divided into Phrygia Prima, or Pacatiana, and Phrygia Secunda until the fourth century. [181:4] It is stated at the end of another epistle that it was "written to Titus ordained the first Bishop of the Church of the Cretians;" but, as the letter itself demonstrates, Paul did not intend that Titus should remain permanently in Crete, [182:1] and it can be shewn that, for centuries afterwards, such a dignitary as "the Bishop of the Church of the Cretians" was utterly unknown.

The seven letters written by James, Peter, Jude, and John, are called General or Catholic epistles. The Epistle of James was addressed "to the twelve tribes scattered abroad" probably in A.D. 61, and its author survived its publication perhaps little more than twelve months. [182:2] Peter, as we have seen, appears to have written his two epistles only a short time before his martyrdom. [182:3] The Epistle of Jude is the production of a later period, as it contains quotations from the Second Epistle of Peter. [182:4] The exact dates of the Epistles of John cannot now be discovered, but they supply internal proof that they must have been written towards the close of the first century. [182:5]

According to some, the Apocalypse, or Revelation of John, was drawn up before the destruction of Jerusalem, and in the time of the Emperor Nero; but the arguments in support of so early an origin are very unsatisfactory. Ancient writers [182:6] attest that it was written in the reign of Domitian towards the close of the first century, and the truth of this statement is established by various collateral evidences.

The divine authority of the four Gospels and of the Acts of the Apostles was, from their first appearance, universally acknowledged in the ancient Church. [182:7] These books were publicly read in the religious assemblies of the primitive Christians, and were placed on a level with the Old Testament Scriptures. [182:8] The epistles of Paul occupied an equally honourable position. [182:9] In the second and third centuries the Epistle to the Hebrews was not, indeed, received among the sacred books by the Church of Rome; [183:1] but at an earlier period its inspiration was acknowledged by the Christians of the great city, for it is quoted as the genuine work of the Apostle Paul by an eminent Roman pastor who flourished in the first century. [183:2] The authority of two of the most considerable of the Catholic epistles—the First Epistle of Peter and the First Epistle of John—was never questioned; [183:3] but, for a time, there were churches which doubted the claims of the five others to be ranked amongst "the Scriptures." [183:4] The multitude of spurious writings which were then abroad suggested to the disciples the necessity of caution, and hence suspicions arose in certain cases where they were destitute of foundation. But these suspicions, which never seem to have been entertained by more than a minority of the churches, gradually passed away; and at length, towards the close of the fourth century, the whole of what are now called the Catholic epistles were received, by unanimous consent, as inspired documents. [183:5] The Apocalypse was acknowledged to be a divine revelation as soon as it appeared; and its credit remained unimpeached until the question of the Millennium began to create discussion. Its authenticity was then challenged by some of the parties who took an interest in the controversy; but it still continued to be regarded as a part of Holy Scripture by the majority of Christians, and there is no book of the New Testament in behalf of which a title to a divine original can be established by more conclusive and ample evidence. [184:1]

It thus appears that, with the exception of a few short epistles which some hesitated to accredit, the New Testament, in the first century, was acknowledged as the Word of God by all the Apostolical Churches. Its various parts were not then included in a single volume; and as a considerable time must have elapsed before copies of every one of them were universally disseminated, it is not to be thought extraordinary if the appearance of a letter, several years after it was written, and in quarters where it had been previously unknown, awakened suspicion or scepticism. But the slender objections, advanced under such circumstances, gradually vanished before the light of additional evidence; and it may safely be asserted that the whole of the documents, now known as the

84

Scriptures of the New Testament, were received, as parts of a divine revelation, by an overwhelming majority of the early Christians. The present division into chapters and verses was introduced at a period comparatively recent; [184:2] but there is reason to believe that stated portions of the writings of the apostles and evangelists were read by the primitive disciples at their religious meetings, and that, for the direction of the reader, as well as for the facility of reference, the arrangement was soon notified in the manuscripts by certain marks of distinction. [184:3] It is well known that in the ancient Churches persons of all classes and conditions were encouraged and required to apply themselves to the study of the sacred records; that even children were made acquainted with the Scriptures; [185:1] and that the private perusal of the inspired testimonies was considered an important means of individual edification. All were invited and stimulated by special promises to meditate upon the mysterious, as well as the plain, passages of the book of Revelation. "Blessed," says the Apostle John, "is he that readeth, and they that hear the words of this prophecy, and keep those things which are written therein." [185:2]

The original manuscripts of the New Testament, which must from the first have been accessible to comparatively few, have all long since disappeared; and it is now impossible to tell whether they were worn away by the corroding tooth of time, or destroyed in seasons of persecution. Copies of them were rapidly multiplied; and though heathen adversaries displayed no small amount of malice and activity, it was soon found impossible to effect their annihilation. It was not necessary that the apostolic autographs [185:3] should be preserved for ever, as the records, when transcribed, still retained the best and clearest proofs of their inspiration. They did not require even the imprimatur of the Church, for they exhibited in every page the stamp of divinity; and as soon as they were published, they commended themselves by the internal tokens of their heavenly lineage to the acceptance of the faithful. "The Word of God is quick and powerful," and every one who peruses the New Testament in a right spirit must feel that it has emanated from the Searcher of hearts. It speaks to the conscience; it has all the simplicity and majesty of a divine communication; it enlightens the understanding; and it converts the soul. No mere man could have invented such a character as the Saviour it reveals; no mere man could have contrived such a system of mercy as that which it announces. The New Testament is always on the side of whatsoever is just, and honest, and lovely, and of good report; it glorifies God; it alarms the sinner; it comforts the saint. "The words of the Lord are pure words, as silver tried in a furnace of earth purified seven times." [186:1]

The excellence of the New Testament is displayed to singular advantage when contrasted with those uninspired productions of nearly the same date which emanated from the companions of the apostles. The only genuine document of this nature which has come down to us, and which appeared in the first century,[186:2] is an epistle to the Corinthians. It was prepared immediately after the Domitian persecution, or about A.D. 96,[186:3] with a view to heal certain divisions which had sprung up in the religious community to which it is addressed; and, though written in the name of the Church of Rome, there is no reason to doubt that it is the composition of Clement, who was then at the head of the Roman presbytery. The advice which it administers is most judicious; and the whole letter breathes the peaceful spirit of a devoted Christian pastor. But it contains passages which furnish conclusive evidence that it has no claims whatever to inspiration; and its illustration of the doctrine of the resurrection is in itself more than sufficient to demonstrate that it could not have been dictated under any supernatural guidance. "There is," says Clement,[186:4] "a certain bird called the phoenix. Of this there is never but one at a time, and that lives five hundred years: and when the time of its dissolution draws near that it must die, it makes itself a nest of frankincense, and myrrh, and other spices, into which, when its time is fulfilled, it enters and dies. But its flesh putrefying breeds a certain worm which, being nourished with the juice of the dead bird, brings forth feathers; and when it is grown to a perfect state, it takes up the nest in which the bones of its parent are, and carries it from Arabia into Egypt to a city called Heliopolis; and flying in open day, in the sight of all men, lays it upon the altar of the Sun, and so returns from whence it came. The priests then search into the records of the time, and find that it returned precisely at the end of five hundred years." [187:1]

In point of education the authors of the New Testament did not generally enjoy higher advantages than Clement; and yet, writing "as they were moved by the Holy Ghost," they were prevented from giving currency, even in a single instance, to such a story as this fable of the phoenix. All their statements will be found to be true, whether tried by the standard of mental or of moral science, of geography, or of natural history. The theology which they teach is at once sound and genial; and those by whom it is appreciated can testify that whilst it invigorates and elevates the intellect, it also pacifies the conscience and purifies the heart.

CHAPTER II

THE DOCTRINE OF THE APOSTOLIC CHURCH

The same system of doctrine is inculcated throughout the whole of the sacred volume. Though upwards of fifteen hundred years elapsed between the commencement and the completion of the canon of Scripture; though its authors were variously educated; though they were distinguished, as well by their tastes, as by their temperaments; and though they lived in different countries and in different ages; all the parts of the volume called the Bible exhibit the clearest indications of unity of design. Each writer testifies to the "one faith," and each contributes something to its illustration. Thus it is that, even at the present day, every book in the canon is "good to the use of edifying." The announcements made to our first parents will continue to impart spiritual refreshment to their posterity of the latest generations; and the believer can now give utterance to his devotional feelings in the language of the Psalms, as appropriately as could the worshipper of old, when surrounded by all the types and shadows of the Levitical ceremonial.

The Old Testament is related to the New as the dawn to the day, or the prophecy to its accomplishment. Jesus appeared merely to consummate the Redemption which "the promises made to the fathers" had announced. "Think not," said he, "that I am come to destroy the law or the prophets, I am not come to destroy but to fulfil." [189:1] The mission of our Lord explained many things which had long remained mysterious; and, in allusion to the great amount of fresh information thus communicated, He is said to have "brought life and immortality to light through the gospel." [189:2]

When the apostles first became disciples of the Son of Mary, their views were certainly very indefinite and circumscribed. Acting under the influence of strong attachment to the Wonderful Personage who exhibited such wisdom and performed so many mighty works, they promptly obeyed the invitation to come and follow Him; and yet when required to tell who was this Great Teacher to whom they were attached by the charm of such a holy yet mysterious fascination, they could do little more than declare their conviction that Jesus was THE CHRIST. [189:3] They knew, indeed, that the Messiah, or the Great Prophet, was to be a redeemer, and a King; [189:4] but they did not understand how their lowly Master was to establish His title to such high offices. [189:5] Though they "looked for redemption," and "waited for the kingdom of God," [189:6] there was much that was vague, as well as much that was visionary, in their notions of the Redemption and the Kingdom. We may well suppose that the views of the multitude were still less correct and perspicuous. Some, perhaps, expected that Christ, as a prophet, would decide the ecclesiastical controversies of the age; [189:7] others, probably, anticipated that, as a Redeemer, he would deliver His countrymen from Roman domination; [189:8] whilst others again cherished the hope that, as a King, he would erect in Judea a mighty monarchy. [189:9] The expectation that he would assert the possession of temporal dominion was long entertained even by those who had been taught to regard Him as a spiritual Saviour. [190:1]

During the interval between the resurrection and ascension, the apostles profited greatly by the teaching of our Lord. "Then opened He their understanding that they might understand the Scriptures," [190:2] shewing that all things were "fulfilled which were written in the law of Moses, and in the Prophets, and in the Psalms" [190:3] concerning Him. The true nature of Christ's Kingdom was now fully disclosed to them; they saw that the history of Jesus was embodied in the ancient predictions; and thus their ideas were brought into harmony with the revelations of the Old Testament. On the day of Pentecost they, doubtless, received additional illumination; and thus, maturely qualified for the duties of their apostleship, they began to publish the great salvation. Even afterwards, their knowledge continued to expand; for they had yet to be taught that the Gentiles also were heirs of the Kingdom of Heaven; [190:4] that uncircumcised believers were to be admitted to all the privileges of ecclesiastical fellowship; [190:5] and that the ceremonial law had ceased to be obligatory. [190:6]

We do not require, however, to trace the progress of enlightenment in the minds of the original heralds of the gospel, that we may ascertain the doctrine of the Apostolic Church; for in the New Testament we have a complete and unerring exposition of the faith delivered to the saints. We have seen that, with a few comparatively trivial exceptions, all the documents dictated by the apostles and evangelists were at once recognised as inspired, [190:7] so that in them, combined with the Jewish Scriptures, we have a perfect ecclesiastical statute-book. The doctrine set forth in the New Testament was cordially embraced in the first century by all genuine believers. And it cannot be too emphatically inculcated that the written Word was of paramount authority among the primitive Christians. The Israelites had traditions which they professed to have received from Moses; but our Lord repudiated these fables, and asserted the supremacy of the book of inspiration. [191:1] In His own discourses He honoured the Scriptures by continually quoting from them; [191:2] and He commanded the Jews to refer to them as the only sure arbiters of his pretensions. [191:3] The apostles followed His example. More than one-half of the sermon preached by Peter on the day of Pentecost consisted of passages selected from the Old Testament. [191:4] The Scriptures, too, inculcate, not only their claims as standards of ultimate appeal, but also their sufficiency to meet all the wants of the faithful; for they are said to be "able to make wise unto salvation," [191:5] and to be "profitable for doctrine, for reproof, for correction, for instruction in righteousness, that the man of God may be perfect, thoroughly furnished unto all good works." [191:6] The sacred records teach, with equal clearness, their own plenary inspiration. Each writer has his peculiarities of style, and yet each uses language which the Holy Spirit dictates. In the New Testament a single word is more than once made the basis of an argument; [191:7] and doctrines are repeatedly established by a critical examination of particular forms of expression, [191:8] When statements advanced by Moses, or David, or Isaiah, are adduced, they are often prefaced with the intimation that thus "the Holy Ghost saith," [191:9] or thus "it is spoken of the Lord." [191:10] The apostles plainly aver that they employ language of infallible authority. "We speak," says Paul, "in the words which the Holy Ghost teacheth," [192:1] "All Scripture is given by inspiration of God." [192:2]

It is of unutterable importance that the Scriptures are the very word of the Lord, for they relate to our highest interests, and were they of less authority, they could not command our entire confidence. The momentous truths which they reveal are in every way worthy to be recorded in memorials given by inspiration of God. Under the ancient economy the sinner was assured of a Redeemer; [192:3] and intimations were not wanting that his deliverance would be wrought out in a way which would excite the wonder of the whole intelligent creation; [192:4] but the New Testament uplifts the veil, and sheds a glorious radiance over the revelation of mercy. According to the doctrine of the Apostolic Church the human race are at once "guilty before God," [192:5] and "dead in trespasses and sins;" [192:6] and as Christ in the days of His flesh called forth Lazarus from the tomb, and made him a monument of His wonder-working power, so by His word He still awakens dead sinners and calls them with an holy calling, that they may be trophies of His grace throughout all eternity. And as the restoration of hearing is an evidence of the restoration of life, so the reception of the word by faith is a sure token of spiritual vitality. "He that heareth my word," said Christ, "and believeth on Him that sent me, hath everlasting life, and shall not come into condemnation, but is passed from death unto life." [192:7]

Faith is to the soul of the believer what the living organs are to his body. It is the ear, the eye, the hand, and the palate of the spiritual man. By faith he hears the voice of the Son of God; [192:8] by faith he sees Him who is invisible; [192:9] by faith he looks unto Jesus; [193:1] by faith he lays hold upon the Hope set before him; [193:2] and by faith he tastes that the Lord is gracious. [193:3] All the promises are addressed to faith; and by faith they are appropriated and enjoyed. By faith the believer is pardoned, [193:4] sanctified, [193:5] sustained, [193:6] and comforted. [193:7] Faith is the substance of things hoped for, the evidence of things not seen; [193:8] for it enables us to anticipate the happiness of heaven, and to realize the truth of God.

The word of the Lord is to the faith of the Christian what the material world is to his bodily senses. As the eye gazes with delight on the magnificent scenery of creation, the eye of faith contemplates with joy unspeakable the exceedingly great and precious promises. And as the eye can look with pleasure only on those objects which it sees, faith can rest with satisfaction only on those things which are written in the book of God's testimony. It has been "written that we might believe that Jesus is the Christ, the Son of God; and that believing we might have life through his name." [193:9]

The Scriptures are not to be regarded as a storehouse of facts, promises, and precepts, without relation or dependency; but a volume in which may be found a collection of glorious truths, all forming one great and well-balanced system. Every part of revelation refers to the Redeemer; and His earthly history is the key by means of which its various announcements may be illustrated and harmonized. In the theology of the New Testament Christ is indeed the "All in all." In addition to many other illustrious titles which He bears, He is represented as "the Lamb of God which taketh away the sin of the world," [193:10] "the End of the Law for righteousness to every one that believeth," [193:11] "the Head of the Church," [194:1] the "King of kings," [194:2] and "the Hope of glory." [194:3] During His public ministry He performed miracles such as had been previously understood to mark the peculiar energy of Omnipotence; for He opened the eyes of the blind; [194:4] He walked upon the waves of the sea; [194:5] He made the storm a calm; [194:6] and He declared to man what was his thought. [194:7] In His capacity of Saviour He exercises attributes which are essentially divine; as He redeems from all iniquity, [194:8] and pardons sin, [194:9] and sanctifies the Church, [194:10] and opens the heart, [194:11] and searches the reins. [194:12] Had Jesus of Nazareth failed to assert His divine dignity, the credentials of His mission would have been incomplete, for the Messiah of the Old Testament is no other than the Monarch of the universe. Nothing can be more obvious than that the ancient prophets invest Him with the various titles and attributes of Deity. He is called "the Lord," [194:13] "Jehovah," [194:14] and "God;" [194:15] He is represented as the object of worship; [194:16] He is set forth as the King's Son who shall daily be praised; [194:17] and He is exhibited as an Almighty and Eternal Friend in whom all that put their trust are blessed. [194:18]

During the public ministry of our Lord the Twelve do not seem to have been altogether ignorant of His exalted dignity; [194:19] and yet the most decisive attestations to His Godhead do not occur until after His resurrection. [194:20] When the apostles surveyed the humble individual with whom they were in daily intercourse, it is not extraordinary that their faith faltered, and that their powers of apprehension failed, as they pondered the prophecies relating to His advent. When they attempted closely to grapple with the amazing truths there presented to their contemplation, and thought of "the Word made flesh," well might they be overwhelmed with a feeling of giddy and dubious wonder. Even after the resurrection had illustrated so marvellously the announcements of the Old

Testament, the disciples still continued to regard them with a species of bewilderment; and our Saviour himself found it necessary to point out in detail their meaning and their fulfilment. "Beginning at Moses and all the prophets he expounded to them in all the Scriptures the things concerning himself." [195:1] The whole truth as to the glory of His person now flashed upon their minds, and henceforth they do not scruple to apply to Him all the lofty titles bestowed of old on the Messiah. The writers of the New Testament say expressly that "Jesus is the Lord," [195:2] and "God blessed for ever;" [195:3] they describe believers as trusting in Him, [195:4] as serving Him, [195:5] and as calling upon His name; [195:6] and they tell of saints and angels, uniting in the celebration of His praise. [195:7] Such testimonies leave no doubt as to their ideas of His dignity. Divine incarnations were recognised in the heathen mythology, so that the Gentiles could not well object to the doctrine of the assumption of our nature by the Son of God; but Christianity asserts its immense superiority to paganism in its account of the design of the union of humanity and Deity in the person of the Redeemer. According to the poets of Greece and Rome, the gods often adopted material forms for the vilest of purposes; but the Lord of glory was made partaker of our flesh and blood, [196:1] that He might satisfy the claims of eternal justice, and purchase for us a happy and immortal inheritance. In the cross of Christ sin appears "exceedingly sinful," and the divine law has been more signally honoured by His sufferings than if all men of all generations had for ever groaned under its chastisements. The Jewish ritual must have made the apostles perfectly familiar with the doctrine of atonement; but they were "slow of heart to believe" that their Master was Himself the Mighty Sacrifice represented in the types of the Mosaic ceremonial [196:2] The evangelist informs us that He expounded this subject after His resurrection, shewing them that "thus it behoved Christ to suffer." [196:3] Still, the crucifixion of the Saviour was to multitudes a "rock of offence." The ambitious Israelite, who expected that the Messiah would go forth conquering and to conquer, and that He would make Palestine the seat of universal empire, could not brook the thought that the Great Deliverer was to die; and the learned Greek, who looked upon all religion with no little scepticism, was prepared to ridicule the idea of the burial of the Son of God; but the very circumstance which awakened such prejudices, suggested to those possessed of spiritual discernment discoveries of stupendous grandeur. Justice demands the punishment of transgressors; mercy pleads for their forgiveness: holiness requires the execution of God's threatenings; goodness insists on the fulfilment of His promises: and all these attributes are harmonized in the doctrine of a Saviour sacrificed. God is "just, and the justifier of him which, believeth in Jesus." [196:4] The Son of Man "by his own blood obtained eternal redemption" [197:1] for His Church; "mercy and truth meet together" in His expiation; and His death is thus the central point to which the eye of faith is now directed. Hence Paul says—"We preach Christ crucified, unto the Jews a stumbling-block, and unto the Greeks foolishness; but unto them which are called, both Jews and Greeks, Christ, the power of God, and the wisdom of God." [197:2]

The doctrine of the Apostolic Church is simple and consistent, as well as spiritual and sublime. The way of redemption it discloses is not an extempore provision of Supreme benevolence called forth by an unforeseen contingency, but a plan devised from eternity, and fitted to display all the divine perfections in most impressive combination. Whilst it recognises the voluntary agency of man, it upholds the sovereignty of God. Jehovah graciously secures the salvation of every heir of the promises by both contriving and carrying out all the arrangements of the "well ordered covenant." His Spirit quickens the dead soul, and works in us "to will and to do of His good pleasure." [197:3] "The Father hath chosen us in Christ before the foundation of the world, that we should be holy and without blame before him in love; having predestinated us unto the adoption of children by Jesus Christ to himself, according to the good pleasure of his will, to the praise of the glory of his grace, wherein he hath made us accepted in the Beloved." [197:4]

The theological term Trinity was not in use in the days of the apostles, but it does not follow that the doctrine now so designated was then unknown; for the New Testament clearly indicates that the Father, the Son, and the Holy Ghost exist in the unity of the Godhead. [197:5] Neither can it be inferred from the absence of any fixed formula of doctrine that the early followers of our Lord did not all profess the same sentiments, for they had "one Lord, one faith, one baptism." [198:1] The document commonly called "the Apostles' Creed" is certainly of very great antiquity, but no part of it proceeded from those to whom it is attributed by its title; [198:2] and its rather bald and dry detail of facts and principles obviously betokens a decline from the simple and earnest spirit of primitive Christianity. Though the early converts, before baptism, made a declaration of their faith, [198:3] there is in the sacred volume no authorised summary of doctrinal belief; and in this fact we have a proof of the far-seeing wisdom by which the New Testament was dictated; as heresy is ever changing its features, and a test of orthodoxy, suited to the wants of one age, would not exclude the errorists of another. It has been left to the existing rulers of the Church to frame such ecclesiastical symbols as circumstances require; and it is a striking evidence of the perfection of the Bible that it has been found capable of furnishing an antidote to every form of heterodoxy which has ever appeared.

It may be added that the doctrine of the Apostolic Church is eminently practical. The great object of the mission of Jesus was to "save His people from their sins;" [198:4] and the tendency of all the teachings of the New Testament is to promote sanctification. But the holiness of the gospel is not a shy asceticism which sits in a cloister in moody melancholy, so that its light never shines before men; but a generous consecration of the heart to God, which leads us to confess Christ in the presence of gainsayers, and which prompts us to delight in works of benevolence. The true Christian should be happy as well as holy; for the knowledge of the highest truth is connected with the purest enjoyment. This "wisdom is better than rubies, and all the things that may be desired are not to be compared to it." [199:1] The Apostle Paul, when a prisoner at Rome, had comforts to which Nero was an utter stranger. Even then he could say—"I have learned in whatsoever state I am therewith to be content. I know both how to be abased, and I know how to abound; everywhere and in all things I am instructed both to be full and to be hungry, both to abound and to suffer need. I can do all things through Christ which strengtheneth me." [199:2] When all around the believer may be dark and discouraging, there may be sunshine in his soul. There are no joys comparable to the joys of a Christian. They are the gifts of the Spirit of God, and the first-fruits of eternal blessedness; they are serene and heavenly, solid and satisfying.

CHAPTER III

THE HERESIES OF THE APOSTOLIC AGE

The Greek word translated heresy [200:1] in our authorised version of the New Testament, did not primarily convey an unfavourable idea. It simply denoted a choice or preference. It was often employed to indicate the adoption of a particular class of philosophical sentiments; and thus it came to signify a sect or denomination. Hence we find ancient writers speaking of the heresy of the Stoics, the heresy of the Epicureans, and the heresy of the Academics. The Jews who used the Greek language did not consider that the word necessarily reflected on the party it was intended to describe; and Josephus, who was himself a Pharisee, accordingly discourses of the three heresies of the Pharisees, the Sadducees, and the Essenes. [200:2] The Apostle Paul, when speaking of his own history prior to his conversion, says, that "after the strictest heresy" of his religion he lived a Pharisee. [200:3] We learn, too, from the book of the Acts, that the early Christians were known as "the heresy of the Nazarenes." [200:4] But very soon the word began to be employed to denote something which the gospel could not sanction; and accordingly, in the Epistle to the Galatians, heresies are enumerated among the works of the flesh. [200:5] It is not difficult to explain why Christian writers at an early date were led to attach such a meaning to a term which had hitherto been understood to imply nothing reprehensible. The New Testament teaches us to regard an erroneous theology as sinful, and traces every deviation from "the one faith" of the gospel to the corruption of a darkened intellect. [201:1] It declares—"He that believeth not is condemned already, because he hath not believed in the name of the only-begotten Son of God; and this is the condemnation, that light is come into the world, and men loved darkness rather than light, because their deeds were evil." [201:2] Thus it was that the most ancient ecclesiastical authors described all classes of unbelievers, sceptics, and innovators, under the general name of heretics. Persons who in matters of religion made a false choice, of whatever kind, were viewed as "vainly puffed up by a fleshly mind," or as under the influence of some species of mental depravity.

It thus appears that heresy, in the first century, denoted every deviation from the Christian faith. Pagans and Jews, as well as professors of apocryphal forms of the gospel, were called heretics. [201:3] But in the New Testament our attention is directed chiefly to errorists who in some way disturbed the Church, and adulterated the doctrine taught by our Lord and His apostles. Paul refers to such characters when he says—"A man that is an heretic, after the first and second admonition, reject;" [201:4] and Peter also alludes to them when he speaks of false teachers who were to appear and "privily bring in damnable heresies." [201:5]

The earliest corrupters of the gospel were unquestionably those who endeavoured to impose the observance of the Mosaic law on the converted Gentiles. Their proceedings were condemned in the Council of Jerusalem, mentioned in the fifteenth chapter of the Acts of the Apostles; and Paul, in his letter to the Galatians, subsequently exposed their infatuation. But evangelical

92

truth had, perhaps, more to fear from dilution with the speculations of the Jewish and pagan literati. [202:1] The apostle had this evil in view when he said to the Colossians— "Beware lest any man spoil you through philosophy and vain deceit, after the tradition of men, after the rudiments of the world, and not after Christ." [202:2] He likewise emphatically attested the danger to be apprehended from it when he addressed to his own son in the faith the impassioned admonition—"O Timothy, keep that which is committed to thy trust, avoiding profane and vain babblings, and oppositions of science falsely so called." [202:3]

There is no reason to doubt that the "science" or "philosophy" of which Paul was so anxious that the disciples should beware, was the same which was afterwards so well known by the designation of Gnosticism. The second century was the period of its most vigorous development, and it then, for a time, almost engrossed the attention of the Church; but it was already beginning to exert a pernicious influence, and it is therefore noticed by the vigilant apostle. Whilst it acknowledged, to a certain extent, the authority of the Christian revelation, it also borrowed largely from Platonism; and, in a spirit of accommodation to the system of the Athenian sage, it rejected some of the leading doctrines of the gospel. Plato never seems to have entertained the sublime conception of the creation of all things out of nothing by the word of the Most High. He held that matter is essentially evil, and that it existed from eternity. [202:4] The false teachers who disturbed the Church in the apostolic age adopted both these views; and the errors which they propagated and of which the New Testament takes notice, flowed from their unsound philosophy by direct and necessary consequence. As a right understanding of certain passages of Scripture depends on an acquaintance with their system, it may here be expedient to advert somewhat more particularly to a few of its peculiar features.

The Gnostics alleged that the present world owes neither its origin nor its arrangement to the Supreme God. They maintained that its constituent parts have been always in existence; and that, as the great Father of Lights would have been contaminated by contact with corrupt matter, the visible frame of things was fashioned, without His knowledge, by an inferior Intelligence. These principles obviously derogated from the glory of Jehovah. By ascribing to matter an independent and eternal existence, they impugned the doctrine of God's Omnipotent Sovereignty; and by representing it as regulated without His sanction by a spiritual agent of a lower rank, they denied His Universal Providence. The apostle, therefore, felt it necessary to enter his protest against all such cosmogonies. He declared that Jehovah alone, as Father, Son, and Holy Ghost, existed from eternity; and that all things spiritual and material arose out of nothing in obedience to the word of the second person of the Godhead. "By Him," says he, "were all things created, that are in heaven and that are in earth, visible and invisible, whether they be thrones or dominions or principalities or powers; all things were created by Him and for Him, and He is before all things, and by Him all things consist." [203:1]

The philosophical system of the Gnostics also led them to adopt false views respecting the body of Christ. As, according to their theory, the Messiah appeared to deliver men from the bondage of evil matter, they could not consistently acknowledge that He himself inhabited an earthly tabernacle. They refused to admit that our Lord was born of a human parent; and, as they asserted that He had a body only in appearance, or that His visible form as man was in reality a phantom, they were at length known by the title of Docetae. [204:1] The Apostle John repeatedly attests the folly and the danger of such speculations. "The Word," says he, "was made flesh and dwelt among us. [204:2] ... Every spirit that confesseth not that Jesus Christ is come in the flesh is not of God. [204:3] ... That which was from the beginning, which we have heard, which we have seen with our eyes, which we have looked upon, and our hands have handled of the Word of Life ... declare we unto you. [204:4] ... Many deceivers are entered into the world who confess not that Jesus Christ is come in the flesh." [204:5]

Reasoning from the principle that evil is inherent in matter, the Gnostics believed the union of the soul and the body to be a calamity. According to their views the spiritual being can never attain the perfection of which he is susceptible so long as he remains connected with his present corporeal organization. Hence they rejected the doctrine of the resurrection of the body. When Paul asks the Corinthians—"How say some among you that there is no resurrection of the dead?" [204:6]—he alludes to the Gnostic denial of this article of the Christian theology. He also refers to the same circumstance when he denounces the "profane and vain babblings" of those who "concerning the truth" had erred, "saying that the resurrection is past already." [204:7] These heretics, it would appear, maintained that an introduction to their Gnosis, or knowledge, was the only genuine deliverance from the dominion of death; and argued accordingly that, in the case of those who had been initiated into the mysteries of their system, the resurrection was "past already."

The ancient Christian writers concur in stating that Simon, mentioned in the Acts of the Apostles, [205:1] and commonly called Simon Magus, was the father of the sects of the Gnostics. [205:2] He was a Samaritan by birth, and after the rebuke he received from Peter, [205:3] he is reported to have withdrawn from the Church, and to have concocted a theology of his own, into which he imported some elements borrowed from Christianity. At a subsequent period he travelled to Rome, where he attracted attention by the novelty of his creed, and the boldness of his pretensions. We are told that, prior to his baptism by Philip, he "had used sorcery, and bewitched the people of Samaria, giving out that himself was some great one;" [205:4] and subsequently he seems to have pursued a similar career. According to a very early authority, nearly all the inhabitants of his native country, and a few persons in other districts, worshipped him as the first or supreme God. [205:5] There is, probably, some exaggeration in this statement; but there seems no reason to doubt that he laid claim to extraordinary powers, maintaining that the same spirit which had been imparted to Jesus, had descended on himself. He is also said to have denied that our Lord had a real body. Some, who did not enrol themselves under his standard, soon partially adopted his principles; and there is cause to think that Hymenaeus, Philetus, Alexander, Phygellus, and Hermogenes, mentioned in the New Testament, [205:6] were all more or less tinctured with the spirit of Gnosticism. Other heresiarchs, not named in the sacred record, are known to have flourished towards the close of the first century. Of these the most famous were Carpocrates, Cerinthus, and Ebion. [206:1] There is a tradition that John, "the beloved disciple," came in contact with Cerinthus, when going into a bath at Ephesus, and retired abruptly from the place, that he might not compromise himself by remaining in the same building with such an enemy of the Christian revelation. [206:2] It is also stated that the same apostle's testimony to the dignity of the

94

Word, in the beginning of his Gospel, was designed as an antidote to the errors of this heresiarch. [206:3]

When the gospel exerts its proper influence on the character it produces an enlightened, genial, and consistent piety; but a false faith is apt to lead, in practice, to one of two extremes, either the asceticism of the Essene, or the sensualism of the Sadducee. Gnosticism developed itself in both these directions. Some of its advocates maintained that, as matter is essentially evil, the corrupt propensities of the body should be kept in constant subjection by a life of rigorous mortification; others held that, as the principle of evil is inherent in the corporeal frame, the malady is beyond the reach of cure, and that, therefore, the animal nature should be permitted freely to indulge its peculiar appetites. To the latter party, as some think, belonged the Nicolaitanes noticed by John in the Apocalypse. [206:4] They are said to have derived their name from Nicolas, one of the seven deacons ordained by the apostles; [206:5] and to have been a class of Gnostics noted for their licentiousness. The origin of the designation may, perhaps, admit of some dispute; but it is certain that those to whom it was applied were alike lax in principle and dissolute in practice, for the Spirit of God has declared His abhorrence as well of the "doctrine," as of "the deeds of the Nicolaitanes." [207:1]

Though the Jews, at the time of the appearance of our Lord, were so much divided in sentiment, and though the Pharisees, the Sadducees, and the Essenes, had each their theological peculiarities, their sectarianism did not involve any complete severance or separation. Notwithstanding their differences of creed, the Pharisees and Sadducees sat together in the Sanhedrim, [207:2] and worshipped together in the temple. All the seed of Abraham constituted one Church, and congregated in the same sacred courts to celebrate the great festivals. In the Christian Church, in the days of the apostles, there was something approaching to the same outward unity. Though, for instance, there were so many parties among the Corinthians—though one said, I am of Paul, and another I am of Apollos, and another I am of Cephas, and another I am of Christ—all assembled in the same place to join in the same worship, and to partake of the same Eucharist. Those who withdrew from the disciples with whom they had been previously associated, appear generally to have relinquished altogether the profession of Christianity. [207:3] Some, at least, of the Gnostics acted very differently. When danger appeared they were inclined to temporize, and to discontinue their attendance on the worship of the Church; but they were desirous to remain still nominally connected with the great body of believers. [207:4] Any form of alliance with such dangerous errorists was, however, considered a cause of scandal; and the inspired teachers of the gospel insisted on their exclusion from ecclesiastical fellowship. Hence Paul declares that he had delivered Hymenaeus and Alexander "unto Satan" that they might learn "not to blaspheme;" [208:1] and John upbraids the Church in Pergamos because it retained in its communion "them that held the doctrine of the Nicolaitanes." [208:2] During the first century the Gnostics seem to have been unable to create anything like a schism among those who had embraced Christianity. Whilst the apostles lived the "science falsely so called" could not pretend to a divine sanction; and though here and there they displayed considerable activity in the dissemination of their principles, they were sternly and effectually discountenanced. It is accordingly stated by one of the earliest ecclesiastical writers that, in the time of Simeon of Jerusalem, who

95

finished his career in the beginning of the second century, "they called the Church as yet a virgin, inasmuch as it was not yet corrupted by vain discourses." [208:3] Other writers concur in bearing testimony to the fact that, whilst the apostles were on earth, false teachers failed "to divide the unity" of the Christian commonwealth, "by the introduction of corrupt doctrines." [208:4]

The gospel affords scope for the healthful and vigorous exercise of the human understanding, and it is itself the highest and the purest wisdom. It likewise supplies a test for ascertaining the state of the heart. Those who receive it with faith unfeigned will delight to meditate on its wonderful discoveries; but those who are unrenewed in the spirit of their minds will render to it only a doubtful submission, and will pervert its plainest announcements. The apostle therefore says—"There must be also heresies among you, that they which are approved may be made manifest among you." [208:5] The heretic is made manifest alike by his deviations from the doctrines and the precepts of revelation. His creed does not exhibit the consistency of truth, and his life fails to display the beauty of holiness. Bible Christianity is neither superstitious nor sceptical, neither austere nor sensual. "The wisdom that is from above is first pure, then peaceable, gentle, and easy to be intreated, full of mercy and good fruits, without partiality and without hypocrisy." [209:1]

SECTION III

THE WORSHIP AND CONSTITUTION OF THE APOSTOLIC CHURCH

CHAPTER I

THE LORD'S DAY—THE WORSHIP OF THE APOSTOLIC CHURCH—ITS SYMBOLIC ORDINANCES AND ITS DISCIPLINE

To the primitive disciples the day on which our Lord rose from the grave was a crisis of intense excitement. The crucifixion had cast a dismal cloud over their prospects; for, immediately before, when He entered Jerusalem amidst the hosannahs of the multitude, they had probably anticipated that He was about to assert His sovereignty as the Messiah: yet, when His body was committed to the tomb, they did not at once sink into despair; and, though filled with anxiety, they ventured to indulge a hope that the third day after His demise would be signalised by some new revelation. [210:1] The report of those who were early at the sepulchre at first inspired the residue of the disciples with wonder and perplexity; [210:2] but, as the proofs of His resurrection multiplied, they became confident and joyful. Ever afterwards the first day of the week was observed by them as the season of holy convocation. [211:1] Those members of the Apostolic Church who had been originally Jews, continued for some time to meet together also on the Saturday; but, what was called "The Lord's Day," [211:2] was regarded by all as sacred to Christ.

It has often been asserted that, during His own ministry, our Saviour encouraged His disciples to violate the Sabbath, and thus prepared the way for its abolition. But this theory is as destitute of foundation as it is dangerous to morality. Even the ceremonial law continued to be binding until Jesus expired upon the cross; and meanwhile He no doubt felt it to be His duty to attend to every jot and tittle of its appointments. [211:3] Thus, it became Him "to fulfil all righteousness." [211:4] He is at pains to shew that the acts of which the Pharisees complained as breaches of the Sabbath could be vindicated by Old Testament authority; [211:5] and that these formalists "condemned the guiltless," [211:6] when they denounced the disciples as doing that which was unlawful. Jesus never transgressed either the letter or the spirit of any commandment pertaining to the holy rest; but superstition had added to the written law a multitude of minute observances; and every Israelite was at perfect liberty to neglect any or all of these frivolous regulations.

The Great Teacher never intimated that the Sabbath was a ceremonial ordinance which was to cease with the Mosaic ritual. It was instituted when our first parents were in Paradise; [211:7] and the precept enjoining its remembrance, being a portion of the Decalogue, [212:1] is of perpetual obligation. Hence,

97

instead of regarding it as a merely Jewish institution, Christ declares that it "was made for MAN," [212:2] or, in other words, that it was designed for the benefit of the whole human family. Instead of anticipating its extinction along with the ceremonial law, He speaks of its existence after the downfal of Jerusalem. When He announces the calamities connected with the ruin of the holy city, He instructs His followers to pray that the urgency of the catastrophe may not deprive them of the comfort of the ordinances of the sacred rest. "Pray ye," said he, "that your flight be not in the winter, neither on the Sabbath-day." [212:3] And the prophet Isaiah, when describing the ingathering of the Gentiles and the glory of the Church in the times of the gospel, mentions the keeping of the Sabbath as characteristic of the children of God. "The sons of the stranger," says he, "that join themselves to the Lord to serve him, and to love the name of the Lord, to be his servants, every one that keepeth the Sabbath from polluting it, and taketh hold of my covenant—even them I will I bring to my holy mountain, and make them joyful in my house of prayer; their burnt-offerings and their sacrifices shall be accepted upon mine altar: [212:4] for mine house shall be called an house of prayer for all people." [212:5]

But when Jesus declared that "the Son of Man is Lord also of the Sabbath," [212:6] He unquestionably asserted His right to alter the circumstantials of its observance. He accordingly abolished its ceremonial worship, gave it a new name, and changed the day of its celebration. He signalised the first day of the week by then appearing once and again to His disciples after His resurrection, [212:7] and by that Pentecostal outpouring of the Spirit [213:1] which marks the commencement of a new era in the history of redemption. As the Lord's day was consecrated to the Lord's service, [213:2] the disciples did not now neglect the assembling of themselves together; [213:3] and the apostle commanded them at this holy season to set apart a portion of their gains for religious purposes. [213:4] It was most fitting that the first day of the week should be thus distinguished under the new economy; for the deliverance of the Church is a more illustrious achievement than the formation of the world; [213:5] and as the primeval Sabbath commemorated the rest of the Creator, the Christian Sabbath reminds us of the completion of the work of the Redeemer. "There remaineth, therefore, the keeping of a Sabbath [213:6] to the people of God, for he that is entered into his rest, he also hath ceased from his own works, as God did from his." [213:7]

As many of the converts from Judaism urged the circumcision of their Gentile brethren, they were likewise disposed to insist on their observance of the Hebrew festivals. The apostles, at least for a considerable time, did not deem it expedient positively to forbid the keeping of such days; but they required that, in matters of this nature, every one should be left to his own discretion. "One man," says Paul, "esteemeth one day above another; another esteemeth every day alike. Let every man be fully persuaded in his own mind." [213:8] It is obvious that the Lord's day is not included in this compromise; for from the morning of the resurrection there appears to have been no dispute as to its claims, and its very title attests the general recognition of its authority. The apostle can refer only to days which were typical and ceremonial. Hence he says elsewhere—"Let no man judge you in meat, or in drink, or in respect of an holyday, or of the new moon, or of the Sabbath days—which are a shadow of things to come, but the body is of Christ." [214:1]

Though the New Testament furnishes no full and circumstantial description of the worship of the Christian Church, it makes such incidental allusions to its various parts, as enable us to form a pretty accurate idea of its general character. Like the worship of the synagogue [214:2] it consisted of prayer, singing, reading the Scriptures, and expounding or preaching. Those who joined the Church, for several years after it was first organized, were almost exclusively converts from Judaism, and when they embraced the Christian faith, they retained the order of religious service to which they had been hitherto accustomed; but by the recognition of Jesus Christ as the Messiah of whom the law and the prophets testified, their old forms were inspired with new life and significance. At first the heathen did not challenge the distinction between the worship of the synagogue and the Church; and thus it was, as has already been intimated, that for a considerable portion of the first century, the Christians and the Jews were frequently confounded.

It has often been asserted, that the Jews had a liturgy when our Lord ministered in their synagogues; but the proof adduced in support of this statement is far from satisfactory; and their prayers which are still extant, and which are said to have been then in use, must obviously have been written after the destruction of Jerusalem. [215:1] It is, however, certain that the Christians in the apostolic age were not restricted to any particular forms of devotion. The liturgies ascribed to Mark, James, and others, are unquestionably the fabrications of later times; [215:2] and had any of the inspired teachers of the gospel composed a book of common prayer, it would, of course, have been received into the canon of the New Testament. Our Lord taught His disciples to pray, and supplied them with a model to guide them in their devotional exercises; [215:3] but there is no evidence whatever that, in their stated services, they constantly employed the language of that beautiful and comprehensive formulary. The very idea of a liturgy was altogether alien to the spirit of the primitive believers. They were commanded to give thanks "in everything," [215:4] to pray "always with all prayer and supplication in the spirit," [215:5] and to watch thereunto "with all perseverance and supplication for all saints;" [215:6] and had they been limited to a form, they would have found it impossible to comply with these admonitions. Their prayers were dictated by the occasion, and varied according to passing circumstances. Some of them which have been recorded, [215:7] had a special reference to the occurrences of the day, and could not have well admitted of repetition. In the apostolic age, when the Spirit was poured out in such rich effusion on the Church, the gift, as well as the grace, of prayer was imparted abundantly, so that a liturgy would have been deemed superfluous, if not directly calculated to freeze the genial current of devotion.

Singing, in which none but Levites were permitted to unite, [216:1] and which was accompanied by instrumental music, constituted a prominent part of the temple service. The singers occupied an elevated platform adjoining the court of the priests; [216:2] and it is somewhat doubtful whether, in that position, they were distinctly heard by the majority of the worshippers within the sacred precincts. [216:3] As the sacrifices, offerings, and other observances of the temple, as well as the priests, the vestments, and even the building itself, had an emblematic meaning, [216:4] it would appear that the singing, intermingled with the music of various instruments of sound, was also typical and ceremonial. It seems to have indicated that the tongue of man cannot sufficiently express the

99

praise of the King Eternal, and that all things, animate and inanimate, owe Him a revenue of glory. The worship of the synagogue was more simple. Its officers had, indeed, trumpets and cornets, with which they published their sentences of excommunication, and announced the new year, the fasts, and the Sabbath; [216:5] but they did not introduce instrumental music into their congregational services. The early Christians followed the example of the synagogue; and when they celebrated the praises of God "in psalms, and hymns, and spiritual songs," [216:6] their melody was "the fruit of the lips." [216:7] For many centuries after this period, the use of instrumental music was unknown in the Church. [217:1]

The Jews divided the Pentateuch and the writings of the Prophets into sections, one of which was read every Sabbath in the synagogue; [217:2] and thus, in the place set apart to the service of the God of Israel, His own will was constantly proclaimed. The Christians bestowed equal honour on the holy oracles; for in their solemn assemblies, the reading of the Scriptures of the Old and New Testament formed a part of their stated worship. [217:3] At the close of this exercise, one or more of the elders edified the congregation, either by giving a general exposition of the passage read, or by insisting particularly on some point of doctrine or duty which it obviously inculcated. If a prophet was present, he, too, had now an opportunity of addressing the auditory. [217:4]

As apostolic Christianity aimed to impart light to the understanding, its worship was uniformly conducted in the language of the people. It, indeed, attested its divine origin by miracles, and it accordingly enabled some to speak in tongues in which they had never been instructed; but it permitted such individuals to exercise their gifts in the church only when interpreters were present to translate their communications. [217:5] Whilst the gift of tongues, possessed by so many of the primitive disciples, must have attracted the attention of the Gentile as well as of the Jewish literati, it must also have made a powerful impression on the popular mind, more especially in large cities; for in such places there were always foreigners to whom these strange utterances would be perfectly intelligible, and for whom a discourse delivered in the speech of their native country would have peculiar charms. But in the worship of the primitive Christians there was no attempt, in the way of embellishment or decoration, to captivate the senses. The Church had no gorgeous temples, no fragrant incense, [218:1] no splendid vestments. For probably the whole of the first century, she celebrated her religious ordinances in private houses, [218:2] and her ministers officiated in their ordinary costume. John, the forerunner of our Saviour, "had his raiment of camel's hair, and a leathern girdle about his loins;" [218:3] but perhaps few of the early Christian preachers were arrayed in such coarse canonicals.

The Founder of the Christian religion instituted only two symbolic ordinances—Baptism and the Lord's Supper. [218:4] It is universally admitted that, in the apostolic age, baptism was dispensed to all who embraced the gospel; but it has been much disputed whether it was also administered to the infant children of the converts. The testimony of Scripture on the subject is not very explicit; for, as the ordinance was in common use amongst the Jews, [218:5] a minute description of its mode and subjects was, perhaps, deemed unnecessary by the apostles and evangelists. When an adult heathen was received into the Church of Israel, it is well known that the little children of the proselyte were admitted along with him; [219:1] and as the Christian Scriptures no where forbid

100

the dispensation of the rite to infants, it may be presumed that the same practice was observed by the primitive ministers of the gospel. This inference is emphatically corroborated by the fact that, of the comparatively small number of passages in the New Testament which treat of its administration, no less than five refer to the baptism of whole households. [219:2] It is also worthy of remark that these five cases are not mentioned as rare or peculiar, but as ordinary specimens of the method of apostolic procedure. It is not, indeed, absolutely certain that there was an infant in any of these five households; but it is, unquestionably, much more probable that they contained a fair proportion of little children, than that every individual in each of them had arrived at years of maturity, and that all these adults, without exception, at once participated in the faith of the head of the family, and became candidates for baptism.

In the New Testament faith is represented as the grand qualification for baptism; [219:3] but this principle obviously applies only to all who are capable of believing; for in the Word of God faith is also represented as necessary to salvation, [219:4] and yet it is generally conceded that little children may be saved. Under the Jewish dispensation infants were circumcised, and were thus recognised as interested in the divine favour, so that, if they be excluded from the rite of baptism, it follows that they occupy a worse position under a milder and more glorious economy. But the New Testament forbids us to adopt such an inference. It declares that infants should be "suffered to come" to the Saviour; [219:5] it indicates that baptism supplies the place of circumcision, for it connects the gospel institution with "the circumcision of Christ;" [220:1] it speaks of children as "saints" and as "in the Lord," [220:2] and, of course, as having received some visible token of Church membership; and it assures them that their sins are forgiven them "for His name's sake." [220:3] The New Testament does not record a single case in which the offspring of Christian parents were admitted to baptism on arriving at years of intelligence; but it tells of the apostles exhorting the men of Judea to repent and to submit to the ordinance, inasmuch as it was a privilege proffered to them and to their children. [220:4] Nay more, Paul plainly teaches that the seed of the righteous are entitled to the recognition of saintship; and that, even when only one of the parents is a Christian, the offspring do not on that account forfeit their ecclesiastical inheritance. "The unbelieving husband," says he, "is sanctified by the wife, and the unbelieving wife is sanctified by the husband, else were your children unclean, but now are they holy." [220:5] This passage demonstrates that the Apostolic Church recognised the holiness of infants, or in other words, that it admitted them to baptism.

The Scriptures furnish no very specific instructions as to the mode of baptism; and it is probable that, in its administration, the primitive heralds of the gospel did not adhere to a system of rigid uniformity. [220:6] Some have asserted that the Greek word translated baptize, [220:7] in our authorised version, always signifies immerse, but it has been clearly shewn [221:1] that this statement is inaccurate, and that baptism does not necessarily imply dipping. In ancient times, and in the lands where the apostles laboured, bathing was perhaps as frequently performed by affusion as immersion; [221:2] and it may be that the apostles varied their method of baptizing according to circumstances. [221:3] The ordinance was intended to convey the idea of washing or purifying; and it is obvious that water may be applied, in many ways, as the means of ablution. In the sacred volume sprinkling is often spoken of as equivalent to washing. [221:4]

As baptism was designed to supersede the Jewish circumcision, the Lord's Supper was intended to occupy the place of the Jewish Passover. [221:5] The Paschal lamb could be sacrificed nowhere except in the temple of Jerusalem, and the Passover was kept only once a year; but the Eucharist could be dispensed wherever a Christian congregation was collected; and at this period it seems to have been observed every first day of the week, at least by the more zealous and devout worshippers. [221:6] The wine, as well as the other element, was given to all who joined in its celebration; and the title of the "Breaking of Bread," [221:7] one of the names by which the ordinance was originally distinguished, supplies evidence that the doctrine of transubstantiation was then utterly unknown. The word Sacrament, as applied to Baptism and the Holy Supper, was not in use in the days of the apostles, and the subsequent introduction of this nomenclature, [222:1] probably contributed to throw an air of mystery around these institutions. The primitive disciples considered the elements employed in them simply as signs and seals of spiritual blessings; and they had no more idea of regarding the bread in the Eucharist as the real body of our Saviour, than they had of believing that the water of baptism is the very blood in which He washed His people from their sins. They knew that they enjoyed the light of His countenance in prayer, in meditation, and in the hearing of His Word; and that He was not otherwise present in these symbolic ordinances.

Whilst, in the Lord's Supper, believers hold fellowship with Christ, they also maintain and exhibit their communion with each other. "We, being many," says Paul, "are one bread and one body, for we are all partakers of that one bread." [222:2] Those who joined together in the observance of this holy institution were thereby pledged to mutual love; but every one who acted in such a way as to bring reproach upon the Christian name, was no longer admitted to the sacred table. Paul, doubtless, refers to exclusion from this ordinance, as well as from intimate civil intercourse, when he says to the Corinthians—"I have written unto you not to keep company, if any man that is called a brother be a fornicator, or covetous, or an idolater, or a railer, or a drunkard, or an extortioner; with such an one no not to eat." [222:3]

In the synagogue all cases of discipline were decided by the bench of elders; [222:4] and it is plain, from the New Testament, that those who occupied a corresponding position in the Christian Church, also exercised similar authority. They are described as having the oversight of the flock, [222:5] as bearing rule, [223:1] as watching for souls, [223:2] and as taking care of the Church of God. [223:3] They are instructed how to deal with offenders, [223:4] and they are said to be entitled to obedience. [223:5] Such representations obviously imply that they were intrusted with the administration of ecclesiastical discipline.

This account of the functions of the spiritual rulers has been supposed by some to be inconsistent with several statements in the apostolic epistles. It has been alleged that, according to these letters, the administration of discipline was vested in the whole body of the people; and that originally the members of the Church, in their collective capacity, exercised the right of excommunication. The language of Paul, in reference to a case of scandal which had occurred among the Christians of Corinth, has been often quoted in proof of the democratic character of their ecclesiastical constitution. "It is reported commonly," says the apostle, "that there is fornication, among you, and such fornication as is not so much as named among the Gentiles, that one should have his father's wife..... Therefore

102

put away from among yourselves that wicked person." [223:6] The admonition was obeyed, and the application of discipline seems to have produced a most salutary impression upon the mind of the offender. In his next letter the apostle accordingly alludes to this circumstance, and observes—"Sufficient to such a man is this punishment, which was inflicted of many." [223:7] These words have been frequently adduced to shew that the government of the Corinthian Church was administered by the whole body of the communicants.

The various statements of Scripture, if rightly understood, must exactly harmonize, and a closer investigation of the case of this transgressor is all that is required to prove that he was not tried and condemned by a tribunal composed of the whole mass of the members of the Church of Corinth. His true history reveals facts of a very different character. For reasons which it would, perhaps, be now in vain to hope fully to explore, he seems to have been a favourite among his fellow-disciples; many of them, prior to their conversion, had been grossly licentious; and, it may be, that they continued to regard certain lusts of the flesh with an eye of comparative indulgence. [224:1] Some of them probably considered the conduct of this offender as only a legitimate exercise of his Christian liberty; and they appear to have manifested a strong inclination to shield him from ecclesiastical censure. Paul, therefore, felt it necessary to address them in the language of indignant expostulation. "Ye are puffed up," says he, "and have not rather mourned that he that hath done this deed might be taken away from among you.....Your glorying is not good. Know ye not that a little leaven leaveneth the whole lump." [224:2] At the same time, as an apostle bound to vindicate the reputation of the Church, and to enforce the rules of ecclesiastical discipline, he solemnly announces his determination to have the offender excommunicated. "I verily," says he, "as absent in body, but present in spirit, have judged already as though I were present, concerning him that hath so done this deed, in the name of our Lord Jesus Christ, when ye are gathered together, and my spirit, with the power of our Lord Jesus Christ, to deliver such an one unto Satan for the destruction of the flesh, that the spirit may be saved in the day of the Lord Jesus." [224:3] To deliver any one to Satan is to expel him from the Church, for whoever is not in the Church is in the world, and "the whole world lieth in the wicked one." [224:4] This discipline was designed to teach the fornicator to mortify his lusts, and it thus aimed at the promotion of his highest interests; or, as the apostle expresses it, he was to be excommunicated "for the destruction of the flesh, [225:1] that the spirit might be saved in the day of the Lord Jesus." It is obvious that the Church of Corinth was now in a state of great disorder. A partisan spirit had crept in amongst its members; [225:2] and it seems probable that those elders [225:3] who were anxious to maintain wholesome discipline were opposed and overborne. The fornicator had in some way contrived to make himself so popular that an attempt at his expulsion would, it was feared, throw the whole society into hopeless confusion. Under these circumstances Paul felt it necessary to interpose, to assert his apostolic authority, and to insist upon the maintenance of ecclesiastical order. Instead, however, of consulting the people as to the course to be pursued, he peremptorily delivers his judgment, and requires them to hold a solemn assembly that they may listen to the public announcement [225:4] of a sentence of excommunication. He, of course, expected that their rulers would concur with him in this decision, and that one of them would officially publish it when they were "gathered together."

When the case is thus stated, it is easy to understand why the apostle required all the disciples to "put away" from among themselves "that wicked person." Had they continued to cherish the spirit which they had recently displayed, they might either have encouraged the fornicator to refuse submission to the sentence, or they might have rendered it comparatively powerless. He therefore reminds them that they too should seek to promote the purity of ecclesiastical fellowship; and that they were bound to cooperate in carrying out a righteous discipline. They were to cease to recognize this fallen disciple as a servant of Christ; they were to withdraw themselves from his society; they were to decline to meet him on the same terms, as heretofore, in social intercourse; and they were not even to eat in his company. Thus would the reputation of the Church be vindicated; for in this way it would be immediately known to all who were without that he was no longer considered a member of the brotherhood.

The Corinthians were awakened to a sense of duty by this apostolic letter, and acted up to its instructions. The result was most satisfactory. When the offender, saw that he was cut off from the Church, and that its members avoided his society, he was completely humbled. The sentence of the apostle, or the eldership, if opposed or neglected by the people, might have produced little impression; but "the punishment which was inflicted of many"—the immediate and entire abandonment of all connexion with him by the disciples at Corinth—overwhelmed him with shame and terror. He felt as a man smitten by the judgment of God; he renounced his sin; and he exhibited the most unequivocal tokens of genuine contrition. In due time he was restored to Church fellowship; and the apostle then exhorted his brethren to readmit him to intercourse, and to treat him with kindness and confidence. "Ye ought," says he, "rather to forgive him and comfort him, lest perhaps such an one should be swallowed up with overmuch sorrow. Wherefore I beseech you that ye would confirm your love toward him." [227:1]

This case of the Corinthian fornicator has been recorded for the admonition and guidance of believers in all generations. It teaches that every member of a Christian Church is bound to use his best endeavours to promote a pure communion; and that he is not guiltless if, prompted by mistaken charity or considerations of selfishness, he is not prepared to co-operate in the exclusion of false brethren. Many an immoral minister has maintained his position, and has thus continued to bring discredit on the gospel, simply because those who had witnessed his misconduct were induced to suppress their testimony; and many a church court has been prevented from enforcing discipline by the clamours or intimidation of an ignorant and excited congregation. The command—"Put away from among yourselves that wicked person," is addressed to the people, as well as to the ministry; and all Christ's disciples should feel that, in vindicating the honour of His name, they have a common interest, and share a common responsibility. Every one cannot be a member of a church court; but every one can aid in the preservation of church discipline. He may supply information, or give evidence, or encourage a healthy tone of public sentiment, or assist, by petition or remonstrance, in quickening the zeal of lukewarm judicatories. And discipline is never so influential as when it is known to be sustained by the approving verdict of a pious and intelligent community. The punishment "inflicted of many"—the withdrawal of the confidence and countenance of a whole church—is a most impressive admonition to a proud sinner.

In the apostolic age the sentence of excommunication had a very different significance from that which was attached to it at a subsequent period. Our Lord pointed out its import with equal precision and brevity when he said—"If thy brother....neglect to hear the church, [228:1] let him be unto thee as an heathen man and a publican." [228:2] The Israelites could have no religious fellowship with heathens, or the worshippers of false gods; and they could have no personal respect for publicans, or Roman tax-gatherers, who were regarded as odious representatives of the oppressors of their country. To be "unto them as an heathen" was to be excluded from the privileges of their church; and to be "unto them as a publican" was to be shut out from their society in the way of domestic intercourse. When the apostle says—"Now we command you, brethren, that ye withdraw yourselves from every brother that walketh disorderly and not after the ordinance [228:3] which he received of us," [228:4] he doubtless designed to intimate that those who were excommunicated should be admitted neither to the intimacy of private friendship nor to the sealing ordinances of the gospel. But it did not follow that the disciples were to treat such persons with insolence or inhumanity. They were not at liberty to act thus towards heathens and publicans; for they were to love even their enemies, and they were to imitate the example of their Father in heaven who "maketh his sun to rise on the evil and on the good, and sendeth rain on the just and on the unjust." [228:5] It is obvious from the address of the apostle to the Thessalonians that the members of the Church were not forbidden to speak to those who were separated from communion; and that they were not required to refuse them the ordinary charities of life. They were simply to avoid such an intercourse as implied a community of faith, of feeling, and of interest. "If any man," says he, "obey not our word by this epistle, note that man, and have no company with him, that he may be ashamed. Yet count him not as an enemy, but admonish him as a brother." [229:1]

How different was this discipline from that which was established, several centuries afterwards, in the Latin Church! The spirit and usages of paganism then supplanted the regulations of the New Testament, and the excommunication of Christianity was converted into the excommunication of Druidism. [229:2] Our Lord taught that "whoever would not hear the church" should be treated as a heathen man and a publican; but the time came when he who forfeited his status as a member of the Christian commonwealth was denounced as a monster or a fiend. Paul declared that the person excommunicated, instead of being counted as an enemy, should be admonished as a brother; but the Latin Church, in a long list of horrid imprecations, [229:3] invoked a curse upon every member of the body of the offender, and commanded every one to refuse to him the civility of the coldest salutation! The early Church acted as a faithful monitor, anxious to reclaim the sinner from the error of his ways: the Latin Church, like a tyrant, refuses to the transgressor even that which is his due, and seeks either to reduce him to slavery, or to drive him to despair.

CHAPTER II

THE EXTRAORDINARY TEACHERS OF THE APOSTOLIC CHURCH; AND ITS ORDINARY OFFICE-BEARERS, THEIR APPOINTMENT, AND ORDINATION

Paul declares that Christ "gave some, apostles; and some, prophets; and some, evangelists; and some, pastors and teachers; for the perfecting of the saints, for the work of the ministry, for the edifying of the body of Christ." [230:1] In another place the same writer, when speaking of those occupying positions of prominence in the ecclesiastical community, makes a somewhat similar enumeration. "God," says he, "hath set some in the church, first, apostles; secondarily, prophets; thirdly, teachers; after that, miracles; then, gifts of healings, helps, governments, diversities of tongues." [230:2]

These two passages, presenting something like catalogues of the most prominent characters connected with the Apostolic Church, throw light upon each other. They mention the ordinary, as well as the extraordinary, ecclesiastical functionaries. Under the class of ordinary office-bearers must be placed those described as "pastors and teachers," "helps," and "governments." The evangelists, such as Timothy, [230:3] Titus, and Philip, [230:4] seem to have had a special commission to assist in organizing the infant Church; [230:5] and, as they were furnished with supernatural endowments, [231:1] they may be considered extraordinary functionaries. The apostles themselves clearly belong to the same denomination. They all possessed the gift of inspiration [231:2] they all received their authority immediately from Christ; [231:3] they all "went in and out with Him" during His personal ministry; and, as they all saw Him after He rose from the dead, they could all attest His resurrection. [231:4] It is plain, too, that the ministrations of "the prophets," as well as of those who wrought "miracles," who possessed "gifts of healings," and who had "diversities of tongues," must also be designated extraordinary.

It is probable that by the "helps," of whom Paul here speaks, he understands the deacons, [231:5] who were originally appointed to relieve the apostles of a portion of labour which they felt to be inconvenient and burdensome. [231:6] The duties of the deacons were not strictly of a spiritual character; these ministers held only a subordinate station among the office-bearers of the Church; and, even in dealing with its temporalities, they acted under the advice and direction of those who were properly entrusted with its government. Hence, perhaps, they were called "helps" or attendants. [231:7]

When these helps and the extraordinary functionaries are left out of the apostolic catalogues, it is rather singular that, in the passage addressed to the Ephesians, we have nothing remaining but "PASTORS AND TEACHERS;" and, in that to the Corinthians, nothing but "TEACHERS" AND "GOVERNMENTS." There are good grounds for believing that these two residuary elements are identical,—the "pastors," mentioned before[232:1] the teachers in one text, being equivalent to the "governments" mentioned after them in the other.[232:2] Nor is it strange that those entrusted with the ecclesiastical government should be styled pastors or shepherds; for they are the guardians and rulers of "the flock of

God." [232:3] Thus, it appears that the ordinary office-bearers of the Apostolic Church were pastors, teachers, and helps; or, teachers, rulers, and deacons.

In the apostolic age we read likewise of elders and bishops; and in the New Testament these names are often used interchangeably.[232:4] The elders or bishops, were the same as the pastors and teachers; for they had the charge of the instruction and government of the Church.[232:5] Hence elders are required to act as faithful pastors under Christ, the Chief Shepherd.[232:6] It appears, too, that whilst some of the elders were only pastors, or rulers, others were also teachers. The apostle says accordingly—"Let the elders that rule well, be counted worthy of double honour, especially those that labour in the word and doctrine".[232:7] We may thus see that the teachers, governments, and helps, mentioned by Paul when writing to the Corinthians, are the same as the "bishops and deacons" of whom he speaks elsewhere. [233:1]

In primitive times there were, generally, a plurality of elders, as well as a plurality of deacons, in every church or congregation; [233:2] and each functionary was expected to apply himself to that particular department of his office which he could manage most efficiently. Some elders possessed a peculiar talent for expounding the gospel in the way of preaching, or, as it was occasionally called, prophesying; [233:3] others excelled in delivering hortatory addresses to the people; others displayed great tact and sagacity in conducting ecclesiastical business, or in dealing personally with offenders, or with penitents; whilst others again were singularly successful in imparting private instruction to catechumens. Some deacons were frequently commissioned to administer to the wants of the sick; and others, who were remarkable for their shrewdness and discrimination, were employed to distribute alms to the indigent. In one of his epistles Paul pointedly refers to the multiform duties of these ecclesiastical office-bearers-"Having then," says he," gifts, differing according to the grace that is given to us, whether prophecy, let us prophesy according to the proportion of faith; or ministry (of the deacon), let us wait on our ministering; or he that teacheth, on teaching; or he that exhorteth, on exhortation; he that giveth, let him do it with simplicity; he that ruleth, with diligence; he that sheweth mercy, with cheerfulness." [233:4] It has been supposed by some that all the primitive elders, or bishops, were preachers; but the records of apostolic times warrant no such conclusion. These elders were appointed simply to "take care of the Church of God;" [233:5] and it was not necessary that each individual should perform all the functions of the pastoral office. Even at the present day a single preacher is generally sufficient to minister to a single congregation. When Paul requires that the elders who rule well, though they may not "labour in the word and doctrine," shall be counted worthy of double honour, [234:1] is language distinctly indicates that there were then persons designated elders who did not preach, and who, notwithstanding, were entitled to respect as exemplary and efficient functionaries. It is remarkable that when the apostle enumerates the qualifications of a bishop, or elder, [234:2] he scarcely refers to oratorical endowments. He states that the ruler of the Church should be grave, sober, prudent, and benevolent; but, as to his ability to propagate his principles, he employs only one word—rendered in our version "apt to teach." [234:3] This does not imply that he must be qualified to preach, for teaching and preaching are repeatedly distinguished in the New Testament; [234:4] neither does it signify that he must become a professional tutor, for, as has already been intimated, all

107

elders are not expected to labour in the word and doctrine; it merely denotes that he should be able and willing, as often as an opportunity occurred, to communicate a knowledge of divine truth. All believers are required to "exhort one another daily," [235:1] "teaching and admonishing one another," [235:2] being "ready always to give an answer to every man that asketh them a reason of the hope that is in them;" [235:3] and those who "watch for souls" should be specially zealous in performing these duties of their Christian vocation. The word which has been supposed to indicate that every elder should be a public instructor occurs in only one other instance in the New Testament; and in that case it is used in a connexion which serves to illustrate its meaning. Paul there states that whilst such as minister to the Lord should avoid a controversial spirit, they should at the same time be willing to supply explanations to objectors, and to furnish them with information. "The servant of the Lord," says he, "must not strive, but be gentle unto all men, apt to teach, patient, in meekness instructing those that oppose themselves, if God peradventure will give them repentance to the acknowledging of the truth." [235:4] Here the aptness to teach refers apparently to a talent for winning over gainsayers by means of instruction communicated in private conversation. [235:5]

But still preaching is the grand ordinance of God, as well for the edification of saints as for the conversion of sinners; and it was, therefore, necessary that at least some of the session or eldership connected with each flock should be competent to conduct the congregational worship. As spiritual gifts were more abundant in the apostolic times than afterwards, it is probable that at first several of the elders [236:1] were found ready to take part in its celebration. By degrees, however, nearly the whole service devolved on one individual; and this preaching elder was very properly treated with peculiar deference. [236:2] He was accordingly soon recognized as the stated president of the presbytery, or eldership.

It thus appears that the preaching elder held the most honourable position amongst the ordinary functionaries of the Apostolic Church. Whilst his office required the highest order of gifts and accomplishments, and exacted the largest amount of mental and even physical exertion, the prosperity of the whole ecclesiastical community depended mainly on his acceptance and efficiency. The people are accordingly frequently reminded that they are bound to respect and sustain their spiritual instructors. "Let him that is taught in the word," says Paul, "communicate unto him that teacheth in all good things." [236:3] "The Scripture saith—Thou shalt not muzzle the ox that treadeth out the corn; and, The labourer is worthy of his reward." [236:4] "So hath the Lord ordained that they which preach the gospel should live of the gospel." [236:5]

The apostles held a position which no ministers after them could occupy, for they were sip pointed by our Lord himself to organize the Church. As they were to carry out instructions which they had received from His own lips, and as they were armed with the power of working miracles, [236:6] they possessed an extraordinary share of personal authority. Aware that their circumstances were peculiar, and that their services would be available until the end of time, [236:7] they left the ecclesiastical government, as they passed away one after another, to the care of the elders who had meanwhile shared in its administration. [237:1] As soon as the Church began to assume a settled form, they mingled with these elders on terms of equality; and, as at the Council of Jerusalem, [237:2] sat with

108

them in the same deliberative assemblies. When Paul addressed the elders of Ephesus for the last time, and took his solemn farewell of them, [237:3] he commended the Church to their charge, and emphatically pressed upon them the importance of fidelity and vigilance. [237:4] In his Second Epistle to Timothy, written in the prospect of his martyrdom, he makes no allusion to the expediency of selecting another individual to fill his place. The apostles had fully executed their commission when, as wise master-builders, they laid the foundation of the Church and fairly exhibited the divine model of the glorious structure; and as no other parties could produce the same credentials, no others could pretend to the same authority. But even the apostles repeatedly testified that they regarded the preaching of the Word as the highest department of their office. It was, not as church rulers, but as church teachers, that they were specially distinguished. "We will give ourselves," said they, "continually to prayer, and to the ministry of the Word." [237:5] "Christ sent me," said Paul, "not to baptize, but to preach the gospel." [238:1] "Unto me, who am less than the least of all saints, is this grace given, that I should preach among the Gentiles the unsearchable riches of Christ." [238:2]

But though, according to the New Testament, the business of ruling originally formed only a subordinate part of the duty of the church teacher, some have maintained that ecclesiastical government pertains to a higher function than ecclesiastical instruction; and that the apostles instituted a class of spiritual overseers to whose jurisdiction all other preachers are amenable. They imagine that, in the Pastoral Epistles, they find proofs of the existence of such functionaries; [238:3] and they contend that Timothy and Titus were diocesan bishops, respectively of Ephesus and Crete. But the arguments by which they endeavour to sustain these views are quite inconclusive. Paul says to Timothy—"I besought thee to abide still at Ephesus, when I went into Macedonia, that thou mightest charge some that they teach no other doctrine;" [239:1] and it has hence been inferred that the evangelist was the only minister in the capital of the Proconsular Asia who was sufficiently authorized to oppose heresiarchs. It happens, however, that in this epistle the writer says also to his correspondent— "Charge them that are rich in this world that they be not high-minded, nor trust in uncertain riches;" [239:2] so that, according to the same method of interpretation, it would follow that Timothy was the only preacher in the place who was at liberty to admonish the opulent. When Paul subsequently stood face to face with the elders of Ephesus [239:3] he told them that it was their common duty to discountenance and resist false teachers; [239:4] and he had therefore now no idea of entrusting that responsibility to any solitary individual. The reason why the service was pressed specially on Timothy is sufficiently apparent. He had been trained up by Paul himself; he was a young minister remarkable for intelligence, ability, and circumspection; and he was accordingly deemed eminently qualified to deal with the errorists. Hence at this juncture his presence at Ephesus was considered of importance; and the apostle besought him to remain there whilst he himself was absent on another mission.

The argument founded on the instructions addressed to Titus is equally unsatisfactory. Paul says to him—"For this cause left I thee in Crete, that thou shouldest set in order the things that are wanting, and ordain [240:1] elders in every city as I had appointed thee;" [240:2] and from these words the inference has been drawn that to Titus alone was committed the ecclesiastical oversight of all the churches of the island. But the words of the apostle warrant no such sweeping conclusion. Apollos, [240:3] and probably other ministers equal in authority to the evangelist, were now in Crete, and were, no doubt, ready to co-operate with him in the business of church organization. Titus, besides, had no right to act without the concurrence of the people; for, in all cases, even when the apostles were officiating, the church members were consulted in ecclesiastical appointments. [240:4] It is probable that the evangelist had much administrative ability, and this seems to have been the great reason why he was left behind Paul in Crete. The apostle expected that, with his peculiar energy and tact, he would stimulate the zeal of the people, as well as of the other preachers; and thus complete, as speedily as possible, the needful ecclesiastical arrangements.

When Paul once said to the high priest of Israel—"Sittest thou to judge me after the law, and commandest me to be smitten contrary to the law" [240:5]—he had no intention of declaring that the dignitary he addressed was the only member of the Jewish council who had the right of adjudication. [240:6] The court consisted of at least seventy individuals, every one of whom had a vote as effective as that of the personage with whom he thus remonstrated. It is said that the high priest at this period was not even the president of the Sanhedrim. [241:1] Paul was perfectly aware of the constitution of the tribunal to which Ananias belonged; and he merely meant to remind his oppressor that the circumstances in which he was placed added greatly to the iniquity of his present procedure. Though only one of the members of a large judicatory he was not the less accountable. Thus too, when Jesus said to Paul himself—"I send thee" to the Gentiles, "to open their eyes, and to turn them from darkness to light, and from the power of Satan unto God" [241:2]—it was certainly not understood that the apostle was to be the only labourer in the wide field of heathendom. The address simply intimated that he was individually commissioned to undertake the service. And though there were other ministers at Ephesus and Crete, Paul reminds Timothy and Titus that he had left them there to perform specific duties, and thus urges upon them the consideration of their personal responsibility. Though surrounded by so many apostles and evangelists, he tells us that there rested on himself daily "the care of all the churches;" [241:3] for he believed that the whole commonwealth of the saints had a claim on his prayers, his sympathy, and his services; and he desired to cherish in the hearts of his young brethren the same feeling of individual obligation. Hence, in these Pastoral Epistles, he gives his correspondents minute instructions respecting all the departments of the ministerial office, and reminds them how much depends on their personal faithfulness. Hence he here points out to them how they are to deport themselves in public and in private; [241:4] as preachers of the Word, and as members of church judicatories; [241:5] towards the rich and the poor, masters and slaves, young men and widows. [242:1] But there is not a single advice addressed to Timothy and Titus in any of these three epistles which may not be appropriately given to any ordinary minister of the gospel, or which necessarily implies that either of these evangelists exercised exclusive ecclesiastical authority in Ephesus or Crete. [242:2]

The legend that Timothy and Titus were the bishops respectively of Ephesus and Crete appears to have been invented about the beginning of the fourth century, and at a time when the original constitution of the Church had been completely, though silently, revolutionized. [242:3] It is obvious that, when the

Pastoral Epistles were written, these ministers were not permanently located in the places with which their names have been thus associated. [242:4] The apostle John resided principally at Ephesus during the last thirty years of the first century; [242:5] so that, according to this tale, the beloved disciple must have been nearly all this time under the ecclesiastical supervision of Timothy! The story otherwise exhibits internal marks of absurdity and fabrication. It would lead us to infer that Paul must have distributed most unequally the burden of official labour; for whilst Timothy is said to have presided over the Christians of a single city, Titus is represented as invested with the care of a whole island celebrated in ancient times for its hundred cities. [243:1] It is well known that long after this period, and when the distinction between the president of the presbytery and his elders was fully established, a bishop had the charge of only one church, so that the account of the episcopate of Titus over all Crete must be rejected as a monstrous fiction.

On the occasion of an ambitious request from James and John, our Lord expounded to His apostles one of the great principles of His ecclesiastical polity. "Jesus called them to him, and saith unto them—Ye know that they which are accounted to rule over the Gentiles exercise lordship over them; and their great ones exercise authority upon them. But so shall it not be among you, but whosoever will be great among you, shall be your minister, and whosoever of you will be chiefest, shall be servant of all. For even the Son of man came not to be ministered unto, but to minister, and to give his life a ransom for many." [243:2] The teaching elder holds the most honourable position in the Church, simply because his office is the most laborious, the most responsible, and the most useful. And no minister of the Word is warranted to exercise lordship over his brethren, for all are equally the servants of the same Divine Master. He is the greatest who is most willing to humble himself, to spend, and to be spent, that Christ may be exalted. Even the Son of man came, not to be ministered unto, but to minister; it was His meat and His drink to do the will of His Father in heaven; He was ready to give instruction to many or to few; at the sea or by the wayside; in the house, the synagogue, or the corn-field; on the mountain or in the desert; when sitting in the company of publicans, or when He had not where to lay His head. He who exhibits most of the spirit and character of the Great Teacher is the most illustrious of Christ's ministers.

The primitive Church was pre-eminently a free society; and, with a view to united action, its members were taught to consult together respecting all matters of common interest. Whilst the elders were required to beware of attempting to domineer over each other, they were also warned against deporting themselves as "lords over God's heritage." [244:1] All were instructed to be courteous, forbearing, and conciliatory; and each individual was made to understand that he possessed some importance. Though the apostles, as inspired rulers of the Christian commonwealth, might have done many things on their own authority, yet, even in concerns comparatively trivial, as well as in affairs of the greatest consequence, they were guided by the wishes of the people. When an apostle was to be chosen in the place of Judas, the multitude were consulted. [244:2] When deputies were required to accompany Paul in a journey to be undertaken for the public service, the apostle did not himself select his fellow-travellers, but the churches concerned, proceeded, by a regular vote, to make the appointment. [244:3] When deacons A or elders were to be nominated, the choice rested with

111

the congregation. [244:4] The records of the apostolic age do not mention any ordinary church functionary who was not called to his office by popular suffrage. [244:5]

But though, in apostolic times, the communicants were thus freely entrusted with the elective franchise, the constitution of the primitive Church was not purely democratic; for while its office-bearers were elected for life, and whilst its elders or bishops formed a species of spiritual aristocracy, the powers of the people and the rulers were so balanced as to check each other's aberrations, and to promote the healthful action of all parts of the ecclesiastical body. When a deacon or a bishop was elected, he was not permitted, without farther ceremony, to enter upon the duties of his vocation. He was bound to submit himself to the presbytery, that they might ratify the choice by ordination; and this court, by refusing the imposition of hands, could protect the Church against the intrusion of incompetent or unworthy candidates. [245:1]

Among the Jews every ordained elder was considered qualified to join in the ordination of others. [245:2] The same principle was acknowledged in the early Christian Church; and when any functionary was elected, he was introduced to his office by the presbytery of the city or district with which he was connected. There is no instance in the apostolic age in which ordination was conferred by a single individual, Paul and Barnabas were separated to the work to which the Lord had called them by the ministers of Antioch; [245:3] the first elders of the Christian Churches of Asia Minor were set apart by Paul and Barnabas; [245:4] Timothy was invested with ecclesiastical authority by "the laying on of the hands of the presbytery;" [245:5] and even the seven deacons were ordained by the twelve apostles acting, for the time, as the presbytery of Jerusalem. [245:6]

Towards the conclusion of the Epistle to the Romans, [245:7] Paul mentions Phoebe, "a servant [245:8] of the Church which is at Cenchrea;" and from this passage some have inferred that the apostles instituted an order of deaconesses. It is scarcely safe to build such an hypothesis on the foundation of a solitary text of doubtful significance. It may be that Phoebe was one of the poor widows supported by the Church; [246:1] and that, as such, she was employed by the elders in various little services of a confidential or benevolent character. It is probable that, at one period, she had been in more comfortable circumstances, and that she had then distinguished herself by her humane and obliging disposition; for Paul refers apparently to this portion of her history when he says, "she hath been a succourer of many, and of myself also." [246:2]

In the primitive age all the members of the same Church were closely associated. As brethren and sisters in the faith, they took a deep interest in each other's prosperity; and they regarded the afflictions of any single disciple as a calamity which had befallen the whole society. Each individual was expected in some way to contribute to the well-being of all. Even humble Phoebe could be the bearer of an apostolic letter to the Romans; and, on her return to Cenchrea, could exert a healthful influence among the younger portion of the female disciples, by her advice, her example, and her prayers. The industrious scribe could benefit the brotherhood by writing out copies of the gospels or epistles; and the pleasant singer, as he joined in the holy psalm, could thrill the hearts of the faithful by his notes of grave sweet melody. By establishing a plurality of both elders and deacons in every worshipping society, the apostles provided more efficiently, as well for its temporal, as for its spiritual interests; and the most useful members of

112

the congregation were thus put into positions in which their various graces and endowments were better exhibited and exercised. One deacon attested his fitness for his office by his delicate attentions to the sick; another, by his considerate kindness to the poor; and another, by his judicious treatment of the indolent, the insincere, and the improvident. One elder excelled as an awakening preacher; another, as a sound expositor; and another, as a sagacious counsellor: whilst another still, who never ventured to address the congregation, and whose voice was seldom heard at the meetings of the eldership, could go to the house of mourning, or the chamber of disease, and there pour forth the fulness of his heart in most appropriate and impressive supplications. Every one was taught to appreciate the talents of his neighbour, and to feel that he was, to some extent, dependent on others for his own edification. The preaching elder could not say to the ruling elders, "I have no need of you;" neither could the elders say to the deacons, "We have no need of you." When the sweet singer was absent, every one admitted that the congregational music was less interesting; when the skilful penman removed to another district, the Church soon began to complain of a scarcity of copies of the sacred manuscripts; and even when the pious widow died in a good old age, the blank was visible, and the loss of a faithful servant of the Church was acknowledged and deplored. "As the body is one, and hath many members, and all the members of that one body, being many, are one body; so also is Christ. And the eye cannot say unto the hand, I have no need of thee: nor again the head to the feet, I have no need of you. And whether one member suffer, all the members suffer with it, or one member be honoured, all the members rejoice with it." [247:1]

CHAPTER III

THE ORGANIZATION OF THE APOSTOLIC CHURCH

The Israelites were emphatically "a peculiar people." Though amounting, in the days of our Lord, to several millions of individuals, they were all the lineal descendants of Abraham; and though two thousand years had passed away since the time of their great progenitor; they had not meanwhile intermingled, to any considerable extent, with the rest of the human family. The bulk of the nation still occupied the land which had been granted by promise to the "father of the faithful;" the same farms had been held by the same families from age to age; and probably some of the proprietors could boast that their ancestors, fifteen hundred years before, had taken possession of the very fields which they now cultivated. They had all one form of worship, one high priest, and one place of sacrifice. At stated seasons every year all the males of a certain age were required to meet together at Jerusalem; and thus a full representation of the whole race was frequently collected in one great congregation.

The written law of Moses was the sacred bond which united so closely the

Church of Israel. The ritual observances of the Hebrews, which had all a typical meaning, are described by the inspired lawgiver with singular minuteness; and any deviation from them was forbidden, not only because it involved an impeachment either of the authority or the wisdom of Jehovah, but also because it was calculated to mar their significance. Under the Mosaic economy the posterity of Abraham were taught to regard each other as members of the same family, interested, as joint heirs, in the blessings promised to their distinguished ancestor. The Israelites were knit together by innumerable ties, as well secular as religious; and when they appeared in one multitudinous assemblage on occasions of peculiar solemnity, [249:1] they presented a specimen of ecclesiastical unity such as the world has never since contemplated.

Some, however, have contended that the Christian community was originally constructed upon very different principles. According to them the word church [249:2] in the New Testament is always used in one of two senses—either as denoting a single worshipping society, or the whole commonwealth of the faithful; and from this they infer that, in primitive times, every Christian congregation was independent of every other. But such allegations, which are exceedingly improbable in themselves, are found, when carefully investigated, to be totally destitute of foundation. The Church of Jerusalem, [249:3] with the tens of thousands of individuals belonging to it, [249:4] must have consisted of several congregations; [249:5] the Church of Antioch, to which so many prophets and teachers ministered, [249:6] was probably in a similar position; and the Church of Palestine [249:7] obviously comprehended a large number of associated churches. When our Saviour prayed that all His people "may be one," [250:1] He evidently indicated that the unity of the Church, so strikingly exhibited in the nation of Israel, should still be studied and maintained; and when Paul describes the household of faith, he speaks of it, not as a loose mass of independent congregations, but as a "body fitly joined together and compacted by that which every joint supplieth." [250:2] The apostle here refers to the vital union of believers by the indwelling of the Holy Ghost; but he apparently alludes also to those "bands" of outward ordinances, and "joints" [250:3] of visible confederation, by which their communion is upheld; for, were the Church split up into an indefinite number of insulated congregations, even the unity of the spirit could neither be distinctly ascertained nor properly cultivated. When oiled by the spirit of Divine love, the machinery of the Church moves with admirable harmony, and accomplishes the most astonishing results; but, when pervaded by another spirit, it is strained and dislocated, and in danger of dashing itself to pieces.

Those who hold that every congregation, however small, is a complete church in itself, are quite unable to explain why the system of ecclesiastical organization should be thus circumscribed. The New Testament inculcates the unity of all the faithful, as well as the unity of particular societies; and the same principle of Christian brotherhood which prompts a number of individuals to meet together for religious fellowship, should also lead a number of congregations in the same locality to fraternize. The twelve may be regarded as the representatives of the doctrine of ecclesiastical confederation; for though they were commanded to go into all the world and to preach the gospel to every creature, yet, as long as circumstances permitted, they continued to co-operate. "When the apostles which were at Jerusalem heard that Samaria had received the

114

word of God, they sent unto them Peter and John;" [251:1] and, at a subsequent period, they concurred in sending "forth Barnabas, that he should go as far as Antioch." [251:2] These facts distinctly prove that they had a common interest in everything pertaining to the well-being of the whole Christian commonwealth; and that, like Paul, they were entrusted with "the care of all the churches." Nor did the early Christian congregations act independently. They believed that union is strength, and they were "knit together" in ecclesiastical relationship. Hence, we read of the brother who was "chosen of the churches" [251:3] to travel with the Apostle Paul. It is now impossible to determine in what way this choice was made—whether at a general meeting of deputies from different congregations, or by a separate vote in each particular society—but, in whatever way the election was accomplished, the appointment of one representative for several churches was itself a recognition of their ecclesiastical unity.

We have seen that the worship of the Church was much the same as the worship of the synagogue, [251:4] and it would seem that its polity also was borrowed from the institutions of the chosen people. [251:5] Every Jewish congregation was governed by a bench of elders; and in every city there was a smaller sanhedrim, or presbytery, consisting of twenty-three members, [251:6] to which the neighbouring synagogues were subject. Jerusalem is said to have had two of these smaller sanhedrims, as it was found that the multitudes of cases arising among so vast a population were more than sufficient to occupy the time of any one judicatory. Appeals lay from all these tribunals to the Great Sanhedrim, or "Council," so frequently mentioned in the New Testament. [252:1] This court consisted of seventy or seventy-two members, made up, perhaps, in equal portions, of chief priests, scribes, and elders of the people, [252:2] The chief priests were probably twenty-four in number—each of the twenty-four courses, into which the sacerdotal order was divided, [252:3] thus furnishing one representative. The scribes were the men of learning, like Gamaliel, [252:4] who had devoted themselves to the study of the Jewish law, and who possessed recondite, as well as extensive information. The elders were laymen of reputed wisdom and experience, who, in practical matters, might be expected to give sound advice. [252:5] It was not strange that the Jews had so profound a regard for their Great Sanhedrim. In the days of our Lord and His apostles it had, indeed, miserably degenerated; but, at an earlier period, its members must have been eminently entitled to respect, as in point of intelligence, prudence, piety, and patriotism, they held the very highest place among their countrymen.

The details of the ecclesiastical polity of the ancient Israelites are now involved in much obscurity; but the preceding statements may be received as a pretty accurate description of its chief outlines. Our Lord himself, in the sermon on the mount, is understood to refer to the great council and its subordinate judicatories; [252:6] and in the Old Testament appeals from inferior tribunals to the authorities in the holy city are explicitly enjoined. [253:1] All the synagogues, not only in Palestine but in foreign countries, obeyed the orders of the Sanhedrim at Jerusalem; [253:2] and it constituted a court of review to which all other ecclesiastical arbiters yielded submission.

In the government of the Apostolic Church we may trace a resemblance to these arrangements. Every Christian congregation, like every synagogue, had its elders; and every city had its presbytery, consisting of the spiritual rulers of the district. In the introductory chapters of the book of the Acts we discover the germ

115

of this ecclesiastical constitution; for we there find the apostles ministering to thousands of converts, and, as the presbytery of Jerusalem, ordaining deacons, exercising discipline, and sending out missionaries. [253:3] The prophets and teachers of Antioch obviously performed the same functions; [253:4] Titus was instructed to have elders established, or a presbytery constituted, in every city of Crete; [253:5] and Timothy was ordained by such a judicatory. [253:6] For the first thirty years after the death of our Lord a large proportion of the ministers of the gospel were Jews by birth, and as they were in the habit of going up to Jerusalem to celebrate the great festivals, they appear to have taken advantage of the opportunity, and to have held meetings in the holy city for consultation respecting the affairs of the Christian commonwealth. Prudence and convenience conspired to dictate this course, as they could then reckon upon finding there a considerable number of able and experienced elders, and as their presence in the Jewish metropolis on such occasions was fitted to awaken no suspicion. [253:7]

We may thus see that the transaction mentioned in the 15th chapter of the Acts admits of a simple and satisfactory explanation. When the question respecting the circumcision of the Gentile converts began to be discussed at Antioch, there were individuals in that city quite as well qualified as any in Jerusalem to pronounce upon its merits; for the Church there enjoyed the ministry of prophets; and Paul, its most distinguished teacher, was "not a whit behind the very chiefest apostles." But the parties proceeded in the matter in much the same way as Israelites were accustomed to act under similar circumstances. Had a controversy relative to any Mosaic ceremony divided the Jewish population of Antioch, they would have appealed for a decision to their Great Sanhedrim; and now, when this dispute distracted the Christians of the capital of Syria, they had recourse to another tribunal at Jerusalem which they considered competent to pronounce a deliverance. [254:1] This tribunal consisted virtually of the rulers of the universal Church; for the apostles, who had a commission to all the world, and elders from almost every place where a Christian congregation existed, were in the habit of repairing to the capital of Palestine. In one respect this judicatory differed from the Jewish council, for it was not limited to seventy members. In accordance with the free spirit of the gospel dispensation, it appears to have consisted of as many ecclesiastical rulers as could conveniently attend its meetings. But the times were somewhat perilous; and it is probable that the ministers of the early Christian Church did not deem it expedient to congregate in very large numbers.

A single Scripture precedent for the regulation of the Church is as decisive as a multitude; and though the New Testament distinctly records only one instance in which a question of difficulty was referred by a lower to a higher ecclesiastical tribunal, this case sufficiently illustrates the character of the primitive polity. A very substantial reason can be given why Scripture takes so little notice of the meetings of Christian judicatories. The different portions of the New Testament were put into circulation as soon as written; and though it was most important that the heathen should be made acquainted with the doctrines of the Church, it was not by any means expedient that their attention should be particularly directed to the machinery by which it was regulated. An accurate knowledge of its constitution would only have exposed it more fearfully to the attacks of persecuting Emperors. Every effort would have been made to discover the times and places of the meetings of pastors and teachers, and to inflict a deadly wound

116

on the Church by the destruction of its office-bearers. Hence, in general, its courts appear to have assembled in profound secrecy; and thus it is that, for the first three centuries, so little is known of the proceedings of these conventions.

It is to be observed that, in the first century, when the rulers of the Church met for consultation, they all sat in the same assembly. When the ecclesiastical constitution was fairly settled, even the Twelve were disposed to waive their personal claims to precedence, and to assume the status of ordinary ministers. We find accordingly that there were then no higher and lower houses of convocation; for "the apostles and elders came together." [255:1] Some, who suppose that James was the first bishop of the holy city, imagine that in his manner of giving the advice adopted at the Synod of Jerusalem, they can detect marks of his prelatic influence. [255:2] But the sacred narrative, when candidly interpreted, merely shews that he acted on the occasion as a judicious counsellor. He was, assuredly, not entitled to dictate to Paul or Peter. The reasoning of those who maintain that, as a matter of right, he expected the meeting to yield to the weight of his official authority, would go to prove, not that he was bishop of the Jewish capital, but that he was the prince of the apostles.

The New Testament history speaks frequently of James, and extends over the whole period of his public career; but it never once hints that he was bishop of Jerusalem, he himself has left behind him an epistle addressed "to the twelve tribes which are scattered abroad," in which he makes no allusion to his possession of any such office. Paul, who was well acquainted with him, and who often visited the mother Church during the time of his alleged episcopate, is equally silent upon the subject. But it is easy to understand how the story originated. The command of our Lord to the apostles, "Go ye unto all the world and preach the gospel to every creature," [256:1] did not imply that their countrymen at home were not to enjoy a portion of their ministrations; and it was probably considered expedient that one of their number should reside in the Jewish capital. This field of exertion seems to have been assigned to James. His colleagues meanwhile travelled to distant countries to disseminate the truth; and as he was the only individual of the apostolic company who could ordinarily be consulted in the holy city, he soon became the ruling spirit among the Christians of that crowded metropolis. In all cases of importance and of difficulty his advice would be sought and appreciated; and his age, experience, and rank as one of the Twelve, would suggest the propriety of his appointment as president of any ecclesiastical meeting he would attend. The precedence thus so generally conceded to him would be remembered in after-times when the hierarchical spirit began to dominate; and would afford a basis for the legend that he was the first bishop of Jerusalem. And as he, perhaps, commonly occupied the chair when the rulers of the Church assembled there at the annual festivals, we can see too why he is also called "bishop of bishops" in documents of high antiquity. [257:1]

During a considerable part of the first century Jerusalem probably contained a much greater number of disciples than any other city in the Roman Empire; and until shortly before its destruction by Titus in A.D. 70, it continued to be the centre of Christian influence. There is every reason to believe that, for some time, all matters in dispute throughout the Church, which could not be settled by inferior judicatories, were decided by the apostles and elders there convened. But the rapid propagation of Christianity, the rise of persecution, and the progress of political events, soon rendered such procedure inconvenient, if not impracticable.

117

Persons of Gentile extraction who lived in distant lands, and who were in humble circumstances, could not be expected to travel for redress of their ecclesiastical grievances to the ancient capital of Palestine; and, when the temple was destroyed, the myriads who had formerly repaired to it to celebrate the sacred feasts, of course discontinued their attendance. The Christian communities throughout the Empire about this period began to assume that form which they present in the following century, the congregations of each province associating together for their better government and discipline. There are not wanting evidences, as we shall now endeavour to show, that the apostles themselves suggested the arrangement.

It has been taken for granted by many that when Paul, on his arrival at Miletus, "sent to Ephesus and called the elders of the Church," [258:1] he convoked a meeting only of the ecclesiastical rulers of the chief city of the Proconsular Asia. But a more attentive examination, of the passage in which the transaction is described may lead us to doubt the correctness of such an interpretation. It is probable that, when the apostle sent to Ephesus, the Christian elders of the surrounding district, as well as of the capital, were requested to meet him at Miletus. Such a conclusion is sustained by the reason assigned for his mode of proceeding at this juncture. Ephesus was a seaport about thirty miles from Miletus, and it is said he did not touch at it on his voyage "because he would not spend the time in Asia, for he hasted, if it were possible for him, to be at Jerusalem the day of Pentecost." [258:2] But, had he merely wished to see the elders of this provincial metropolis, his visit to it need have created no delay, for he might have gone to it as quickly as the messenger who was the bearer of his communication. He seems, however, to have felt that, had he appeared there, he would have given offence had he not also favoured the Christian communities in its neighbourhood with his presence; and as he could not afford to spend so much time in Asia as would thus have been required, he adopted the expedient of inviting all the elders of the district to repair to him in the place where he now sojourned. [258:3] From Ephesus, the capital, his invitation could be readily transmitted to other provincial cities. The address which he delivered to the assembled elders certainly conveys the impression that they did not all belong to the metropolis, and its very first sentence suggests such an inference. "When they were come to him, he said unto them, Ye know from the first day that I came into Asia after what manner I have been with you at all seasons." [259:1] The evangelist informs us that he had spent only two years and three months at Ephesus, [259:2] and yet he here tells his audience that "by the space of three years" he had not ceased to warn every one night and day with tears. [259:3] He says also "I know that ye all among whom I have gone preaching the kingdom of God, shall see my face no more," [259:4]—thereby intimating that his auditors were not resident in one locality. We have also distinct evidence that when Paul formerly ministered at Ephesus, there were Christian societies throughout the province, for in his First Epistle to the Corinthians written from that city, [259:5] he sends his correspondents the salutations of "the Churches of Asia." [259:6] These Churches must obviously have been united by the ties of Christian fellowship; and the apostle must have been in close communication with them when he was thus employed as the medium of conveyance for the expression of their evangelical attachment.

In other parts of the New Testament we may discern traces of consocation among the primitive Churches. Thus, Paul, their founder, sends to "the Churches of Galatia" [259:7] a common letter in which he requires them to "serve one another," [259:8] and to "bear one another's burdens." [259:9] Without some species of united action, the Galatians could not well have obeyed such admonitions. Peter also, when writing to the disciples "scattered throughout Pontus, Galatia, Cappadocia, Asia, and Bithynia," [259:10] represents them as an associated body. "The elders," says he, "which are among you I exhort, who am also an elder....feed the flock of God which is among you taking the oversight thereof." [260:1] This "flock of God," which was evidently equivalent to the "Church of God," [260:2] was spread over a large territory; and yet the apostle suggests that the elders were conjointly charged with its supervision. Had the Churches scattered throughout so many provinces been a multitude of independent congregations, Peter would not have described them as one "flock" of which these rulers had the oversight.

But, though the elders of congregations in adjoining provinces could maintain ecclesiastical intercourse, and meet together at least occasionally or by delegates, it was otherwise with Churches in different countries. Even these, however, cultivated the communion of saints; for there are evidences that they corresponded with each other by letters or deputations. The attentive reader of the inspired epistles must have observed how the apostles contrived to keep open a door of access to their converts by means of itinerating preachers; [260:3] and the same agency seems to have been continued in succeeding generations. Disciples travelling into strange lands were furnished with "epistles of commendation" [260:4] to the foreign Churches; and Christian teachers, who had these credentials, were permitted freely to officiate in the congregations which they visited. It is an extraordinary fact that, during the lives of the apostles, there were preachers, in whom they had no confidence, who were yet in full standing, and who went from place to place addressing apostolic Churches. Having found their way into the ministry in a particular locality, they set out to other regions provided with their "letters of commendation;" and, on the strength of these testimonials, they were readily recognised as heralds of the cross. The apostles deemed it prudent to advise their correspondents not to rest satisfied with the certificates of these itinerant evangelists, but to try them by a more certain standard. "If there come any unto you," says John, "and bring not this doctrine, receive him not into your house, neither bid him God speed." [261:1]— "Beloved, believe not every spirit, but try the spirits whether they are of God, because many false prophets are gone out into the world." [261:2] Strange as it may now appear, even some of the apostles had personal enemies among the primitive preachers, and yet when these proclaimed the truth, they were suffered to proceed without interruption. "Some indeed," says Paul, "preach Christ even of envy and strife; and some also of good will. The one preach Christ of contention, not sincerely, supposing to add affliction to my bonds; but the other of love, knowing that I am set for the defence of the gospel. What then? notwithstanding, every way, whether in pretence or in truth, Christ is preached; and I therein do rejoice, yea, and will rejoice." [261:3]

The preceding statements may enable us to appreciate the unity of the Apostolic Church. This unity was not perfect; for there were false brethren who stirred up strife, and false teachers who fomented divisions. But these elements of discord no more disturbed the general unity of the Church than the presence of a few empty or blasted ears of corn affects the productiveness of an abundant harvest. As a body, the disciples of Christ were never so united as in the first century. Heresy had yet made little impression; schism was scarcely known; and charity, exerting her gentle influence with the brotherhood, found it comparatively easy to keep the unity of the spirit in the bond of peace. The members of the Church had "one Lord, one faith, one baptism." But their unity was very different from uniformity. They had no canonical hours, no clerical costume, no liturgies. The prayers of ministers and people varied according to circumstances, and were dictated by their hopes and fears, their wants and sympathies. When they met for worship, the devotional exercises were conducted in a language intelligible to all; when the Scriptures were read in their assemblies, every one heard in his own tongue the wonderful works of God. The unity of the Apostolic Church did not consist in its subordination to any one visible head or supreme pontiff; for neither Peter nor Paul, James nor John pretended to be the governor of the household of faith. Its unity was not like the unity of a jail where all the prisoners must wear the same dress, and receive the same rations, and dwell in cells of the same construction, and submit to the orders of the same keeper; but like the unity of a cluster of stalks of corn, all springing from one prolific grain, and all rich with a golden produce. Or it may be likened to the unity of the ocean, where all the parts are not of the same depth, or the same colour, or the same temperature; but where all, pervaded by the same saline preservative, ebb and flow according to the same heavenly laws, and concur in bearing to the ends of the earth the blessings of civilisation and of happiness.

CHAPTER IV

THE ANGELS OF THE SEVEN CHURCHES

The Apocalypse is a book of symbols. The light which we obtain from it may well remind us of the instruction communicated to the Israelites by the ceremonies of the law. The Mosaic institutions imparted to a Jew the knowledge of an atonement and a Saviour; but he could scarcely have undertaken to explain, with accuracy and precision, their individual significance, as their meaning was not fully developed until the times of the Messiah. So is it with "the Revelation of Jesus Christ which God gave unto him to shew unto his servants things which must shortly come to pass," and which "he sent and signified by his angel unto his servant John." [263:1] The Church here sees, as "through a glass darkly," the transactions of her future history; and she can here distinctly discern the ultimate triumph of her principles, so that, in days of adversity, she is encouraged and sustained; but she cannot speak with confidence of the import of much of this mysterious record; and it would seem as if the actual occurrence of the events foretold were to supply the only safe key for the interpretation of some of its strange imagery.

120

In the beginning of this book we have an account of a glorious vision presented to the beloved disciple. He was instructed to write down what he saw, and to send it to the Seven Churches in Asia, "unto Ephesus, and unto Smyrna, and unto Pergamos, and unto Thyatira, and unto Sardis, and unto Philadelphia, and unto Laodicea." [264:1] A vision so extraordinary as that which he describes, must have left upon his mind a permanent and most vivid impression. "I saw," says he, "seven golden candlesticks, and in the midst of the seven candlesticks one like unto the Son of Man clothed with a garment down to the foot, and girt about the paps with a golden girdle. His head and his hair were white like wool, as white as snow; and his eyes were as a flame of fire; and his feet like unto fine brass, as if they burned in a furnace; and his voice as the sound of many waters— and he had in his rigid hand seven stars, and out of his mouth went a sharp two-edged sword, and his countenance was as the sun shineth in his strength." [264:2]

In the foreground of this picture the Son of God stands conspicuous. His dress corresponds to that of the Jewish high priest, and the whole description of His person has obviously a reference, either to His own divine perfections, or to His offices as the Saviour of sinners. He himself is the expositor of two of the most remarkable of the symbols. "The seven stars," says He, "are the angels of the Seven Churches, and the seven candlesticks which thou sawest, are the Seven Churches." [264:3]

But though the symbol of the stars has been thus interpreted by Christ, the interpretation itself has been the subject of considerable discussion. Much difficulty has been experienced in identifying the angels of the Seven Churches; and there have been various conjectures as to the station which they occupied, and the duties which they performed. According to some they were literally angelic beings who had the special charge of the Seven Churches. [264:4] According to others, the angel of a Church betokens the collective body of ministers connected with the society. But such explanations are very far from satisfactory. The Scriptures nowhere teach that each Christian community is under the care of its own angelic guardian; neither is it to be supposed that an angel represents the ministry of a Church, for one symbol would not be interpreted by another symbol of dubious signification. It seems clear that the angel of the Church is a single individual, and that he must have been a personage well known to the body with which he was connected at the time when the Apocalypse was written.

It has often been asserted that the title "The angel of the Church" is borrowed from the designation of one of the ministers of the synagogue. [265:1] This point, however, has never been fairly demonstrated. In later times there was, no doubt, in the synagogue an individual known by the name of the legate, or the angel; but there is no decisive evidence that an official with such a designation existed in the first century. In the New Testament we have repeated references to the office-bearers of the synagogue; we are told of the rulers [265:2] or elders, the reader, [265:3] and the minister [265:4] or deacon; but the angel is never mentioned. Philo and Josephus are equally silent upon the subject. It is, therefore, extremely doubtful whether a minister with this title was known among the Jews in the days of the apostles. Even granting, what is so very problematical, that there were in the synagogues in the first century individuals distinguished by the designation of angels, it is still exceedingly doubtful whether the angels of the Seven Churches borrowed their names from these functionaries. If so, the angel of the Church must have occupied the same position as the angel of the synagogue, for the adoption of the same title indicated the possession of the same office. But it was the duty of the angel of the synagogue to offer up the prayers of the assembly; [266:1] and as, in all the synagogues, there was worship at the same hour, [266:2] he could, of course, be the minister of only one congregation. If then the angel of the Church discharged the same functions as the angel of the synagogue, it would follow that, towards the termination of the first century, there was only one Christian congregation in each of the seven cities of Ephesus, Smyrna, Pergamos, Thyatira, Sardis, Philadelphia, and Laodicea. It may, however, be fairly questioned whether the number of disciples in every one of these places was then so limited as such an inference would suggest. In Laodicea, and perhaps in one or two of the other cities, [266:3] there may have been only a single congregation; but it is scarcely probable that all the brethren in Ephesus still met together in one assembly. About forty years before, the Word of God "grew mightily and prevailed" [266:4] in that great metropolis; and, among its inhabitants, Paul had persuaded "much people" [266:5] to become disciples of Christ. But if the angel of the Church derived his title from the angel of the synagogue, and if the position of these two functionaries was the same, we are shut up to the conclusion that there was now only one congregation in the capital of the Proconsular Asia. The angel could not be in two places at the same time; and, as it was his duty to offer up the prayers of the assembled worshippers, it was impossible for him to minister to two congregations.

These considerations abundantly attest the futility of the imagination that the angel of the Church was a diocesan bishop. The office of the angel of the synagogue had, in fact, no resemblance whatever to that of a prelate. The rank of the ancient Jewish functionary seems to have been similar to that of a precentor in some of our Protestant churches; and when set forms of prayer were introduced among the Israelites, it was his duty to read them aloud in the congregation. The angel was not the chief ruler of the synagogue; he occupied a subordinate position; and was amenable to the authority of the bench of elders. [267:1] It is in vain then to attempt to recognise the predecessors of our modern diocesans in the angels of the Seven Churches. Had bishops been originally called angels, they never would have parted with so complimentary a designation. Had the Spirit of God in the Apocalypse bestowed upon them such a title, it never would have been laid aside. When, about a century after this period, we begin to discover distinct traces of a hierarchy, an extreme anxiety is discernible to find for it something like a footing in the days of the apostles; but, strange to say, the earliest prelates of whom we read are not known by the name of angels. [267:2] If such a nomenclature existed in the time of the Apostle John, it must have passed away at once and for ever! No trace of it can be detected even in the second century. It is thus apparent that, whatever the angels of the Seven Churches may have been, they certainly were not diocesan bishops.

The place where these angels are to be found in the apocalyptic scene also suggests the fallacy of the interpretation that they are the chief pastors of the Seven Churches. The stars are seen, not distributed over the seven candlesticks, but collected together in the hand of Christ. Though the angels seem to be in someway related to the Churches, the relation is such that they may be separated without inconvenience. What, then, can these angels be? How do they happen to possess the name they bear? Why are they gathered into the right hand of the Son of Man? All these questions admit of a very plain and satisfactory solution.

An angel literally signifies a messenger, and these angels were simply the messengers of the Seven Churches. John had long resided at Ephesus; and now that he was banished to the Isle of Patmos "for the word of God and for the testimony of Jesus Christ," it would appear that the Christian communities among which he had ministered so many years, sent trusty deputies to visit him, to assure him of their sympathy, and to tender to him their friendly offices. In primitive times such angels were often sent to the brethren in confinement or in exile. Thus, Paul, when in imprisonment at Rome, says to the Philippians—"Ye have well done that ye did communicate with my affliction ... I am full, having received of Epaphroditus the things which were sent from you." [268:1] Here, Epaphroditus is presented to us as the angel of the Church of Philippi. This minister seems, indeed, to have now spent no small portion of his time in travelling between Rome and Macedonia. Hence Paul observes—"I supposed it necessary to send to you Epaphroditus, my brother and companion in labour and fellow-soldier, but your messenger and he that ministered to my wants." [269:1] In like manner, the individuals selected to convey, to the poor saints in Jerusalem, the contributions of the Gentile converts in Greece and Asia Minor, are called "the messengers of the Churches." [269:2] The practice of sending messengers to visit and comfort the saints in poverty, in confinement, or in exile, may be traced for centuries in the history of the Church. It also deserves notice that, in other parts of the New Testament as well as in the Apocalypse, an individual sent on a special errand is repeatedly called an angel. Thus, John the Baptist, who was commissioned to announce the approach of the Messiah, is styled God's angel, [269:3] or messenger, and the spies, sent to view the land of Canaan, are distinguished by the same designation. [269:4]

Towards the close of the first century the Apostle John must have been regarded with extraordinary veneration by his Christian brethren. He was the last survivor of a band of men who had laid the foundations of the New Testament Church; and he was himself one of the most honoured members of the little fraternity, for he had enjoyed peculiarly intimate fellowship with his Divine Master. Our Lord, "in the days of His flesh," had permitted him to lean upon His bosom; and he has been described by the pen of inspiration as "the disciple whom Jesus loved." [269:5] All accounts concur in representing him as most amiable and warm-hearted; and as he had now far outlived the ordinary term of human existence, the snows of age must have imparted additional interest to a personage otherwise exceedingly attractive. It is not to be supposed that such a man was permitted in apostolic times to pine away unheeded in solitary exile. The small island which was the place of his banishment was not far from the Asiatic metropolis, and the other six cities named in the Apocalypse were all in the same district as Ephesus. It was, therefore, by no means extraordinary that seven messengers from seven neighbouring Churches, to all of which he was well known, are found together in Patmos on a visit to the venerable confessor.

This explanation satisfies all the conditions required by the laws of interpretation. Whilst it reveals a concern for the welfare of John quite in keeping with the benevolent spirit of apostolic times, it is also simple and sufficient. In prophetic language a star usually signifies a ruler, and it is probable that the angels sent to Patmos were selected from among the elders, or rulers, of the

Churches with which they were respectively connected; for, it is well known that, at an early period, elders, or presbyters, were frequently appointed to act as messengers or commissioners. [270:1] We may thus perceive, too, why the letters are addressed to the angels, for in this case they were the official organs of communication between the apostle and the religious societies which they had been deputed to represent. It is obvious that the instructions contained in the epistles were designed, not merely for the angels individually, but for the communities of which they were members; and hence the exhortation with which each of them concludes—"He that hath an ear, let him hear what the Spirit saith unto the Churches." [270:2] When the apostle was honoured with the vision, he was directed to write out an account of what he saw, and to "send it unto the Seven Churches which are in Asia;" [270:3] and this interpretation explains how he transmitted the communication; for, as Christ is said to have "sent and signified" His Revelation "by his angel unto his servant John," [271:1] so John, in his turn, conveyed it by the seven angels to the Seven Churches. It was, no doubt, thought that the messengers undertook a most perilous errand when they engaged to visit a distinguished Christian minister who had been driven into banishment by a jealous tyrant; but they are taught by the vision that they are under the special care of Him who is "the Prince of the kings of the earth;" for the Saviour appears holding them in His right hand as He walks in the midst of the seven golden candlesticks. When bearing consolation to the aged minister, each one of them could enjoy the comfort of the promise—"Can a woman forget her sucking child that she should not have compassion on the son of her womb? Yea, they may forget, yet will not I forget thee. Behold, I have graven thee upon the palms of my hands." [271:2]

It has often been thought singular that only seven Churches of the Proconsular Asia are here addressed, as it is well known that, at this period, there were several other Christian societies in the same province. Thus, in the immediate neighbourhood of Laodicea were the Churches of Colosse and Hierapolis; [271:3] and in the vicinity of Ephesus, perhaps the Churches of Tralles and Magnesia. But the seven angels mentioned by John may have been the only ecclesiastical messengers in Patmos at the time of the vision; and they may have been the organs of communication with a greater number of Churches than those which they directly represented. Seven was regarded by the Jews as the symbol of perfection; and it is somewhat remarkable that, on another occasion noticed in the New Testament, [271:4] we find exactly seven messengers deputed by the Churches of Greece and Asia Minor to convey their contributions to the indigent disciples in Jerusalem. There are, too, grounds for believing that these seven religious societies, in their varied character and prospects, are emblems of the Church universal. The instructions addressed to the disciples in these seven cities of Asia were designed for the benefit of "THE CHURCHES" of all countries as well as of all succeeding generations; and the whole imagery indicates that the vision is to be thus interpreted. The Son of Man does not confine His care to the Seven Churches of Asia, for He who appears walking in the midst of the seven golden candlesticks is the same who said of old to the nation of Israel—"I will set up my tabernacle among you, and my soul shall not abhor you, and I will walk among you, and will be your God, and ye shall be my people." [272:1] In the vision, the "countenance" of the Saviour is said to have been "as the sun shineth in his strength;" [272:2] and the prayer of the Church

124

catholic is—"God be merciful unto us, and bless us, and cause his face to shine upon us, that that thy way may be known upon earth, thy saving health among all nations." [272:3]

The preceding statements demonstrate the folly of attempting to construct a system of ecclesiastical polity from such a highly-figurative portion of Scripture as the Apocalypse. In the angel of the Church some have believed they have discovered the moderator of a presbytery; others, the bishop of a diocese; and others, the minister of an Irvingite congregation. But the basis on which all such theories are founded is a mere blunder as to the significance of an ecclesiastical title. The angels of the Seven Churches were neither moderators, nor diocesans, nor precentors, but messengers sent on an errand of love to an apostle in tribulation.

PERIOD II

FROM THE DEATH OF THE APOSTLE JOHN TO THE CONVERSION OF CONSTANTINE, A.D. 100 TO A.D. 312

SECTION I

THE HISTORY OF THE CHURCH

CHAPTER I

THE GROWTH OF THE CHURCH

The dawn of the second century was full of promise to the Church. On the death of Domitian in A.D. 96, the Roman Empire enjoyed for a short time [275:1] the administration of the mild and equitable Nerva. This prince repealed the sanguinary laws of his predecessor, and the disciples had a respite from persecution. Trajan, who succeeded him, [275:2] and who now occupied the throne, seemed not unwilling to imitate his policy, so that, in the beginning of his reign, the Christians had no reason to complain of imperial oppression. All accounts concur in stating that their affairs, at this period, presented a most hopeful aspect. They yet displayed a united front, for they had hitherto been almost entirely free from the evils of sectarianism; and now, that they were relieved from the terrible incubus of a ruthless tyranny, their spirits were as buoyant as ever; for though intolerance had thinned their ranks, it had also exhibited their constancy and stimulated their enthusiasm. Their intense attachment to the evangelical cause stood out in strange and impressive contrast with the apathy of polytheism. A heathen repeated, not without scepticism, the tales of his mythology, and readily passed over from one form of superstition to another; but the Christian felt himself strong in the truth, and was prepared to peril all that was dear to him on earth rather than abandon his cherished principles. Well might serious pagans be led to think favourably of a creed which fostered such decision and magnanimity.

The wonderful improvement produced by the gospel on the lives of multitudes by whom it was embraced, was, however, its most striking and cogent recommendation. The Christian authors who now published works in its defence, to many of which they gave the designation of apologies, and who sought, by means of these productions, either to correct the misrepresentations of its enemies, or to check the violence of persecution, always appeal with special confidence to this weighty testimonial. A veteran profligate converted into a

126

sober and exemplary citizen was a witness for the truth whose evidence it was difficult either to discard or to depreciate. Nor were such vouchers rare either in the second or third century. A learned minister of the Church could now venture to affirm that Christian communities were to be found composed of men "reclaimed from ten thousand vices," [276:1] and that these societies, compared with others around them, were "as lights in the world." [276:2] The practical excellence of the new faith is attested, still more circumstantially, by another of its advocates who wrote about half a century after the age of the apostles. "We," says he, "who formerly delighted in vicious excesses are now temperate and chaste; we, who once practised magical arts, have consecrated ourselves to the good and unbegotten God; we, who once prized gain above all things, give even what we have to the common use, and share it with such as are in need; we, who once hated and murdered one another, who, on account of difference of customs, would have no common hearth with strangers, now, since the appearance of Christ, live together with them; we pray for our enemies; we seek to persuade those who hate us without cause to live conformably to the goodly precepts of Christ, that they may become partakers with us, of the joyful hope of blessings from God, the Lord of all." [277:1] When we consider that all the old superstitions had now become nearly effete, we cannot be surprised at the signal triumphs of a system which could furnish such noble credentials.

Whilst Christianity demonstrated its divine virtue by the good fruits which it produced, it, at the same time, invited all men to study its doctrines and to judge for themselves. Those who were disposed to examine its internal evidences were supplied with facilities for pursuing the investigation, as the Scriptures of the New Testament were publicly read in the assemblies of the faithful, and copies of them were diligently multiplied, so that these divine guides could be readily consulted by every one who really wished for information. The importance of the writings of the apostles and evangelists suggested the propriety of making them available for the instruction of those who were ignorant of Greek; and versions in the Latin, the Syriac, and other languages [277:2] soon made their appearance. Some compositions are stripped of their charms when exhibited in translations, as they owe their attractiveness to the mere embellishments of style or expression; but the Word of God, like all the works of the High and the Holy One, speaks with equal power to every kindred and tongue and people. When correctly rendered into another language, it is still full of grace and truth, of majesty and beauty. In whatever dialect it may be clothed, it continues to awaken the conscience and to convert the soul. Its dissemination at this period either in the original or in translations, contributed greatly to the extension of the Church; and the gospel, issuing from this pure fountain, at once revealed its superiority to all the miserable dilutions of superstition and absurdity presented in the systems of heathenism.

When accounting for the rapid diffusion of the new faith in the second and third centuries, many have laid much stress on the miraculous powers of the disciples; but the aid derived from this quarter seems to have been greatly over-estimated. The days of Christ and His apostles were properly the times of "wonders and mighty deeds;" and though the lives of some, on whom extraordinary endowments were conferred, probably extended far into the second century, it is remarkable that the earliest ecclesiastical writers are almost, if not altogether, silent upon the subject of contemporary miracles. [278:1]

127

Supernatural gifts perhaps ceased with those on whom they were bestowed by the inspired founders of the Church; [278:2] but many imagined that their continuance was necessary to the credit of the Christian cause, and were, therefore, slow to admit that these tokens of the divine recognition had completely disappeared. It must be acknowledged that the prodigies attributed to this period are very indifferently authenticated as compared with those reported by the pen of inspiration. [278:3] In some cases they are described in ambiguous or general terms, such as the narrators might have been expected to employ when detailing vague and uncertain rumours; and not a few of the cures now dignified with the title of miracles are of a commonplace character, such as could have been accomplished without any supernatural interference, and which Jewish and heathen quacks frequently performed. [279:1] No writer of this period asserts that he himself possessed the power either of speaking with tongues, [279:2] or of healing the sick, or of raising the dead. [279:3] Legend now began to supply food for popular credulity; and it is a suspicious circumstance that the greater number of the miracles which are said to have happened in the second and third centuries are recorded for the first time about a hundred years after the alleged date of their occurrence. [279:4] But Christianity derived no substantial advantage from these fictitious wonders. Some of them were so frivolous as to excite contempt, and others so ridiculous as to afford matter for merriment to the more intelligent pagans. [279:5]

The gospel had better claims than any furnished by equivocal miracles; and, though it still encountered opposition, it now moved forward in a triumphant career. In some districts it produced such an impression that it threatened the speedy extinction of the established worship. In Bithynia, early in the second century, the temples of the gods were well-nigh deserted, and the sacrificial victims found very few purchasers. [280:1] The pagan priests now took the alarm; the power of the magistrate interposed to prevent the spread of the new doctrine; and spies were found willing to dog the steps and to discover the meeting-places of the converts. Many quailed before the prospect of death, and purchased immunity from persecution by again repairing to the altars of idolatry. But, notwithstanding all the arts of intimidation and chicanery, the good cause continued to prosper. In Rome, in Antioch, in Alexandria, and in other great cities, the truth steadily gained ground; and, towards the end of the second century, it had acquired such strength even in Carthage—a place far removed from the scene of its original proclamation—that, according to the statement of one of its advocates, its adherents amounted to a tenth of the inhabitants. [280:2] About the same period Churches were to be found in various parts of the north of Africa between Egypt and Carthage; and, in the East, Christianity soon acquired a permanent footing in the little state of Edessa, [280:3] in Arabia, in Parthia, and in India. In the West, it continued to extend itself throughout Greece and Italy, as well as in Spain and France. In the latter country the Churches of Lyons and Vienne attract attention in the second century; and in the third, seven eminent missionaries are said to have formed congregations in Paris, Tours, Arles, Narbonne, Toulouse, Limoges, and Clermont. [281:1] Meanwhile the light of divine truth penetrated into Germany; and, as the third century advanced, even the rude Goths inhabiting Moesia and Thrace were partially brought under its influence. The circumstances which led to the conversion of these barbarians are somewhat remarkable. On the occasion of one of their predatory incursions into the Empire, they carried away captive some Christian presbyters; but the parties thus unexpectedly reduced to bondage did not neglect the duties of their spiritual calling, and commended their cause so successfully to those by whom they had been enslaved, that the whole nation eventually embraced the gospel. [281:2] Even the barriers of the ocean did not arrest the progress of the victorious faith. Before the end of the second century the religion of the cross seems to have reached Scotland; for though Tertullian certainly speaks rhetorically when he says that "the places of Britain inaccessible to the Romans were subject to Christ," [281:3] his language at least implies that the message of salvation had already been proclaimed with some measure of encouragement in Caledonia.

Though no contemporary writer has furnished us with anything like an ecclesiastical history of this period, it is very clear, from occasional hints thrown out by the early apologists and controversialists, that the progress of the Church must have been both extensive and rapid. A Christian author, who flourished about the middle of the second century, asserts that there was then "no race of men, whether of barbarians or of Greeks, or bearing any other name, either because they lived in waggons without fixed habitations, or in tents leading a pastoral life, among whom prayers and thanksgivings were not offered up to the Father and Maker of all things through the name of the crucified Jesus." [282:1] Another father, who wrote shortly afterwards, observes that, "as in the sea there are certain habitable and fertile islands, with wholesome springs, provided with roadsteads and harbours, in which those who are overtaken by tempests may find refuge—in like manner has God placed in a world tossed by the billows and storms of sin, congregations or holy churches, in which, as in insular harbours, the doctrines of truth are sheltered, and to which those who desire to be saved, who love the truth, and who wish to escape the judgment of God, may repair." [282:2] These statements indicate that the gospel must soon have been very widely disseminated. Within less than a hundred years after the apostolic age places of Christian worship were to be seen in the chief cities of the Empire; and early in the third century a decision of the imperial tribunal awarded to the faithful in the great Western metropolis a plot of ground for the erection of one of their religious edifices. [282:3] At length about A.D. 260 the Emperor Gallienus issued an edict of toleration in their favour; and, during the forty years which followed, their numbers so increased that the ecclesiastical buildings in which they had hitherto assembled were no longer sufficient for their accommodation. New and spacious churches now supplanted the old meeting-houses, and these more fashionable structures were soon filled to overflowing. [282:4] But the spirit of the world now began to be largely infused into the Christian communities; the Church was distracted by its ministers struggling with each other for pre-eminence; and even the terrible persecution of Diocletian which succeeded, could neither quench the ambition, nor arrest the violence of contending pastors.

If we stand, only for a moment, on the beach, we may find it impossible to decide whether the tide is ebbing or flowing. But if we remain there for a few hours, the question will not remain unsettled. The sea will meanwhile either retire into its depths, or compel us to retreat before its advancing waters. So it is with the Church. At a given date we may be unable to determine whether it is aggressive, stationary, or retrograde. But when we compare its circumstances at distant intervals, we may easily form a judgment. From the first to the fourth century, Christianity moved forward like the flowing tide; and yet, perhaps, its advance, during any one year, was not very perceptible. When, however, we contrast its weakness at the death of the Apostle John with its strength immediately before the commencement of the last imperial persecution, we cannot but acknowledge its amazing progress. At the termination of the first century, its adherents were a little flock, thinly scattered over the empire. In the reign of Diocletian, such was even their numerical importance that no prudent statesman would have thought it safe to overlook them in the business of legislation. They held military appointments of high responsibility; they were to be found in some of the most honourable civil offices; they were admitted to the court of the sovereign; and in not a few cities they constituted a most influential section of the population. The wife of Diocletian, and his daughter Valeria, are said to have been Christians. The gospel had now passed over the boundaries of the empire, and had made conquests among savages, some of whom had, perhaps, scarcely ever heard of the majesty of Rome. But it did not establish its dominion unopposed, and, in tracing its annals, we must not neglect to notice the history of its persecutions.

CHAPTER II

THE PERSECUTIONS OF THE CHURCH

The persecutions of the early Church form an important and deeply interesting portion of its history. When its Great Author died on the accursed tree, Christianity was baptized in blood; and for several centuries its annals consist largely of details of proscription and of suffering. God might have introduced the gospel amongst men amidst the shouts of applauding nations, but "He doeth all things well;" and He doubtless saw that the way in which its reign was actually inaugurated, was better fitted to exhibit His glory, and to attest its excellence. Multitudes, who might otherwise have trifled with the great salvation, were led to think of it more seriously, when they saw that it prompted its professors to encounter such tremendous sacrifices. As the heathen bystanders gazed on the martyrdom of a husband and a master, and as they observed the unflinching fortitude with which he endured his anguish, they often became deeply pensive. They would exclaim—"The man has children, we believe—a wife he has, unquestionably—and yet he is not unnerved by these ties of kindred: he is not turned from his purpose by these claims of affection. We must look into the affair—we must get at the bottom of it. Be it what it may, it can be no trifle which makes one ready to suffer and willing to die for it." [284:1] The effects produced on spectators by the heroism of the Christians cannot have escaped the notice of the heathen magistrates. The Church herself was well aware of the credit she derived from these displays of the constancy of her children; and hence, in an address to the persecutors which appeared about the beginning of the third century, the ardent writer boldly invites them to proceed with the work of butchery. "Go on," says he tauntingly, "ye good governors, so much better in the eyes of the people if ye sacrifice the Christians to them—rack, torture, condemn, grind us to powder—our numbers increase in proportion as you mow us down. The blood of Christians is their harvest seed—that very obstinacy with which you upbraid us, is a teacher. For who is not incited by the contemplation of it to inquire what there is in the core of the matter? and who, that has inquired, does not join us? and who, that joins us, does not long to suffer?" [285:1]

In another point of view the perils connected with a profession of the gospel exercised a wholesome influence. Comparatively few undecided characters joined the communion of the Church; and thus its members, as a body, displayed much consistency and steadfastness. The purity of the Christian morality was never seen to more advantage than in those days of persecution, as every one who joined the hated sect was understood to possess the spirit of a martyr. And never did the graces of the religion of the cross appear in more attractive lustre than when its disciples were groaning under the inflictions of imperial tyranny. As some plants yield their choicest odours only under the influence of pressure, it would seem as if the gospel reserved its richest supplies of patience, strength, and consolation, for times of trouble and alarm. Piety never more decisively asserts its celestial birth than when it stands unblenched under the frown of the persecutor, or calmly awaits the shock of death. In the second and third centuries an unbelieving world often looked on with wonder as the Christians submitted to torment rather than renounce their faith. Nor were spectators more impressed by the amount of suffering sustained by the confessors and the martyrs, than by the spirit with which they endured their trials. They approached their tortures in no temper of dogged obstinacy or sullen defiance. They rejoiced that they were counted worthy to suffer in so good a cause. They manifested a self-possession, a meekness of wisdom, a gentleness, and a cheerfulness, at which the multitude were amazed. Nor were these proofs of Christian magnanimity confined to any one class of the sufferers. Children and delicate females, illiterate artisans and poor slaves, sometimes evinced as much intrepidity and decision as hoary-headed pastors. It thus appeared that the victims of intolerance were upheld by a power which was divine, and of which philosophy could give no explanation.

We form a most inadequate estimate of the trials of the early Christians, if we take into account only those sufferings they endured from the hands of the pagan magistrates. Circumstances which seldom came under the eye of public observation not unfrequently kept them for life in a state of disquietude. Idolatry was so interwoven with the very texture of society that the adoption of the new faith sometimes abruptly deprived an individual of the means of subsistence. If he was a statuary, he could no longer employ himself in carving images of the gods; if he was a painter, he could no more expend his skill in decorating the high places of superstition. To earn a livelihood, he must either seek out a new sphere for the exercise of his art, or betake himself to some new occupation. If the Christian was a merchant, he was, to a great extent, at the mercy of those with whom he transacted business. When his property was in the hands of dishonest heathens, he was often unable to recover it, as the pagan oaths administered in the courts of justice prevented him from appealing for redress to the laws of the empire. [287:1] Were he placed in circumstances which enabled him to surmount this difficulty, he could not afford to exasperate his debtors; as they could have so

131

easily retaliated by accusing him of Christianity. The wealthy disciple could not accept the office of a magistrate, for he would have thus only betrayed his creed; neither could he venture to aspire to any of the honours of the state, as his promotion would most certainly have aggravated the perils of his position. Our Saviour had said—"I am come to set a man at variance against his father, and the daughter against her mother, and the daughter-in-law against her mother-in-law; and a man's foes shall be they of his own household." [287:2] These words were now verified with such woeful accuracy that the distrust pervading the domestic circle often imbittered the whole life of the believer. The slave informed against his Christian master; the husband divorced his Christian wife; and children who embraced the gospel were sometimes disinherited by their enraged parents. [287:3] As the followers of the cross contemplated the hardships which beset them on every side, well might they have exclaimed in the words of the apostle— "If in this life only we have hope in Christ, we are of all men most miserable." [287:4]

In the first century the very helplessness of the Church served partially to protect it from persecution. Its adherents were then almost all in very humble circumstances; and their numbers were not such as to inspire the sovereign with any political anxiety. When they were harassed by the unbelieving Jews, the civil magistrate sometimes interposed, and spread over them the shield of toleration; and though Nero and Domitian were their persecutors, the treatment they experienced from two princes so generally abhorred for cruelty elicited a measure of public sympathy. [288:1] At length, however, the Roman government, even when administered by sovereigns noted for their political virtues, began to assume an attitude of decided opposition; and, for many generations, the disciples were constantly exposed to the hostility of their pagan rulers.

The Romans acted so far upon the principle of toleration as to permit the various nations reduced under their dominion to adhere to whatever religion they had previously professed. They were, no doubt, led to pursue this policy by the combined dictates of expediency and superstition; for whilst they were aware that they could more easily preserve their conquests by granting indulgence to the vanquished, they believed that each country had its own tutelary guardians. But they looked with the utmost suspicion upon all new systems of religion. Such novelties, they conceived, might be connected with designs against the state; and should, therefore, be sternly discountenanced. Hence it was that Christianity so soon met with opposition from the imperial government. For a time it was confounded with Judaism, and, as such, was regarded as entitled to the protection of the laws; but when its true character was ascertained, the disciples were involved in all the penalties attached to the adherents of an unlicensed worship.

Very early in the second century the power of the State was turned against the gospel. About A.D. 107, the far-famed Ignatius, the pastor of Antioch, is said to have suffered martyrdom. Soon afterwards our attention is directed to the unhappy condition of the Church by a correspondence between the celebrated Pliny, and the Emperor Trajan. It would seem that in Bithynia, of which Pliny was governor, the new faith was rapidly spreading; and that those who derived their subsistence from the maintenance of superstition, had taken the alarm. The proconsul had, therefore, been importuned to commence a persecution; and as existing statutes supplied him with no very definite instructions respecting the

132

method of procedure, he deemed it necessary to seek directions from his Imperial master. He stated, at the same time, the course which he had hitherto pursued. If individuals arraigned before his judgment-seat, and accused of Christianity, refused to repudiate the obnoxious creed, they were condemned to death; but if they abjured the gospel, they were permitted to escape unscathed. Trajan approved of this policy, and it now became the law of the Empire.

In his letter to his sovereign [289:1] Pliny has given a very favourable account of the Christian morality, and has virtually admitted that the new religion was admirably fitted to promote the good of the community, he mentions that the members of the Church were bound by solemn obligations to abstain from theft, robbery, and adultery; to keep their promises, and to avoid every form of wickedness. When such was their acknowledged character, it may appear extraordinary that a sagacious prince and a magistrate of highly cultivated mind concurred in thinking that they should be treated with extreme rigour. We have here, however, a striking example of the military spirit of Roman legislation. The laws of the Empire made no proper provision for the rights of conscience; and they were based throughout upon the principle that implicit obedience is the first duty of a subject. Neither Pliny nor Trajan could understand why a Christian should not renounce his creed at the bidding of the civil governor. In their estimation, "inflexible obstinacy" in confessing the Saviour was a crime which deserved no less a penalty than death.

Though the rescript of Trajan awarded capital punishment to the man who persisted in acknowledging himself a Christian, it also required that the disciples should not be inquisitively sought after. The zeal of many of the enemies of the Church was, no doubt, checked by this provision; as those who attempted to hunt down the faithful expressly violated the spirit of the imperial enactment. But still, some Christians now suffered the penalty of a good confession. Pliny himself admits that individuals who were brought before his own tribunal, and who could not be induced to recant, were capitally punished; and elsewhere the law was not permitted to remain in abeyance. About the close of the reign of Trajan, Simeon, the senior minister of Jerusalem, now in the hundred and twentieth year of his age, fell a victim to its severity. This martyr was, probably, the second son of Mary, the mother of our Lord. He is, perhaps, the same who is enumerated in the Gospels [290:1] among the brethren of Christ; and the chronology accords with the supposition that he was a year younger than our Saviour. [290:2] His relationship to Jesus, his great age, and his personal excellence secured for him a most influential position in the mother Church of Christendom; and hence, by writers who flourished afterwards, and who expressed themselves in the language of their generation, he has been called the second bishop of Jerusalem.

Though the rescript of Trajan served for a time to restrain the violence of persecution, it pronounced the profession of Christianity illegal; so that doubts, which had hitherto existed as to the interpretation of the law, could no longer be entertained. The heathen priests, and others interested in the support of idolatry, did not neglect to proclaim a fact so discouraging to the friends of the gospel. The law, indeed, still presented difficulties, for an accuser who failed to substantiate his charge was liable to punishment; but the wily adversaries of the Church soon contrived to evade this obstacle. When the people met together on great public occasions, as at the celebration of their games, or festivals, and when the interest in the sports began to flag, attempts were often made to provide them with a new and more exciting pastime by raising the cry of "The Christians to the Lions;" and as, at such times, the magistrates had been long accustomed to yield to the wishes of the multitude, many of the faithful were sacrificed to their clamours. Here, no one was obliged to step forward and hold himself responsible for the truth of an indictment; and thus, without incurring any danger, personal malice and blind bigotry had free scope for their indulgence. In the reign of Hadrian, the successor of Trajan, the Christians were sadly harassed by these popular ebullitions; and at length Quadratus and Aristides, two eminent members of the Church at Athens, presented apologies to the Emperor in which they vividly depicted the hardships of their position. Serenius Granianus, the Proconsul of Asia, also complained to Hadrian of the proceedings of the mob; and, in consequence, that Prince issued a rescript requiring that the magistrates should in future refuse to give way to the extempore clamours of public meetings.

Antoninus Pius, who inherited the throne on the demise of Hadrian, was a mild Sovereign; and under him the faithful enjoyed comparative tranquillity; but his successor Marcus Aurelius, surnamed the Philosopher, pursued a very different policy. Marcus is commonly reputed one of the best of the Roman Emperors; at a very early period of life he gave promise of uncommon excellence; and throughout his reign he distinguished himself as an able and accomplished monarch. But he was proud, pedantic, and self-sufficient; and, like every other individual destitute of spiritual enlightenment, his character presented the most glaring inconsistencies; for he was at once a professed Stoic, and a devout Pagan. This Prince could not brook the contempt with which the Christians treated his philosophy; neither could he tolerate the idea that they should be permitted to think for themselves. He could conceive how an individual, yielding to the stern law of fate, could meet death with unconcern; but he did not understand how the Christians could glory in tribulation, and hail even martyrdom with a song of triumph. Had he calmly reflected on the spirit displayed by the witnesses for the truth, he might have seen that they were partakers of a higher wisdom than his own; but the tenacity with which they adhered to their principles, only mortified his self-conceit, and roused his indignation. It is remarkable that this philosophic Emperor was the most systematic and heartless of all the persecutors who had ever yet oppressed the Church. When Nero lighted up his gardens with the flames which issued from the bodies of the dying Christians, he wished to transfer to them the odium of the burning of Rome, and he acted only with the caprice and cunning of a tyrant; and when Domitian promulgated his cruel edicts, he was haunted with the dread that the proscribed sect would raise up a rival Sovereign; but Marcus Aurelius could not plead even such miserable apologies. He hated the Christians with the cool acerbity of a Stoic; and he took measures for their extirpation which betrayed at once his folly and his malevolence. Disregarding the law of Trajan which required that they should not be officiously sought after, he encouraged spies and informers to harass them with accusations. He caused them to be dragged before the tribunals of the magistrates; and, under pain of death, to be compelled to conform to the rites of idolatry. With a refinement of cruelty unknown to his predecessors, he employed torture for the purpose of forcing them to recant. If, in their agony, they gave way, and consented to sacrifice to the gods, they were released; if they remained firm, they were permitted to die in torment. In his reign we read of new and hideous forms of punishment—evidently instituted for the purpose of aggravating pain and terror.

The Christians were stretched upon the rack, and their joints were dislocated; their bodies, when lacerated with scourges, were laid on rough sea-shells, or on other most uncomfortable supports; they were torn to pieces by wild beasts; or they were roasted alive on heated iron chairs. Ingenuity was called to the ignoble office of inventing new modes and new instruments of torture.

One of the most distinguished sufferers of this reign was Justin, surnamed the Martyr. [293:1] He was a native of Samaria; but he had travelled into various countries, and had studied various systems of philosophy, with a view, if possible, to discover the truth. His attention had at length been directed to the Scriptures, and in them he had found that satisfaction which he could not obtain elsewhere. When in Rome about A.D. 165, he came into collision with Crescens, a Cynic philosopher, whom he foiled in a theological discussion. His unscrupulous antagonist, annoyed by this discomfiture, turned informer; and Justin, with some others, was put to death. Shortly afterwards Polycarp, the aged pastor of Smyrna, was committed to the flames. [293:2] This venerable man, who had been acquainted in his youth with the Apostle John, had long occupied a high position as a prudent, exemplary, and devoted minister. Informations were now laid against him, and orders were given for his apprehension. At first he endeavoured to elude his pursuers; but when he saw that escape was impossible, he surrendered himself a prisoner. After all, he would have been permitted to remain unharmed had he consented to renounce the gospel. In the sight of an immense throng who gloated over the prospect of his execution, the good old man remained unmoved. When called on to curse Christ he returned the memorable answer—"Eighty and six years have I served Him, and He has done me nothing but good; and how could I curse Him my Lord and Saviour?" "I will cast you to the wild beasts," said the Proconsul, "if you do not change your mind." "Bring the wild beasts hither," replied Polycarp, "for change my mind from the better to the worse I will not." "Despise you the wild beasts?" exclaimed the magistrate—"I will subdue your spirit by the flames." "The flames which you menace endure but for a time and are soon extinguished," calmly rejoined the prisoner, "but there is a fire reserved for the wicked, whereof you know not; the fire of a judgment to come and of punishment everlasting." These answers put an end to all hope of pardon; a pile of faggots was speedily collected; and Polycarp was burned alive.

Towards the end of the reign of Marcus Aurelius, or about A.D. 177, the Churches of Lyons and Vienne [294:1] in France endured one of the most horrible persecutions recorded in the annals of Christian martyrdom. A dreadful pestilence, some years before, had desolated the Empire; and the pagans seem to have been impressed with the conviction that the new religion had provoked the visitation. The mob in various cities became, in consequence, exasperated; and demanded, with loud cries, the extirpation of the hated sectaries. In the south of France a considerable time appears to have elapsed before the ill-will of the multitude broke out into open violence. At first the disciples in Lyons and Vienne were insulted in places of public concourse; they were then pelted with stones and forced to shut themselves up in their own houses; they were subsequently seized and thrown into prison; and afterwards their slaves were put to the torture, and compelled to accuse them of crimes of which they were innocent. Pothinus, the pastor of Lyons, now upwards of ninety years of age, was brought before the governor, and so roughly handled by the populace that he died two

135

days after he was thrown into confinement. The other prisoners were plied with hunger and thirst, and then put to death with wanton and studied cruelty. Two of the sufferers, Blandina, a female, and Ponticus, a lad of fifteen, displayed singular calmness and intrepidity. For several days they were obliged to witness the tortures inflicted on their fellow-disciples, that they might, if possible, be intimidated by the appalling spectacle. After passing through this ordeal, the torture was applied to themselves. Ponticus soon sunk under his sufferings; but Blandina still survived. When she had sustained the agony of the heated iron chair, she was put into a net and thrown to a wild bull that she might be trampled and torn by him; and she continued to breathe long after she had been sadly mangled by the infuriated animal. While subjected to these terrible inflictions, she exhibited the utmost patience; no boasts escaped her lips; no murmurs were uttered by her; and even in the paroxysms of her anguish she was seen to be full of faith and courage. But such touching exhibitions of the spirit of the gospel failed to repress the fury of the excited populace. Their hatred of the gospel was so intense that they resolved to deprive the disciples who survived this reign of terror of the melancholy satisfaction of paying the last tribute of respect to the remains of their martyred brethren. They, accordingly, burned the dead bodies, and then cast the ashes into the Rhone. "Now," said they, "we will see whether they will rise again, and whether God can help them, and deliver them out of our hands." [296:1]

Under the brutal and bloody Commodus, the son and heir of Marcus Aurelius, the Christians had some repose. Marcia, his favourite concubine, was a member of the Church; [296:2] and her influence was successfully exerted in protecting her co-religionists. But the penal statutes were still in force, and they were not everywhere permitted to remain a dead letter. In this reign [296:3] we meet with some of the earliest indications of that zeal for martyrdom which was properly the spawn of the fanaticism of the Montanists. In a certain district of Asia, a multitude of persons, actuated by this absurd passion, presented themselves in a body before the proconsul Arrius Antoninus; and proclaimed themselves Christians. The sight of such a crowd of victims appalled the magistrate; and, after passing judgment on a few, he is said to have driven the remainder from his tribunal, exclaiming— "Miserable men, if you wish to kill yourselves, you have ropes or precipices."

The reigns of Pertinax and Julian, the Emperors next in succession after Commodus, amounted together only to a few months; and the faithful had meanwhile to struggle with many discouragements; [296:4] but these short-lived sovereigns were so much occupied with other matters, that they could not afford time for legislation on the subject of religion. Septimius Severus, who now obtained the Imperial dignity, was at first not unfriendly to the Church; and a cure performed on him by Proculus, a Christian slave, [297:1] has been assigned as the cause of his forbearance; but, as his reign advanced, he assumed an offensive attitude; and it cannot be denied that the disciples suffered considerably under his administration. As the Christians were still obliged to meet at night to celebrate their worship, they were accused of committing unnatural crimes in their nocturnal assemblies; and though these heartless calumnies had been triumphantly refuted fifty or sixty years before, they were now revived and circulated with fresh industry. [297:2] About this period, Leonides, the father of the learned Origen, was put to death. By a law,

136

promulgated probably in A.D. 202, the Emperor interdicted conversions to Christianity; and at a time when the Church was making vigorous encroachments on heathenism, this enactment created much embarrassment and anxiety. Some of the governors of provinces, as soon as they ascertained the disposition of the Imperial court, commenced forthwith a persecution; and there were magistrates who proceeded to enforce the laws for the base purpose of extorting money from the parties obnoxious to their severity. Sometimes individuals, and sometimes whole congregations purchased immunity from suffering by entering into pecuniary contracts with corrupt and avaricious rulers; and by the payment of a certain sum obtained certificates [297:3] which protected them from all farther inquisition. [297:4] The purport of these documents has been the subject of much discussion. According to some they contained a distinct statement to the effect that those named in them had sacrificed to the gods, and had thus satisfied the law; whilst others allege that, though they guaranteed protection, they neither directly stated an untruth, nor compromised the religious consistency of their possessors. But it is beyond all controversy that the more scrupulous and zealous Christians uniformly condemned the use of such certificates. Their owners were known by the suspicious designation of "Libellatici," or "the Certified;" and were considered only less criminal than the "Thurificati," or those who had actually apostatised by offering incense on the altars of paganism. [298:1]

About this time the enforcement of the penal laws in a part of North Africa, probably in Carthage, led to a most impressive display of some of the noblest features of the Christian character. Five catechumens, or candidates for baptism, among whom were Perpetua and Felicitas, [298:2] had been put under arrest. Perpetua, who was only two and twenty years of age, was a lady of rank and of singularly prepossessing appearance. Accustomed to all the comforts which wealth could procure, she was ill fitted, with a child at the breast, to sustain the rigours of confinement—more especially as she was thrown into a crowded dungeon during the oppressive heat of an African summer. But, with her infant in her arms, she cheerfully submitted to her privations; and the thought that she was persecuted for Christ's sake, converted her prison into a palace. Her aged father, who was a pagan, was overwhelmed with distress because, as he conceived, she was bringing deep and lasting disgrace upon her family by her attachment to a proscribed sect; and as she was his favourite child, he employed every expedient which paternal tenderness and anxiety could dictate to lead her to a recantation. When she was conducted to the judgment-seat with the other prisoners, the old gentleman appeared there, to try the effect of another appeal to her; and the presiding magistrate, touched with pity, entreated her to listen to his arguments, and to change her resolution. But, though deeply moved by the anguish of her aged parent, all these attempts to shake her constancy were in vain. At the place of execution she sung a psalm of victory, and, before she expired, she exhorted her brother and another catechumen, named Rusticus, to continue in the faith, to love each other, and to be neither affrighted nor offended by her sufferings. Her companion Felicitas exhibited quite as illustrious a specimen of Christian heroism. When arrested, she was far advanced in pregnancy, and during her imprisonment, the pains of labour came upon her. Her cries arrested the attention of the jailer, who said to her—"If your present sufferings are so great, what will you do when you are thrown to the wild beasts? You did not consider this when you refused to sacrifice." With undaunted spirit

137

Felicitas replied—"It is I that suffer now, but then there will be Another with me, who will suffer for me, because I shall suffer for His sake." The prisoners were condemned to be torn by wild beasts on the occasion of an approaching festival; and when they had passed through this terrible ordeal, they were despatched with the sword.

After the death of Septimius Severus, the Christians experienced some abatement of their sufferings. Caracalla and Elagabalus permitted them to remain almost undisturbed; and Alexander Severus has been supposed by some to have been himself a believer. Among the images in his private chapel was a representation of Christ, and he was obviously convinced that Jesus possessed divine endowments; but there is no proof that he ever accepted unreservedly the New Testament revelation. He was simply an eclectic philosopher who held that a portion of truth was to be found in each of the current systems of religion; and who undertook to analyse them, and extract the spiritual treasure. The Emperor Maximin was less friendly to the Church; and yet his enmity was confined chiefly to those Christian ministers who had been favourites with his predecessor; so that he cannot be said to have promoted any general persecution. Under Gordian the disciples were free from molestation; and his successor, Philip the Arabian, was so well affected to their cause that he has been sometimes, though erroneously, represented as the first Christian Emperor. [300:1] The death of this monarch in A.D. 249 was, however, soon followed by the fiercest and the most extensive persecution under which the faithful had yet groaned. The more zealous of the pagans, who had been long witnessing with impatience the growth of Christianity, had become convinced that, if the old religion were to be upheld, a mighty effort must very soon be made to strangle its rival. Various expedients were meanwhile employed to prejudice the multitude against the gospel. Every disaster which occurred throughout the Empire was attributed to its evil influence; the defeat of a general, the failure of a harvest, the overflowing of the Tiber, the desolations of a hurricane, and the appearance of a pestilence, were all ascribed to its most inauspicious advancement. The public mind was thus gradually prepared for measures of extreme severity; and Decius, who now became emperor, aimed at the utter extirpation of Christianity. All persons suspected of attachment to the gospel were summoned before the civil authorities; and if, regardless of intimidation, they refused to sacrifice, attempts were made to overcome their constancy by torture, by imprisonment, and by starvation. When all such expedients failed, the punishment of death was inflicted. Those who fled before the day appointed for their appearance in presence of the magistrates, forfeited their property; and were forbidden, under the penalty of death, to return to the district. The Church in many places had now enjoyed peace for thirty years, and meanwhile the tone of Christian principle had been considerably lowered. It was not strange, therefore, that, in these perilous days, many apostatised. [301:1] The conduct of not a few of the more opulent Christians of Alexandria has been graphically described by a contemporary. "As they were severally called by name, they approached the unholy offering; some, pale and trembling, as if they were going, not to sacrifice, but to be sacrificed to the gods; so that they were jeered by the mob who thronged around them, as it was plain to all that they were equally afraid to sacrifice and to die. Others advanced more briskly, carrying their effrontery so far as to avow that they never had been Christians." [301:2] Multitudes now withdrew into deserts or mountains, and there perished with cold and hunger. The prisons were everywhere crowded with Christians; and the magistrates were occupied with the odious task of oppressing and destroying the most meritorious of their fellow-citizens. The disciples were sent to labour in the mines, branded on the forehead, subjected to mutilation, and reduced to the lowest depth of misery. In this persecution the pastors were treated with marked severity, and during its continuance many of them suffered martyrdom. Among the most distinguished victims were Fabian bishop of Rome, Babylas bishop of Antioch, and Alexander bishop of Jerusalem. [302:1]

The reign of Decius was short; [302:2] but the hardships of the Church did not cease with its termination, as Gallus adopted the policy of his predecessor. Though Valerian, the successor of Gallus, for a time displayed much moderation, he eventually relinquished this pacific course; and, instigated by his favourite Macrianus, an Egyptian soothsayer, began about A.D. 257 to repeat the bloody tragedy which, in the days of Decius, had filled the Empire with such terror and distress. At first the pastors were driven into banishment, and the disciples forbidden to meet for worship. But more stringent measures were soon adopted. An edict appeared announcing that bishops, presbyters, and deacons were to be put to death; that senators and knights, who were Christians, were to forfeit their rank and property; and that, if they still refused to repudiate their principles, they were to be capitally punished; whilst those members of the Church who were in the service of the palace, were to be put in chains, and sent to labour on the imperial estates. [302:3] In this persecution, Sixtus bishop of Rome, and Cyprian bishop of Carthage, [302:4] were martyred.

On the accession of Gallienus in A.D. 260, the Church was once more restored to peace. Gallienus, though a person of worthless character, was the first Emperor who protected the Christians by a formal edict of toleration. He commanded that they should not only be permitted to profess their religion unmolested, but that they should again be put in possession of their cemeteries [303:1] and of all other property, either in houses or lands, of which they had been deprived during the reign of his predecessor. This decree was nearly as ample in its provisions as that which was issued in their favour by the great Constantine upwards of half a century afterwards.

But, notwithstanding the advantages secured by this imperial law, the Church still suffered occasionally in particular districts. Hostile magistrates might plead that certain edicts had not been definitely repealed; and, calculating on the connivance of the higher functionaries, might perpetrate acts of cruelty and oppression. The Emperor Aurelian had even resolved to resume the barbarous policy of Decius and Valerian; and, in A.D. 275, had actually prepared a sanguinary edict; but, before it could be executed, death stepped in to arrest his violence, and to prevent the persecution. Thus, as has already been intimated, for the last forty years of the third century the Christians enjoyed, almost uninterruptedly, the blessings of toleration. Spacious edifices, frequented by crowds of worshippers, and some of them furnished with sacramental vessels of silver or gold, [303:2] were to be seen in all the great cities of the Empire. But, about the beginning of the fourth century, the prospect changed. The pagan party beheld with dismay the rapid extension of the Church, and resolved to make a tremendous effort for its destruction. This faction, pledged to the maintenance of idolatry, now caused its influence to be felt in all political transactions; and the treatment of the Christians once more became a question on which statesmen were divided. Diocletian, who was made Emperor in A.D. 285, continued for many years afterwards to act upon the principle of toleration; but at length he was induced, partly by the suggestions of his own superstitious and jealous temper, and partly by the importunities of his son-in-law Galerius, to enter upon another course. The persecution commenced in the army, where all soldiers refusing to sacrifice forfeited their rank, and were dismissed the service. [304:1] But other hostile demonstrations soon followed. In the month of February A.D. 303, the great church of Nicomedia, the city in which the Emperor then resided, was broken open; the copies of the Scriptures to be found in it were committed to the flames; and the edifice itself was demolished. The next day an edict appeared interdicting the religious assemblies of the faithful; commanding the destruction of their places of worship; ordering all their sacred books to be burned; requiring those who held offices of honour and emolument to renounce their principles on pain of the forfeiture of their appointments; declaring that disciples in the humbler walks of life, who remained steadfast, should be divested of their rights as citizens and free-men; and providing that even slaves, so long as they continued Christians, should be incapable of manumission. [304:2] Some time afterwards another edict was promulgated directing that all ecclesiastics should be seized and put in chains. When the jails were thus filled with Christian ministers, another edict made its appearance, commanding that the prisoners should by all means be compelled to sacrifice. At length a fourth edict, of a still more sweeping character and extending to the whole body of Christians, was published. In accordance with this decree proclamation was made throughout the streets of the cities, and men, women, and children, were enjoined to repair to the heathen temples. The city gates were guarded that none might escape; and, from lists previously prepared, every individual was summoned by name to present himself, and join in the performance of the rites of paganism. [305:1] At a subsequent period all provisions sold in the markets, in some parts of the empire, were sprinkled with the water or the wine employed in idolatrous worship, that the Christians might either be compelled to abstinence, or led to defile themselves by the use of polluted viands. [305:2]

Throughout almost the whole Church the latter part of the third century was a period of spiritual decay; and many returned to heathenism during the sifting time which now followed. Not a few incurred the reproach of their more consistent and courageous brethren by surrendering the Scriptures in their possession; and those who thus purchased their safety were stigmatised with the odious name of traditors. Had the persecutors succeeded in burning all the copies of the Word of God, they would, without the intervention of a miracle, have effectually secured the ruin of the Church; but their efforts to destroy the sacred volume proved abortive; for the faithful seized the earliest opportunity of replacing the consumed manuscripts. The holy book was prized by them more highly than ever, and Bible burning only gave a stimulus to Bible transcription. Still, however, sacred literature sustained a loss of no ordinary magnitude in this wholesale destruction of the inspired writings, and there is not at present in existence a single codex of the New Testament of higher antiquity than the Diocletian persecution. [305:3]

It has been computed that a greater number of Christians perished under Decius than in all the attacks which had previously been made upon them; but their sufferings under Diocletian were still more formidable and disastrous. Paganism felt that it was now engaged in a death struggle; and this, its last effort to maintain its ascendency, was its most protracted and desperate conflict. It has been frequently stated that the Diocletian persecution was of ten years' duration; and, reckoning from the first indications of hostility to the promulgation of an edict of toleration, it may certainly be thus estimated; but all this time the whole Church was not groaning under the pressure of the infliction. The Christians of the west of Europe suffered comparatively little; as there the Emperor Constantius Chlorus, and afterwards his son Constantine, to a great extent, preserved them from molestation. In the East they passed through terrific scenes of suffering; for Galerius and Maximin, the two stern tyrants who governed that part of the empire on the abdication of Diocletian, endeavoured to overcome their steadfastness by all the expedients which despotic cruelty could suggest. A contemporary, who had access to the best sources of information, has given a faithful account of the torments they endured. Vinegar mixed with salt was poured on the lacerated bodies of the dying; some were roasted on huge gridirons; some, suspended aloft by one hand, were then left to perish in excruciating agony; and some, bound to parts of different trees which had been brought together by machinery, were torn limb from limb by the sudden revulsion of the liberated branches. [306:1] But, even in the East, this attempt to overwhelm Christianity was not prosecuted from its commencement to its close with unabated severity. Sometimes the sufferers obtained a respite; and again, the work of blood was resumed with fresh vigour. Though many were tempted for a season to make a hollow profession of paganism, multitudes met every effort to seduce them in a spirit of indomitable resolution. At length tyranny became weary of its barren office, and the Church obtained peace. In A.D. 311, Galerius, languishing under a loathsome disease, and perhaps hoping that he might be relieved by the God of the Christians, granted them toleration. Maximin subsequently renewed the attacks upon them; but at his death, which occurred in A.D. 313, the edict in favour of the Church, which Constantine and his colleague Licinius had already published, became law throughout the empire.

It is often alleged that the Church, before the conversion of Constantine, passed through ten persecutions; but the statement gives a very incorrect idea of its actual suffering. It would be more accurate to say that, for between two and three hundred years, the faithful were under the ban of imperial proscription. During all this period they were liable to be pounced upon at any moment by bigoted, domineering, or greedy magistrates. There were not, indeed, ten persecutions conducted with the systematic and sanguinary violence exhibited in the times of Diocletian or of Decius; but there were perhaps provinces of the empire where almost every year for upwards of two centuries some Christians suffered for the faith. [307:1] The friends of the confessors and the martyrs were not slow to acknowledge the hand of Providence, as they traced the history of the emperors by whom the Church was favoured or oppressed. It was remarked that the disciples were not worn out by the barbarities of a continuous line of persecutors; for an unscrupulous tyrant was often succeeded on the throne by an equitable or an indulgent sovereign. Thus, the Christians had every now and then a breathing-time during which their hopes were revived and their numbers recruited. It was observed, too, that the princes, of whose cruelty they had reason to complain, generally ended their career under very distressing circumstances.

An ecclesiastical writer who is supposed to have flourished towards the commencement of the fourth century has discussed this subject in a special treatise, in which he has left behind him a very striking account of "The Deaths of the Persecutors." [308:1] Their history certainly furnishes a most significant commentary on the Divine announcement that "the Lord is known by the judgment which he executeth." [308:2] Nero, the first hostile emperor, perished ignominiously by his own hand. Domitian, the next persecutor, was assassinated. Marcus Aurelius died a natural death; but, during his reign, the Empire suffered dreadfully from pestilence and famine; and war raged, almost incessantly, from its commencement to its close. The people of Lyons, who now signalised themselves by their cruelty to the Christians, did not escape a righteous retribution; for about twenty years after the martyrdom of Pothinus and his brethren, the city was pillaged and burned. [308:3] Septimius Severus narrowly escaped murder by the hand of one of his own children. Decius, whose name is associated with an age of martyrdom, perished in the Gothic war. Valerian, another oppressor, ended his days in Persia in degrading captivity. The Emperor Aurelian was assassinated. Diocletian languished for years the victim of various maladies, and is said to have abruptly terminated his life by suicide. Galerius, his son-in-law, died of a most horrible distemper; and Maximin took away his own life by poison. [308:4] The interpretation of providences is not to be rashly undertaken; but the record of the fate of persecutors forms a most extraordinary chapter in the history of man; and the melancholy circumstances under which so many of the enemies of religion have finished their career, have sometimes impressed those who have been otherwise slow to acknowledge the finger of the Almighty.

The persecutions of the early Church originated partly in selfishness and superstition. Idolatry afforded employment to tens of thousands of artists and artisans—all of whom had thus a direct pecuniary interest in its conservation; whilst the ignorant rabble, taught to associate Christianity with misfortune, were prompted to clamour for its overthrow. Mistaken policy had also some share in the sufferings of the Christians; for statesmen, fearing that the disciples in their secret meetings might be hatching treason, viewed them with suspicion and treated them with severity. But another element of at least equal strength contributed to promote persecution. The pure and spiritual religion of the New Testament was distasteful to the human heart, and its denunciations of wickedness in every form stirred up the malignity of the licentious and unprincipled. The faithful complained that they suffered for neglecting the worship of the gods, whilst philosophers, who derided the services of the established ritual, escaped with impunity. [309:1] But the sophists were not likely ever to wage an effective warfare against immorality and superstition. Many of themselves were persons of worthless character, and their speculations were of no practical value. It was otherwise with the gospel. Its advocates were felt to be in earnest; and it was quickly perceived that, if permitted to make way, it would revolutionize society. Hence the bitter opposition which it so soon awakened.

It might have been expected that the sore oppression which the Church endured for so many generations would have indelibly imprinted on the hearts of her children the doctrine of liberty of conscience. As the early Christians expostulated with their pagan rulers, they often described most eloquently the folly of persecution. "How unjust is it," said they, "that freemen should be driven to sacrifice to the gods, when in all other instances a willing mind is required as an indispensable qualification for any office of religion?" [310:1] "It appertains to man's proper right and natural privilege that each should worship that which he thinks to be God....Neither is it the part of religion to compel men to religion, which ought to be adopted voluntarily, not of compulsion, seeing that sacrifices are required of a willing mind. Thus, even if you compel us to sacrifice, you shall render no sacrifice thereby to your gods, for they will not desire sacrifices from unwilling givers, unless they are contentious; but God is not contentious." [310:2] When, however, the Church obtained possession of the throne of the empire, she soon ignored these lessons of toleration; and, snatching the weapons of her tormentors, she attempted, in her turn, to subjugate the soul by the dungeon, the sword, and the faggot. For at least thirteen centuries after the establishment of Christianity by Constantine, it was taken for granted almost everywhere that those branded with the odious name of heretics were unworthy the protection of the laws; and that, though good and loyal citizens, they ought to be punished by the civil magistrate. This doctrine, so alien to the spirit of the New Testament, has often spread desolation and terror throughout whole provinces; and has led to the deliberate murder of a hundredfold more Christians than were destroyed by pagan Rome. Even the fathers of the Reformation did not escape from the influence of an intolerant training; but that Bible which they brought forth from obscurity has been gradually imparting a milder tone to earthly legislation; and various providences have been illustrating the true meaning of the proposition that Christ's kingdom is "not of this world." [311:1] In all free countries it is now generally admitted that the weapons of the Church are not carnal, and that the jurisdiction of the magistrate is not spiritual. "God alone is Lord of the conscience;" and it is only by the illumination of His Word that the monitor within can be led to recognise His will, and submit to His authority.

CHAPTER III

FALSE BRETHREN AND FALSE PRINCIPLES IN THE CHURCH: SPIRIT AND CHARACTER OF THE CHRISTIANS

Some have an idea that the saintship of the early Christians was of a type altogether unique and transcendental. In primitive times the Spirit was, no doubt, poured out in rich effusion, and the subjects of His grace, when contrasted with the heathen around them, often exhibited most attractively the beauty of holiness; but the same Spirit still dwells in the hearts of the faithful, and He is now as able, as He ever was, to enlighten and to save. As man, wherever he exists, possesses substantially the same organic conformation, so the true children of God, to whatever generation they belong, have the same divine lineaments. The age of miracles has passed away, but the reign of grace continues, and, at the present day, there may, perhaps, be found amongst the members of the Church as noble examples of vital godliness as in the first or second century.

There was a traitor among the Twelve, and it is apparent from the New Testament that, in the Apostolic Church, there were not a few unworthy members. "Many walk," says Paul, "of whom I have told you often, and now tell you, even weeping, that they are the enemies of the cross of Christ, whose end is destruction, whose god is their belly, and whose glory is in their shame, who mind earthly things." [312:1] In the second and third centuries the number of such false brethren did not diminish. To those who are ignorant of its saving power, Christianity may commend itself, by its external evidences, as a revelation from God; and many, who are not prepared to submit to its authority, may seek admission to its privileges. The superficial character of much of the evangelism now current appeared in times of persecution; for, on the first appearance of danger, multitudes abjured the gospel, and returned to the heathen superstitions. It is, besides, a fact which cannot be disputed that, in the third century, the more zealous champions of the faith felt it necessary to denounce the secularity of many of the ministers of the Church. Before the Decian persecution not a few of the bishops were mere worldlings, and such was their zeal for money-making, that they left their parishes neglected, and travelled to remote districts where, at certain seasons of the year, they might carry on a profitable traffic [313:1]. If we are to believe the testimony of the most distinguished ecclesiastics of the period, crimes were then perpetrated to which it would be difficult to find anything like parallels in the darkest pages of the history of modern Christianity. The chief pastor of the largest Church in the Proconsular Africa tells, for instance, of one of his own presbyters who robbed orphans and defrauded widows, who permitted his father to die of hunger and treated his pregnant wife with horrid brutality. [313:2] Another ecclesiastic, of still higher position, speaks of three bishops in his neighbourhood who engaged, when intoxicated, in the solemn rite of ordination. [313:3] Such excesses were indignantly condemned by all right-hearted disciples, but the fact, that those to whom they were imputed were not destitute of partisans, supplies clear yet melancholy proof that neither the Christian people nor the Christian ministry, even in the third century, possessed an unsullied reputation.

Meanwhile the introduction of a false standard of piety created much mischief. It had long been received as a maxim, among certain classes of philosophers, that bodily abstinence is necessary to those who would attain more exalted wisdom; and the Gentile theology, especially in Egypt and the East, had endorsed the principle. It was not without advocates among the Jews, as is apparent from the discipline of the Essenes and the Therapeutae. At an early period its influence was felt within the pale of the Church, and before the termination of the second century, individual members here and there were to be found who eschewed certain kinds of food and abstained from marriage. [314:1] The pagan literati, who now joined the disciples in considerable numbers, did much to promote the credit of this adulterated Christianity. Its votaries, who were designated ascetics and philosophers [314:2] did not withdraw themselves from the world, but, whilst adhering to their own regimen, still remained mindful of their social obligations. Their self-imposed mortification soon found admirers, and an opinion gradually gained ground that these abstinent disciples cultivated a higher form of piety. The adherents of the new discipline silently increased, and

144

by the middle of the third century, a class of females who led a single life, and who, by way of distinction, were called virgins, were in some places regarded by the other Church members with special veneration. [314:3] Among the clergy also celibacy was now considered a mark of superior holiness. [314:4] But, in various places, pietism about this time assumed a form which disgusted all persons of sober judgment and ordinary discretion. The unmarried clergy and the virgins deemed it right to cultivate the communion of saints after a new fashion, alleging that, in each other's society, they enjoyed peculiar advantages for spiritual improvement. It was not, therefore, uncommon to find a single ecclesiastic and one of the sisterhood of virgins dwelling in the same house and sharing the same bed! [315:1] All the while the parties repudiated the imputation of any improper intercourse, but in some cases the proofs of profligacy were too plain to be concealed, and common sense refused to credit the pretensions of such an absurd and suspicious spiritualism. The ecclesiastical authorities felt it necessary to interfere, and compel the professed virgins and the single clergy to abstain from a degree of intimacy which was unquestionably not free from the appearance of evil.

About the time that the advocates of "whatsoever things are of good report" were protesting against the improprieties of these spiritual brethren and sisters, Paul and Antony, the fathers and founders of Monachism, commenced to live as hermits. Paul was a native of Egypt, and the heir of a considerable fortune; but, driven at first by persecution from the abodes of men, he ultimately adopted the desert as the place of his chosen residence. Antony, in another part of the same country, guided by a mistaken spirit of self-renunciation, divested himself of all his property; and also retired into a wilderness. The biographies of these two well-meaning but weak-minded visionaries, which have been written by two of the most eminent divines of the fourth century, [316:1] are very humiliating memorials of folly and fanaticism. These solitaries spent each a long life in a cave, macerating the body with fasting, and occupying the mind with the reveries of a morbid imagination. In an age of growing superstition their dreamy pietism was mistaken by many for sanctity of uncommon excellence; and the admiration bestowed on them, tempted others, in the beginning of the following century, to imitate their example. Soon afterwards, societies of these sons of the desert were established; and, in the course of a few years, a taste for the monastic life spread, like wild-fire, over the whole Church.

It is a curious fact that the figure of the instrument of torture on which our Lord was put to death, occupied a prominent place among the symbols of the ancient heathen worship. From the most remote antiquity the cross was venerated in Egypt and Syria; it was held in equal honour by the Buddhists of the East, [316:2] and, what is still more extraordinary, when the Spaniards first visited America, the well-known sign was found among the objects of worship in the idol temples of Anahuac. [316:3] It is also remarkable that, about the commencement of our era, the pagans were wont to make the sign of a cross upon the forehead in the celebration of some of their sacred mysteries. [317:1] A satisfactory explanation of the origin of such peculiarities in the ritual of idolatry can now scarcely be expected; but it certainly need not excite surprise if the early Christians were impressed by them, and if they viewed them as so many unintentional testimonies to the truth of their religion. The disciples displayed, indeed, no little ingenuity in their attempts to discover the figure of a cross in

145

almost every object around them. They could recognise it in the trees and the flowers, in the fishes and the fowls, in the sails of a ship and the structure of the human body; [317:2] and if they borrowed from their heathen neighbours the custom of making a cross upon the forehead, they would of course be ready to maintain that they thus only redeemed the holy sign from profanation. Some of them were, perhaps, prepared, on prudential grounds, to plead for its introduction. Heathenism was, to a considerable extent, a religion of bowings and genuflexions; its votaries were, ever and anon, attending to some little rite or form; and, because of the multitude of these diminutive acts of outward devotion, its ceremonial was at once frivolous and burdensome. When the pagan passed into the Church, he, no doubt, often felt, for a time, the awkwardness of the change; and was frequently on the point of repeating, as it were automatically, the gestures of his old superstition. It may, therefore, have been deemed expedient to supersede more objectionable forms by something of a Christian complexion; and the use of the sign of the cross here probably presented itself as an observance equally familiar and convenient. [318:1] But the disciples would have acted more wisely had they boldly discarded all the puerilities of paganism; for credulity soon began to ascribe supernatural virtue to this vestige of the repudiated worship. As early as the beginning of the third century, it was believed to operate like a charm; and it was accordingly employed on almost all occasions by many of the Christians. "In all our travels and movements," says a writer of this period, "as often as we come in or go out, when we put on our clothes or our shoes, when we enter the bath or sit down at table, when we light our candles, when we go to bed, or recline upon a couch, or whatever may be our employment, we mark our forehead with the sign of the cross." [318:2]

But whilst not a few of the Christians were beginning to adopt some of the trivial rites of paganism, they continued firmly to protest against its more flagrant corruptions. They did not hesitate to assail its gross idolatry with bold and biting sarcasms. "Stone, or wood, or silver," said they, "becomes a god when man chooses that it should, and dedicates it to that end. With how much more truth do dumb animals, such as mice, swallows, and kites, judge of your gods? They know that your gods feel nothing; they gnaw them, they trample and sit on them; and if you did not drive them away, they would make their nests in the very mouth of your deity." [319:1] The Church of the first three centuries rejected the use of images in worship, and no pictorial representations of the Saviour were to be found even in the dwellings of the Christians. They conceived that such visible memorials could convey no idea whatever of the ineffable glory of the Son of God; and they held that it is the duty of His servants to foster a spirit of devotion, not by the contemplation of His material form, but by meditating on His holy and divine attributes as they are exhibited in creation, providence, and redemption. So anxious were they to avoid even the appearance of anything like image-worship, that when they wished to mark articles of dress or furniture with an index of their religious profession, they employed the likeness of an anchor, or a dove, or a lamb, or a cross, or some other object of an emblematical character. [319:2] "We must not," said they, "cling to the sensuous but rise to the spiritual. The familiarity of daily sight lowers the dignity of the divine, and to pretend to worship a spiritual essence through earthly matter, is to degrade that essence to the world of sense." [319:3] Even so late as the beginning of the fourth century the practice of displaying paintings in places of worship was prohibited by ecclesiastical authority. A canon which bears upon this subject, and which was enacted by the Council of Elvira held about A.D. 305, is more creditable to the pious zeal than to the literary ability of the assembled fathers. "We must not," said they, "have pictures in the church, lest that which is worshipped and adored be painted on the walls." [320:1]

It has been objected to the Great Reformation of the sixteenth century that it exercised a prejudicial influence on the arts of painting and statuary. The same argument might have been urged against the gospel itself in the days of its original promulgation. Whilst the early Church entirely discarded the use of images in worship, its more zealous members looked with suspicion upon all who assisted in the fabrication of these objects of the heathen idolatry. [320:2] The excuse that the artists were labouring for subsistence, and that they had themselves no idea of bowing down to the works of their own hands, did not by any means satisfy the scruples of their more consistent and conscientious brethren. "Assuredly," they exclaimed, "you are a worshipper of idols when you help to promote their worship. It is true you bring to them no outward victim, but you sacrifice to them, your mind. Your sweat is their drink-offering. You kindle for them the light of your skill." [320:3] By denouncing image-worship the early Church, no doubt, to some extent interfered with the profits of the painter and the sculptor; but, in another way, it did much to purify and elevate the taste of the public. In the second and third centuries the playhouse in every large town was a centre of attraction; and whilst the actors were generally persons of very loose morals, their dramatic performances were perpetually pandering to the depraved appetites of the age. It is not, therefore, wonderful that all true Christians viewed the theatre with disgust. Its frivolity was offensive to their grave temperament; they recoiled from its obscenity; and its constant appeals to the gods and goddesses of heathenism outraged their religious convictions. [321:1] In their estimation, the talent devoted to its maintenance was miserably prostituted; and whilst every actor was deemed unworthy of ecclesiastical fellowship, every church member was prohibited, by attendance or otherwise, from giving any encouragement to the stage. The early Christians were also forbidden to frequent the public shows, as they were considered scenes of temptation and pollution. Every one at his baptism was required to renounce "the devil, his pomp, and his angels" [321:2]—a declaration which implied that he was henceforth to absent himself from the heathen spectacles. At this time, statesmen, poets, and philosophers were not ashamed to appear among the crowds who assembled to witness the combats of the gladiators, though, on such occasions, human life was recklessly sacrificed. But here the Church, composed chiefly of the poor of this world, was continually giving lessons in humanity to heathen legislators and literati. It protested against cruelty, as well to the brute creation as to man; and condemned the taste which could derive gratification from the shedding of the blood either of lions or of gladiators. All who sanctioned by their presence the sanguinary sports of the amphitheatre incurred a sentence of excommunication. [322:1]

At this time, though an increasing taste for inactivity and solitude betokened the growth of a bastard Christianity, and though various other circumstances were indicative of tendencies to adulterate religion, either by reducing it to a system of formalism, or by sublimating it into a life of empty contemplation, there were still abundant proofs of the existence of a large amount of healthy and vigorous piety. The members of the Church, as a body, were distinguished by their exemplary morals; and about the beginning of the third century, one of their advocates, when pleading for their toleration, could venture to assert that, among the numberless culprits brought under the notice of the magistrates, none were Christians. [322:2] Wherever the gospel spread, its social influence was most salutary. Its first teachers applied themselves discreetly to the redress of prevalent abuses; and time gradually demonstrated the effectiveness of their plans of reformation. When they appeared, polygamy was common; [322:3] and had they assailed it in terms of unmeasured severity, they would have defeated their own object by rousing up a most formidable and exasperated opposition. It would have been argued by the Jews that they were reflecting on the patriarchs; and it would have been said by the Roman governors that they were interfering with matters which belonged to the province of the civil magistrate. They were obliged, therefore, to proceed with extreme caution. In the first place, they laid it down as a principle that every bishop and deacon must be "the husband of one wife," [323:1] or, in other words, that no polygamist could hold office in their society. They thus, in the most pointed way, inculcated sound views respecting the institution of marriage; for they intimated that whoever was the husband of more than one wife was not, in every respect, "a pattern of good works," and was consequently unfit for ecclesiastical promotion. In the second place, in all their discourses they proceeded on the assumption that the union of one man and one woman is the divine arrangement. [323:2] Throughout the whole of the New Testament, wherever marriage is mentioned, no other idea is entertained. It is easy to see what must have been the effect of this method of procedure. It soon came to be understood that no good Christian could have at one time more than one wife; and at length the polygamist was excluded from communion by a positive enactment. [323:3]

Every disciple who married a heathen was cut off from Church privileges. The apostles had condemned such an alliance, [323:4] and it still continued to be spoken of in terms of the strongest reprobation. Nothing, it was said, but discomfort and danger could be anticipated from the union; as parties related so closely, and yet differing so widely on the all-important subject of religion, could not permanently hold cordial intercourse. A writer of this period has given a vivid description of the trials of the female who made such an ill-assorted match. Whilst she is about to be engaged in spiritual exercises, her husband will probably contrive some scheme for her annoyance; and her zeal may be expected to awaken his jealousy, and provoke his opposition. "If there be a prayer-meeting, the husband will devote this day to the use of the bath; if a fast is to be observed, the husband has a feast at which he entertains his friends; if a religious ceremony is to be attended, never does household business fall more upon her hands. And who would allow his wife, for the sake of visiting the brethren, to go from street to street the round of strange and especially of the poorer class of cottages? ... If a stranger brother come to her, what lodging in an alien's house? If a present is to be made to any, the barn, the storehouse are closed against her." [324:1]

The primitive heralds of the gospel acted with remarkable prudence in reference to the question of slavery. According to some high authorities, bondsmen constituted one-half [324:2] of the entire population of the Roman Empire; and as the new religion was designed to promote the spiritual good of man, rather than the improvement of his civil or political condition, the apostles

148

did not deem it expedient, in the first instance, to attempt to break up established relations. They did not refuse to receive any one as a member of the Church because he happened to be a slave-owner; neither did they reject any applicant for admission because he was a slave. The social position of the individual did not at all affect his ecclesiastical standing; for bond and free are "all one in Christ Jesus." [324:3] In the Church the master and the servant were upon a footing of equality; they joined in the same prayers; they sat down, side by side, at the same communion table; and they saluted each other with the kiss of Christian recognition. A slave-owner might belong to a congregation of which his slave was the teacher; and thus, whilst in the household, the servant was bound to obey his master according to the flesh, in the Church the master was required to remember that his minister was "worthy of double honour." [325:1]

The spirit of the gospel is pre-eminently a spirit of freedom; but the inspired founders of our religion did not fail to remember that we may be partakers of the glorious liberty of the children of God, whilst we are under the yoke of temporal bondage. Whilst, therefore, they did not hesitate to speak of emancipation as a blessing, and whilst they said to the slave—"If thou mayest be made free, use it rather;" [325:2] they at the same time declared it to be his duty to submit cheerfully to the restraints of his present condition. "Let every man," said they, "abide in the same calling wherein he was called; for he that is called in the Lord, being a servant, is the Lord's freeman." [325:3] They were most careful to teach converted slaves that they were not to presume upon their church membership; and that they were not to be less respectful and obedient when those to whom they were in bondage were their brethren in the Lord. "Let as many servants as are under the yoke," says the apostle, "count their own masters worthy of all honour, that the name of God and his doctrine be not blasphemed. And they that have believing masters, let them not despise them, because they are brethren, but rather do them service, because they are faithful and beloved, partakers of the benefit." [325:4]

The influence of Christianity on the condition of the slave was soon felt. The believing master was more humane than his pagan neighbour; [325:5] his bearing was more gentle, conciliatory, and considerate; and the domestics under his care were more comfortable. [325:6] There was a disposition among pious slave-owners to let the oppressed go free, and when they performed such an act of mercy, and both parties were in communion with the Church, the congregation was assembled to witness the consummation of the happy deliverance. [326:1] Thus, multitudes of bondsmen in all parts of the Roman Empire were soon taught to regard the gospel as their best benefactor.

Whilst Christianity, in the spirit of its Great Founder, was labouring to improve the tone of public sentiment, and to undo heavy burdens, it exhibited other most attractive characteristics. Wherever a disciple travelled, if a church existed in the district, he felt himself at home. The ecclesiastical certificate which he carried along with him, at once introduced him to the meetings of his co-religionists, and secured for him all the advantage of membership. The heathen were astonished at the cordiality with which the believers among whom they resided greeted a Christian stranger. He was saluted with the kiss of peace; ushered into their assembly; and invited to share the hospitality of the domestic board. If he was sick, they visited him; if he was in want, they made provision for his necessities. The poor widows were supported at the expense of the Church;

and if any of the brethren were carried captive by predatory bands of the barbarians who hovered upon the borders of the Empire, contributions were made to purchase their liberation from servitude. [326:2] To those who were without the Church, its members appeared as one large and affectionate family. The pagan could not comprehend what it was that so closely cemented their brotherhood; for he did not understand how they could be attracted to each other by love to a common Saviour. He was almost induced to believe that they held intercourse by certain mysterious signs, and that they were affiliated by something like the bond of freemasonry. Even statesmen observed with uneasiness the spirit of fraternity which reigned among the Christians; and, though the disciples could never be convicted of any political designs, suspicions were often entertained that, after all, they might form a secret association, on an extensive scale, which might one day prove dangerous to the established government.

But Christianity, like the sun, shines on the evil and the good; and opportunities occurred for shewing that its charities were not confined within the limits of its own denomination. There were occasions on which its very enemies could not well refuse to admit its excellence; for in seasons of public distress, its adherents often signalised themselves as by far the most energetic, benevolent, and useful citizens. At such times its genial philanthropy appeared to singular advantage when contrasted with the cold and selfish spirit of polytheism. Thus, in the reign of the Emperor Gallus, when a pestilence spread dismay throughout North Africa, [327:1] and when the pagans shamefully deserted their nearest relatives in the hour of their extremity, the Christians stepped forward, and ministered to the wants of the sick and dying without distinction. [327:2] Some years afterwards, when the plague appeared in Alexandria, and when the Gentile inhabitants left the dead unburied and cast out the dying into the streets, the disciples vied with each other in their efforts to alleviate the general suffering. [327:3] The most worthless men can scarcely forget acts of kindness performed under such circumstances. Forty years afterwards, when the Church in the capital of Egypt was overtaken by the Diocletian persecution, their pagan neighbours concealed the Christians in their houses, and submitted to fines and imprisonment rather than betray the refugees. [328:1]

The fact that the heathen were now ready to shelter the persecuted members of the Church is itself of importance as a sign of the times. When the disciples first began to rise into notice in the great towns, they were commonly regarded with aversion; and, when the citizens were assembled in thousands at the national spectacles, no cry was more vociferously repeated than that of "The Christians to the lions." But this bigoted and intolerant spirit was fast passing away; and when the state now set on foot a persecution, it could not reckon so extensively on the support of popular antipathy. The Church had attained such a position that the calumnies once repeated to its prejudice could no longer obtain credence; the superior excellence of its system of morals was visible to all; and it could point on every side to proofs of the blessings it communicated. It could demonstrate, by a reference to its history, that it produced kind masters and dutiful servants, affectionate parents and obedient children, faithful friends and benevolent citizens. On all classes, whether rich or poor, learned or unlearned, its effects were beneficial. It elevated the character of the working classes, it vastly improved the position of the wife, it comforted the afflicted, and it taught even senators wisdom. Its doctrines, whether preached to the half-naked Picts or the polished Athenians, to the fierce tribes of Germany or the literary coteries of Alexandria, exerted the same holy and happy influence. It promulgated a religion obviously fitted for all mankind. There had long since been a prediction that its dominion should extend "from sea to sea and from the river unto the ends of the earth;" and its progress already indicated that the promise would receive a glorious accomplishment.

CHAPTER IV

THE CHURCH OF ROME IN THE SECOND CENTURY

The great doctrines of Christianity are built upon the facts of the life of our Lord. These facts are related by the four evangelists with singular precision, and yet with a variety of statement, as to details, which proves that each writer delivered an independent testimony. The witnesses all agree when describing the wonderful history of the Captain of our Salvation; and they dwell upon the narrative with a minuteness apparently corresponding to the importance of the doctrine which the facts establish or illustrate. Hence it is that, whilst they scarcely notice, or altogether omit, several items of our Saviour's biography, they speak particularly of His birth and of His miracles, of His death and of His resurrection. Thus, all the great facts of the gospel are most amply authenticated.

It is not so with the system of Romanism; as nothing can be weaker than the historical basis on which it rests. The New Testament demonstrates that Peter was not the Prince of the Apostles; for it records the rebuke which our Lord delivered to the Twelve when they strove among themselves "which of them should be accounted the greatest." [329:1] It also supplies evidence that neither Peter nor Paul founded the Church of Rome; as, before that Church had been visited by the Apostle of the Gentiles, its faith was "spoken of throughout the whole world;" [329:2] and the apostle of the circumcision was meanwhile labouring in another part of the Empire. [330:1] When writing to the Romans in A.D. 57, Paul greets many members of the Church, and mentions the names of a great variety of individuals; [330:2] but, throughout his long epistle, Peter is not once noticed. Had he been connected with that Christian community, he would, beyond doubt, have been prominently recognised.

There is, indeed, a sense in which Peter may, perhaps, be said to have founded the great Church of the West; for it is possible that some of the "strangers of Rome," [330:3] who heard his celebrated sermon on the day of Pentecost, were then converted by his ministry; and it may be that these converts, on their return home, proceeded to disseminate the truth, and to organize a Christian society, in the chief city of the Empire. This, however, is mere matter of conjecture; and it is now useless to speculate upon the subject; as, in the absence of historical materials to furnish us with information, the question must remain involved in impenetrable mystery. It is certain that the Roman Church was established long before it was visited by an apostle; and it is equally clear that its members were distinguished, at an early period, by their Christian excellence. When Paul was prisoner for the first time in the great city, he was freely permitted to exercise his ministry; but, subsequently, when there during the Neronian persecution, he was, according to the current tradition, seized and put to death. [330:4] Peter's martyrdom took place, as we have seen, [330:5] perhaps about a year afterwards; but the legend describing it contains very improbable details, and the facts have obviously been distorted and exaggerated.

For at least seventy years after the death of the apostle of the circumcision, nothing whatever is known of the history of the Roman Church, except the names of some of its leading ministers. It was originally governed, like other Christian communities, by the common council of the presbyters, who, as a matter of order, must have had a chairman; but though, about a hundred years after the martyrdom of Peter, when the presidents began to be designated bishops, an attempt was made to settle their order of succession, [331:1] the result was by no means satisfactory. Some of the earliest writers who touch incidentally upon the question are inconsistent with themselves; [331:2] whilst they flatly contradict each other. [331:3] In fact, to this day, what is called the episcopal succession in the ancient Church of Rome is an historical riddle. At first no one individual seems to have acted for life as the president, or moderator, of the presbytery; but as it was well known that, at an early date, several eminent pastors had belonged to it, the most distinguished names found their way into the catalogues, and each writer appears to have consulted his own taste or judgment in regulating the order of succession. Thus, it has probably occurred that their lists are utterly irreconcileable. All such genealogies are, indeed, of exceedingly dubious credit, and those who deem them of importance must always be perplexed by the candid acknowledgment of the father of ecclesiastical history. "How many," says he, "and who, prompted by a kindred spirit, were judged fit to feed the churches established by the apostles, it is not easy to say, any farther than may be gathered from the statements of Paul." [331:4]

About A.D. 139, Telesphorus, who was then at the head of the Roman presbytery, is said to have been put to death for his profession of the gospel; but the earliest authority for this fact is a Christian controversialist who wrote upwards of forty years afterwards; [332:1] and we are totally ignorant of all the circumstances connected with the martyrdom. The Church of the capital, which had hitherto enjoyed internal tranquillity, began in the time of Hyginus, who succeeded Telesphorus, to be disturbed by false teachers. Valentine, Cerdo, and other famous heresiarchs, now appeared in Rome; [332:2] and laboured with great assiduity to disseminate their principles. The distractions created by these errorists seem to have suggested the propriety of placing additional power in the hands of the presiding presbyter. [332:3] Until this period every teaching elder had been accustomed to baptize and administer the Eucharist on his own responsibility; but it appears to have been now arranged that henceforth none should act without the sanction of the president, who was thus constituted the centre of ecclesiastical unity. According to the previous system, some of the presbyters, who were themselves, perhaps, secretly tainted with unsound doctrine, might have continued to hold communion with the heretics; and it might have been exceedingly difficult to convict them of any direct breach of ecclesiastical law; but now their power was curtailed; and a broad line of demarcation was established between true and false churchmen. Thus, Rome was the city in which what has been called the Catholic system was first organized. Every one who was in communion with the president, or bishop, was a catholic; [332:4] every one who allied himself to any other professed teacher of the Christian faith was a sectary, a schismatic, or a heretic. [333:1]

The study of the best forms of government was peculiarly congenial to the Roman mind; and the peace enjoyed under the Empire, as contrasted with the miseries of the civil wars in the last days of the Republic, pleaded, no doubt, strongly in favour of a change in the ecclesiastical constitution. But though this portion of the history of the Church is involved in much obscurity, there are indications that the transference of power from the presbyters to their president was not accomplished without a struggle. Until this period the Roman elders appear to have generally succeeded each other as moderators of presbytery in the order of their seniority; [333:2] but it was now deemed necessary to adopt another method of appointment; and it is not improbable that, at this time, a division of sentiment as to the best mode of filling up the presidential chair, was the cause of an unusually long vacancy. According to some, no less than four years [333:3] passed away between the death of Hyginus and the choice of his successor Pius; and even those who object to this view of the chronology admit that there was an interval of a twelvemonth. [333:4] The plan now adopted seems to have been to choose the bishop by lot out of a leet of selected candidates. [333:5] Thus, to use the phraseology current towards the end of the second century, the new chief pastor "obtained the lot of the episcopacy." [334:1]

The changes introduced at Rome were probably far from agreeable to many of the other Churches throughout the Empire; and Polycarp, the venerable pastor of Smyrna, who was afterwards martyred, and who was now nearly eighty years of age, appears to have been sent to the imperial city on a mission of remonstrance. The design of this remarkable visit is still enveloped in much mystery, for with the exception of an allusion to a question confessedly of secondary consequence, [334:2] ecclesiastical writers have passed over the whole subject in suspicious silence; but there is every reason to believe that Polycarp was deputed to complain of the incipient assumptions of Roman prelacy. [334:3] Anicetus, who then presided over the Church of the capital, prudently bestowed very flattering attentions on the good old Asiatic pastor; and, though there is no evidence that his scruples were removed, he felt it to be his duty to assist in opposing the corrupt teachers who were seeking to propagate their errors among the Roman disciples. The testimony to primitive truth delivered by so aged and eminent a minister produced a deep impression, and gave a decided check to the progress of heresy in the metropolis of the Empire. [334:4]

But though the modified prelacy now established encountered opposition, the innovation thus inaugurated in the great city was sure to exert a most extensive influence. Rome was then, not only the capital, but the mistress of a large portion of the world. She kept up a constant communication with every part of her dominions in Asia, Africa, and Europe; strangers from almost every clime were to be found among her teeming population; and intelligence of whatever occurred within her walls soon found its way to distant cities and provinces. The Christians in other countries would be slow to believe that their brethren at head-quarters had consented to any unwarrantable distribution of Church power, for they had hitherto displayed their zeal for the faith by most decisive and illustrious

153

testimonies. Since the days of Nero they had sustained the first shock of every persecution, and nobly led the van of the army of martyrs. Telesphorus, the chairman of the presbytery, had recently paid for his position with his life; their presiding pastor was always specially obnoxious to the spirit of intolerance; and if they were anxious to strengthen his hands, who could complain? The Roman Church had the credit of having enjoyed the tuition of Peter and Paul; its members had long been distinguished for intelligence and piety; and it was not to be supposed that its ministers would sanction any step which they did not consider perfectly capable of vindication. There were other weighty reasons why Christian societies in Italy, as well as elsewhere, should regard the acts of the Church of the imperial city with peculiar indulgence. It was the sentinel at the seat of government to give them notice of the approach of danger, [335:1] and the kind friend to aid them in times of difficulty. The wealth of Rome was prodigious; and though as yet "not many mighty" and "not many noble" had joined the proscribed sect, it had been making way among the middle classes; and there is cause to think that at this time a considerable number of the rich merchants of the capital belonged to its communion. It was known early in the second century as a liberal benefactor; and, from a letter addressed to it about A.D. 170, it would appear that even the Church of Corinth was then indebted to its munificence. "It has ever been your habit," says the writer, "to confer benefits in various ways, and to send assistance to the Churches in every city. You have relieved the wants of the poor, and afforded help to the brethren condemned to the mines. By a succession of these gifts, Romans, you preserve the customs of your Roman ancestors." [336:1]

The influence of the Roman Church throughout the West soon became conspicuous. Here, as in many other instances, commerce was the pioneer of religion; and as the merchants of the capital traded with all the ports of their great inland sea, it is not improbable that their sailors had a share in achieving some of the early triumphs of the gospel. Carthage, now one of the most populous cities in the Empire, is said to have been indebted for Christianity to Rome; [336:2] and by means of the constant intercourse kept up between these two commercial marts, the mother Church contrived to maintain an ascendancy over her African daughter. Thus it was that certain Romish practices and pretensions so soon found advocates among the Carthaginian clergy. [336:3] In other quarters we discover early indications of the extraordinary deference paid to the Church of the city "sitting upon many waters." Towards the close of the second century, Irenaeus, a disciple of Polycarp, was pastor of Lyons; and from this some have rather abruptly drawn the inference that the Christian congregations then existing in the south of France were established by missionaries from the East; but it is at least equally probable that the young minister from Asia Minor was in Rome before he passed to the more distant Gaul; and it is certain that he is the first father who speaks of the superior importance of the Church of the Italian metropolis. His testimony to the position which it occupied about eighty years after the death of the Apostle John shews clearly that it stood already at the head of the Western Churches. The Church of Rome, says he, is "very great and very ancient, and known to all, founded and established by the two most glorious Apostles Peter and Paul." [337:1] "To this Church in which Catholics [337:2] have always preserved apostolic tradition, every Catholic Church should, because it is more potentially apostolical, [337:3] repair." [337:4]

154

The term Catholic, which occurs for the first time in a document written about this period, [337:5] was probably coined at Rome, and implied, as already intimated, that the individual so designated was in communion with the bishop. The presiding pastors in the great city began now, in token of fraternity and recognition, to send the Eucharist to their brethren elsewhere by trusty messengers, [337:6] and thus the name was soon extended to all who maintained ecclesiastical relations with these leading ministers. Sectaries were almost always the minority; and in many places, where Christianity was planted, they were utterly unknown. The orthodox might, therefore, not inappropriately be styled members of the Catholic or general Church, inasmuch as they formed the bulk of the Christian population, and were to be found wherever the new religion had made converts. And though the heretics pleaded tradition in support of their peculiar dogmas, it was clear that their statements could not stand the test of examination. Irenaeus, in the work from which the words just quoted are extracted, very fairly argues that no such traditions as those propagated by the sectaries were to be found in the most ancient and respectable Churches. No Christian community in Western Europe could claim higher antiquity than that of Rome; and as it had been taught by Paul and Peter, none could be supposed to be better acquainted with the original gospel. Because of its extent it already required a larger staff of ministers than perhaps any other Church; and thus there were a greater number of individuals to quicken and correct each other's recollections. It might be accordingly inferred that the traditions of surrounding Christian societies, if true, should correspond to those of Rome; as the great metropolitan Church might, for various reasons, be said to be more potentially primitive or apostolical, and as its traditions might be expected to be particularly accurate. The doctrines of the heretics, which were completely opposed to the testimony of this important witness, should be discarded as entirely destitute of authority.

We can only conjecture the route by which Irenaeus travelled to the south of France when he first set out from Asia Minor; but we have direct evidence that he had paid a visit to the capital shortly before he wrote this memorable eulogium on the Roman Church. About the close of the dreadful persecution endured in A.D. 177 by the Christians of Lyons and Vienne, he had been commissioned to repair to Italy with a view to a settlement of the disputes created by the appearance of the Montanists. As he was furnished with very complimentary credentials, [339:1] we may presume that he was handsomely treated by his friends in the metropolis; and if he returned home laden with presents to disciples whose sufferings had recently so deeply moved the sympathy of their brethren, it is not strange that he gracefully seized an opportunity of extolling the Church to which he owed such obligations. His account of its greatness is obviously the inflated language of a panegyrist; but in due time its hyperbolic statements received a still more extravagant interpretation; and, on the authority of this ancient father, the Church of Rome was pompously announced as the mistress and the mother of all Churches.

It has been mentioned in a former chapter [339:2] that the celebrated Marcia who, until shortly before his death, possessed almost absolute control over the Emperor Commodus, made a profession of the faith. Her example, no doubt, encouraged other personages of distinction to connect themselves with the Roman Church; and, through the medium of these members of his flock, the

155

bishop Eleutherius must have had an influence such as none of his predecessors possessed. It is beyond doubt that Marcia, after consulting with Victor, the successor of Eleutherius, induced the Emperor to perform acts of kindness to some of her co-religionists. [339:3] The favour of the court seems to have puffed up the spirit of this naturally haughty churchman; and though, as we have seen, there is cause to suspect that certain ecclesiastical movements in the chief city had long before excited much ill-suppressed dissatisfaction, the Christian commonwealth was now startled for the first time by a very flagrant exhibition of the arrogance of a Roman prelate. [340:1] Because the Churches of Asia Minor celebrated the Paschal feast in a way different from that observed in the metropolis, [340:2] Victor cut them off from his communion. But this attempt of the bishop of the great city to act as lord over God's heritage was premature. Other churches condemned the rashness of his procedure; his refusal to hold fellowship with the Asiatic Christians threatened only to isolate himself; and he seems to have soon found it expedient to cultivate more pacific councils.

At this time the jurisdiction of Victor did not properly extend beyond the few ministers and congregations to be found in the imperial city. A quarter of a century afterwards even the bishop of Portus, a seaport town at the mouth of the Tiber about fifteen miles distant from the capital, acknowledged no allegiance to the Roman prelate. [340:3] The boldness of Victor in pronouncing so many foreign brethren unworthy of Catholic communion may at first, therefore, appear unaccountable. But it is probable that he acted, in this instance, in conjunction with many other pastors. Among the Churches of Gentile origin there was a deep prejudice against what was considered the judaizing of the Asiatic Christians in relation to the Paschal festival, and a strong impression that the character of the Church was compromised by any very marked diversity in its religious observances. There is, however, little reason to doubt that Victor was to some extent prompted by motives of a different complexion. Fifty years before, the remarkable words addressed to the apostle of the circumcision—"Thou art Peter, and upon this Rock I will build my Church" [341:1]—were interpreted at Rome in the way in which they are now understood commonly by Protestants; for the brother of the Roman bishop Pius, [341:2] writing about A.D. 150, teaches that the Rock on which the Church is built is the Son of God; [341:3] but ingenuity was already beginning to discover another exposition, and the growing importance of the Roman bishopric suggested the startling thought that the Church was built on Peter! [341:4] The name of the Galilean fisherman was already connected with the see of Victor; and it was thus easy for ambition or flattery to draw the inference that Victor himself was in some way the heir and representative of the great apostle. The doctrine that the bishop was necessary as the centre of Catholic unity had already gained currency; and if a centre of unity for the whole Church was also indispensable, who had a better claim to the pre-eminence than the successor of Peter? When Victor fulminated his sentence of excommunication against the Asiatic Christians he probably acted under the partial inspiration of this novel theory. He made an abortive attempt to speak in the name of the whole Church—to assert a position as the representative or president of all the bishops of the Catholic world [342:1]—and to carry out a new system of ecclesiastical unity. The experiment was a failure, simply because the idea looming in the imagination of the Roman bishop had not yet obtained full possession of the mind of Christendom.

Prelacy had been employed as the cure for Church divisions, but the remedy had proved worse than the disease. Sects meanwhile continued to multiply; and they were, perhaps, nowhere so abundant as in the very city where the new machinery had been first set up for their suppression. Towards the close of the second century their multitude was one of the standing reproaches of Christianity. What was called the Catholic Church was now on the brink of a great schism; and the very man, who aspired to be the centre of Catholic unity, threatened to be the cause of the disruption. It was becoming more and more apparent that, when the presbyters consented to surrender any portion of their privileges to the bishop, they betrayed the cause of ecclesiastical freedom; and even now indications were not wanting that the Catholic system was likely to degenerate into a spiritual despotism.

CHAPTER V

THE CHURCH OF ROME IN THE THIRD CENTURY

Though very few of the genuine productions of the ministers of the ancient Church of Rome are still extant, [343:1] multitudes of spurious epistles attributed to its early bishops have been carefully preserved. It is easy to account for this apparent anomaly. The documents now known as the false Decretals, [343:2] and ascribed to the Popes of the first and immediately succeeding centuries, were suited to the taste of times of ignorance, and were then peculiarly grateful to the occupants of the Roman see. As evidences of its original superiority they were accordingly transmitted to posterity, and ostentatiously exhibited among the papal title-deeds. But the real compositions of the primitive pastors of the great city supplied little food for superstition; and must have contained startling and humiliating revelations which laid bare the absurdity of claims subsequently advanced. These unwelcome witnesses were, therefore, quietly permitted to pass into oblivion.

It has been said, however, that Truth is the daughter of Time, and the discovery of monuments long since forgotten, or of writings supposed to have been lost, has often wonderfully verified and illustrated the apologue. The reappearance, within the last three hundred years, of various ancient records and memorials, has shed a new light upon the history of antiquity. Other testimonies equally valuable will, no doubt, yet be forthcoming for the settlement of existing controversies.

In A.D. 1551, as some workmen in the neighbourhood of Rome were employed in clearing away the ruins of a dilapidated chapel, they found a broken mass of sculptured marble among the rubbish. The fragments, when put together, proved to be a statue representing a person of venerable aspect sitting in a chair, on the back of which were the names of various publications. It was ascertained, on more minute examination, that, some time after the establishment of

Christianity by Constantine, [344:1] this monument had been erected in honour of Hippolytus—a learned writer and able controversialist, who bad been bishop of Portus in the early part of the third century, and who had finished his career by martyrdom, about A.D. 236, during the persecution under the Emperor Maximin. Hippolytus is commemorated as a saint in the Romish Breviary; [344:2] and the resurrection of his statue, after it had been buried for perhaps a thousand years, created quite a sensation among his papal admirers. Experienced sculptors, under the auspices of the Pontiff, Pius IV., restored the fragments to nearly their previous condition; and the renovated statue was then duly honoured with a place in the Library of the Vatican.

Nearly three hundred years afterwards, or in 1842, a manuscript which had been found in a Greek monastery at Mount Athos, was deposited in the Royal Library at Paris. This work, which has been since published, [345:1] and which is entitled "Philosophumena, or a Refutation of all Heresies," has been identified as the production of Hippolytus. It does not appear in the list of his writings mentioned on the back of the marble chair; but any one who inspects its contents can satisfactorily account for its exclusion from that catalogue. It reflects strongly on the character and principles of some of the early Roman bishops; and as the Papal see was fast rising into power when the statue was erected, it was obviously deemed prudent to omit an invidious publication. The writer of the "Philosophumena" declares that he is the author of one of the books named on that piece of ancient sculpture, and various other facts amply corroborate his testimony. There is, therefore, no good reason to doubt that a Christian bishop who lived about fifteen miles from Rome, and who flourished little more than one hundred years after the death of the Apostle John, composed the newly discovered Treatise. [345:2]

In accordance with the title of his work, Hippolytus here reviews all the heresies which had been broached up till the date of its publication. Long prior to the reappearance of this production, it was known that one of the early Roman bishops had been induced to countenance the errors of the Montanists; [345:3] and it would seem that Victor was the individual who was thus deceived; [345:4] but it had not been before suspected that Zephyrinus and Callistus, the two bishops next to him in succession, [345:5] held unsound views respecting the doctrine of the Trinity. Such, however, is the testimony of their neighbour and contemporary, the bishop of Portus. The witness may, indeed, be somewhat fastidious, as he was himself both erudite and eloquent; but had there not been some glaring deficiency in both the creed and the character of the chief pastor of Rome, Hippolytus would scarcely have described Zephyrinus as "an illiterate and covetous man," [346:1] "unskilled in ecclesiastical science," [346:2] and a disseminator of heretical doctrine. According to the statement of his accuser, he confounded the First and Second Persons of the Godhead, maintaining the identity of the Father and the Son. [346:3]

Callistus, who was made bishop on the death of Zephyrinus, must have possessed a far more vigorous intellect than his predecessor. Though regarded by the orthodox Hippolytus with no friendly eye, it is plain that he was endowed with an extraordinary share of energy and perseverance. He had been originally a slave, and he must have won the confidence of his wealthy Christian master Carpophores, for he had been intrusted by him with the care of a savings bank. The establishment became insolvent, in consequence, as Hippolytus alleges, of the mismanagement of its conductor; and many widows and others who had committed their money to his keeping, lost their deposits. When Carpophorus, by whom he was now suspected of embezzlement, determined to call him to account, Callistus fled to Portus—in the hope of escaping by sea to some other country. He was, however, overtaken, and, after an ineffectual attempt to drown himself, was arrested, and thrown into prison. His master, who was placable and kind-hearted, speedily consented to release him from confinement; but he was no sooner at large, than, under pretence of collecting debts due to the savings bank, he went into a Jewish synagogue during the time of public worship, and caused such disturbance that he was seized and dragged before the city prefect. The magistrate ordered him first to be scourged, and then to be transported to the mines of Sardinia. He does not appear to have remained long in exile; for, about this time, Marcia procured from the Emperor Commodus an order for the release of the Christians who had been banished to that unhealthy island; and Callistus, though not included in the act of grace, contrived to prevail upon the governor to set him at liberty along with the other prisoners. He now returned to Rome, where he appears to have acquired the reputation of a changed character. In due time he procured an appointment to one of the lower ecclesiastical offices; and as he possessed much talent, he did not find it difficult to obtain promotion. When Zephyrinus was advanced to the episcopate, Callistus, who was his special favourite, became one of the leading ministers of the Roman Church; and exercised an almost unbounded sway over the mind of the superficial and time-serving bishop. The Christians of the chief city were now split up into parties, some advocating the orthodox doctrine of the Trinity, and others abetting a different theory. Callistus appears to have dexterously availed himself of their divisions; and, by inducing each faction to believe that he espoused its cause, managed, on the death of Zephyrinus, to secure his election to the vacant dignity.

When Callistus had attained the object of his ambition, he tried to restore peace to the Church by endeavouring to persuade the advocates of the antagonistic principles to make mutual concessions. Laying aside the reserve which he had hitherto maintained, he now took up an intermediate position, in the hope that both parties would accept his own theory of the Godhead. "He invented," says Hippolytus, "such a heresy as follows. He said that the Word is the Son and is also the Father, being called by different names, but being one indivisible spirit; and that the Father is not one and the Son another (person), but that they both are one and the same.... The Father, having taken human flesh, deified it by uniting it to Himself,... and so he said that the Father had suffered with the Son." [348:1]

Though Callistus, as well as Hippolytus, is recognised as a saint in the Romish Breviary, [348:2] it is thus certain that the bishop of Portus regarded the bishop of Rome as a schemer and a heretic. It is equally clear that, at this period, all bishops were on a level of equality, for Hippolytus, though the pastor of a town in the neighbourhood of the chief city, did not acknowledge Callistus as his metropolitan. The bishop of Portus describes himself as one of those who are "successors of the apostles, partakers with them of the same grace both of principal priesthood and doctorship, and reckoned among the guardians of the Church." [348:3] Hippolytus testifies that Callistus was afraid of him, [348:4] and if both were members of the same synod, [348:5] well might the heterodox prelate stand in awe of a minister who possessed co-ordinate authority, with greater honesty and superior erudition. But still, it is abundantly plain, from the admissions of the "Philosophumena," that the bishop of Rome, in the time of the author of this treatise, was beginning to presume upon his position. Hippolytus complains of his irregularity in receiving into his communion some who had been "cast out of the Church" of Portus "after judicial sentence." [348:6] Had the bishop of the harbour of Rome been subject to the bishop of the capital, he would neither have expressed himself in such a style, nor preferred such an accusation.

Various circumstances indicate, as has already been suggested, that the bishop of Rome, in the time of the Antonines, was chosen by lot; but we may infer from the "Philosophumena" that, early in the third century, another mode of appointment had been adopted. [349:1] It is obvious that he now owed his advancement to the suffrages of the Church members, for Hippolytus hints very broadly that Callistus pursued a particular course with a view to promote his popularity and secure his election. It is beyond doubt that, about A.D. 236, Fabian was chosen bishop of Rome by the votes of the whole brotherhood, and there is on record a minute account of certain extraordinary circumstances which signalised the occasion. "When all the brethren had assembled in the church for the purpose of choosing their future bishop, and when the names of many worthy and distinguished men had suggested themselves to the consideration of the multitude, no one so much as thought of Fabian who was then present. They relate, however, that a dove gliding down from the roof, straightway settled on his head, as when the Holy Spirit, like a dove, rested upon the head of our Saviour. On this, the whole people, as if animated by one divine impulse, with great eagerness, and with the utmost unanimity, exclaimed that he was worthy; and, taking hold of him, placed him forthwith on the bishop's chair." [349:2]

Some time after the resurrection of the statue of Hippolytus, another revelation was made in the neighbourhood of Rome which has thrown much light upon its early ecclesiastical history. In the latter part of the sixteenth century, the unusual appearance of some apertures in the ground, not far from the Papal capital, awakened curiosity, and led to the discovery of dark subterranean passages of immense extent filled with monuments and inscriptions. These dismal regions, after having been shut up for about eight hundred years, were then again re-opened and re-explored.

The soil for miles around Rome is undermined, and the long labyrinths thus created are called catacombs. [350:1] The galleries are often found in stories two or three deep, communicating with each other by stairs; and it has been thought that formerly some of them were partially lighted from above. They were originally gravel-pits or stone-quarries, and were commenced long before the reign of Augustus. [350:2] The enlargement of the city, and the growing demand for building materials, led then to new and most extensive excavations. In the preparation of these vast caverns, we may trace the presiding care of Providence. As America, discovered a few years before the Reformation, furnished a place of refuge to the Protestants who fled from ecclesiastical intolerance, so the catacombs, re-opened shortly before the birth of our Lord, supplied shelter to the Christians in Rome during the frequent proscriptions of the second and third centuries. When the gospel was first propagated in the imperial city, its adherents belonged chiefly to the lower classes; and, for reasons of which it is now impossible to speak with certainty, [350:3] it seems to have been soon very generally embraced by the quarrymen and sand-diggers. [350:4] Thus it was that when persecution raged in the capital, the Christian felt himself comparatively safe in the catacombs. The parties in charge of them were his friends; they could give him seasonable intimation of the approach of danger; and among these "dens and caves of the earth," with countless places of ingress and egress, the officers of government must have attempted in vain to overtake a fugitive.

At present their appearance is most uncomfortable; they contain no chamber sufficient for the accommodation of any large number of worshippers; and it has even been questioned whether human life could be long supported in such gloomy habitations. But we have the best authority for believing that some of the early Christians remained for a considerable time in these asylums. [351:1] Wells of water have been found in their obscure recesses; fonts for baptism have also been discovered; and it is beyond doubt that the disciples met here for religious exercises. As early as the second century these vaults became the great cemetery of the Church. Many of the memorials of the dead which they contained have long since been transferred to the Lapidarian Gallery in the Vatican; and there, in the palace of the Pope, the venerable tombstones testify, to all who will consult them, how much modern Romanism differs from ancient Christianity.

Though many of these sepulchral monuments were erected in the fourth and fifth centuries, they indicate a remarkable freedom from superstitions with which the religion of the New Testament has been since defiled. These witnesses to the faith of the early Church of Rome altogether repudiate the worship of the Virgin Mary, for the inscriptions of the Lapidarian Gallery, all arranged under the papal supervision, contain no addresses to the mother of our Lord. [352:1] They point only to Jesus as the great Mediator, Redeemer, and Friend. It is also worthy of note that the tone of these voices from the grave is eminently cheerful. Instead of speaking of masses for the repose of souls, or representing departed believers as still doomed to pass through purgatory, they describe the deceased as having entered immediately into the abodes of eternal rest. "Alexander," says one of them, "is not dead, but lives beyond the stars, and his body rests in this tomb." "Here," says another, "lies Paulina, in the place of the blessed." "Gemella," says a third, "sleeps in peace." "Aselus," says a fourth, "sleeps in Christ." [352:2]

We learn from the testimony of Hippolytus that, during the episcopate of Zephyrinus, Callistus was "set over the cemetery." [352:3] This was probably considered a highly important trust, as, in those perilous times, the safety of the Christians very much depended on the prudence, activity, and courage of the individual who had the charge of their subterranean refuge. [352:4] The new curator seems to have signalised himself by the ability with which he discharged the duties of his appointment; he probably embellished and enlarged some of these dreary caves; and hence a portion of the catacombs was designated "The Cemetery of Callistus." Hippolytus, led astray by the ascetic spirit beginning so strongly to prevail in the commencement of the third century, was opposed to all second marriages, so that he was sadly scandalized by the exceedingly liberal views of his Roman brother on the subject of matrimony; and he was so ill-informed as to pronounce them novel. "In his time," says he indignantly, "bishops, presbyters, and deacons, though they had been twice or three times married, began to be recognised as God's ministers; and if any one of the clergy married, it was determined that such a person should remain among the clergy, as not having sinned." [353:1] We cannot tell how many of the ancient bishops of the great city were husbands; [353:2] we have certainly no distinct evidence that

161

even Callistus took to himself a wife; but we have the clearest proof that the primitive Church of Rome did not impose celibacy on her ministers; and, in support of this fact, we can produce the unimpeachable testimony of her own catacombs. There is, for instance, a monument "To Basilus the Presbyter, and Felicitas his wife;" and, on another tombstone, erected about A.D. 472, or only four years before the fall of the Western Empire, there is the following singular record—"Petronia, a deacon's wife, the type of modesty. In this place I lay my bones: spare your tears, dear husband and daughters, and believe that it is forbidden to weep for one who lives in God." [353:3] "Here," says another epitaph, "Susanna, the happy daughter of the late Presbyter Gabinus, lies in peace along with her father." [353:4] In the Lapidarian Gallery of the papal palace, the curious visitor may still read other epitaphs of the married ministers of Rome.

Though the gospel continued to make great progress in the metropolis, there was perhaps no city of the Empire in which it encountered, from the very first, such steady and powerful opposition. The Sovereign, being himself the Supreme Pontiff of Paganism, might be expected to resent, as a personal indignity, any attempt to weaken its influence; and the other great functionaries of idolatry, who all resided in the capital, were of course bound by the ties of office to resist the advancement of Christianity. The old aristocracy disliked everything in the shape of religious innovation, for they believed that the glory of their country was inseparably connected with an adherence to the worship of the gods of their ancestors. Thus it was that the intolerance of the state was always felt with peculiar severity at the seat of government. Exactly in the middle of the third century a persecution of unusual violence burst upon the Roman Church. Fabian, whose appointment to the bishopric took place, as already related, under such extraordinary circumstances, soon fell a victim to the storm. After his martyrdom, the whole community over which he presided seems to have been paralysed with terror; and sixteen months passed away before any successor was elected; for Decius, the tyrant who now ruled the Roman world, had proclaimed, his determination rather to suffer a competitor for his throne than a bishop for his chief city. [354:1] A veritable rival was quickly forthcoming to prove the falsehood of his gasconade; for when Julius Valens appeared to dispute his title to the Empire, Decius was obliged, by the pressure of weightier cares, to withdraw his attention from the concerns of the Roman Christians. During the lull in the storm of persecution, Cornelius was chosen bishop; but after an official life of little more than a year, he was thrown into confinement. His death in prison was, no doubt, occasioned by harsh treatment. The episcopate of his successor Lucius was even shorter than his own, for he was martyred about six months after his election. [355:1] Stephen, who was now promoted to the vacant chair, did not long retain possession of it; for though we have no reliable information as to the manner of his death, it is certain that he occupied the bishopric only between four and five years. His successor Xystus in less than twelve months finished his course by martyrdom. [355:2] Thus, in a period of eight years, Rome lost no less than five bishops, at least four of whom were cut down by persecution: of these Cornelius and Stephen, by far the most distinguished, were interred in the cemetery of Callistus.

There is still extant the fragment of a letter written by Cornelius furnishing a curious statistical account of the strength of the Roman Church at this period.

[355:3] According to this excellent authority it contained forty-six presbyters, seven deacons, seven sub-deacons, forty-two acolyths, fifty-two others who were either exorcists, readers, or door-keepers, and upwards of fifteen hundred besides, who were in indigent circumstances, and of whom widows constituted a large proportion. All these poor persons were maintained by the liberality of their fellow-worshippers. Rome, as we have seen, was the birthplace of prelacy; and other ecclesiastical organisms unknown to the New Testament may also be traced to the same locality, for here we read for the first time of such officials as the acolyths. [355:4] We may infer from the details supplied by the letter of Cornelius, that there were now fourteen congregations [355:5] of the faithful in the great city; and its Christian population has been estimated at about fifty thousand. No wonder that the chief pastor of such a multitude of zealous disciples all residing in his capital, awakened the jealousy of a suspicious Emperor.

A schism, which continued for generations to exert an unhappy influence, commenced in the metropolis during the short episcopate of Cornelius. The leader of this secession was Novatian, a man of blameless character, [356:1] and a presbyter of the Roman Church. In the Decian persecution many had been terrified into temporary conformity to paganism; and this austere ecclesiastic maintained, that persons who had so sadly compromised themselves, should, on no account whatever, be re-admitted to communion. When he found that he could not prevail upon his brethren to adopt this unrelenting discipline, he permitted himself to be ordained bishop in opposition to Cornelius; and became the founder of a separate society, known as the sect of the Novatians. As he denied the validity of the ordinance previously administered, he rebaptized his converts, and exhibited otherwise a miserably contracted spirit; but many sympathised with him in his views, and Novatian bishops were soon established in various parts of the Empire.

Immediately after the rise of this sect, a controversy relative to the propriety of rebaptizing heretics brought the Church of Rome into collision with many Christian communities in Africa and Asia Minor. The discussion, which did not eventuate in any fresh schism, is chiefly remarkable for the firm stand now made against the assumptions of the great Bishop of the West. When Stephen, who was opposed to rebaptism, discovered that he could not induce the Asiatics and Africans to come over to his sentiments, he rashly tried to overbear them by declaring that he would shut them out from his communion; but his antagonists treated the threat merely as an empty display of insolence. "What strife and contention hast thou awakened in the Churches of the whole world, O Stephen," said one of his opponents, "and how great sin hast thou accumulated when thou didst cut thyself off from so many flocks! Deceive not thyself, for he is truly the schismatic who has made himself an apostate from the communion of the unity of the Church. For whilst thou thinkest that all may be excommunicated by thee, thou hast excommunicated thyself alone from all." [357:1]

When the apostle of the circumcision said to his Master—"Thou art the Christ, the Son of the living God," Jesus replied—"Blessed art thou, Simon Bar-jona, for flesh and blood hath not revealed it unto thee, but my Father which is in heaven." To this emphatic acknowledgment of the faith of His disciple, our Lord added the memorable words—"And I say also unto thee, that thou art Peter, and upon this rock I will build my church, and the gates of hell shall not prevail

163

against it." [357:2] As the word Peter signifies a stone, [357:3] this address admits of a very obvious and satisfactory exposition. "Thou art," said Christ to the apostle, "a lively stone [357:4] of the spiritual structure I erect; and upon this rock on which thy faith is established, as witnessed by thy good confession, I will build my Church; and though the rains of affliction may descend, and the floods of danger may come, and the winds of temptation may blow, and beat upon this house, it shall remain immoveable, [358:1] because it rests upon an impregnable foundation." But a different interpretation was already gaining wide currency; for though Peter had been led to deny Christ with oaths and imprecations, the rapid growth and preponderating wealth of the Roman bishopric, of which the apostle was supposed to be the founder, had now induced many to believe that he was the Rock of Salvation, the enduring basis on which the living temple of God was to be reared! Tertullian and Cyprian, in the third century the two most eminent fathers of the West, countenanced the exposition; [358:2] and though both these writers were lamentably deficient in critical sagacity, men of inferior standing were slow to impugn the verdict of such champions of the faith. Thus it was that a false gloss of Scripture was already enthralling the mind of Christendom; and Stephen boldly renewed the attempt at domination commenced by his predecessor Victor. His opponents deserved far greater credit for the sturdy independence with which they upheld their individual rights than for the scriptural skill with which they unmasked the sophistry of a delusive theory; for all their reasonings were enervated and vitiated by their stupid admission of the claims of the chair of Peter as the rock on which the Church was supposed to rest. [358:3] This second effort of Rome to establish her ascendancy was, indeed, a failure; but the misinterpretation of Holy Writ, by which it was encouraged, was not effectively corrected and exposed; and thus the great Western prelate was left at liberty, at another more favourable opportunity, to wrest the Scriptures for the destruction of the Church.

From the middle of the third century, the authority of the Roman bishops advanced apace. The magnanimity with which so many of them then encountered martyrdom elicited general admiration; and the divisions caused by the schism of Novatian supplied them with a specious apology for enlarging their jurisdiction. The argument from the necessity of unity, which was urged so successfully for the creation of a bishop upwards of a hundred years before, could now be adduced with equal plausibility for the erection of a metropolitan; and, from this date, these prelates undoubtedly exercised archiepiscopal power. Seventy years afterwards, or at the Council of Nice, [359:1] the ecclesiastical rule of the Primate of Rome was recognised by the bishops of the ten suburbicarian provinces, including no small portion of Italy. [359:2]

For the last forty years of the third century the Church was free from persecution, and, during this long period of repose, the great Western see enjoyed an unwonted measure of outward prosperity. Its religious services were now conducted with increasing splendour, and distressed brethren in very distant countries shared the fruits of its munificence. In the reign of Gallienus, when the Goths burst into the Empire and devastated Asia Minor, the bishop of Rome transmitted a large sum of money for the release of the Christians who had fallen into the hands of the barbarians. [359:3] A few years afterwards, when Paul of Samosata was deposed for heresy, and when, on his refusal to surrender the property of the Church of Antioch, an application was made to the Emperor

Aurelian for his interference, that prince submitted the matter in dispute to the decision of Dionysius of Rome and the other bishops of Italy. [360:1] This reference, in which the position of the Roman prelate was publicly recognised, perhaps for the first time, by a Roman Emperor, was calculated to add vastly to the importance of the metropolitan see in public estimation. When Christianity was established about fifty years afterwards by Constantine, the bishop of the chief city was thus, to a great extent, prepared for the high position to which he was suddenly promoted.

None of the early bishops of Rome were distinguished for their mental accomplishments; and though they are commonly reputed the founders of the Latin Church, it would appear that, for nearly two hundred years, they all wrote and spoke the Greek language. The name Pope, which they have since appropriated, was now common to all pastors. [360:2] For the first three centuries almost every question relating to them is involved in much mystery; and, as we approach the close of this period, the difficulty of unravelling their perplexed traditions rather increases than diminishes. Even the existence of some who are said to have now flourished has been considered doubtful. [360:3] It is alleged that the see was vacant for upwards of three years and a half during the Diocletian persecution in the beginning of the fourth century; [360:4] but even this point has not been very clearly ascertained. The Roman bishopric was by far the most important in the Church; and the obscurity which overhangs its early history, cannot but be embarrassing to those who seek to establish a title to the ministry by attempting to trace it up through such dark annals.

On looking back over the first three centuries, we may remark how much the chairman of the Roman eldership, about the time of the death of the Apostle John, differed from the prelate who filled his place two hundred years afterwards. The former was the servant of the presbyters, and appointed to carry out their decisions; the latter was their master, and entitled to require their submission. The former presided over the ministers of, perhaps, three or four comparatively poor congregations dispirited by recent persecution; the latter had the charge of at least five-and-twenty flourishing city churches, [361:1] together with all the bishops in all the surrounding territory. In eventful times an individual of transcendent talent, such as Pepin or Napoleon, has adroitly bolted into a throne; but the bishop of Rome was indebted for his gradual elevation and his ultimate ascendancy neither to extraordinary genius nor superior erudition, but to a combination of circumstances of unprecedented rarity. His position furnished him with peculiar facilities for acquiring influence. Whilst the city in which he was located was the largest in the world, it was also the most opulent and the most powerful. He was continually coming in contact with men of note in the Church from all parts of the Empire; and he had frequent opportunities of obliging these strangers by various offices of kindness. He thus, too, possessed means of ascertaining the state of the Christian interest in every land, and of diffusing his own sentiments under singularly propitious circumstances. When he was fast rising into power, it was alleged that he was constituted chief pastor of the Church by Christ himself; and a text of Scripture was quoted which was supposed to endorse his title. For a time no one cared to challenge its application; for meanwhile his precedence was but nominal, and those, who might have been competent to point out the delusion, had no wish to give offence, by attacking the fond conceit of a friendly and prosperous prelate. But when the scene changed,

165

and when the Empire found another capital, the acumen of the bishop of the rival metropolis soon discovered a sounder exposition; and Chrysostom of Constantinople, at once the greatest preacher and the best commentator of antiquity, ignored the folly of Tertullian and of Cyprian. "Upon the rock," says he, "that is, upon the faith of the apostle's confession," [362:1] the Church is built. "Christ said that he would build His Church on Peter's confession." [362:2] Soon afterwards, the greatest divine connected with the Western Church, and the most profound theologian among the fathers, pointed out, still more distinctly, the true meaning of the passage. "Our Lord declares," says Augustine, "On this rock I will found my Church, because Peter had said: Thou art the Christ, the Son of the living God. On this rock, which thou hast confessed, He declares I will build my Church, for Christ was the rock on whose foundation Peter himself was built; for other foundation hath no man laid than that which is laid, which is Christ Jesus." [362:3] In the Italian capital, the words on which the power of the Papacy is understood to rest are exhibited in gigantic letters within the dome of St Peter's; but their exhibition only proves that the Church of Rome has lost the key of knowledge; for, though she would fain appeal to Scripture, she shews that she does not understand the meaning of its testimony; and, closing her eyes against the light supplied by the best and wisest of the fathers, she persists in adhering to a false interpretation.

166

SECTION II

THE LITERATURE AND THEOLOGY OF THE CHURCH

CHAPTER I

THE ECCLESIASTICAL WRITERS

By "the Fathers" we understand the writers of the ancient Christian Church. The name is, however, of rather vague application, for though generally employed to designate only the ecclesiastical authors of the first six centuries, it is extended, occasionally, to distinguished theologians who flourished in the middle ages.

The fathers of the second and third centuries have a strong claim on our attention. Living on the verge of apostolic times, they were acquainted with the state of the Church when it had recently passed from under the care of its inspired founders; and, as witnesses to its early traditions, their testimony is of peculiar value. But the period before us produced comparatively few authors, and a considerable portion of its literature has perished. There have been modern divines, such as Calvin and Baxter, who have each left behind a more voluminous array of publications than now survives from all the fathers of these two hundred years. Origen was by far the most prolific of the writers who flourished during this interval, but the greater number of his productions have been lost; and yet those which remain, if translated into English, would amount to nearly triple the bulk of our authorised version of the Bible. His extant works are, however, more extensive than all the other memorials of this most interesting section of the history of the Church.

Among the earliest ecclesiastical writers after the close of the first century is Polycarp of Smyrna. He is said to have been a disciple of the Apostle John, and hence he is known as one of the Apostolic Fathers. [365:1] An epistle of his addressed to the Philippians, and designed to correct certain vices and errors which had been making their appearance, is still preserved. It seems to have been written towards the middle of the second century; [365:2] its style is simple; and its general tone worthy of a man who had enjoyed apostolic tuition. Its venerable author suffered martyrdom about A.D. 167, [365:3] at the advanced age of eighty-six. [365:4]

Justin Martyr was contemporary with Polycarp. He was a native of Samaria, and a Gentile by birth; he had travelled much; he possessed a well-cultivated mind; and he had made himself acquainted with the various systems of philosophy which were then current. He could derive no satisfaction from the wisdom of the pagan theorists; but, one day, as he walked, somewhat sad and pensive, near the sea shore, a casual meeting with an aged stranger led him to turn his thoughts to the Christian revelation. The individual, with whom he had this solitary and important interview, was a member and, perhaps, a minister of the Church. After pointing out to Justin the folly of mere theorising, and recommending him to study the Old Testament Scriptures, as well on account of their great antiquity as their intrinsic worth, he proceeded to expatiate on the nature and excellence of the gospel. [366:1] The impression now made upon the mind of the young student was never afterwards effaced; he became a decided Christian; and, about A.D. 165, finished his career by martyrdom.

Justin is the first writer whose contributions to ecclesiastical literature are of considerable extent. Some of the works ascribed to him are unquestionably the productions of others; but there is no reason to doubt the genuineness of his Dialogue with Trypho the Jew, and of the two Apologies addressed to the Emperors, [366:2] Though the meeting with Trypho is said to have occurred at Ephesus, it is now perhaps impossible to determine whether it ever actually took place, or whether the Dialogue is only the report of an imaginary discussion. It serves, however, to illustrate the mode of argument then adopted in the controversy between the Jews and the disciples, and throws much light upon the state of Christian theology. Antoninus Pius and Marcus Aurelius appear to have been the Emperors to whom the Apologies are addressed. In these appeals to Imperial justice the calumnies against the Christians are refuted, whilst the simplicity of their worship and the purity of their morality are impressively described.

Justin, even after his conversion, still wore the philosopher's cloak, and continued to cherish an undue regard for the wisdom of the pagan sages. His mind never was completely emancipated from the influence of a system of false metaphysics; and thus it was that, whilst his views of various doctrines of the gospel remained confused, his allusions to them are equivocal, if not contradictory. But it has been well remarked that conscience, rather than science, guided many of the fathers; and the case of Justin demonstrates the truth of the observation. He possessed an extensive knowledge of the Scriptures; and though his theological views were not so exact or so perspicuous as they might have been, had he been trained up from infancy in the Christian faith, or had he studied the controversies which subsequently arose, it is beyond doubt that his creed was substantially evangelical. He had received the truth "in the love of it," and he counted not his life dear in the service of his Divine Master.

The Epistle to Diognetus, frequently included amongst the works of Justin, is apparently the production of an earlier writer. Its author, who styles himself "a disciple of apostles," designed by it to promote the conversion of a friend; his own views of divine truth are comparatively correct and clear; and in no uninspired memorial of antiquity are the peculiar doctrines of the gospel exhibited with greater propriety and beauty. Appended also to the common editions of the works of Justin are the remains of a few somewhat later writers, namely, Tatian, Athenagoras, Theophilus, and Hernias. Tatian was a disciple of Justin; [367:1] Athenagoras was a learned man of Athens; Theophilus is said to have been one of the pastors of Antioch; and of Hermas nothing whatever is known. The tracts of these authors relate almost entirely to the controversy between Christianity and Paganism. Whilst they point out the folly and falsehood of the accusations so frequently preferred against the brethren, they press the gospel upon the acceptance of the Gentiles with much earnestness, and support its claims by a great variety of arguments.

The tract known as the Epistle of Barnabas was probably composed in A.D.135. [367:2] It is the production apparently of a convert from Judaism who took special pleasure in allegorical interpretations of Scripture. Hermas, the author of the little work called Pastor, or The Shepherd, is a writer of much the same character. He was, in all likelihood, the brother of Pius, [368:1] who flourished about the middle of the second century, and who was, perhaps, the first or second individual who was officially designated Bishop of Rome. The writings of Papias, said to have been pastor of Hierapolis in the time of Polycarp, are no longer extant. [368:2] The works of Hegesippus, of a somewhat later date, and treating of the subject of ecclesiastical history, have also disappeared. [368:3]

Irenaeus of Lyons is the next writer who claims our special notice. He was originally connected with Asia Minor; and in his youth he is said to have enjoyed the tuition of Polycarp of Smyrna. We cannot tell when he left his native country, or what circumstances led him to settle on the banks of the Rhone; but we know that, towards the termination of the reign of Marcus Aurelius, he was appointed by the Gallic Christians to visit the Roman Church on a mission of importance. The Celtic language, still preserved in the Gaelic or Irish, was then spoken in France, [368:4] and Irenaeus found it necessary to qualify himself for the duties of a preacher among the heathen by studying the barbarous dialect. His zeal, energy, and talent were duly appreciated; soon after the death of the aged Pothinus he became the chief pastor of Lyons; and for many years he exercised considerable influence throughout the whole of the Western Church. When the Paschal controversy created such excitement, and when Victor of Rome threatened to rend the Christian commonwealth by his impetuous and haughty bearing, Irenaeus interposed, and to some extent succeeded in moderating the violence of the Italian prelate. He was the author of several works, [369:1] but his only extant production is a treatise "Against Heresies." It is divided into five books, four of which exist only in a Latin version; [369:2] and it contains a lengthened refutation of the Valentinians and other Gnostics.

Irenaeus is commonly called the disciple of Polycarp; but it is reported that he was also under the tuition of a less intelligent preceptor, Papias of Hierapolis. [369:3] This teacher, who has been already mentioned, and who was the author of a work now lost, entitled, "The Explanations of the Discourses of the Lord," is noted as the earliest ecclesiastical writer who held the doctrine of the personal reign of Christ at Jerusalem during the millennium. "These views," says Eusebius, "he appears to have adopted in consequence of having misunderstood the apostolic narratives.... For he was a man of very slender intellect, as is evident from his discourses." [369:4] His pupil Irenaeus possessed a much superior capacity; but even his writings are not destitute of puerilities; and it is not improbable that he derived some of the errors to be found in them from his weak-minded teacher. [369:5]

Irenaeus is supposed to have died in the beginning of the third century; and, shortly before that date, by far the most vigorous and acute writer who had yet appeared among the fathers, began to attract attention. This was the celebrated TERTULLIAN. He was originally a heathen, [370:1] and he appears in early life to have been engaged in the profession of a lawyer. At that time, as afterwards, there was constant intercourse between Rome and Carthage; [370:2] Tertullian seems to have been well acquainted with both these great cities; and he had probably resided for several years in the capital of the Empire. [370:3] But most of his public life was, perhaps, spent in Carthage, the place of his birth. In the beginning of the third century clerical celibacy was beginning to be fashionable; and yet Tertullian, though a presbyter, [370:4] was married; for two of his tracts are addressed To his Wife; and it is apparent from his works that then no law of the Church prohibited ecclesiastics from entering into wedlock.

The extant productions of this writer are numerous; and, if rendered into our language, would form a very portly volume. But though several parts of them have found translators, the whole have never yet appeared in English; and, of some pieces, the most accomplished scholar would scarcely undertake to furnish at once a literal and an intelligible version. [370:5] His style is harsh, his transitions are abrupt, and his inuendos and allusions most perplexing. He must have been a man of very bilious temperament, who could scarcely distinguish a theological opponent from a personal enemy; for he pours forth upon those who differ from him whole torrents of sarcasm and invective. [371:1] His strong passion, acting upon a fervid imagination, completely overpowered his judgment; and hence he deals so largely in exaggeration, that, as to many matters of fact, we cannot safely depend upon his testimony. His tone is dictatorial and dogmatic; and, though we cannot doubt his piety, we must feel that his spirit is somewhat repulsive and ungenial. Whilst he was sadly deficient in sagacity, he was very much the creature of impulse; and thus it was that he was so superstitious, so bigoted, and so choleric. But he was, beyond question, possessed of erudition and of genius; and when he advocates a right principle, he can expound, defend, and illustrate it with great ability and eloquence.

Tertullian is commonly known as the earliest of the Latin fathers. [371:2] The writer who first attempted to supply the rulers of the world with a Christian literature in their own tongue encountered a task of much difficulty. It was no easy matter to conduct theological controversies in a language which was not remarkable for flexibility, and which had never before been employed in such discussions; and Tertullian seems to have often found it necessary to coin unwonted forms of expression, or rather to invent an ecclesiastical nomenclature. The ponderous Latin, hitherto accustomed to speak only of Jupiter and the gods, engages somewhat awkwardly in its new vocation; and yet contrives to proclaim, with wonderful power, the great thoughts for which it must now find utterance. Several years after his appearance as an author, Tertullian lapsed into Montanism—a species of heresy peculiarly attractive to a man of his rugged and austere character. Some of his works bear clear traces of this change of sentiment; but others furnish no internal evidences warranting us to pronounce decisively respecting the date of their composition. It is remarkable that though he identified himself with a party under the ban of ecclesiastical proscription, his works still continued to be held in high repute, and to be perused with avidity by those who valued themselves on their zeal for orthodoxy. It is recorded of one of the most influential of the Catholic bishops of the third century that he read a portion of them daily; and, when calling for his favourite author, he is reported to have said—"Give me the Master." [372:1]

Tertullian flourished at a period when ecclesiastical usurpation was beginning to produce some of its bitter fruits, and when religion was rapidly degenerating from its primitive purity. [372:2] His works, which treat of a great variety of topics interesting to the Christian student, throw immense light on the state of the Church in his generation. His best known production is his Apology, in which he pleads the cause of the persecuted disciples with consummate talent, and urges upon the state the equity and the wisdom of toleration. He expounds the doctrine of the Trinity more lucidly than any preceding writer; he treats of Prayer, of Repentance, and of Baptism; he takes up the controversy with the Jews; [372:3] and he assails the Valentinians and other heretics. But the way of salvation by faith seems to have been very indistinctly apprehended by him, so that he cannot be safely trusted as a theologian. He had evidently no clear conception of the place which works ought to occupy according to the scheme of the gospel; and hence he sometimes speaks as if pardon could be purchased by penance, by fasting, or by martyrdom.

Clement of Alexandria was contemporary with Tertullian. Like him, he was a Gentile by birth; but we know nothing of the circumstances connected with his conversion. In early times Alexandria was one of the great marts of literature and science; its citizens were noted for their intellectual culture; and, when a Church was formed there, learned men began to pass over to the new religion in considerable numbers. It was, in consequence, deemed expedient to establish an institute where catechumens of this class, before admission to baptism, could be instructed in the faith by some well qualified teacher. The plan of the seminary seems to have been gradually enlarged; and it soon supplied education to candidates for the ministry. Towards the close of the second century, Pantaenus, a distinguished scholar, had the charge of it; and Clement, who had been his pupil, became his successor as its president. Some of the works of this writer have perished, and his only extant productions are a discourse entitled "What rich man shall be saved?" his Address to the Greeks or Gentiles, his Paedagogue, and his Stromata. The hortatory Address is designed to win over the pagans from idolatry; the Paedagogue directs to Jesus, or the Word, as the great Teacher, and supplies converts with practical precepts for their guidance; whilst in the Stromata, or Miscellanies, we have a description of what he calls the Gnostic or perfect Christian. He here takes occasion to attack those who, in his estimation, were improperly designated Gnostics, such as Basilides, Valentine, Marcion, and others.

Clement, as is apparent from his writings, was extensively acquainted with profane literature. But he formed quite too high an estimate of the value of the heathen philosophy, whilst he allegorized Scripture in a way as dangerous as it was absurd. By the serpent which deceived Eve, according to Clement, "pleasure, an earthly vice which creeps upon the belly, is allegorically represented." [374:1] Moses, speaking allegorically, if we may believe this writer, called the Divine Wisdom the tree of life planted in paradise; by which paradise we may understand the world, in which all the works of creation were called into being. [374:2] He even interprets the ten commandments allegorically. Thus, by adultery, he understands a departure from the true knowledge of the Most High, and by murder, a violation of the truth respecting God and His eternal existence. [374:3] It is easy to see how Scripture, by such a system of interpretation, might be tortured into a witness for any extravagance.

In the early part of the third century Hippolytus of Portus exerted much influence by his writings. It was long believed that, with the exception of some fragments and a few tracts of little consequence, the works of this father had ceased to exist; but, as stated in a preceding chapter, [374:4] one of his most important publications, the "Philosophumena, or Refutation of all Heresies," has been recently recovered. The re-appearance of this production after so many centuries of oblivion is an extraordinary fact; and its testimony relative to historical transactions of deep interest connected with the early Church of Rome, has created quite a sensation among the students of ecclesiastical literature.

Hippolytus was the disciple of Irenaeus, and one of the soundest theologians of his generation. His works, which are written in Greek, illustrate his learning, his acuteness, and his eloquence. His views on some matters of ecclesiastical discipline were, indeed, too rigid; and, by a writer of the fifth century, [375:1] he has been described as an abettor of Novatianism; but his zeal and piety are universally admitted. He is said to have lost his life in the cause of Christianity; and though he attests the heretical teaching of two of her chief pastors, the Church of Rome still honours him as a saint and a martyr.

Minucius Felix was the contemporary of Hippolytus. He was a Roman lawyer, and a convert from paganism. In his Dialogue, entitled "Octavius," the respective merits of Christianity and heathenism are discussed with much vivacity. In point of style this little work is surpassed by none of the ecclesiastical writings of the period.

Another and a still more distinguished author, contemporary with Hippolytus, was ORIGEN. He was born at Alexandria about A.D. 185; his father Leonides, who was a teacher of rhetoric, was a member of the Church; and his son enjoyed the advantages of an excellent elementary education. Origen, when very young, was required daily to commit prescribed portions of the Word of God to memory; and the child soon became intensely interested in the study of the sacred oracles. The questions which he proposed to his father, as he repeated his appointed tasks, displayed singular precocity of intellect; and Leonides rejoiced exceedingly as he observed from time to time the growing indications of his extraordinary genius. But, before Origen reached maturity, his good parent fell a victim to the intolerance of the imperial laws. In the persecution under Septimius Severus, when the young scholar was about seventeen years of age, Leonides was put into confinement, and then beheaded. He had a wife and seven children who were likely to be left destitute by his death; but Origen, who was his first born, afraid lest his constancy should be overcome by the prospect of a beggared family, wrote a letter to him when he was in prison to encourage him to martyrdom. "Stand steadfast, father," said the ardent youth, "and take care not to desert your principles on our account." At this crisis he would have exposed himself to martyrdom, had not his mother hid his clothes, and thus prevented him from appearing in public.

When Leonides was put to death his property was confiscated, and his family reduced to poverty. But Origen now attracted the notice of a rich and noble lady of Alexandria, who received him into her house, and became his patron. He did not, however, remain long under her roof; as he was soon able to earn a maintenance by teaching. He continued, meanwhile, to apply himself with amazing industry to the acquisition of knowledge; and at length he began to be regarded as one of the most learned of the Christians. So great was his celebrity as a divine that, more than once during his life, whole synods of foreign bishops solicited his advice and interference in the settlement of theological controversies.

Whilst Origen, by intense study, was constantly adding to his intellectual treasures, he also improved his mind by travelling. When about twenty-six years of age he made a journey to Rome; and he subsequently visited Arabia, Palestine, Syria, Asia Minor, and Greece. As he passed through Palestine in A.D. 228, when he was in the forty-third year of his age, he was ordained a presbyter by some of the bishops of that country. He was now teacher of the catechetical school of Alexandria—an office in which he had succeeded Clement—and his ordination by the foreign pastors gave great offence to Demetrius, his own bishop. It has been said that this haughty churchman was galled by the superior reputation of the great scholar; and Origen, on his return to Egypt, was exposed to an ecclesiastical persecution. An indiscreet act of his youth was now converted into a formidable accusation, [377:1] whilst some incautious speculations in which he had indulged were urged as evidences of his unsoundness in the faith. His ordination was pronounced invalid; he was deprived of his appointment as president of the catechetical school; and he was excommunicated as a heretic. He now retired to Caesarea, where he appears to have spent the greater portion of the remainder of his life. The sentence of excommunication was announced by Demetrius to the Churches abroad; but though it was approved at Rome and elsewhere, it was not recognised in Palestine, Phoenice, Arabia, and Achaia. At Caesarea, Origen established a theological seminary such as that over which he had so long presided at Alexandria; and, in this institute, some of the most eminent pastors of the third century received their education.

This great man throughout life practised extraordinary self-denial. His clothing was scarcely sufficient to protect him from the cold; he slept on the ground; he confined himself to the simplest fare; and for years he persisted in going barefoot. [377:2] But his austerities did not prevent him from acquiring a world-wide reputation. Pagan philosophers attended his lectures, and persons of the highest distinction sought his society. When Julia Mammaea, the mother of Alexander Severus, invited him to visit her, and when, in compliance with this summons, he proceeded to Antioch [377:3] escorted by a military guard, he must have been an object of no little curiosity to the Imperial courtiers. It could now no longer be said that the Christians were an illiterate generation; as, in all that brilliant throng surrounding the throne of the Master of the Roman world, there was not, perhaps, one to be compared, with the poor catechist of Alexandria for varied and profound scholarship. But his theological taste was sadly vitiated by his study of the pagan philosophy. Clement, his early instructor, led him to entertain far too high an opinion of its excellence; and a subsequent teacher, Ammonius Saccas, the father of New Platonism, thoroughly imbued his mind with many of his own dangerous principles. According to Ammonius all systems of religion and philosophy contain the elements of truth; and it is the duty of the wise man to trace out and exhibit their harmony. The doctrines of Plato formed the basis of his creed, and it required no little ingenuity, to shew how all other theories quadrated with the speculations of the Athenian sage. To establish his views, he was obliged to draw much on his imagination, and to adopt modes of exegesis the most extravagant and unwarrantable. The philosophy of Ammonius exerted a very pernicious influence upon Origen, and seduced him into not a few of those errors which have contributed so greatly to lower his repute as a theologian.

Origen was a most prolific author; and, if all his works were still extant, they would be far more voluminous than those of any other of the fathers. But most of his writings have been lost; and, in not a few instances, those which remain have reached us either in a very mutilated form, or in a garbled Latin version. His treatise "Against Celsus," which was composed when he was advanced in life, and which is by far the most valuable of his existing works, has come down to us in a more perfect state than, perhaps, any of his other productions. It is a defence of Christianity in reply to the publication of a witty heathen philosopher who wrote against it in the time of the Antonines. [378:1] Of his celebrated "Hexapla," to which he is said to have devoted much of his time for eight and twenty years, only some fragments have been preserved. This great work appears to have been undertaken to meet the cavils of the Jews against the Septuagint—the Greek translation of the Old Testament in current use in the days of the apostles, and still most appreciated by the Christians. The unbelieving Israelites now pronounced it a corrupt version; and, that all might have an opportunity of judging for themselves, Origen exhibited the text in six consecutive columns—the first, containing the original Hebrew—the second, the same in Greek letters—and the third, fourth, fifth, and sixth, four of the most famous of the Greek translations, including the Septuagint. [379:1] The labour employed in the collation of manuscripts, when preparing this work, was truly prodigious. The expense, which must also have been great, is said to have been defrayed by Ambrosius, a wealthy Christian friend, who placed at the disposal of the editor the constant services of seven amanuenses. By his "Hexapla" Origen did much to preserve the purity of the sacred text, and he may be said to have thus laid the foundations of the science of Scripture criticism.

This learned writer cannot be trusted as an interpreter of the inspired oracles. Like the Jewish Cabbalists, of whom Philo, whose works he had diligently studied, [379:2] is a remarkable specimen, he neglects the literal sense of the Word, and betakes himself to mystical expositions. [379:3] In this way the divine record may be made to support any crotchet which happens to please the fancy of the commentator. Origen may, in fact, be regarded as the father of Christian mysticism; and, in after-ages, to a certain class of visionaries, especially amongst the monks, his writings long continued to present peculiar attractions.

On doctrinal points his statements are not always consistent, so that it is extremely difficult to form anything like a correct idea of his theological sentiments. Thus, on the subject of the Trinity, he sometimes speaks most distinctly in the language of orthodoxy, whilst again he employs phraseology which rather savours of the creed of Sabellius or of Arius. In his attempts to reconcile the gospel and his philosophy, he miserably compromised some of the most important truths of Scripture. The fall of man seems to be not unfrequently repudiated in his religious system; and yet, occasionally, it is distinctly recognized. [380:1] He maintained the pre-existence of human souls; he held that the stars are animated beings; he taught that all men shall ultimately attain happiness; and he believed that the devils themselves shall eventually be saved. [380:2] It is abundantly clear that Origen was a man of true piety. His whole life illustrates his self-denial, his single-mindedness, his delight in the Word of God, and his zeal for the advancement of the kingdom of Christ. In the Decian persecution he suffered nobly as a confessor; and the torture which he then endured seems to have hastened his demise. But with all his learning he was obviously deficient in practical sagacity; and though both his genius and his eloquence were of a high order, he possessed scarcely even an average share of prudence and common sense. His writings diffused, not the genial light of the

Sun of Righteousness, but the mist and darkness of a Platonized Christianity. Though he induced many philosophers to become members of the Church, the value of these accessions was greatly deteriorated by the daring spirit of speculation which they were still encouraged to cultivate. Of his Christian courage, his industry, and his invincible perseverance, there can be no doubt. He closed a most laborious career at Tyre, A.D. 254, in the seventieth year of his age.

About the time of the death of Origen, a Latin author, whose writings are still perused with interest, was beginning to attract much notice. CYPRIAN of Carthage, before his conversion to Christianity, was a professor of rhetoric and a gentleman of property. When he renounced heathenism, he is supposed to have reached the mature age of forty-five or forty-six; and as he possessed rank, talent, and popular eloquence, he was deemed no ordinary acquisition to the Church. About two years after his baptism, the chief pastor of the metropolis of the Proconsular Africa was removed by death; and Cyprian, by the acclamations of the Christian people, was called to the vacant office. At that time there seem to have been only eight presbyters, [381:1] or elders, connected with the bishopric of Carthage; but the city contained probably some hundreds of thousands of a population; and, though the episcopal dignity was not without its perils, it did not want the attractions of wealth and influence. The advancement of Cyprian gave great offence to the other elders, who appear to have conceived that one of themselves, on the ground of greater experience and more lengthened services, had a better title to promotion. Though the new bishop was sustained by the enthusiastic support of the multitude, the presbytery contrived, notwithstanding, to give him considerable annoyance. Five of them, constituting a majority, formed themselves into a regular opposition; and for several years the Carthaginian Church was distracted by the struggles between the bishop and his eldership.

The pastorate of Cyprian extended over a period of about ten years; but meanwhile persecution raged, and the bishop was obliged to spend nearly the one-third of his episcopal life in retirement and in exile. From his retreat he kept up a communication by letters with his flock. [382:1] The worship and constitution of the Church about the middle of the third century may be ascertained pretty clearly from the Cyprianic correspondence. Some of the letters addressed to the Carthaginian bishop, as well as those dictated by him, are still extant; and as he maintained an epistolary intercourse with Rome, Cappadocia, and other places, the documents known as the Cyprianic writings, [382:2] are amongst the most important of the ancient ecclesiastical memorials. This eminent pastor has also left behind him several short treatises on topics which were then attracting public attention. Among these may be mentioned his tracts on "The Unity of the Church," "The Lord's Prayer," "The Vanity of Idols," "The Grace of God," "The Dress of Virgins," and "The Benefit of Patience."

The writings of Cyprian have long been noted for their orthodoxy; and yet it must be admitted that his hierarchical prejudices stunted his charity and obscured his intellectual vision. Tertullian was his favourite author; and it is evident that he possessed much of the contracted spirit and of the stiff formalism of the great Carthaginian presbyter. He speaks in more exalted terms of the authority of bishops than any preceding writer. It is not improbable that the attempts of his discontented elders to curb his power inflamed his old aristocratic hauteur, and thus led to a reaction; and that, supported by the popular voice, he

175

was tempted absurdly to magnify his office, and to stretch his prerogative beyond the bounds of its legitimate exercise. His name carried with it great influence, and from his time episcopal pretensions advanced apace.

Cyprian was martyred about A.D. 258 in the Valerian persecution. As he was a man of rank, and perhaps personally related to some of the imperial officers at Carthage, he seems to have been treated, when a prisoner, with unusual respect and indulgence. On the evening before his death an elegant supper was provided for him, and he was permitted to enjoy the society of a numerous party of his friends. When he reached the spot where he was to suffer, he was subjected to no lingering torments; for his head was severed from his body by a single stroke of the executioner. [383:1]

The only other writer of note who flourished after Cyprian, in the third century, [383:2] was Gregory, surnamed Thaumaturgus, or The Wonder-Worker. He belonged to a pagan family of distinction; and, when a youth, was intended for the profession of the law; but, becoming acquainted with Origen at Caesarea in Palestine, he was induced to embrace the Christian faith, and relinquish flattering prospects of secular promotion. He became subsequently the bishop of Neo-Caesarea in Pontus. When he entered on his charge he is said to have had a congregation of only seventeen individuals; but his ministry must have been singularly successful; for, according to tradition, all the inhabitants of the city, with seventeen exceptions, were, at the time of his death, members of the Church. The reports respecting him are obviously exaggerated, and no credit can be attached to the narrative of his miracles. [384:1] He wrote several works, of which his "Panegyric on Origen," and his "Paraphrase on Ecclesiastes," are still extant. The genuineness of some other tracts ascribed to him may be fairly challenged.

The preceding account of the fathers of the second and third centuries may enable us to form some idea of the value of these writers as ecclesiastical authorities. Most of them had reached maturity before they embraced the faith of the gospel, so that, with a few exceptions, they wanted the advantages of an early Christian education. Some of them, before their conversion, had bestowed much time and attention on the barren speculations of the pagan philosophers; and, after their reception into the bosom of the Church, they still continued to pursue the same unprofitable studies. Cyprian, one of the most eloquent of these fathers, had been baptized only about two years before he was elected bishop of Carthage; and, during his comparatively short episcopate, he was generally in a turmoil of excitement, and had, consequently, little leisure for reading or mental cultivation. Such a writer is not entitled to command confidence as an expositor of the faith once delivered to the saints. Even in our own day, with all the facilities supplied by printing for the rapid accumulation of knowledge, no one would expect much spiritual instruction from an author who would undertake the office of an interpreter of Scripture two years after his conversion from heathenism. The fathers of the second and third centuries were not regarded as safe guides even by their Christian contemporaries. Tatian was the founder of a sect of extreme Teetotallers. [383:1] Tertullian, who, in point of learning, vigour, and genius, stands at the head of the Latin writers of this period, was connected with a party of gloomy fanatics. Origen, the most voluminous and erudite of the Greek fathers, was excommunicated as a heretic. If we estimate these authors, as they were appreciated by the early Church of Rome, we must pronounce their writings of little value. Tertullian, as a Montanist, was under the ban of the Roman bishop.

Hippolytus could not have been a favourite with either Zephyrinus or Callistus, for he denounced both as heretics. Origen was treated by the Roman Church as a man under sentence of excommunication. Stephen deemed even Cyprian unworthy of his ecclesiastical fellowship, because the Carthaginian prelate maintained the propriety of rebaptizing heretics.

Nothing can be more unsatisfactory, or rather childish, than the explanations of Holy Writ sometimes given by these ancient expositors. According to Tertullian, the two sparrows mentioned in the New Testament [383:2] signify the soul and the body; [383:3] and Clemens Alexandrinus gravely pleads for marriage [383:4] from the promise-"Where two or three are gathered together in my name, there am I in the midst of them." [383:5] Cyprian produces, as an argument in support of the doctrine of the Trinity, that the Jews observed "the third, sixth, and ninth hours" as their "fixed and lawful seasons for prayer." [383:6] Origen represents the heavenly bodies as literally engaged in acts of devotion. [386:1] If these authorities are to be credited, the Gihon, one of the rivers of Paradise, was no other than the Nile. [386:2] Very few of the fathers of this period were acquainted with Hebrew, so that, as a class, they were miserably qualified for the interpretation of the Scriptures. Even Origen himself must have had a very imperfect knowledge of the language of the Old Testament. [386:3] In consequence of their literary deficiencies, the fathers of the second and third centuries occasionally commit the most ridiculous blunders. Thus, Irenaeus tells us that the name Jesus in Hebrew consists of two letters and a half, and describes it as signifying "that Lord who contains heaven and earth!" [386:4] This father asserts also that the Hebrew word Adonai, or the Lord, denotes "utterable and wonderful." [386:5] Clemens Alexandrinus is not more successful as an interpreter of the sacred tongue of the chosen people; for he asserts that Jacob was called Israel "because he had seen the Lord God," [386:6] and he avers that Abraham means "the elect father of a sound!" [386:7] Justin Martyr errs egregiously in his references to the Old Testament; as he cites Isaiah for Jeremiah, [386:8] Zechariah for Malachi, [386:9] Zephaniah for Zechariah, [386:10] and Jeremiah for Daniel. [386:11] Irenaeus repeats, as an apostolic tradition, that when our Lord acted as a public teacher He was between forty and fifty years of age; [387:1] and Tertullian affirms that He was about thirty years of age at the time of His crucifixion. [387:2] The opinion of this same writer in reference to angels is still more extraordinary. He maintains that some of these beings, captivated by the beauty of the daughters of men, came down from heaven and married them; and that, out of complaisance to their brides, they communicated to them the arts of polishing and setting precious stones, of preparing cosmetics, and of using other appliances which minister to female vanity. [387:3] His ideas upon topics of a different character are equally singular. Thus, he affirms that the soul is corporeal, having length, breadth, height, and figure. [387:4] He even goes so far as to say that there is no substance which is not corporeal, and that God himself is a body. [387:5]

It would seem as if the Great Head of the Church permitted these early writers to commit the grossest mistakes, and to propound the most foolish theories, for the express purpose of teaching us that we are not implicitly to follow their guidance. It might have been thought that authors, who flourished on the borders of apostolic times, knew more of the mind of the Spirit than others who appeared in succeeding ages; but the truths of Scripture, like the phenomena

177

of the visible creation, are equally intelligible to all generations. If we possess spiritual discernment, the trees and the flowers will display the wisdom and the goodness of God as distinctly to us as they did to our first parents; and, if we have the "unction from the Holy One," we may enter into the meaning of the Scriptures as fully as did Justin Martyr or Irenaeus. To assist us in the interpretation of the New Testament, we have at command a critical apparatus of which they were unable to avail themselves. Jehovah is jealous of the honour of His Word, and He has inscribed in letters of light over the labours of its most ancient interpreters— "CEASE YE FROM MAN." The "opening of the Scriptures," so as to exhibit their beauty, their consistency, their purity, their wisdom, and their power, is the clearest proof that the commentator is possessed of "the key of knowledge." When tried by this test, Thomas Scott or Matthew Henry is better entitled to confidence than either Origen or Gregory Thaumaturgus. The Bible is its own safest expositor. "The law of the Lord is perfect, converting the soul; the testimony of the Lord is sure, making wise the simple."

CHAPTER II

THE IGNATIAN EPISTLES AND THEIR CLAIMS.
THE EXTERNAL EVIDENCE

The Epistles attributed to Ignatius have attracted greater notice, and have created more discussion, than any other uninspired writings of the same extent in existence. The productions ascribed to this author, and now reputed genuine by the most learned of their recent editors, might all be printed on the one-fourth of a page of an ordinary newspaper; and yet, the fatigue of travelling thousands of miles has been encountered, [389:1] for the special purpose of searching after correct copies of these highly-prized memorials. Large volumes have been written, either to establish their authority, or to prove that they are forgeries; and, if collected together, the books in various languages to which they have given birth, would themselves form a considerable library. Recent discoveries have thrown new light on their pretensions, but though the controversy has now continued upwards of three hundred years, it has not hitherto reached a satisfactory termination. [390:1]

The Ignatian letters owe almost all their importance to the circumstance that they are alleged to have been written on the confines of the apostolic age. As very few records remain to illustrate the ecclesiastical history of that period, it is not strange that epistles, purporting to have emanated from one of the most distinguished ministers who then flourished, should have excited uncommon attention. But doubts regarding their genuineness have always been entertained by candid and competent scholars. The spirit of sectarianism has entered largely into the discussion of their claims; and, whilst certain distinct references to the subject of Church polity, which they contain, have greatly enhanced their value in the estimation of one party, the same passages have been quoted, by those who repudiate their authority, as so many decisive proofs of their fabrication. The annals of literature furnish, perhaps, scarcely any other case in which ecclesiastical prejudices have been so much mixed up with a question of mere criticism.

The history of the individual to whom these letters have been ascribed, has been so metamorphosed by fables, that it is now, perhaps, impossible to ascertain its true outlines. There is a tradition that he was the child whom our Saviour set in the midst of His disciples as a pattern of humility; [390:2] and as our Lord, on the occasion, took up the little personage in His arms, it has been asserted that Ignatius was therefore surnamed Theophorus, that is, borne or carried by God. [390:3] Whatever may be thought as to the truth of this story, it probably gives a not very inaccurate view of the date of his birth; for he was, in all likelihood, far advanced in life [391:1] at the period when he is supposed to have written these celebrated letters. According to the current accounts, he was the second bishop of Antioch at the time of his martyrdom; and as his age would lead us to infer that he was then the senior member of the presbytery, [391:2] the tradition may have thus originated. It is alleged that when Trajan visited the capital of Syria in the ninth year of his reign, or A.D. 107, Ignatius voluntarily presented himself before the imperial tribunal, and avowed his Christianity. It is added, that he was in consequence condemned to be carried a prisoner to Rome, there to be consigned to the wild beasts for the entertainment of the populace. On his way to the Western metropolis, he is said to have stopped at Smyrna. The legend represents Polycarp as then the chief pastor of that city; and, when there, Ignatius is described as having received deputations from the neighbouring churches, and as having addressed to them several letters. From Smyrna he is reported to have proceeded to Troas; where he dictated some additional epistles, including one to Polycarp. The claims of these letters to be considered his genuine productions have led to the controversy which we are now to notice.

The story of Ignatius exhibits many marks of error and exaggeration; and yet it is no easy matter to determine how much of it should be pronounced fictitious. Few, perhaps, will venture to assert that the account of his martyrdom is to be rejected as altogether apocryphal; and still fewer will go so far as to maintain that he is a purely imaginary character. There is every reason to believe that, very early in the second century, he was connected with the Church of Antioch; and that, about the same period, he suffered unto death in the cause of Christianity. Pliny, who was then Proconsul of Bithynia, mentions that, as he did not well know, in the beginning of his administration, how to deal with the accused Christians, he sent those of them who were Roman citizens to the Emperor, that he might himself pronounce judgment. [392:1] It is possible that the chief magistrate of Syria pursued the same course; and that thus Ignatius was transmitted as a prisoner into Italy. But, upon some such substratum of facts, a mass of incongruous fictions has been erected. The "Acts of his Martyrdom," still extant, and written probably upwards of a hundred years after his demise, cannot stand the test of chronological investigation; and have evidently been compiled by some very superstitious and credulous author. According to these Acts, Ignatius was condemned by Trajan at Antioch in the ninth [392:2] year of his reign; but it has been contended that, not until long afterwards, was the Emperor in the Syrian capital. [392:3] In the "Acts," Ignatius is described as presenting himself before his sovereign of his own accord, to proclaim his Christianity—a piece of foolhardiness for which it is difficult to discover any reasonable apology. The report of the interview between Ignatius and Trajan, as given in this document, would, if believed, abundantly warrant the conclusion that the martyr must have entirely lost the humility for which he is said to have obtained credit when a child; as his conduct, in the presence of the Emperor, betrays no small amount of boastfulness and presumption. The account of his transmission to Rome, that he might be thrown to wild beasts, presents difficulties with which even the most zealous defenders of his legendary history have found it impossible to grapple. He was sent away, say they, to the Italian metropolis that the sight of so distinguished a victim passing through so many cities on his way to a cruel death might strike terror into the hearts of the Christian inhabitants. But we are told that he was conveyed from Syria to Smyrna by water, [393:1] so that the explanation is quite unsatisfactory; and, had the journey been accomplished by land, it would still be insufficient, as the disciples of that age were unhappily only too familiar with spectacles of Christian martyrdom. Our perplexity increases as we proceed more minutely to investigate the circumstances under which the epistles are reported to have been composed. Whilst Ignatius is said to have been hurried with great violence and barbarity from the East to the West, he is at the same time represented, with strange inconsistency, as remaining for many days together in the same place, [393:2] as receiving visitors from the churches all around, and as writing magniloquent epistles. What is still more remarkable, though he was pressed by the soldiers to hasten forward, and though a prosperous gale speedily carried his vessel into Italy, [394:1] one of these letters is supposed to outstrip the rapidity of his own progress, and to reach Rome before himself and his impatient escort!

Early in the fourth century at least seven epistles attributed to Ignatius were in circulation, for Eusebius of Caesarea, who then flourished, distinctly mentions so many, and states to whom they were addressed. From Smyrna the martyr is said to have written four letters—one to the Ephesians, another to the Magnesians, a third to the Trallians, and a fourth to the Romans. From Troas he is reported to have written three additional letters—one to Polycarp, a second to the Smyrnaeans, and a third to the Philadelphians. [394:2] At a subsequent period eight more epistles made their appearance, including two to the Apostle John, one to the Virgin Mary, one to Maria Cassobolita, one to the Tarsians, one to the Philippians, one to the Antiochians, and one to Hero the deacon. Thus, no less than fifteen epistles claim Ignatius of Antioch as their author.

It is unnecessary to discuss the merits of the eight letters unknown to Eusebius. They were probably all fabricated after the time of that historian; and critics have long since concurred in rejecting them as spurious. Until recently, those engaged in the Ignatian controversy were occupied chiefly with the examination of the claims of the documents mentioned by the bishop of Caesarea. Here, however, the strange variations in the copies tended greatly to complicate the discussion. The letters of different manuscripts, when compared together, disclosed extraordinary discrepancies; for, whilst all the codices contained much of the same matter, a letter in one edition was, in some cases, about double the length of the corresponding letter in another. Some writers contended for the genuineness of the shorter epistles, and represented the larger

180

as made up of the true text extended by interpolations; whilst others pronounced the larger letters the originals, and condemned the shorter as unsatisfactory abridgments. [395:1] But, though both editions found most erudite and zealous advocates, many critics of eminent ability continued to look with distrust upon the text, as well of the shorter, as of the larger letters; whilst not a few were disposed to suspect that Ignatius had no share whatever in the composition of any of these documents.

In the year 1845 a new turn was given to this controversy by the publication of a Syriac version of three of the Ignatian letters. They were printed from a manuscript deposited in 1843 in the British Museum, and obtained, shortly before, from a monastery in the desert of Nitria in Egypt. The work was dedicated by permission to the Archbishop of Canterbury, and the views propounded in it were understood to have the sanction of the English metropolitan. [395:2] Dr Cureton, the editor, has since entered more fully into the discussion of the subject in his "Corpus Ignatianum" [395:3]—a volume dedicated to His Royal Highness the Prince Albert, in which the various texts of all the epistles are exhibited, and in which the claims of the three recently discovered letters, as the only genuine productions of Ignatius, are ingeniously maintained. In the Syriac copies, [396:1] these letters are styled "The Three Epistles of Ignatius, Bishop, and Martyr," and thus the inference is suggested that, at one time, they were the only three epistles in existence. Dr Cureton's statements have obviously made a great impression upon the mind of the literary public, and there seems at present to be a pretty general disposition in certain quarters [396:2] to discard all the other epistles as forgeries, and to accept those preserved in the Syriac version as the veritable compositions of the pastor of Antioch.

It must be obvious from the foregoing explanations that increasing light has wonderfully diminished the amount of literature which once obtained credit under the name of the venerable Ignatius. In the sixteenth century he was reputed by many as the author of fifteen letters: it was subsequently discovered that eight of them must be set aside as apocryphal: farther investigation convinced critics that considerable portions of the remaining seven must be rejected: and when the short text of these epistles was published, [396:3] about the middle of the seventeenth century, candid scholars confessed that it still betrayed unequivocal indications of corruption. [396:4] But even some Protestant writers of the highest rank stoutly upheld their claims, and the learned Pearson devoted years to the preparation of a defence of their authority. [397:1] His "Vindiciae Ignatianae" has long been considered by a certain party as unanswerable; and, though the publication has been read by very few, [397:2] the advocates of what are called "High-Church principles" have been reposing for nearly two centuries under the shadow of its reputation. The critical labours of Dr Cureton have somewhat disturbed their dream of security, as that distinguished scholar has adduced very good evidence to shew that about three-fourths of the matter [397:3] which the Bishop of Chester spent a considerable portion of his mature age in attempting to prove genuine, is the work of an impostor. It is now admitted by the highest authorities that four of the seven short letters must be given up as spurious; and the remaining three, which are addressed respectively to Polycarp, to the Ephesians, and to the Romans, and which are found in the Syriac version, are much shorter even than the short epistles which had already appeared under the same designations. The Epistle to Polycarp, the shortest of

181

the seven letters in preceding editions, is here presented in a still more abbreviated form; the Epistle to the Romans wants fully the one-third of its previous matter; and the Epistle to the Ephesians has lost nearly three-fourths of its contents. Nor is this all. In the Syriac version a large fragment of one of the four recently rejected letters reappears; as the new edition of the Epistle to the Romans contains two entire paragraphs to be found in the discarded letter to the Trallians.

It is only due to Dr Cureton to acknowledge that his publications have thrown immense light on this tedious and keenly agitated controversy. But, unquestionably, he has not exhausted the discussion. Instead of abruptly adopting the conclusion that the three letters of the Syriac version are to be received as genuine, we conceive he would have argued more logically had he inferred that they reveal one of the earliest forms of a gross imposture. We are persuaded that the epistles he has edited, as well as all the others previously published, are fictitious; and we shall endeavour to demonstrate, in the sequel of this chapter, that the external evidence in their favour is most unsatisfactory.

When discussing the testimonies from the writers of antiquity in their support, it is not necessary to examine any later witness than Eusebius. The weight of his literary character influenced all succeeding fathers, some of whom, who appear never to have seen these documents, refer to them on the strength of his authority. [398:1] In his "Ecclesiastical History," which was published as some think about A.D. 325, he asserts that Ignatius wrote seven letters, and from these he makes a few quotations. [398:2] But his admission of the genuineness of a correspondence, bearing date upwards of two hundred years before his own appearance as an author, is an attestation of very doubtful value. He often makes mistakes respecting the character of ecclesiastical memorials; and in one memorable case, of far more consequence than that now under consideration, he has blundered most egregiously; for he has published, as genuine, the spurious correspondence between Abgarus and our Saviour. [399:1] He was under strong temptations to form an unduly favourable judgment of the letters attributed to Ignatius, inasmuch as, to use the words of Dr Cureton, "they seemed to afford evidence to the apostolic succession in several churches, an account of which he professes to be one of the chief objects of his history." [399:2] His reference to them is decisive as to the fact of their existence in the early part of the fourth century; but those who adopt the views propounded in the "Corpus Ignatianum," are not prepared to bow to his critical decision; for, on this very occasion, he has given his sanction to four letters which they pronounce apocryphal.

The only father who notices these letters before the fourth century, is Origen. He quotes from them twice; [399:3] the citations which he gives are to be found in the Syriac version of the three epistles; [399:4] and it would appear from his writings that he was not acquainted with the seven letters current in the days of Eusebius. [399:5] Those to which he refers were, perhaps, brought under his notice when he went to Antioch on the invitation of Julia Mammaea, the mother of the Emperor; as, for reasons subsequently to be stated, it is probable that they were manufactured in that neighbourhood not long before his visit. If presented to him at that time by parties interested in the recognition of their claims, they were, under the circumstances, exactly such documents as were likely to impose upon him; for the student of Philo, and the author of the "Exhortation to Martyrdom," could not but admire the spirit of mysticism by which they are

182

pervaded, and the anxiety to die under persecution which they proclaim. Whilst, therefore, his quotation of these letters attests their existence in his time, it is of very little additional value. Again and again in his writings we meet with notices of apocryphal works unaccompanied by any intimations of their spuriousness. [400:1] He asserts that Barnabas, the author of the epistle still extant under his name, [400:2] was the individual mentioned in the Acts of the Apostles as the companion of Paul; and he frequently quotes the "Pastor" of Hermas [400:3] as a book given by inspiration of God. [400:4] Such facts abundantly prove that his recognition of the Ignatian epistles is a very equivocal criterion of their genuineness.

Attempts have been made to shew that two other writers, earlier than Origen, have noticed the Ignatian correspondence; and Eusebius himself has quoted Polycarp and Irenaeus as if bearing witness in its favour. Polycarp in early life was contemporary with the pastor of Antioch; and Irenaeus is said to have been the disciple of Polycarp; and, could it be demonstrated that either of these fathers vouched for its genuineness, the testimony would be of peculiar importance. But, when their evidence is examined, it is found to be nothing to the purpose. In the Treatise against Heresies, Irenaeus speaks, in the following terms, of the heroism of a Christian martyr—"One of our people said, when condemned to the beasts on account of his testimony towards God—As I am the wheat of God, I am also ground by the teeth of beasts, that I may be found the pure bread of God." [400:5] These words of the martyr are found in the Syriac Epistle to the Romans, and hence it has been inferred that they are a quotation from that letter. But it is far more probable that the words of the letter were copied out of Irenaeus, and quietly appropriated, by a forger, to the use of his Ignatius, with a view to obtain credit for a false document. The individual who uttered them is not named by the pastor of Lyons; and, after the death of that writer, a fabricator might put them into the mouth of whomsoever he pleased without any special danger of detection. The Treatise against Heresies obtained extensive circulation; and as it animadverted on errors which had been promulgated in Antioch, [401:1] it, no doubt, soon found its way into the Syrian capital. [401:2] But who can believe that Irenaeus describes Ignatius, when he speaks of "one of our people?" The martyr was not such an insignificant personage that he could be thus ignored. He was one of the most eminent Christians of his age—the companion of apostles—and the presiding minister of one of the most influential Churches in the world. Irenaeus is obviously alluding to some disciple who occupied a very different position. He is speaking, not of what the martyr wrote, but of what he said—not of his letters, but of his words. Any reader who considers the situation of Irenaeus a few years before he published this treatise, can have no difficulty in understanding the reference. He had witnessed at Lyons one of the most terrible persecutions the disciples ever had endured; and, in the letter to the Churches of Asia and Phrygia, he had graphically described its horrors. [401:3] He there tells how his brethren had been condemned to be thrown to wild beasts, and he records with simplicity and pathos the constancy with which they suffered. But in such an epistle he could not notice every case which had come under his observation, and he here mentions a new instance of the Christian courage of some believer unknown to fame, when he states—"one of our people when condemned to the beasts, said,

183

'As I am the wheat of God, I am also ground by the teeth of beasts, that I may be found the pure bread of God.'"

The Treatise against Heresies supplies the clearest evidence that Irenaeus was quite ignorant of the existence of the Ignatian epistles. These letters contain pointed references to the errorists of the early Church, and had they been known to the pastor of Lyons, he could have brought them to bear with most damaging effect against the heretics he assailed. Ignatius was no ordinary witness, for he had heard the truth from the lips of the apostles; he had spent a long life in the society of the primitive disciples; and he filled one of the most responsible stations that a Christian minister could occupy. The heretics boldly affirmed that they had tradition on their side, [402:1] and therefore the testimony of Ignatius, as of an individual who had received tradition at the fountain-head, would have been regarded by Irenaeus as all-important. And the author of the Treatise against Heresies was not slow to employ such evidence when it was in any way available. He plies his antagonists with the testimony of Clement of Rome, [402:2] of Polycarp [402:3] of Papias, [402:4] and of Justin Martyr. [402:5] But throughout the five books of his discussion he never adduces any of the words of the pastor of Antioch. He never throws out any hint from which we can infer that he was aware of the existence of his Epistles. [402:6] He never even mentions his name. Could we desire more convincing proof that he had never heard of the Ignatian correspondence?

The only other witness now remaining to be examined is Polycarp. It has often been affirmed that he distinctly acknowledges the authority of these letters; and yet, when honestly interrogated, he will be found to deliver quite a different deposition. But, before proceeding to consider his testimony, let us inquire his age when his epistle was written. It bears the following superscription:— "Polycarp, and the elders who are with him, to the Church of God which is at Philippi." At this time, therefore, though the early Christians paid respect to hoary hairs, and were not willing to permit persons without experience to take precedence of their seniors, Polycarp must have been at the head of the presbytery. But, at the death of Ignatius, when according to the current theory he dictated this letter, he was a young man of six and twenty. [403:1] Such a supposition is very much out of keeping with the tone of the document. In it he admonishes the widows to be sober; [403:2] he gives advice to the elders and deacons; [403:3] he expresses his great concern for Valens, an erring brother, who had once been a presbyter among them; [403:4] and he intimates that the epistle was written at the urgent request of the Philippians themselves. [403:5] Is it at all probable that Polycarp, at the age of six and twenty, was in a position to warrant him to use such a style of address? Are we to believe he was already so well known and so highly venerated that a Christian community on the other side of the Aegean Sea, and the oldest Church in all Greece, would apply to him for advice and direction? We must be prepared to admit all this, before we can acknowledge that his epistle refers to Ignatius of Antioch.

Let us attend now to that passage in the letter to the Philippians where he is supposed to speak of the Syrian pastor. "I exhort all of you that ye obey the word of righteousness, and exercise all patience, which ye have seen set forth before your eyes, not only in the blessed Ignatius, and Zosimus, and Rufus, but also in others of you." [404:1] These words would suggest to an ordinary reader that Polycarp is here speaking, not of Ignatius of Antioch, but of an Ignatius of

184

Philippi. If this Ignatius did not belong to the Philippian Church, why, when addressing its members, does he speak of Ignatius, Zosimus, Rufus, and "others of you?" Ignatius of Antioch could not have been thus described. But who, it may be asked, were Zosimus and Rufus here mentioned as fellow-sufferers with Ignatius? They were exactly in the position which the words of Polycarp literally indicate; they were men of Philippi; and, as such, they are commemorated in the "Martyrologies." [404:2] It is impossible, therefore, to avoid the conclusion that the Ignatius of Polycarp was also a Philippian.

It appears, then, that this testimony of the pastor of Smyrna has been strangely misunderstood. Ignatius, as is well known, was not a very uncommon name; and it would seem that several martyrs of the ancient Church bore this designation. Cyprian, for example, tells us of an Ignatius in Africa who was put to death for the profession of Christianity in the former part of the third century. [405:1] It is apparent from the words of Polycarp that there was also an Ignatius of Philippi, as well as an Ignatius of Antioch.

It may, however, be objected that the conclusion of this letter clearly points to Ignatius of Antioch, inasmuch as Polycarp there speaks apparently of Syria, and of some one interested about Ignatius who might shortly visit that country. [405:2] Some critics of high name have maintained that this portion of the epistle is destitute of authority, and that it has been added by a later hand to countenance the Ignatian forgery. [405:3] But every candid and discriminating reader may see that the charge is destitute of foundation. An Ignatian interpolator would not have so mismanaged his business. He would not have framed an appendix which, as we shall presently shew, testifies against himself. The passage to which such exception has been taken is unquestionably the true postscript of the letter, for it bears internal marks of genuineness.

In this postscript Polycarp says—"What you know certainly both of Ignatius himself, and of those who are with him, communicate." [405:4] Here is another proof that the Ignatius of Polycarp is not Ignatius of Antioch. The Syrian pastor is said to have been hurried with the utmost expedition to Rome that he might be thrown to the beasts before the approaching termination of the public spectacles; and it is reported that when he reached the great city, he was forthwith consigned to martyrdom. [406:1] But, though letters had been meanwhile passing between Philippi and Smyrna, this Ignatius is understood to be still alive. It would appear, too, that Zosimus and Rufus, previously named as his partners in tribulation, continued to be his companions. Polycarp, therefore, must be speaking of the "patience" of confessors who were yet "in bonds," [406:2] and not of a man who had already been devoured by the lions.

Other parts of this postscript are equally embarrassing to those who contend for the authority of the Ignatian Epistles. Thus, Polycarp says—"The Epistles of Ignatius which were sent to you by him, and whatever others we have by us, we have sent to you." [406:3] If these words apply to Ignatius of Antioch, it follows that he must have written several letters to the Philippians; and yet it in now almost universally admitted that even the one extant epistle addressed to them in his name is an impudent fabrication. Again, Polycarp states—"Ye have written to me, both ye and Ignatius, that when any one goes to Syria, he can carry my letters to you." [406:4] But no such suggestion is to be found, either in the Syriac version of the Three Epistles, or in the larger edition known to Eusebius. Could we desire clearer proof that Polycarp must here be speaking of another Ignatius, and another correspondence?

The words which we have last quoted deserve an attentive consideration. Were a citizen of New York, in the postscript of a letter to a citizen of London, to suggest that his correspondent should take an opportunity of writing to him, when any common friend went to Jerusalem, the Englishman might well feel perplexed by such a communication. Why should a letter from London to New York travel round by Palestine? Such an arrangement would not, however, be a whit more absurd than that seemingly pointed out in this postscript. Philippi and Smyrna were not far distant, and there was considerable intercourse between them; but Syria was in another quarter of the Empire, and Polycarp could have rarely found an individual passing to Antioch from "the chief city" of a "part of Macedonia," and travelling to and fro by Smyrna. This difficulty admits, however, of a very simple and satisfactory solution. We have no entire copy of the epistle in the original Greek, [407:1] and the text of the old Latin version in this place is so corrupt that it is partially unintelligible; [407:2] but as the context often guides us in the interpretation of a manuscript where it is blotted or torn, so here it may enable us to spell out the meaning. The insertion of one letter and the change of another in a single word [407:3] will render the passage intelligible. If we read Smyrna for Syria, the obscurity vanishes. Polycarp then says to the Philippians— "Ye have written to me, both ye and Ignatius, that, when any one goes to Smyrna, he can carry my letters to you." The postscript, thus understood, refers to the desire of his correspondents, that he should write frequently, and that, when a friend went from Philippi to Smyrna, he should not be permitted to return without letters.

As it can be thus shewn that the letter of Polycarp, when tested by impartial criticism, refuses to accredit the Epistles ascribed to Ignatius of Antioch, it follows that, with the single exception of Origen, no father of the first three centuries has noticed this correspondence. Had these letters, at the alleged date of their appearance, attracted such attention as they would themselves lead us to believe, is it possible that no writer for upwards of a century after the demise of their reputed author, would have bestowed upon them even a passing recognition? They convey the impression that, when Ignatius was on his way to Rome, all Asia Minor was moved at his presence—that Greece caught the infection of excitement—and that the Western capital itself awaited, with something like breathless anxiety, the arrival of the illustrious martyr. Strange, indeed, then that even his letter to the Romans is mentioned by no Western father until between two and three hundred years after the time of its assumed publication! Nor were Western writers wanting who would have sympathised with its spirit. It would have been quite to the taste of Tertullian, and he could have quoted it to shew that some of the peculiar principles of Montanism had been held by a man of the apostolic era. Nor can it be said that had the letter then been in existence, it was likely to have escaped his observation. He had lived for years in Rome, and we have good reason to believe that he was a presbyter of the Church of the Imperial city. A man of his inquiring spirit, and literary habits, must have been well acquainted with the Epistle had it obtained currency in Italy. But in not one of his numerous treatises does he ever speak of it, or even name its alleged author. [409:1] Hippolytus of Portus is another writer who might have been expected to know something of this production. He lived within a few miles of Rome, and he was conversant with the history of its Church and with its ecclesiastical memorials. He, as well as Tertullian, could have sympathised with

186

the rugged and ascetic spirit pervading the Ignatian correspondence. But, even in his treatise against all heresies, he has not fortified his arguments by any testimony from these letters. He had evidently never heard, of the now far famed documents. [409:2]

The conclusion to be drawn from these facts must be sufficiently obvious. The Ignatian Epistles began to be fabricated in the time of Origen; and the first edition of them appeared, not at Troas or Smyrna, but in Syria or Palestine. At an early period festivals were kept in honour of the martyrs; and on his natal day, [409:3] why should not the Church of Antioch have something to tell of her great Ignatius? The Acts of his Martyrdom were probably written in the former part of the third century—a time when the work of ecclesiastical forgery was rife [409:4]—and the Epistle to the Romans, which is inserted in these Acts, is in all likelihood of earlier date than any of the other letters. The Epistle to the Ephesians, perhaps, next made its appearance, and then followed the Epistle to Polycarp. These letters gradually crept into circulation as "The Three Epistles of Ignatius, Bishop, and Martyr." There is every reason to believe that, as edited by Dr Cureton, they are now presented to the public in their original language, as well as in their original form. Copies of these short letters are not known to be extant in any manuscript either Greek or Latin. Dr Cureton has not attempted any explanation of this emphatic fact. If the Epistle to the Romans, in its newly discovered form, is genuine, how does it happen that there are no previous traces of its existence in the Western Church? How are we to account for the extraordinary circumstance that the Church of Rome can produce no copy of it in either Greek or Latin? She had every reason to preserve such a document had it ever come into her possession; for, even considered as a pious fraud of the third century, the address "to her who sitteth at the head in the place of the country of the Romans," [410:1] is one of the most ancient testimonies to her early pre-eminence to be found in the whole range of ecclesiastical literature. Why should she have permitted it to be supplanted by an interpolated document? Can any man, who adopts the views of Dr Cureton, fairly answer such an inquiry?

It is plain that the mistake or corruption of a word in the postscript of the Epistle of Polycarp has had much to do with this Ignatian imposture. In some worn or badly written manuscript, Syria was perhaps read instead of Smyrna, and the false reading probably led to the incubation of the whole brood of Ignatian letters. The error, whether of accident or design, was adopted by Eusebius, [411:1] and from him passed into general currency. We may thus best account for the strange multiplication of these Ignatian epistles. It was clear that the Ignatius spoken of by Polycarp had written more letters than what first appeared, [411:2] and thus the epistles to the Smyrnaeans, the Magnesians, the Trallians, and the Philadelphians, in due time emerged into notice. At a subsequent date the letters to the Philippians, the Antiochians, the Virgin Mary, and others, were forthcoming.

The variety of forms assumed by this Ignatian fraud is not the least remarkable circumstance connected with its mysterious history. All the seven Epistles mentioned by Eusebius exist in a Longer and a Shorter Recension; whilst the Syriac version exhibits three of them in a reduced size, and a third edition. It is a curious fact that other spurious productions display similar transformations. "A great number of spurious or interpolated works of the early ages of Christianity," says Dr Cureton, "are found in two Recensions, a Shorter and a

187

Longer, as in the instance of the Ignatian Epistles. Thus, we find the two Recensions of the Clementines, the two Recensions of the Acts of St Andrew, ... the Acts of St Thomas, the Journeying of St John, the Letter of Pilate to Tiberius." [411:3] It is still more suspicious that some of these spurious writings present a striking similarity in point of style to the Ignatian Epistles. [412:1] The standard coin of the realm is seldom put into the crucible, but articles of pewter or of lead are freely melted down and recast according to the will of the modeller. We cannot add a single leaf to a genuine flower, but an artificial rose may be exhibited in quite another form by a fresh process of manipulation. Such, too, has been the history of ancient ecclesiastical records. The genuine works of the fathers have come down to us in a state of wonderful preservation; and comparatively few attempts have been made, by interpolation or otherwise, to interfere with their integrity; [412:2] but spurious productions seem to have been considered legitimate subjects for the exercise of the art of the fabricator; and hence the strange discrepancies in their text which have so often puzzled their editors.

CHAPTER III

THE IGNATIAN EPISTLES AND THEIR CLAIMS.
THE INTERNAL EVIDENCE

The history of the Ignatian Epistles may well remind us of the story of the Sibylline Books. A female in strange attire is said to have appeared before Tarquin of Rome, offering to sell nine manuscripts which she had in her possession; but the king, discouraged by the price, declined the application. The woman withdrew; destroyed the one-third of her literary treasures; and, returning again into the royal presence, demanded the same price for what were left. The monarch once more refused to come up to her terms; and the mysterious visitor retired again, and burnt the one-half of her remaining store. Her extraordinary conduct excited much astonishment; and, on consulting with his augurs, Tarquin was informed that the documents which she had at her disposal were most valuable, and that he should by all means endeavour to secure such a prize. The king now willingly paid for the three books, not yet committed to the flames, the full price originally demanded for all the manuscripts. The Ignatian Epistles have experienced something like the fate of those Sibylline oracles. In the sixteenth century, fifteen letters were brought out from beneath the mantle of a hoary antiquity, and offered to the world as the productions of the pastor of Antioch. Scholars refused to receive them on the terms required, and forthwith eight of them were admitted to be forgeries. In the seventeenth century, the seven remaining letters, in a somewhat altered form, again came forth from obscurity, and claimed to be the works of Ignatius. Again, discerning critics refused to acknowledge their pretensions; but curiosity was roused by this second apparition, and many expressed an earnest desire to obtain a sight of the real epistles. Greece, Syria, Palestine, and Egypt were ransacked in search of them, and at length three letters are found. The discovery creates general gratulation; it is confessed that four of the Epistles, so lately asserted to be genuine, are apocryphal; and it is boldly said that the three now forthcoming are above challenge. [414:1] But Truth still refuses to be compromised, and sternly disowns these claimants for her approbation. The internal evidence of these three epistles abundantly attests that, like the last three books of the Sibyl, they are only the last shifts of a grave imposture. [414:2]

The candid investigator, who compares the Curetonian version of the letters with that previously in circulation, must acknowledge that Ignatius, in his new dress, has lost nothing of his absurdity and extravagance. The passages of the Epistles, which were formerly felt to be so objectionable, are yet to be found here in all their unmitigated folly. Ignatius is still the same anti-evangelical formalist, the same puerile boaster, the same dreaming mystic, and the same crazy fanatic. These are weighty charges, and yet they can be substantiated. But we must enter into details, that we may fairly exhibit the spirit, and expose the falsehood of these letters.

I. The style of the Epistles is certainly not above suspicion. On the ground of style alone, it is, unquestionably, somewhat hazardous to pronounce a decisive judgment upon any document; but, if such an element is ever to be taken into consideration, it cannot, in this case, be overlooked. It is well known that, of the seven epistles mentioned by Eusebius, there was one which scholars of the highest reputation always regarded with extreme dubiety. In style it appeared to them so different from the rest of the letters, and so unlike what might have been expected from an apostolic minister, that some who were prepared to admit the genuineness of the other documents, did not hesitate to declare it a forgery. We allude to the Epistle to Polycarp. Even Archbishop Ussher and Cardinal Bona [415:1] concurred in its condemnation. It so happens, however, that it is one of the three letters recently re-edited; and it appears that, of the three, it has been the least altered. If then such a man as Ussher be considered a safe and sufficient judge of the value of an ancient ecclesiastical memorial, the Epistle to Polycarp, published by Dr Cureton, must be pronounced spurious. Their editor urges that the letters to the Ephesians and Romans, as expurgated in the Syriac version, now closely resemble the Epistle to Polycarp in style; and if so, may we not fairly infer that, had they been presented, in their new form, to the learned Primate of Armagh, consistency would have bound him to denounce them as also forgeries?

II. The way in which the Word of God is ignored in these Epistles argues strongly for their spuriousness. Every one acquainted with the early fathers must have observed their frequent use of the sacred records. A considerable portion of a chapter is sometimes introduced in a quotation. [416:1] Hence it has been remarked that were all the copies of the Bible lost and the writings of these fathers preserved, a large share of the Holy Volume might thus be recovered. But Ignatius would contribute nothing to the work of restoration; as, in the whole of the three letters, not a single verse of Scripture is given at length. They, no doubt, occasionally use Bible phraseology, as without it an ecclesiastical document could not well be written; but not one promise is quoted, and not one testimony from the Word is repeated for the edification of the faithful. [416:2] An apostolical

189

pastor on his way to martyrdom would have written very differently. He would have reminded his brethren of the "lively oracles," and he would have mentioned some of those precious assurances which now contributed to his own spiritual refreshment. He would have told them to have "no confidence in the flesh;" [416:3] to take unto themselves "the sword of the Spirit which is the Word of God;" [416:4] and to lay aside every weight and the sin which did so easily beset them, "looking unto Jesus." [416:5] But, instead of adopting such a course, this Ignatius addresses them in the style of a starched and straitlaced churchman. "Let your treasures," says he, "be your good works. Let your baptism be to you as armory." "Look to the bishop that God also may look upon you. I will be instead of the souls of those who are subject to the bishop, and the presbyters and the deacons." [416:6] What intelligent Christian can believe that a minister, instructed by Paul or Peter, and filling one of the most important stations in the apostolic Church, was verily such an ignorant driveller?

III. The chronological blunders in these Epistles betray their forgery. In the "Acts of the Martyrdom of Ignatius," he and Polycarp are represented as "fellow-scholars" of the Apostle John, [417:1] and the pastor of Smyrna is supposed to be, in point of age, at least as venerable a personage as the pastor of Antioch. The letter to Polycarp is evidently written under the same impression. Ignatius there says to him—"I praise God that I have been deemed worthy of thy countenance, which in God I long after." When these words are supposed to have been penned, Polycarp was only about six and twenty years of age; [417:2] and the Church of Smyrna, with which he was connected, did not occupy a very prominent place in the Christian commonwealth. Is it probable that a man of the mature faith and large experience of Ignatius would have thus addressed so youthful a minister? It also seems passing strange that the aged martyr should commit all the widows of the community to his special guardianship, and should think it necessary to add— "It is becoming to men and women who marry, that they marry by the counsel of the bishop." Was an individual, who was himself not much advanced beyond boyhood, the most fitting person to give advice as to these matrimonial engagements? A similar mistake as to age is made in the case of Onesimus, who is supposed to be bishop of Ephesus. This minister, who is understood to be mentioned in the New Testament. [417:3] is said at an early date to have been pastor of the Church of the metropolis of the Proconsular Asia; and the Ignatian forger obviously imagined that he was still alive when his hero passed through Smyrna on his way to the Western capital. But Onesimus perished in the Domitian persecution, [418:1] so that Ignatius is made to write to a Christian brother who had been long in his grave. [418:2] The fabricator proceeds more cautiously in his letter to the Romans. How marvellous that this old gentleman, who is willing to pledge his soul for every one who would submit to the bishop, does not find it convenient to name the bishop of Rome! The experiment might have been somewhat hazardous. The early history of the Roman Church was better known than that of any other in the world, and, had he here made a mistake, the whole cheat might have been at once detected. Though his erudition was so great that he could tell "the places of angels," [418:3] he evidently did not dare to commit himself by giving us a piece of earthly information, and by telling us who was at the head of the Church of the Great City in the ninth year of the reign of Trajan. But the same prudence does not prevail throughout the Epistle. He here obviously speaks of the Church of Rome, not as she existed a few years after the death of Clement, but of the same Church as she was known after the death of Victor. In the beginning of the second century the Church of the Syrian capital would not have acknowledged the precedence of her Western sister. On the fall of Jerusalem, the Church of Antioch was herself the first Christian community in the Empire. She had a higher antiquity, a more distinguished prestige, and perhaps a more numerous membership than any other Church in existence. In the Syrian metropolis the disciples had first been called Christians; there, Barnabas and Paul had been separated to the work to which the Lord had called them; there, Peter had preached; and there, prophets had laboured. But a century had brought about a wonderful change. The Church of Rome had meanwhile obtained the first place among Christian societies; and, before the middle of the third century, "the See of Peter" was honoured as the centre of catholic unity. Towards the close of the second century, many persons of rank and power joined her communion, [419:1] and her political influence was soon felt to be so formidable that even the Roman Emperor began to be jealous of the Roman bishop. [419:2] But the Ignatian forger did not take into account this ecclesiastical revolution. Hence he here incautiously speaks in the language of his own age, and writing "to her who sitteth at the head in the place of the country of the Romans," he says to her with all due humility—"I am not commanding you like Peter and Paul" [419:3]—"Ye have taught others"—"It is easy for you to do whatsoever you please."

IV. Various words in these Epistles have a meaning which they did not acquire until long after the time of Ignatius. Thus, the term employed in the days of the Apostles to denote purity, or chastity, here signifies celibacy. [419:4] Even in the commencement of the third century those who led a single life were beginning to be considered Christians of a superior type, as contrasted with those who were married; and clerical celibacy was becoming very fashionable. [420:1] The Ignatian fabricator writes under the influence of the popular sentiment. "The house of the Church" at Antioch, of which Paul of Samosata kept possession after his deposition about A.D. 269, [420:2] seems to have been a dwelling appropriated to the use of the ecclesiastical functionaries, [420:3] and the schemer who wrote the first draft of these letters evidently believed that the ministers of Christ should be a brotherhood of bachelors. Hence Ignatius is made thus to address Polycarp and his clergy—"Labour together one with another; make the struggle together one with another; run together one with another; suffer together one with another; sleep together one with another; rise together one with another." Polycarp and others of the elders of Smyrna were probably married; [420:4] so that some inconvenience might have attended this arrangement.

The word bishop is another term found in these Epistles, and employed in a sense which it did not possess at the alleged date of their publication. Every one knows that, in the New Testament, it does not signify the chief pastor of a Church; but, about the middle of the second century, as will subsequently appear, [421:1] it began to have this acceptation. Clement of Rome, writing a few years before the time of the martyrdom of Ignatius, uses the words bishop and presbyter interchangeably. [421:2] Polycarp, in his own Epistle, dictated, perhaps, forty years after the death of the Syrian pastor, still adheres to the same phraseology. In the Peshito version of the New Testament, executed probably in the former half of the second century, [421:3] the same terminology prevails.

191

[421:4] Ignatius, however, is far in advance of his generation. When new terms are introduced, or when new meanings are attached to designations already current, it seldom happens that an old man changes his style of speaking. He is apt to persevere, in spite of fashion, in the use of the phraseology to which he has been accustomed from his childhood. But Ignatius is an exception to all such experience, for he repeats the new nomenclature with as much flippancy as if he had never heard any other. [421:5] Surely this minister of Antioch must be worthy of all the celebrity he has attained, for he can not only carry on a written correspondence with the dead, but also anticipate by half a century even the progress of language!

V. The puerilities, vapouring, and mysticism of these letters proclaim their forgery. We would expect an aged apostolic minister, on his way to martyrdom, to speak as a man in earnest, to express himself with some degree of dignity, and to eschew trivial and ridiculous comparisons. But, when treating of a grave subject, what can be more silly or indecorous than such language as the following—"Ye are raised on high by the engine of Jesus Christ, which is the cross, and ye are drawn by the rope, which is the Holy Ghost, and your pulley is your faith." [422:1] Well may the Christian reader exclaim, with indignation, as he peruses these words, Is the Holy Ghost then a mere rope? Is that glorious Being who worketh in us to will and to do according to His own good pleasure, a mere piece of tackling pertaining to the ecclesiastical machinery, to be moved and managed according to the dictation of Bishop Ignatius? [422:2] But the frivolity of this impostor is equalled by his gasconade. He thus tantalises the Romans with an account of his attainments—"I am able to write to you heavenly things, but I fear lest I should do you an injury." .....

"I am able to know heavenly things, and the places of angels, and the station of powers that are visible and invisible." Where did he gather all this recondite lore? Certainly not from the Old or New Testament. May we not safely pronounce this man to be one who seeks to be wise above what is written, "intruding into those things which he hath not seen, vainly puffed up by his fleshly mind?" [422:3] He seems, indeed, to have himself had some suspicion that such was his character, for he says, again, to his brethren of the Western metropolis—"I know many things in God, but I moderate myself that I may not perish through boasting; for now it is becoming to me that I should fear the more abundantly, and should not look to those that puff me up." Let us now hear a specimen of the mysticism of this dotard. "There was hidden from the Ruler of this world the virginity of Mary, and the birth of our Lord, and the three mysteries of the shout, which were done in the quietness of God by means of the star, and here by the manifestation of the Son magic began to be dissolved." [423:1] Who can undertake to expound such jargon? What are we to understand by "the quietness of God?" Who can tell how "the three mysteries of the shout" were "done by means of the star?"

VI. The unhallowed and insane anxiety for martyrdom which appears throughout these letters is another decisive proof of their fabrication. He who was, in the highest sense, the Faithful Witness betrayed no fanatic impatience for the horrid tragedy of crucifixion; and, true to the promptings of his human nature, he prayed, in the very crisis of His agony—"O my Father, if it be possible, let this cup pass from me." [423:2] The Scriptures represent the most exalted saints as shrinking instinctively from suffering. In the prophecy announcing the

192

violent death of Peter, it is intimated that even the intrepid apostle of the circumcision would feel disposed to recoil from the bloody ordeal. "When thou shalt be old," said our Lord to him, "thou shalt stretch forth thy hands, and another shall gird thee, and carry thee whither thou wouldest not." [423:3] Paul mentions with thankfulness how, on a critical occasion, the Lord stood with him, and "delivered" him "out of the mouth of the lion." [423:4] Long after the apostolic age, the same spirit continued to be cherished, and hence we are told of Polycarp that, even when bowed down by the weight of years, he felt it right to retire out of the way of those who sought his destruction. The disciples, whom he had so long taught, took the same view of Christian duty; and accordingly, in the Epistle of the Church of Smyrna, which records his martyrdom, the conduct of those who "present themselves of their own accord to the trial" is emphatically condemned. [424:1] "We do not," say the believers of Smyrna, "commend those who offer themselves to persecution, seeing the gospel teaches no such thing." [424:2] But a man who is supposed to have enjoyed far higher advantages than Polycarp—a minister who is said to have been contemporary with all the apostles—a ruler of the Church who is understood to have occupied a far more prominent and influential position than the pastor of Smyrna—is exhibited in the legend of his martyrdom as appearing "of his own free will" [424:3] at the judgment-seat of the Emperor, and as manifesting the utmost anxiety to be delivered into the mouth of the lion. In the commencement of the second century the Churches of Rome and Ephesus doubtless possessed as much spiritual enlightenment as any other Churches in the world, and it is a libel upon their Christianity to suppose that they could have listened with any measure of complacency to the senseless ravings to be found even in the recent edition of the Ignatian Letters. [424:4] The writer is made to assure the believers in these great cities that he has an unquenchable desire to be eaten alive, and he beseeches them to pray that he may enjoy this singular gratification. "I hope," says he, "through your prayers that I shall be devoured by the beasts in Rome." [425:1] ... "I beg of you, be not with me in the love that is not in its season. Leave me, that I may be for the beasts, that by means of them I may be worthy of God.... With provoking provoke ye the beasts that they may be a grave for me, and may leave nothing of my body, that not even when I am fallen asleep may I be a burden upon any man.... I rejoice in the beasts which are prepared for me, and I pray that they may be quickly found for me, and I will provoke them that they may quickly devour me." [425:2] Every man jealous for the honour of primitive Christianity should be slow to believe that an apostolic preacher addressed such outrageous folly to apostolic Churches.

When reviewing the external evidence in support of these Epistles, we have had occasion to shew that they were probably fabricated in the former part of the third century. The internal evidence corroborates the same conclusion. Ecclesiastical history attests that during the fifty years preceding the death of Cyprian, [425:3] the principles here put forward were fast gaining the ascendency. As early as the days of Tertullian, ritualism was rapidly supplanting the freedom of evangelical worship; baptism was beginning to be viewed as an "armour" of marvellous potency; [425:4] the tradition that the great Church of the West had been founded by Peter and Paul was now extensively propagated; and there was an increasing disposition throughout the Empire to recognise the precedence of "her who sitteth at the head in the place of the country of the

Romans." It is apparent from the writings of Cyprian that in some quarters the "church system" was already matured. The language ascribed to Ignatius—"Be careful for unanimity, than which there is nothing more excellent" [426:1]—then expressed a prevailing sentiment. To maintain unity was considered a higher duty than to uphold truth, and to be subject to the bishop was deemed one of the greatest of evangelical virtues. Celibacy was then confounded with chastity, and mysticism was extensively occupying the place of scriptural knowledge and intelligent conviction. And the admiration of martyrdom which presents itself in such a startling form in these Epistles was one of the characteristics of the period. Paul taught that a man may give his body to be burned and yet want the spirit of the gospel; [426:2] but Origen does not scruple to describe martyrdom as "the cup of salvation," the baptism which cleanses the sufferer, the act which makes his blood precious in God's sight to the redemption of others. [426:3] Do not all these circumstances combined supply abundant proof that these Epistles were written in the time of this Alexandrian father? [426:4]

It is truly wonderful that men, such as Dr Cureton, have permitted themselves to be befooled by these Syriac manuscripts. It is still more extraordinary that writers, such as the pious and amiable Milner, [426:5] have published, with all gravity, the rhapsodies of Ignatius for the edification of their readers. It would almost appear as if the name Bishop has such a magic influence on some honest and enlightened Episcopalians, that when the interests of their denomination are supposed to be concerned, they can be induced to close their eyes against the plainest dictates of common sense and the clearest light of historical demonstration. In deciding upon matters of fact the spirit of party should never be permitted to interfere. Truth is the common property of the catholic Church; and no good and holy cause can require the support of an apocryphal correspondence.

It is no mean proof of the sagacity of the great Calvin, that, upwards of three hundred years ago, he passed a sweeping sentence of condemnation on these Ignatian Epistles. At the time, many were startled by the boldness of his language, and it was thought that he was somewhat precipitate in pronouncing such a decisive judgment. But he saw distinctly, and he therefore spoke fearlessly. There is a far more intimate connexion than many are disposed to believe between sound theology and sound criticism, for a right knowledge of the Word of God strengthens the intellectual vision, and assists in the detection of error wherever it may reveal itself. Had Pearson enjoyed the same clear views of gospel truth as the Reformer of Geneva, he would not have wasted so many precious years in writing a learned vindication of the nonsense attributed to Ignatius. Calvin knew that an apostolic man must have been acquainted with apostolic doctrine, and he saw that these letters must have been the productions of an age when the pure light of Christianity was greatly obscured. Hence he denounced them so emphatically: and time has verified his deliverance. His language respecting them has been often quoted, but we feel we cannot more appropriately close our observations on this subject than by another repetition of it. "There is nothing more abominable than that trash which is in circulation under the name of Ignatius." [428:1]

194

CHAPTER IV

THE GNOSTICS, THE MONTANISTS, AND THE MANICHAEANS

When Christianity made its appearance in the world, it produced a profound sensation. It spread on all sides with great rapidity; it was at once felt to be a religion for the common people; and some individuals of highly cultivated minds soon acknowledged its authority. For a time its progress was impeded by the persecutions of Nero and Domitian; but, about the beginning of the second century, it started upon a new career of prosperous advancement, and quickly acquired such a position that the most distinguished scholars and philosophers could no longer overlook its pretensions. In the reigns of Trajan and Hadrian, a considerable number of men of learning were already in its ranks; but it would appear that, on the whole, it derived very equivocal aid from the presence of these new adherents. Not a few of the literati who joined its standard attempted to corrupt it; and one hundred and twenty years after the death of the Apostle John, the champions of orthodoxy had to contend against no less than thirty-two heresies. [429:1]

Of those who now adulterated the gospel, the Gnostics were by far the most subtle, the most active, and the most formidable. The leaders of the party were all men of education; and as they were to be found chiefly in the large cities, the Church in these centres of influence was in no small degree embarrassed and endangered by their speculations. Some of the peculiarities of Gnosticism have been already noticed; [430:1] but as the second century was the period when it made most progress and awakened most anxiety, we must here advert more distinctly to its outlines. The three great antagonists of the gospel were the Grecian philosophy, the heathen mythology, and a degenerate Judaism; and Gnosticism may be described as an attempt to effect a compromise between Christianity and these rivals. As might have been expected, the attempt met with much encouragement; for many, who hesitated to accept the new religion unconditionally, were constrained to acknowledge that it exhibited many indications of truth and divinity; and they were, therefore, prepared to look on it with favour when presented to them in an altered shape and furnished with certain favourite appendages. The Gnostics called themselves believers; and their most celebrated teachers would willingly have remained in the bosom of the Church; but it soon appeared that their principles were subversive of the New Testament revelation; and they were accordingly excluded from ecclesiastical fellowship.

Gnosticism assumed a variety of forms, and almost every one of its teachers had his own distinctive creed; but, as a system, it was always known by certain remarkable features. It uniformly ignored the doctrine that God made all things out of nothing; [430:2] and, taking for granted the eternity of matter, it tried to account, on philosophical principles, for the moral and spiritual phenomena of the world which we inhabit. The Gnosis, [430:3] or knowledge, which it supplied, and from which it derived its designation, was a strange congeries of wild speculations. The Scriptures describe the Most High as humbling Himself to behold the things that are on earth, [431:1] as exercising a constant providence over all His creatures, as decking the lilies of the valley, and as numbering the very hairs of our heads; but Gnosticism exhibited the Supreme God as separated by an immeasurable interval from matter, and as having no direct communication with anything thus contaminated. The theory by means of which many of its adherents endeavoured to solve the problem of the origin of evil, [431:2] and to trace the connexion between the finite and the infinite, was not without ingenuity. They maintained that a series of Aeons, or divine beings, emanated from the Primal Essence; but, as sound issuing from a given point gradually becomes fainter until it is finally lost in silence, each generation of Aeons, as it receded from the great Fountain of Spiritual Existence, lost somewhat of the vigour of divinity; and at length an Aeon was produced without power sufficient to maintain its place in the Pleroma, or habitation of the Godhead. This scheme of a series of Aeons of gradually decreasing excellence was apparently designed to shew how, from an Almighty and Perfect Intelligence, a weak and erring being might be generated. There were Gnostics who carried the principle of attenuation so far as to teach that the inhabitants of the celestial world were distributed into no less than three hundred and sixty-five heavens, [431:3] each somewhat inferior to the other. According to some of these systems, an Aeon removed by many emanations from the source of Deity, and, in consequence, possessed of comparatively little strength, passed over the bounds of the Pleroma, and imparted life to matter. Another Power, called the Demiurge, was now produced, who, out of the materials already in existence, fashioned the present world. The human race, ushered, under such circumstances, upon the stage of time, are ignorant of the true God, and in bondage to corrupt matter. But all men are not in a state of equal degradation. Some possess a spiritual nature; some, a physical or animal nature; and some, only a corporeal or carnal nature. Jesus now appeared, and, at His baptism in the Jordan, Christ, a powerful Aeon, joined Him, that He might be fitted for redeeming souls from the ignorance and slavery in which they are entangled. This Saviour taught the human family the knowledge of the true God. Jesus was seized and led to crucifixion, and the Aeon Christ now departed from Him; but, as His body was composed of the finest ethereal elements, and was, in fact, a phantom, He did not really suffer on the accursed tree. Many of the Gnostics taught that there are two spheres of future enjoyment. They held that, whilst the spiritual natures shall be restored to the Pleroma, the physical or animal natures shall be admitted to an inferior state of happiness; and that such souls as are found to be incapable of purification shall be consigned to perdition or annihilation.

Whilst, according to all the Gnostics, the Demiurge, or maker of this world, is far inferior to the Supreme Deity, these system-builders were by no means agreed as to his position and his functions. Some of them regarded him as an Aeon of inferior intelligence who acted in obedience to the will of the Great God; others conceived that he was no other than the God of the Jews, who, in their estimation, was a Being of somewhat rugged and intractable character; whilst others contended that he was an Evil Power at open war with the righteous Sovereign of the universe. The Gnostics also differed in their views respecting matter. Those of them who were Egyptians, and who had been addicted to the study of the Platonic philosophy, held matter to be inert until impregnated with life; but the Syrians, who borrowed much from the Oriental theology, taught that it was eternally subject to a Lord, or Ruler, who had been perpetually at variance with the Great God of the Pleroma.

Two of the most distinguished Gnostic teachers who flourished in the early part of the second century were Saturninus of Antioch and Basilides of Alexandria. [433:1] Valentine, who appeared somewhat later, and who is supposed to have first excited attention at Rome about A.D. 140, was still more celebrated. He taught that in the Pleroma there are fifteen male and fifteen female Aeons, whom he professed to distinguish by their names; and he even proceeded to point out how they are distributed into married pairs. Some have supposed that certain deep philosophical truths were here concealed by him under the veil of allegory. As he, like others of the same class, conveyed parts of his Gnosis only into the ears of the initiated, it may be that the explanation of its symbols was reserved for those who were thus made acquainted with its secret wisdom. It has been alleged that he personified the attributes of God, and that the Aeons, whom he names and joins together, are simply those divine perfections which, when combined, are fitted to produce the most remarkable results. Thus, he associated Profundity and Thought, Intelligence and Truth, Reason and Life. [433:2] His system seems to have had many attractions for his age, as his disciples, in considerable numbers, were soon to be found both in the East and in the West.

When Valentine was at Rome, Marcion, another heresiarch of the same class, was also in the great metropolis. [433:3] This man is said to have been born in Pontus, and though some of the fathers have attempted to fix a stain upon his early reputation, his subsequent character seems to have been irreproachable. [434:1] There is reason to think that he was one of the most upright and amiable of the Gnostics. These errorists were charged by their orthodox antagonists with gross immorality; and there was often, perhaps, too much ground for the accusation; for some of them, such as Carpocrates, [434:2] avowed and encouraged the most shameless licentiousness; but others, such as Marcion, were noted for their ascetic strictness. All the more respectable Gnostics appear to have recommended themselves to public confidence by the austerity of their discipline. They enjoined rigorous fasting, and inculcated abstinence from wine, flesh-meat, and marriage. The Oriental theology, as well as the Platonic philosophy, sanctioned such a mode of living; and, therefore, those by whom it was practised were in a favourable position for gaining the public ear when they came forward as theological instructors.

Gnosticism may appear to us a most fantastic system; but, in the second century, it was dreaded as a very formidable adversary by the Church; and the extent to which it spread attests that it possessed not a few of the elements of popularity. Its doctrine of Aeons, or Divine Emanations, was quite in accordance with theories which had then gained extensive currency; and its account of the formation of the present world was countenanced by established modes of thinking. Many who cherished a hereditary prejudice against Judaism were gratified by the announcement that the Demiurge was no other than the God of the Israelites; and many more were flattered by the statement that some souls are essentially purer and better than others. [435:1] The age was sunk in sensuality; and, as it was the great boast of the heresiarchs that their Gnosis secured freedom from the dominion of the flesh, multitudes, who secretly sighed for deliverance, were thus induced to test its efficacy. But Gnosticism, in whatever form it presented itself, was a miserable perversion of the gospel. Some of its teachers entirely rejected the Old Testament; others reduced its history to a myth; whilst all mutilated and misinterpreted the writings of the apostles and evangelists. Like the Jewish Cabbalists, who made void the law of God by expositions which fancy suggested and tradition embalmed, the Gnostics by their far-fetched and unnatural comments, threw an air of obscurity over the plainest passages of the New Testament. Some of them, aware that they could derive no support from the inspired records, actually fabricated Gospels, and affixed to them the names of apostles or evangelists, in the hope of thus obtaining credit for the spurious documents. [435:2] Whilst Gnosticism in this way set aside the authority of the Word of God, it also lowered the dignity of the Saviour; and even when Christ was most favourably represented by it, He was but an Aeon removed at the distance of several intermediate generations from the Supreme Ruler of the universe. The propagators of this system altogether misconceived the scope of the gospel dispensation. They substituted salvation by carnal ordinances for salvation by faith; they represented man in his natural state rather as an ignoramus than a sinner; and, whilst they absurdly magnified their own Gnosis, they entirely discarded the doctrine of a vicarious atonement.

Shortly after the middle of the second century the Church began to be troubled by a heresy in some respects very different from Gnosticism. At that time the persecuting spirit displayed by Marcus Aurelius filled the Christians throughout the Empire with alarm, and those of them who were given to despondency began to entertain the most gloomy anticipations. An individual, named Montanus, who laid claim to prophetic endowments, now appeared in a village on the borders of Phrygia; and though he seems to have possessed a rather mean capacity, his discipline was so suited to the taste of many, and the predictions which he uttered so accorded with prevailing apprehensions, that he soon created a deep impression. When he first came forward in the character of a Divine Instructor he had been recently converted to Christianity; and he seems to have strangely misapprehended the nature of the gospel. When he delivered his pretended communications from heaven, he is said to have wrought himself up into a state of frenzied excitement. His countrymen, who had been accustomed to witness the ecstasies of the priests of Bacchus and Cybele, saw proofs of a divine impulse in his bodily contortions; and some of them at once acknowledged his extraordinary mission. By means of two wealthy female associates, named Priscilla and Maximilla, who also professed to utter prophecies, Montanus was enabled rapidly to extend his influence. His fame spread abroad on all sides; and, in a few years, he had followers in Europe and in Africa, as well as in Asia.

It cannot be said that this heresiarch attempted to overturn the creed of the Church. He was neither a profound thinker nor a logical reasoner; and he certainly had not maturely studied the science of theology. But he possessed an ardent temperament, and he seems to have mistaken the suggestions of his own fanaticism for the dictates of inspiration. The doctrine of the personal reign of Christ during the millennium appears to have formed a prominent topic in his ministrations. [437:1] He maintained that the discipline of the Church had been left incomplete by the apostles, and that he was empowered to supply a better code of regulations. According to some he proclaimed himself the Paraclete; but, if so, he most grievously belied his assumed name, for his system was far better fitted to induce despondency than to inspire comfort. All his precepts were

198

conceived in the sour and contracted spirit of mere ritualism. He insisted upon long fasts; he condemned second marriages; [437:2] he inveighed against all who endeavoured to save themselves by flight in times of persecution; and he asserted that such as had once been guilty of any heinous transgression should never again be admitted to ecclesiastical fellowship. Whilst he promulgated this stern discipline, he at the same time delivered the most dismal predictions, announcing, among other things, the speedy catastrophe of the Roman Empire. He also gave out that the Phrygian village where he ministered was to become the New Jerusalem of renovated Christianity.

But the Church was still too strongly impregnated with the free spirit of the gospel to submit to such a prophet as Montanus. He had, however, powerful advocates, and even a Roman bishop at one time gave him countenance. [437:3] Though his discipline commended itself to the morose and pharisaical, it was rejected by those who rightly understood the mystery of godliness. Several councils were held to discuss its merits, and it was emphatically condemned. [438:1] The signal failure of some of the Montanist predictions had greatly lowered the credit of the party; Montanus was pronounced a false prophet; and though the sect was supported by Tertullian, the most vigorous writer of the age, it gradually ceased to attract notice. [438:2]

About a century after the appearance of Montanus, another individual, in a more remote part of Asia, acquired great notoriety as a heresiarch. The doctrine of two First Principles, a good deity and an evil deity, had been long current in the East. Even in the days of Isaiah we may trace its existence, for there is a most significant allusion to it in one of his prophecies, in which Jehovah is represented as saying—"I am the Lord, and there is none else, there is no God beside me.... I form the light, and create darkness; I make peace, and create evil: I the Lord do all these things." [438:3] About the fifth century before Christ, the Persian theology had been reformed by Zoroaster, and the subordination of the two Principles to one God, the author of both, had been acknowledged as an article of the established creed. In the early part of the third century of the Christian era, there was a struggle between the adherents of the old and the new faith of Parsism; and the supporters of the views of Zoroaster had been again successful. But a considerable party still refused to relinquish the doctrine of the independence of the two Principles; and some of these probably joined themselves to Mani, a Persian by birth, who, in the latter half of the third century, became distinguished as the propagator of a species of mongrel Christianity. This man, who was born about A.D. 240, possessed genius of a high order. Though he finished his career when he was only thirty-seven years of age, he had already risen to eminence among his countrymen, and attracted the notice of several successive sovereigns. He is said to have been a skilful physician, an accomplished painter, and an excellent astronomer, as well as an acute metaphysician. Like Montanus, he laid claim to a divine commission, and alleged that he was the Paraclete who was promised to guide into all truth. He maintained that there are two First Principles of all things, light and darkness: God, in the kingdom of light, and the devil, in the kingdom of darkness, have existed from eternity. Mani thus accounted for the phenomena of the world around us—"Over the kingdom of light," said this heresiarch, "ruled God the Father, eternal in His sacred race, glorious in His might, the truth by His very essence.... But the Father himself, glorious in His majesty; incomprehensible in

His greatness, has united with Himself blessed and glorious Aeons, in number and greatness surpassing estimation." [439:1] He taught that Christ appeared to liberate the light from the darkness, and that he himself was now deputed to reveal the mysteries of the universe, and to assist men in recovering their freedom. He rejected a great portion of the canon of Scripture, and substituted certain writings of his own, which his followers were to receive as of divine authority. His disciples, called Manichees or Manichaeans, assumed the name of a Church, and were divided into two classes, the Elect and the Hearers. The Elect, who were comparatively few, were the sacred order. They alone were made acquainted with the mysteries, or more recondite doctrines, of the sect; they practised extreme abstinence; they subsisted chiefly upon olives; [439:2] and they lived in celibacy. They were not to kill, or even wound, an animal; neither were they to pull up a vegetable, or pluck a flower. The Hearers were permitted to share in the business and pleasures of the world, but they were taught only the elements of the system. After death, according to Mani, souls do not pass immediately into the world of light. They must first undergo a two-fold purification; one, by water in the moon; another, by fire in the sun.

Mani had provoked the enmity of the Magians; and, at their instigation, he was consigned, about A.D. 277, by order of the Persian monarch, to a cruel and ignominious death. But the sect which he had organized did not die along with him. His system was well fitted to please the Oriental fancy; its promise of a higher wisdom to those who obtained admission into the class of the Elect encouraged the credulity of the auditors; and, to such as had not carefully studied the Christian revelation, its hypothesis of a Good and of an Evil Deity accounted rather plausibly for the mingled good and evil of our present existence. The Manichaeans were exposed to much suffering in the country where they first appeared; and, as a sect of Persian origin, they were oppressed by the Roman government; but they were not extinguished by persecution, and, far down in the middle ages, they still occasionally figure in the drama of history.

Synods and councils may pass resolutions condemnatory of false doctrine, but it is somewhat more difficult to counteract the seduction of the principles from which heresies derive their influence. The Gnostics, the Montanists, and the Manichaeans, owed much of their strength to fallacies and superstitions with which the Christian teachers of the age were not fully prepared to grapple; and hence it was that, whilst the errorists themselves were denounced by ecclesiastical authority, a large portion of their peculiar leaven found its way into the Church, and gradually produced an immense change in its doctrine and discipline. A notice of the more important of the false sentiments and dangerous practices which the heretics propagated and the catholics adopted, may enable us to estimate the amount of the damage which the cause of truth now sustained.

The Montanists recognised the distinction of venial and mortal sins. They held that a professed disciple, who was guilty of what they called mortal sin, should never again be admitted to sealing ordinances. [441:1] It is apparent from the writings of Hippolytus, the famous bishop of Portus, that, in the early part of the third century, some of the most influential of the catholics cordially supported this principle. Soon afterwards it was openly advocated by a powerful party in the Church of Borne, and its rejection by Cornelius, then at the head of that community, led to the schism of Novatian. But the distinction of venial and mortal sins, upon which it proceeded, was even now generally acknowledged.

This distinction, which lies at the basis of the ancient penitential discipline, was already beginning to vitiate the whole catholic theology. Some sins, it is true, are more heinous than others, but the comparative turpitude of transgressions depends much on the circumstances in which they are committed. The wages of every sin is death, [441:2] and it is absurd to attempt to give a stereotyped character to any one violation of God's law by classing it, in regard to the extent of its guilt, in a particular category. Christianity regards sin, in whatever form, as a spiritual poison; and instead of seeking to solve the curious problem—how much of it may exist in the soul without the destruction of spiritual life?—it wisely instructs us to guard against it in our very thoughts, and to abstain from even the "appearance of evil." [442:1] "When lust," or indwelling depravity of any description, "has conceived, it bringeth forth sin; and sin, when it is finished, bringeth forth death." [442:2] Experience has demonstrated that the admission of the distinction of venial and mortal sins is most perilous to the best interests of the Christian community; for, whilst it is without foundation in the inspired statutebook, it must inevitably lead to the neglect or careless performance of many duties which the Most High has solemnly enjoined.

The Platonic philosophy taught the necessity of a state of purification after death; [442:3] and a modification of this doctrine formed part of at least some of the systems of Gnosticism. [442:4] It is inculcated by Tertullian, the great champion of Montanism; [442:5] and we have seen how, according to Mani, departed souls must pass, first to the moon, and then to the sun, that they may thus undergo a twofold purgation. Here, again, a tenet originally promulgated by the heretics, became at length a portion of the creed of the Church. The Manichaeans, as well as the Gnostics, rejected the doctrine of the atonement, and as faith in the perfection of the cleansing virtue of the blood of Christ declined, a belief in Purgatory became popular. [442:6]

The Gnostics, with some exceptions, insisted greatly on the mortification of the body; and the same species of discipline was strenuously recommended by the Montanists and the Manichaeans. All these heretics believed that the largest measure of future happiness was to be realised by those who practised the most rigid asceticism. Mani admitted that an individual without any extraordinary amount of self-denial, might reach the world of Light, for he held out the hope of heaven to his Hearers; but he taught that its highest distinctions were reserved for the Elect, who scrupulously refrained from bodily indulgence. The Church silently adopted the same principle; and the distinction between precepts and counsels, which was soon introduced into its theology, rests upon this foundation. By precepts are understood those duties which are obligatory upon all; by counsels, those acts, whether of charity or abstinence, which are expected from such only as aim at superior sanctity. [443:1] The Elect of the Manichaeans, as well as many of the Gnostics, [443:2] declined to enter into wedlock, and the Montanists were disposed to confer double honour on the single clergy. [443:3] The Church did not long stand out against the fascinations of this popular delusion. Her members almost universally caught up the impression that marriage stands in the way of the cultivation of piety; and bishops and presbyters, who lived in celibacy, began to be regarded as more holy than their brethren. This feeling continued to gain strength; and from it sprung that vast system of monasticism which spread throughout Christendom, with such amazing rapidity, in the fourth century.

It thus appears that asceticism and clerical celibacy have been grafted on Christianity by Paganism. Hundreds of years before the New Testament was written, Buddhism could boast of multitudes of monks and eremites. [443:4] The Gnostics, in the early part of the second century, celebrated the praises of a single life; and the Elect of the Manichaeans were all celibates. Meanwhile marriage was permitted to the clergy of the catholic Church. Well might the apostle exhort the disciples to beware of those ordinances which have "a shew of wisdom in will-worship, and humility, and neglecting of the body," [444:1] as the austerities of the cloister are miserable preparatives for the enjoyments of a world of purity and love. Christianity exhibited startling tokens of degeneracy when it attempted to nourish piety upon the spawn of the heathen superstitions. The gospel is designed for social and for active beings; as it hallows all the relations of life, it also teaches us how to use all the good gifts of God; and whilst celibacy and protracted fasting may only generate misanthropy and melancholy, faith, walking in the ways of obedience, can purify the heart, and induce the peace that passeth all understanding.

CHAPTER V

THE DOCTRINE OF THE CHURCH

For some time after the apostolic age, the doctrine of the Church remained unchanged. Those who had been taught the gospel by the lips of its inspired heralds could not have been readily induced to relinquish any of its distinctive principles. It must, indeed, be admitted that the purity of the evangelical creed was soon deteriorated by the admixture of dogmas suggested by bigotry and superstition; but, it may safely be asserted that, throughout the whole of the period now before us, its elementary articles were substantially maintained by almost all the Churches of the Empire.

Though there was still a pretty general agreement respecting the cardinal points of Christianity, it is not to be thought strange that the early writers occasionally expressed themselves in a way which would now be considered loose or inaccurate. Errorists, by the controversies they awakened, not unfrequently created much perplexity and confusion; but, in general, the truth eventually issued from discussion with renovated credit; for, in due time, acute and able advocates came forward to prove that the articles assailed rested on an impregnable foundation. During these debates it was found necessary to distinguish the different shades of doctrine by the establishment of a fixed terminology. The disputants were obliged to define with precision the expressions they employed; and thus various forms of speech ceased to have an equivocal meaning. But, in the second or third century, theology had not assumed a scientific form; and the language of orthodoxy was, as yet, unsettled. Hence, when treating of doctrinal questions, those whose views were substantially correct sometimes gave their sanction to the use of phrases which were afterwards condemned as the symbols of heterodoxy. [446:1]

About the beginning of the third century all adults who were admitted to baptism were required to make a declaration of their faith by assenting to some such formula as that now called "The Apostles' Creed;" [446:2] and though no general council had yet been held, the chief pastors of the largest and most influential Churches maintained, by letters, an official correspondence, and were in this way well acquainted with each other's sentiments. A considerable number of these epistles, or at least of extracts from them, are still extant; [446:3] and there is thus abundant proof of the unity of the faith of the ecclesiastical rulers. But, in treating of this subject, it is necessary to be more specific, and to notice particularly the leading doctrines which were now commonly received.

Before entering directly on this review, it is proper to mention that the Holy Scriptures were held in the highest estimation. The reading of them aloud formed part of the stated service of the congregations, and one or other of the passages brought, at the time, under the notice of the auditory, usually constituted the groundwork of the preacher's discourse. Their perusal was recommended to the laity; [447:1] the husband and wife talked of them familiarly as they sat by the domestic hearth; [447:2] and children were accustomed to commit them to memory. [447:3] As many of the disciples could not read, and as the expense of manuscripts was considerable, copies of the sacred books were not in the hands of all; but their frequent rehearsal in the public assemblies made the multitude familiar with their contents, and some of the brethren possessed an amount of acquaintance with these records which, even at the present day, would be deemed most extraordinary. Eusebius speaks of several individuals who could repeat, at will, any required passage from either the Old or New Testament. On a certain occasion the historian happened to be present when one of these walking concordances poured forth the stores of his prodigious memory. "I was struck with admiration," says he, "when I first beheld him standing amidst a large crowd, and reciting certain portions of Holy Writ. As long as I could only hear his voice, I supposed that he was reading, as is usual in the congregations; but, when I came close up to him, I discovered that, employing only the eyes of his mind, he uttered the divine oracles like some prophet." [447:4]

It was not extraordinary that the early Christians were anxious to treasure up Scripture in the memory, for in all matters of faith and practice the Written Word was regarded as the standard of ultimate appeal. No human authority whatever was deemed equal to the award of this divine arbiter. "They who are labouring after excellency," says a father of this period, "will not stop in their search after truth, until they have obtained proof of that which they believe from the Scriptures themselves." [448:1] Nor was there any dispute as to the amount of confidence to be placed in the language of the Bible. The doctrine of its plenary inspiration—a doctrine which many in modern times either openly or virtually deny—was now received without abatement or hesitation. Even Origen, who takes such liberties when interpreting the sacred text, admits most fully that it is all of divine dictation. "I believe," says he, "that, for those who know how to draw virtue from the Scriptures, every letter in the oracles of God has its end and its work, even to an iota and particle of a letter. And, as among plants, there is not one but has its peculiar virtue, and as they only who have a knowledge of botanical science can tell how each should be prepared and applied to a useful purpose; so it is that he who is a holy and spiritual botanist of the Word of God, by gathering up each atom and element will find the virtue of that Word, and acknowledge that there is nothing in all that is written that is superfluous." [448:3]

It has been already stated [448:3] that little difference of sentiment existed in the early Church respecting the books to be included in the canon of the New Testament. All, with the exception of the Gnostics and some other heretics, recognized the claims of the four Gospels, [448:4] of the Acts of the Apostles, of the Epistles of Paul, of the First Epistle of Peter, and of the First Epistle of John. Though, for a time, some Churches hesitated to acknowledge the remaining epistles, their doubts seem to have been gradually dissipated. At first the genuineness of the Apocalypse was undisputed; but, after the rise of the Montanists, who were continually quoting it in proof of their theory of a millennium, some of their antagonists foolishly questioned its authority. At an early period two or three tracts [449:1] written by uninspired men were received as Scripture by a number of Churches. They were never, however, generally acknowledged; and at length, by common consent, they were excluded from the canon. [449:2]

The code of heathen morality supplied a ready apology for falsehood, [449:3] and its accommodating principles soon found too much encouragement within the pale of the Church. Hence the pious frauds which were now perpetrated. Various works made their appearance with the name of some apostolic man appended to them, [449:4] their fabricators thus hoping to give currency to opinions or to practices which might otherwise have encountered much opposition. At the same time many evinced a disposition to supplement the silence of the Written Word by the aid of tradition. But though the writers of the period sometimes lay undue stress upon the evidence of this vague witness, they often resort to it merely as an offset against statements professedly derived from the same source which were brought forward by the heretics; and they invariably admit that the authority of Scripture is entitled to override the authority of tradition. "The Lord in the Gospel, reproving and rebuking, declares," says Cyprian, "ye reject the commandment of God that ye may keep your own tradition. [450:1] .... Custom should, not be an obstacle that the truth prevail not and overcome, for a custom without truth is error inveterate." [450:2] "What obstinacy is that, or what presumption, to prefer human tradition to divine ordinances, and not to perceive that God is displeased and provoked, as often as human tradition relaxes and sets aside the divine command." [450:3] During this period—the uncertainty of any other guide than the inspired record was repeatedly demonstrated; for, though Christians were removed at so short a distance from apostolic times, the traditions of one Church sometimes diametrically contradicted those of another. [450:4]

There is certainly nothing like uniformity in the language employed by the Christian writers of this era when treating of doctrinal subjects; and yet their theology seems to have been essentially the same. All apparently admit the corruption of human nature. Justin Martyr speaks of a "concupiscence in every man, evil in all its tendencies, and various in its nature," [450:5] whilst Tertullian mentions original sin under the designation of "the vice of our origin." [450:6] Our first parent, says he, "having been seduced into disobedience by Satan was

204

delivered over to death, and transmitted his condemnation to the whole human race which was infected from his seed." [450:7] Though the ancient fathers occasionally describe free will in terms which apparently ignore the existence of indwelling depravity, [451:1] their language should not be too strictly interpreted, as it only implies a strong protest against the heathen doctrine of fate, and a recognition of the principle that man is a voluntary agent. Thus it is that Clemens Alexandrinus, one of the writers who asserts most decidedly the freedom of the will, admits the necessity of a new birth unto righteousness. "The Father," says he, "regenerates by the Spirit unto adoption all who flee to Him." [451:2] "Since the soul is moved of itself, the grace of God demands from it that which it has, namely, a ready temper as its contribution to salvation. For the Lord wishes that the good which He confers on the soul should be its own, since it is not without sensation, so that it should be impelled like a body." [451:3]

No fact is more satisfactorily attested than that the early disciples rendered divine honours to our Saviour. In the very beginning of the second century, a heathen magistrate, who deemed it his duty to make minute inquiries respecting them, reported to the Roman Emperor that, in their religious assemblies, they sang "hymns to Christ as to a God." [451:4] They were reproached by the Gentiles, as well as by the Jews, for worshipping a man who had been crucified. [451:5] When the accusation was brought against them, they at once admitted its truth, and they undertook to shew that the procedure for which they were condemned was perfectly capable of vindication. [452:1] In the days of Justin Martyr there were certain professing Christians, probably the Ebionites, [452:2] who held the simple humanity of our Lord, but that writer represents the great body of the disciples as entertaining very different sentiments. "There are some of our race," says he, "who confess that He was the Christ, but affirm that He was a man born of human parents, with whom I do not agree, neither should I, even if very many, who entertain the same opinion as myself, were to say so; since we are commanded by Christ to attend, not to the doctrines of men, but to that which was proclaimed by the blessed prophets, and taught by Himself." [452:3]

When Justin here expresses his dissent from those who described our Lord as "a man born of human parents," he obviously means no more than that he is not a Humanitarian, for, in common with the early Church, he held the doctrine of the two natures in Christ. The fathers who now flourished, when touching upon the question of the union of humanity and deity in the person of the Redeemer, do not, it is true, express themselves always with as much precision as writers who appeared after the Eutychian controversy in the fifth century; but they undoubtedly believed that our Lord was both God and man. [453:1] Even already the subject was pressed on their attention by various classes of errorists who were labouring with much assiduity to disseminate their principles. The Gnostics, who affirmed that the body of Jesus was a phantom, shut them up to the necessity of shewing that He really possessed all the attributes of a human being; whilst, in meeting objectors from a different quarter, they were compelled to demonstrate that He was also the Jehovah of the Old Testament. The Ebionites were not the only sectaries who taught that Jesus was a mere man. The same doctrine was inculcated by Theodotus, a native of Byzantium, who settled at Rome about the end of the second century. This individual, though by trade a tanner, possessed no small amount of learning, and created some disturbance in the Church of the Western capital by the novelty and boldness of his speculations.

In the end he is said to have been excommunicated by Victor, the Roman bishop. Some time afterwards, his sentiments were adopted by Artemon, whose disciples, named Artemonites, elected a bishop of their own, [453:2] and existed for some time at Rome as a distinct community.

But by far the most distinguished of these ancient impugners of the proper deity of the Messiah was the celebrated Paul of Samosata, who flourished shortly after the middle of the third century. Paul occupied the bishopric of Antioch, the second see in Christendom; and was undoubtedly a man of superior talent. According to his views, the Divine Logos is not a distinct Person, but the Reason of God; and Jesus was the greatest of the sons of men simply because the Logos dwelt in Him after a higher manner, or more abundantly, than in any other of the posterity of Adam. [454:1] But though this prelate had great wealth, influence, and eloquence, his heterodoxy soon raised a storm of opposition which he could not withstand. The Christians of Antioch in the third century could not quietly tolerate the ministrations of a preacher who insinuated that the Word is not truly God. He appears to have possessed consummate address, and when first arraigned, his plausible equivocations and sophistries imposed upon his judges; but, at a subsequent council, held about A.D. 269 in the metropolis of Syria, he was so closely pressed by Malchion, one of his own presbyters, that he was obliged reluctantly to acknowledge his real sentiments. He was, in consequence, deposed from his office by a unanimous vote of the Synod. A circular letter [454:2] announcing the decision was transmitted to the leading pastors of the Church all over the Empire, and this ecclesiastical deliverance seems to have received their universal sanction. [454:3]

The theological term translated Trinity, [454:4] was in use as early as the second century; for, about A.D. 180, it is employed by Theophilus, who is supposed to have been one of the predecessors of Paul of Samosata in the Church of Antioch. [454:5] Speaking of the formation of the heavenly bodies on the fourth day of creation, as described in the first chapter of Genesis, this writer observes—"The three days which preceded the luminaries are types of the Trinity, [454:6] of God, and His Word, and His Wisdom." Here, as elsewhere in the works of the fathers of the early Church, the third person of the Godhead is named under the designation of Wisdom. [455:1] Though this is the first mention of the word Trinity to be found in any ecclesiastical document now extant, it is plain that the doctrine is of far higher antiquity. Justin Martyr repeatedly refers to it, and Athenagoras, who flourished in the reign of Marcus Aurelius, treats of it with much clearness. "We speak," says he, "of the Father as God, and the Son as God, and the Holy Ghost, shewing at the same time their power in unity, and their distinction in order." [455:2] "We who look upon this present life as worth little or nothing, and are conducted through it by the sole principle of knowing God and the Word proceeding from Him, of knowing what is the unity of the Son with the Father, what the Father communicates to the Son, what is the Spirit, what is the union of this number of Persons, the Spirit, the Son, and the Father, and in what way they who are united are divided—shall we not have credit given us for being worshippers of God?" [455:3]

The attempts made in the latter half of the second century to pervert the doctrine of Scripture relative to the Father, Son, and Holy Spirit, probably led to the appearance of the word Trinity in the ecclesiastical nomenclature; for, when controversy commenced, some such symbol was required to prevent the necessity of constant and tedious circumlocution. One of the most noted of the parties dissatisfied with the ordinary mode of speaking respecting the Three Divine Persons, and desirous of changing the current creed, was Praxeas, a native of Asia Minor. After having acquired much credit by his fortitude and courage in a time of persecution, he had also signalised himself by his zeal against the Montanists. He now taught that the Son and Holy Ghost are not distinct Persons, but simply modes or energies of the Father; and as those who adopted his sentiments imagined that they thus held more strictly than others the doctrine of the existence of a single Ruler of the universe, they styled themselves Monarchians. [456:1] According to their views the first and second Persons of the Godhead are identical; and, as it apparently followed from this theory, that the Father suffered on the cross, they received the name of Patripassians. [456:2] Praxeas travelled from Asia Minor to Rome, and afterwards passed over into Africa, where he was strenuously opposed by the famous Tertullian. Another individual, named Noetus, attracted some notice about the close of the second century by the peculiarity of his speculations in reference to the Godhead. "Noetus," says a contemporary, "calls the same both Son and Father, for he speaks thus—'When the Father had not been born, He was rightly called Father, but when it pleased Him to undergo birth, then by birth He became the Son of Himself, and not of another.' Thus he professes to establish the principle of Monarchianism." [456:3] But, perhaps, the attempts of Sabellius to modify the established doctrine made the deepest impression. This man, who was an ecclesiastic connected with Ptolemais in Africa, [456:4] maintained that there is no foundation for the ordinary distinction of the Persons of the Trinity, and that the terms Father, Son, and Holy Spirit, merely indicate different manifestations of the Supreme Being, or different phases under which the one God reveals Himself. From him the doctrine of those who confound the Persons of the Godhead still bears the name of Sabellianism.

It has been sometimes said that the Church borrowed its idea of a Trinity from Plato, but this assertion rests upon no historical basis. Learned men have found it exceedingly difficult to give anything like an intelligible account of the Trinity of the Athenian philosopher, [457:1] and it seems to have had only a metaphysical existence. It certainly had nothing more than a fanciful and verbal resemblance to the Trinity of Christianity. Had the doctrine of the Church been derived from the writings of the Grecian sage, it would not have been inculcated with so much zeal and unanimity by the early fathers. Some of them were bitterly opposed to Platonism, and yet, though none denounced it more vehemently than Tertullian, [457:2] we cannot point to any one of them who speaks of the Three Divine Persons more clearly or copiously. The heretic thinks, says he, "that we cannot believe in one God in any other way than if we say that the very same Person is Father, Son, and Holy Ghost.... These persons assume the number and arrangement of the Trinity to be a division of the Unity; whereas the Unity, which derives a Trinity from itself, is not destroyed by it, but has its different offices performed. They, therefore, boast that two and three Gods are preached by us, but that they themselves are worshippers of one God; as if the Unity, when improperly contracted, did not create heresy, and a Trinity, when properly considered, did not constitute truth." [457:3]

Every one at all acquainted with the ecclesiastical literature of this period must acknowledge that the disciples now firmly maintained the doctrine of the

Atonement. The Gnostics and the Manichaeans discarded this article from their systems, as it was entirely foreign to the spirit of their philosophy; but, though the Church teachers enter into scarcely any explanation of it, by attempting to shew how the violated law required a propitiation, they proclaim it as a glorious truth which should inspire all the children of God with joy and confidence. Clemens Alexandrinus gives utterance only to the common faith when he declares—"Christians are redeemed from corruption by the blood of the Lord." "The Word poured forth His blood for us to save human nature." "The Lord gave Himself a victim for us." [458:1] The early writers also mention faith as the means by which we are to appropriate the benefits of the Redeemer's sacrifice. Thus, Justin Martyr represents Christ as "purifying by His blood those who believe on Him." [458:2] Clemens Alexandrinus, in like manner, speaks of "the one mode of salvation by faith in God," [458:3] and says that "we have believed in God through the voice of the Word." [458:4] In the "Letter to Diognetus" the doctrine of justification by faith through the imputed righteousness of the Saviour is beautifully exhibited. "For what else," says the writer, "could cover our sins but His righteousness? In whom was it a possible that we, the lawless and the unholy, could be justified, save by the Son of God alone? Oh sweet exchange! oh unsearchable wisdom! oh unexpected benefits! that the sin of many should be hidden by One righteous, and the righteousness of One justify many sinners." [458:5]

The Church of the second and third centuries was not agitated by any controversies relative to grace and predestination. Few, probably, were disposed to indulge in speculations on these subjects; and some of the ecclesiastical writers, in the heat of controversial discussion, are occasionally tempted to make use of language which it would be difficult to reconcile with the declarations of the New Testament. All of them, however, either explicitly or virtually, admit the necessity of grace; and some distinctly enunciate the doctrine of election. "We stand in especial need of divine grace, and right instruction, and pure affection," says Clemens Alexandrinus, "and we require that the Father should draw us towards himself." "God, who knows the future as if it was already present, knows the elect according to His purpose even before the creation." [459:1] "Your power to do," says Cyprian, "will be according to the increase of spiritual grace.... What measure we bring thither of faith to hold, so much do we drink in of grace to inundate. Hereby is strength given." [459:2] It is worthy of note that those writers, who speak most decidedly of the freedom of the will, also most distinctly proclaim their faith in the perfection of the Divine Sovereignty. Thus, Justin Martyr urges, as a decisive proof of the impious character of their theology, that the heathen philosophers repudiated the doctrine of a particular providence; [459:3] and all the ancient fathers are ever ready to recognise the superintending guardianship of God in the common affairs of life.

But though the creed of the Church was still to some extent substantially sound, it must be admitted that it was already beginning to suffer much from adulteration. One hundred years after the death of the Apostle John, spiritual darkness was fast settling down upon the Christian community; and the fathers, who flourished towards the commencement of the third century, frequently employ language for which they would have been sternly rebuked, had they lived in the days of the apostles and evangelists. Thus, we find them speaking of "sins cleansed by repentance," [460:1] and of repentance as "the price at which the

Lord has determined to grant forgiveness." [460:2] We read of "sins cleansed by alms and faith," [460:3] and of the martyr, by his sufferings, "washing away his own iniquities." [460:4] We are told that by baptism "we are cleansed from all our sins," and "regain that Spirit of God which Adam received at his creation and lost by his transgression." [460:5] "The pertinacious wickedness of the Devil," says Cyprian, "has power up to the saving water, but in baptism he loses all the poison of his wickedness." [460:6] The same writer insists upon the necessity of penance, a species of discipline unknown to the apostolic Church, and denounces, with terrible severity, those who discouraged its performance. "By the deceitfulness of their lies," says he, they interfere, "that satisfaction be not given to God in His anger..... All pains are taken that sins be not expiated by due satisfactions and lamentations, that wounds be not washed clean by tears." [460:7] It may be said that some of these expressions are rhetorical, and that those by whom they were employed did not mean to deny the all-sufficiency of the Great Sacrifice; but had these fathers clearly apprehended the doctrine of justification by faith in Christ, they would have recoiled from the use of language so exceedingly objectionable.

There are many who imagine that, had they lived in the days of Tertullian or of Origen, they would have enjoyed spiritual advantages far higher than any to which they have now access. But a more minute acquaintance with the ecclesiastical history of the third century might convince them that they have no reason to complain of their present privileges. The amount of material light which surrounds us does not depend on our proximity to the sun. When our planet is most remote from its great luminary, we may bask in the splendour of his effulgence; and, when it approaches nearer, we may be involved in thick darkness. So it is with the Church. The amount of our religious knowledge does not depend on our proximity to the days of primitive Christianity. The Bible is the sun of the spiritual firmament; and this divine illuminator, like the glorious orb of day, pours forth its light with equal brilliancy from generation to generation. The Church may retire into "chambers of imagery" erected by her own folly; and there, with the light shut out from her, may sink into a slumber disturbed only, now and then, by some dream of superstition; or, with the light still shining on her, her eye may be dim or disordered, and she may stumble at noonday. But the light is as pure as in the days of the apostles; and, if we have eyes to profit by it, we may "understand more than the ancients." The art of printing has supplied us with facilities for the study of the Scriptures which were denied to the fathers of the second century; and the ecclesiastical documents, relative to that age, which have been transmitted to us from antiquity, contain, perhaps, the greater part of even the traditionary information which was preserved in the Church. If we are only "taught of God," we are in as good a position for acquiring a correct acquaintance with the way of salvation as was Polycarp or Justin Martyr. What an encouragement for every one to pray—"Open thou mine eyes, that I may behold wondrous things out of thy law. I am a stranger in the earth: hide not thy commandments from me!" [461:11]

SECTION III

THE WORSHIP AND CONSTITUTION OF THE CHURCH

CHAPTER I

THE WORSHIP OF THE CHURCH

The religion of the primitive Christians must have appeared exceedingly strange to their pagan contemporaries. The heathen worship was little better than a solemn show. Its victims adorned with garlands, its incense and music and lustral water, its priests arrayed in white robes, and its marble temples with gilded roofs, were fitted, rather to fascinate the senses, than to improve the heart or expand the intellect. Even the Jewish ritual, in the days of its glory, must have had a powerful effect on the imagination. As the Israelites assembled from all quarters at their great festivals—as they poured in thousands and tens of thousands into the courts of their ancient sanctuary—as they surveyed the various parts of a structure which was one of the wonders of the world—as they beheld the priests in their holy garments—and as they gazed on the high priest himself, whose forehead glittered with gold whilst his breastplate sparkled with precious stones—they must have felt that they mingled in a scene of extraordinary splendour. But, when Christianity made its appearance in the world, it presented none of these attractions. Its adherents were stigmatized as atheists, [463:1] because they had no altars, no temples, and no sacrifices. They held their meetings in private dwellings; their ministers wore no peculiar dress; and, by all who sought merely the gratification of the eye or of the ear, the simple service in which they engaged must have been considered very bald and uninteresting. But they rejoiced exceedingly in its spiritual character, as they felt that they could thus draw near to God, and hold sweet and refreshing communion with their Father in heaven.

It is probable that, during a considerable part of the second century, the Christians had comparatively few buildings set apart for public worship. At a time when they congregated to celebrate the rites of their religion at night or before break of day, it is not to be supposed that they were anxious to obtrude their conventicles on the notice of their persecutors. But as they increased in numbers, and as the State became somewhat more indulgent, they gradually acquired confidence; and, about the beginning of the third century, the form of their ecclesiastical structures seems to have been already familiar to the eyes of the heathen. [463:2] Shortly after that period, their meeting-houses in Rome were well known; and, in the reign of Alexander Severus, they ventured to dispute with one of the city trades the possession of a piece of ground on which they were

210

desirous to erect a place of worship. [463:3] When the case came for adjudication before the Imperial tribunal, the sovereign decided in their favour, and thus virtually placed them under the shield of his protection. When the Emperor Gallienus, about A.D. 260, issued an edict of toleration, church architecture advanced apace, and many of the old buildings, which were now falling into decay, were superseded by edifices at once more capacious and more tasteful. The Christians at this time began to emulate the magnificence of the heathen temples, and even to ape their arrangements. Thus it is that some of our churches at the present day are nearly fac-similes of the ancient religious edifices of paganism. [464:1]

In addition to the administration of baptism and the Lord's Supper, the worship of the early Church consisted of singing, prayer, reading the Scriptures, and preaching. In the earliest notice of the Christians of the second century which occurs in any pagan writer, their psalmody, with which they commenced their religious services, [464:2] is particularly mentioned; for, in his celebrated letter to the Emperor Trajan, Pliny states that they met together, before the rising of the sun, to "sing hymns to Christ as to a God." It is highly probable that the "hymns" here spoken of were the Psalms of the Old Testament. Many of these inspired effusions celebrate the glories of Immanuel, and as, for obvious reasons, the Messianic Psalms would be used more frequently than any others, it is not strange that the disciples are represented as assembling to sing praise to Christ. But it would appear that the Church at this time was not confined to the ancient Psalter. Hymns of human composition were occasionally employed; [464:3] and one of these, to be found in the writings of Clement of Alexandria, [464:4] was, perhaps, sung in the early part of the third century by the Christians of the Egyptian capital. Influential bishops sometimes introduced them by their own authority, but the practice was regarded with suspicion, and seems to have been considered irregular. Hence Paul of Samosata, in the Council of Antioch held A.D. 269, was blamed for discontinuing the Psalms formerly used, and for establishing a new and very exceptionable hymnology. [465:1]

In the church, as well as in the synagogue, the whole congregation joined in the singing; [465:2] but instrumental music was never brought into requisition. The early Christians believed that the organs of the human voice are the most appropriate vehicles for giving utterance to the feelings of devotion; and viewing the lute and the harp as the carnal ordinances of a superannuated dispensation, they rejected their aid in the service of the sanctuary. Long after this period one of the most eminent of the ancient fathers describes the music of the flutes, sackbuts, and psalteries of the temple worship as only befitting the childhood of the Church. "It was," says he, "permitted to the Jews, as sacrifice was, for the heaviness and grossness of their souls. God condescended to their weakness, because they were lately drawn off from idols; but now, instead of instruments, we may use our own bodies to praise Him withal." [465:3]

The account of the worship of the Church, given by a Christian writer who flourished about the middle of the second century, is exceedingly instructive. "On the day which is called Sunday," says Justin Martyr, "there is a meeting together in one place of all who dwell either in towns or in the country; and the memoirs of the apostles, or the writings of the prophets are read, as long as the time permits. When the reading ceases, the president delivers a discourse, in which he makes an application and exhorts to the imitation of these good things. We then

211

rise all together and pray. Then ... when we cease from prayer, bread is brought, and wine and water; and the president, in like manner, offers up prayers and thanksgivings according to his ability; [466:1] and the people express their assent by saying Amen." [466:2] It is abundantly clear from this statement that the presiding minister was not restricted to any set form of supplication. As he prayed "according to his ability," his petitions could neither have been dictated by others nor taken from a liturgy. Such a practice as the reading of prayers seems, indeed, to have been totally unknown in the Church during the first three centuries. Hence Tertullian represents the Christians of his generation as praying "looking up with hands spread open, ... and without a prompter because from the heart." [466:3] In his "Treatise on Prayer" Origen recommends the worshipper to address God with stretched out hands and uplifted eyes. [466:4] The erect body with the arms extended was supposed to represent the cross, [466:5] and therefore this attitude was deemed peculiarly appropriate for devotion. [466:6] On the Lord's day the congregation always stood when addressing God. [466:7] At this period forms of prayer were used in the heathen worship, [467:1] and in some cases the pagans adhered with singular tenacity to their ancient liturgies; [467:2] but the Church did not yet require the aid of such auxiliaries. It is remarkable that, though in the account of the losses sustained during the Diocletian persecution, we read frequently of the seizure of the Scriptures, and of the ecclesiastical utensils, we never meet with any allusion to the spoliation of prayer-books. [467:3] There is, in fact, no evidence whatever that such helps to devotion were yet in existence. [467:4]

The worship was now conducted in a dialect which was understood by the congregation; and though the officiating minister was at perfect liberty to select his phraseology, it is probable that he did not think it necessary to aim at great variety in the mere language of his devotional exercises. So long as a petition was deemed suitable, it perhaps continued to be repeated in nearly the same words, whilst providential interpositions, impending persecutions, and the personal condition of the flock, would be continually suggesting some fresh topics for thanksgiving, supplication, and confession. The beautiful and comprehensive prayer taught by our Lord to His disciples was never considered out of place; and, as early as the third century, it was, at least in some districts, used once at every meeting of the faithful. [468:1] The apostle had taught the brethren that intercessions should be made "for kings and for all that are in authority," [468:2] and the primitive disciples did not neglect to commend their earthly rulers to the care of the Sovereign of the universe. [468:3] But still it is clear that even such petitions did not run in the channel of any prescribed formulary.

From the very days of the apostles the reading of the Scriptures constituted an important part of public worship. This portion of the service was, at first perhaps, conducted by one of the elders, but, in some places, towards the close of the second century, it was committed to a new official, called the Reader. [468:4] The presiding minister seems to have been permitted originally to choose whatever passages he considered most fitting for the occasion, as well as to determine the amount of time which was to be occupied in the exercise; but, at length, an order of lessons was prepared, and then the Reader was expected to confine himself to the Scriptures pointed out in his calendar. [468:5] This arrangement, which was obviously designed to secure a more uniform attention to the several parts of the inspired canon, came only gradually into general operation; and it frequently happened that the order of lessons for one church was very different from that used in another. [468:6]

Whilst the constant reading, in the vernacular tongue, of considerable portions of Scripture at public worship, promoted the religious instruction of the people, the mode of preaching which now prevailed contributed to make them still more intimately acquainted with the sacred records. The custom of selecting a text as the basis of a discourse had not yet been introduced; but, when the reading closed, the minister proceeded to expatiate on that section of the Word which had just been brought under the notice of the congregation, and pointed out, as well the doctrines which it recognised, as the practical lessons which it inculcated. The entire presbytery was usually present in the congregation every Lord's day, and when one or other of the elders had made a few comments, [469:1] the president added some remarks of an expository and hortatory character; but, frequently, he received no assistance in this part of the service. The method of reading and elucidating Scripture, now pursued, was eminently salutary; for, whilst it stored the memory with a large share of biblical knowledge, the whole Word of God, in the way of earnest appeal, was brought into close contact with the heart and conscience of each individual.

So long as pristine piety flourished, the people listened with devout attention to the observations of the preacher; but, as a more secular spirit prevailed, he began to be treated, rather as an orator, than a herald from the King of kings. Before the end of the third century, the house of prayer occasionally resounded with the plaudits of the theatre. Such exhibitions were, indeed, condemned at the time by the ecclesiastical authorities, but the very fact that in the principal church of one of the chief cities of the Empire, the bishop, as he proceeded with his sermon, was greeted with stamping of feet, clapping of hands, and waving of handkerchiefs, [469:2] supplied melancholy evidence of the progress of spiritual degeneracy. In the days of the Apostle Paul such demonstrations would have been universally denounced as unseemly and unseasonable.

During the first three centuries there was nothing in the ordinary costume of a Christian minister to distinguish him from any of his fellow-citizens; [470:1] but, it would appear, that when the pastor officiated in the congregation, he began, at an early date, to wear some peculiar piece of apparel. In an old document, purporting to have been written shortly after the middle of the second century, he is described, at the period of his advancement to the episcopal chair, as "clothed with the dress of the bishops." [470:2] As the third century advanced, there was a growing disposition to increase the pomp of public worship; in some places vessels of silver or of gold were used at the dispensation of the, Lord's Supper; [470:3] and it is highly probable that, about this time, some few decorations were assumed by those who took part in its administration. But still the habit used by ecclesiastics at divine service was distinguished by its comparative simplicity, and differed very little from the dress commonly worn by the mass of the population.

What a change must have passed over the Church from the period before us to the dawn of the Reformation! Now, the making of images was forbidden, and no picture was permitted to appear even on the walls of the sacred edifice: [470:4] then, a church frequently suggested the idea of a studio, or a picture-gallery. Now, the whole congregation joined heartily in the psalmody: then, the mute crowd listened to the music of the organ accompanied by the shrill voices of

213

a chorus of thoughtless boys. Now, prayers, in the vernacular tongue and suited to the occasion, were offered with simplicity and earnestness; then, petitions, long since antiquated, were muttered in a dead language. Now, the Word was read and expounded in a way intelligible to all: then, a few Latin extracts from it were mumbled over hastily; and, if a sermon followed, it was, perhaps, a eulogy on some wretched fanatic, or an attack on some true evangelist. There are writers who believe that the Church was meanwhile going on in a career of hopeful development; but facts too clearly testify that she was moving backwards in a path of cheerless declension. Now, the Church "holding forth the Word of life" was commending herself to philosophers and statesmen: then, she had sunk into premature dotage, and her very highest functionaries were lisping the language of infidelity.

CHAPTER II

BAPTISM

When the venerable Polycarp was on the eve of martyrdom, he is reported to have said that he had served Christ "eighty and six years." [472:1] By the ancient Church these words seem to have been regarded as tantamount to a declaration of the length of his life, and as implying that he had been a disciple of the Saviour from his infancy. [472:2] The account of his martyrdom indicates that he was still in the enjoyment of a green old age, [472:3] and as very few overpass the term of fourscore years and six, we are certainly not at liberty to infer, without any evidence, and in the face of probabilities, that he had now attained a greater longevity. A contemporary father, who wrote about the middle of the second century, informs us, that there were then many persons of both sexes, some sixty, and some seventy years of age, who had been "disciples of Christ from childhood," [472:4] and the pastor of Smyrna is apparently included in the description. If he was eighty-six at the time of his death, he must have been about threescore and ten when Justin Martyr made this announcement.

No one could have been considered a disciple of Jesus who had not received baptism, and it thus appears that there were many aged persons, living about A.D. 150, to whom, when children, the ordinance had been administered. We may infer, also, that Polycarp, when an infant, had been in this way admitted within the pale of visible Christianity. Infant baptism must, therefore, have been an institution of the age of the apostles. This conclusion is corroborated by the fact that Justin Martyr speaks of baptism as supplying the place of circumcision. "We," says he, "who through Christ have access to God, have not received that circumcision which is in the flesh, but that spiritual circumcision which Enoch, and others like him, observed. And this, because we have been sinners, we do, through the mercy of God, receive by baptism." [473:1] Justin would scarcely

214

have represented the initiatory ordinance of the Christian Church as supplying so efficiently the place of the Jewish rite, had it not been of equally extensive application. The testimony of Irenaeus, the disciple of Polycarp, throws additional light upon this argument. "Christ," says he, "came to save all persons by Himself; all, I say, who by Him are regenerated unto God—infants, and little ones, and children, and youths, and aged persons: therefore He went through the several ages, being made an infant for infants, that He might sanctify infants; [473:2] and, for little ones, He was made a little one, to sanctify them of that age also." [473:3] Irenaeus elsewhere speaks of baptism as our regeneration or new birth unto God, [473:4] so that his meaning in this passage cannot well be disputed. He was born on the confines of the apostolic age, and when he mentions the regeneration unto God of "infants, and little ones, and children," he alludes to their admission by baptism to the seal of salvation.

The celebrated Origen was born about A.D. 185, and we have as strong circumstantial evidence as we could well desire that he was baptized in infancy. [474:1] Both his parents were Christians, and as soon as he was capable of receiving instruction, he began to enjoy the advantages of a pious education. He affirms, not only that the practice of infant baptism prevailed in his own age, but that it had been handed down as an ecclesiastical ordinance from the first century. "None," says he, "is free from pollution, though his life upon the earth be but the length of one day, and for this reason even infants are baptized, because by the sacrament of baptism the pollution of our birth is put away." [474:2] "The Church has received the custom of baptizing little children from the apostles." [474:3]

The only writer of the first three centuries who questions the propriety of infant baptism is Tertullian. The passage in which he expounds his views on this subject is a most transparent specimen of special pleading, and the extravagant recommendations it contains sufficiently attest that he had taken up a false position. "Considering," says he, "every one's condition and disposition, and also his age, the delay of baptism is more advantageous, but especially in the case of little children. For what necessity is there that the sponsors be brought into danger? Because they may fail to fulfil their promises by death, or may be deceived by the child's proving of a wicked disposition. Our Lord says indeed— 'Do not forbid them to come unto me.' Let them come, therefore, whilst they are growing up, let them come whilst they are learning, whilst they are being taught where it is they are coming, let them be made Christians when they are capable of knowing Christ. Why should their innocent age make haste to the remission of sins? Men proceed more cautiously in worldly things; and he that is not trusted with earthly goods, why should he be trusted with divine? Let them know how to ask salvation, that you may appear to give it to one that asketh. For no less reason unmarried persons ought to be delayed, because they are exposed to temptations, as well virgins that are come to maturity, as those that are in widowhood and have little occupation, until they either marry or be confirmed in continence. They who know the weight of baptism will rather dread its attainment than its postponement." [475:1]

In the apostolic age all adults, when admitted to baptism, answered for themselves. Had additional sponsors been required for the three thousand converts who joined the Church on the day of Pentecost, [475:2] they could not have been procured. The Ethiopian eunuch and the Philippian jailor [475:3] were their own sponsors. Until long after the time when Tertullian wrote, there were, in the case of adults, no other sponsors than the parties themselves. But when an infant was dedicated to God in baptism, the parents were required to make a profession of the faith, and to undertake to train up their little one in the way of righteousness. [476:1] It is to this arrangement that Tertullian refers when he says—"What necessity is there that the sponsors be brought into danger? Because even they may fail to fulfil their promises by death, or may be deceived by the child's proving of a wicked disposition."

It is plain, from his own statements, that infant baptism was practised in the days of this father; and it is also obvious that it was then said to rest on the authority of the New Testament. Its advocates, he alleges, quoted in its defence the words of our Saviour—"Suffer the little children to come unto me and forbid them not." [476:2] And how does Tertullian meet this argument? Does he venture to say that it is contradicted by any other Scripture testimony? Does he pretend to assert that the appearance of parents, as sponsors for their children, is an ecclesiastical innovation? Had this acute and learned controversialist been prepared to encounter infant baptism on such grounds, he would not have neglected his opportunity. But, instead of pursuing such a line of reasoning, he merely exhibits his weakness by resorting to a piece of miserable sophistry. When our Lord said—"Suffer the little children to come unto me and forbid them not," He illustrated His meaning as He "took them up in His arms, put His hands upon them, and blessed them;" [476:3] so that the gloss of Tertullian—"Let them come whilst they are growing up, let them come whilst they are learning"—is a palpable misinterpretation. Nor is this all. The Carthaginian father must have known that there were frequent instances in the days of the apostles of the baptism of whole households; and yet he maintains that the unmarried, especially young widows, cannot with safety be admitted to the ordinance. Had he been with Paul and Silas at Philippi he would thus scarcely have consented to the baptism of Lydia; and he would certainly have protested against the administration of the rite to all the members of her family. [477:1]

Though Tertullian may not have formally separated from the Church when he wrote the tract in which this passage occurs, it is evident that he had already adopted the principles of the Montanists. These errorists held that any one who had fallen into heinous sin after baptism could never again be admitted to ecclesiastical fellowship; and this little book itself supplies proof that its author now supported the same doctrine. He here declares that the man "who renews his sins after baptism" is "destined to fire;" and he intimates that martyrdom, or "the baptism of blood," can alone "restore" such an offender. [477:2] It was obviously the policy of the Montanists to discourage infant baptism, and to retain the mass of their adherents, as long as possible, in the condition of catechumens. Hence Tertullian here asserts that "they who know the weight of baptism will rather dread its attainment than its postponement." [477:3] But neither the apostles, nor the early Church, had any sympathy with such a sentiment. They represent baptism as a privilege—as a sign and seal of God's favour—which all should thankfully embrace. On the very day on which Peter denounced the Jews as having with wicked hands crucified his Master, he assisted in the baptism of three thousand of these transgressors. "Repent," says he, "and be baptized every one of you in the name of Jesus Christ for the remission of sins, and ye shall receive the gift of the Holy Ghost, for the promise is unto you and to your children." [478:1]

Tertullian would have given them no such encouragement. But the Montanists believed that their Phrygian Paraclete was commissioned to supersede the apostolic discipline. When the African father attacked infant baptism he obviously acted under this conviction; and whilst seeking to set aside the arrangements of the Church of his own age, he felt no scruple in venturing at the same time to subvert an institute of primitive Christianity.

We have the clearest evidence that, little more than twenty years after the death of Tertullian, the whole Church of Africa recognised the propriety of this practice. About the middle of the third century a bishop of that country, named Fidus, appears to have taken up the idea that, when administering the ordinance, he was bound to adhere to the very letter of the law relative to circumcision, [478:2] and that therefore he was not at liberty to baptize the child before the eighth day after its birth. When the case was submitted to Cyprian and an African Synod, consisting of sixty-six bishops, they unanimously decided that these scruples were groundless; and, in an epistle addressed to the pastor who entertained them, the Assembly thus communicated the result of its deliberations—"As regards the case of infants who, you say, should not be baptized within the second or third day after their birth, and that respect should be had to the law of the ancient circumcision, whence you think that one newly born should not be baptized and sanctified within the eighth day, we all in our council thought very differently.... If even to the most grievous offenders, ... when they afterwards believe, remission of sins is granted, and no one is debarred from baptism and grace, how much more ought not an infant to be debarred who, being newly born, has in no way sinned, except that being born after Adam in the flesh, he has by his first birth contracted the contagion of the old death; who is on this very account more easily admitted to receive remission of sins, in that, not his own, but another's sins are remitted to him." [479:1]

Whilst it is thus apparent that the baptism of infants was the established order of the Church, it is equally clear that the particular mode of administration was not considered essential to the validity of the ordinance. It was usually dispensed by immersion or affusion, [479:2] but when the health of the candidate might have been injured by such an ordeal, sprinkling was deemed sufficient. Aspersion was commonly employed in the case of the sick, and was known by the designation of clinic or bed baptism. Cyprian points out to one of his correspondents the absurdity of the idea that the extent to which the water is applied can affect the character of the institution. "In the saving sacrament," says he, "the contagion of sin is not washed away just in the same way as is the filth of the skin and body in the ordinary ablution of the flesh, so that there should be need of saltpetre and other appliances, and a bath and a pool in which the poor body may be washed and cleansed.... It is apparent that the sprinkling of water has like force with the saving washing, and that when this is done in the Church, where the faith both of the giver and receiver is entire, [480:1] all holds good and is consummated and perfected by the power of the Lord, and the truth of faith." [480:2]

Cyprian is here perfectly right in maintaining that the essence of baptism does not consist in the way in which the water is administered; but much of the language he employs in speaking of this ordinance cannot be commended as sober and scriptural. He often confounds it with regeneration, and expresses himself as if the mere rite possessed a mystic virtue. "The birth of Christians,"

217

says he, "is in baptism." [480:3] "The Church alone has the life-giving water." [480:4] "The water must first be cleansed and sanctified by the priest, that it may be able, by baptism therein, to wash away the sins of the baptized." [480:5] Tertullian and other writers of the third century make use of phraseology equally unguarded. [480:6] When the true character of the institute was so far misunderstood, it is not extraordinary that it began to be tricked out in the trappings of superstition. The candidate, as early as the third century, was exorcised before baptism, with a view to the expulsion of evil spirits; [480:7] and, in some places, after the application of the water, when the kiss of peace was given to him, a mixture of milk and honey was administered, [480:8] He was then anointed, and marked on the forehead with the sign of the cross. [480:9] Finally, the presiding minister, by the laying on of hands, bestowed the benediction. [480:10] Tertullian endeavours to explain some of these ceremonies. "The flesh," says he, "is washed, that the soul may be freed from spots; the flesh is anointed, that the soul may be consecrated; the flesh is marked (with the sign of the cross), that the soul may be guarded; the flesh is overshadowed by the imposition of hands, that the soul may be enlightened by the Spirit." [481:1]

It is not improbable that the baptismal service constituted the first germ of a Church liturgy. As the ordinance was so frequently celebrated, it was found convenient to adhere to the same form, not only in the words of administration, [481:2] but also in the accompanying prayers; and thus each pastor soon had his own baptismal office. But when heresies spread, and when, in consequence, measures were taken to preserve the unity of the Catholic faith, a uniform series of questions—prepared, perhaps, by councils and adopted by the several ministers—was addressed to all catechumens. Thus, the baptismal services were gradually assimilated; and, as the power of the hierarchy increased, one general office, in each district, superseded all the previously-existing formularies.

Baptism, as dispensed in apostolic simplicity, is a most significant ordinance; but the original rite was soon well-nigh hidden behind the rubbish of human inventions. The milk and honey, the unction, the crossing, the kiss of peace, and the imposition of hands, were all designed to render it more imposing; and, still farther to deepen the impression, it was already administered in the presence of none save those who had themselves been thus initiated. [481:3] But the foolishness of God is wiser than man. Nothing is more to be deprecated than any attempt to improve upon the institutions of Christ. Baptism, as established by the Divine Founder of our religion, is a visible exhibition of the gospel; but, as known in the third century, it had much of the character of one of the heathen mysteries. It was intended to confirm faith: but it was now contributing to foster superstition. How soon had the gold become dim, and the most fine gold been changed!

CHAPTER III

THE LORD'S SUPPER

Baptism and the Lord's Supper may be regarded as a typical or pictorial summary of the great salvation. In Baptism the gospel is exhibited subjectively—renewing the heart and cleansing from all iniquity: in the Lord's Supper it is exhibited objectively—providing a mighty Mediator, and a perfect atonement. Regeneration and Propitiation are central truths towards which all the other doctrines of Christianity converge, and in marking them out by corresponding symbols, the Head of the Church has been graciously pleased to signalize their importance.

The Scriptures are able to make us wise unto salvation and thoroughly furnished unto all good works; but we are not at liberty to adulterate these records either by addition or subtraction. If they should be preserved exactly as they issued from the pen of inspiration, it is clear that the visible ordinances in which they are epitomized should also be maintained in their integrity. He who tampers with a divinely-instituted symbol is obviously to some extent obnoxious to the malediction [483:1] pronounced upon the man who adds to, or takes away from, the words of the book of God's prophecy.

Had the original form of administering the Lord's Supper been rigidly maintained, the Church might have avoided a multitude of errors; but very soon the spirit of innovation began to disfigure this institute. The mode in which it was observed, and the views which were entertained respecting it by the Christians of Rome, about the middle of the second century, are minutely described by Justin Martyr. "There is brought," says he, "to that one of the brethren who is president, bread and a cup of wine mixed with water. And he, having received them, gives praise and glory to the Father of all things.... And when he has finished his praises and thanksgiving, all the people who are present express their assent saying Amen, which in the Hebrew tongue signifies so be it. The president having given thanks, and the people having expressed their assent, those whom we call deacons give to each of those who are present a portion of the bread which has been blessed, and of the wine mixed with water; and carry away some for those who are absent. And this food is called by us the Eucharist, of which no one may partake unless he believes that which we teach is true, and is baptized, ... and lives in such a manner as Christ commanded. For we receive not these elements as common bread or common drink. But even as Jesus Christ our Saviour ... had both flesh and blood for our salvation, even so we are taught that the food which is blessed ... by the digestion of which our blood and flesh are nourished, is the flesh and blood of that Jesus who was made flesh. For the apostles in the memoirs composed by them, which are called gospels, have related that Jesus thus commanded them, that having taken bread and given thanks He said—'Do this in remembrance of me, this is my body;' and that, in like manner, having taken the cup and given thanks, He said, 'This is my blood;' and that He distributed them to these alone." [484:1]

The writer does not here mention the posture of the disciples when communicating, but it is highly probable that they still continued to sit [485:1] in

219

accordance with the primitive pattern. As they received the ordinance in the same attitude as that in which they partook of their common meals, the story that their religious assemblies were the scenes of unnatural feasting, may have thus originated. [485:2] For the first three centuries, kneeling at the Lord's Supper was unknown; and it is not until about a hundred years after the death of the Apostle John, that we read of the communicants standing. [485:3] Throughout the whole of the third century, this appears to have been the position in which they partook of the elements. [485:4]

The bread and wine of the Eucharist were now supplied by the worshippers, who made "oblations" according to their ability, [485:5] as well for the support of the ministers of the Church, as for the celebration of its ordinances. There is no reason to believe that the bread, used at this period in the holy Supper, was unfermented; for, though our Lord distributed a loaf, or cake, of that quality when the rite was instituted, the early Christians seem to have considered the circumstance accidental; as unleavened bread was in ordinary use among the Jews at the time of the Passover. The disciples appear to have had less reason for mixing the wine with water, and they could have produced no good evidence that such was the beverage used by Christ when He appointed this commemoration. In the third century superstition already recognized a mystery in the mixture. "We see," says Cyprian, "that in the water the people are represented, but that in the wine is exhibited the blood of Christ. When, however, in the cup water is mingled with wine, the people are united to Christ, and the multitude of the faithful are coupled and conjoined to Him on whom they believe." [486:1] The bread was not put into the mouth of the communicant by the administrator, but was handed to him by a deacon; and it is said that, the better to shew forth the unity of the Church, all partook of one loaf made of a size sufficient to supply the whole congregation. [486:2] The wine was administered separately, and was drunk out of a cup or chalice. As early as the third century an idea began to be entertained that the Eucharist was necessary to salvation, and it was, in consequence, given to infants. [486:3] None were now suffered to be present at its celebration but those who were communicants; [486:4] for even the catechumens, or candidates for baptism, were obliged to withdraw before the elements were consecrated.

The Passover was kept only once a year, but the Eucharist, which was the corresponding ordinance of the Christian dispensation, was observed much more frequently. Justin intimates that it was administered every Lord's day, and other fathers of this period bear similar testimony. Cyprian speaks even of its daily celebration. [486:5] The New Testament has promulgated no precise law upon the subject, and it is probable that only the more zealous disciples communicated weekly. On the Paschal week it was observed with peculiar solemnity, and by the greatest concourse of worshippers.

The term sacrament was now applied to both Baptism and the Lord's Supper; but it was not confined to these two symbolic ordinances. [487:1] The word transubstantiation was not introduced until upwards of a thousand years after the death of our Saviour; [487:2] and the doctrine which it indicates was not known to any of the fathers of the first three centuries. They all concur in describing the elements, after consecration, as bread and wine; they all represent them as passing through the usual process of digestion; and they all speak of them as symbols of the body and blood of Christ. In this strain Justin Martyr discourses of "that bread which our Christ has commanded us to offer in remembrance of His being made flesh, ... and of that cup which He commanded those that celebrate the Eucharist to offer in remembrance of His blood." [487:3] According to Clement of Alexandria the Scripture designates wine "a mystic symbol of the holy blood." [487:4] Origen, as if anticipating the darkness which was to overspread the Church, expresses himself very much in the style of a zealous Protestant. He denounces as "simpletons" [487:5] those who attributed a supernatural power to the Eucharistic elements, and repeatedly affirms that the words used at the institution of the Lord's Supper are to be interpreted spiritually. "The meat," says he, "which is sanctified by the Word of God and prayer, as it is material, goes into the stomach, ... but, by reason of prayer made over it, it is profitable according to the proportion of faith, and is the cause that the understanding is enlightened and attentive to what is profitable; and it is not the substance of bread, but the word pronounced upon it, which is profitable to him who eats it in a way not unworthy of the Lord." [488:1] Cyprian uses language scarcely less equivocal, for he speaks of "that wine whereby the blood of Christ is set forth," [488:2] and asserts that it "was wine which He called His blood." [488:3]

Christ has said—"Where two or three are gathered together in my name, there am I in the midst of them;" [488:4] and, true to His promises, He is really present with His people in every act of devotion. Even when they draw near to Him in secret, or when they read His word, or when they meditate on His mercy, as well as when they listen to His gospel preached in the great congregation, He manifests Himself to them not as He does unto the world. But in the Eucharist He reveals His character more significantly than in any of His other ordinances; for He here addresses Himself to all the senses, as well as to the soul. In the words of institution they "hear His voice;" when the elements are presented to them, they perceive as it were "the smell of His garments;" with their hands they "handle of the Word of Life;" and they "taste and see that the Lord is good." But some of the early Christian writers were by no means satisfied with such representations. They appear to have entertained an idea that Christ was in the Eucharist, not only in richer manifestations of His grace, but also in a way altogether different from that in which He vouchsafes His presence in prayer, or praise, or any other divine observance. They conceived that, as the soul of man is united to his body, the Logos, or Divine nature of Christ, pervades the consecrated bread and wine, so that they may be called His flesh and blood; and they imagined that, in consequence, the sacred elements imparted to the material frame of the believer the germ of immortality. [489:1] Irenaeus declares that "our bodies, receiving the Eucharist, are no longer corruptible, but possessed of the hope of eternal life." [489:2] This misconception of the ordinance was the fruitful source of superstition. The mere elements began to be regarded with awful reverence; the loss of a particle of the bread, or of a drop of the wine, was considered a tremendous desecration; and it was probably the growth of such feelings which initiated the custom of standing at the time of participation. But still there were fathers who were not carried away with the delusion, and who knew that the disposition of the worshipper was of far more consequence than the care with which he handled the holy symbols. "You who frequent our sacred mysteries," says Origen, "know that when you receive the body of the Lord, you take care with all due caution and veneration, that not even the smallest particle of the consecrated gift shall fall to the ground and be wasted. [489:3] If, through inattention, any part thus falls, you justly account yourselves guilty. If then, with good reason, you use so much caution in preserving His body, how can you esteem it a lighter sin to slight the Word of God than to neglect His body?" [489:4]

"The words of the Lord are pure words, as silver tried in a furnace of earth purified seven times." [489:5] The history of Baptism and the Lord's Supper demonstrates that, when speaking of the ordinances of religion, it is exceedingly dangerous to depart, even from the phraseology, which the Holy Spirit has dictated. In the second century Baptism was called "regeneration" and the Eucharistic bread was known by the compendious designation of "the Lord's body." Such language, if typically understood, could create no perplexity; but all by whom it was used could scarcely be expected to give it a right interpretation, and thus many misconceptions were speedily generated. In a short time names, for which there is no warrant in the Word of God, were applied to the Lord's Supper; and false doctrines were eventually deduced from these ill-chosen and unauthorised designations. Thus, before the close of the second century, it was called an offering, and a sacrifice, [490:1] and the table at which it was administered was styled the altar. [490:2] Though these terms were now used rhetorically, in after-ages they were literally interpreted; and in this way the most astounding errors gradually gained currency. Meanwhile other topics led to keen discussion; but there was a growing disposition to shroud the Eucharist in mystery; and hence, for many centuries, the question as to the manner of Christ's presence in the ordinance awakened no controversy.

CHAPTER IV

CONFESSION AND PENANCE

When the Evangelist Matthew is describing the ministry of John the Baptist, he states that there "went out to him Jerusalem, and all Judea, and all the region round about Jordan; and were baptized of him in Jordan, confessing their sins." [491:1] The ministry of Paul at Ephesus produced similar results; for it is said that "fear fell" on all the Jews and Greeks dwelling in that great capital, "and many that believed came, and confessed, and shewed their deeds," [491:2]

The confession here mentioned obviously flowed spontaneously from deep religious convictions. It was not a private admission of guilt made to an ecclesiastical functionary; but a public acknowledgment of acts which weighed heavily on the consciences of individuals, and which they felt constrained to recapitulate and to condemn. Men awakened to a sense of their sins deemed it due to themselves and to society, to state how sincerely they deplored their past career; and, no doubt, their words often produced a profound impression on the multitudes to whom they were addressed. These confessions of sin were connected with a confession of faith in Christ, and were generally associated with the ordinance of baptism. They were not required from all, but were only tendered in cases where there had been notorious and flagrant criminality; and they must have been of a very partial character, only embracing such transgressions as the party had some urgent reason for specializing.

In the time of the apostles those who embraced the gospel were immediately baptized. Thus, the three thousand persons who were converted on the day of Pentecost, were forthwith received into the bosom of the Church; and the Philippian jailor, "the same hour of the night" [493:1] when he hearkened to "the word of the Lord," "was baptized, he and all his, straightway." But, soon, afterwards, the Christian teachers began to proceed with greater formality; and, about the middle of the second century, candidates were not admitted to the ordinance until they had passed through a certain course of probation. "As many," says Justin Martyr, "as are persuaded and believe that the things which we teach and declare are true, and promise that they are determined to live accordingly, are taught to pray, and to beseech God with fasting to grant them remission of their past sins, while we also pray and fast with them. We then lead them to a place where there is water, and there they are regenerated in the same manner as we also were; for they are then washed in that water in the name of God the Father and Lord of the universe, and of our Saviour Jesus Christ, and the Holy Spirit." [493:2]

These confessions and penitential exercises were repeated and enlarged when persons who had lapsed into gross sin, and who had, in consequence, forfeited their position as members of the Church, sought readmission to ecclesiastical fellowship. It would be difficult, on scriptural grounds, to vindicate the system of discipline enforced on such occasions; and yet it is evident that it was established, at least in some quarters, as early as the beginning of the third century. Tertullian gives a very striking account of the course pursued by those called penitents about that period. "Confession of sins," says he, "lightens their burden, as much as the dissembling of them increases it; for confession savours of making amends, dissembling, of stubbornness. ..... Wherefore confession is the discipline of a man's prostrating and humbling himself, enjoining such a conversation as invites mercy. It restrains a man even as to the matter of dress and food, requiring him to lie in sackcloth and ashes, to hide his body in filthy garments, to afflict his soul with sorrow, to exchange for severe treatment the sins in which he indulged; for the rest to use simple things for meat and drink, that is, for the sake of the soul, and not to please the appetite: for the most part also to quicken prayer by fasts, to groan, to weep, and to moan day and night before the Lord his God; to throw himself on the ground before the presbyters, and to fall on his knees before the beloved of God; to enjoin all the brethren to bear the message of his prayer for mercy—all these things does confession that it may commend repentance." [493:1]

When a man is overwhelmed with grief, the state of his mind will often be revealed by the loss of his appetite. He will think little of his dress and personal accommodation; and though he may give no utterance to his feelings, his general appearance will betray to the eye of an observer the depths of his affliction. The mourner not unfrequently takes a melancholy satisfaction in surrounding himself with the symbols of sorrow; and we read, accordingly, in Scripture how, in

223

ancient times and in Eastern countries, he clothed himself in sackcloth and sat in ashes. [493:2] There is a wonderful sympathy between the body and the mind; and as grief affects the appetite, so occasional abstinence from food may foster a serious and contrite spirit. Hence fasting has been so commonly associated with penitential exercises.

Fasting is not to be regarded as one of the ordinary duties of a disciple of Christ,[494:1] but rather as a kind of discipline in which he may feel called on to engage under special circumstances.[494:2] When oppressed with a consciousness of guilt, or when anxious for divine direction on a critical occasion, or when trembling under the apprehension of impending judgments, he may thus seek to "afflict his soul," that he may draw near with deeper humility and reverence into the presence of the Divine Majesty. But, in such a case, every one should act according to the dictates of his own enlightened convictions. As the duty is extraordinary, the self-denial to be practised must be regulated by various contingencies; and no one can well prescribe to another its amount or duration.

According to the Mosaic law, only one day in the year—the great day of atonement—was required to be kept as a national fast.[494:3] There is now no divine warrant for so observing any corresponding day, and for upwards of a hundred years after the death of our Lord, there is no evidence that any fixed portion of time was thus appropriated under the sanction of ecclesiastical authority. But towards the close of the second century the termination of the Paschal week was often so employed—the interval, between the hour on Friday when our Lord expired and the morning of the first day of the week, being spent in total abstinence.[494:4] About the same time some partially abstained from food on what were called stationary days, or the Wednesday and Friday of each week.[494:5] At this period some began also to observe Xerophagiae, or days on which they used neither flesh nor wine. [495:1] Not a few saw the danger of this ascetic tendency; but, whilst it betokened zeal, it had also "a show of wisdom," [495:2] and it silently made great progress. Towards the close of the third century the whole Church was already pervaded by its influence.

Fasting has been well described as "the outward shell" of penitential sorrow, and is not to be confounded with its spiritual elements. It is its accidental accompaniment, and not one of its true and essential features. A man may "bow down his head as a bulrush," or fast, or clothe himself in sackcloth, when he is an utter stranger to that "repentance to salvation not to be repented of." The hypocrite may put on the outward badges of mourning merely with a view to regain a position in the Church, whilst the sincere penitent may "anoint his head and wash his face," and reveal to the eye of the casual spectator no tokens of contrition. As repentance is a spiritual exercise, it can only be recognised by spiritual signs; and the rulers of the ancient Church committed a capital error when they proposed to test it by certain dietary indications. Their penitential discipline was directly opposed to the genuine spirit of the gospel; and it was the fountain from whence proceeded many of the superstitions which, like a river of death, soon overspread Christendom. Whilst repentance was reduced to a mechanical round of bodily exercises, the doctrine of a free salvation was practically repudiated.

In connexion with the appearance of a system of penitential discipline, involving in some cases a penance of several years' continuance, [495:3] the distinction of venial and mortal sins now began to be recognised. Venial sins were

224

transgressions which any sincere believer might commit, whilst mortal sins were such as were considered incompatible with the genuine profession of Christianity. Penance was prescribed only to those who had been guilty of mortal sins. Its severity and duration varied with the character of the offence, and was soon regulated according to an exact scale arranged by the rulers of the Church in their ecclesiastical conventions.

About the middle of the third century a new arrangement was introduced, with a view to promote the more exact administration of penitential discipline. During the Decian persecution which occurred at this time, many were induced by fear to abandon the profession of the gospel; and, on the return of better days, those who sought restoration to Christian privileges were so numerous that, in the larger churches, it was deemed expedient to require the lapsed, in the first instance, to address themselves to one of the presbyters appointed for their special examination. The business of this functionary, who was known by the designation of the Penitentiary [496:1] was to hear the confessions of the penitents, to ascertain the extent and circumstances of their apostasy, and to announce the penance required from each by the existing ecclesiastical regulations. The disclosures made to the Penitentiary did not supersede the necessity of public confession; it was simply the duty of this minister to give to the lapsed such instructions as his professional experience enabled him to supply, including directions as to the fasts they should observe, and the sins they should openly acknowledge. Under the guidance of the Penitentiaries the system of discipline for transgressors seems to have been still farther matured; and at length, in the beginning of the fourth century, the penitents were divided into various classes, according to their supposed degrees of unworthiness. The members of each class were obliged to occupy a particular position in the place of worship when the congregation assembled for religious exercises. [497:1]

It must be obvious from these statements that the institution known as Auricular Confession had, as yet, no existence. In the early Church the disciples, under ordinary circumstances, were neither required nor expected, at stated seasons, to enter into secret conference with any ecclesiastical searcher of consciences. When a professing Christian committed a heinous transgression by which religion was scandalized, he was obliged, before being re-admitted to communion, to express his sorrow in the face of the congregation; and the revelations made to the Penitentiary did not relieve him from this act of humiliation. It must also be apparent that the whole system of penance is an unauthorized addition to the ordinances of primitive Christianity. Of such a system we do not find even a trace in the New Testament; and under its blighting influence, the religion of the Church gradually became little better than a species of refined heathenism.

The spiritual darkness now settling down upon the Christian commonwealth might be traced in the growing obscurity of the ecclesiastical nomenclature. The power and the form of godliness began to be confounded, and the same term was employed to denote penance and repentance. [497:2] Bodily mortification was mistaken for holiness, and celibacy for sanctity. [497:3] Other errors of an equally grave character became current, for the penitent was described as making satisfaction for his sins by his fasts and his outward acts of self abasement, [497:4] and thus the all-sufficiency of the great atonement was openly ignored. Thus, too, the doctrine of a free salvation to transgressors could no longer be proclaimed, for pardon was clogged with conditions as burdensome to the sinner, as they were alien to the spirit of the New Testament. The doctrine that "a man is justified by faith without the deeds of the law," [498:1] reveals the folly of the ancient penitential discipline. Our Father in heaven demands no useless tribute of mortification from His children; He merely requires us to "bring forth fruits meet for repentance." [498:2] "Is not this the fast that I have chosen?" saith the Lord, "to loose the bands of wickedness, to undo the heavy burdens, and to let the oppressed go free, and that ye break every yoke? Is it not to deal thy bread to the hungry, and that thou bring the poor that are cast out to thy house? when thou seest the naked, that thou cover him; and that thou hide not thyself from thine own flesh? Then shall thy light break forth as the morning, and thine health shall spring forth speedily; and thy righteousness shall go before thee: the glory of the Lord shall be thy reward." [498:3]

CHAPTER V

THE CONSTITUTION OF THE CHURCH IN THE SECOND CENTURY

Justin Martyr, who had travelled much, and who was probably as well acquainted with the state of the Church about the middle of the second century as most of his contemporaries, has left behind him an account of the manner in which its worship was then conducted. This account, which has already been submitted to the reader, [499:1] represents one individual as presiding over each Christian community, whether in the city or the country. Where the Church consisted of a single congregation, and where only one of the elders was competent to preach, it is easy to understand how the society was regulated. In accordance with apostolic arrangement, the presbyter, who laboured in the Word and doctrine, was counted worthy of double honour, [499:2] and was recognized as the stated chairman of the solemn assembly. His brother elders contributed in various ways to assist him in the supervision of the flock; but its prosperity greatly depended on his own zeal, piety, prudence, and ability. Known at first as the president, and afterwards distinguished by the title of the bishop, he occupied very much the same position as the minister of a modern parish.

Where a congregation had more than one preaching elder, the case was different. There, several individuals were in the habit of addressing the auditory, [500:1] and it was the duty of the president to preserve order; to interpose, perhaps, by occasional suggestions; and to close the exercise. When several congregations with a plurality of preaching elders existed in the same city, the whole were affiliated; and a president, acknowledged by them all, superintended their united movements.

It must be admitted that much obscurity hangs over the general condition of the Christian commonwealth in the first half of the second century; but it so happens that two authentic and valuable documents which still remain, one of which was written about the beginning and the other about the close of this period, throw much light upon the question of Church government. These documents are the "Epistle of Clement to the Corinthians," and the "Epistle of Polycarp to the Philippians." As to the matters respecting which they bear testimony, we could not desire more competent witnesses than the authors of these two letters. The one lived in the West; the other, in the East. Clement, who is mentioned by the Apostle Paul, [500:2] was a presbyter of the Church of Rome; Polycarp, who, in his youth, had conversed with the Apostle John, was a presbyter of the Church of Smyrna. Clement died about the close of the first century, and his letter to the Corinthians was written three or four years before, that is, immediately after the Domitian persecution; Polycarp survived until a somewhat advanced period of the second century, and his letter to the Philippians was probably written fifty or sixty years after the date of the Epistle of Clement. [500:3]

Towards the termination of the first century a spirit of discord disturbed the Church of Corinth; and the Church of Rome, anxious to restore peace, addressed a fraternal letter to the distracted community. The Epistle was drawn up by Clement, who was then the leading minister of the Italian capital; but, as it is written in the name of the whole brotherhood, and as it had, no doubt, obtained their sanction, it obviously possesses all the authority of a public and official correspondence. From it the constitution of the Church of Corinth, and, by implication, of the Church of Rome, may be easily ascertained: and it furnishes abundant proof that, at the time of its composition, both these Christian societies were under presbyterial government. Had a prelate then presided in either Church, a circumstance so important would not have been entirely overlooked, more especially as the document is of considerable length, and as it treats expressly upon the subject of ecclesiastical polity. It appears that some members of the community to which it is addressed had acted undutifully towards those who were over them in the Lord, and it accordingly condemns in very emphatic terms a course of proceeding so disreputable. "It is shameful, beloved," says the Church of Rome in this letter, "it is exceedingly shameful and unworthy of your Christian profession, to hear that the most firm and ancient Church of the Corinthians should, by one or two persons, be led into a sedition against its elders." [501:1] "Let the flock of Christ be in peace with THE ELDERS THAT ARE SET OVER IT." [502:1] Having stated that the apostles ordained those to whom the charge of the Christian Church was originally committed, it is added, that they gave directions in what manner, after the decease of these primitive pastors, "other chosen and approved men should succeed to their ministry." [502:2] The Epistle thus continues—"Wherefore we cannot think that those may justly be thrown out of their ministry who were either ordained by them (the apostles), or afterwards by other approved men with the approbation of the whole Church, and who have, with all lowliness and innocency, ministered to the flock of Christ in peace and without self-interest, and have been for a long time commended by all. For it would be no small sin in us, should we cast off those from the ministry who holily and without blame fulfil the duties of it. Blessed are those elders who, having finished their course before these times, have obtained a fruitful and perfect dissolution." [502:3] Towards the conclusion of the letter, the parties who had created this confusion in the Church of Corinth have the following admonition addressed to them—"Do ye, therefore, who laid the foundation of the sedition, submit yourselves unto your elders, and be instructed unto repentance, bending the knees of your hearts." [502:4]

In the preservation of this precious letter we are bound to recognize the hand of Providence. [502:5] Its instructions were so highly appreciated by the ancient Christians that it continued to be publicly read in many of their churches for centuries afterwards. [502:6] It is universally acknowledged to be genuine; it breathes the benevolent spirit of a primitive presbyter; and it is distinguished by its sobriety and earnestness. It was written upon the verge of the apostolic age, and it is the production of a pious, sensible, and aged minister who preached for years in the capital of the Empire. The Church of Rome has since advanced the most extravagant pretensions, and has appealed in support of them to ecclesiastical tradition; but here, an elder of her own—one who had conversed with, the apostles—and one whom she delights to honour [503:1]—deliberately comes forward and ignores her assumptions! She fondly believes that Clement was an early Pope, but the good man himself admits that he was only one of the presbyters. Had there then been a bishop of Corinth, this letter would unquestionably have exhorted the malcontents to submit to his jurisdiction; or had there been a bishop of Rome, it would not have failed to dilate upon the benefits of episcopal government. But, as to the existence of any such functionary in either Church, it preserves throughout a most intelligible silence. It says that the apostles ordained the first-fruits of their conversions, not as bishops and presbyters and deacons, but as "bishops and deacons over such as should afterwards believe;" [503:2] and it is apparent that, when it was written, the terms bishop and presbyter were still used interchangeably. [503:3]

The Epistle of Polycarp bears equally decisive testimony. It was drawn up perhaps about the middle of the second century, [503:4] and though the last survivor of the apostles was now dead for many years, no general change had meanwhile taken place in the form of church government. This document purports to be the letter of "Polycarp and the elders who are with him [504:1] to the Church of God which is at Philippi;" but it does not recognize a bishop as presiding over the Christian community to which it is addressed. The Church was still apparently in much the same state as when Paul wrote to "the saints in Christ Jesus which are at Philippi, with the bishops and deacons;" [504:2] for Polycarp was certainly not aware of the existence of any new office-bearers; and he accordingly exhorts his correspondents to be "subject to the presbyters and deacons." [504:3] "Let the presbyters," says he, "be compassionate, merciful to all, bringing back such as are in error, seeking out all those that are weak, not neglecting the widow or the fatherless, or the poor; but providing always what is good in the sight of God and men; abstaining from all wrath, respect of persons, and unrighteous judgment; being far from all covetousness; not ready to believe anything against any; not severe in judgment, knowing that we are all debtors in point of sin." [504:4]

It is stated by the most learned of the fathers of the fourth century that the Church was at first "governed by the common council of the, presbyters;" [504:5] and these two letters prove most satisfactorily the accuracy of the representation. They shew that, throughout the whole of the apostolic age, this species of polity continued. But the Scriptures ordain that "all things be done decently and in

228

order;" [504:6] and, as a common council requires an official head, or mayor, to take the chair at its meetings, and to act on its behalf, so the ancient eldership, or presbytery, must have had a president or moderator. It would appear that the duty and honour of presiding commonly devolved on the senior member of the judicatory. We may thus account for those catalogues of bishops, reaching back to the days of the apostles, which are furnished by some of the writers of antiquity. From the first, every presbytery had its president; and as the transition from the moderator to the bishop was the work of time, the distinction at one period was little more than nominal. Hence, writers who lived when the change was taking place, or when it had only been recently accomplished, speak of these two functionaries as identical. But in their attempts to enumerate the bishops of the apostolic era, they encountered a practical difficulty. The elders who were at first set over the Christian societies were all ordained, in each church, on the same occasion, [505:1] and were, perhaps, of nearly the same age, so that neither their date of appointment, nor their years, could well determine the precedence; and it is probable that, in general, no single individual continued permanently to occupy the office of moderator. There may have been instances in which a stated president was chosen, and yet it is remarkable that not even one such case can be clearly established by the evidence of contemporary documents. When all the other apostles departed from Jerusalem, James appears to have remained in the holy city, so that we may reasonably presume he always acted, when present, as chairman of the mother presbytery; and accordingly, the writers of succeeding ages have described him as the first bishop of the Jewish metropolis; but so little consequence was originally attached to the office of moderator, [505:2] that, in as far as the New Testament is concerned, the situation held by this distinguished man can be inferred only from some very obscure and doubtful intimations. [505:3] In Rome, and elsewhere, the primitive elders at first, perhaps, filled the chair alternately. Hence the so-called episcopal succession is most uncertain and confused at the very time when it should be sustained by evidence the most decisive and perspicuous. The lists of bishops, commencing with the ministry of the apostles, and extending over the latter half of the first century, are little better than a mass of contradictions. The compilers seem to have set down, almost at random, the names of some distinguished men whom they found connected with the different churches, and thus the discrepancies are nearly as numerous as the catalogues. [506:1]

But when Clement dictated the Epistle to the Corinthians most of the elders, ordained by the apostles or evangelists about the middle of the first century, must have finished their career; and there is little reason to doubt that this eminent minister was then the father of the Roman presbytery. The superscription of the letter to the Philippians supplies direct proof that, at the time when it was written, Polycarp likewise stood at the head of the presbytery of Smyrna. [506:2] Other circumstances indicate that the senior presbyter now began to be regarded as the stated president of the eldership. Hilary, one of the best commentators of the ancient Church, [506:3] bears explicit testimony to the existence of such an arrangement. "At first," says he, "presbyters were called bishops, so that when the one (who was called bishop) passed away, the next in order took his place." [507:1] "Though every bishop is a presbyter, every presbyter is not a bishop, for he is bishop who is first among the presbyters." [507:2] As soon as the regulation, recognizing the claims of seniority was proposed, its advocates were, no doubt, prepared to recommend it by arguments which possessed at least considerable plausibility. The Scriptures frequently inculcate respect for age, and when the apostle says—"Likewise, ye younger, submit yourselves unto the elder," [507:3] he seems, from the connexion in which the words occur, to refer specially to the deportment of junior ministers. [507:4] In the lists of the Twelve to be found in the New Testament the name of Peter appears first; [507:5] and if, as is believed, he was more advanced in years than any of his brethren, [507:6] it is easy to understand why this precedence has been given to him; for, in all likelihood, he usually acted as president of the apostolic presbytery. Even the construction of corporate bodies in the Roman Empire might have suggested the arrangement; for it is well known that, in the senates of the cities out of Italy, the oldest decurion, under the title principalis, acted as president. [508:1] Did we, therefore, even want the direct evidence already quoted, we might have inferred, on other grounds, that, at an early date, the senior member generally presided wherever an eldership was erected.

As a point of such interest relating to the constitution of the ancient Church should be carefully elucidated, it may be necessary to fortify the statement of Hilary by some additional evidence. It is not to be supposed that this candid and judicious commentator ventured, without due authority, to describe the original order of succession in the presidential chair; and he had, no doubt, access to sources of information which have long ceased to be available; but the credit of the fact for which he vouches does not rest upon the unsustained support of his solitary attestation. Whilst his averment is recommended by internal marks of probability, and whilst it is countenanced by several scriptural intimations, it is also corroborated by a large amount of varied and independent testimony. We shall now exhibit some of the most striking portions of the confirmatory proof.

I. The language applied in ancient documents to the primitive presidents of the Churches illustrates the accuracy of this venerable commentator. In one of the earliest extant notices of these ecclesiastical functionaries, a bishop is designated "the old man." [508:2] The age of the individual who is thus distinguished was not a matter of accident; for each of his brethren in the same position, all over the Church, was called "father" [508:3] on the ground of his seniority. The official title "Pope," which has the same meaning, had also the same origin. It was given at first to every president of the eldership, because he was, in point of fact, the father, or senior member, of the judicatory. It soon, no doubt, ceased to convey this meaning, but it still remained as a memorial of the primitive regimen.

II. It is a remarkable fact that, in none of the great sees before the close of the second century, do we find any trace of the existence of a young, or even of a middle-aged bishop. When Ignatius of Antioch was martyred, he was verging on fourscore; Polycarp of Smyrna finished his career at the age of eighty-six; Pothinus of Lyons fell a victim to persecution when he was upwards of ninety; [509:1] Narcissus of Jerusalem must have been at least that age when he was first placed in the presidential chair; [509:2] one of his predecessors, named Justus, appears to have been about one hundred and ten when he reached the same dignity; [509:3] and Simeon of Jerusalem died when he had nearly completed the patriarchal age of one hundred and twenty. As an individual might become a member of the presbytery when comparatively young, [509:4] such extraordinary longevity among the bishops of the second century can be best explained by accepting the testimony of Hilary.

230

III. The number of bishops now found within a short period in the same see has long presented a difficulty to many students of ecclesiastical history. Thus, at Rome in the first forty years of the second century there were five or six bishops, [509:5] and yet only one of them suffered martyrdom. Within twelve or fifteen years after the death of Polycarp, there were several bishops in Smyrna. [510:1] But the Church of Jerusalem furnishes the most wonderful example of this quick succession of episcopal dignitaries. Simeon, one of the relatives of our Lord, is reported to have become the presiding pastor after the destruction of the city by Titus, and to have been martyred about the close of the reign of Trajan, or in A.D. 116; and yet, according to the testimony of Eusebius, [510:2] no less than thirteen bishops in succession occupied his place before the end of the year A.D. 134. He must have been set at the head of the Church when he was above threescore and ten; [510:3] and dying, as already stated, at the extreme age of one hundred and twenty, he probably left behind him a considerable staff of very aged elders. These may have become presidents in the order of their seniority; and as they would pass rapidly away, we may thus account for the extraordinary number of the early chief pastors of the ancient capital of Palestine. [510:4]

At this time, or about A.D. 135, the original Christian Church of Jerusalem was virtually dissolved. The Jews had grievously provoked Hadrian by their revolt under the impostor Barchochebas; and the Emperor, in consequence, resolved to exclude the entire race from the precincts of the holy city. The faithful Hebrews, who had hitherto worshipped there under the ministry of Simeon and his successors, still observed the Mosaic law, and were consequently treated as Jews, so that they were now obliged to break up their association, and remove to other districts. A Christian Church, composed chiefly of Gentile converts, was soon afterwards established in the same place; and the new society elected an individual, named Marcus, as their bishop, or presiding elder. Marcus was, probably, in the decline of life when he was placed at the head of the community; and on his demise, [511:1] as well as long afterwards, the old rule of succession seems to have been observed. During the sixty years immediately after his appointment, there were fifteen bishops at Jerusalem [511:2]—a fact which apparently indicates that, on the occurrence of a vacancy, the senior elder still continued to be advanced to the episcopal chair. This conclusion is remarkably corroborated by the circumstance that Narcissus, who was bishop of the ancient capital of Judea at the end of these sixty years, was, as has been already mentioned, upwards of fourscore and ten when he obtained his ecclesiastical promotion.

The episcopal roll of Jerusalem has no recorded parallel in the annals of the Christian ministry, for there were no less than twenty-eight bishops in the holy city in a period of eighty years. Even the Popes have never followed each other with such rapidity. The Roman Prelate, when elevated to St. Peter's chair, has almost invariably been far advanced in years, and the instances are not a few in which Pontiffs have fallen victims to poison or to open violence; and yet their history, even in the worst of times, exhibits nothing equal to the frequency of the successions indicated by this ancient episcopal registry. [512:1] It would appear from it that there were more bishops in Jerusalem in the second century than there have been Archbishops of Canterbury for the last four hundred years! [512:2] Such facts demonstrate that those who then stood at the head of the mother Church of Christendom, must have reached their position by means of

231

some order of succession very different from that which is now established. Hilary furnishes at once a simple and an adequate explanation. The senior minister was the president, or bishop; and as, when placed in the episcopal chair, he had already reached old age, it was not to be expected that he could long retain a situation which required some exertion and involved much anxiety. Hence the startling amount of episcopal mortality.

As the Church of Jerusalem may be said to have been founded by our Lord himself, it could lay claim to a higher antiquity than any other Christian community in existence; and it long continued to be regarded by the disciples all over the Empire with peculiar interest and veneration. [512:3] When re-established about the close of the reign of Hadrian, it was properly a new society; but it still enjoyed the prestige of ancient associations. Its history has, therefore, been investigated by Eusebius with special care; he tells us that he derived a portion of his information from its own archives; [512:4] and, though he enters into details respecting very few of the early Churches, he notices it with unusual frequency, and gives an accredited list of the names of its successive chief pastors. [513:1] About this period it was obviously considered a model which other Christian societies of less note might very safely imitate. It is, therefore, all the more important if we are able to ascertain its constitution, as we are thus prepared to speak with a measure of confidence respecting the form of ecclesiastical government which prevailed throughout the second century. The facts already stated, when coupled with the positive affirmation of the Roman Hilary, place the solution of the question, as nearly as possible, upon the basis of demonstration; for, if we reject the conclusion that, during a hundred years after the death of the Apostle John, the senior member of the presbytery of Jerusalem was the president or moderator, we may in vain attempt to explain, upon any Round statistical principles, how so many bishops passed away in succession within so limited periods, and how, at several points along the line, and exactly where they might have been expected, [513:2] we find individuals in occupation of the chair who had attained to extreme longevity.

IV. The statement of Hilary illustrates the peculiar cogency of the argumentation employed by the defenders of the faith who flourished about the close of the second century. This century was pre-eminently the age of heresies, and the disseminators of error were most extravagant and unscrupulous in their assertions. The heresiarchs, among other things, affirmed that the inspired heralds of the gospel had not committed their whole system to written records; that they had entrusted certain higher revelations only to select or perfect disciples; and that the doctrine of Aeons, which they so assiduously promulgated, was derived from this hidden treasure of ecclesiastical tradition. [514:1] To such assertions the champions of orthodoxy were prepared to furnish a triumphant reply, for they could shew that the Gnostic system was inconsistent with Scripture, and that its credentials, said to be derived from tradition, were utterly apocryphal. They could appeal, in proof of its falsehood, to the tradition which had come down to themselves from the apostles, and which was still preserved in the Churches "through the successions of the elders." [514:2] They could farther refer to those who stood at the head of their respective presbyteries as the witnesses most competent to give evidence. "We are able," says Irenaeus, "to enumerate those whom the apostles established as bishops in the Churches, [514:3] together with their successors down to our own times, who neither taught

232

any such doctrine as these men rave about, nor had any knowledge of it. For if the apostles had been acquainted with recondite mysteries which they were in the habit of teaching to the perfect disciples apart and without the knowledge of the rest, they would by all means have communicated them to those to whom they entrusted the care of the Church itself, since they wished that those whom they left behind them as their successors, and to whom they gave their own place of authority, should be quite perfect and irreproachable in all things." [514:4]

Had the succession to the episcopal chair been regulated by the arrangements of modern times, there would have been little weight in the reasoning of Irenaeus. The declaration of the bishop respecting the tradition of the Church over which he happened to preside would have possessed no special value. But it was otherwise in the days of this pastor of Lyons. The bishop was generally one of the oldest members of the community with which he was connected, and had been longer conversant with its ecclesiastical affairs than any other minister. His testimony to its traditions was, therefore, of the highest importance. In a few of the great Churches, as we have elsewhere shewn, [515:1] the senior elder now no longer succeeded, as a matter of course, to the episcopate; but age continued to be universally regarded as an indispensable qualification for the office, [515:2] and, when Irenaeus wrote, the law of seniority appears to have been still generally maintained. It was, therefore, with marked propriety that he appealed to the evidence of the bishops; as they, from their position, were most competent to expose the falsehood of the fables of Gnosticism.

V. It is well known that, in some of the most ancient councils of which we have any record, the senior bishop officiated as moderator [515:3] and, long after age had ceased to determine the succession to the episcopal chair, the recognition of its claims, under various forms, may be traced in ecclesiastical history. In Spain, so late as the fourth century, the senior chief pastor acted as president when the bishops and presbyters assembled for deliberation [515:4] In Africa the same rule was observed until the Church of that country was overwhelmed by the northern barbarians. In Mauritania and Numidia, even in the fifth century, the senior bishop of the province, whoever he might be, was acknowledged as metropolitan. [516:1] In the usages of a still later age we may discover vestiges of the ancient regulation, for the bishops sat, in the order of their seniority, in the provincial synods. [516:2] Still farther, where the bishop of the chief city of the province was the stated metropolitan, the ecclesiastical law still retained remembrancers of the primitive polity; as, when this dignitary died, the senior bishop of the district performed his functions until a successor was regularly appointed. [516:3]

Though the senior presbyter presided in the meetings of his brethren, and was soon known by the name of bishop, it does not appear that he originally possessed any superior authority. He held his place for life, but as he was sinking under the weight of years when he succeeded to it, he could not venture to anticipate an extended career of official distinction. In all matters relating either to discipline, or the general interests of the brotherhood, he was expected to carry out the decisions of the eldership, so that, under his presidential rule, the Church was still substantially governed by "the common council of the presbyters."

The allegation that presbyterial government existed in all its integrity towards the end of the second century does not rest on the foundation of obscure intimations or doubtful inferences. It can be established by direct and conclusive testimony. Evidence has already been adduced to shew that the senior presbyter of Smyrna continued to preside until the days of Irenaeus, and there is also documentary proof that meanwhile he possessed no autocratical authority. The supreme power was still vested in the council of the elders. This point is attested by Hippolytus, who was now just entering on his ecclesiastical career, and who, in one of his works, a fragment of which has been preserved, describes the manner in which the rulers of the Church dealt with the heretic Noetus. The transaction probably occurred about A.D. 190. [517:1] "There are certain others," says Hippolytus, "who introduce clandestinely a strange doctrine, being disciples of one Noetus, who was by birth a Smyrnean, and lived not long ago. This man, being puffed up, was led to forget himself, being elated by the vain fancy of a strange spirit. He said that Christ is himself the Father, and that the Father himself had been born, and had suffered and died....When the blessed presbyters heard these things, they summoned him and examined him before the Church. He, however, denied, saying at first that such were not his sentiments. But afterwards, when he had intrigued with some, and had found persons to join him in his error, he took courage, and at length resolved to stand by his dogma. The blessed presbyters again summoned him, and administered a rebuke. But he withstood them, saying—'Why, what evil am I doing in glorifying Christ?' To whom the presbyters replied—'We also truly acknowledge one God; we acknowledge Christ; we acknowledge that the Son suffered as He did suffer, that He died as He did die, and that He rose again the third day, and that He is at the right hand of the Father, and that He is coming to judge the quick and the dead; and we declare those things which we have been taught.' Then they rebuked him, and cast him out of the Church." [517:2]

About the time to which these words refer a change was made in the ecclesiastical constitution. The senior minister ceased to preside over the eldership; and the Church was no longer governed, as heretofore, by the "blessed presbyters." It would appear that the synods which were held all over the Church for the suppression of the Montanist agitation, and in connexion with the Paschal controversy, [518:1] adopted a modified episcopacy. As parties already in the presidential chair were, no doubt, permitted to hold office during life, this change could not have been accomplished instantaneously; but various circumstances concur to prove that it took place about the period now indicated. The following reasons, among others, may be adduced in support of this view of the history of the ecclesiastical revolution.

I. The Montanists, towards the termination of the second century, created much confusion by their extravagant doctrines and their claims to inspiration. These fanatics were in the habit of disturbing public worship by uttering their pretended revelations, and as they were often countenanced by individual elders, the best mode of protecting the Church from their annoyance soon became a question of grave and pressing difficulty. Episcopacy, as shall afterwards be shewn, [518:2] had already been introduced in some great cities, and about this time the Churches generally agreed to follow the influential example. It was, no doubt, thought that order could be more effectually preserved were a single individual armed with independent authority. Thus, the system of government by presbyters was gradually and silently subverted.

II. It is well known that the close of the second century is a transition period

234

in the history of the Church. A new ecclesiastical nomenclature now appeared; [519:1] the bishops acquired increased authority; and, early in the third century, they were chosen in all the chief cities by popular suffrage. The alteration mentioned by Hilary may, therefore, have been the immediate precursor of other and more vital changes.

III. Though Eusebius passes over in suspicious silence the history of all ecclesiastical innovations, his account of the bishops of Jerusalem gives good reason for believing that the law abolishing the claim of seniority came into operation about the close of the second century. He classes together the fifteen chief pastors who followed each other in the holy city immediately after its restoration by Hadrian, [519:2] and then goes on to give a list of others, their successors, whose pastorates were of the ordinary duration. He mentions likewise that the sixteenth bishop was chosen by election. [519:3] May we not here distinctly recognize the close of one system, and the commencement of another? As the sixteenth bishop was appointed about A.D. 199, the law had, probably, been then only recently enacted.

IV. Eusebius professes to trace the episcopal succession from the days of the apostles in Rome, Alexandria, Antioch, and Jerusalem; and it has often been shewn that the accuracy of these four lists is extremely problematical; but it is remarkable that in other Churches the episcopal registry cannot be carried up higher than the end of the second century. The roll of the bishops of Carthage is there discontinued, [519:4] and the episcopal registry of Spain there also abruptly terminates. But the history of the Church of Caesarea affords the most extraordinary specimen of this defalcation. Caesarea was the civil metropolis of Palestine, and a Christian Church existed in it from the days of Paul and Peter. [520:1] Its bishop in the early part of the fourth century was the friend of the Emperor Constantine and the father of ecclesiastical history. Eusebius enjoyed all needful facilities for investigating the annals of his own Church; and yet, strange to say, he commences its episcopal registry about the close of the second century! [520:2] What explanation can be given of this awkward circumstance? Had Eusebius taken no notice of any of the bishops of his own see, we could appreciate his modesty; but why should he overlook those who nourished before the time of Victor of Rome, and then refer to their successors with such marked frequency? [520:3] May we not infer, either that he deemed it inexpedient to proclaim the inconvenient fact that the bishops of Caesarea were as numerous as the bishops of Jerusalem; or that he found it impossible to recover the names of a multitude of old men who had only a nominal precedence among their brethren, and who had passed off the stage, one after another, in quick succession?

V. A statement of Eutychius, who was patriarch of Alexandria in the tenth century, and who has left behind him a history of his see from the days of the apostles, supplies a remarkable confirmation of the fact that, towards the close of the second century, a new policy was inaugurated. According to this writer there was, with the exception of the occupant of the episcopal chair of Alexandria, "no bishop in the provinces of Egypt" before Demetrius. [520:4] As Demetrius became bishop of Alexandria about A.D. 190, Christianity must have now made extensive progress in the country; [520:5] for it had been planted there perhaps one hundred and fifty years before; but it would seem that meanwhile, with the one exception, the Churches still remained under presbyterial government. Demetrius was a prelate of great influence and energy; and, during his long episcopate of forty-three years, [521:1] he succeeded in spreading all over the land the system of which he had been at one time the only representative.

It is not, indeed, to be supposed that the whole Church, prompted by a sudden and simultaneous impulse, agreed, all at once, to change its ecclesiastical arrangements. Another polity, as has already been intimated, at first made its appearance in places of commanding influence; and its advocates now, no doubt, most assiduously endeavoured to recommend its claims by appealing to the fruits of experience. The Church of Rome, as will subsequently appear, took the lead in setting up a mitigated form of prelacy; the Churches of Antioch and Alexandria followed; and, soon afterwards, other Christian communities of note adopted the example. That this subject may be fairly understood, a few chapters must now be employed in tracing the rise and progress of the hierarchy.

CHAPTER VI

THE RISE OF THE HIERARCHY CONNECTED WITH THE
SPREAD OF HERESIES

Eusebius, already so often quoted, and known so widely as the author of the earliest Church history, flourished in the former half of the fourth century. This distinguished father was a spectator of the most wonderful revolution recorded in the annals of the world. He had seen Christianity proscribed, and its noblest champions cut down by a brutal martyrdom; and he had lived to see a convert to the faith seated on the throne of the Caesars, and ministers of the Church basking in the sunshine of Imperial bounty. He was himself a special favourite with Constantine; as bishop of Caesarea, the chief city of Palestine, he had often access to the presence of his sovereign; and in a work which is still extant, professing to be a Life of the Emperor, he has well-nigh exhausted the language of eulogy in his attempts to magnify the virtues of his illustrious patron.

Eusebius may have been an accomplished courtier, but certainly he is not entitled to the praise of a great historian. The publication by which he is best known would never have acquired such celebrity, had it not been the most ancient treatise of the kind in existence. Though it mentions many of the ecclesiastical transactions of the second and third centuries, and supplies a large amount of information which would have otherwise been lost, it must be admitted to be a very ill-arranged and unsatisfactory performance. Its author does not occupy a high position either as a philosophic thinker, a judicious observer, or a sound theologian. He makes no attempt to point out the germs of error, to illustrate the rise and progress of ecclesiastical changes, or to investigate the circumstances which led to the formation of the hierarchy. Even the announcement of his Preface, that his purpose is "to record the successions of the holy apostles," or, in other words, to exhibit some episcopal genealogies, proclaims how much he was mistaken as to the topics which should have been noticed most prominently in his narrative. It is somewhat doubtful whether his history was expressly written, either for the illumination of his own age, or for the instruction of posterity; and its appearance, shortly after the public recognition of Christianity by the State, [523:1] is fitted to generate a suspicion that it was intended to influence the mind of Constantine, and to recommend the episcopal order to the consideration of the great proselyte.

About six or seven years after the publication of this treatise a child was born who was destined to attain higher distinction, both as a scholar and a writer, than the polished Eusebius. This was Jerome—afterwards a presbyter of Rome, and a father whose productions challenge the foremost rank among the memorials of patristic erudition. Towards the close of the fourth century he shone the brightest literary star in the Church, and even the proud Pope Damasus condescended to cultivate his favour. At one time he contemplated the composition of a Church history, [523:2] and we have reason to regret that the design was never executed, as his works demonstrate that he was in possession of much rare and important information for which we search in vain in the pages of the bishop of Caesarea.

No ancient writer has thrown more light on the history of the hierarchy than Jerome. His remarks upon the subject frequently drop incidentally from his pen, and must be sought for up and down throughout his commentaries and epistles; but he speaks as an individual who was quite familiar with the topics which he introduces; and, whilst all his statements are consistent, they are confirmed and illustrated by other witnesses. As a presbyter, he seems to have been jealous of the honour of his order; and, when in certain moods, he is obviously very well disposed to remind the bishops that their superiority to himself was a mere matter of human arrangement. One of his observations relative to the original constitution of the Christian commonwealth has been often quoted. "Before that, by the prompting of the devil, there were parties in religion, and it was said among the people, I am of Paul, and I of Apollos, and I of Cephas, the Churches were governed by the common council of the presbyters. But, after that each, one began to reckon those whom he baptized as belonging to himself and not to Christ, it was DECREED THROUGHOUT THE WHOLE WORLD that one elected from the presbyters should be set over the rest, that he should have the care of the whole Church, that the seeds of schisms might be destroyed." [524:1]

Because Jerome in this place happens to use language which occurs in the First Epistle of Paul to the Corinthians, we are not to understand him as identifying the date of that letter with the origin of prelacy. Such a conclusion would be quite at variance with the tenor of this passage. The words, "I am of Paul, and I of Apollos, and I of Cephas," [525:1] are used by him rhetorically; he was accustomed to repeat them when describing schisms or contentions; and he has employed them on one memorable occasion in relation to a controversy of the fourth century. [525:2] The divisions among the Corinthians, noticed by Paul, were trivial and temporary; the Church at large was not disturbed by them; but Jerome speaks of a time when the whole ecclesiastical community was so agitated that it was threatened with dismemberment. The words immediately succeeding those which we have quoted clearly shew that he dated the origin of prelacy after the days of the apostles. "Should any one think that the identification of bishop and presbyter, the one being a name of age and the other of office, is not a doctrine of Scripture, but our own opinion, let him refer to the words of the

237

apostle saying to the Philippians-'Paul and Timotheus, the servants of Jesus Christ, to all the saints in Christ Jesus which are at Philippi, with the bishops and deacons, Grace to you and peace,' [525:3] and so forth. Philippi is one city of Macedonia, and truly in one city, there cannot be, as is thought, more than one bishop; but because, at that time, they called the same parties bishops and presbyters, therefore he speaks of bishops as of presbyters without making distinction. Still this may seem doubtful to some unless confirmed by another testimony. In the Acts of the Apostles it is written [526:1] that when the apostle came to Miletus he 'sent to Ephesus and called the elders of the same Church,' to whom then, among other things, he said—'Take heed to yourselves and to all the flock over which the Holy Ghost has made you bishops, [526:2] to feed the Church of the Lord which He has purchased with His own blood.' And attend specially to this, how, calling the elders of the one city Ephesus, he afterwards addressed the same as bishops. Whoever is prepared to receive that Epistle which is written to the Hebrews under the name of Paul, [526:3] there also the care of the Church is divided equally among more than one, since he writes to the people—'Obey them that have the rule over you and submit yourselves, for they are they who watch for your souls as those who must give account, that they may not do it with grief, since this is profitable for you.' [526:4] And Peter, who received his name from the firmness of his faith, in his Epistle speaks, saying— 'The elders, therefore, who are among you, I exhort, who am also an elder, and a witness of the sufferings of Christ, and who am a partaker of his glory which shall be revealed, feed that flock of the Lord which is among you, not by constraint but willingly.' [527:1] We may thus shew that anciently bishops and presbyters were the same; but, by degrees, THAT THE PLANTS OF DISSENSION MIGHT BE ROOTED UP, all care was transferred to one. As, therefore, the presbyters know that, in accordance with the custom of the Church, they are subject to him who has been set over them, so the bishops should know that they are greater than the presbyters, rather by custom, than by the truth of an arrangement of the Lord." [527:2]

Jerome here explains himself in language which admits of no second interpretation; for all these proofs, adduced to shew that the Church was originally under presbyterial government, are of a later date than the First Epistle to the Corinthians. The Epistle to the Philippians contains internal evidence that it was dictated during Paul's first imprisonment at Rome; the Epistle to the Hebrews appeared after his liberation; and the First Epistle of Peter was written in the old age of the apostle of the circumcision. [527:3] Nor is this even the full amount of his testimony to the antiquity of the presbyterian polity. On another occasion, after mentioning some of the texts which have been given, he goes on to make quotations from the Second and Third Epistles of John—which are generally dated towards the close of the first century [527:4]—and he declares that prelacy had not made its appearance when these letters were written. Having produced authorities from Paul and Peter, he exclaims—"Do the testimonies of such men seem small to you? Let the Evangelical Trumpet, the Son of Thunder, whom Jesus loved very much, who drank the streams of doctrine from the bosom of the Saviour, sound in your ears—'The elder, unto the elect lady and her children, whom I love in the truth;' [528:1] and, in another epistle—'The elder to the very dear Caius, whom I love in the truth.' [528:2] But what was done afterwards, when one was elected who was set over the rest, was for a cure of schism; lest every one, insisting upon his own will, should rend the Church of God." [528:3]

We have already seen [528:4] that extant documents, written about the close of the first century and the middle of the second, bear similar testimony as to the original constitution of the Church. The "Epistle of Clement to the Corinthians" cannot be dated earlier than the termination of the reign of Domitian, for it refers to a recent persecution, [528:5] it describes the community to which it in addressed as "most ancient," it declares that others now occupied the places of those who had been ordained by the apostles, and it states that this second generation of ministers had been long in possession of their ecclesiastical charges. [528:6] Candid writers, of almost all parties, acknowledge that this letter distinctly recognizes the existence of government by presbyters. [528:7] The evidence of the letter of Polycarp [528:8] is not less explicit. Jerome, therefore, did not speak without authority when he affirmed that prelacy was established after the days of the apostles, and as an antidote against schism.

The apostolic Church was comparatively free from divisions; and, whilst the inspired heralds of the gospel lived, it could not be said that "there were parties in religion." The heretics who appeared were never able to organize any formidable combinations; they were inconsiderable in point of numbers; and, though not wanting in activity, those to whom our Lord had personally entrusted the publication of His Word, were ready to oppose them, so that all their efforts were effectually checked or defeated. The most ancient writers acknowledge that, during the early part of the second century, the same state of things continued. According to Hegesippus, who outlived Polycarp about fifteen or twenty years, [529:1] the Church continued until the death of Simeon of Jerusalem, in A.D. 116, [529:2] "as a pure and uncorrupted virgin." "If there were any at all," says he, "who attempted to pervert the right standard of saving doctrine, they were yet skulking in dark retreats; but when the sacred company of the apostles had, in various ways, finished their career, AND THE GENERATION OF THOSE WHO HAD BEEN PRIVILEGED TO HEAR THEIR INSPIRED WISDOM HAD PASSED AWAY, then at length the fraud of false teachers produced a confederacy of impious errors." [529:3] The date of the appearance of these parties is also established by the testimony of Celsus, who lived in the time of the Antonines, and who was one of the most formidable of the early antagonists of Christianity. This writer informs us that, though in the beginning the disciples were agreed in sentiment, they became, in his days, when "spread out into a multitude, divided and distracted, each aiming to give stability to his own faction." [530:1]

The statements of Hegesippus and Celsus are substantiated by a host of additional witnesses. Justin Martyr, [530:2] Irenaeus, [530:3] Clemens Alexandrinus, [530:4] Cyprian, [530:5] and others, all concur in representing the close of the reign of Hadrian, or the beginning of the reign of Antoninus Pius, as the period when heresies burst forth, like a flood, upon the Church. The extant ecclesiastical writings of the succeeding century are occupied chiefly with their refutation. No wonder that the best champions of the faith were embarrassed and alarmed. They had hitherto been accustomed to boast that Christianity was the cement which could unite all mankind, and they had pointed triumphantly to its influence in bringing together the Jew and the Gentile, the Greek and the barbarian, the master and the slave, the learned and the illiterate. They had looked forward with high expectation to the days of its complete ascendency,

239

when, under its gentle sway, all nations would exhibit the spectacle of one great and happy brotherhood. How, then, must they have been chagrined by the rise and spread of heresies! They saw the Church itself converted into a great battle-field, and every man's hand turned against his fellow. In almost all the populous cities of the Empire, as if on a concerted signal, the errorists commenced their discussions. The Churches of Lyons, [531:1] of Rome, of Corinth, of Athens, of Ephesus, of Antioch, and of Alexandria, resounded with the din of theological controversy. Nor were the heresiarchs men whom their opponents could afford to despise. In point of genius and of literary resources, many of them were fully equal to the most accomplished of their adversaries. Their zeal was unwearied, and their tact most perplexing. Mixing up the popular elements of the current philosophy with a few of the facts and doctrines of the gospel, they produced a compound by which many were deceived. How did the friends of the Church proceed to grapple with these difficulties? They, no doubt, did their utmost to meet the errorists in argument, and to shew that their theories were miserable perversions of Christianity. But they did not confine themselves to the use of weapons drawn from their own heavenly armoury. Not a few presbyters were themselves tainted with the new opinions; some of them were even ringleaders of the heretics; [531:2] and, in an evil hour, the dominant party resolved to change the constitution of the Church, and to try to put down disturbance by means of a new ecclesiastical organization. Believing, with many in modern times, that "parity breedeth confusion," and expecting, as Jerome has expressed it, "that the seeds of schisms might be destroyed," they sought to invigorate their administration by investing the presiding elder with authority over the rest of his brethren. The senior presbyters, the last survivors of a better age, were all sound in the faith; and, as they were still at the head of the Churches in the great cities, it was thought that by enlarging their prerogatives, and by giving them the name of bishops, they would be the better able to struggle energetically with the dangers of their position. The principle that, whoever would not submit to the bishop should be cast out of the Church, was accordingly adopted; and it was hoped that in due time peace would be restored to the spiritual commonwealth.

About the same period arrangements were made in some places for changing the mode of advancement to the presidential chair, so that, in no case, an elder suspected of error could have a chance of promotion. [532:1] An immense majority of the presbyters were yet orthodox; and by being permitted to depart, as often as they pleased, from the ancient order of succession, and to nominate any of themselves to the episcopate, they could always secure the appointment of an individual representing their own sentiments. In some of the larger Churches, where their number was considerable, they appear to have usually selected three or four candidates; and then to have permitted the lot to make the ultimate decision. [532:2] But the ecclesiastical revolution could not stop here. Jealousy quickly appeared among the presbyters; and, during the excitement of elections, the more popular candidates would not long be willing to limit the voting to the presbytery. The people chose their presbyters and deacons, and now that the office of moderator possessed substantial power, and differed so much from what it was originally, why should not all the members of the Church be allowed to exercise their legitimate influence? Such a claim could not be well resisted. Thus it was that the bishops were ultimately chosen by popular suffrage. [533:1]

Some have imagined that they have discovered inconsistency in the statements of Jerome relative to prelacy. They allege, in proof, that whilst he describes the Church as governed, until the rise of "parties in religion," by the common council of the presbyters, he also speaks of bishops as in existence from the days of the apostles. "At Alexandria," says he, "from Mark the Evangelist, [by whom the Church there is said to have been founded] to Heraclas and Dionysius the bishops, [who flourished in the third century] the presbyters always named as bishop one chosen from among themselves and placed along with them [533:2] in a higher position." [533:3] It must appear, however, on due consideration, that here there is no inconsistency whatever. In the Epistle where this passage occurs Jerome is asserting the ancient dignity of presbyters, and shewing that they originally possessed prerogatives of which they had more recently been deprived. In proof of this he refers to the Church of Alexandria, one of the greatest sees in Christendom, where for upwards of a century and a half after the days of the Evangelist Mark, the presbyters appointed their spiritual overseers, and performed all the ceremonies connected with their official investiture. But it does not therefore follow that meanwhile these overseers had always possessed exactly the same amount of authority. The very fact mentioned by Jerome suggests a quite different inference, as it proves that whilst the power of the presbyters had been declining, that of the bishops had increased. In the second century the presbyters inaugurated bishops; in the days of Jerome they were not permitted even to ordain presbyters.

Jerome says, indeed, that, in the beginning, the Alexandrian presbyters nominated their bishops, but we are not to conclude that the parties chosen were always known distinctively by the designation which he here gives to them. He evidently could not have intended to convey such an impression, as in the same Epistle he demonstrates, by a whole series of texts of Scripture, that the titles bishop and presbyter were used interchangeably throughout the whole of the first century. By bishops he obviously understands the presidents of the presbyteries, or the officials who filled the chairs which those termed bishops subsequently occupied. In their own age these primitive functionaries were called bishops and presbyters indifferently; but they partially represented the bishops of succeeding times, and they always appeared in the episcopal registries as links of the apostolical succession, so that Jerome did not deem it necessary to depart from the current nomenclature. His meaning cannot be mistaken by any one who attentively marks his language, for he has stated immediately before, that episcopal authority properly commenced when the Church began to be distracted by the spirit of sectarianism. [534:1]

In this passage, however, the learned father bears unequivocal testimony to the fact that, from the earliest times, the presbytery had an official head or president. Such an arrangement was known in the days of the apostles. But the primitive moderator was very different from the bishop of the fourth century. He was the representative of the presbytery—not its master. Christ had said to the disciples—"Whosoever will be great among you, let him be your minister; and whosoever will be chief among you, let him be your servant." [535:1] Such a chief was at the head of the ancient presbytery. Without a president no Church court could transact business; and it was the duty of the chairman to preserve order, to bear many official burdens, to ascertain the sentiments of his brethren, to speak in their name, and to act in accordance with the dictates of their collective

241

wisdom. [535:2] The bishop of after-times rather resembled a despotic sovereign in the midst of his counsellors. He might ask the advice of the presbyters, and condescend to defer to their recommendations; but he could also negative their united resolutions, and cause the refractory quickly to feel the gravity of his displeasure.

Though Jerome tells us how, for the destruction of the seeds of schisms, "it was decreed throughout the whole WORLD that one elected from the presbyters should be set over the rest," we are not to suppose that the decree was carried out, all at once, into universal operation. General councils were yet unknown, and the decree must have been sanctioned at different times and by distant Church judicatories. Such a measure was first thought of shortly before the middle of the second century, but it was not very extensively adopted until about fifty years afterwards. The history of its origin must now be more minutely investigated.

CHAPTER VII

PRELACY BEGINS IN ROME

Any attentive reader who has marked the chronology of the early bishops of Rome, as given by Eusebius, [537:1] may have observed that the pastorates of those who flourished during the first forty years of the second century were all of comparatively short duration. Clement is commonly reputed to have died about A.D. 100; [537:2] he was followed by Evaristus, Alexander, Xystus, and Telesphorus; and Hyginus, who was placed at the head of the Church in A.D. 139, and who died in A.D. 142, was the fifth in succession. Thus, the five ministers next in order after Clement occupied the post of president only forty-two years, and, with the exception of Hyginus, whose official career was very brief, each appears to have held the situation for nearly an equal period. [538:1] But, on the death of Hyginus, a pastorate of unusual length commences, as Pius, by whom he was followed, continued fifteen years in office—a term considerably more extended than that of any of his five predecessors. Reckoning from the date of the advancement of Pius, we find also a decided increase in the average length of the life of the president for the remainder of the century; as, of the ten individuals in all who were at the head of the Roman Church during its revolution, the five who followed next after Clement lived only forty-two years, whilst their five successors lived fifty-nine years. Thus, there is at least some ostensible ground for the inquiry whether any arrangement was made, about the time of Hyginus, which may account for these statistics.

The origin of the Church of Rome, like the origin of the city, is buried in obscurity; and a very few facts constitute the whole amount of our information respecting it during the first century of its existence. About the time of Hyginus the twilight of history begins to dawn upon it. Guided by the glimmerings of intelligence thus supplied, we shall endeavour to illustrate tins dark passage in its annals. The following statements may contribute somewhat to the explanation of transactions which have hitherto been rarely noticed by modern ecclesiastical writers.

I. A change in the organization of the Church about the time of Hyginus, will account for the increase in the average length of the lives of the Roman bishops. [539:1] If the alteration, mentioned by Hilary, was now made in the mode of succession to the presidential chair, such a result must have followed. Under the new regime, the recommendation of large experience would still have much weight in the choice of a bishop, but he would frequently enter on his duties at a somewhat earlier age, and thus the ordinary duration of his official career would be considerably extended. [539:2]

II. The time of Hyginus exactly answers to the description of the period when, according to the testimony of Jerome, prelacy commenced. The heretics then exhibited extraordinary zeal, so that "parties in religion" were springing up all over the Empire. The Church of Rome is said to have hitherto escaped the contagion of false doctrine, [539:3] but now errorists from all quarters began to violate its purity and to disturb its peace. Valentine, Cerdo, Marcion, and Marcus appeared about this time in the Western capital. [540:1] Some of these men were noted for their genius and learning; and there is every reason to believe that they created no common ferment. They were assiduous in the dissemination of their principles, and several of them resorted to very extraordinary and unwarrantable expedients for strengthening their respective factions. An ancient writer represents them as conducting their adherents to water, and as baptizing them "in the name of the Unknown Father of the universe; in the Truth, the mother of all; and in Him who descended on Jesus." "Others again," says the same authority, "repeated Hebrew names to inspire the initiated with the greater awe." [540:2] These attempts at proselytism were not unsuccessful. Valentine, in particular, made many converts, and after his death, when Irenaeus wrote a refutation of his heresy, his disciples must still have been numerous. [540:3]

The account given by Jerome of the state of the Christian interest when it was deemed necessary to set up episcopacy, is not so completely supplemented by the condition of the Church at any other period. Never certainly did the brethren at Rome more require the services of a skilful and energetic leader, than when the Gnostic chiefs settled in the great metropolis. Never could it be said with so much truth of their community, in the language of the Latin father, that "every one reckoned those whom he baptized as belonging to himself and not to Christ;" [541:1] for, as we have just seen, some, when baptizing their disciples, used even new forms of initiation. Never, assuredly, had the advocates of expediency a better opportunity for pleading in favour of a decree ordaining that "one chosen from among the presbyters should be put over the rest, and that the whole care of the Church should be committed to him, that the seeds of schisms should be taken away." [541:2]

III. The testimony of Hilary, who was contemporary with Jerome, exactly accords with the views here promulgated as to the date of this occurrence. This writer, who was also a minister of the Roman Church, was obviously acquainted with a tradition that a change had taken place at an early period in the mode of ecclesiastical government. His evidence is all the more valuable as it contains internal proofs of derivation from an independent source; for, whilst it

243

corroborates the statement of Jerome, it supplies fresh historical details. According to his account, "after that churches were erected in all places and offices established, an arrangement was adopted different from that which prevailed at the beginning." [541:3] By "the beginning" he understands the apostolic age, or the time when the New Testament was written. [541:4] He then goes on to say, in explanation, that it was found necessary to change the mode of appointing the chairman of the eldership, and that he was now promoted to the office by election, and not by seniority. [541:5] Whilst his language indicates distinctly that this alteration was made after the days of the apostles, it also implies a date not later than the second century; for, though it was "after the beginning," it was at a time when churches had been only recently "erected in all places, and offices established." The period of the spread of heresies at Rome, at the commencement of the reign of Antoninus Pius, and when Hyginus closed his career, answers these conditions.

IV. As Rome was the head-quarters of heathenism, it was also the place where the divisions of the Church must have proved most disastrous. There, the worship of the State was celebrated in all its magnificence; there, the Emperor, the Pontifex Maximus of the gods, surrounded by a splendid hierarchy of priests and augurs, presided at the great festivals; and there, thousands and tens of thousands, prompted by interest or by prejudice, were prepared to struggle for the maintenance of the ancient superstition. Already, the Church of Rome had often sustained the violence of persecution; but, notwithstanding the bloody trials it had undergone, it had continued steadily to gain strength; and a sagacious student of the signs of the times might even now have looked forward to the day when Christianity and paganism, on nearly equal terms, would be contending for mastery in the chief city of the Empire. But the proceedings of the heretics were calculated to dissipate all the visions of ecclesiastical ascendency. If the Roman Christians were split up into fragments by sectarianism, the Church, in one of its great centres of influence, would be incalculably injured. And yet, how could the crisis be averted? How could heresy be most effectually discountenanced? How could the unity of the Church be best maintained? In times of peril the Romans had formerly been wont to set up a Dictator, and to commit the whole power of the commonwealth to one trusty and vigorous ruler. During the latter days of the Republic, the State had been almost torn to pieces by contending factions; and now, under the sway of the Emperors, it enjoyed comparative repose. It seems to have occurred to the brethren at Rome that they should try the effects of a similar change in the ecclesiastical constitution. By committing the government of the Church, in this emergency, almost entirely into the hands of one able and resolute administrator, they, perhaps, hoped to contend successfully against the dangers by which they were now encompassed.

V. A recent calamity of a different character was calculated to abate the jealousy which such a proposition might have otherwise awakened. It appears that Telesphorus, the immediate predecessor of Hyginus, suffered a violent death. [543:1] Telesphorus is the first bishop of Rome whose title to martyrdom can be fairly established; and not one of his successors during the remainder of the second century forfeited his life for his religion. The death of the presiding pastor, as a victim to the intolerance of heathenism, must have thrown the whole Church into a state of confusion and perplexity; and when Hyginus was called upon to occupy the vacant chair, well might he enter upon its duties with deep anxiety. The appearance of heresy multiplied the difficulties of his office. It might now be asked with no small amount of plausibility—Is the presiding presbyter to have no special privileges? If his mind is to be harassed continually by errorists, and if his life is to be imperilled in the service of the Church, should he not be distinguished above his brethren? Without some such encouragement will not the elders at length refuse to accept a situation which entails so much responsibility, and yet possesses so little influence? Such questions, urged under such circumstances, must have been felt to be perplexing.

VI. As there was now constant intercourse between the seat of government and all the provinces of the Empire, it would seem that the Church of the metropolis soon contrived to avail itself of the facilities of its position for keeping up a correspondence with the Churches of other countries. [544:1] In due time the results became apparent. Every event of interest which occurred in any quarter of the Christian world was known speedily in the capital; no important religious movement could be well expected to succeed without the concurrence and co-operation of the brethren at Rome; and its ministers gradually acquired such influence that they were able, to some extent, to control the public opinion of the whole ecclesiastical community. On this occasion they, perhaps, did not find it difficult to persuade their co-religionists to enter into their views. In Antioch, in Alexandria, in Ephesus, and elsewhere, as well as in Italy, the heretics had been displaying the most mischievous activity; [544:2] and it is not improbable that the remedy now proposed by the ruling spirits in the great city had already suggested itself to others. During the summer months vessels were trading to Rome from all the coasts of the Mediterranean, so that Christian deputies, without much inconvenience, could repair to head-quarters, and, in concert with the metropolitan presbyters, make arrangements for united action. If the champions of orthodoxy were nearly as zealous as the errorists, [544:3] they must have travelled much during these days of excitement. But had not the idea of increasing the power of the presiding pastor originated in Rome, or had it not been supported by the weighty sanction of the Church of the capital, it is not to be supposed that it would have been so readily and so extensively adopted by the Churches in other parts of the Empire.

VII. Though we know little of the early history of the Roman see, it would seem that, on the death of Hyginus, there was a vacancy of unusual length; and circumstances, which meanwhile took place, argue strongly in favour of the conclusion that, about this time, the change in the ecclesiastical constitution indicated by Jerome actually occurred. According to some, the interval between the death of Hyginus and the commencement of the episcopate of Pius, his immediate successor, was of several years' duration; [545:1] but it is clear that the chair must have been vacant for at least about a twelvemonth. [545:2] How are we to account for this interregnum? We know that subsequently, in the times of Decius and of Diocletian, there were vacancies of quite as long continuance; but then the Church was in the agonies of martyrdom, and the Roman Christians were prevented by the strong arm of imperial tyranny from filling up the bishopric. Now no such calamity appears to have threatened; and the commotions created by the heretics supply evidence that persecution was asleep. This long vacancy must be otherwise explained. If Hyginus had been invested with additional authority, and if he soon afterwards died, it is not to be wondered at that his removal was the signal for the renewal of agitation. Questions which, perhaps, had not hitherto been mooted, now arose. How was the vacant place to be supplied? Was the senior presbyter, no matter how ill adapted for the crisis, to be allowed to take quiet possession? If other influential Churches required to be consulted, some time would thus be occupied; so that delay in the appointment was unavoidable.

During this interval the spirit of faction was busily at work. The heretic Marcion sought admission into the Roman presbytery; [546:1] and Valentine, who appears to have been now recognized as an elder, [546:2] no doubt supported the application. The presbytery itself was probably divided, and there is good reason to believe that even Valentine had hopes of obtaining the presidential chair! His pretensions, at this period of his career, were sufficiently imposing. Though he may have been suspected of unsoundness in the faith, he had not yet committed himself by any public avowal of his errors; and as a man of literary accomplishment, address, energy, and eloquence, he had few compeers. No wonder, with so many disturbing elements in operation, that the see remained so long vacant.

Some would willingly deny that Valentine was a candidate for the episcopal chair of Rome, but the fact can be established by evidence the most direct and conclusive. Tertullian, who had lived in the imperial city, and who was well acquainted with its Church history, expressly states that "Valentine hoped for the bishopric, because he excelled in genius and eloquence, but indignant that another, who had the superior claim of a confessor, obtained the place, he deserted the Catholic Church" [546:3] The Carthaginian father does not, indeed, here name the see to which the heresiarch unsuccessfully aspired, but his words shut us up to the conclusion that he alluded to Rome. [546:4] And we can thus discover at least one reason why the history of this vacancy has been involved in so much mystery. In a few more generations the whole Church would have felt compromised by any reflection cast upon the orthodoxy of the great Western bishopric. [547:1] How sadly would many have been scandalized had it been proclaimed abroad that the arch-heretic Valentine had once hoped to occupy the chair of St Peter!

VIII. Two letters which are still extant, and which are supposed to have been addressed by Pius, the immediate successor of Hyginus, to Justus, bishop of Vienne in Gaul, supply corroborative evidence that the presiding pastor had recently obtained additional authority. Though the genuineness of these documents has been questioned, the objections urged against them have not been sufficient to prevent critics and antiquarians of all parties from appealing to their testimony. [547:2] It is not improbable that they are Latin translations from Greek originals, and we may thus account for a few words to be found in them which were introduced at a later period. [547:3] Their tone and spirit, which are entirely different from the spurious productions ascribed to the same age, plead strongly in their favour as trustworthy witnesses. The writer makes no lofty pretensions as a Roman bishop; he speaks of himself simply as at the head of an humble presbytery; and it would be difficult to divine the motive which could have tempted an impostor to fabricate such unpretending compositions. Though given as the veritable Epistles of Pius by the highest literary authorities of Borne, they are certainly ill calculated to prop up the cause of the Papacy. If their claims are admitted, they must be regarded as among the earliest authentic records in which the distinction between the terms bishop and presbyter is unequivocally recognized; and it is obvious that if alterations in the ecclesiastical constitution were made under Hyginus, they must have prepared the way for such a change in the terminology. In one of these Epistles Pius gives the following piece of advice to his correspondent:—"Let the elders and deacons respect you, not as a greater, but as the servant of Christ." [548:1] This letter purports to have been written when its author anticipated the approach of death; and the individual to whom it is directed seems to have been just placed in the episcopal chair. Had Pius believed that Justus had a divine right to rule over the presbyters, would he have tendered such an admonition? A hundred years afterwards, Cyprian of Carthage, when addressing a young prelate, would certainly have expressed himself very differently. He would, probably, have complained of the presumption of the presbyters, have boasted of the majesty of the episcopate, and have exhorted the new bishop to remember his apostolical dignity. But, in the middle of the second century, such language would have been strangely out of place. Pius is writing to an individual, just entering on an office lately endowed with additional privileges, who could not yet afford to make an arbitrary use of his new authority. He, therefore, counsels him to moderation, and cautions him against presuming on his power. "Beware," says he, "in your intercourse with your presbyters and deacons, of insisting too much on the duty of obedience. Let them feel that your prerogative is not exercised capriciously, but for good and necessary purposes. Let the elders and deacons regard you, not so much in the light of a superior, as the servant of Christ."

In another portion of this letter a piece of intelligence is communicated, which, as coming from Pius, possesses peculiar interest. When the law was enacted altering the mode of succession to the presidency, it may be supposed that the proceeding was deemed somewhat ungracious towards those aged presbyters who might have soon expected, as a matter of right, to obtain possession of the seat of the moderator. The death of Telesphorus, the predecessor of Hyginus, as a martyr, was, indeed, calculated to abate an anxiety to secure the chair; for the whole Church was thus painfully reminded that it was a post of danger, as well as of dignity; but still, when, on the occurrence of the first vacancy, Pius was promoted over the heads of older men, he may, on this ground, have felt, to some extent, embarrassed by his elevation. We may infer, however, from this letter, that the few senior presbyters, with whose advancement the late arrangement interfered, did not long survive this crisis in the history of the Church; for the bishop of Rome here informs his Gallic brother of their demise. "Those presbyters," says he, "who were taught by the apostles, [549:1] and who have survived to our own days, with whom we have united in dispensing the word of faith, have now, in obedience to the call of the Lord, gone to their eternal rest." [550:1] Such a notice of the decease of these venerable colleagues is precisely what might have been expected, under the circumstances, in a letter from Pius to Justus.

IX. The use of the word bishop, as denoting the president of the presbytery, marks an era in the history of ecclesiastical polity. New terms are not coined without necessity; neither, without an adequate cause, is a new meaning annexed to an ancient designation. When the name bishop was first used as descriptive of the chief pastor, there must have been some special reason for such an application of the title; and the rise of the hierarchy furnishes the only satisfactory explanation.[550:2] If then we can ascertain when this new

247

nomenclature first made its appearance, we can also fix the date of the origin of prelacy. Though the documentary proof available for the illustration of this subject is comparatively scanty, it is sufficient for our purpose; and it clearly shews that the presiding elder did not begin to be known by the title of bishop until about the middle of the second century. Polycarp, who seems to have written about that time,[550:3] still uses the terminology employed by the apostles. Justin Martyr, the earliest father who has left behind him memorials amounting in extent to anything like a volume, often speaks of the chief minister of the Church, and designates him, not the bishop, but the president. [551:1] His phraseology is all the more important as he lived for some time in Rome, and as he undoubtedly adopted the style of expression once current in the great city. But another writer, who was his contemporary, and who also resided in the capital, incidentally supplies evidence that the new title was then just coming into use. The author of the book called "Pastor," when referring to those who were at the head of the presbyteries, describes them as "THE BISHOPS, that is, THE PRESIDENTS OF THE CHURCHES." [551:2] The reason why he here deems it necessary to explain what he means by bishops cannot well be mistaken. The name, in its new application, was not yet familiar to the public ear; and it therefore required to be interpreted by the more ancient designation. Could we tell when this work of Hermas was written, we could also perhaps name the very year when the president of the eldership was first called bishop. [551:3] It is now pretty generally admitted that the author was no other than the brother of Pius of Rome, [551:4] the immediate successor of Hyginus, so that he wrote exactly at the time when, as appears from other evidences, the transition from presbytery to prelacy actually occurred. His words furnish a very strong, but an undesigned, attestation to the novelty of the episcopal regimen.

X. But, perhaps, the most pointed, and certainly the most remarkable testimony to the fact that a change took place in the constitution of the Roman Church in the time of Hyginus is furnished from a quarter where such a voucher might have been, least of all, anticipated. We allude to the Pontifical Book. This work has been ascribed to Damasus, the well-known bishop of the metropolis of the West, who flourished in the fourth century, but much of it is unquestionably of later origin; and though many of its statements are apocryphal, it is often quoted as a document of weight by the most distinguished writers of the Romish communion. [552:1] Its account of the early popes is little better than a mass of fables; but some of its details are evidently exaggerations, or rather caricatures, of an authentic tradition; and a few grains of truth may be discovered here and there in a heap of fictions and anachronisms. This part of the production contains one brief sentence which has greatly puzzled the commentators, [552:2] as it is strangely out of keeping with the general spirit of the narrative, and as it contradicts, rather awkwardly, the pretensions of the popedom. According to this testimony, Hyginus "ARRANGED THE CLERGY AND DISTRIBUTED THE GRADATIONS." [552:3] Peter himself is described by Romanists as organizing the Church; but here, one of his alleged successors, upwards of seventy years after his death, is set forth as the real framer of the hierarchy. [553:1] The facts already adduced prove that this obscure announcement rests upon a sound historical foundation, and that it vaguely indicates the alterations now introduced into the ecclesiastical constitution. If Hilary and Jerome be employed as its interpreters, the truth may be easily eliminated. At a synod held in Rome,

Hyginus brought under the notice of the meeting the confusion and scandal created by the movements of the errorists; and, with a view to correct these disorders, the council agreed to invest the moderator of each presbytery with increased authority, to give him a discretionary power as the general superintendent of the Church, and to require the other elders, as well as the deacons, to act under his advice and direction. A new functionary was thus established, and, under the old name of bishop or overseer, a third order was virtually added to the ecclesiastical brotherhood. Hence Hyginus, who, no doubt, took a prominent part in the deliberations of the convocation, is said to have "arranged the clergy and distributed the gradations."

The change in the ecclesiastical polity which now occurred led to results equally extensive and permanent, and yet it has been but indistinctly noticed by the writers of antiquity. Nor is it so strange that we have no contemporary account of this ecclesiastical revolution. The history of other occurrences and innovations is buried in profound obscurity. We can only ascertain by inference what were the reasons which led to the general adoption of the sign of the cross, to the use of the chrism in baptism, to standing at the Lord's Supper, to the institution of lectors, acolyths, and sub-deacons, and to the establishment of metropolitans. Though the Paschal controversy agitated almost the whole Church towards the close of the second century, and though Tertullian wrote immediately afterwards, he does not once mention it in any of his numerous extant publications. [554:1] Owing to peculiar circumstances the rise of prelacy can be more minutely traced than that of, perhaps, any other of the alterations which were introduced during the first three centuries. At the time the change which it involved was probably considered not very important; but, as the remaining literary memorials of the period are few and scanty, the reception which it experienced can now only be conjectured. The alteration was adopted as an antidote against the growth of heresy, and thus originating in circumstances of a humiliating character, there would be little disposition, on the part of ecclesiastical writers, to dwell upon its details. Soon afterwards the pride of churchmen began to be developed; and it was then found convenient to forget that all things originally did not accord with existing arrangements, and that the hierarchy itself was but a human contrivance. Prelacy soon advanced apace, and every bishop had an interest in exalting "his order." It is only wonderful that so much truth has oozed out from witnesses so prejudiced, and that the Pontifical Book contains so decisive a deposition. And the momentous consequences of this apparently slight infringement upon the primitive polity cannot be overlooked. That very Church which, in its attempts to suppress heresy, first departed from divine arrangements, was soon involved in doctrinal error, and eventually became the great foster-mother of superstition and idolatry.

It may at first seem extraordinary that the ecclesiastical transformation was so rapidly accomplished; but, when the circumstances are more attentively considered, this view of the subject presents no real difficulty. At the outset, the principle now sanctioned produced very little alteration on the general aspect of the spiritual commonwealth. At this period a Church, in most places, consisted of a single congregation; and as one elder labouring in the word and doctrine was generally deemed sufficient to minister to the flock, only a slight modification took place in the constitution of such a society. The preaching elder, who was entitled by authority of Scripture [555:1] to take precedence of elders who only ruled, had always been permitted to act as moderator; but, on the ground of the new arrangement, the pastor probably began to assume an authority over his session which he had never hitherto ventured to exercise. In the beginning of the reign of Antoninus Pius the number of towns with several Christian congregations must have been but small; and if five or six leading cities approved of the system now inaugurated at Rome, its general adoption was thus secured. The statements of Jerome and Hilary attest that the matter was submitted to a synod; and the remarkable interregnum which followed the death of Hyginus can be best accounted for on the hypothesis that meanwhile the ministers of the great metropolis found it necessary to consult the rulers of other influential and distant Churches. If the measure had the sanction of these foreign brethren, they were of course prepared to resort to it at home on the demise of their presiding presbyter. Heretics were now disturbing the Church all over the Empire, so that the same arguments could be everywhere used in favour of the new polity. We find, too, that there was a vacancy in the presidential chair at Antioch about the time of the death of Hyginus; and that, in the course of the next year, a similar vacancy occurred at Alexandria. [555:2] If the three most important Churches then in Christendom, with the sanction of a very few others of less note, almost simultaneously adopted the new arrangement, the question was practically settled. There were probably not more than twenty cities to be found with more than one Christian congregation; and places of inferior consequence would speedily act upon the example of the large capitals. But unquestionably the system now introduced gradually effected a complete revolution in the state of the Church. The ablest man in the presbytery was commonly elevated to the chair, so that the weight of his talents, and of his general character, was added to his official consequence. The bishop soon became the grand centre of influence and authority, and arrogated to himself the principal share in the administration of all divine ordinances.

When this change commenced, the venerable Polycarp was still alive, and there are some grounds for believing that, when far advanced in life, he was induced to undertake a journey to Rome on a mission of remonstrance. This view is apparently corroborated by the fact that his own Church of Smyrna did not now adopt the new polity; for we have seen [556:1] that, upwards of a quarter of a century after his demise, it still continued under presbyterial government. Irenaeus was obviously well acquainted with the circumstances which occasioned this extraordinary visit of Polycarp to Rome; but had he not come into collision with the pastor of the great city in the controversy relating to the Paschal Feast, we might never have heard of its occurrence. Even when he mentions it, he observes a mysterious silence as to its main design. The Paschal question awakened little interest in the days of Polycarp, and among the topics which he discussed with Anicetus when at Rome, it confessedly occupied a subordinate position. [556:2] "When," says Irenaeus, "the most blessed Polycarp came to Rome in the days of Anicetus, and when as to certain other matters they had a little controversy, they were immediately agreed on this point (of the Passover) without any disputation." [557:1] What the "certain other matters" were which created the chief dissatisfaction, we are left obscurely to conjecture; but we may presume that they must have been of no ordinary consequence, when so eminent a minister as Polycarp, now verging on eighty years of age, felt it necessary to make a lengthened journey by sea and land with a view to their adjustment. He

250

obviously considered that Anicetus was at least influentially connected with arrangements which he deemed objectionable; and he plainly felt that he could hope to obtain their modification or abandonment only by a personal conference with the Roman pastor. And intimations are not wanting that he was rather doubtful whether Anicetus would be disposed to treat with him as his ecclesiastical peer, for he seems to have been in some degree appeased when the bishop of the capital permitted him to preside in the Church at the celebration of the Eucharist. [557:2] This, certainly, was no extraordinary piece of condescension; as Polycarp, on various grounds, was entitled to take precedence of his Roman brother; [557:3] and the reception given to the "apostolic presbyter" was only what might have fairly been expected in the way of ministerial courtesy. [557:4] Why has it then been mentioned as an exhibition of the episcopal humility of Anicetus? Apparently because he had been previously making some arrogant assumptions. He had been, probably, presuming on his position as a pastor of the "new order," and his bearing had perhaps been so offensive that Polycarp had been commissioned to visit him on an errand of expostulation. But by prudently paying marked deference to the aged stranger; and, it may be, by giving a plausible account of some proceedings which had awakened anxiety; he appears to have succeeded in quieting his apprehensions. That the presiding minister of the Church of Smyrna was engaged in some such delicate mission is all but certain, as the design of the journey would not otherwise have been involved in so profound secrecy. The very fact of its occurrence is first noticed about forty years afterwards, when the haughty behaviour of another bishop of Rome provoked Irenaeus to call up certain unwelcome reminiscences which it must have suggested.

Though the journey of Polycarp betokens that he must have been deeply dissatisfied with something which was going forward in the great metropolis, we can only guess at its design and its results; and it is now impossible to ascertain whether the alterations introduced there encountered any very formidable opposition: but it is by no means improbable that they were effected without much difficulty. The disorders of the Church imperatively called for some strong remedy; and it perhaps occurred to not a few that a distracted presbytery, under the presidency of a feeble old man, was but ill fitted to meet the emergency. They would accordingly propose to strengthen the executive government by providing for the appointment of a more efficient moderator, and by arming him with additional authority. The people would be gratified by the change, for, though in Rome and some other great cities, where its effects would be felt most sensibly, they, no doubt, met before this time in separate congregations, yet they had still much united intercourse; and as, on such occasions, their edification depended mainly on the gifts of the chairman of the eldership, they would gladly join in advancing the best preacher in the presbytery to the office of president. At this particular crisis the alteration may not have been unacceptable to the elders themselves. To those of them who were in the decline of life, there was nothing very inviting in the prospect of occupying the most prominent position in a Church threatened by persecution and torn by divisions, so that they may have been not unwilling to waive any claim to the presidency which their seniority implied; whilst the more vigorous, sanguine, and aspiring, would hail an arrangement which promised at no distant day to place one of themselves in a position of greatly increased dignity and influence. Whilst all were agreed that the times demanded the appointment of the ablest member of presbytery as moderator, none, perhaps, foresaw the danger of adding permanently to the prerogatives of so potent a chairman. It was never anticipated that the day would come when the new law would be regarded as any other than a human contrivance; and when the bishops and their adherents would contend that the presbyters, under no circumstances whatever, had a right to reassume that power which they now surrendered. The result, however, has demonstrated the folly of human wisdom. The prelates, who were originally set up to save the Church from heresy, became themselves at length the abetters of false doctrine; and whilst they thus grievously abused the influence with which they were entrusted, they had the temerity to maintain that they still continued to be exclusively the fountains of spiritual authority.

It is not to be supposed that prelacy was set up at once in the plenitude of its power. Neither is it to be imagined that the system was simultaneously adopted by Christians all over the world. Jerome informs us that it was established "by little and little;" [559:1] and he thus apparently refers, as well to its gradual spread, as to the almost imperceptible growth of its pretensions. We have shewn, in a preceding chapter, [560:1] that in various cities, such as Smyrna, Caesarea, and Jerusalem, the senior presbyter continued to be the president until about the close of the second century; and there the Church seems to have been meanwhile governed by "the common council of the presbyters." [560:2] Evidence can be adduced to prove that, in many places, even at a much later period, the episcopal system was still unknown. [560:3] But its advocates were active and influential, and they continued to make steady progress. The consolidation of the Catholic system contributed vastly to its advancement. The leading features of this system must now be illustrated.

CHAPTER VIII

THE CATHOLIC SYSTEM

The word catholic, which signifies universal or general, came into use towards the end of the second century. Its introduction indicates a new phase in the history of the ecclesiastical community. For upwards of a hundred years after its formation, the Church presented the appearance of one great and harmonious brotherhood, as false teachers had hitherto failed to create any considerable diversity of sentiment; but when many of the literati began to embrace the gospel, the influence of elements of discord soon became obvious. These converts attempted to graft their philosophical theories on Christianity; not a few of the more unstable of the brethren, captivated by their ingenuity and eloquence, were tempted to adopt their views; and though the great mass of the disciples repudiated their adulterations of the truth, the Christian commonwealth was

252

distracted and divided. Those who banded themselves together to maintain the unity of the Church were soon known by the designation of Catholics. "After the days of the apostles," says one of the fathers, "when heresies had burst forth, and were striving under various names to tear piecemeal and divide the Dove and the Queen of God, [561:1] did not the apostolic people require a name of their own whereby to mark the unity of those that were uncorrupted? .... Therefore our people, when named Catholic, are separated by this title from those denominated heretics." [562:1]

The Catholic system, being an integral portion of the policy which invested the presiding elder with additional authority, rose contemporaneously with Prelacy. When Gnosticism was spreading so rapidly, and creating so much scandal and confusion, schism upon schism appeared unavoidable. How was the Church to be kept from going to pieces? How could its unity be best conserved? How could it contend most successfully against its subtle and restless disturbers? Such were the problems which now occupied the attention of its leading ministers. It was thought that all these difficulties would be solved by the adoption of the Catholic system. Were the Church, it was said, to place more power in the hands of individuals, and then to consolidate its influence, it could bear down more effectively upon the errorists. Every chief pastor of the Catholic Church was the symbol of the unity of his own ecclesiastical district; and the associated bishops represented the unity of the whole body of the faithful. According to the Catholic system when strictly carried out, every individual excommunicated by one bishop was excommunicated by all, so that when a heresiarch was excluded from fellowship in one city, he could not be received elsewhere. The visible unity of the Church was the great principle which the Catholic system sought to realise. "The Church," says Cyprian, "which is catholic and one, is not separated or divided, but is in truth connected and joined together by the cement of bishops mutually cleaving to each other." [562:2]

The funds of the Church were placed very early in the hands of the president of the eldership, [563:1] and though they may not have been at his absolute disposal, he, no doubt, soon found means of sustaining his authority by means of his monetary influence. But the power which he possessed, as the recognized centre of ecclesiastical unity, to prevent any of his elders or deacons from performing any official act of which he disapproved, constituted one of the essential features of the Catholic system. "The right to administer baptism," says Tertullian, "belongs to the chief priest, that is, the bishop: then to the presbyters and the deacons, [563:2] yet not without the authority of the bishop, for the honour of the Church, which being preserved, peace is preserved." [563:3] Here, the origin of Catholicism is pretty distinctly indicated; for the prerogatives of the bishop are described, not as matters of divine right, but of ecclesiastical arrangement. [563:4] They were given to him "for the honour of the Church," that peace might be preserved when heretics began to cause divisions.

Though the bishop could give permission to others to celebrate divine ordinances, he was himself their chief administrator. He was generally the only preacher; he usually dispensed baptism; [563:5] and he presided at the observance of the Eucharist. At Rome, where the Catholic system was maintained most scrupulously, his presence seems to have been considered necessary to the due consecration of the elements. Hence, at one time, the sacramental symbols were carried from the cathedral church to all the places of Christian worship throughout the city. [564:1] With such minute care did the Roman chief pastor endeavour to disseminate the doctrine that whoever was not in communion with the bishop was out of the Church.

The establishment of a close connexion, between certain large Christian associations and the smaller societies around them, constituted the next link in the organization of the Catholic system. These communities, being generally related as mother and daughter churches, were already prepared to adapt themselves to the new type of ecclesiastical polity. The apostles, or their immediate disciples, had founded congregations in most of the great cities of the Empire; and every society thus instituted, now distinguished by the designation of the principal [564:2] or apostolic Church, became a centre of ecclesiastical unity. Its presiding minister sent the Eucharist to the teachers of the little flocks in his vicinity, to signify that he acknowledged them as brethren; [564:3] and every pastor who thus enjoyed communion with the principal Church was recognized as a Catholic bishop. This parent establishment was considered a bulwark which could protect all the Christian communities surrounding it from heresy, and they were consequently expected to be guided by its traditions. "It is manifest," says Tertullian, "that all doctrine, which agrees with these apostolic Churches, THE WOMBS AND ORIGINALS OF THE FAITH, [564:4] must be accounted true, as without doubt containing that which the Churches have received from the apostles, the apostles from Christ, Christ from God: and that all other doctrine must be judged at once to be false, which savours of things contrary to the truth of the Churches, and of the apostles, and of Christ, and of God....Go through the apostolic Churches, in which the very seats of the apostles, at this very day, preside over their own places, [565:1] in which their own authentic writings are read, speaking with the voice of each, and making the face of each present to the eye. Is Achaia near to you? You have Corinth. If you are not far from Macedonia, you have Philippi, you have the Thessalonians. [565:2] If you can travel into Asia, you have Ephesus. But if you are near to Italy you have Rome, where we also have an authority close at hand." [565:3]

But the Catholic system was not yet complete. In every congregation the bishop or pastor was the centre of unity, and in every district the principal or apostolic Church bound together the smaller Christian societies; but how were the apostolic Churches themselves to be united? This question did not long remain without a solution. [565:4] Had the Church of Jerusalem, when the Catholic system was first organized, still occupied its ancient position, it might have established a better title to precedence than any other ecclesiastical community in existence. It had been, beyond all controversy, the mother Church of Christendom. But it had been recently dissolved, and a new society, composed, to a great extent, of new members, was now in process of formation in the new city of Aelia. Meanwhile the Church of Rome had been rapidly acquiring strength, and its connexion with the seat of government pointed it out as the appropriate head of the Catholic confederation. If the greatest convenience of the greatest number of Churches were to be taken into account, it had claims of peculiar potency, for it was easily accessible by sea or land from all parts of the Empire, and it had facilities for keeping up communication with the provinces to which no other society could pretend. Nor were these its only recommendations. It had, as was alleged, been watered by the ministry of two or three [556:1] of the apostles, so that, even as an apostolic Church, it had high pretensions. In addition to all

254

this, it had, more than once, sustained with extraordinary constancy the first and fiercest brunt of persecution; and if its members had so signalized themselves in the army of martyrs, why should not its bishop lead the van of the Catholic Church? Such considerations urged in favour of a community already distinguished by its wealth, as well as by its charity, were amply sufficient to establish its claim as the centre of Catholic unity. If, as is probable, the arrangement was concocted in Rome itself, they must have been felt to be irresistible. Hence Irenaeus, writing about A.D. 180, speaks of it even then as the recognized head of the Churches of the Empire. "To this Church," says he, "because it is more potentially principal, it is necessary that every Catholic Church should go, as in it the apostolic tradition has by the Catholics been always preserved." [567:1]

Many Protestant writers have attempted to explain away the meaning of this remarkable passage, but the candid student of history is bound to listen respectfully to its testimony. When we assign to the words of Irenaeus all the significance of which they are susceptible, they only attest the fact that, in the latter half of the second century, the Church of Rome was acknowledged as the most potent of all the apostolic Churches. And in the same place the grounds of its pre-eminence are enumerated pretty fully by the pastor of Lyons. It was the most ancient Church in the West of Europe; it was also the most populous; like a city set upon a hill, it was known to all; and it was reputed to have had for its founders the most illustrious of the inspired heralds of the cross, the apostle of the Gentiles, and the apostle of the circumcision. [567:2] It was more "potentially principal," because it was itself the principal of the apostolic or principal Churches.

It has been already stated that every principal bishop, [567:3] or presiding minister of an apostolic Church, sent the Eucharist to the pastors around him as a pledge of their ecclesiastical fellowship; and it would appear that the bishop of Rome kept up intercourse with the other bishops of the apostolic Churches by transmitting to them the same symbol of catholicity. [567:4] The sacred elements were doubtless conveyed by confidential churchmen, who served, at the same time, as channels of communication between the great prelate and the more influential of his brethren. By this means the communion of the whole Catholic Church was constantly maintained.

When the Catholic system was set up, and the bishop of Rome recognized as its Head, he was not supposed to possess, in his new position, any arbitrary or despotic authority. He was simply understood to hold among pastors the place which had previously been occupied by the senior elder in the presbytery—that is, he was the president or moderator. The theoretical parity of all bishops, the chief pastor of Rome included, was a principle long jealously asserted. [568:1] But the prelate of the capital was the individual to whom other bishops addressed themselves respecting all matters affecting the general interests of the ecclesiastical community; he collected their sentiments; and he announced the decisions of their united wisdom. It was, however, scarcely possible for an official in his circumstances either to satisfy all parties, or to keep within the limits of his legitimate power. When his personal feelings were known to run strongly in a particular channel, the minority, to whom he was opposed, would at least suspect him of attempting domination. Hence it was that by those who were discontented with his policy he was tauntingly designated, as early as the beginning of the third century, The Supreme Pontiff, and The Bishop of Bishops. [568:2] These titles cannot now be gravely quoted as proofs of the existence of the claims which they indicate; for they were employed ironically by malcontents who wished thus either to impeach his partiality, or to condemn his interference. But they supply clear evidence that his growing influence was beginning to be formidable, and that he already stood at the head of the ministers of Christendom.

The preceding statements enable us to understand why the interests of Rome and of the Catholic Church have always been identified. The metropolis of Italy has, in fact, from the beginning been the heart of the Catholic system. In ancient times Roman statesmen were noted for their skill in fitting up the machinery of political government: Roman churchmen have laboured no less successfully in the department of ecclesiastical organization. The Catholic system is a wonderful specimen of constructive ability; and there is every reason to believe that the same city which produced Prelacy, also gave birth, about the same time, to this masterpiece of human contrivance. The fact may be established, as well by other evidences, as by the positive testimony of Cyprian. The bishop of Carthage, who flourished only about a century after it appeared, was connected with that quarter of the Church in which it originated. We cannot, therefore, reasonably reject the depositions of so competent a witness, more especially when he speaks so frequently and so confidently of its source. When he describes the Roman bishopric as "the root and womb of the Catholic Church," [569:1] his language admits of no second interpretation. He was well aware that the Church of Jerusalem was the root and womb of all the apostolic Churches; and when he employs such phraseology, he must refer to some new phase of Christianity which had originated in the capital of the Empire. In another place he speaks of "the see of Peter, and the principal Church, whence the unity of the priesthood took its rise." [569:2] Such statements shut us up to the conclusion that Rome was the source and centre from which Catholicism radiated.

This system could have been only gradually developed, and nearly half a century appears to have elapsed before it acquired such maturity that it attained a distinctive designation. [570:1] But, as it was currently believed to be admirably adapted to the exigencies of the Church, it spread with much rapidity; and, in less than a hundred years after its rise, its influence may be traced in almost all parts of the Empire. We may thus explain a historical phenomenon which might otherwise be unaccountable. Towards the close of the second and throughout the whole of the third century, ecclesiastical writers connected with various and distant provinces refer with peculiar respect to the Apostle Peter, and even appeal to Scripture [570:2] with a view to his exaltation. Their misinterpretations of the Word reveal an extreme anxiety to obtain something like an inspired warrant for their catholicism. The visible unity of the Church was deemed by them essential to its very existence, and the Roman see was the actual key-stone of the Catholic structure. Hence every friend of orthodoxy imagined it to be, as well his duty as his interest, to uphold the claims of the supposed representative of Peter, and thus to maintain the cause of ecclesiastical unity. It might have been anticipated under such circumstances that Scripture would be miserably perverted, and that the see, which was believed to possess as its heritage the prerogatives of the apostle of the circumcision, would be the subject of extravagant laudation.

Ambition has been often represented as the great principle which guided the policy of the early Roman bishops, but there is no evidence that, as a class, they were inferior in piety to other churchmen, and the readiness with which some of them suffered for the faith attests their Christian sincerity and resolution. Ambition, doubtless, soon began to operate; but their elevation was not so much the result of any deep-laid scheme for their aggrandizement, as of a series of circumstances pushing them into prominence, and placing them in a most influential position. The efforts of heretics to create division led to a reaction, and tempted the Church to adopt arrangements for preserving union by which its liberties were eventually compromised. The bishop of Rome found himself almost immediately at the head of the Catholic league, and there is no doubt that, before the close of the second century, he was acknowledged as the chief pastor of Christendom. About that time we see him writing letters to some of the most distinguished bishops of the East [571:1] directing them to call councils; and it does not appear that his epistles were deemed unwarranted or officious. Unity of doctrine was speedily connected with unity of discipline, and an opinion gradually prevailed that the Church Catholic should exhibit universal uniformity. When Victor differed from the Asiatic bishops relative to the mode of observing the Paschal festival, he was only seeking to realize the idea of unity; and, as the Head of the Catholic Church, he might have carried out against them his threat of excommunication, had he not in this particular case been moving in advance of public opinion. When Stephen, sixty years afterwards, disputed with Cyprian and others concerning the rebaptism of heretics, he was still endeavouring to work out the same unity; and the bishop of Carthage found himself involved in contradictions when he proceeded at once to assert his independence, and to concede to the see of Peter the honour which, as he admitted, it could legitimately challenge. [572:1]

The theory of Catholicism is based on principles thoroughly fallacious. Assuming that visible unity is essential to the Church on earth, it sanctions the startling inference that whoever is not connected with a certain ecclesiastical society must be out of the pale of salvation. The most grinding spiritual tyranny ever known has been erected on this foundation. And yet how hollow is the whole system! It is no more necessary that all the children of God in this world should belong to the same visible Church than that all the children of men should be connected with the same earthly monarchy. All believers are "one in Christ;" they have all "one Lord, one faith, one baptism;" but "the kingdom of God cometh not with observation," and the unity of the saints on earth can be discerned only by the eye of Omniscience. They are all sustained by the same living bread which cometh down from heaven, but they may receive their spiritual provision as members of ten thousand separated Churches. All who truly love the Saviour are united to Him by a link which can never be broken; and no ecclesiastical barrier can either exclude them from His presence here, or shut them out from His fellowship hereafter. But a number of men might as well propose to appropriate all the light of the sun or all the winds of heaven, as attempt to form themselves into a privileged society with a monopoly of the means of salvation.

The Church of Rome is understood to be the spiritual Babylon of the Apocalypse, and yet one point of correspondence between the type and the antitype seems to have been hitherto overlooked. The great city of Babylon commenced with the erection of Babel, and the builders said—"Go to, let us build us a city, and a tower whose top may reach unto heaven, and let us make us a name, lest we be scattered abroad upon the face of the whole earth." [573:1] Civil unity was avowedly the end designed by these architects. Amongst other purposes contemplated by the famous tower, it appears to have been intended to

257

serve as a centre of catholicity—a great rallying point or landmark—by which every citizen might be guided homewards when he lost his way in the plain of Shinar. It is a curious fact that in the "Pastor of Hermas," perhaps the first work written in Rome after the establishment of Prelacy, the Church is described under the similitude of a tower! [573:2] When Hyginus "established the gradations," the hierarchy at once assumed that appearance. And the see of Peter, the centre of Catholic unity, was now to be the great spiritual landmark to guide the steps of all true churchmen. The ecclesiastical builders prospered for a time, but when Constantine had finished a new metropolis in the East, some symptoms of disunion revealed themselves. When the Empire was afterwards divided, jealousies increased; the builders could not well understand one another's speech; and the Church at length witnessed the great schism of the Greeks and the Latins. In due time the Reformation interfered still more vexatiously with the building of the ecclesiastical Babel. But this more recent schism has given a mighty impulse to the cause of freedom, of civilization, and of truth; for the Protestants, scattered abroad over the face of the whole earth, have been spreading far and wide the light of the gospel. The builders of Babel still continue their work, but their boasted unity is gone for ever; and now, with the exception of their political manoeuvring, their highest achievements are literally in the department of stone and mortar. They may found costly edifices, and they may erect spires pointing, like the tower of Babel, to the skies, but they can no longer reasonably hope to bind together the liberated nations with the chains of a gigantic despotism, or to induce worshippers of all kindreds and tongues to adopt the one dead language of Latin superstition. The signs of the times indicate that the remnant of the Catholic workmen must soon "leave off to build the city." The final overthrow of the mystical Babylon will usher in the millennium of the Church, and the present success of Protestant missions is premonitory of the approaching doom of Romish ritualism. It is written—"I saw another angel fly in the midst of heaven, having the everlasting gospel to preach unto them that dwell on the earth, and to every nation, and kindred, and tongue, and people, saying with a loud voice, Fear God, and give glory to him; for the hour of his judgment is come: and worship him that made heaven, and earth, and the sea, and the fountains of waters. And there followed another angel, saying, Babylon is fallen, is fallen, that great city, because she made all nations drink of the wine of the wrath of her fornication." [574:1]

CHAPTER IX

PRIMITIVE EPISCOPACY AND PRESBYTERIAN ORDINATION

It has been already stated that, except in a few great cities where there were several Christian congregations, the introduction of Episcopacy produced a very slight change in the appearance of the ecclesiastical community. In towns and villages, where the disciples constituted but a single flock, they had commonly only one teaching elder; and as, in accordance with apostolic rule, [575:1] this labourer in the word and doctrine was deemed worthy of double honour, he was already the most prominent and influential member of the brotherhood. The new arrangement merely clothed him with the name of bishop, and somewhat augmented his authority. Having the funds of the Church at his disposal, he had special influence; and though he could not well act without the sanction of his elders, he could easily contrive to negative any of their resolutions which did not meet his approval.

It is abundantly clear that this primitive dignitary was ordinarily the pastor of only a single congregation. "If, before the multitude increase, there should be a place having a few faithful men in it, to the extent of twelve, who shall be able to make a dedication to pious uses for a bishop, let them write to the Churches round about the place," says an ancient canon, "that three chosen men.... may come to examine with diligence him who has been thought worthy of this degree.... If he has not a wife, it is a good thing; but if he has married a wife, having children, let him abide with her, continuing steadfast in every doctrine, able to explain the Scriptures well." [576:1] This humble functionary was assisted in the management of his little flock by two or three elders. "If the bishop has attended to the knowledge and patience of the love of God," says another regulation, "let him ordain two presbyters, when he has examined them, or rather three." [576:2] The bishop, the elders, and the deacons, all assembled in one place every Lord's day for congregational worship. An old ecclesiastical law accordingly prescribes the following arrangement—"Let the seat of the bishop be placed in the midst, and let the presbyters sit on each side of him, and let the deacons stand by them,... and let it be their care that the people sit a with all quietness and order in the other part of the church." [576:3] Thus, except in the case of a few large towns, the primitive bishop was simply the parochial minister. Towards the close of the second century, the bishop and the teacher were designations of the same import. Speaking of those at the head of the Churches, Irenaeus describes them as distinguished by their superior or inferior ability in sermonizing; [576:4] and a well-informed writer, who flourished as late as the fourth century, mentions preaching as the bishop's peculiar function. [576:5] In the apostolic age every one who had popular gifts was permitted to edify the congregation by their exercise; [576:6] and, long afterwards, any elder, who was qualified to speak in the Church, was at liberty to address his fellow-worshippers. When Origen, prior to his ordination as a presbyter, ventured to expound the Scriptures publicly at the request of the bishops of Palestine, Demetrius, his own ecclesiastical superior, denounced his conduct as irregular; but the parties, by whom the learned Alexandrian had been invited to lecture, boldly vindicated the proceeding. He (Demetrius) has asserted, said they, "that this was never before either heard or done, that laymen should deliver discourses in the presence of bishops. We know not how it happens that he is here evidently so far from the truth. For, indeed, wherever there are found those qualified to benefit the brethren, they are exhorted by the holy bishops to address the people." [577:1] But still the bishop himself was the stated and ordinary preacher; and when he was sick or absent, the flock could seldom expect a sermon. When present, he always administered the Lord's Supper with his own hands, and dispensed in person the rite of baptism. He also occupied the chair at the meetings of the

259

presbytery, and presided at the ordination of the elders and deacons of his congregation.

Though Christians formed but a fraction, and often but a small fraction of the population, their bishops were thickly planted. Thus, Cenchrea, the port of Corinth, had an episcopal overseer, [577:2] as well as Corinth itself; the bishop of Portus and the bishop of Ostia were only two miles asunder; [577:3] and, of the eighty-seven bishops who met at Carthage, about A.D. 256, to discuss the question of the rebaptism of heretics, many, such as Mannulus, Polianus, Dativus, and Secundinus, [577:4] were located in small towns or villages. Though, probably, some of these pastors had not the care of more than twenty or thirty Christian families, each had the same rank and authority as the bishop of Carthage. "It remains," said Cyprian at the opening of the council, "that we severally declare our opinion on this same subject, judging no one, nor depriving any one of the right of communion if he differ from us. For no one of us sets himself up as a bishop of bishops, or by tyrannical terror forces his colleagues to a necessity of obeying; inasmuch as every bishop in the free use of his liberty and power has the right of forming his own judgment." [578:1] In other quarters of the Church its episcopal guardians were equally numerous. Hence it is said of the famous Paul of Samosata, bishop of Antioch, that, to sustain his reputation, he instigated "the bishops of the adjacent rural districts and towns" to praise him in their addresses to the people. [578:2] Even so late as the middle of the third century, the jurisdiction of the greatest bishops was extremely limited. Cyprian of Carthage, in point of position the second prelate in the Western Church, presided over only eight or nine presbyters; [578:3] and Cornelius of Rome, confessedly the most influential ecclesiastic in Christendom, had the charge of probably not more than fourteen congregations. [578:4]

There were commonly several elders and deacons connected with every worshipping society, and though these, as well as the bishops, began, towards the close of the second century, to be called clergymen, [578:5] and were thus taught to cherish the idea that the Lord was their inheritance, it would be quite a mistake to infer that they all subsisted on their official income. Not a few of them probably derived their maintenance from secular employments, some of them being tradesmen or artizans, and others in stations of greater prominence. Hyacinthus, an elder of the Church of Rome in the time of bishop Victor, appears to have held a situation in the Imperial household, [579:1] and Tertullian complains that persons engaged in trades directly connected with the support of idolatry were promoted to ecclesiastical offices. [579:2] There was a time when even an apostle laboured as a tent-maker, but as the hierarchical spirit acquired strength, and as the Church increased in wealth and numbers, there was a growing impression that all its office-bearers were degraded by such services. Cyprian speaks with extreme bitterness of a deceased elder who had appointed a brother elder the executor of his will, declaring that the clergy "should in no way be called off from their holy ministrations nor tied down by secular troubles and business." [579:3] But the common sense of the Church revolted against such high-flown spiritualism, as in many districts where the disciples were still few and indigent, they could not afford a suitable support for all entrusted with the performance of ecclesiastical duties. Hence, before the recognition of Christianity by Constantine, even bishops in some countries were permitted by trade to eke out a scanty maintenance. "Let not bishops, elders, and deacons leave their places for the sake of trading," says a council held in the beginning of the fourth century, "nor travelling about the provinces let them be found dealing in fairs. However, to provide a living for themselves, let them send either a son, or a freedman, or a servant, or a friend, or any one else: and if they wish to trade, let them do so within their province." [580:1]

It is clear, from the New Testament, that, in the apostolic age, ordination was performed by "the laying on of the hands of the presbytery," and this mode of designation to the ministry appears to have continued until some time in the third century. We are informed by the most learned of the fathers, in a passage to which the attention of the reader has already been invited, [580:2] that "even at Alexandria, from Mark the Evangelist until Heraclas and Dionysius the bishops, the presbyters were always in the habit of naming bishop one chosen from among themselves and placed in a higher degree, in the same manner as if an army should make an emperor, or the deacons choose from among themselves one whom they knew to be industrious and call him archdeacon." [580:3] As Jerome here mentions various important facts of which we might have otherwise remained ignorant, and as this statement throws much light upon the ecclesiastical history of the early Church, it is entitled to special notice.

In the letter where this passage occurs the writer is extolling the dignity of presbyters, and is endeavouring to shew that they are very little inferior to bishops. He admits, indeed, that, in his own days, they had ceased to ordain; but he intimates that they once possessed the right, and that they retained it in all its integrity until the former part of the preceding century. Some have thought that Jerome has here expressed himself indefinitely, and that he did not know the exact date at which the arrangement he describes ceased at Alexandria. But his testimony, when fairly analysed, can scarcely be said to want precision; for he obviously speaks of Heraclas and Dionysius as bishops by anticipation, alleging that a custom which anciently existed among the elders of the Egyptian metropolis was maintained until the time when these ecclesiastics, who afterwards successively occupied the episcopal chair, sat together in the presbytery. The period, thus pointed out, can be easily ascertained. Demetrius, bishop of Alexandria, after a long official life of forty-three years, died about A.D. 232, [581:1] and it is well known that Heraclas and Dionysius were both members of his presbytery towards the close of his episcopal administration. It was, therefore, shortly before his demise that the new system was introduced. In certain parts of the Church the arrangement mentioned by Jerome probably continued somewhat longer. Cyprian apparently hints at such cases of exception when he says that in "almost all the provinces," [581:2] the neighbouring bishops assembled, on the occasion of an episcopal vacancy, at the new election and ordination. It may have been that, in a few of the more considerable towns, the elders still continued to nominate their president.

When the erudite Roman presbyter informs us that "even at Alexandria" [581:3] the elders formerly made their own bishop, his language obviously implies that such a mode of creating the chief pastor was not confined to the Church of the metropolis of Egypt. It existed wherever Christianity had gained a footing, and he mentions this particular see, partly, because of its importance—being, in point of rank, the second in the Empire—and partly, perhaps, because the remarkable circumstances in its history, leading to the alteration which he specifies, were known to all his well-informed contemporaries. Jerome does not say that the Alexandrian presbyters inducted their bishop by imposition of hands, [582:1] or set him apart to his office by any formal ordination. His words apparently indicate that they did not recognize the necessity of any special rite of investiture; that they made the bishop by election; and that, when once acknowledged as the object of their choice, he was at liberty to enter forthwith on the performance of his episcopal duties. When the Roman soldiers made an emperor they appointed him by acclamation, and the cheers which issued from their ranks as he stood up before the legions and as he was clothed with the purple by one of themselves, constituted the ceremony of his inauguration. The ancient archdeacon was still one of the deacons; [582:2] as he was the chief almoner of the Church, he required to possess tact, discernment, and activity; and, in the fourth century, he was nominated to his office by his fellow-deacons. Jerome assures us that, until the time of Heraclas and Dionysius, the elders made a bishop just in the same way as in his own day the soldiers made an emperor, or as the deacons chose one whom they knew to be industrious, and made him an archdeacon.

In one of the letters purporting to have been written by Pius, bishop of Rome, to Justus of Vienne, shortly after the middle of the second century, there is a passage which supplies a singularly striking confirmation of the testimony of Jerome. Even were we to admit that the genuineness of this epistle cannot be satisfactorily established, it must still be acknowledged to be a very ancient document, and were it of somewhat later date than its title indicates, it should at least be received as representing the traditions which prevailed respecting the ecclesiastical arrangements of an early antiquity. In this communication Pius speaks of his episcopal correspondent of Vienne as "constituted by the brethren and clothed with the dress of the bishops." [583:1] By "the brethren," as is plain from another part of the letter, [583:2] he understands the presbytery. And as the soldiers made a sovereign by saluting him emperor, and arraying him in the purple; so the elders made a president by clothing him with a certain piece of dress, and calling him bishop. Thus, the statement of Jerome is exactly corroborated by the evidence of this witness.

We may infer from the letter of Pius that in Gaul and Italy, as well as in Egypt, the elders were in the habit of making their own bishop. [583:3] There is not a particle of evidence to shew that any other arrangement originally existed. The declaration of so competent an authority as Jerome backed by the attestation of this ancient epistle may be regarded as perfectly conclusive. [583:4] But other proofs of the same fact are not wanting. For a long period the bishop continued to be known by the title of "the elder who presides"-a designation which obviously implies that he was still only one of the presbyters. When the Paschal controversy created such excitement, and when Victor of Rome threatened to renounce the communion of those who held views different from his own, Irenaeus of Lyons wrote a letter of remonstrance to the haughty churchman in which he broadly reminded him of his ecclesiastical position. "Those, presbyters before Soter who governed the Church over which you now preside, I mean," said he, "Anicetus, and Pius, Hyginus with Telesphorus and Xystus, neither did themselves observe, nor did they permit those after them to observe it.... But those very presbyters before you who did not observe it, sent the Eucharist to those of Churches which did." [584:1] Irenaeus here endeavours to teach the bishop of Rome a lesson of humility by reminding him repeatedly that he and his predecessors were but presbyters.

262

The pastor of Lyons speaks even still more distinctly respecting the status of the bishops who flourished in his generation. Thus, he says—"We should obey those presbyters in the Church who have the succession from the apostles, and who, with the succession of the episcopate, have received the certain gift of truth according to the good pleasure of the Father: but we should hold as suspected or as heretics and of bad sentiments the rest who depart from the principal succession, and meet together wherever they please.... From all such we must keep aloof, but we must adhere to those who both preserve, as we have already mentioned, the doctrine of the apostles, and exhibit, with the order of the presbytery, sound teaching and an inoffensive conversation." [585:1] "The order of the presbytery" obviously signifies the official character conveyed by "the laying on of the hands of the presbytery," and yet such was the ordination of those who, in the time of Irenaeus, possessed "the succession from the apostles" and "the succession of the episcopate."

Some imagine that no one can be properly qualified to administer divine ordinances who has not received episcopal ordination, but a more accurate acquaintance with the history of the early Church is all that is required to dissipate the delusion. The preceding statements clearly shew that, for upwards of one hundred and fifty years after the death of our Lord, all the Christian ministers throughout the world were ordained by presbyters. The bishops themselves were of "the order of the presbytery," and, as they had never received episcopal consecration, they could only ordain as presbyters. The bishop was, in fact, nothing more than the chief presbyter. [585:2] A father of the third century accordingly observes—"All power and grace are established in the Church where elders preside, who possess the power, as well of baptizing, as of confirming and ordaining." [585:3]

An old ecclesiastical law, recently presented for the first time to the English reader, [586:1] throws much light on a portion of the history of the Church long buried in great obscurity. This law may well remind us of those remains of extinct classes of animals which the naturalist studies with so much interest, as it obviously belongs to an era even anterior to that of the so-called apostolical canons. [586:2] Though it is part of a series of regulations once current in the Church of Ethiopia, there is every reason to believe that it was framed in Italy, and that its authority was acknowledged by the Church of Rome in the time of Hippolytus. [586:3] It marks a transition period in the history of ecclesiastical polity, and whilst it indirectly confirms the testimony of Jerome relative to the custom of the Church of Alexandria, it shews that the state of things to which the learned presbyter refers was now superseded by another arrangement. This curious specimen of ancient legislation treats of the appointment and ordination of ministers. "The bishop," says this enactment, "is to be elected by all the people.... And they shall choose ONE OF THE BISHOPS AND ONE OF THE PRESBYTERS, ... AND THESE SHALL LAY THEIR HANDS UPON HIS HEAD AND PRAY." [586:4] Here, to avoid the confusion arising from a whole crowd of individuals imposing hands in ordination, two were selected to act on behalf of the assembled office-bearers; and, that the parties entitled to officiate might be fairly represented, the deputies were to be a bishop and a presbyter. [587:1] The canon illustrates the jealousy with which the presbyters in the early part of the third century still guarded some of their rights and privileges. In the matter of investing others with Church authority, they yet maintained their original position, and though many bishops might be present when another was inducted into office, they would permit only one of the number to unite with one of themselves in the ceremony of ordination. Some at the present day do not hesitate to assert that presbyters have no right whatever to ordain, but this canon supplies evidence that in the third century they were employed to ordain bishops.

It thus appears that the bishop of the ancient Church was very different from the dignitary now known by the same designation. The primitive bishop had often but two or three elders, and sometimes a single deacon, [587:2] under his jurisdiction: the modern prelate has frequently the oversight of several hundreds of ministers. The ancient bishop, surrounded by his presbyters, preached ordinarily every Sabbath to his whole flock: the modern bishop may spend an entire lifetime without addressing a single sermon, on the Lord's day, to many who are under his episcopal supervision. The early bishop had the care of a parish: the modern bishop superintends a diocese. The elders of the primitive bishop were not unfrequently decent tradesmen who earned their bread by the sweat of their brow: [587:3] the presbyters of a modern prelate have generally each the charge of a congregation, and are supposed to be entirely devoted to sacred duties. Even the ancient city bishop had but a faint resemblance to his modern namesake. He was the most laborious city minister, and the chief preacher. He commonly baptized all who were received into the Church, and dispensed the Eucharist to all the communicants. He was, in fact, properly the minister of an overgrown parish who required several assistants to supply his lack of service.

The foregoing testimonies likewise shew that the doctrine of apostolical succession, as now commonly promulgated, is utterly destitute of any sound historical basis. According to some, no one is duly qualified to preach and to dispense the sacraments whose authority has not been transmitted from the Twelve by an unbroken series of episcopal ordinations. But it has been demonstrated that episcopal ordinations, properly so called, originated only in the third century, and that even the bishops of Rome, who flourished prior to that date, were "of the order of the presbytery." All the primitive bishops received nothing more than presbyterian ordination. It is plain, therefore, that the doctrine of the transmission of spiritual power from the apostles through an unbroken series of episcopal ordinations flows from sheer ignorance of the actual constitution of the early Church.

But the arrangements now described were gradually subverted by episcopal encroachments, and a separate chapter must be devoted to the illustration of the progress of Prelacy.

CHAPTER X

THE PROGRESS OF PRELACY

We cannot tell when the president of the presbytery began to hold office for life; but it is evident that the change, at whatever period it occurred, must have added considerably to his power. The chairman of any court is the individual through whom it is addressed, and, without whose signature, its proceedings cannot be properly authenticated. He acts in its name, and he stands forth as its representative. He may, theoretically, possess no more power than any of the other members of the judicatory, and he may be bound, by the most stringent laws, simply to carry out the decisions of their united wisdom; but his very position gives him influence; and, if he holds office for life, that influence may soon become formidable. If he is not constantly kept in check by the vigilance and determination of those with whom he is associated, he may insensibly trench upon their rights and privileges. In the second century the moderator of the city eldership was invariably a man advanced in years, who, instead of being watched with jealousy, was regarded with affectionate veneration; and it is not strange if he was often permitted to stretch his authority beyond the exact range of its legitimate exercise.

Evidence has already been adduced to shew that, on the rise of Prelacy, the presidential chair was no longer inherited by the members of the city presbytery in the order of seniority. The individuals considered most competent for the situation were now nominated by their brethren; and as the Church, especially in great towns, was sadly distracted by the machinations of the Gnostics, it was deemed expedient to arm the moderator with additional authority. As a matter of necessity, the official who was furnished with these new powers required a new name; for the title of president by which he was already known, and which continued long afterwards in current use, [590:1] did not now fully indicate his importance. It was, therefore, gradually supplanted by the designation of bishop, or overseer. Whilst this functionary was nominated by the presbyters, he might be also set aside by them, so that he felt it necessary to consult their wishes and to use his discretionary power with modesty and moderation; but, when he began to be elected by general suffrage, his authority was forthwith established on a broader and firmer foundation. He was now emphatically the man of the people; and from this date he possessed an influence with which the presbytery itself was incompetent to grapple.

As early as the middle of the second century the bishop, at least in some places, was entrusted with the chief management of the funds of the Church; [590:2] and probably, about fifty years afterwards, a large share of its revenues was appropriated to his personal maintenance. [590:3] His superior wealth soon added immensely to his influence. He was thus enabled to maintain a higher position in society than any of his brethren; and he was at length regarded as the great fountain of patronage and preferment. Long before Christianity enjoyed the sanction of the state, the chief pastors of the great cities began to attract attention by their ostentatious display of secular magnificence. Origen, who flourished in the former half of the third century, strongly condemns their vanity and

265

ambition; and though perhaps his ascetic temperament prompted him to indulge somewhat in the language of exaggeration, the testimony of so respectable a witness cannot be rejected as untrue. "We," says he, "proceed so far in the affectation of pomp and state, as to outdo even bad rulers among the pagans; and, like the emperors, surround ourselves with a guard that we may be feared and made difficult of access, particularly to the poor. And in many of our so-called Churches, especially in the large towns, may be found presiding officers of the Church of God who would refuse to own even the best among the disciples of Jesus while on earth as their equals." [591:1] In these remarks the writer had doubtless a particular reference to his own Church of Alexandria; but it is well known that elsewhere some bishops in the third century assumed a very lofty bearing. It is related of the celebrated Paul of Samosata, the bishop of Antioch, that he acted as a secular judge, that he appeared in public surrounded by a crowd of servants, and that he took special pleasure in pomp and parade; and yet, had he not lapsed into heresy, there is no evidence that his overweening pride would have brought down upon him the vengeance of ecclesiastical discipline. In the third century the chief pastor of the Western metropolis must have been known to the great officers of government, and perhaps to the Emperor himself. Decius must have regarded the Roman bishop as a somewhat formidable personage when he declared that he would sooner tolerate a rival candidate for the throne, and when he proclaimed his determination to annihilate the very office. [591:2]

It was not strange that dignitaries who affected so much state soon contrived to surround themselves with a whole host of new officials. Within little more than a century after the rise of Prelacy the number of grades of ecclesiastics was nearly trebled. In addition to the bishop, the presbyters, and the deacons, there were also, in A.D. 251, in the Church of Rome lectors, sub-deacons, acolyths, exorcists, and janitors. [592:1] The lectors, who read the Scriptures to the congregation [592:2] and who had charge of the sacred manuscripts, attract our attention as distinct office-bearers about the close of the second century. The sub-deacons are said to have had the care of the sacramental cups; the acolyths attended to the lamps of the sacred edifice; the exorcists [592:3] professed by their prayers to expel evil spirits out of the bodies of those about to be baptized; and the janitors performed the more humble duties of porters or door-keepers. At a subsequent period each of these functionaries was initiated into office by a special form of ordination or investiture. It was laid down as a principle that no one could regularly become a bishop who had not previously passed through all these inferior orders; [592:4] but when the multitude wished all at once to elevate a layman to the rank of a bishop or a presbyter, ecclesiastical routine was compelled to yield to the pressure of popular enthusiasm. [592:5]

The great city in which Prelacy originated appears to have been the place where these new offices made their first appearance. Rome, true to her mission as "the mother of the Catholic Church," conceived and brought forth nearly all the peculiarities of the Catholic system. The lady seated on the seven hills was already regarded with great admiration, and surrounding Churches silently copied the arrangements of their Imperial parent. In the East, at least one of the orders now instituted by the great Western prelate, that is, the order of acolyths, was not adopted for centuries afterwards. [593:1]

The city bishops were well aware of the vast accession of influence they

266

acquired in consequence of their election by the people, and did not fail to insist upon the circumstance when desirous to illustrate their ecclesiastical title. Any one who peruses the letters of Cyprian may remark the frequency, as well as the transparent satisfaction, with which he refers to the mode of his appointment. Who, he seems to say, could doubt his right to act as bishop of Carthage, seeing that he had been chosen by "the suffrage of the whole fraternity"—by "the vote of the people?" [593:2] The members of the Church enthusiastically acknowledged such appeals to their sympathy and support, and in cases of emergency promptly rallied round the individuals whom they had themselves elevated to power. But as all the other church officers were meanwhile likewise chosen by common suffrage, the bishops soon betrayed an anxiety to appropriate the distinction, and began, under various pretexts, to interfere with the free exercise of the popular franchise. In one of his epistles Cyprian excuses himself to the Christians of Carthage because he had ventured to ordain a reader without their approval. He pleads that the peculiar circumstances of the case and the extraordinary merits of the candidate must be accepted as his apology. "In clerical ordinations," says he, "my custom is to consult you beforehand, dearest brethren, and in common deliberation to weigh the character and merits of each. But testimonies of men need not be awaited when anticipated by the sentence of God." [593:3] The sanction of the people should have been obtained before the ordination; but, as persecution now raged, it is suggested that it would have been inconvenient to lay the matter before them; and Cyprian argues that the informality was pardonable, inasmuch as the Almighty himself had given His suffrage in favour of the new lector; for Aurelius, though only a youth, had nobly submitted to the torture rather than renounce the gospel.

The ordination of Aurelius under such circumstances was not, however, a solitary case; and there is certainly something suspicious in the frequency with which the bishop of Carthage apologizes to the clergy and people for neglecting to consult them on the appointment of church officers. In another of his letters he announces to the presbyters and deacons that, "on an urgent occasion" he had "made Saturus a reader, and Optatus the confessor a sub-deacon." [594:1] Again, he tells the same parties, and "the whole people," that "Celerinus, renowned alike for his courage and his character, has been joined to the clergy, not by human suffrage, but by the divine favour;" [594:2] and at another time he informs them that he had been "admonished and instructed by a divine vouchsafement to enrol Numidicus in the number of the Carthaginian presbyters." [594:3] These cases were, no doubt, afterwards quoted as precedents for the non-observance of the law; and from time to time new pretences were discovered for evading its provisions. In this way the rights of the people were gradually abridged; and in the course of two or three centuries, the bishops almost entirely ignored their interference in the election of presbyters and deacons, as well as of the inferior clergy.

New canons relative to ordination were promulgated probably about the time when the city presbyters ceased to have the exclusive right of electing their own bishop. The altered circumstances of the Church led to the establishment of these regulations. The election of the chief pastor of a great town was often a scene of much excitement, and as several of the elders might be regarded as candidates for the office, it was obviously unseemly that any of them should preside on the occasion. It was accordingly arranged that some of the neighbouring bishops should be present to superintend the proceedings. The successful candidate now began to be formally invested with his new dignity by the imposition of hands; and at first, perhaps, one of the bishops, assisted by one of the presbyters of the place, performed this ceremony. [595:1] But the elders soon ceased to take part in the ordination. At the election, the people and the clergy sometimes took opposite sides; and, in the contest, the ecclesiastical party was not unfrequently completely overborne. It occasionally happened, as in the case of Cyprian, [595:2] that one of the elders was chosen in opposition to the wishes of the majority of the presbytery; or, as in the case of Fabian of Rome, [595:3] that a layman was all at once elevated to the episcopal chair; and, at such times, the disappointed presbyters did not care to join in the inauguration. The bishops availed themselves of the pretexts thus furnished to dispense with their services altogether. At length the power of admitting to the ministry by the laying on of hands began to be challenged as the peculiar prerogative of the episcopal order.

In many places, perhaps before the middle of the third century, elders were no longer permitted to take part in the consecration of bishops; but Prelacy had not yet completely established itself upon the ruins of the more ancient polity. Sometimes the presbytery itself still discharged the functions of the bishop. After the martyrdom of Fabian in A.D. 250, the Church of Rome remained upwards of a year under its care, [596:1] as the see was meanwhile vacant; and about the same period we find Cyprian, when in exile, requesting his presbyters and deacons to execute both his duties and their own. [596:2] It was still admitted that elders were competent to ordain elders and deacons, as well as to confirm and to baptize; and the bishop continued to recognise them as his "colleagues" and his "fellow-presbyters." [596:3] It is clear, however, that the relations between them and their episcopal chief were now very vaguely defined, and that the ambiguous position of the parties led to mutual complaints of ambition and usurpation. The Epistles of Cyprian supply evidence that the bishop of Carthage, during a great part of his episcopate, was engaged with his presbyters in a struggle for power; [596:4] and though he asserted that he was contending for nothing more than his legitimate authority, he was sometimes obliged to abate his pretensions. In one case he complains that, "without his permission or knowledge," his presbyter Novatus "of his own factiousness and ambition" had "made Felicissimus his follower a deacon;" [596:5] but still he does not venture to impeach the validity of the act, or refuse to recognise the standing of the new ecclesiastic. Felicissimus seems to have been ordained in a small meeting-house in the neighbourhood of Carthage; and as Novatus, who probably presided on the occasion, appears to have proceeded in conjunction with the majority of the presbytery, they no doubt considered that, under these circumstances, the sanction of the bishop was by no means indispensable. The manifestation of such a spirit of independence was, however, exceedingly galling to their imperious prelate.

From the manner in which Cyprian expresses himself we may infer that he would not have been dissatisfied had Novatus and the elders who acted with him obtained his permission to ordain the deacon Felicissimus. But about this period the bishops were beginning to look with extreme jealousy on all presbyterian ordinations, and were commencing a series of encroachments on the rights of their episcopal brethren in rural districts. These country bishops, [597:1] who

268

wore simply ministers of single congregations, and who were generally poor and uninfluential, soon succumbed to the great city dignitaries. By a council held at Ancyra in A.D. 314, or very shortly after the close of the Diocletian persecution, they were forbidden to perform duties which they had hitherto been accustomed to discharge, for one of its canons declares that "country bishops must not ordain presbyters or deacons; neither must city presbyters in another parish without the written permission of the bishop." [597:2]

This canon illustrates the strangely anomalous condition of the Church at the period of its adoption. It takes no notice of country elders, as the proceedings of such an humble class of functionaries probably awakened no jealousy; and it degrades country bishops, who unquestionably belonged to the episcopal order, by placing them in a position inferior to that of city presbyters. About sixty years before, or in the middle of the third century, three of these country bishops were deemed competent to ordain a bishop of Rome; [598:1] but now they are deprived of the right of ordaining even elders and deacons. It is easy to understand why city presbyters were still permitted, under certain conditions, to exercise this privilege. As they constituted the council of the city chief pastor, their influence was considerable; and as they had, until a recent date, been accustomed even to take part in his own consecration, it was deemed inexpedient to tempt so formidable a class of churchmen to make common cause with the country bishops by stripping both at once of their ancient prerogatives. The country bishops, as the weaker party, were first subjected to a process of spoliation. But the recognition of Christianity by Constantine gave an immense impulse to the progress of the hierarchy, and the city presbyters were soon afterwards deprived of the privilege now wrested from the country bishops.

The current of events had placed the Church, about the middle of the third century, in a position which it could not long maintain. As the growth of Christianity in towns was steady and rapid, the bishop there rose quickly into wealth and power; but, among the comparatively poor and thinly-scattered population of the country, his condition remained nearly stationary. When Cyprian, in A.D. 256, addressed the eighty-seven bishops assembled in the Council of Carthage, and told them that they were all on an equality, he might have felt that the doctrine of episcopal parity, as then understood, must be given up as indefensible if assailed by the skill of a vigorous logician. Who could believe that the bishop of Carthage held exactly the same official rank as every one of his episcopal auditors? He was the chief pastor of a flourishing metropolis; he had several congregations under his care, and several of his presbyters were preachers; [599:1] but many of the bishops before him were ministers of single congregations and without even one elder competent to deliver a sermon, [599:2] In point of ministerial gifts and actual influence some of the presbyters of Carthage were, no doubt, far superior to many of the bishops of the council. And who could affirm that Paul of Samosata, the chief pastor of the capital of the Eastern Empire, was quite on a level with every one of the village bishops around him whom he bribed to celebrate his praises? No wonder that it was soon found necessary to remodel the episcopal system. The city bishops had a show of equity in their favour when they asserted their superiority, and their brethren in rural districts were too feeble and dependent effectively to resist their own degradation.

The ecclesiastical title metropolitan came into use about the time of the

269

Council of Nice in A.D. 325. [599:3] and there is reason to believe that the territorial jurisdiction it implied was then first distinctly defined and generally established; but the changes of the preceding three quarters of a century, had been preparing the way for the new arrangement. Many of the country bishops had meanwhile been reduced to a condition of subserviency, whilst a considerable number of the chief pastors in the great cities had been recognized as the constant presidents of the synods which met in their respective capitals. It is easy to see how these prelates acquired such a position. Talent, if exerted, must always assert its ascendency; and it is probable that the metropolitan bishops were generally more able and accomplished than the majority of their brethren. They could fairly plead that zeal for the good of the Church prompted them to take a lead in ecclesiastical affairs, and their place of residence supplied them with facilities for communicating with other pastors of which they often deemed it prudent to avail themselves. When the synod met in the metropolis, the bishop of the city was wont to entertain many of the members as his guests; and, as he was elevated above most, if not all, of those with whom he acted, in point of wealth, social standing, address, and knowledge of the world, he was usually called on to occupy the chair of the moderator. In process of time that which was originally conceded as a matter of courtesy passed into an admitted right. So long as the metropolitan bishop was inducted into office by mere presbyters, the circumstances of his investiture pointed out to him the duty of humility; but when the most distinguished chief pastors of the province deemed it an honour to take part in his consecration, he immediately increased his pretensions. Thus it is that the change in the mode of episcopal inauguration forms a new era in the history of ecclesiastical assumption.

About the middle of the third century various circumstances conspired to augment the authority of the great bishops. In the Decian and Valerian persecutions the chief pastors were specially marked out for attack, and the heroic constancy with which some of the most eminent encountered a cruel death vastly enhanced the reputation of their order. In a few years several bishops of Rome were martyred; Cyprian of Carthage endured the same fate: Alexander of Jerusalem, and Babylas of Antioch, also laid down their lives for their religion. [600:1] At the same time the schism of Novatian at Rome, and the schism of Felicissimus at Carthage threatened the Church with new divisions, and the same arguments which were used, upwards of a hundred years before, for increasing the power of the president of the eldership, could now be urged with equal pertinency for adding to the authority of the president of the synod. In point of fact perhaps the earliest occasion on which the bishop of Rome executed discipline in his archiepiscopal capacity was immediately connected with the schism of Novatian; for we have no record of any exercise of such power until Cornelius, at the head of a council held in the Imperial city, deposed the pastors who had officiated at the consecration of his rival. [601:1] From this date the Roman metropolitan probably presided at all the ordinations of the bishops in his vicinity.

To prevent the recurrence of schisms such as had now happened at Rome and Carthage, it was, in all likelihood, arranged about this period, at least in some quarters of the Church, that the presence or sanction of the stated president of the provincial synod should be necessary to the validity of all episcopal consecrations. There were still, however, many districts in which the provincial synod had no fixed chairman. Hence an ancient canon directs that at the ordination of a member of the hierarchy, "one of the principal bishops shall pray to God over the approved candidate." [601:2] By a "principal bishop" we are to understand the chief pastor of a principal or apostolic church; [601:3] but in some provinces several such churches were to be found, and this regulation attests that there no single ecclesiastic had yet acquired an unchallenged precedence. As the close of the third century approached, the ecclesiastical structure exhibited increasing uniformity; and one dignitary in each region began to be known as the stated president of the episcopal body. In one of the so-called apostolical canons, framed probably before the Council of Nice, this arrangement is embodied. "The bishops of every nation," says the ordinance, "ought to know who is the first among them, and him they ought to esteem as their head, and not do any great thing without his consent. ... But neither let him do anything without the consent of all." [602:1]

This canon is apparently couched in terms of studied ambiguity, for the expression "the first among the bishops of every nation" admits of various interpretations. In many cases it probably meant the senior bishop of the district; in others, it perhaps denoted the chief pastor of the chief city of the province; and in others again, it may have indicated the prelate of a great metropolis who had contrived to establish his authority over a still more extensive territory. The rise of the city bishops had completely destroyed that balance of power which originally existed in the Church; and much commotion preceded the settlement of a new ecclesiastical equilibrium. During the last forty years of the third century the Christians enjoyed almost uninterrupted peace; the chief pastors were meanwhile perpetually engaged in contests for superiority; and about this time the bishops of Rome, of Alexandria, and of Antioch, rapidly extended their influence. So rampant was the usurping spirit of churchmen that even the violence of the Diocletian persecution was not sufficient to check them in their career of ambition. A contemporary writer, who was himself a member of the episcopal order, bears testimony to this melancholy fact. "Some," said he, "who were reputed our pastors, contemning the law of piety, were, under the excitement of mutual animosities, fomenting nothing else but disputes and threatenings and rivalry and reciprocal hostility and hatred, as they contentiously prosecuted their ambitious designs for sovereignty." [601:2]

What a change had passed over the Christian commonwealth in the course of little more than two hundred years! When the Apostle John died, the city church was governed by the common council of the elders, and their president simply announced and executed the decisions of his brethren: now, the president was transformed into a prelate who, by gradual encroachments, had stripped the presbytery of a large share of its authority. At the close of the first century the Church of Rome was, perhaps, less influential than the Church of Ephesus, and the very name of its moderator at that period is a matter of disputed and doubtful tradition; but the Diocletian persecution had scarcely terminated when the bishop of the great metropolis was found sitting in a council in the palace of the Lateran, and claiming jurisdiction over eight or ten provinces of Italy! These revolutions were not effected without much opposition. The strife between the presbyters and the bishops was succeeded by a general warfare among the possessors of episcopal power, for the constant moderator of the synod was as anxious to increase his authority as the constant moderator of the presbytery.

271

About the close of the third century the Church appears to have been sadly scandalised by the quarrels of the bishops, and Eusebius accordingly intimates that, in the reign of terror which so quickly followed, they suffered a righteous retribution for their misconduct.

Discussions respecting questions of Church polity are often exceedingly distasteful to persons of contracted views but of genuine piety, for they cannot understand how the progress of vital godliness can be influenced by forms of ecclesiastical government. [603:1] About this period such sentiments were probably not uncommon, and much of the apathy with which innovations were contemplated may thus be easily explained. Besides, if the early bishop was a man of ability and address, his influence in his own church was nearly overwhelming; for as he was the ordinary, if not the only, preacher, he thus possessed the most effective means of recommending any favourite scheme, and of giving a decided tone to public opinion. When a parochial charge became vacant by the demise of the chief pastor, the election of a successor was often vigorously contested; and when an influential presbyter was defeated, he sometimes exhibited his mortification by contending for the rights of his order, and by disputing the pretensions of his successful rival. But as such opposition was obviously dictated by the spirit of faction, it was commonly brief, ill-sustained, and abortive. The young, talented, and aspiring presbyters must have been strongly tempted to encourage the growth of episcopal prerogative, for each might one day hope to occupy the place of dignity, and thus to reap the fruits of present encroachments. The bishops seem to have resisted more strenuously the establishment of metropolitan ascendency. An ecclesiastical regulation of great antiquity, [604:1] condemned their translation from one parish to another, so that when the episcopate was gained, all farther prospects of promotion were extinguished, for the place of first among the bishops was either inherited by seniority or claimed by the prelate of the chief city. Hence it was that the pastors withstood so firmly all infringements on their theoretical parity; and hence those "ambitious disputes," [604:2] and those "collisions of bishops with bishops," [604:3] even amidst the fires of martyrdom, over which the historian of the Church professes his anxiety to cast the veil of oblivion.

CHAPTER XI

SYNODS—THEIR HISTORY AND CONSTITUTION

The apostles, and the other original heralds of the gospel, sought primarily the conversion of unbelievers. The commission given to Paul points out distinctly the grand design of their ministry. When the great persecutor of the saints was himself converted on his way to Damascus, our Lord addressed to him the memorable words—"I have appeared unto thee for this purpose, to make thee a minister and a witness both of these things which thou hast seen, and of those

272

things in the which I will appear unto thee; delivering thee from the people, and from the Gentiles, unto whom now I send thee, to open their eyes, and to turn them from darkness to light, and from the power of Satan unto God, that they may receive forgiveness of sins, and inheritance among them which are sanctified by faith that is in me." [605:1]

When a few disciples were collected in a particular locality, it not unfrequently happened that they remained for a time without any proper ecclesiastical organization. [605:2] But the Christian cause, under such circumstances, could not be expected to flourish; and therefore, as soon as practicable, the apostles and evangelists did not neglect to make arrangements for the increase and edification of these infant communities. To provide, as well for the maintenance of discipline, as for the preaching of the Word, they accordingly proceeded to ordain elders in every city where the truth had gained converts. These elders afterwards ordained deacons in their respective congregations; and thus, in due time, the Church was regularly constituted.

In the first century Christian societies were formed only here and there throughout the Roman Empire; and, at its close, the gospel had scarcely penetrated into some of the provinces. It is not to be expected that we can trace any general confederation of the churches established during this period, and it would be vain to attempt to demonstrate their incorporation; as their distance, their depressed condition, and the jealousy with which they were regarded by the civil government, [606:1] rendered any extensive combination utterly impossible. At a time when the disciples met together for worship in secret and before break of day, it is not to be supposed that their pastors deemed it expedient to undertake frequent journeys on the business of the Church, or assembled in multitudinous councils. But though, in the beginning of the second century, there was no formal bond of union connecting the several Christian communities throughout the world, they meanwhile contrived in various ways to cultivate an unbroken fraternal intercourse. Recognising each other as members of the same holy brotherhood, they maintained an epistolary correspondence, in which they treated of all matters pertaining to the common interest. When the pastor of one church visited another, his status was immediately acknowledged; and even when an ordinary disciple emigrated to a distant province, the ecclesiastical certificate which he carried along with him secured his admission to membership in the strange congregation. Thus, all the churches treated each other as portions of one great family; all adhered to much the same system of polity and discipline; and, though there was not unity of jurisdiction, there was the "keeping of the unity of the Spirit in the bond of peace."

In modern times many ecclesiastical historians [607:1] have asserted that synods commenced about the middle of the second century. But the statement is unsupported by a single particle of evidence, and a number of facts may be adduced to prove that it is altogether untenable. There is no reason to doubt that synods, at least on a limited scale, met in the days of the apostles, and that the Church courts of a later age were simply the continuation and expansion of those primitive conventions. We know very little respecting the history of the Christian commonwealth during the former half of the second century, for the extant memorials of the Church of that period are exceedingly few and meagre; and as the proceedings of most of the synods which were then held did not perhaps attract much notice, [607:2] it is not remarkable that they have shared the fate of

273

almost all the other ecclesiastical transactions of the same date, and that they have been buried in oblivion. [607:3] It is nowhere intimated by any ancient authority that synodical meetings commenced fifty years after the death of the beloved disciple, and the earliest writers who touch upon the subject speak of them as of apostolic original. Irenaeus, the pastor of Lyons, had probably reached manhood when, according to Mosheim and others, synods were at first formed; he enjoyed the instructions of Polycarp, the disciple of the Apostle John; he was beyond question one of the best informed Christian ministers of his generation; and yet he obviously considered that these ecclesiastical assemblies were in existence in the first century. Speaking of the visit of Paul to Miletus when he sent to Ephesus and called the elders of the Church, [608:1] he says that the apostle then convoked "the bishops and presbyters of Ephesus and of the other adjoining cities" [608:2]—plainly indicating that he summoned a synodical meeting. Had an assembly of this kind been a novelty in the days of Irenaeus, the pastor of Lyons would not have given such a version of a passage in the inspired narrative. Cyprian flourished shortly after the time when, according to the modern theory, councils began to meet in Africa, but the bishop of Carthage himself unquestionably entertained higher views of their antiquity. He declared that conformably to "the practice received from divine tradition and apostolic observance," [608:3] "all the neighbouring bishops of the same province met together" among the people over whom a pastor was to be ordained; [608:4] and he did not here merely give utterance to his own impressions, for a whole African synod concurred in his statement. Subsequent writers of unimpeachable credit refer to the canons of councils of which we otherwise know nothing, and though we cannot now ascertain the exact time when these courts assembled, there is no reason to doubt that at least some of them were convened before the middle of the second century. Thus, when Jerome ascribes the origin of Prelacy to an ecclesiastical decree, he alludes evidently to some synodical convention of an earlier date than any of the meetings of which history has preserved a record. [609:1]

Did we even want the direct testimony just adduced as to the government of synods in the former part of the second century, we might on other grounds infer that this species of polity then existed; for apostolic example suggested its propriety, and the spirit of fraternity so assiduously cherished by the early rulers of the Church must have prompted them to meet together for the discussion and settlement of ecclesiastical questions in which they felt a common interest. But whilst Christianity was still struggling for existence, it was not in a condition to form widely spread organizations. It is probable that the business of the early Church courts was conducted with the utmost secrecy, that they were attended by but few members, and that they were generally composed of those pastors and elders who resided in the same district and who could conveniently assemble on short notice. Their meetings, in all likelihood, were summoned at irregular intervals, and were held, to avoid suspicion, sometimes in one city and sometimes in another; and, except when an exciting question awakened deep and general anxiety, the representatives of the Churches of a whole province rarely, perhaps, ventured on a united convention. Our ignorance of the councils of the early part of the second century arises simply from the fact that no writer appeared during that interval to register their acts; and we have now no means of accurately filling up this blank in the history. But we have good grounds for believing that Gnosticism now formed the topic of discussion in several synods. [609:2] The errorists, we know, were driven out of the Church in all places; and how can we account for this general expulsion, except upon the principle of the united action of ecclesiastical judicatories? Jerome gives us to understand that their machinations led to a change in the ecclesiastical constitution, and that this change was effected by a synodical decree adopted all over the world [610:1]—thereby implying that presbyterial government was already in universal operation. Montanism appeared whilst Gnosticism was yet in its full strength, and this gloomy fanaticism created intense agitation. Many of the pastors, as well as of the people, were bewildered by its pretensions to inspiration, and by the sanctimony of its ascetic discipline. It immediately occupied the attention of the ecclesiastical courts, and its progress was, no doubt, arrested by their emphatic condemnation of its absurdities. It is certain that their interference was judicious and decided. "When the faithful held frequent meetings in many places throughout Asia on account of this affair, and examined the novel doctrines, and pronounced them profane, and rejected them as heresy," the Montanist prophets "were in consequence driven out of the Church and excluded from communion." [610:2]

The words just quoted are from the pen of an anonymous writer who flourished towards the end of the second or beginning of the third century; [610:3] and, though they supply the earliest distinct notice of synodical meetings, they do not even hint that such assemblies were of recent original. The Paschal controversy succeeded the Montanist agitation, and convulsed the whole Church from East to West by its frivolous discussions. The mode of keeping the Paschal festival had for nearly fifty years been a vexed question, but about the close of the second century it began to create bitter contention. Eusebius has given us an account of the affair, and his narrative throws great light upon the state of the ecclesiastical community at the time of its occurrence. "For this cause," says he, "there were synods and councils of bishops, and all, with according judgment, published in epistles an ecclesiastical decree.... There is still extant a letter from those who at that time were called together in Palestine, over whom presided Theophilus, bishop of the parish of Caesarea, and Narcissus, bishop of the parish of Jerusalem. There is also another letter from those who were convoked at Rome [611:1] concerning the same question, which shews that Victor was then bishop. There is too a letter from the bishops of Pontus, over whom Palmas, as the senior pastor, presided. There is likewise a letter from the parishes in Gaul of which Irenaeus was president. And another besides from the Churches in Osroene and the cities in that quarter." [611:2]

It is obvious from this statement that, before the termination of the second century, synodical government was established throughout the whole Church; for we here trace its operation in France, in Mesopotamia or Osroene, in Italy, Pontus, and Palestine. This passage also illustrates the progress of the changes which were taking place about the period under review in the constitution of ecclesiastical judicatories. As the president of the presbytery was at first the senior elder, so the president of the synod was at first the senior pastor. At this time the primitive arrangement had not been altogether superseded, for at the meeting of the bishops of Pontus, Palmas, as being the oldest member present, was called to occupy the chair of the moderator. But elsewhere this ancient regulation had been set aside, and in some places no new principle had yet been

275

adopted. At the synod of Palestine the jealousy of two rivals for the presidency led to a rather awkward compromise. Caesarea was the seat of government, and on that ground its bishop could challenge precedence of every other in the district, but the Church of Jerusalem was the mother of the entire Christian community, and its pastor, now a hundred years of age, [612:1] considered that he was entitled to fill the place of dignity. For the sake of peace the assembled fathers agreed to appoint two chairmen, and accordingly Theophilus of Caesarea and Narcissus of Jerusalem presided jointly in the synod of Palestine. In the synod of Rome there was no one to dispute the pretensions of Bishop Victor. As the chief pastor of the great metropolitan Church, he seems, as a matter of course, to have taken possession of the presidential office.

A few years after the Paschal controversy the celebrated Tertullian became entangled in the errors of Montanism, and in vindication of his own principles published a tract "Concerning Fasts," in which there is a passing reference to the subject of ecclesiastical convocations. "Among the Greek nations," says he, "these councils of the whole Church are held in fixed places, in which, whilst certain important questions are discussed, the representation of the whole Christian name is also celebrated with great solemnity. And how worthy is this of a faith which expects to have its converts gathered from all parts to Christ? See how good and how pleasant a thing it is for brethren to dwell together in unity! You do not well know how to sing this, except when you are holding communion with many. But those conventions, after they have been first employed in prayers and fasting, know how to mourn with the mourners, and thus at length to rejoice with those that rejoice." [612:2]

Greek was now spoken throughout a great part of the Roman Empire, and at this period it continued to be used even by the chief pastors of the Italian capital, so that when Tertullian here mentions the Greek nations, [613:1] he employs an expression of somewhat doubtful significance. But it is probable that he refers chiefly to the mother country and its colonies on the other side of the Aegean Sea, or to Greece and Asia Minor. It is apparent from the apostolic epistles, most of which are addressed to Churches within their borders, that the gospel, at an early date, spread extensively and rapidly in these countries; and it is highly probable that, at least in some districts, its adherents would have now made a considerable figure in any denominational census. They were thus, perhaps, emboldened to erect their ecclesiastical courts upon a broader basis, as well as to hold their meetings with greater publicity, than heretofore; and, as these assemblies were attended, not only by the pastors and the elders, but also by many deacons and ordinary church members who were anxious to witness their deliberations, Tertullian alleges, in his own rhetorical style of expression, that in them "the representation of the whole Christian name was celebrated with great solemnity." [613:2] These Greek councils commenced with a period of fasting—a circumstance by which they seem to have been distinguished from similar meetings convened elsewhere, and as they thus supplied him with an argument in favour of one of the grand peculiarities of the discipline of Montanism, it is obviously for this reason they are here so prominently noticed. If, as he contends, these fasts were kept so religiously by the representatives of the Church when in attendance on some of their most solemn assemblies, there might, after all, be a warrant for the observance of that more rigid abstinence which he now inculcated. But though this passage of Tertullian is the only authority adduced to

276

prove that councils originated in Greece, it is plain that it gives no sanction whatever to any such theory. Neither does it afford the slightest foundation for the inference that, at the time when it was written, these ecclesiastical convocations were unknown in Africa and Italy. We have direct proof that before this period they not only met in Rome, but that the bishop of the great city had been in the habit of requesting his brother pastors in other countries to hold such assemblies. [614:1] There is, too, satisfactory evidence that they were now not unknown at Carthage, [614:2] and Tertullian himself elsewhere apparently refers to the proceedings of African synods. [614:3] He must have been well aware that they had recently assembled in various parts of the West to pronounce judgment in the Paschal controversy; for the decisions of the Gallic and Roman synods mentioned by Eusebius seem to have been published all over the Church; and the reason why he refers to the convocations of the Greeks was, not because such meetings were not held in other lands, but because these, from their peculiar method of procedure in the way of fasting, [614:4] supplied, as he conceived, a very apposite argument in support of the discipline which he was so desirous to recommend.

If historians have erred in stating that synods commenced in Greece, they have been still more egregiously mistaken in asserting that the once famous Amphictyonic Council suggested their establishment, and furnished the model for their construction. In the second century of the Christian era the Council of the Amphictyons was shorn of its glory, and though it then continued to meet, [615:1] it had long ceased to be either an exponent of the national mind, or a free and independent assembly. It is not to be imagined that the Christian community, in the full vigour of its early growth, would all at once have abandoned its apostolic constitution, and adopted a form of government borrowed from an effete institute. Synods, which now formed so prominent a part of the ecclesiastical polity, could claim a higher and holier original. They were obviously nothing more than the legitimate development of the primitive structure of the Church, for they could be traced up to that meeting of the apostles and elders at Jerusalem which relieved the Gentile converts from the observance of the rite of circumcision.

The most plausible argument in support of the theory that the Amphictyonic Council suggested the establishment of synodical conventions is based upon the alleged fact that these ecclesiastical meetings were at first held in spring and autumn, or exactly at the times when the Greek political deputies were accustomed to assemble. [615:2] But this statement, when closely examined, is found to be quite destitute of evidence. Tertullian does not say that the Greek synods met twice a year, and we know that, at least half a century afterwards, they assembled only annually. This fact is attested by Firmilian of Cappadocia in his celebrated letter to Cyprian. "It is of necessity arranged among us," says he, "that we elders and presidents meet every year [616:1] to set in order the things entrusted to our charge, that if there be any matters of grave moment they may be settled by common advice." [616:2] The author of this epistle lived in the very country where synods are supposed to have assembled so much more frequently half a century before, so that his evidence demonstrates the fallacy of the hypothesis framed by some modern historians.

About the beginning of the third century, or at the time when Tertullian wrote, it would seem that the members of the Greek synods had an arrangement

277

which was not then generally adopted. The Greek councils met together "in fixed places." There is reason to believe that these "fixed places" were, commonly speaking, the metropolitan cities of the respective provinces. But still, as we have seen, the pastors and elders had not yet generally agreed to the regulation that the chief pastor of the metropolitan city should be the constant moderator of the provincial synod. In the case of the bishop of Rome the rule was, no doubt, already established; but, in other instances, the senior pastor present was, as yet, invited to fill the office of president. The constant meeting of the synod in the principal town of the province tended, however, to increase the influence of its bishop; and he was at length almost everywhere acknowledged as the proper chairman. [616:3] At the Council of Nice in A.D. 325 his rights were formally secured by ecclesiastical enactment. About the same date synods appear to have commenced to assemble with greater frequency. "Let there be a meeting of the bishops twice a year," says the thirty-seventh of the so-called Apostolical Canons, "and let them examine amongst themselves the decrees concerning religion, and settle the ecclesiastical controversies which may have occurred. One meeting is to be held in the fourth week of the Pentecost, and the other on the 12th day of the month of October." [617:1]

As soon as the light of historical records begins to illustrate the condition of any portion of the ancient Church, its synodical government may be discovered; and though the literary memorials of the third century are comparatively few, they are abundantly sufficient to demonstrate that, as early as the middle of that period, ecclesiastical courts upon a tolerably extensive scale were everywhere established. About that time the controversy relative to the propriety of rebaptizing heretics created much agitation, and the subject was keenly discussed in the synods which met for its consideration. Nowhere is any hint given that these courts were of recent formation. Though meeting in so many places in the East and West, and in countries so far apart, they are invariably represented as the ancient order of ecclesiastical regimen. They all appear, too, as co-ordinate and independent judicatories; and though the Roman bishop, as the chief pastor of the Catholic Church, endeavoured to induce them to adopt uniform decisions, his attempts to dictate to the brethren in Spain, Africa, and other countries, were firmly and indignantly repulsed. There were fundamental principles which they were all understood to acknowledge; these principles were generally embodied in the divine Statute-book; it was admitted that the decisions of every council which adhered to them were entitled to universal reverence; but, though the reservation was scarcely compatible with the genius of catholicity, each provincial convention claimed the right of forming its own judgment of the acts of other courts, and of adopting or rejecting them accordingly.

The most influential synods which were held before the establishment of Christianity by Constantine were those which met in the latter part of the third century to try the case of the famous Paul of Samosata, the bishop of Antioch. The charge preferred against him was the denial of the proper deity of the Son of God, and as he was an individual of much ability and address, as well as, in point of rank, one of the greatest prelates in existence, his case awakened uncommon interest. Christianity had recently obtained the sanction of a legal toleration, [618:1] and therefore churchmen now ventured to travel from different provinces to sit in judgment on this noted heresiarch. In the councils which assembled at Antioch were to be found, not only the pastors of Syria, but also those of various

278

places in Palestine and Asia Minor. Even Dionysius, bishop of the capital of Egypt, was invited to be present, but he pleaded his age and infirmities as an apology for his non-attendance. [618:2] In a council which assembled A.D. 269, [618:3] Paul was deposed and excommunicated; and the sentence, which was announced by letter to the chief pastors of Rome, Alexandria, and other distinguished sees, was received with general approbation.

All the information we possess respecting the councils of the first three centuries is extremely scanty, so that it is no easy matter exactly to ascertain their constitution; but we have no reason to question the correctness of the statement of Firmilian of Cappadocia, who was himself a prominent actor in several of the most famous of these assemblies, and who affirms that they were composed of "elders and presiding pastors." [619:1] We have seen that bishops and elders anciently united even in episcopal ordinations, and these ministers, when assembled on such occasions, constituted ecclesiastical judicatories. A modern writer, of high standing in connexion with the University of Oxford, has affirmed that "bishops alone had a definitive voice in synods," [619:2] but the testimonies which he has himself adduced attest the inaccuracy of the assertion. The presbyter Origen, at an Arabian synod held about A.D. 229, sat with the bishops, and was, in fact, the most important and influential member of the convention. About A.D. 230, Demetrius of Alexandria "gathered a council of bishops and of certain presbyters, which decreed that Origen should remove from Alexandria." [619:3] About the middle of the third century, "during the vacancy of the see of Rome, the presbyters of the city took part in the first Roman council on the lapsed." [619:4] At the council of Eliberis, held about A.D. 305, no less than twenty-six presbyters sat along with the bishops. [619:5] In some cases deacons, [619:6] and even laymen, were permitted to address synods, [619:7] but ancient documents attest that they were never regarded as constituent members. Whilst the bishops and elders sat together, and thus proclaimed their equality as ecclesiastical judges, [619:8] the people and even the deacons were obliged to stand at these meetings. The circular letter of the council of Antioch announcing the deposition of Paul of Samosata is written in the name of "bishops, and presbyters, and deacons, and the Churches of God," [620:1] but there is reason to believe that the latter are added merely as a matter of prudence, and in testimony of their cordial approval of the ecclesiastical verdict. The heresiarch had left no art unemployed to acquire popularity, and it was necessary to shew that he had lost the influence upon which he had been calculating. It is obvious that the pastors and elders alone were permitted to adjudicate, for why were they assembled from various quarters to uphold the doctrine and discipline of the Church, if the people who were themselves tainted with heresy or guilty of irregularity, had the liberty of voting? Under such circumstances, the decision would have been substantially, not the decree of the Church rulers, but of the multitude of the particular city in which they happened to congregate.

The theory of some modern ecclesiastical historians, who hold that all the early Christian congregations were originally independent, cannot bear the ordeal of careful investigation. Whilst it directly conflicts with the testimony of Jerome, who declares that the churches were at first "governed by the common council of the presbyters," it is otherwise destitute of evidence. As soon as the light of ecclesiastical memorials begins to guide our path, we find everywhere presbyteries and synods in existence. Congregationalism has no solid foundation either in Scripture or antiquity. The eldership, the most ancient court of the Church, commenced with the first preaching of the gospel; and in the account of the meeting of the Twelve to induct the deacons into office, we have the record of the first ordination performed by the laying on of the hands of the presbytery of Jerusalem. A few years afterwards the representatives of several Christian communities assembled in the holy city and "ordained decrees" for the guidance of the Jewish and Gentile Churches. The continuous development of the same form of ecclesiastical regimen has now been illustrated. This polity was obviously based upon the principle that "in the multitude of counsellors there is safety." [621:1] At the meetings of the elders, information was multiplied, the intellect was sharpened, the brethren were made better acquainted with each other, and the Christian cause enjoyed the benefit of the decisions of their collective wisdom. The members had been previously elected to office by the voice of the people, so that the Church had pre-eminently a free constitution. And it is no mean proof as well of the intrepidity as of the zeal of the early Christian ministers that, at a time when their religion was proscribed, they sometimes undertook lengthened journeys for the purpose of meeting in ecclesiastical judicatories. They thus nobly asserted the principle that Christ has established in His Church a government with which the civil magistrate has no right whatever to intermeddle. It has been said that the early Christian councils "changed nearly the whole form of the Church," and that by them "the influence and authority of the bishops were not a little augmented." [621:2] But this is obviously quite a mistaken view of their native tendency. The face of the Church was, indeed, changed at an early period, but it was simply because these councils yielded with too much facility to the spirit of innovation. Had they been always conducted in accordance with primitive arrangements, they could have crushed in the bud the aspirations of clerical ambition. But when the city ministers were rapidly accumulating wealth, their brethren in rural districts remained poor; and when councils began to meet on a scale of increased magnitude, the village and country pastors, who could not afford the expenses of lengthened journeys, were unable to attend. Meanwhile Prelacy established itself in the great towns, and the influence of the city bishops began gradually to preponderate in all ecclesiastical assemblies. When the prelates had once secured their ascendency in these conventions, they made use of the machinery for their own purposes. The people were deprived of many of their rights and privileges; the elders were stripped of their proper status; the village and rural bishops were extinguished; and at length the ancient presbytery itself disappeared. The city dignitaries became the sole depositories of ecclesiastical power, and the Church lost nearly every vestige of its freedom. But, long after the beginning of the fourth century, many remnants of the primitive polity still survived as memorials of its departed excellence.

CHAPTER XII

THE CEREMONIES AND DISCIPLINE OP THE CHURCH AS ILLUSTRATED BY CURRENT CONTROVERSIES AND DIVISIONS

Whilst the Christian community was contending against the Gnostics, it was not without other controversies which were fitted to prejudice its claims in the sight of the heathen. The destruction of the temple of Jerusalem by Titus had prevented the sticklers for the Mosaic law from practising many of their ancient ceremonies: but there were parts of their ritual, such as circumcision, to which they still adhered, as these could be observed when the altar and the sanctuary no longer existed. In the reign of Hadrian a division of sentiment relative to the continued obligation of the Levitical code led to a great change in the mother Church of Christendom. About A.D. 132, an adventurer, named Barchochebas, pretending to be the Messiah and aiming at temporal dominion, appeared in Palestine; the Jews, in great numbers, flocked to his standard; and the rebel chief contrived for three years to maintain a bloody war against the strength of the Roman legions. The Israelitish race, by their conduct at this juncture, grievously provoked the emperor; and when he had rebuilt Jerusalem, under the name of Aelia Capitolina, he threatened them with the severest penalties should they appear either in the city or the suburbs. Some of the Jewish Christians of the place, anxious, no doubt, to escape the proscription, now resolved to give up altogether the observance of circumcision. Others, however, objected to this course, and persisted in maintaining the permanent obligation of the Mosaic ritual. The dissentients, called Nazarenes, formed themselves into a separate community, which obtained adherents elsewhere, and which subsisted for several centuries. At first they differed from other Christians chiefly in their adherence to the initiatory ordinance of Judaism, but eventually they adopted erroneous principles in regard to the person of our Lord, and were in consequence ranked amongst heretics. [624:1]

In the history of the Church, the Nazarenes occupy a somewhat singular and unique position. Their name was one of the earliest designations by which the followers of our Saviour were known, [624:2] and though by many they have been called the First Dissenters, they might have very fairly pleaded that they were the lineal descendants of the most ancient stock of Christians in the world. The rite for which they contended had been practised in the Church of Jerusalem since its very establishment; the ministers by whom they had been taught had probably been instructed by the apostles themselves; and all the elders at the time connected with the holy city seem to have joined the secession. It is alleged that a number of Christians of Gentile origin, uniting with those of their brethren of Jewish descent who now agreed to relinquish the Hebrew ceremonies, chose an individual, named Marcus, for their chief pastor, and that at this period the succession in the line of the circumcision "failed." [624:3] This statement cannot signify that some dire calamity had at once swept away all the old presbytery of Jerusalem. It obviously indicates that none of its members had joined the party whose principles had obtained the ascendency. And yet, though the adherents of

281

Marcus might have been charged with innovation, they acted under the sanction of apostolical authority. They very properly refused to continue any longer in bondage to the beggarly elements of a ritual which had long since been superseded. Though the seceders might have urged that they were of apostolical descent, and that they were supported by ancient custom, it must be admitted, after all, that they were but a company of deluded and narrow-minded bigots. The evangelical pastors of the primitive Church repudiated their zeal for ritualism, and gave the right hand of fellowship to Marcus and his newly-organized community. The history of the mother Church of Christendom in the early part of the second century is thus fraught with lessons of the gravest wisdom. We may see from it that the true successors of the apostles were not those who occupied their seats, or who were able to trace from them a ministerial lineage, but those who inherited their spirit, who taught their doctrines, and who imitated their example.

Though, in this instance, the disciples at Jerusalem nobly emancipated themselves from the yoke of circumcision, it appears, from a controversy which created much confusion about sixty years afterwards, that the whole Church was disposed, to some extent, to conform to another Judaic ordinance. The embers of this dispute had been for some time smouldering, before they attracted much notice; but, about the termination of the second century, they broke out into a flame which spread from Rome to Jerusalem. The name of Easter [625:1] was yet unknown, and the Paschal feast appears, at least in some places, to have been then only recently established; but at an early period there was a sprinkling of Jewish Christians in almost every Church throughout the Empire, and they had at length induced their fellow-disciples to mark the seasons of the Passover and Pentecost [626:1] by certain special observances. The Passover was regarded as the more solemn feast, and, strange as it may now appear, was kept at the time by the Christians in much the same way in which it had been celebrated by the Jews before the fall of Jerusalem. A lamb was shut up on a certain day; it was afterwards roasted; and then eaten by the brotherhood. [626:2] The time when this ceremony was to be observed, and some other circumstantials, now formed topics of earnest and protracted discussion. One party, known as the Quarto-decimans, or Fourteenth Day Men, held that the Paschal feast was to be kept exactly at the time when the Jews had been accustomed to eat the Passover, that is, on the fourteenth day of the first month of the Jewish year; [626:3] and they celebrated the festival of the resurrection on the seventeenth day of the month, that is, on the third day after partaking of the Paschal lamb, whether that happened to be the first day of the week or otherwise. The other party strenuously maintained that the eating of the Paschal lamb ought to be postponed until the night preceding the first Lord's day next following the fourteenth day of the first month. They considered that this next Lord's day should be recognized as the festival of our Saviour's resurrection, and that the whole of the preceding week until the close should be kept as a fast not to be interrupted by the eating of the Passover.

The most determined Quarto-decimans were to be found in Asia Minor, and at their head was Polycrates, the chief pastor of Ephesus. At the head of the other party was Victor, bishop of Rome. The Church over which he presided did not originally observe any such appointment, [627:1] but some of its members of Jewish extraction were probably, on that account, dissatisfied; and about the time of the establishment of the Catholic system, the matter seems to have been settled by a compromise. It appears to have been then arranged that the festival should be kept; but to avoid the imputation of symbolizing with the Jews, it was agreed that the Friday of the Paschal week and the Lord's day following, or the day on which our Saviour suffered and the day on which He rose from the dead, should be the great days of observance. This arrangement was pretty generally accepted by those connected with what now began to be called the Catholic Church: but some parties pertinaciously refused to conform. Victor, as the head of the Catholic confederation, no doubt deemed it his duty to exact obedience from all its members; and, deeply mortified because the Asiatic Churches persisted in their own usages, shut them out from his communion. But it was soon evident that the Church was not prepared for such an exercise of authority, for the Asiatics refused to yield; and as some of Victor's best friends protested against the imprudence of his procedure, the ecclesiastical thunderbolt proved an impotent demonstration.

The Paschal controversy was far from creditable to any of the parties concerned. The eating of a lamb on a particular day was a fragment of an antiquated ceremonial, and as the ordinance itself had been superseded, the time of its observance was not a legitimate question for debate. Each party is said to have endeavoured to fortify its own position by quoting the names of Paul or Peter or Philip or John; but had any one of these apostles risen from the dead and appeared in the ecclesiastical arena, he would, no doubt, have rebuked all the disputants for their trivial and unholy wrangling. We have here a notable proof of the absurdity of appealing to tradition. Within a hundred years after the death of the last survivor of the Twelve its testimony was most discordant, for the tradition of the Western Churches, as propounded by Victor, expressly contradicted the tradition of the Eastern Churches, as attested by Polycrates. It is clear that in this case the apostles must have been misrepresented. Peter and Paul certainly never taught the members of the Church of Rome to eat the Paschal lamb, for the Jewish temple continued standing until after both these eminent ministers had finished their career, and meanwhile the eating of the Passover was confined to those who went up to worship at Jerusalem. Philip and John may have continued to keep the feast according to the ancient ritual until shortly before the ruin of the holy city; and if, afterwards, they permitted the converts from Judaism to kill a lamb and to have a social repast at the same season of the year, they could have attached no religious importance to such an observance. But now that both parties were heated by the spirit of rivalry and contention, they extracted from tradition a testimony which it did not supply. Vague reports and equivocal statements, handed down from ages preceding, were compelled to convey a meaning very different from that which they primarily communicated; and thus the voice of one tradition could be readily employed to neutralize the authority of another.

It is a curious fact that the custom which now created such violent excitement gradually passed into desuetude. At present there are few places [629:1] where the eating of the Paschal lamb is continued. But otherwise the practice for which Victor contended eventually prevailed, as the Roman mode of celebration was established by the authority of the Council of Nice. What is called Easter Sunday is still observed in many Churches as the festival of the resurrection. But the institution of such a festival is unnecessary, as each

283

returning Lord's day should remind the Christian that his Saviour has risen from the dead and become the first-fruits of them that sleep. [629:2]

This Paschal controversy generated no schism, but other disputes, which subsequently occurred, did not terminate so peacefully. About the middle of the third century disagreements respecting matters of discipline rent the Churches of Carthage and Rome. At Carthage, the malecontents sought for greater laxity; at Rome, they contended for greater strictness. At that time the confessors and the martyrs, or those who had persevered in their adherence to the faith under pains and penalties, and those who had suffered for it unto death, were held in the highest veneration. They had been even permitted in some places to dictate to the existing ecclesiastical rulers by granting what were called tickets of peace [629:3] to the lapsed, that is, to those who had apostatized in a season of persecution, and who had afterwards sought readmission to Church communion. These certificates, or tickets of peace, were understood to entitle the parties in whose favour they were drawn up to be admitted forthwith to the Lord's Supper. But it sometimes happened that a confessor or a martyr was himself far from a paragon of excellence, [630:1] as mere obstinacy, or pride, or self-righteousness, may occasionally hold out as firmly as a higher principle; and a man may give his body to be burned who does not possess one atom of the grace of Christian charity. There were confessors and martyrs in the third century who held very loose views on the subject of Church discipline, and who gave tickets of peace without much inquiry or consideration. [630:2] In some instances they did not condescend so far as to name the parties to whom they supplied recommendations, but directed that a particular individual "and his friends" [630:3] should be restored to ecclesiastical fellowship. Cyprian of Carthage at length determined to set his face against this system of testimonials. He alleged that the ticket of a martyr was no sufficient proof of the penitence of the party who tendered it, and that each application for readmission to membership should be decided on its own merits, by the proper Church authorities. The bishop was already obnoxious to some of the presbyters and people of Carthage; and, in the hope of undermining his authority, his enemies eagerly seized on his refusal to recognize these certificates. They endeavoured to create a prejudice against him by alleging that he was acting dictatorially, and that he was not rendering due honour to those who had so nobly imperilled or sacrificed their lives in the service of the gospel. To a certain extent their opposition was successful; and, as much sickness prevailed about the time, Cyprian was obliged to concede so far as to consent to give the Eucharist, on the tickets of peace, to those who had lapsed, and who were apparently approaching dissolution. But, soon afterwards, strengthened by the decision of an African Synod, he returned to his original position, and the parties now became hopelessly alienated. The leader of the secession was a deacon of the Carthaginian Church, named Felicissimus, and from him the schism which now occurred has received its designation. The Separatists chose a presbyter, named Fortunatus, as their bishop, and thus in the capital of the Proconsular Africa a new sect was organized. But the secession, which was based upon a principle thoroughly unsound, soon dwindled into insignificance, and rapidly passed into oblivion.

The schism which occurred about the same time at Rome was of a more formidable and permanent character. It had long been the opinion of a certain party in the Church that persons who had committed certain heinous sins should never again be readmitted to ecclesiastical fellowship. [631:1] Those who held this principle did not pretend to say that these transgressions were unpardonable; it was admitted that the offenders might obtain forgiveness from God, but it was alleged that the Church on earth could never feel warranted to receive them to communion. Cornelius, who was then the bishop of Rome, supported a milder system and contended that those who were not hopelessly excluded from the peace of God should not be inexorably debarred from the visible pledges of His affection. The leader of the stricter party was Novatian, a Roman presbyter of pure morals and considerable ability, who has left behind him one of the best treatises in defence of the Trinity which the ecclesiastical literature of antiquity can supply. This individual was ordained bishop in opposition to Cornelius; and, for a time, some of the most distinguished pastors of the age found it difficult to decide between these two claimants of the great bishopric. The high character of Novatian, and the supposed tendency of his discipline to preserve the credit and promote the purity of the Church, secured him considerable support: the sect which derived its designation from him spread into various countries; and, for several generations, the Novatians could challenge comparison, as to soundness in the faith and propriety of general conduct, with those who assumed the name of Catholics.

The agitation caused by the Novatian schism had not yet subsided when another controversy respecting the propriety of rebaptizing those designated heretics created immense excitement. Cyprian at the head of one party maintained that the baptism of heretical ministers was not to be recognized, and that the ordinance must again be dispensed to such sectaries as sought admission to catholic communion; whilst Stephen of Rome as strenuously affirmed that the rite was not to be repeated. It is rather singular that the Italian prelate, on this occasion, pleaded for the more liberal principle; but various considerations conspired to prompt him to pursue this course. When heresies were only germinating, and when what was afterwards called the Catholic Church was yet but in process of formation, no question as to the necessity of rebaptizing those to whom the ordinance had already been dispensed by any reputed Christian minister, seems to have been mooted. In the time of Hyginus of Rome, even the baptism of the leading ministers of the Gnostics was acknowledged by the chief pastor of the Western metropolis. [633:1] The Church of Rome had ever since continued to act upon the same system; and her determination to adhere to it had been fortified, rather than weakened, by recent occurrences. As the Novatians had set out on the principle of rebaptizing all who joined them, [633:2] Stephen recoiled from the idea of deviating from the ancient practice to follow in their footsteps. But Cyprian, who was naturally of a very imperious temper, and who had formed most extravagant notions of the dignity of the Catholic Church, could not brook the thought that the ministers connected with the schism of Felicissimus could dispense any baptism at all. He imagined that the honour of the party to which he belonged would be irretrievably compromised by such an admission, and he was sustained in these views by a strong party of African and Asiatic bishops. On this occasion Stephen repeated the experiment made about sixty years before by his predecessor Victor, and attempted to reduce his antagonists to acquiescence by excluding them from his fellowship. But this second effort to enforce ecclesiastical conformity was equally unsuccessful. It only provoked an outburst of indignation, as the parties in favour of rebaptizing

285

refused to give way. This controversy led, however, to the broad assertion of a principle which might not otherwise have been brought out so distinctly, for it was frequently urged during the course of the discussion that all pastors stand upon a basis of equality, and that the bishop of a little African village had intrinsically as good a right to think and to act for himself as the bishop of the great capital of the Empire.

It is very clear that at this time the unity of the Church did not consist in the uniformity of its discipline and ceremonies. The believers at Jerusalem continued to practise circumcision nearly a century after the establishment of Gentile Churches in which such a rite was unknown. On the question of rebaptizing heretics the Churches of Africa and Asia Minor were diametrically opposed to the Church of Rome and other communities in the West. As to the mode of observing the Paschal feast a still greater diversity existed. According to the testimony of Irenaeus there was nothing approaching to uniformity in the practice of the various societies with which he was acquainted. "The dispute," said he, "is not only respecting the day, but also respecting the manner of fasting. For some think that they ought to fast only one day, some two, some more days; some compute their day as consisting of forty hours night and day; [634:1] and this diversity existing among those that observe it, is not a matter that has just sprung up in our times, but long ago among those before us." [634:2] When Cyprian refused to admit the lapsed to the Lord's Supper on the strength of the tickets of peace furnished by the confessors and the martyrs, he departed from the course previously adopted in Carthage; and when Novatian excluded them altogether from communion, he acted on a principle which was not then novel. There was at that time, in fact, quite as much diversity in discipline and ceremonies among Christians as is now to be found in evangelical Protestant Churches.

It must be admitted that, as we descend from the apostolic age, the spirit of the dominant body in the Church betrays a growing want of Christian charity. There soon appeared a disposition, on the part of some, to monopolize religion, and to disown all who did not adopt their ecclesiastical Shibboleth. When the great mass of Christians became organized into what was called the Catholic Church, the chief pastors branded with the odious name of heretics all who did not belong to their association. The Nazarenes originally held all the great doctrines of the gospel, but they soon found themselves in the list of the proscribed, and they gradually degenerated into abettors of very corrupt principles. Those members of the Church of Carthage who joined Felicissimus acted upon principles which the predecessors even of Cyprian had sanctioned, and yet the African prelate denounced them as beyond the pale of divine mercy. Novatian was not less orthodox than Cornelius; but because he contended for a system of discipline which, though not unprecedented, was deemed by his rival too austere, and because he organized a party to support him, he also was stigmatized with the designation of heretic. The Quarto-decimans, as well as those who contended for Catholic rebaptism, would doubtless have been classed in the same list, had they not formed numerous and powerful confederations. Thus it was that those called Catholics were taught to cherish a contracted spirit, and to look upon all, except their own party, as out of the reach of salvation. Their false conceptions of what properly constituted the Church involved them in many errors and tended to vitiate their entire theology. But this subject is too important

286

to be discussed in a few cursory remarks, and must be reserved for consideration in a separate chapter.

CHAPTER XIII

THE THEORY OF THE CHURCH, AND THE HISTORY OF ITS PERVERSION

CONCLUDING OBSERVATIONS

"I am the good Shepherd," said Jesus: "the good Shepherd giveth his life for the sheep.... My sheep hear my voice, and I know them, and they follow me: and I give unto them eternal life, and they shall never perish." [636:1] The sheep here spoken of are the true children of God. They constitute that blessed community of which it is written—"Christ loved the Church, and gave himself for it, that he might sanctify and cleanse it with the washing of water by the word, that he might present it to himself a glorious Church, not having spot or wrinkle or any such thing, but that it should be holy and without blemish." [636:2]

The society thus described is, in the highest sense, "the holy Catholic Church." Its members are to be found wherever genuine piety exists, and they are all united to Christ by the bond of the Holy Spirit. Their Divine Overseer has promised to be with them "alway unto the end of the world," [636:3] to keep them "through faith unto salvation," [636:4] and to sustain them even against the violence of "the gates of hell." [636:5] Though they are scattered throughout different countries, and separated by various barriers of ecclesiastical division, they have the elements of concord. Could they be brought together, and divested of their prejudices, and made fully acquainted with each other's sentiments, they would speedily incorporate; for they possess "the unity of the Spirit," [637:1] "the unity of the faith," [637:2] and "the unity of the knowledge of the Son of God." [637:3] But these heirs of promise cannot be distinguished by the eye of sense; their true character can be known infallibly only to the Great Searcher of hearts; and for this, among other reasons, the spiritual commonwealth to which they belong is usually designated "the Church invisible." [637:4]

The visible Church is composed, to a considerable extent, of very different materials. It embraces the whole mixed multitude of nominal Christians, including not a few who exhibit no evidence whatever of vital godliness. Our Lord describes it in one of His parables when He says—"The kingdom of heaven is like unto a net which was cast into the sea, and gathered of every kind; which, when it was full, they drew to shore, and sat down, and gathered the good into vessels, but cast the bad away. So shall it be at the end of the world: the angels shall come forth, and sever the wicked from among the just, and shall cast them into the furnace of fire: there shall be wailing and gnashing of teeth." [637:5]

In the first century the profession of Christianity was perilous as well as

287

unpopular, so that the number of spurious disciples was comparatively small; and so long as the brethren enjoyed the ministrations of inspired teachers, all attempts to alienate them from each other, or to create schisms, had little success. But still, even whilst the apostles were on earth, some of the Churches planted and watered by themselves were involved in error and agitated by the spirit of division. "It hath been declared unto me of you," says Paul to the Corinthians, "that there are contentions among you. Now this I say, that every one of you saith, I am of Paul, and I of Apollos, and I of Cephas, and I of Christ." [638:1] The same writer had occasion to mourn over the apostasy of the Churches of Galatia. "I marvel," said he, "that ye are so soon removed from him that called you into the grace of Christ unto another gospel.... O foolish Galatians, who hath bewitched you that ye should not obey the truth?" [638:2] The Church of Sardis in the lifetime of the Apostle John had sunk into an equally deplorable condition, and hence he was commissioned to declare to it—"I know thy works, that thou hast a name that thou livest, and art dead." [638:3]

The circumstances which led to the organization of the Catholic system have already been detailed, and it has been shewn that the great design of the arrangement was to secure the visible unity of the ecclesiastical commonwealth. The Catholic confederation was supposed to comprehend all the faithful; and it was, no doubt, expected that, not long after its establishment, it would have rung the death knell of schism and sectarianism. According to its fundamental principle, whoever was not in communion with the bishop was out of the Church. To be out of the Church was soon considered as tantamount to be without God and without hope, so that this test condemned all who in any way dissented from the dominant creed as beyond the pale of salvation. Its assumptions, involving a decision of such grave importance and of such dubious authority, were acknowledged with some difficulty; and the question as to the extent and character of the Church seems to have led to considerable discussion; [639:1] but the horror of heresy which so generally prevailed strengthened the pretensions of the hierarchy, and at length every candidate for baptism was required to declare, as one of the articles of his faith—"I believe in the holy Catholic Church." [639:2]

According to one interpretation the sentiment embodied in this profession was perfectly unobjectionable. If by the holy Catholic Church we understand the Church invisible composed of all the true children of God, it must be conceded that every devout student of the Scriptures is bound to express his belief in its existence and its excellence. This Church is precious in the eyes of the Lord; it is the habitation of His Spirit; it is the heir of His great and glorious promises. But the holy Catholic Church, in the current ecclesiastical phraseology of the third century, had a very different signification. It denoted the great mass of disciples associated under the care of the Catholic bishops, as distinguished from all the minor sects throughout the Empire which made a profession of Christianity. A sincere and intelligent believer might well have scrupled to give such a title to the mixed society thus claiming its application.

It is quite true that there is no salvation out of the Church, if by the Church is meant that elect company which Christ died to redeem and sanctify; but the Word of God does not warrant us to assert that the eternal well-being of man depends on his connexion with any earthly society. Even in the days of the apostles, some who were subjected to a sentence of excommunication were the excellent of the earth. "I wrote unto the Church," says John, "but Diotrephes, who loveth to have the pre-eminence among them, receiveth us not. Wherefore, if I come, I will remember his deeds which he doeth, prating against us with malicious words, and not content therewith, neither doth he himself receive the brethren, and forbiddeth them that would, and casteth them out of the Church." [640:1] This Diotrephes seems to have been some wayward and domineering presbyter who took the lead among his fellow-elders, and who induced them by the influence of commanding talent, combined, it may be, with superior worldly station, to support him in his wilfulness. [640:2] But it would be very foolish to suppose that the brethren who were thus cast out of the Church were thereby eternally undone, for such certainly was not the judgment of the beloved disciple. Faith in Christ, and not a relation to any visible society, secures a title to heaven. Thousands, as well as the thief on the cross, have been admitted into paradise who have never been baptized, [640:3] and we might point out numberless cases in which individuals, in the wonderful providence of God, have been led to a saving knowledge of the truth who have never had an opportunity of joining a congregation of Christian worshippers. But those who now assumed the name of Catholics were continually dwelling upon the importance of a connexion with their own association; and, assuming that they were the Church, they appropriated to themselves whatever they could find in Scripture in commendation of its excellence. The promises addressed to the Church in the book of inspiration refer, however, not to any local and visible community, but to the "Church of the first-born which are written in heaven;" [641:1] and the Catholics, by misapplying them, were led to form very extravagant notions of the advantages of the position which they occupied. The ascription of the attributes of the Church invisible to their own association was, in fact, the fundamental misconception on which a vast fabric of error was erected. By reason of the indwelling of the Spirit in all believers the Church invisible is catholic, or universal, that is, it is to be found wherever vital Christianity exists; for the same reason it is holy, every member of it being a living temple of Jehovah; it is also one, as one Spirit animates all the saints and unites them to God and to each other; and it is perpetual, or indestructible, for the Most High has promised never to leave Himself without witnesses among men, and all His redeemed ones shall remain as trophies of His grace throughout all eternity. But these attributes were represented as belonging to the Church visible, and this radical mistake became the parent of monstrous delusions. The ecclesiastical writers who flourished towards the end of the second and beginning of the third century exhibit a considerable amount of inconsistency and vacillation when they touch upon the subject; [641:2] but, half a century afterwards, the language currently employed is much bolder and more decided. At that time Cyprian does not hesitate to express himself in the strongest terms of high-church exclusiveness. "All," says he, "are adversaries of the Lord and antichrist who are found to have departed from the charity and unity of the Catholic Church." [641:3] "You ought to know that the bishop is in the Church and the Church in the bishop, and if any be not with the bishop, that he is not in the Church." [641:4] "The house of God is one, and there cannot be salvation for any except in the Church." [641:5] "He can no longer have God for a Father, who has not the Church for a mother." [642:1]

Though the Catholics were a compact body, forming the bulk of the Christian population, their system failed to absorb all the professors of the gospel, or perhaps even greatly to check the tendency towards ecclesiastical

289

separation. In their controversies with seceders and schismatics, their own principles were more distinctly defined; and, as they soon found that they were quite an overmatch for any individual sect, their tone gradually became more decided and dictatorial. But the theological position from which they started was a sophism; and, like the movements of a traveller who has mistaken his way, every step of their progress was an advance in a wrong direction. Some of the more prominent errors to which their theory led may here be enumerated.

I. The theory of the Catholic Church recognized an odious ecclesiastical monopoly. Pastors and teachers are "for the perfecting of the saints, for the work of the ministry, for the edifying of the body of Christ;" [642:2] and yet a sinner may be saved without their instrumentality. The truth when spoken by a layman, or when read in a private chamber, may prove quite as efficacious as when proclaimed from the pulpit of a cathedral. That kingdom of God which "cometh not with observation" is built up by "the Word of His grace;" [642:3] and so long as the Word exists, and so long as the Spirit applies it to enlighten and sanctify and comfort God's children, the Church is imperishable. The evangelical labours of the pious master of a merchant vessel have often been blessed abundantly; and among the tens of thousands afloat upon the broad waters, who seldom enjoy any ecclesiastical ministrations, may be found some of the highest types of Christian excellence. Though regularly ordained pastors are necessary to the growth and well-being of the Church, such facts shew that they are not essential to its existence. But, according to the Catholic system, they are the veins and arteries through which its very life-blood circulates. All grace belongs to the visible society called the Catholic Church, and of this grace the Catholic ministers have the exclusive distribution. Without their intervention, as the dispensers of divine ordinances, no one can hope to inherit heaven. No other ministers whatever can be instrumental in conferring any saving benefit. Was it extraordinary that individuals who were supposed to be entrusted with such tremendous influence soon began to be regarded with awful reverence? If the services which they rendered were necessary to salvation, and if these services could be performed by none else, they were possessed of absolute authority, and it was to be expected that they would forthwith begin to act as "lords over God's heritage."

Under the Mosaic economy none save the descendants of a single individual were permitted to present the sacrifices or to enter the holy place. In the celebration of the most solemn rites of their religion the Jewish people were kept at a mysterious distance from the presence of the Divine Majesty, and were taught to regard the officiating ministers as mediators between God and themselves. This arrangement was symbolical, as all the priests were types of the Great Intercessor. But every believer may now enjoy the nearest access to his Maker, for the Saviour has made all His people "kings and priests unto God." [643:1] The ministers of the gospel do not constitute a privileged fraternity entitled by birth to exercise certain functions and to claim certain immunities. They should be appointed by the people as well as for them, and no service which they perform implies that they have nearer access to the Divine Presence than the rest of the worshippers. In the New Testament they are never designated priests, [644:1] neither is their intervention between God and the sinner described as indispensable. But Catholicism invested them with a factitious consequence, representing them as inheriting peculiar rights and privileges by ecclesiastical descent from the apostles. According to Cyprian, "Christ says to the apostles, and thereby to all prelates who by vicarious ordination are successors of the apostles. 'He that heareth you, heareth me.'" [644:2] About the commencement of the third century the pastors of the Church began to be called priests, [644:3] and this change in the ecclesiastical nomenclature betokens the influence of Catholic principles on the current theology. The Jewish sacrificial system had now ceased, and the Hebrew Christians were perhaps disposed to transfer to their new ministers the titles of the sons of Levi; but, had not the alteration been in accordance with the spirit of the times, it could not have been accomplished. It was, however, justified by Catholicism, as that system set forth the clergy in the light of mediators between God and the people. This misconception of the nature of the Christian ministry generated a multitude of errors. If ministers are priests they must offer sacrifice, and must be entrusted with the work of atonement. It is true, indeed, that the monstrous dogma of transubstantiation was not yet broached, but it cannot be denied that forms of expression which were exceedingly liable to misinterpretation, now began to be adopted. Thus, the Eucharist was styled "a sacrifice," [645:1] and the communion-table "the altar." [645:2] At first such phraseology was not intended to be literally understood, [645:3] but its tendency, notwithstanding, was most pernicious, as it fostered false views of a holy ordinance, and laid the foundation of the most senseless superstition ever imposed on human credulity.

Every genuine pastor has a divine call to the sacred office, and no act of man can supply the place of this spiritual vocation. God alone can provide a true minister, [645:4] for He alone can bestow the gifts and the graces which are required. Ordination is simply the form in which the existing Church rulers endorse the credentials of the candidate, and sanction his appearance in the character of an ecclesiastical functionary. But these rulers may themselves be incompetent or profane, so that their approval may be worthless; or, by mistake, they may permit wolves in sheep's clothing to take charge of the flock of Christ. The simple fact, therefore, that an individual holds a certain position in any section of the visible Church, is no decisive evidence that he is a true shepherd. Such, however, was not the doctrine of Catholicism. Whoever was accredited by the existing ecclesiastical authorities was, according to this system, the chosen of the Lord. When certain parties who had joined Novatian were induced to retrace their steps, they made the following penitential declaration in presence of a large congregation assembled in the Western metropolis—"We acknowledge Cornelius bishop of the most holy Catholic Church chosen by God Almighty and Christ our Lord." [646:1] Cyprian asserted that, as he was bishop of Carthage, he must necessarily have a divine commission. Nothing, indeed, can exceed the arrogance with which this imperious prelate expressed himself when speaking of his ecclesiastical authority. To challenge his conduct was, in his estimation, tantamount to blasphemy; and, to dispute his prerogatives, a contempt of the Divine Majesty. Once, in a time of persecution, he retired from Carthage, and he was, in consequence, upbraided by some as a coward; but when a fellow-bishop, Papianus, ventured to ask an explanation of a course of proceeding which apparently betokened indecision, Cyprian treated the inquiry as an insult, and poured out upon his correspondent a whole torrent of invectives and reproaches. He is God's bishop, and no one is to attempt, by the breath of suspicion, to stain the lustre of his episcopal dignity. "I perceive by your letter," says he, "that you believe the same things of me, and persist in what you believed.... This is not to believe in God, this is to be a rebel against Christ and against His gospel.... Do you suppose that the priests of God are without His cognizance ordained in the Church? For if you believe that those who are ordained are unworthy and incestuous, what else is it but to believe that, not by God, or through God, are His bishops appointed in the Church." [646:2] After indulging at great length in the language of denunciation, he adds, in a strain of irony—"Vouchsafe at length and deign to pronounce on us, and to confirm our episcopate by the authority of your hearing, that God and Christ may give you thanks, that through you a president and ruler has been restored as well to their altar as to their people." [647:1]

II. The Catholic system encouraged its adherents to cultivate very bigoted and ungenerous sentiments. They were taught to regard themselves as the "peculiar people," and to look on all others, however excellent, as without claim to the title or privileges of Christians. How different the spirit of the inspired heralds of the gospel! When Peter saw that the Holy Ghost was poured out on men uncircumcised, he recognized the divine intimation by acknowledging the believing Gentiles as his brethren in Christ. Conceiving that God himself had thus settled the question of their Church membership, "he commanded them to be baptized in the name of the Lord." [647:2] But men who professed to derive their authority from the apostle, now showed how grievously they misunderstood the benign and comprehensive genius of his ecclesiastical polity. The dominant party among the disciples had not long assumed the name of Catholics when they sadly belied the designation, for nothing could be more illiberal or uncatholic than their Church principles. All evidences of piety, no matter how decided, if found among the Nazarenes, or the Novatians, or the friends of Felicissimus, were rejected by them as apocryphal. The brightest manifestations of godliness, if exhibited outside their own denomination, only roused their jealousy or provoked their uncandid and malicious criticisms. The Catholic bishops acted as if they moved within something like a charmed circle, and as if a curse rested upon everything not under their own influence. Their proceedings often displayed alike their folly and inconsistency. Tertullian, for example, was a Montanist, and yet he was the writer from whom Cyprian himself derived a large share of his theological instruction. "Give me the master," the bishop of Carthage is reported to have said, when he called for his favourite author. [648:1] Thus, an individual who, according to Cyprian's own principles, was beyond the pale of hope, was the teacher with whom he was daily holding spiritual fellowship! The bigotry of the party must appear all the more intolerable when we consider that some of those who differed from them taught the cardinal doctrines of the gospel, as zealously and as fully as themselves. The Novatians seceded from their communion merely on the ground of a question of discipline, and yet the Catholics could not believe that any grace could exist among these ancient Puritans. The Novatians in their lives might exhibit much of the beauty of holiness, and they might shed their blood in the cause of Christianity, [648:2] but all this availed them nothing in the estimation of their narrow-minded antagonists. "Let no one think," says Cyprian, "that they can be good men who leave the Church." [648:3] "He can never attain to the kingdom who leaves her with whom the kingdom shall be." [648:4] "He cannot be a martyr who is not in the Church." [648:5] Every man not blinded by prejudice might well have suspected the soundness of a theory which could only be sustained by such brazen recklessness of assertion.

III. Nothing, however, more clearly revealed the anti-evangelical character of the Catholic system than its interference with the claims of the Word of God. The gospel commends itself by the light of its own evidence. The official rank of the preacher cannot add to its truth, neither can the corrupt motives which may prompt him to proclaim it, impair its authority. As a revelation from heaven, it possesses a title to consideration irrespective of any individual, or any Church; and God honours His own communication even though it may be delivered by a very unworthy messenger. [649:1] "Some indeed," says Paul, "preach Christ even of envy and strife, and some also of good-will.... What then? Notwithstanding, every way, whether in pretence or in truth, Christ is preached; and I therein do rejoice, yea, and will rejoice." [649:2] But Catholicism taught its partizans to cherish very different feelings, for they were instructed to believe that the gospel itself was without efficacy when promulgated by a minister who did not belong to their own party. They could not challenge a single flaw in the creed of Novatian, [649:3] and yet they strongly maintained that his preaching was useless, and that the baptism he dispensed was worthless as the ablution of a heathen. "You should know," says Cyprian, "that we ought not even to be curious as to what Novatian teaches, since he teaches out of the Church. Whosoever he be, and whatsoever he be, he is not a Christian who is not in the Church of Christ." [649:4] "When the Novatians say—'Dost thou believe remission of sins and eternal life by the Holy Church?' they lie in their interrogatory, since they have no Church." [649:5]

Strange infatuation! Who could have anticipated that one hundred and fifty years after the death of the Apostle John, such miserable and revolting bigotry would have been current? The Scriptures teach us that, in the salvation of sinners, ministers are as nothing, and the gospel everything. "Whosoever," says Paul, "shall call upon the name of the Lord shall be saved.... Faith cometh by hearing, and hearing by the Word of God." [650:1] Cyprian did not understand such doctrine. He imagined that the Word of God had no power except when issuing from the lips of the ministers of his own communion. The Catholic Church must put its seal upon the gospel to give it currency. Without this stamp it was all in vain to announce it to a world lying in wickedness. The Catholic pastor might be a man without ability; he might be comparatively ignorant; and he might be of more than suspicious integrity; and yet the King of the Church was supposed to look down with complacency on all the official acts of this wretched hireling, whilst no dew of heavenly influence rested on the labours of a pious and accomplished Novatian minister! When men like Cyprian were prepared to acknowledge such folly, it was not strange that a darkness which might be felt soon settled down upon Christendom.

* * * * *

In the preceding pages the history of the ancient Church for the first three centuries has passed under review, and a few general observations may now be not inappropriately appended to this concluding chapter. The details here furnished supply ample evidence that Christianity was greatly corrupted long before the conversion of Constantine. It is true, indeed, that much of the superstition which has since so much disfigured the Church was yet unknown. During the first three centuries we find no recognition of the mediatorship of Mary, or of the dogma of her immaculate conception, [650:2] or of the worship of images, or of the celebration of divine service in an unknown tongue, or of the doctrine of the infallibility of the Roman bishop. But the germs of many dangerous errors were distinctly visible, and when the sun of Imperial favour

293

began to shine upon the Christians, these errors rapidly reached maturity. The Eucharistic bread and wine were viewed with superstitious awe, and language was applied to them which was calculated to bewilder and to confound. A system of penitential discipline alien to the spirit of the New Testament was already in existence; rites and ceremonies unknown in the apostolic age had now made their appearance; and in the great towns a crowd of functionaries, whom Paul and Peter would have refused to own, added to the pomp of public worship. Some imagine that in the times of Tertullian and of Cyprian we may find the purest faith in the purest form, but a more intimate acquaintance with the history of the period is quite sufficient to dispel the delusion. A little consideration may, indeed, convince us that, in the second or third century, we could scarcely expect to see either the most brilliant displays of the light of truth or the most attractive exhibitions of personal holiness. The waters of life gushed forth, clear as crystal, from the Rock of Ages; but, as their course was through the waste wilderness of a degenerate world, they were soon defiled by its pollutions; and it was not until the desert began "to rejoice and blossom as the rose," that the stream flowed smoothly in the channel it had wrought, and partially recovered its native purity. At the present day we would not be warranted in expecting as high a style of Christianity in a convert from idolatry as in one who had been trained up from infancy under the care of enlightened and godly parents. By judicious culture the graces of the Spirit, as well as the fruits of the earth, may be improved; but when a section of the open field of immorality and ignorance is first added to the garden of the Lord, it may not forthwith possess all the fertility and loveliness of the more ancient plantation. [652:1] A large portion of the early disciples had once been heathens; they had to struggle against evil habits and inveterate prejudices; they were surrounded on all sides by corrupting influences; and, as they had not the same means of obtaining an exact and comprehensive knowledge of the gospel as ourselves, we cannot reasonably hope to find among them any very extraordinary measure either of spiritual wisdom or of consistent piety.

When the Church towards the middle of the second century was sorely harassed by divisions, its situation was extremely critical and embarrassing. Christianity had appeared among men bearing the olive branch of peace, and had proposed to supersede the countless superstitions of the heathen by a faith which would bind the human race together in one great and harmonious family. How mortified, then, must have been its friends when Basilides, Marcion, Valentine, Cerdo, Mark, and many others began to propagate their heresies, and when it appeared as if the divisions of the Church were to be as numerous as the religions of paganism! Had the ministers of the gospel girded themselves for the emergency; had they boldly encountered the errorists, and vanquished them with weapons drawn from the armoury of the Word; they would have approved themselves worthy of their position, and acquired strength for future conflicts. But whilst they did not altogether neglect an appeal to Scripture, they were tempted in an evil hour to think of sequestrating their own freedom that they might overwhelm heresy with the vigour of an ecclesiastical despotism. By investing their chairman with arbitrary power and by making communion with this functionary the criterion of discipleship, they at once sanctioned a perilous arrangement and endorsed a vicious principle. From this date we may trace the commencement of a career of defection. The bishop and the Church began to supplant Christ and a knowledge of the gospel. Bigotry advanced apace, and conscience found itself in bondage.

The establishment of the hierarchical system, though imparting, as was thought, greater unity to the structure of the Church, did not really invigorate its constitution. The spiritual commonwealth is very different from any merely earthly organization, for it has no statute-book but the Bible, and it owes explicit obedience to no ruler but the King of Zion. Freedom of conscience, in obedience to the Word, is the heritage of all its members; and every one of them is bound to exercise the privilege, and to resist its violation. Its unity appears, not in adhesion to any visible head, but in cordial submission to its one great Lord and Sovereign. When a change was made in its primitive framework, its essential unity was impaired. After the elders had handed over a considerable share of their authority to their president, they could not be expected to take such a deep interest in its government as when they were themselves individually responsible for its official administration. They still, indeed, acted as his counsellors, but as they no longer held the independent footing they had once occupied, they could neither speak nor act so freely and so energetically as before. Thus, whilst one member of the ecclesiastical body was permitted to attain an unnatural magnitude, others ceased to perform their proper functions, and the whole eventually became diseased and misshapen. And the new arrangement entirely failed in checking the growth of the errorists. After its adoption heresies sprung up as rapidly as ever, and the multitude of its sects continued to be the scandal of Christianity even in the time of Constantine. [654:1] Their suppression is to be attributed, not to the potency of Prelacy, but to the stern intolerance of the Imperial laws. By the rigid enforcement of conformity the Catholic Church at length reigned without a rival.

It is easy to see from the extant ecclesiastical writings of the third century that the doctrine of the visible unity of the Church as represented by the Catholic hierarchy already formed a prominent part of the current creed. As there is "one God, one Christ, and one Holy Ghost," it was affirmed that there could be but "one bishop in the Catholic Church." [654:2] This theory seemed somewhat inconsistent with the fact that there were many bishops in almost every province of the Empire; but the ingenuity of churchmen attempted a solution of the difficulty. It was alleged that the whole episcopacy should be regarded as one, and that each bishop constituted an integral part of the grand unit. "The episcopacy is one," says Cyprian, "it is a whole in which each enjoys full possession." [654:3] "There is one Church from Christ throughout the whole world divided into many members, and one episcopate diffused throughout an harmonious multitude of many bishops." [654:4]

We have seen that the Roman prelate was already recognized as the centre of ecclesiastical unity. A misunderstood passage in the Gospel of Matthew [654:5] was supposed to sanction this ecclesiastical primacy. "There is," said the bishop of Carthage, "one God, and one Christ, and one Church, and one chair founded by the Word of the Lord on the Rock." [654:6] Though the Roman chief pastor might be considered theoretically only the first among the Catholic bishops, his zeal for uniformity had now more than once interrupted the peace of the Christian community. The erection of a new capital and the subsequent dismemberment of the Empire considerably affected his position; but, within a certain sphere, he steadily endeavoured to carry out the idea of Catholic unity. The doctrine reached its highest point of development after the lapse of upwards of a thousand years. Then, the bishop of Rome had become a sovereign prince, and was the acknowledged ruler of a vast and magnificent hierarchy. Then, he swayed his spiritual sceptre over all the tribes of Western Christendom. Then, verily, uniformity had its day of triumph; for, with some rare exceptions, wherever the stranger travelled throughout Europe, he found the same order of divine service, and saw the ministers of the sanctuary arrayed in the same costume, and practising even the same gestures. Then, wherever he entered a sacred edifice, he heard the same language, and listened to the same prayers expressed in the very same phraseology. But what was meanwhile the real condition of the Church? Was there love without dissimulation, and the keeping of the unity of the Spirit in the bond of peace? Nothing of the kind. Never could it be said with greater truth of the people of the West that they were "foolish, disobedient, deceived, serving divers lusts and pleasures, living in malice and envy, hateful and hating one another." There were wars and rumours of wars; nation rose up against nation and kingdom against kingdom; and the Pope was generally the cause of the contention. The very man who claimed to be the centre of Catholic unity was the grand fomenter of ecclesiastical and political disturbance. The Sovereign Pontiff, and the Catholic princes with whom he was engaged in deadly feuds, were equally faithless, restless, and implacable. Freedom of thought was proscribed, and the human mind was placed under the most exacting and intolerable tyranny by which it was ever oppressed.

The mutilation of this Dagon of hierarchical unity is one of the many glorious results of the great Reformation. The sooner the remaining fragments of this idol be crushed to atoms, the better for the peace and freedom of Christendom. The unity of the Church cannot be achieved by the iron rod of despotism, neither can the communion of saints be promoted by the sacrifice of their rights and privileges. "Where the Spirit of the Lord is, there is liberty." [656:1] Christ alone can draw all men unto Him. The real unity of His Church is, not any merely ecclesiastical cohesion, but a unity of faith, of hope, and of affection. It is the fellowship of Christian freemen walking together in the fear of the Lord, and in the comfort of the Holy Ghost. It is the attraction of all hearts to one heavenly Saviour, and the submission of all wills to one holy law. Looking at the past condition or the present aspect of society, we may think the difficulties in the way of such unity altogether insurmountable; but it will, in due time, be brought about by Him "who doeth great things and unsearchable, marvellous things without number." Its realization will present the most delightful and impressive spectacle that the earth has ever seen. "Every valley shall be exalted, and every mountain and hill shall be made low; and the crooked shall be made straight, and the rough places plain; and the glory of the Lord shall be revealed, and all flesh shall see it together." [656:2] "Thy watchmen shall lift up the voice, with the voice together shall they sing; for they shall see eye to eye, when the Lord shall bring again Zion." [656:3] "And the Lord shall be King over all the earth; in that day shall there be one Lord, and His name one." [656:4] AMEN.

THE END

[3:1] Mr Merivale, in his "History of the Romans under the Empire," (vol. iv. p. 450,) estimates the population in the time of Augustus at eighty-five millions, but in this reckoning he does not include Palestine, and perhaps some of his calculations are rather low. Greswell computes the population of Palestine at ten millions, and that of the whole empire at one hundred and twenty millions. ("Dissertations upon an Harmony of the Gospels," vol. iv. p. 11, 493.)

[7:1] See the article [Greek: Hetairai] in Smith's "Dictionary of Greek and Roman Antiquities."

[8:1] "We despise," says an early Christian writer, "the supercilious looks of philosophers, whom we have known to be the corrupters of innocence, adulterers, and tyrants, and eloquent declaimers against vices of which they themselves are guilty."—Octavius of Minucius Felix.

[9:1] "De Republ.," ii.

[9:2] In the "Octavius of Minucius Felix" (c. 25), we meet with the following startling challenge—"Where are there more bargains for debauchery made, more assignations concerted, or more adultery devised than by the priests amidst the altars and shrines of the gods?" This, of course, refers to the state of things in the third century, but there is no reason to believe that it was now much better. Tertullian speaks in the same manner ("Apol". c. 15). See also "Juvenal," sat. vi. 488, and ix. 23.

[10:1] "Origen. Contra Celsum," lib. i. c. 49.

[10:2] Mat. xxii. 23.

[10:3] Luke ii. 25, 36.

[11:1] See Matt. v. 18; John v. 39, and x. 35.

[11:2] See Josephus against Apion, i. § 8. Origen says that the Hebrews had twenty-two sacred books corresponding to the number of letters in their alphabet. Opera, ii. 528. It would appear from Jerome that they reckoned in the following manner: they considered the Twelve Minor Prophets only one book; First and Second Samuel, one book; First and Second Kings, one book; First and Second Chronicles, one book; Ezra and Nehemiah, one book; Jeremiah and Lamentations, one book; the Pentateuch, five books; Judges and Ruth, one book; thus, with the other ten books of Joshua, Esther, Job, Psalms, Proverbs, Ecclesiastes, Canticles, Isaiah, Ezekiel, and Daniel, making up twenty-two. The most learned Roman Catholic writers admit that what are called the apocryphal books were never acknowledged by the Jewish Church. See, for example, Dupin's "History of Ecclesiastical Writers," Preliminary Dissertation, section ii. See also Father Simon's "Critical History of the Old Testament," book. i. chap. viii.

[11:3] Matt, xxiii. 15.

[12:1] Many proofs of this occur in the Acts. See Acts x. 2, xiii. 43, xvi. 14, xvii.4.

[12:2] See Cudworth's "Intellectual System," i. 318, &c. Edition, London, 1845. Warburton has adduced evidence to prove that this doctrine was imparted to the initiated in the heathen mysteries. "Divine Legation of Moses," i. 224. Edit., London, 1837.

[12:3] Gal. iv. 4.

[12:4] Gen. xlix. 10; Dan. ix. 25; Haggai ii. 6, 7.

[12:5] Virgil. Ec. iv. Suetonius. Octavius, 94. Tacitus. Histor. v. 13.

[13:1] Haggai ii. 7.

[13:2] Dan. vii. 14.

[14:1] See Supplementary Note at the end of this chapter on the year of Christ's Birth.

[14:2] Luke ii. 6, 7.

[15:1] Luke i. 11, 19.

[15:2] Luke. 26, 31.

[15:3] Luke ii. 13, 14.

[15:4] Matt. ii. 9.

[15:5] Matt. ii. 12.

[15:6] Matt. ii. 3. The evangelist does not positively assert that the wise men met Herod at Jerusalem. On their arrival in the holy city he was probably at Jericho—distant about a day's journey—for Josephus states that he died there. ("Antiq." xvii. 6. § 5. and 8. § 1.) We may infer, therefore, that he "heard" of the strangers on his sick-bed, and "privily called" them to Jericho. The chief priests and scribes were, perhaps, summoned to attend him at the same place.

[16:1] Matt. ii. 16. The estimates formed at a subsequent period of the number of infants in the village of Bethlehem and its precincts betray a strange ignorance of statistics. "The Greek Church canonised the 14,000 innocents," observes the Dean of St Paul's, "and another notion, founded on a misrepresentation of Revelations (xiv. 3), swelled the number to 144,000. The former, at least, was the common belief of our Church, though even in our liturgy the latter has in some degree been sanctioned by retaining the chapter of Revelations as the epistle for the day. Even later, Jeremy Taylor, in his 'Life of Christ,' admits the 14,000 without scruple, or rather without thought."—Milman's History of Christianity, i. p. 113, note.

[16:2] Matt. ii. 11.

[16:3] Luke ii. 38. It is a curious fact that in the year 751 of the city of Rome, the year of the Birth of Christ according to the chronology adopted in this volume, the passover was not celebrated as usual in Judea. The disturbances which occurred on the death of Herod had become so serious on the arrival of the paschal day, that Archelaus was obliged to disperse the people by force of arms in the very midst of the sacrifices. So soon did Christ begin to cause the sacrifice and the oblation to cease. See Greswell's "Dissertations," i. p 393, 394, note.

[17:1] Luke ii. 40.

[17:2] Luke ii. 52.

[17:3] Mark vi. 3.

[17:4] John vii. 15.

[18:1] Luke ii. 46, 47.

[18:2] Luke iv. 16.

[18:3] Luke iii. 21-23. "It became Him, being in the likeness of sinful flesh, to go through these appointed rites and purifications which belonged to that flesh. There is no more strangeness in His having been baptized by John, than in His keeping the Passover. The one rite, as the other, belonged to sinners, and among the transgressors He was numbered."—ALFORD, Greek Testament, Note on Matt. iii. 13-17.

[18:4] See Greswell's "Dissertations upon an Harmony of the Gospels," vol. i.

p. 362, 363. John probably commenced his ministry about the feast of Tabernacles, A.D. 27.

[18:5] See Josephus, "Antiq." xviii, 5, § 2.

[19:1] Matt. iv. 23.

[19:2] Matt. iv. 24, 25.

[19:3] Isaiah xlv. 15.

[19:4] 1 Kings viii. 10-12.

[19:5] John v. 13, vi. 15, viii. 59, xii. 36; Mark i. 45, vii. 24.

[19:6] Mark ii. 1, 2; Matt. xiv. 13, 14, 21, xv. 32, 38, 39.

[20:1] Matt. iv. 13. Hence it is said to have been "exalted unto heaven" in the way of privilege. Matt. xi. 23; Luke x. 15. It was the residence as well of Peter and Andrew (Matt. xvii. 24), as of James, John (Mark i. 21, 29), and Matthew (Mark ii. 1, 14, 15), and there also dwelt the nobleman whose son was healed by our Lord (John iv. 46). It was on the borders of the Sea of Galilee, so that by crossing the water He could at once reach the territory of another potentate, and withdraw Himself from the multitudes drawn together by the fame of His miracles. See Milman's "History of Christianity," i. 188.

[21:1] John i. 46.

[22:1] Luke xxiv. 32.

[22:2] Matt. vii. 29.

[23:1] According to Mr Greswell our Lord adopted this method of teaching about eighteen months after the commencement of His ministry, and the Parable of the Sower was the first delivered. "Exposition of the Parables," Vol. i. p. 2.

[23:2] Isa. xxxv. 5, 6.

[23:3] See John v. 13, ix. 1, 6, 25, 36.

[23:4] Mark ii. 6, 7, 10, 11, iii. 5, 22.

[24:1] John vi. 9.

[24:2] Matt. xiv. 24, 25.

[24:3] Mark iv. 39; Matt. viii. 26, 27.

[24:4] John ix. 16.

[24:5] Matt. xxi. 19. Neander has shown that this was a typical action pointing to the rejection of the Jews. See his "Life of Christ." Bohn's Edition.

[24:6] John ii. 9.

[24:7] Matt. ix. 28, 29; Mark vi. 5, ix. 23, 24.

[25:1] John viii. 12.

[26:1] Several of the early fathers imagined that it continued only a year. Some of them, such as Clemens Alexandrinus, drew this conclusion from Isaiah lxi. 1, "To preach the acceptable year of the Lord." See Kaye's "Clement of Alexandria," p. 347.

[26:2] John ii. 13, v. 1, vi. 4, xii. 1. Eusebius argues from the number of high priests that our Lord's ministry did not embrace four entire years. "Ecc. Hist." i. c. x.

[26:3] He lived, therefore, about thirty-three years. According to Malto Brun ("Universal Geography," book xxii.), "the mean duration of human life is between thirty and forty years," and, in the same chapter, he computes it at thirty-three years. It would thus appear that, at the time of His death, our Lord was, in point of age, a fitting representative of the species.

[26:4] Luke iv. 44, viii. 1; Matt. ix. 35.

[27:1] John iii. 1, 2.

[27:2] Matt. xxvi. 63-66.

[27:3] Matt, xxvii. 38.

[27:4] Matt, xxvii. 24; John xviii. 38.

[27:5] Mark xv. 10, 15.

[28:1] Acts ii. 23.

[28:2] Matt. xxvi. 38; Mark xiv. 33.

[28:3] Luke xxii. 44.

[28:4] Matt. xxvii. 46.

[28:5] Luke xxii. 43.

[28:6] Luke xxiii. 44; Mark xv. 33.

[29:1] Matt. xxvii. 51, 52.

[29:2] Matt. xxvii. 54.

[29:3] John x. 18.

[29:4] Ps. xvi. 10; Acts ii. 31.

[29:5] John ii. 19; Mark viii. 31; Luke xviii, 33.

[29:6] John xiv. 19; 1 Thess. iv. 14.

[29:7] Rom. i. 4; 1 Cor. xv. 14, 17; 1 Pet. i. 3; Rev. i. 18.

[29:8] John xix. 33, 34.

[29:9] Matt. xxvii. 60.

[30:1] Matt. xxvii. 66.

[30:2] Matt. xxviii. 2, 4.

[30:3] Matt. xxviii. 11.

[30:4] Matt. xxviii. 12, 13, 15.

[30:5] Rev. i. 5.

[30:6] Acts x. 40, 41.

[30:7] John xiv. 22.

[31:1] Acts i. 3.

[31:2] Luke xxiv. 27.

[31:3] Matt, xxviii. 19.

[31:4] Luke xxiv. 50, 51.

[32:1] John i. 10-12.

[36:1] Isa. liii. 3.

[36:2] John vii. 39.

[36:3] Acts i. 15.

[37:1] 1 Cor. xv. 6.

[37:2] See Matt. xv. 31; John ii. 23, vii. 31, viii. 30.

[37:3] See Joshua xv. 25.

[37:4] Hence called Iscariot, that is, Ish Kerioth, or, a man of Kerioth. See Alford, Greek Test., Matt. x. 4.

[37:5] Acts ii. 7.

[37:6] Compare Matt. ix. 9, 10, and Mark ii. 14, 15.

[37:7] "As St John never mentions Bartholomew in the number of the apostles, so the other evangelists never take notice of Nathanael, probably because the same person under two several names; and as in John, Philip and Nathanael are joined together in their coming to Christ, so in the rest of the evangelists, Philip and Bartholomew are constantly put together without the least variation."—Cave's Lives of the Apostles. Life of Bartholomew. Compare Matt. x. 3; Acts i. 13; and John i. 45, xxl. 2.

[38:1] Compare Matt. x. 3, and Acts i. 13.

[38:2] John xi. 16, xxi. 2.

[38:3] Mark xv. 40. He was in some way related to our Lord, and hence called His brother (Gal. i. 19). But though Mary, the mother of our Saviour, had evidently several sons (see Matt. i. 20, 25, compared with Matt. xiii. 55; Mark vi. 3; Matt. xii. 46, 47), they were not disciples when the apostles were appointed, and none of them consequently could have been of the Twelve. (See John vii. 5). The other sons of Mary, who must all have been younger than Jesus, seem to have been converted about the time of the resurrection. Hence they are found among the disciples before the day of Pentecost (Acts i. 14).

[38:4] Mark iii. 17.

[38:5] Matt. x. 2.

[38:6] John i. 42.

[38:7] Matt. x. 4; Mark iii. 18; Luke vi. 15; Acts i. 13. Some think that Kananites is equivalent to Zelotes, whilst others contend that it in derived from a village called Canan. See Alford, Greek Test., Matt. x. 4; and Greswell's; "Dissertations," vol. ii. p. 128. Some MSS. have [Greek: Kananaios].

[38:8] Mark vi. 7. "Although no two of these catalogues (of the Twelve) agree precisely in the order of the names, they may all be divided into three quaternions, which are never interchanged, and the leading names of which are the same in all. Thus the first is always Peter, the fifth Philip, the ninth James the son of Alpheus, and the twelfth Judas Iscariot. Another difference is that Matthew and Luke's Gospel gives the names in pairs, or two and two, while Mark enumerates them singly, and the list before us (in the Acts) follows both, these methods, one after the other."—Alexander on the Acts, vol. i. p. 19.

[39:1] Gal. i. 19.

[39:2] Acts i. 13. See also Jude v. 1.

[39:3] Upon this subject see the conjectures of Greswell, "Dissertation," vol. ii. p. 120.

[39:4] John i. 35, 40.

[39:5] From the great minuteness of the statements in the passage, it has been conjectured that the evangelist himself was the second of the two disciples mentioned in John i. 35-37.

[39:6] John iii. 30.

[39:7] Matt. xix. 27.

[40:1] Mark i. 20.

[40:2] Luke xix. 2.

[40:3] Luke xix. 2.

[40:4] Mark ii. 15.

[40:5] John vii. 52.

[40:6] John xi. 16. See also v. 8.

[41:1] John xx. 25.

[41:2] John xx. 28.

[41:3] Some writers have asserted that he is a different person from James "the Lord's brother" mentioned Gal. i. 19, but the statement rests upon no solid foundation. Compare John vii. 5; 1 Cor. xv. 7; Acts i. 14, xv. 2, 13. See also note p. 38 [38:3] of this chapter.

[41:4] John i. 47.

[41:5] Mark v. 37, ix. 2; Matt. xxvi. 37.

[41:6] Acts xii. 2, 3. "It is remarkable that, so far as we know, one of these inseparable brothers (James and John) was the first, and one the last, that died of the apostles."—Alexander on the Acts, i. 443.

[41:7] See Greswell's "Dissertations," vol. ii. p. 115.

[42:1] Matt. xx. 20, 21.

[42:2] Some writers have asserted that Philip and Nathanael were learned men, but of this there is no good evidence. See Cave's "Lives of the Apostles," Philip and Bartholomew.

[42:3] Greswell makes it nine months. See his "Harmonia Evangelica," p. xxiv. xxvi.

[42:4] Matt. x. 5, 6.

[42:5] See Vitringa "De Synagoga Vetere," p. 577, and Mosheim's "Commentaries," by Vidal, vol. i. 120-2, note.

[43:1] This is the calculation of Greswell. "Harmonia Evangelica," p. xxvi. xxxi. Robinson makes the interval considerably shorter. See his "Harmony of the Four Gospels in Greek."

[43:2] They received new powers at the close of their first missionary excursion. See Luke x. 19.

[43:3] Selden in his treatise "De Synedriis" supplies some curious information on this subject. See lib. ii. cap. 9, § 3. See also some singular speculations respecting it in Baumgarten's "Theologischer Commentar zum Pentateuch," i. 153, 351. Some of the fathers speak of seventy-two disciples and of seventy-two nations and tongues. See Stieren's "Irenaeus," i. p. 544, note, and Epiphanius, tom. i. p. 50, Edit. Coloniae, 1682; compared with Greswell's "Dissertations," ii. p.7.

[43:4] Gen. x. 32.

[44:1] The following tabular view of the names of the descendants of Shem, Ham, and Japheth, mentioned in the 10th chapter of Genesis, will illustrate this statement:—

SHEM. | HAM.

Elam.Asshur.Arphaxad, Lud. Aram, |Cush, Mizraim, Phut. Canaan,
　　　　　　Salah, Uz, |Seba, Ludim, Sidon,
　　　　　　Eber, Hul, |Havilah, Anamim, Heth,
　　　　　　Peleg, Gether,|Sabtah, Lehabim, Jebusite,
　　　　　　Joktan, Mash. |Raamah, Naphtuhim, Amorite,
　　　　　　Almodad, |Sabtechab,Pathrusim, Girgasite,
　　　　　　Sheleph, |Sheba, Caslubim, Hivite,
　　　　　　Hazarmaveth, |Dedan, Caphtorim, Arkite,
　　　　　　Jerah, |Nimrod. Philistim. Sinite,
　　　　　　Hadoram, | Arvadite,
　　　　　　Uzal, | Zemarite,
　　　　　　Diklah, | Hamathite.
　　　　　　Obal, |
　　　　　　Abimael, |
　　　　　　Sheba, |
　　　　　　Ophir, |
　　　　　　Havilah, |
　　　　　　Jobab. |
　　　　　　　　JAPHETH.
Gomer, Magog. Madai. Javan, Tubal. Meshech. Tiras.

Ashkenaz, Elishah,
Riphath, Tarshish,
Togarmah. Kittim,
   Dodanim.

It often happens that one branch of a family is exceedingly prolific whilst another is barren. So it seems to have been with the descendants of the three sons of Noah. Thus, Elam, Ashur, and others, appear each to have founded only one nation, whilst Arphaxad and his posterity founded eighteen.

[45:1] Luke x. 1.

[45:2] John iv. 39.

[45:3] Mark vii. 24, 26, 30, 31.

[45:4] This is the opinion of Dr Robinson. See His "Harmony." See also Luke ix. 51, 52, x. 33.

[45:5] Luke x. 13, 17, 18.

[45:6] Matt. xv. 24.

[46:1] Rev. xxi. 14.

[46:2] It is certain that some were called apostles who were not of the number of the Twelve. See Acts xiv. 4. In 1 Cor. xv. 5, 7, both "the Twelve," and "all the apostles," are mentioned, and it may be that the Seventy are included under the latter designation. Such was the opinion of Origen—[Greek: epeita tois eterois para tous dôdeka apostolois pasi, tacha tois ebdomêkoita]. "Contra Celsum," lib. ii. 65. See also "De Recta in Deum Fide," sec. i., Opera, tom. i. p. 806.

[46:3] Luke x. 9, 16, 19, 24.

[46:4] Eph. ii. 20. See also Eph. iii. 5. It is evident, especially from the latter passage, that the prophets here spoken of belong to the New Testament Church.

[47:1] Acts xv. 6, xxi. 18.

[47:2] 1 Pet. v. 1; 2 John v. 1; 3 John v. 1. It is remarkable that Papias, one of the very earliest of the fathers, actually speaks of the apostles simply as the elders. See Euseb. book iii. chap. 39.

[47:3] Thus, Simon Zelotes is said to have travelled into Egypt and thence passed into Mesopotamia and Persia, where he suffered martyrdom; whilst, according to others, he travelled through Egypt to Mauritania and thence to Britain, where he was crucified. See Cave's "Lives of the Apostles," Life of Simon the Zealot. No weight can be attached to such legends. Origen states that the Apostle Thomas laboured in Parthia, and Andrew in Scythia. "In Genesim," Opera, tom. ii. p. 24.

[47:4] Acts vi. 6.

[48:1] Matt. vii. 16.

[48:2] Acts xxvi. 16; Luke x. 2; 1 Tim. i. 12.

[48:3] Such was Valentine, the most formidable of the Gnostic heresiarchs, said to be a disciple of Theodas, the companion of Paul. Clem. Alex. Strom. vii. Paul of Samosata and Arius were able to boast, at least as much as their antagonists, of their apostolic descent.

[49:1] 1 John iv. 1, 6.

[49:2] 2 John 10, 11.

[49:3] Gal. i. 8, 9.

[50:1] Luke x. 16.

[50:2] 2 Cor. iii. 1-3.

[51:1] Acts i. 3.

[51:2] Luke xxiv. 46, 47.

[52:1] Acts ii. 41.

[52:2] Acts ii. 44, 45.

[53:1] See Acts iv. 34. Barnabas was probably obliged to go to Cyprus to complete the sale.

[53:2] Acts vi. 1.

[54:1] Acts vi. 2, 3.

[54:2] Acts i. 15, 23. They selected two, and not knowing which to prefer, they decided finally by lot.

[54:3] Acts vi. 6.

[55:1] Acts iv. 18.

[55:2] Acts iv. 19.

[55:3] That is, A.D. 34, dating the crucifixion A.D. 31. Tillemont, but on entirely different grounds, assigns the same date to the martyrdom of Stephen. See "Memoires pour servir à L'Histoire Ecclesiastique des six premiers siecles," tome prem. sec. par. p. 420. Stephen's martyrdom probably occurred about the feast of Tabernacles.

[55:4] Daniel ix. 27. A day in prophetic language denotes a year. Ezek. iv. 4, 5. A prophetic week, or seven days, is, therefore, equivalent to seven years.

[56:1] "The one week, or Passion-week, in the midst of which our Lord was crucified A.D. 31, began with His public ministry A.D. 28, and ended with the martyrdom of Stephen A.D. 34."—Hales' Chronology, ii. p. 518. Faber and others, who hold that the one week terminated with the crucifixion, are obliged to adopt the untenable hypothesis that John the Baptist and our Lord together preached seven years. The view here taken is corroborated by the statement in Dan. ix. 27—"In the midst of the week he shall cause the sacrifice and the oblation to cease,"—as Christ by one sacrifice of Himself "perfected for ever them that are sanctified."

[56:2] Matt, xxviii. 19.

[57:1] Acts viii. 6, 12.

[57:2] John iv. 9.

[57:3] Acts viii. 1.

[57:4] Luke xxiv. 47; Acts i. 4.

[57:5] Acts i. 8.

[57:6] Acts viii. 27-38.

[57:7] Acts x. 19, 30, 32.

[57:8] Acts x. 1.

[58:1] Acts x. 2.

[58:2] Acts xxi. 39.

[58:3] Strabo, xiv. p. 673.

[58:4] Rom. xi. 13; 1 Tim. ii. 7; 2 Tim. i. 11.

[58:5] Matt. x. 5, 6.

[59:1] 1 Cor. xv. 8.

[59:2] Rom. i. 1.

[59:3] Acts xxii. 3.

[59:4] Acts xxii. 3.

[59:5] Acts xxvi. 5.

[59:6] Acts vii. 58.

[60:1] Acts xxvi. 10. [Greek: psêphon]. See Alford on Acts xxvi. 10, and Acts viii. 1. See also "The Life and Epistles of St Paul" by Conybeare and Howson, i. 85.

Edlt., London, 1852. Paul says that "all the Jews" knew his manner of life from his youth—a declaration from which we may infer that he was a person of note. See Acts xxvi. 4. There is a tradition that he aspired to be the son-in-law of the high priest. Epiphanius, "Ad Haer.," 1, 2, § 16 and § 25.

[60:2] Acts ix. 2, and xxii. 5.

[60:3] Acts ix. 3-21.

[60:4] Gal. i. 17, 18.

[60:5] This date may be established thus:—Stephen, as has been shewn, was martyred A.D. 34. See note, p. 55 of this chapter. Paul seems to have been converted in the same year, and therefore, if he returned to Damascus three years afterwards, he must have been in that city in A.D. 37. It would appear, from another source of evidence, that this is the true date. The Emperor Tiberius died A.D. 37, and Aretas immediately afterwards seems to have obtained possession of Damascus. He was in possession of it when Paul was now there. See 2 Cor. xi. 32, 33. It is probable that he remained master of the place only a very short time.

[60:6] Gal. i. 12.

[60:7] 2 Cor. xi. 5.

[61:1] Acts ix. 17, 18.

[61:2] Acts xiii. 1, 2.

[61:3] Simeon or Niger, according to Epiphanius, was one of the Seventy. "Haeres," 20, sec. 4. Luke, the writer of the Book of the Acts, is said to have been one of the Seventy, and some have asserted that he is the same as Lucius of Cyrene, mentioned Acts xiii. 1.

[61:4] Ananias, by whom he was baptized, was, according to the Greek martyrologies, one of the Seventy. See Burton's "Lectures," i. 88, note. It is evident that Ananias was a person of note among the Christians of Damascus.

[62:1] Acts ix. 23.

[62:2] See Josephus' "Antiquities," xviii. 5.

[62:3] See Burton's "Lectures," i. 116, 117.

[62:4] 2 Cor. xi. 32, 33.

[62:5] Acts ix. 26, 27.

[62:6] This statement rests on the authority of a monk of Cyprus, named Alexander, a comparatively late writer. See Burton's "Lectures," i. 56, note.

[62:7] Acts xxii. 21.

[63:1] Acts ix. 29, 30.

[63:2] Gal. i. 21.

[63:3] Acts xv. 23, 41.

[63:4] Acts xi. 25, 26.

[64:1] Griesbach, Lachmann, Alford, and other critics of great note, here prefer [Greek: Hellênas] to [Greek: Hellênistas], but the common rending is better supported by the authority of manuscripts, and more in accordance with Acts xiv. 27, where Paul and Barnabas are represented, long afterwards, as declaring to the Church of Antioch how God "had opened the door of faith unto the Gentiles." See an excellent vindication of the textus receptus in the Journal of Sacred Literature for January 1857, No. VIII., p. 285, by the Rev. W. Kay, M.A., Principal of Bishop's College, Calcutta.

[64:2] Acts xi. 20.

[65:1] John xix. 19-22.

[65:2] Acts xi. 27-30.

[66:1] It is obvious from Acts ix. 31, xxvi. 20, and Gal. i. 22, that such churches now existed.

[66:2] Acts xii. 3, 24, 25.

[66:3] Clem. Alex. Strom, vi. p. 742, note; Edit. Potter. Eusebius, v. 18.

[66:4] "Antiquities," xix. c. 8, § 2, xx. c. 2, § 5.

[66:5] Acts xii. 20-23.

[66:6] From the comparative table of chronology appended to Wieseler's "Chronologie des apostolischen Zeitalters," it appears that the date given in the text is adopted by no less than twenty of the highest chronological authorities, including Ussher, Pearson, Spanheim, Tillemont, Michaelis, Hug, and De Wette. It is also adopted by Burton. Wieseler himself, apparently on insufficient grounds, adopts A.D. 45.

[67:1] Though Peter was taught, by the case of Cornelius, that "God also to the Gentiles had granted repentance unto life" (Acts xi. 18), and though he doubtless felt himself a debtor, both to the Greeks and to the Jews, yet still he continued to cherish the conviction that his mission was, primarily to his kinsmen according to the flesh. James and John had the same impression. See Gal. ii. 9; James i. 1; 1 Pet. i. 1.

[68:1] Acts xii. 2.

[68:2] Acts xxii. 17-21.

[68:3] I here partially adopt the translation of Conybeare and Howson. Their work is one of the most valuable contributions to sacred literature which has appeared in the present century.

[68:4] The Second Epistle to the Corinthians was written about fourteen years after this, or towards the close of A.D. 57. See Chap. IX. of this Section. The Jews often reckoned current time as if it were complete.

[68:5] 2 Cor. xii. 2-4.

[68:6] Exodus iii. 2-10.

[68:7] Isaiah vi. 1, 2, 8, 9.

[70:1] Acts xiii. 1-3.

[70:2] Acts iv. 36.

[71:1] Deut. xxxiii. 10.

[72:1] Rom. i. 1.

[73:1] Gen. xlviii. 13-15.

[73:2] Lev. viii. 18, and iv. 4.

[73:3] Num. xxvii. 18.

[74:1] 1 Tim. v. 17.

[74:2] This portion of the apostolic history may illustrate 1 Tim. iv. 14, for Paul had official authority conferred on him "by prophecy," or in consequence of a revelation made, perhaps, through one of the prophets of Antioch, "with the laying on of the hands of the Presbytery." Something similar, probably, occurred in the case of Timothy. But, in ordinary circumstances, the rulers of the Church must judge of a divine call to the ministry from the gifts and graces of the candidate for ordination.

[75:1] Acts xiii. 4.

[75:2] Acts xiii. 4.

[75:3] Acts iv. 36.

[75:4] Until this date we read of "Barnabas and Saul," now of "Paul and Barnabas." Paul was the Roman, and Saul the Hebrew name of the great apostle.

His superior qualifications had now full scope for development, and accordingly, as he takes the lead, he is henceforth, generally named before Barnabas.

[75:5] 2 Cor. xi. 26,—[Greek: potamôn].

[76:1] Acts xv. 38.

[76:2] Acts xv. 39.

[76:3] Acts xiv. 6.

[76:4] Acts xiv. 23.

[76:5] [Greek: Cheirotonêsantes de autois kat' ekklêsian presbuterous].—The interpretation given in the text is sanctioned by the highest authorities. See Rothe's "Anfange der Christlichen Kirche," p. 150; Alford on Acts xiv. 23; Burton's "Lectures," i. 150; Baumgarten's "Acts of the Apostles," Acts xiv. 23; Litton's "Church of Christ," p. 595.

[76:6] Acts xiv. 27.

[76:7] They set out on the mission probably in A.D. 44, and returned to Antioch in A.D. 50. The Council of Jerusalem took place the year following.

[77:1] Acts xiii. 48.

[77:2] Acts xiv. 13.

[77:3] Acts xiii. 6-8.

[77:4] Acts xiii. 50.

[77:5] Acts xiv. 2.

[78:1] Acts xiv. 19.

[78:1] 2 Tim. iii. 10, 11.

[79:1] Acts xv. 1.

[79:2] This inference was indeed admitted. See Acts xv. 5, 24.

[79:3] Gal. v. 2-4, vi. 13, 14.

[79:4] Acts xvi. 31; John iii. 36.

[80:1] Luke xxiii. 43.

[80:2] Ps. ii. 12.

[80:3] Acts xv. ii.

[81:1] Acts xv. 2.

[81:2] Acts xv. 23, 24, 41.

[81:3] Acts xvi. 4.

[81:4] Paul and Barnabas, with the other deputies, were sent "to Jerusalem unto the apostles and elders" (Acts xv. 2); "when they were come to Jerusalem, they were received of the church, and of the apostles and elders" (Acts xv. 4); and the decrees are said to have been ordained "of the apostles and elders which were at Jerusalem" (Acts xvi. 4); but not one of these statements necessarily implies that these rulers were exclusively elders of the Church of Jerusalem.

[82:1] It has been argued by Burton ("Lectures," vol. i. p. 122), that the first visit of Paul to Jerusalem after his conversion took place about the time of one of the great festivals, as he is said, on the occasion, to have "disputed against the Grecians" (Acts ix. 29), who were likely then to have been very numerous in the city. If he arrived now at the time of the same festival, the interval must have been precisely fourteen years.

[82:2] Gal. ii. 1. Some make these fourteen years to include the three years mentioned Gal. i. 18, but this interpretation does violence to the languages of the apostle. The system of chronology here adopted requires no such forced expositions. Paul came to Jerusalem three years after his conversion, that is, in A.D. 37; and fourteen years after, that is, in A.D. 51, he was at this Synod.

307

[82:3] Acts ix. 26.

[83:1] Acts xxi. 20.

[83:2] Acts xxi. 21.

[83:3] Acts xv. 5.

[83:4] Gal. ii. 4. It is here taken for granted that the visit to Jerusalem, mentioned in the second chapter of the Epistle to the Galatians, is the same as that described in the fifteenth of Acts. Paul says that he went up "by revelation" (Gal. ii. 2),—a statement from which it appears that he was divinely instructed to adopt this method of settling the question.

[83:5] Gal. ii. 12.

[83:6] Gal. ii. 2.

[83:7] Acts xvi. 4, xxi. 25.

[84:1] Acts xv. 12.

[84:2] Acts xv. 22.

[84:3] Acts xv. 23.

[84:4] The expression here used—"the multitude" ([Greek: to plêthos])—is repeatedly applied in the New Testament to the Sanhedrim, a court consisting of not more than seventy-two members. See Luke xxiii. 1; Acts xxiii. 7. There were probably more individuals present at this meeting.

[84:5] Acts xv. 2.

[84:6] 1 Cor. xii. 28; Eph. iv. 11.

[84:7] In Acts xi. 27, we read of "prophets" who came "from Jerusalem unto Antioch."

[84:8] Acts xv. 23. "The apostles, and elders, and brethren."

[84:9]The context may appear to be favourable to this interpretation, for the two deputies now chosen—"Judas surnamed Barsabas, and Silas"—who are said to have been "chief men among the brethren" (ver. 22), are likewise described as "prophets also themselves" (ver. 32). In Acts xviii. 27, "the brethren" appear to be distinguished from "the disciples."

[85:1] This reading, which is adopted by Mill in the Prolegomena to his New Testament, as well as by Lachmann, Neander, Alford, and Tregelles, is supported by the authority of the Codex Vaticanus, the Codex Alexandrinus, the Codex Ephraemi, and the Codex Bezae. It is likewise to be found in by far the most valuable cursive MS. yet known. It is confirmed also by the early testimony of Irenaeus, and by the Latin of the Codex Bezae, a version more ancient than the Vulgate, as well as by the Vulgate itself. The reading in the textus receptus may be accounted for by the growth of the doctrine of apostolical succession; as, when the hierarchy was in its glory, transcribers could not understand how the apostles and elders could be fellow presbyters.

[85:2] It is worthy of note that Peter, fourteen or fifteen years afterwards, speaks in the style here indicated. Thus he says—"The elders which are among you, I exhort, who am also an elder" ([Greek: sumpresbuteros]).—(l Pet. v. 1.)

[85:3] Acts xv. 28.

[86:1] Gal. iii. 2.

[86:2] Acts xv. 8-10.

[86:3] Acts xi. 15, 17.

[86:4] This style of speaking was used by councils in after-ages, and often in cases when it was singularly inappropriate.

[87:1] Acts xv. 29.

[87:2] See 1 Cor. x. 23, 31, 32.

[88:1] "Since the eating of such food, as Paul expressly teaches (1 Cor. x. 19, 33), was not sinful in itself, and yet to be avoided out of tenderness to those who thought it so, the abstinence here recommended must be understood in the same manner."—Alexander on the Acts, ii. 84.

[89:1] Gal. ii. 12.

[89:2] Gal. ii. 9.

[89:3] Gal. ii. 13.

[90:1] Acts xvi. 9.

[90:2] Acts xvi. 12.

[91:1] "The Jus Italicum raised provincial land to the same state of immunity from taxation which belonged to land in Italy."—Conybeare and Howson, i. 302, note.

[91:2] Not the Strymon. See Conybeare and Howson, i. 316.

[91:3] Acts xvi. 14.

[91:4] Acts xvi. 14.

[92:1] Acts xvi. 16-18.

[92:2] They may have perceptive powers of which we can form no conception, and may thus discern the approach of particular events as distinctly an we can now calculate the ebb and flow of the tides, or the eclipses of the sun and moon.

[92:3] Matt. viii. 28, 29; Mark i. 24, 25; Luke iv. 34, 35.

[93:1] Acts xvi. 18.

[93:2] Acts xvi. 19.

[93:3] In some parts of the Empire magistrates and men of rank acted gratuitously, but a large portion of the priests subsisted on the emoluments of office.

[94:1] Acts xvi. 24.

[94:2] Acts xvi. 25.

[95:1] Acts xvi. 26.

[95:2] Acts xvi. 28. "By a singular historical coincidence, this very city of Philippi, or its neighbourhood, had been signalised within a hundred years, not only by the great defeat of Brutus and Cassius, but by the suicide of both, and by a sort of wholesale self-destruction on the part of their adherents."—Alexander on the Acts, ii. 122, 123.

[96:1] Acts xvi. 29, 30.

[97:1] Acts xvi. 31.

[98:1] Acts xvi. 33, 34.

[98:2] Acts xvi. 35.

[98:3] Paul says that he was "free born" (Acts xxii. 28). It was unlawful to scourge a Roman citizen, or even, except in extraordinary cases, to imprison him without trial. He had also the privilege of appeal to the Emperor.

[98:4] Acts xvi. 37.

[99:1] Acts xvi. 39.

[99:2] Acts xvi. 40.

[99:3] Phil. iv. 14-16.

[100:1] Acts xvii. 4.

[100:2] Acts xvii. 7.

[100:3] Acts xvii. 8. [Greek: etaraxan—tous politarchas]. It has been remarked that the name here given to the magistrates (politarchs), does not occur in ancient literature; but it is a curious and important fact that a Greek inscription, on an arch still to be seen at this place, demonstrates the accuracy of the sacred historian. This arch supplies evidence that it was erected about the time when the Republic was passing into the Empire, and that it was in existence when Paul now preached there. It appears from it that the magistrates of Thessalonica were called politarchs, and that they were seven in number. What is almost equally striking is that three of the names in the inscription are Sopater, Gaius, and Secundus, the same as those of three of Paul's friends in this district. Conybeare and Howson, i. 360.

[101:1] Acts xvii. 11.

[102:1] Acts xvii. 16.

[102:2] Acts xvii. 17.

[102:3] See Conybeare and Howson, i. 241.

[102:4] See Alford on Acts xiii. 9, and xxiii. 1.

[102:5] 2 Cor. x. 10.

[102:6] 2 Cor. x. 10.

[102:7] Acts xvii. 18.

[103:1] [Greek: Adikei Sôkratês—etera de kaina daimonia eispherôn.]—Xen. Mem. i. 1.

[103:2] Acts xvii. 19, 20. It is very evident that he was not arraigned before the court of Areopagus as our English translation seems to indicate.

[104:1] Acts xvii. 22, 23. This translation obviously conveys the meaning of the original more distinctly than our English version. See Alford, ii. 178; and Conybeare and Howson, i. 406.

[104:2] It is a curious fact that the impostor Apollonius of Tyana, who was the contemporary of the apostle, speaks of Athens as a place "where altars are raised to the unknown Gods." "Life," by Philostratus, book vi. c. 3. See also Pausanias, Attic, i. 4.

[105:1] See Cudworth's "Intellectual System, with Notes by Mosheim," i. 513, 111. Edition, London, 1845.

[105:2] See Mosheim's "Commentaries on the Affairs of the Christians before Constantine," by Vidal, i. 42.

[105:3] Acts xvii. 24.

[105:4] See Alford on Acts xvii. 26.

[105:5] Acts xvii. 26.

[105:6] Acts xvii. 25, 26.

[106:1] Acts xvii. 29.

[106:2] Acts xvii. 31.

[106:3] Cudworth, with Notes by Mosheim, ii. 120, and Mosheim's "Commentaries," by Vidal, i. 42.

[106:4] Acts xvii. 32.

[106:5] Acts xvii. 21.

[107:1] Acts xvii. 34.

[107:2] These writings, which made their appearance not earlier than the fourth or fifth century, were held in great reputation, particularly by the Mystics, in the Middle Ages.

[107:3] Burton's "Lectures," i. 183.

[108:1] 1 Cor. ii. 1, 2, 4, 5.

[109:1] Strabo, lib. viii. vol. i., p. 549; Edit. Oxon. 1807.

[109:2] Acts xviii. 6.

[109:3] Acts xviii. 8.

[109:4] 1 Cor. i. 26.

[109:5] Rom. xvi. 23. This epistle was written from Corinth.

[109:6] Acts xviii. 8.

[109:7] 1 Cor. i. 14; Rom. xvi. 23.

[109:8] Acts xviii. 2, 26; Rom. xvi. 3; 1 Cor. xvi. 19; 2 Tim. iv. 19.

[110:1] Acts xviii. 2.

[110:2] "Rabbi Judah saith, 'He that teacheth not his son a trade, doth the same as if he taught him to be a thief;' and Rabban Gamaliel saith, 'He that hath a trade in his hand, to what is he like? He is like a vineyard that is fenced.'"—See Alford on Acts, xviii. 3.

[110:3] Acts xviii. 3.

[111:1] Epiphanius, "Haer.," xxx. 16.

[111:2] Acts xviii. 11.

[112:1] Acts xviii. 9, 10.

[112:2] See 1 Cor. i. 11, and xi. 20, 21; and 2 Cor. xii. 21, and xiii. 2.

[112:3] See 1 Cor. vi. 9-11.

[112:4] Acts xviii. 12.

[112:5] Acts xviii. 13.

[113:1] Acts xviii. 14-16.

[113:2] Acts xviii. 17.

[113:3] 1 Thess. v. 12, 13.

[113:4] 2 Thess. ii. 2.

[113:5] 2 Thess. ii. 3-12.

[113:6] 1 Thess. i. 9.

[114:1] [Greek: Tas paradoseis].

[114:2] 2 Thess. ii. 15. Paul is here speaking, not of what had been handed down from preceding generations, but of what had been established by his own apostolic authority, so that the rendering "traditions" in our English version is a peculiarly unhappy translation.

[115:1] Acts xviii. 18.

[115:2] See Conybeare and Howson, i. 454.

[115:3] Acts xviii. 19.

[116:1] Acts xviii. 24.

[116:2] Acts xviii. 25.

[116:3] Acts xviii. 26.

[116:4] It is worthy of note that she is named before Aquila in Acts xviii. 18; Rom. xvi. 3; and 2 Tim. iv. 19.

[116:5] 1 Cor. xiv. 34, 35; 1 Tim. ii. 12.

[117:1] Acts xviii. 24.

[117:2] Acts xviii. 27.

[117:3] Acts xviii. 27, 28.

[117:4] 1 Cor. iii. 4-6.

[118:1] Acts xviii. 22.

[118:2] Acts xviii. 23.

[118:3] Acts xvi. 6.

[118:4] Acts xix. 8.

[118:5] Acts xix. 9.

[119:1] That this epistle was written after the second visit appears from Gal. iv. 13. Mr Ellicott asserts that "the first time" is here the preferable translation of [Greek: to proteron], and yet, rather inconsistently, adds, that "no historical conclusions can safely be drawn from this expression alone." See his "Critical and Grammatical Commentary on Galatians," iv. 13.

[119:2] Gal. i. 6, iii. 1.

[120:1] Gal. ii. 16, iv. 1-4, v. 1.

[120:2] 1 Cor. xvi. 7; 2 Cor. xii. 14, xiii. 1.

[120:3] The Acts take no notice of various parts of his early career as a preacher. Compare Acts ix. 20-26 with Gal. i. 17.

[120:4] 2 Cor. xi. 25.

[120:5] 2 Cor. xi. 26.

[120:6] Titus i. 5.

[120:7] See Titus i. 6-11, ii. 1, 7, 8, 15, iii. 8-11. The reasons assigned in support of a later date for the writing of this epistle do not appear at all satisfactory. Paul directs the evangelist (Titus iii. 12) to come to him to Nicopolis, for he had "determined there to winter." This Nicopolis was in Greece, in the province of Achaia, and we know that Paul wintered there in A.D. 57-58. Acts xx. 2, 3. See Schaff's "Apostolic Church," i. 390.

[120:8] 2 Cor. ii. 13, vii. 6, 13, viii. 6, 16, 23, xii. 18; Gal. ii. 1, 3.

[121:1] Acts xix. 10.

[121:2] See Col. iv. 13, 15, 16. These churches were not, however, founded by Paul. See Col. ii. 1.

[121:3] "This was the largest of the Greek temples. The area of the Parthenon at Athens was not one fourth of that of the temple of Ephesus."—Smith's Dictionary of Greek and Roman Geography, Art. EPHESUS.

[121:4] Conybeare and Howson, ii. 72.

[121:5] Acts xix. 35.

[122:1] Conybeare and Howson, ii. 73. Minucius Felix in his Octavius speaks of Diana as represented "at Ephesus with many distended breasts ranged in tiers."

[122:2] Conybeare and Howson, ii. 13.

[122:3] His Life, written by Philostratus about A.D. 210, is full of lying wonders. His biographer mentions his visit to Ephesus, book iv. 1.

[123:1] Acts xix. 11, 12.

[123:2] Acts xix. 16, 17.

[123:3] The piece of silver here mentioned was worth about tenpence, so that the estimated value of the books burned was about £2000.

[123:4] Acts xix. 19, 20.

[123:5] It was written not long before Paul left Ephesus, and probably about the time of the Passover. 1 Cor. v. 7, xvi. 5-8.

[123:6] 1 Cor. i. 11.

[123:7] 1 Cor. v. 1.

[123:8] 1 Cor. xv. 12. This passage supplies evidence that errorists very soon made their appearance in the Christian Church, and furnishes an answer to those chronologists who date all the Pastoral Epistles after Paul's release from his first imprisonment, on the ground that the Gnostics had no existence at an earlier period.

[124:1] Acts xix. 24.

[124:2] Conybeare and Howson, ii. 74.

[124:3] Acts xix. 25.

[125:1] Acts xix. 25-27.

[125:2] Acts xix. 28.

[125:3] See Conybeare and Howson, ii. 79-81.

[125:4] Acts xix. 29.

[125:5] See Hackett's "Commentary on the Acts of the Apostles," p. 273.

[125:6] Acts xix. 31.

[126:1] Acts xx. 34. The Asiarchs "derived their title from the name of the province, as the corresponding officers in Cyprus, Syria, and Lydia, were called Cypriarchs, Syriarchs, Lydiarchs. Those of Asia are said to have been ten in number.... As the games and sacrifices over which these Asiarchs presided, were provided at their own expense, they were always chosen from the richest class, and may be said to represent the highest rank of the community."—Alexander on the Acts, ii. 210.

[126:2] 2 Tim. iv. 14.

[126:3] Acts xix. 34. It has been observed that, according to the ideas of the heathen, this unintermitted cry was, in itself, an act of worship; and hence we may understand why it was so long continued, but it is surely a notable example of "vain repetitions." See Hackett, p. 275.

[127:1] Acts xix. 40.

[127:2] Acts xix. 32.

[127:3] Our English version "robbers of churches" is obviously incorrect.

[127:4] Acts xix. 37. It is plain from this passage that the apostle, when referring to the Gentile worship, avoided the use of language calculated to give unnecessary offence.

[128:1] 1 Cor. xvi. 8.

[128:2] Acts xx. 1.

[128:3] Rom. xv. 19.

[128:4] See Acts xix. 22.

[128:5] 1 Tim. i. 3.

[128:6] 1 Tim. i. 2.

[129:1] According to the chronology adopted in our English Bible, all the Pastoral Epistles were written after Paul's release from his first imprisonment, and this theory has recently been strenuously advocated by Conybeare and Howson, Alford, and Ellicott; but their reasonings are exceedingly unsatisfactory. For, I. The statement of Conybeare and Howson that "the three epistles were nearly contemporaneous with each other" is a mere assertion resting on no solid foundation; as resemblance in style, especially when all the letters were dictated by the same individual, can be no evidence as to date. II. There is direct evidence that heresies, such as those described in these epistles, existed in the Church long before Paul's first imprisonment. See 1 Cor. iii. 18, 19, xv. 12; 2 Cor. xi. 4, 13, 14, 15, 22, compared with 1 Tim. i. 3, 7. III. The early Churches were very soon organised, as appears from Acts xiv. 23; 1 Thess. v. 12, 13; so that the state of ecclesiastical organisation described in the First Epistle to Timothy and the Epistle to Titus is no proof of the late date of these letters. IV. But the grand argument in support of the early date, and one with which the advocates of the later chronology have never fairly grappled, is derived from the fact that Paul

313

never was in Ephesus after the time mentioned in Acts xx. When he wrote to Timothy he intended shortly to return thither. See 1 Tim. i. 3, iii. 14, 15. It is evident that when the apostle addressed the elders of Ephesus (Acts xx. 25) and told them they should "see his face no more," he considered himself as speaking prophetically. It is clear, too, that his words were so understood by his auditors (Acts xx. 38), and that the evangelist, who wrote them down several years afterwards, was still under the same impression. I agree, therefore, with Wieseler, and others, in assigning an early date to the First Epistle to Timothy and the Epistle to Titus.

[130:1] 2 Cor. xi. 9, 24-28, 32, 33, xii. 2, 7-9. The Second Epistle to the Corinthians was written late in A.D. 57.

[130:2] 2 Cor. ii. 4.

[130:3] [Greek: eis tên Hellada], i.e., Achaia.

[130:4] Acts xx. 2, 3.

[130:5] Rom. xvi. 1, 2, 23.

[130:6] Rom. i. 8.

[130:7] Rom. xvi. 7, 11.

[130:8] Rom. xvi. 3.

[130:9] Acts xix. 21; Rom. i. 10, 11, xv. 23, 24.

[131:1] Acts xx. 3.

[131:2] Acts xx. 6.

[131:3] Acts xx. 6.

[131:4] Acts xx. 17-35.

[131:5] Acts xx. 36-38.

[131:6] Acts xxi. 8.

[131:7] Acts xx. 23, xxi. 10, 11.

[131:8] [Greek: hepiskeuaramenoi]—the reading adopted by Lachmann and others. The word "carriages" used in the authorised version for baggage, or luggage, is now unintelligible to the English reader. The word "carriage" is also used in our translation in Judges xviii. 21, and 1 Sam. xvii. 22, for something to be carried.

[131:9] Acts xxi. 15.

[132:1] Acts ii. 45.

[132:2] Rom. xv. 26.

[132:3] 1 Cor. xvi. 3; 2 Cor. viii. 19.

[132:4] Acts xx. 4.

[133:1] Prov. xviii. 10.

[133:2] Acts xxi. 17.

[133:3] Acts xxi. 24.

[133:4] "It was customary among the Jews for those who had received deliverance from any great peril, or who from other causes desired publicly to testify their dedication to God, to take upon themselves the vow of a Nazarite.... No rule is laid down (Numb. vi.) as to the time during which this life of ascetic rigour was to continue; but we learn from the Talmud and Josephus that thirty days was at least a customary period. During this time the Nazarite was bound to abstain from wine, and to suffer his hair to grow uncut. At the termination of the period, he was bound to present himself in the temple, with certain offerings, and his hair was then cut off and burnt upon the altar. The offerings required were beyond the means of the very poor, and consequently it was thought an act of

314

piety for a rich man to pay the necessary expenses, and thus enable his poorer countrymen to complete their vow." —Conybeare and Howson, ii. 250, 251.

[133:5] Acts xxi. 26.

[134:1] Acts xxi. 29.

[134:2] Acts xxi. 30.

[134:3] Acts xxi. 30.

[134:4] Acts xxiii. 26.

[134:5] Acts xxi. 32.

[134:6] Acts xxi. 33, 34. There were barracks in the tower of Antonia.

[135:1] Acts xxi. 38. "Assassins is in the original a Greek inflection of the Latin word Sicarii, so called from Sica, a short sword or dagger, and described by Josephus as a kind of robbers who concealed short swords beneath their garments, and infested Judea in the period preceding the destruction of Jerusalem."—Alexander on the Acts, ii. 289.

[135:2] Acts xxii. 2.

[135:3] Acts xxii. 22-24.

[136:1] Acts xxiii. 6.

[136:2] Acts xxiii. 7.

[136:3] Acts xxiii. 10.

[136:4] Acts xxiii. 12, 21.

[136:5] Acts xxiii. 16, 23, 30.

[136:6] "Per omnem saevitiam ac libidinem jus regium servili ingenio exercuit."—Hist. v. 9.

[136:7] Josephus' "Antiq." xx. c. 7. § 1,2.

[137:1] Acts xxiv. 25.

[137:2] Acts xxiv. 27.

[137:3] See some account of him in Josephus' "Antiq," xx. c. 8, §. 9, 10.

[138:1] Acts. xxv. 11.

[138:2] Acts xxv. 12.

[138:3] Acts xxv. 13. Festus appears to have been Procurator from the beginning of the autumn of A.D. 60 to the summer of A.D. 62. Felix was recalled A.D. 60. See Conybeare and Howson, Appendix ii. note (C).

[139:1] Josephus' "Wars," ii. c. 12, § 8; "Antiq." xx. c. 5, § 2.

[139:2] Acts xxv. 23.

[139:3] Acts xxvi. 6.

[140:1] Acts xxvi. 22.

[140:2] Acts xxvi. 24.

[140:3] Acts xxvi. 27.

[140:4] Acts xxvi. 28. Some would translate [Greek: en oligô] "in short," instead of "almost."

[140:5] Acts xxvi. 29.

[141:1] Acts xxvi. 30-32.

[141:2] Eph. vi. 22; Phil. ii. 1, 2; Col. i. 24, iv. 8; Philem. 7, compared with 2 Cor i. 3, 4.

[141:3] Acts ix. 15, 16.

[142:1] Acts xxvii. 20. This part of the history of the apostle has been illustrated with singular ability by James Smith, Esq. of Jordanhill in his "Voyage and Shipwreck of St Paul."

[142:2] Acts xxvii. 5, 6.

[142:3] Acts xxviii. 1. That Melita is Malta has been conclusively established by Smith in his "Voyage and Shipwreck of St Paul." "Dissertation," ii.

[142:4] Acts xxviii. 11. "With regard to the dimensions of the ships of the ancients, some of them must have been quite equal to the largest merchantman of the present day. The ship of St Paul had, in passengers and crew, 276 persons on board, besides her cargo of wheat, and as they were carried on by another ship of the same class, she must also have been of great size. The ship in which Josephus was wrecked contained 600 people."—Smith's Voyage and Shipwreck of St Paul, p. 147.

[143:1] Acts xxviii. 13.

[143:2] Acts xxvii. 17.

[143:3] Acts xxvii. 29. "The ancient vessels did not carry, in general, so large anchors as those which we employ; and hence they had often a greater number of them. Athenaeus mentions a ship which had eight iron anchors." Hackett, p. 372.

[143:4] Acts xxvii. 27.

[143:5] "When the Lively, frigate, unexpectedly fell in with this very point, the quarter-master on the look-out, who first observed it, states, in his evidence at the court-martial, that, at the distance of a quarter of a mile the land could not be seen."—Smith's Voyage and Shipwreck of St Paul, pp. 89, 90.

[144:1] Hackett, p. 371.

[144:2] Acts xxvii. 28.

[144:3] Conybeare and Howson, ii. 351.

[144:4] Acts xxvii. 39.

[144:5] Acts xxvii 41.

[144:6] Smith's "Voyage and Shipwreck of St Paul," p. 102.

[144:7] Smith's "Voyage and Shipwreck of St Paul," p. 92.

[144:8] Acts xxvii. 41.

[145:1] Smith's "Voyage and Shipwreck of St Paul," p. 104.

[145:2] Conybeare and Howson make the population more than 2,000,000 (ii. 376). Merivale reduces it to something less than 700,000 (iv. 520). In Smith's "Dictionary of Greek and Roman Geography" it is stated as upwards of 2,000,000. Greswell makes it about 1,000,000 ("Dissertations," iv. 46). Dean Milman reckons it from 1,000,000 to 1,500,000 ("History of Latin Christianity," i. 23).

[145:3] Merivale, iv. 391.

[145:4] Rev. xvii. 1.

[146:1] Merivale, iv. 412.

[146:2] Merivale, iv. 414-420.

[146:3] Rev. xviii. 11.

[146:4] Acts xxviii. 14.

[147:1] Acts xxviii. 14.

[147:2] Acts xxviii. 15.

[147:3] Acts xxviii. 15.

[147:4] Called in our English version "the captain of the guard." The celebrated Burrus was at this time (A.D. 61) the Praetorian Prefect. Wieseler, p. 393. See also Greswell's "Dissertations," iv. p. 199.

[147:5] Acts xxviii. 16.

[148:1] Acts xxviii. 17.

[148:2] Acts xxviii. 23.

316

[148:3] Acts xxviii. 24.

[148:4] Acts xxviii. 31.

[148:5] Conybeare and Howson, ii. 296.

[149:1] Philem. 9.

[149:2] 2 Cor. x. 10.

[149:3] See Conybeare and Howson, ii. 428.

[149:4] Phil. ii. 25; Philem. 2.

[149:5] Eph. vi. 13, 14, 16, 17.

[149:6] Phil. iv. 3. When speaking of a "true yoke-fellow," he may here refer to the way in which he was himself unequally yoked.

[149:7] See Acts xxvi. 1, 29.

[149:8] Eph. iv. 1.

[150:1] [Greek: en olô tô praitôriô]—"We never find the word employed for the Imperial house at Rome; and we believe the truer view to be—that it denotes here, not the palace itself, but the quarters of that part of the Imperial guards which was in immediate attendance on the Emperor."-Conybeare and Howson, ii. 428.

[150:2] Phil. i. 12-14.

[150:3] Philem. 18, 19.

[150:4] Col. iv. 7.

[150:5] Col. ii. 8, 16, 18, 23.

[150:6] Eph. vi. 21, 22.

[151:1] Eph. i. 1.

[151:2] Col. iv. 16.

[151:3] Phil. i. 3-7.

[152:1] Phil. ii. 24; Philem. 22.

[152:2] Phil. i. 23-25.

[152:3] Rom. xv. 24, 28.

[153:1] [Greek: epi to terma tês duseôs]—Epist. to the Corinthians v. Clement in the same place mentions that Paul was seven times in bonds. See also Greswell, "Dissertations," vol. iv. p. 225-228.

[153:2] See Cave's "Fathers," i. 147. Oxford, 1840.

[153:3] [Greek: ton phelonên]. Some think that he wished for the cloak to protect him against the cold of winter. See 2 Tim. iv. 21.

[153:4] In the "Life of St Columba" by Adamnan (Dublin, 1857), the learned editor, Dr Reeves, has given an interesting account of an ancient leather book-case in his own possession. See "Life of St Columba," p. 115. If Paul referred to a case, it was probably to one of a larger description.

[153:5] 2 Tim. iv. 13. It is probable that, in the anticipation of his death, he wished to give the documents as a legacy to some of his friends. Among them may have been Scripture autographs.

[153:6] 2 Tim. iv. 20. [Greek: apelipon]. The translation "they left," instead of "I left," is given up even by Dr Davidson, though he rejects the idea of a second imprisonment. See his "Introduction to the New Testament," iii. 53.

[153:7] Miletum, or Miletus, in Crete, is mentioned by Homer. "Iliad," ii. 647.

[154:1] Acts xii. 6-9.

[154:2] Heb. xiii. 23, 24. In this epistle he apparently refers to his late imprisonment. Heb. x. 34, but the reading of the textus receptus is here rejected by many of our highest critical authorities, such as Griesbach, Lachmann,

317

Tischendorf, and Scholz. Respecting the second imprisonment, see also Eusebius, ii. c. 22.

[155:1] 2 Tim. iv. 20.

[155:2] Phil. ii. 24.

[155:3] 2 Tim. iv. 13.

[155:4] Philem. 22.

[155:5] Heb. xiii. 23.

[155:6] 2 Tim. iv. 20.

[155:7] 2 Tim. iv. 16, ii. 9.

[155:8] This may refer to some powerful defence of Christianity which he had made before the Gentile tribunal of Nero.

[155:9] 2 Tim. iv. 16, 17.

[156:1] 2 Tim. iv. 6-8.

[156:2] "Euseb. Hist." ii. 25.

[156:3] Euseb. ii. 25. See the Note of Valesius on the words [Greek: katha ton auton kairon]. See also Davidson's "Introduction to the New Testament," iii. 361.

[156:4] 2 Tim. iv. 11.

[156:5] Tertullian "De Praescrip," c. 36. Euseb. ii. 25. See also Lactantius, or the work ascribed to him, "De Mort. Persecutorum," c. 2.

[156:6] According to Gregory Nazianzen, Judea was the sphere of Peter. "Oratio." 25, tom. i. 438. If so, Paul when visiting Jerusalem was likely to meet with him.

[157:1] 1 Pet. v. 13.

[157:2] Rev. xvii. 5, xviii. 2, 10, 21.

[157:3] Euseb. ii. 15.

[157:4] 1 Pet. iv. 12.

[157:5] 2 Tim. iv. 11.

[157:6] 1 Pet. v. 13.

[157:7] 1 Pet. v. 12.

[157:8] Acts xv. 40, xvi. 19, 25, xvii. 4, 10, xviii. 5; 1 Thess. i. 1; 2 Thess. i. 1.

[158:1] 1 Pet. v. 12.

[158:2] The Jews at this time were wont to call Rome by the name of Babylon. It was not, therefore, strange that Peter, being a Jew, used this phraseology. See Wordsworth's "Lectures on the Apocalypse," p. 345, and the authorities there quoted.

[158:3] 2 Pet. i. 12, iii. 1.

[158:4] These words apparently suggest that the preceding letter was written not long before.

[159:1] 2 Pet. i. 13. 14.

[159:2] Gal. iv. 17, 21, vi. 12; Col. ii. 16-18.

[159:3] 1 Pet. i. 1.

[159:4] 2 Pet. iii. 16.

[159:5] As Heb. vi. 4-6, vii. 1-3, ix. 17.

[160:1] 2 Pet. iii. 16.

[160:2] Euseb. iii. 1.

[160:3] Euseb. iii. 1.

[160:4] Prudentius, "Peristeph. in Pass. Petr. et Paul." Hymn xii. Augustine, serm. 28. "De Sanctis." The testimony of earlier witnesses represents them as dying "about the same time." See Euseb. ii. c. 25.

[161:1] Phil. iv. 22.

[161:2] Caius, a Roman presbyter who flourished about the beginning of the third century, refers to the Vatican and the Ostian Way as the places where they suffered. Routh's "Reliquiae," ii. p. 127.

[162:1] Hab. ii. 3.

[163:1] John i. 11.

[163:2] John xix. 15.

[163:3] Acts iv. 3, v. 18.

[164:1] Acts xii. 2, 3.

[164:2] See Acts xvii. 5, xviii. 12.

[165:1] Acts xviii. 2. Suetonius in Claud. (c. 25), says—"Judaeos impulsore Chresto assidue tumultuantes Roma expulit." The words Christus and Chrestus seem to have been often confounded, and it has been thought that the historian here refers to some riotous proceedings among the Jews in Rome arising out of discussions relative to Christianity. These disturbances took place about A.D. 53. It is remarkable that even in the beginning of the third century the Christians were sometimes called Chrestiani. Hence Tertullian says—"Sed et cum perperam Chrestianus pronunciatur a vobis, nam nec nominis certa est notitia penes vos, de suavitate vel benignitate compositum est." "Apol." c. iii. See also "Ad Nationes," lib. i. c. 3.

[165:2] See Greswell's "Dissertations," iv. p. 233.

[165:3] Eusebius, ii. 23.

[166:1] "Certi enim esse debemus, si quos latet per ignorantiam literature secularis, etiam ostiorum deos apud Romanos, Cardeam a cardinibus appellatam, et Forculum a foribus, et Limentinum a limine, et ipsum Janum a janua." Tertullian, "De Idololatria," c. 15. See also the same writer "Ad Nationes," ii. c. 10, 15; and "De Corona," 13.

[166:2] 2 Tim. iii. 12. Cyprian touches upon the same subject in his Treatise on the "Vanity of Idols," c. 2.

[167:1] The Christians were familiar with the idea of the conflagration of the world, and there is much plausibility in the conjecture that, as they gazed on the burning city, they may have given utterance to expressions which were misunderstood, and which awakened suspicion. "Some," says Dean Milman, "in the first instance, apprehended and examined, may have made acknowledgments before a passionate and astonished tribunal, which would lead to the conclusion that, in the hour of general destruction, they had some trust, some security, denied to the rest of mankind; and this exemption from common misery, if it would not mark them out in some dark manner, as the authors of the conflagration, at all events would convict them of that hatred of the human race so often advanced against the Jews."—Milman's History of Christianity, ii. 37, 38.

[167:2] Tacitus, "Annal." xv. 44.

[167:3] Heb. xii. 4.

[167:4] Heb. x. 25.

[168:1] 1 Pet. iv. 12.

[168:2] 1 Pet. iv. 17.

[168:3] Tertullian, "Ad Nationes," i. 7.

[168:4] See "De Mortibus Persecutorum," c. 2, and Sulpitius Severus, lib. ii. p. 139; Edit. Leyden, 1635.

[168:5] Dan. ix. 27.

[169:1] Matt. xxiv. 2, 15, 16, 34; Mark xiii. 2, 14, 30; Luke xxi. 6, 20, 21, 24, 32.

[169:2] See Euseb. iii. 31.

[169:3] Acts xvii. 7.

[169:4] Euseb. iii. 20.

[169:5] Matt. xiii. 55. See Greswell's "Dissertations," ii. 114, 121, 122.

[170:1] Matt, xxvii. 57; Mark xv. 43.

[170:2] Acts xiii. 7.

[170:3] Phil. iv. 22.

[170:4] Dio Cassius, lxvii. 14.

[170:5] Euseb. iii. 18.

[171:1] Rev. i. 9.

[171:2] Tertullian, "De Praescrip. Haeret." c. 36.

[171:3] See Mosheim, Cent. i. part i. ch. 5.

[171:4] According to Baronius ("Annal." ad. an. 92, 98) John was six years in Patmos, or from A.D. 92 to A.D. 98. Other writers think that he was set at liberty some time before the death of Domitian, or about A.D. 95. According to this reckoning, had he been six years in exile, he must have been banished A.D. 89. This conclusion derives some countenance from the "Chronicon" of Eusebius, which represents the tyrant in the eighth and ninth years of his reign, or about A.D. 89, as proscribing and putting to death very many of his subjects. If the visions of the Apocalypse were vouchsafed to John in A.D. 89, the interval between their revelation and the establishment of the Pope as a temporal prince is found to be 755-89, or exactly 666 years. See Rev. xiii. 18. There is another very curious coincidence in this case; for the interval between the fall of the Western Empire, and the establishment of the Bishop of Rome as a temporal prince, is 755-476=279 complete, or 280 current years, that is, 40 prophetic weeks. But it so happens that the period of human gestation is 40 weeks, and this would lead to the inference that the Man of Sin was conceived as soon as the Western Empire fell. See 2 Thess. ii. 7, 8. I am not aware that these remarkable coincidences have yet been noticed, and I therefore submit them to the consideration of the students of prophecy.

[172:1] See Burton's "Lectures," i. 361.

[172:2] 2 John 1; 3 John 1.

[172:3] 1 Pet. v. 1; Philem. 1.

[172:4] Acts xx. 28.

[172:5] Mark iii. 17.

[172:6] Jerome, "Comment. on Galatians," vi. 10.

[172:7] See Vitringa, "Observationes Sacrae," lib. iv. c. 7, 8.

[173:1] Rev. iii. 16.

[173:2] Rev. iii. 2.

[173:3] Rev. ii. 5.

[173:4] Claudia, the wife of Pudens, supposed to be mentioned 2 Tim. iv. 21, is said to have been a Briton by birth. See Fuller's "Church History of Britain," vol. i. p. 11; Edit. London, 1837.

[173:5] Euseb. ii. 16.

[173:6] Acts ii. 10.

[174:1] Acts ii. 9, 11.

[174:2] See in Cave's "Fathers," Bartholomew, Matthew, and Thomas.

[175:1] 1 Cor. vi. 9-11.

320

[175:2] Prov. xviii. 24.

[177:1] John xiv. 26.

[177:2] John xvi. 13.

[177:3] See Irenaeus, "Adv. Haeres.," iii. 1; and Euseb. vi. 14.

[177:4] It is probable that these three Gospels were written nearly at the same time. When Luke wrote, he does not seem to have been aware of the existence of any other Gospel. See Luke i. 4.

[177:5] Origen, "Dial, de Recta in Deum Fide," sec. i. tom. i. p. 806; Edit. Delarue. Paris, 1733. See Whitby's "Preface to Luke." There is good reason to believe that the "young man" mentioned Mark xiv. 51, 52, was no other than Mark himself (Davidson's "Introduction to the New Testament," i. 139); and if so, we have thus additional evidence that the evangelist had enjoyed the advantages of our Lord's ministry. He has always been reputed the founder of the Church of Alexandria, and the testimony of Origen to the fact that he was one of the Seventy is therefore of special value; as the Alexandrian presbyter was, no doubt, well acquainted with the traditions of the Church of the Egyptian metropolis.

[178:1] Acts i. 21.

[178:2] Luke i. 2.

[178:3] Matt. ix. 9, x. 3.

[178:4] Mark xiv. 71.

[178:5] Luke xxiv. 25.

[178:6] John xxi. 23.

[178:7] Matt. xxviii. 19.

[179:1] Mark ix. 15.

[179:2] Luke x. 1.

[179:3] John xiv., xv., xvi., xvii.

[179:4] See Horne's "Introduction," ii. 173. Sixth Edition.

[180:1] See Baumgarten on Acts, vii., viii., ix., xiii.

[180:2] Period i. sec. i. chap. 7, 8, 9.

[180:3] Horne, iv. 359.

[181:1] See Wordsworth "On the Canon," Lectures viii. ix.

[181:2] Prov. xxx. 5.

[181:3] This designation is not found in the most ancient manuscripts. Thus, in the very ancient "Recension of the Four Gospels in Syriac," recently edited by Dr Cureton, we have simply—"Gospel of Mark"—"Gospel of John," &c. See p. 6, Preface. See also any ordinary edition of the Greek Testament.

[181:4] Horne, ii. 174.

[182:1] Titus iii. 12.

[182:2] Some, however, assign to it a much earlier date. See Davidson's "Introduction to the New Testament," iii. 320.

[182:3] See Period i. sec. i. chap. 10, p. 158.

[182:4] See Wordsworth "On the Canon," p. 273.

[182:5] See Davidson's "Introduction," iii. 464, 491.

[182:6] Irenaeus, v. 30. Euseb. iii. 18.

[182:7] See Wordsworth "On the Canon," p. 157, 160, 249.

[182:8] Justin Martyr, ap. i. 67.

[182:9] 2 Pet. iii. 16

[183:1] Wordsworth "On the Canon," p. 205.

[183:2] "The allusions to the Epistle to the Hebrews are so numerous that it is not too much to say that it was wholly transfused into Clement's mind."—Westcott on the Canon, p. 32. See also Euseb. iii. 38.

[183:3] Wordsworth "On the Canon," p. 249.

[183:4] "The word ([Greek: graphê]) translated Scripture, which properly means simply a writing, occurs fifty times in the New Testament; and in all these fifty places, it is applied to the writings of the Old and New Testament, and to no other."—Wordsworth, p. 185, 186.

[183:5] Wordsworth, p. 249, 250.

[184:1] See Davidson's "Introduction," iii. 540-550.

[184:2] See Horne's "Introduction," ii. 168. The author of the present division into chapters is said to have been Hugo de Sancto Caro, a learned writer who flourished about the middle of the thirteenth century. The New Testament was first divided into verses by Robert Stephens in 1551. The Geneva Bible was the first English version of the Scriptures into which these divisions of Stephens were introduced.

[184:3] Horne, ii. 169.

[185:1] John v. 39; 2 Tim. iii. 15.

[185:2] Rev. i. 3. See also 2 Peter i. 19.

[185:3] Paul's epistles were often written with the hand of another. See Rom. xvi. 22; 2 Thess. iii. 17.

[186:1] Ps. xii. 6.

[186:2] The epistle to Diognetus may have been written in the first century, but it is commonly referred to a later date.

[186:3] He speaks of the Church of Corinth at the time as "most ancient" (§ 47), and refers apparently to the Domitian persecution. See Euseb. iii. 15, 16.

[186:4] Tertullian also illustrates the resurrection by the story of the phoenix, "De Resurrec. Carn." c. 13.

[187:1] Clement's "Epistle to the Corinthians," § 25. The fragment of the second epistle is not generally considered genuine.

[189:1] Matt. v. 17.

[189:2] 2 Tim. i. 10.

[189:3] Matt. xvi. 16; John i. 41.

[189:4] Luke xxiv. 19, 21; John i. 49.

[189:5] Matt. xvi. 21, 22; John xii. 34.

[189:6] Mark xv. 43; Luke ii. 38.

[189:7] John iv. 20-25.

[189:8] John xix. 12.

[189:9] Matt. ii. 2, 3, xx. 21; John vi. 15.

[190:1] Acts i. 6.

[190:2] Luke xxiv. 45.

[190:3] Luke xxiv. 44.

[190:4] Acts x. 34, 35.

[190:5] Acts xi. 3, 17.

[190:6] Heb. x. 1, 14, 18.

[190:7] Period i. sec. ii. chap. 1.

[191:1] Mark vii. 7-9.

[191:2] Matt. iv. 1-10, xii. 3, 5, 7; Mark xii. 26.

[191:3] John v. 39.

[191:4] Acts ii. 14-36.
[191:5] 2 Tim. iii. 15.
[191:6] 2 Tim. iii. 16, 17.
[191:7] Matt. xxii. 43, 45; Gal. iii. 16; Heb. ii. 8, 11.
[191:8] John x. 34, 35; Heb. viii. 13.
[191:9] Acts xxviii. 25; Heb. iii. 7.
[191:10] Heb. i. 1, 2; Matt. i. 22, ii. 15.
[192:1] 1 Cor. ii. 13.
[192:2] 2 Tim. iii. 16.
[192:3] Gen. iii. 15; Ps. cxxx. 7, 8; Dan. ix. 24.
[192:4] Ps. xcviii. 1-4; Isa. ix. 6.
[192:5] Rom. iii. 19.
[192:6] Eph. ii. 1.
[192:7] John v. 24.
[192:8] Rev. iii. 20.
[192:9] Heb. xi. 27.
[193:1] Heb. xii. 2.
[193:2] Heb. vi. 18.
[193:3] 1 Pet. ii. 3.
[193:4] Rom. v. 1.
[193:5] Acts xv. 9.
[193:6] 1 John v. 4.
[193:7] Rom. v. 2.
[193:8] Heb. xi. 1.
[193:9] John xx. 31.
[193:10] John i. 29.
[193:11] Rom. x. 4.
[194:1] Eph. v. 23.
[194:2] Rev. xvii. 14.
[194:3] Col. i. 27.
[194:4] Ps. cxlvi. 8, compared with John ix. 32, 33.
[194:5] Job ix. 8, compared with Matt. xiv. 25.
[194:6] Ps. cvii. 29, compared with Luke viii. 24.
[194:7] Amos iv. 13, compared with Matt. xii. 25, and John ii. 24, 25.
[194:8] Tit. ii. 14.
[194:9] Mark ii. 5-10.
[194:10] Eph. v. 26.
[194:11] Acts xvi. 14; Luke xxiv. 45.
[194:12] Rev. ii. 23.
[194:13] Mal. iii. i.
[194:14] Isa. xl. 3, and vi. 1, compared with John xii. 38-41.
[194:15] Isa. xl. 3, 9; Ps. xlv. 6.
[194:16] Ps. ii. 12.
[194:17] Ps. lxxii. 15.
[194:18] Ps. ii. 12, compared with Ps. cxlvi. 3, 5, and Isa. xxvi. 4.
[194:19] John i. 49; Matt. xvi. 16, 17.
[194:20] Such as John xx. 28, xxi. 17.
[195:1] Luke xxiv. 27.
[195:2] 1 Cor. xii. 3.

323

[195:3] Rom. ix. 5.

[195:4] Eph. i. 12, 13; Matt. xii. 21.

[195:5] Col. iii. 24.

[195:6] Acts ix. 14; 1 Cor. i. 2.

[195:7] Rev. v. 11-13. Though modern criticism has shaken the credit of some passages usually quoted in support of the Deity of Christ, such as 1 Tim. iii. 16, it is remarkable that it has discovered others equally strong not now in the received text. See Lachmann's text of Col. ii. 2, and 1 Pet. iii. 15.

[196:1] Heb. ii. 14.

[196:2] Matt. xvi. 22.

[196:3] Luke xxiv. 46.

[196:4] Rom. iii. 26.

[197:1] Heb. ix. 12.

[197:2] 1 Cor. i. 24.

[197:3] Phil. ii. 13.

[197:4] Eph. i. 4-6.

[197:5] Matt, xxviii. 19; John x. 30, xv. 26.

[198:1] Eph. iv. 5.

[198:2] See Bingham, iii. 323-327.

[198:3] Acts viii. 37; 1 Pet. iii. 21.

[198:4] Matt. i. 21.

[199:1] Prov. viii. 11.

[199:2] Phil. iv. 11-14.

[200:1] "[Greek: Hairesis] autem Graecé, ab electione dicitur: quòd scilicet eam sibi unusquisque eligat disciplinam, quam putat esse meliorem."— Hieronymus in Epist. ad Galat. c. 5. See also Tertullian, "De Praescrip." c. 6.

[200:2] "Life," Section 2; "Antiq." xiii. 5, 9.

[200:3] Acts xxvi. 5.

[200:4] Acts xxiv. 5.

[200:5] Gal. v. 20.

[201:1] Eph. iv. 17, 18; Col. i. 13.

[201:2] John iii. 18, 19.

[201:3] Mosheim has overlooked this fact, and has, in consequence, been betrayed into some false criticism when treating on this subject.

[201:4] Titus iii. 10.

[201:5] 2 Pet. ii. 1.

[202:1] Every one acquainted with the works of Philo Judaeus must be aware that Jewish literature was now largely impregnated with pagan philosophy.

[202:2] Col. ii. 8.

[202:3] 1 Tim. vi. 20.

[202:4] See Burton's "Inquiry into the Heresies of the Apostolic Age," pp. 314, 315. Also Mosheim's "Dissertation" appended to Cudworth, iii. 171.

[203:1] Col. i. 16, 17.

[204:1] From [Greek: dokeô], I appear.

[204:2] John i. 14.

[204:3] 1 John iv. 3.

[204:4] 1 John i. 1-3.

[204:5] 2 John 7.

[204:6] 1 Cor. xv. 12.

[204:7] 2 Tim. ii. 16-18.

[205:1] Acts viii. 9.

[205:2] Irenaeus, i. 23; Eusebius, ii. 13.

[205:3] Acts viii. 20-23.

[205:4] Acts viii. 9.

[205:5] Justin Martyr, "Apol." ii. 69. Edit. Paris, 1615.

[205:6] 1 Tim. i. 20; 2 Tim. i. 15, ii. 17, iv. 14.

[206:1] Irenaeus, i. 25, 26; Tertullian, "De Praescrip. Haeret." 33; Epiphanius, "Haer." xxx. 2, lxix. 23.

[206:2] Irenaeus, iii. 3, 4.

[206:3] Irenaeus, iii. 11.

[206:4] Rev. ii. 6, 15.

[206:5] Acts vi. 5. Others conceive, however, that the name Nicolaitanes is merely equivalent to Balaamites (as Balaam in Hebrew is nearly equivalent to Nicolas in Greek, each word signifying Ruler, or Conqueror of the people), and that the apostle does not here refer to any party already known by this designation, but to all who, like Balaam, were seducers of God's people. See Neander, "General History," ii. 159. Edinburgh edition, 1847.

[207:1] Rev. ii. 6, 15.

[207:2] Acts xxiii. 1, 6.

[207:3] 1 John ii. 19.

[207:4] Compare Jude 19, and Heb. x. 25.

[208:1] 1 Tim. i. 20.

[208:2] Rev. ii. 15.

[208:3] Hegesippus in Euseb., iv. 22.

[208:4] Eusebius, iv. 22.

[208:5] 1 Cor. xi. 19.

[209:1] James iii. 17.

[210:1] Luke xxiv. 21.

[210:2] Luke xxiv. 17, 22, 23.

[211:1] Acts xx. 7.

[211:2] Rev. i. 10, [Greek: hê kurtakê hêmera]. The day was ever afterwards distinguished by this designation. See a letter from Dionysius of Corinth in Eusebius, iv. 23. See also Kaye's "Clement of Alexandria," p. 418. The first day of the week is called "the Christian Sabbath" in the Ethiopic version of the "Apostolical Constitutions." See Platt's "Didascalia," p. 99. But these Constitutions are of comparatively late origin.

[211:3] Matt. v. 17-19.

[211:4] Matt. iii. 15.

[211:5] Matt. xii. 3-5; Mark ii. 25, 26.

[211:6] Matt. xii. 7.

[211:7] Gen. ii. 3.

[212:1] Exod. xx. 1-17.

[212:2] Mark ii. 27.

[212:3] Matt. xxiv. 20.

[212:4] See Heb. xiii. 10, 15, 16; Ps. li. 17.

[212:5] Isa. lvi. 6, 7. Compare with Isa. ii. 2.

[212:6] Mark ii. 28.

[212:7] John xx. 19, 26. According to the current style of speaking," after eight days" means the eighth day after. See Matt, xxvii. 63.

[213:1] Acts ii. 1. That the day of Pentecost was the first day of the week appears from Lev. xxiii. 11, 15. The same inference may be drawn from John xviii. 28, and xix. 31, compared with Lev. xxiii. 5, 6. See also Schaff's "History of the Apostolic Church," i. p. 230, note, and the authorities there quoted.

[213:2] In the same way the Eucharist is called the Lord's Supper: [Greek: Kuriakon deipnon] (1 Cor. xi. 20). Thus also we speak of the Lord's house, and the Lord's people.

[213:3] Heb. x. 25.

[213:4] 1 Cor. xvi. 1, 2.

[213:5] Isa. lxv. 17, 18.

[213:6] [Greek: Sabbatiamos]. See Owen "On the Hebrews," iv. 9.

[213:7] Heb. iv. 9, 10.

[213:8] Rom. xiv. 5.

[214:1] Col. ii. 16, 17.

[214:2] The ordinary temple service could scarcely be called congregational. It was almost exclusively ceremonial and typical, consisting of sacrificing, burning incense, and offering various oblations. The worshippers generally prayed apart. See Luke i. 10, xviii. 10, 11.

[215:1] See these eighteen prayers in Prideaux's "Connexions," i. 375, and note. Bingham admits (Orig. iv. 194), that these are their "most ancient" forms of devotion; and, of course, if they were written after the fall of Jerusalem, it follows that the Jews had no liturgy in the days of our Lord. Had they then been limited to fixed forms, He would scarcely have upbraided the Scribes and Pharisees for hypocritically "making long prayer" Matt, xxiii. 14.

[215:2] See Palmer's "Origines Liturgicae," i. pp. 44-92; and Clarkson's "Discourse concerning Liturgies;" "Select Works," p. 342.

[215:3] Matt. vi. 9-13.

[215:4] 1 Thess. v. 18.

[215:5] Eph. vi. 18.

[215:6] Eph. vi. 18.

[215:7] Acts i. 24, 25, iv. 24-30.

[216:1] See Lightfoot's "Temple Service," ch. vii. sec. 2; "Works," ix. 56.

[216:2] Lightfoot's "Prospect of the Temple," ch. xxxiii.; "Works," ix. 384.

[216:3] The multitudes who assembled at the great festivals in the temple could not well unite in one service. The wall of the building was more than half a mile in circumference. See Lightfoot, ix. 217. There were various courts and divisions in the building.

[216:4] Heb. ix. 9-12, x. 1; John ii. 19-21; 1 Pet. ii. 5.

[216:5] Vitringa, "De Synagoga," p. 203.

[216:6] Eph. v. 19. According to some, the Psalms were divided into these three classes.

[216:7] Heb. xiii. 15.

[217:1] Bingham, ii. 482-484.

[217:2] Luke iv. 16, 17.

[217:3] Col. iv. 16; 1 Thess. v. 27.

[217:4] 1 Cor. xiv. 29. It would appear from this that only two or three persons were permitted to speak at a meeting. By him that "sitteth by" (verse 30), a doctor or teacher is meant. See Vitringa, "De Synagoga," p. 600, and Matt. v. 1.

[217:5] 1 Cor. xiv. 27. The gift of "interpretation of tongues" (1 Cor. xii. 10) was quite as wonderful as the gift of "divers kinds of tongues" (1 Cor. xii. 10).

[218:1] Censers were introduced into the Church about the fourth or fifth century. Bingham, ii. 454, 455.

[218:2] 1 Cor. xvi. 19; Col. iv. 15; Philem. 2.

[218:3] Matt. iii. 4.

[218:4] The rite of confirmation, as now practised, has no sanction in the New Testament. The "baptisms" and "laying on of hands," mentioned Heb. vi. 2, are obviously the "divers washings" of the Jews, and the imposition of hands on the heads of victims. The laying on of the apostles' hands conferred miraculous gifts. Had the apostle referred to Christian baptism in Heb. vi. 2, he would have used the singular number.

[218:5] Lightfoot affirms that the use of baptism among the Israelites was as ancient as the days of Jacob. He appeals in support of this view to Gen. xxxv. 2. "Works," iv. 278.

[219:1] Lightfoot's "Works," iv. 409, 410. Edit. London, 1822.

[219:2] Acts x. 2, 44-48, xvi. 15, 33, xviii. 8; 1 Cor. i. 16.

[219:3] Acts viii. 37.

[219:4] Mark xvi. 16; John iii. 18.

[219:5] Matt. xix. 14; Luke xviii. 15. In the New Testament children are described as uniting with their Christian parents in prayer (Acts xxi. 5). Were not these children baptized? They were no doubt brought up "in the nurture and admonition of the Lord" (Eph. vi. 4).

[220:1] Col. ii. 11, 12, 13.

[220:2] Col. i. 2, iii. 20; Eph. vi. 1, 4.

[220:3] 1 John ii. 12.

[220:4] Acts ii. 38, 39.

[220:5] 1 Cor. vii. 14. The absurdity of the interpretation according to which holy is here made to signify legitimate, is well exposed by Dr Wilson in his treatise on "Infant Baptism," p. 513. London, 1848.

[220:6] This would, indeed, have been almost, if not altogether, impossible. They would probably act somewhat differently at the river Jordan and in such a place as the jail at Philippi.

[220:7] [Greek: Baptizô].

[221:1] Dr Wilson has demonstrated the incorrectness of Dr Carson's statements on this subject. See his "Infant Baptism," p. 96.

[221:2] Wilson's "Infant Baptism," p. 157. In Titus iii. 5, 6, there is something like a reference to this mode of baptism: "The washing of regeneration and renewing of the Holy Ghost which he shed (or poured out) on us abundantly." [Greek: Ou execheen eph' hêmas plousiôs].

[221:3] In some cases, as at Jerusalem on the day of Pentecost, they do not seem to have had the means of immersing their converts. See also Acts x. 47. The text John iii. 23, indicates the difficulty of baptizing by dipping.

[221:4] Isa. lii. 15; Ezek. xxxvi. 25; I Pet. i. 2; Heb. ix. 10; Rev. i. 5.

[221:5] 1 Cor. v. 7, 8.

[221:6] Acts xx. 7.

[221:7] Acts xx. 7; 1 Cor. x. 16.

[222:1] It was in use before the end of the second century. See Kaye's "Tertullian," p. 431, 451.

[222:2] 1 Cor. x. 17.

[222:3] 1 Cor. v. 11.

[222:4] See Lightfoot's "Works," iii. 242, and xi. 179. Vitringa "De Synagoga," p. 550.

[222:5] Acts xx. 28.

[223:1] Heb. xiii. 17.

[223:2] Heb. xxi. 17.

[223:3] 1 Tim. iii. 5.

[223:4] 1 Tim. v. 19, 20.

[223:5] Heb. xiii. 17.

[223:6] 1 Cor. v. 1,13.

[223:7] 2 Cor. ii. 6.

[224:1] See Period I. section i. chap. v. p. 88.

[224:2] 1 Cor. v. 2, 6.

[224:3] 1 Cor. V. 3-5.

[224:4] 1 John v. 19, [Greek: en tô ponêrô].

[225:1] In the above passage respecting delivering unto Satan there may be a reference to Job ii. 6, 7, and it may be that some bodily affliction rested on the offender. In that case there would be here an exercise of supernatural power on the part of Paul. According to Tertullian, to deliver to Satan was simply to excommunicate. "De ceteris dixit qui illis traditis Satanae, id est, extra ecclesiam projectis, erudiri haberent blasphemandum non esse."—"De Pudicitia," c. xiii.

[225:2] 1 Cor. i. 11,12.

[225:3] That the Church of Corinth at this time was organized in the same way as other Christian communities is evident from various allusions in the first epistle. See 1 Cor. iv. 15, vi. 5, xii. 27, 28. Crispus, mentioned Acts xviii. 8, was, no doubt, one of the eldership. There is a reference to the elders in 1 Cor. xiv. 30. See Vitringa, "De Synagoga," p. 600.

[225:4] In the apostolic age, censures were pronounced in presence of the whole church. See 1 Tim. v. 20. It is to be noted that Paul himself does not excommunicate the offender. He merely delivers his apostolic judgment that the thing should be done, and calls upon the Corinthians to do it; but he expects them to proceed in due order, the rulers and the people performing their respective parts.

[227:1] 2 Cor. ii. 7, 8. The mode of proceeding here indicated is illustrated by what took place in the Church of Rome about the middle of the third century. There certain penitents first appeared before the presbytery to express their contrition, and then it was arranged that "this whole proceeding should be communicated to the people, that they might see those established in the Church, whom they had so long seen and mourned wandering and straying."—Cyprian, Epist. xlvi. p. 136. Edit. Baluzius, Venice, 1728.

[228:1] That "the church" here signifies the eldership, see Vitringa, "De Synagoga," p. 724.

[228:2] Matt, xviii. 15, 17.

[228:3] In our English version the original word [Greek:(paradosin)] is improperly rendered tradition.

[228:4] Thess. iii. 6.

[228:5] Matt. v. 45.

[229:1] 2 Thess. iii. 14, 15.

[229:2] For an account of the excommunication of the Druids, see Caesar, "De Bello Gallico," vi. 13. Many things in the Latin excommunication are doubtless borrowed from paganism.

[229:3] As an example of this, see an old form of excommunication in Collier's "Ecclesiastical History," ii. 273. Edit. London, 1840.

[230:1] Eph. iv. 11, 12.

[230:2] 1 Cor. xii. 28.

[230:3] 2 Tim. iv. 5.

[230:4] Acts xxi. 8, viii. 5.

[230:5] 1 Tim. i 3, v. 1, 7, 17; Tit. i. 5.

[231:1] Acts viii. 13; 2 Tim. i. 6. This latter text is often quoted, though erroneously, as if it referred to the ordination of Timothy. The ordainer usually laid on only his right hand. See "Con. Carthag." iv. can. iii. iv. In conferring extraordinary endowments both hands were imposed. See Acts xix. 6.

[231:2] John xiv. 26, xvi. 13, xx. 22.

[231:3] Matt. x. 1, xxviii. 18, 19.

[231:4] John xx. 26, xxi. 1; Acts i. 3; 1 Cor. ix. 1.

[231:5] Such is the opinion of Chrysostom and others. See Alford on this passage.

[231:6] Acts vi. 2-4.

[231:7] In the Peshito version helps and governments are translated helpers and governors.

[232:1] It is remarkable that the lay council of the modern synagogue are called Parnasim or Pastors. See Vitringa, "De Synagoga," pp. 578, 635.

[232:2] Mr Alford observes that in 1 Cor. xii. 28, "we must not seek for a classified arrangement"—the arrangement being "rather suggestive than logical." Hence "helps" are mentioned before "governments." In the same way in Eph. iv. 11, "pastors" precede "teachers."

[232:3] Acts xx. 28; 1 Pet. v. 2.

[232:4] Acts xx. 17, 28; Titus i. 5, 7; 1 Pet. v. 1, 2.

[232:5] 1 Tim. iii. 1, 2, 5.

[232:6] 1 Pet. v. 1, 2, 4 The identity of elders and pastors is more distinctly exhibited in the original here, and in Acts xx. 17, 28, as the word translated feed signifies literally to act as a shepherd or pastor.

[232:7] 1 Tim. v. 17. Mr Ellicott, in his work on the "Pastoral Epistles," thus speaks of this passage—"The concluding words, [Greek: en logô kai didask.], certainly seem to imply two kinds of ruling presbyters, those who preached and taught and those who did not."

[233:1] Compare 1 Cor. xii. 28, and Philip, i. 1; 1 Tim. iii. 1-8.

[233:2] Acts vi. 3, xiv. 23; Titus i. 5; James v. 14.

[233:3] 1 Cor. xiv. 1, 5, 6, 31.

[233:4] Section Rom. xii. 6-8.

[233:5] 1 Tim, iii. 5. Lightfoot says that, "in every synagogue there was a civil triumvirate, that is, three magistrates who judged of matters in contest arising within that synagogue."—"Works," xi.179. The same writer declares that "in every synagogue there were elders that ruled in civil affairs, and elders that laboured in the word and doctrine."—"Works," iii. 242, 243.

[234:1] [Greek: diplês timês]. Those who adduce this passage to prove that the apostle here defines the pecuniary remuneration of elders involve themselves in much difficulty; for, if limited to the matter of payment, and literally interpreted, it would lead to the inference that, irrespective of the amount of service rendered, all the elders should receive the same compensation; and that no church teacher,

329

though the father of a large family, should be allowed more than twice the gratuity of a poor widow! Compare I Tim. v. 3, and 17. The "double honour" of I Tim. v. 17, is evidently equivalent to the "all honour" of 1 Tim. vi. 1. In the latter case there can be no reference to payment. Paul obviously means to say that the claims of elders should be fully recognized; and in the following verse (1 Tim. v. 18) he refers pointedly to the temporal support to which church teachers are entitled.

[234:2] 1 Tim. iii. 2-7.

[234:3] [Greek: didaktikon].

[234:4] Matt. iv. 23; Acts v. 42, xv. 35.

[235:1] Heb. iii. 13.

[235:2] Col. iii. 16.

[235:3] 1 Pet. iii. 15.

[235:4] 2 Tim. ii. 24, 25.

[235:5] Even a female, though not permitted to speak in the Church, had often this aptness for teaching. Such was the case with the excellent Priscilla, Acts xviii. 26. The aged women were required to be "teachers of good things," Titus ii. 3.

[237:1] In the Church of Corinth several speakers were in the habit of addressing the same meeting. 1 Cor. xiv. 26, 27, 29, 31.

[237:2] 1 Tim. v. 17.

[237:3] Gal. vi. 6.

[237:4] 1 Tim. v. 18.

[237:5] 1 Cor. ix. 14.

[237:6] Matt. x. 1; 1 Cor. xiv. 18.

[237:7] "The place which the apostles occupied while they lived is now filled, not by a living order of ministers, but by their own inspired writings, which constitute, or ought to constitute, the supreme authority in the Church of God.... The New Testament Scriptures, as they are the only real apostolate now in existence, so, are sufficient to supply to us the place of the inspired Twelve."—Litton's Church of Christ, p. 410.

[237:1] "While it is clearly recorded that the apostles instituted the orders of presbyters and deacons, it is not so clearly recorded, indeed it is not recorded at all, that they instituted the order of bishops."—Litton, p. 426. Such a testimony from a Fellow of Oxford is creditable alike to his candour and his intelligence.

[237:2] Acts xv. 6, xvi. 4, xxi. 18, 25.

[237:3] Acts xx. 17, 25.

[237:4] Acts xx. 29-31.

[237:5] Acts vi. 4. "Here," says Mr Litton, "no mention is made of government or of ordination, as the special prerogative of the apostolic office; and if it were not dangerous to lay too much stress upon a single passage, it might from this one be plausibly inferred that the special function of the apostles, as representatives of the ordinary Christian ministry, has descended, not to bishops, but to presbyters, to whom it specially pertains to give themselves to prayer and the ministry of the Word."—Litton's Church of Christ, p. 407. It is certainly not dangerous to lay as much stress upon any Scripture as it will legitimately bear, and the inference hero drawn is in accordance with the rules of the most exact logic.

[238:1] 1 Cor. i. 17.

[238:2] Eph. iii. 8. In dealing with individuals, the apostles seldom challenged obedience on the ground of their divine authority. When they are represented as directing the movements of ministers, the language generally implies simply that the parties in question undertook certain services at their instigation or request, or by their advice. Thus, Paul says that he besought Timothy to abide in Ephesus, that he left Titus in Crete, and that he sent Epaphroditus to the Philippians (1 Tim. i. 3; Titus i. 5; Philip. ii. 25). But Paul himself is said to have been sent forth to Tarsus by the brethren (Acts ix. 30). When Mark refused to accompany Paul and Silas into Asia Minor he did not therefore forfeit his ecclesiastical status (Acts xiii. 13, xv. 37-39). Apart from their special commission, the apostles were entitled to deference from other ministers on account of their superior age and experience; and Paul sometimes refers to this claim. See Philem. 8, 9. On the same ground all who have recently entered the ministry are bound to yield precedence to aged pastors, and to respect their advice. See 1 Pet. v. 5.

[238:3] It can scarcely be necessary to remind the reader that the postscripts to these epistles setting forth that Timothy was "ordained the first bishop of the church of the Ephesians," and that Titus was "ordained the first bishop of the Church of the Cretians," are spurious. See Period i. sec. ii. chap. i. p. 181.

[239:1] 1 Tim. i. 3. Paul says (1 Cor. iv. 17) to the Corinthians—"I have sent unto you Timotheus .... who shall bring you into remembrance of my ways which be in Christ;" and, according to the mode of reasoning employed by some, we might infer from this text that Timothy was bishop of Corinth. "It is a suspicious circumstance," says Dr Burton, "that several persons who are mentioned in the New Testament, are said to have been bishops of the places connected with their names. Thus Cornelius is said to have been bishop of Caesarea, and to have succeeded Zacchaeus, though it is highly improbable that either of them filled such an office."—"Lectures," i., p. 182.

[239:2] 1 Tim. vi. 17.

[239:3] See Period i. sect. i. chap, ix. p. 131.

[239:4] Acts xx. 30, 31.

[240:1] The word [Greek: katastêsês], here translated "ordain," should rather be rendered constitute, or establish.

[240:2] Titus i. 5.

[240:3] Titus iii. 13.

[240:4] Acts vi. 3, xiv. 23; 2 Cor. viii. 19, 23.

[240:5] Acts xxiii. 3.

[240:6] "The whole Sanhedrim were the judges, and sitting to judge him according to the law."—Alford on Acts xxiii. 3.

[241:1] See Prideaux's "Connections," part ii. books 1 and 8.

[241:2] Acts xxvi. 17, 18. See also, as another illustration, Matt. xvi. 19.

[241:3] 2 Cor. xi. 28.

[241:4] 1 Tim. iv. 12, 13; 2 Tim. ii. 22, 23; Titus ii. 7, 8.

[241:5] 1 Tim. ii. 1, 2, iv. 16, v. 19, 20, 22; 2 Tim. ii. 2, 15, iv. 2, 5; Titus iii, 8, 9.

[242:1] 1 Tim. v. 5, 16, vi. 1, 2, 9, 17; Titus ii. 6, 9, 10.

[242:2] One of the most remarkable instances of an appeal to the sense of individual obligation in a case where many were concerned may be found in Gal. vi. 1.

[242:3] Whitby, in his "Preface to the Epistle to Titus," says candidly of the allegation that Timothy and Titus were bishops respectively of Ephesus and Crete—"Now, of this matter, I confess I can find nothing in any writer of the first three centuries, nor any intimation that they bore that name."

[242:4] 1 Tim. i. 3; 2 Tim. iv. 10, 12, 21; Titus i. 5, iii. 12.

[242:5] Hence Fulgentius speaks of "cathedra Joannis Evangelistae Ephesi." Lib. "De Trinitate," c. 1. Contradictory traditions sometimes happily annihilate each other.

[243:1] Homer, "Iliad," ii. v. 156.

[243:2] Mark x. 42-45.

[244:1] 1 Pet. v. 3.

[244:2] Acts i. 15, 21-23, 26.

[244:3] 2 Cor. viii. 19, 23. See also 1 Cor xvi. 3.

[244:4] Acts vi. 3, xiv. 23. See also 1 Tim. iii. 10, compared with 1 John iv. 1.

[244:5] Clemens Romanus states that, in the apostolic age, ecclesiastical appointments were made "with the approbation of the whole church." "Epist. to Corinthians," § 44.

[245:1] Acts vi. 6; 1 Tim. v. 22.

[245:2] See Selden, "De Synedriis," lib. i. c. 14.

[245:3] Acts xiii. 1-3.

[245:4] Acts xiv. 23.

[245:5] 1 Tim. iv. 14. That the preposition [Greek: meta] here indicates the instrumental cause, see Acts xiii. 17, xiv. 27.

[245:6] Acts vi. 6. Some have thought it strange that Paul gives no instructions to Titus respecting the ordination of deacons in Crete. See Titus i. 8. This was unnecessary, as the elders, when ordained, could afterwards ordain deacons.

[245:7] Rom. xvi. 1.

[245:8] [Greek: diakonon].

[246:1] 1 Tim. v. 3, 4, 9.

[246:2] Rom. xvi 2.

[247:1] 1 Cor. xii. 12, 21, 26.

[249:1] Such as we find described in Deut. xxxi. 10-12.

[249:2] In Greek [Greek: ekklêsia]. The reference in the text is to its ecclesiastical use, for in the New Testament it sometimes signifies a mob. See Acts xix. 32.

[249:3] Acts xi. 22, xv. 4.

[249:4] Acts xxi. 20, [Greek: posai muriades]—literally, "how many tens of thousands."

[249:5] One of these is mentioned Acts xii. 12.

[249:6] Acts xiii. 1.

[249:7] Acts ix. 31. The true reading here is, "Then had the church ([Greek: ekklêsia]) rest throughout all Judea and Galilee and Samaria." This reading is supported by the most ancient manuscripts, including ABC; by the Vulgate, and nearly all the ancient versions; including the old Syriac, Coptic, Sahidic, Ethiopian, Arabic of Erpenius, and Armenian; and by the most distinguished critics, such as Kuinoel, Lachmann, Tischendorf, Alford, and Tregelles. It is likewise sustained by the authority of what is believed to be by far the most valuable cursive MS. in existence. See Scrivener's "Codex Augiensis," Introd. lxviii., and p. 425. Cambridge, 1859.

[250:1] John xvii. 21.

[250:2] Eph. iv. 16.

[250:3] See Col. ii. 19.

[251:1] Acts viii. 14.

[251:2] Acts xi. 22. "No notion is more at variance with the spirit of apostolic Christianity than that of societies of Christians existing in the same neighbourhood, but not in communion with each other, and not under a common government."—Litton, p. 450.

[251:3] 2 Cor. viii. 19.

[251:4] Period I. sec. iii. chap. i. p. 214.

[251:5] "That the Church did really derive its polity from the synagogue is a fact upon the proof of which, in the present state of theological learning, it is needless to expend many words."—Litton's Church of Christ, p. 254.

[251:6] See Selden, "De Synedriis," lib. ii. c. 5; Lightfoot's "Works," iii. 242, and xi. 179. Josephus says that Moses appointed only seven judges in every city. "Antiq." book iv. c. 8, § 14. See also "Wars of the Jews," ii. c. 20, § 5.

[252:1] Luke xxii. 66; Acts v. 21, vi. 15. See also Prideaux, part ii. book vii., and Lightfoot's "Works," ix. 342.

[252:2] Matt. xvi. 21, xxvi. 59; Mark xv. 1. See also Lightfoot's "Works," iv. 223.

[252:3] 1 Chron. xxiv. 4, 7-18.

[252:4] Acts v. 34.

[252:5] As they represented the people, and were probably twenty-four in number, there may be a reference to them in Rev. iv. 4.

[252:6] Matt. v. 22.

[253:1] Deut. xvii. 8-10; 2 Chron. xix. 8-11; Ps. cxxii. 5.

[253:2] Acts ix. 1, 2, 14.

[253:3] Acts ii. 14, 41, 42, iv. 4, 32, 33, 35, v. 14, 42, vi. 6, 7, viii. 14.

[253:4] Acts xiii. 1, 3.

[253:5] Titus i. 5.

[253:6] 1 Tim. iv. 14.

[253:7] In the same way the Puritans, in the reign of Queen Elizabeth, frequently held meetings in London during the sittings of Parliament. See Collier, vii. 33, 64.

[254:1] For a more particular account of the constitution of the meeting mentioned in the 15th chapter of the Acts, see Period I. sec. i. chap. v. p. 82.

[255:1] Acts xv. 6.

[255:2] Acts xv. 19. "James, according to the somewhat pompous rendering in our English version, says—'Wherefore my sentence is'—in the original—[Greek: dio elô krina]—a common formula by which the members of the Greek assemblies introduced the expression of their individual opinion, as appears from its repeated occurrence in Thucydides, with which may be compared the corresponding Latin phrase (sic censeo) of frequent use in Cicero's orations."—Alexander on the Acts, ii. p. 83.

[256:1] Mark xvi. 15.

[257:1] See the spurious epistle of Clement to James, prefixed to the Clementine Homilies. Cotelerius, "Pat. Apost." vol. i. p. 617.

[258:1] Acts xx. 17.

[258:2] Acts xx. 16.

[258:3] The view here taken is corroborated by the authority of Irenaeus, iii. c. 14, § 2:—"In Mileto enim convocatis episcopis et presbyteris, qui erant ab Epheso, et a reliquis proximis civitatibus," &c.

[259:1] Acts xx. 18.

[259:2] Acts xix. 8, 10.

[259:3] Acts xx. 31.

[259:4] Acts xx. 25. Demetrius says to the craftsmen—"Ye see and hear that not alone at Ephesus, but almost throughout all Asia, this Paul hath persuaded and turned away much people." Acts xix. 26.

[259:5] See Period I. sec. i. chap. viii. p. 123.

[259:6] 1 Cor. xvi. 19.

[259:7] Gal. i. 2.

[259:8] Gal. v. 13.

[259:9] Gal. vi. 2.

[259:10] 1 Pet. i. 1.

[260:1] 1 Pet. v. i, 2.

[260:2] In Acts xx. 28, these designations are identical. The exhortation in 1 Pet. v. 5—"Yea, all of you be subject one to another"—is obviously addressed to ministers, and implies their mutual subordination. This command can be acted upon only by ministers who are confederated and who hold the same ecclesiastical status. Lachmann adopts a somewhat different reading of this verse without changing the sense, for he puts a semi-period after [Greek: allêlois]. According to his Larger Edition of the Greek Testament, the commencement of the verse should be rendered thus—"Likewise ye younger (presbyters) submit yourselves unto the elder, AND ALL TO ONE ANOTHER." I here suppose presbyters to be understood, as the apostle is speaking to them in all the preceding part of the chapter.

[260:3] 2 Cor. viii. 5, 18, 22; Phil. ii. 25, 28; Col. iv. 7-9; 2 Tim. iv. 9-12.

[260:4] 2 Cor. iii. 1.

[261:1] 2 John 10.

[261:2] 1 John iv. 1.

[261:3] Phil. i. 15-18.

[263:1] Rev. i. 1.

[264:1] Rev. i. 11.

[264:2] Rev. i. 12-16.

[264:3] Rev. i. 20.

[264:4] This was the opinion of Gregory Nazianzen, as well as others. There is an ingenious article on this subject in the "Bibliotheca Sacra" for April 1855. Its author, the Rev. Isaac Jennings, advocates the view propounded in this chapter.

[265:1] This is the opinion of Prideaux, Vitringa, and many others. See Prid. "Connec." part. i. book vi.; and Vitringa, "De Synagoga," lib. iii. par. 2, cap. 3.

[265:2] Acts xiii. 15.

[265:3] Luke iv. 16.

[265:4] Luke iv. 20.

[266:1] Prideaux, part i. book vi. vol. i. p. 385. Edit. London, 1716.

[266:2] "The hours of public devotions in them on their synagogue days were, as to morning and evening prayers, the same hours in which the morning and evening sacrifices were offered up at the temple."—Prideaux, part i. book vi.

[266:3] Maurice, in his work on Diocesan Episcopacy in reply to Clarkson, admits (p. 257) that in our Saviour's time, Laodicea had "but few inhabitants." Philadelphia is described by Strabo as a place with a small population.

[266:4] Acts xix. 20.

[266:5] Acts xix. 26.

[267:1] Prideaux speaks of the angel of the synagogue, in relation to the rulers, as "next to them, or perchance one of them."—Part i. book vi. vol. i. p. 385.

[267:2] It appears never to have occurred to Tertullian that the angels of the Churches were bishops. He obviously considered the angel of the Church an invisible intelligence. Thus he says of Paul—"Lusit igitur et de suo spiritu, et de ecclesiae angelo, et de virtute Domini, si quod de consilio eorum pronunciaverat rescidit."—De Pudicitia, c. xiv. ad finem. See also Tertullian "De Baptismo," c. vi. Such, too, was the opinion of Origen.—"De Principiis," lib. i. c. 8, and "De Oratione," 11. The fact that, long after the hierarchy was formed, in two or three rare cases a bishop is called an angel, in reference to the angels of the Apocalypse, is nothing to the purpose. See Bingham, i. 79.

[268:1] Phil. iv. 14, 18.

[269:1] Phil. ii. 25.

[269:2] 2 Cor. viii. 23, [Greek: apostoloi ekklêsiôn]. In after-times it was deemed proper that those messengers should be of the clerical order.—See Cyprian, epist. xxiv., lxxv., and lxxix.

[269:3] Luke vii. 27, [Greek: ton angelon mou].

[269:4] James ii, 25, [Greek: tous angelous].

[269:5] John xxi. 7, 20.

[270:1] Thus Hippolytus speaks of a certain elder, named Hyacinthus, who was sent to the governor of Sardinia with a letter for the release of the Christians banished there. "Philosophumena," p. 288. The legate of the bishop of Rome is a species of memorial of the angel of the ancient Church.

[270:2] Rev. ii. 7, 11, 17, 29, iii. 6, 13, 22.

[270:3] Rev. i. 11.

[271:1] Rev. i. 1.

[271:2] Isa. xlix. 15, 16.

[271:3] The Christians of Hierapolis are mentioned Col. iv. 13.

[271:4] Acts xx. 4.

[272:1] Lev. xxvi. 11, 12.

[272:2] Rev. i. 16.

[272:3] Ps. lxvii. 1, 2.

[275:1] A.D. 96 to A.D. 98.

[275:2] A.D. 98 to A.D. 117.

[276:1] Origen, "Contra Celsum," i. § 67. See also i. § 26.

[276:2] Origen, "Contra Celsum," iii. § 29.

[277:1] Justin Martyr, "Apol." ii. 61. Edit, Paris, 1615.

[277:2] The Peshito, or old Syriac version, is supposed to have been made in the first half of the second century.—Westcott "On the Canon," pp. 264, 265. There are traces of the existence of a Latin version in the time of Tertullian, or before the close of the second century.—Ibid., p. 275. "Two versions into the dialects of Upper and Lower Egypt—the Thebaic (Sahidic) and Memphitic—date from the close of the third century."—Ibid. pp. 415, 416.

[278:1] See Middleton's "Inquiry," pp. 3, 9.

[278:2] See Kaye's "Tertullian," pp. 98-101. Edition, Cambridge, 1826.

[278:3] Tertullian states that the Emperor Marcus Aurelius became friendly to the Christians, in consequence of a remarkable interposition of Providence in favour of his army, in a war with the Marcomanni and the Quadi. It was alleged that, in answer to the prayers of a body of Christian soldiers, afterwards known as the Thundering Legion, the imperial troops were relieved by rain, whilst a thunderstorm confounded the enemy. It is quite certain that the Roman army was rescued from imminent peril by a seasonable shower; but it is equally clear that the emperor attributed his deliverance, not to the God of the Christians, but to Jupiter Pluvius, and that a certain section of the Roman soldiers was known long before by the name of the Thundering Legion. There is no evidence that Marcus Aurelius ever became friendly to the Christians. See Lardner. "Heathen Testimonies," "Works," vii. 176-188.

[279:1] See Middleton's "Inquiry," p. 84. Edition, Dublin, 1749. Bishop Kaye has remarked that, in the writings of Tertullian, "the only power of the exercise of which specific instances are alleged, was that of exorcising evil spirits." "Kaye's Tertullian," p. 461. From the symptoms mentioned it would appear that the individuals with whom the exorcists succeeded were epileptics.

[279:2] Irenaeus, who seems to have been not unfavourable to the Montanists, speaks of the gift of tongues as possessed by some in his age, and yet he himself, as a missionary, was obliged to struggle with the difficulties of a foreign language. "Adv. Haeres," v., c. 6, and "Praef." ad. 1.

[279:3] When Theophilus of Antioch, towards the end of the second century, was invited by Autolycus to point out a single person who had been raised from the dead, he did not accept the challenge. See Kaye's "Justin Martyr," p. 217.

[279:4] Middleton's "Inquiry," Preface, p. iv.

[279:5] Middleton, pp. 22, 23.

[280:1] Plinii, "Epist." lib. x. epist. 97.

[280:2] Tertullian, "Ad Scapulam," c. 5.

[280:3] "Spicilegium Syriacum" by Cureton, p. 31. The correspondence between Abgar and our Lord, given by Eusebius, is manifestly spurious.

[281:1] Gregory of Tours, "Hist. Francorum," lib. i. c. 28.

[281:2] Sozomen, "Hist. Eccles." ii. 6, and Philostorgius, "Hist. Eccles." ii. 5.

[281:3] "Adversus Judaeos," c. 7.

[282:1] Justin Martyr, "Dialogue with Trypho," Opera, p. 345.

[282:2] Theophilus, "Ad Autolycum," lib. ii. See also Origen, "In Matthaeum," Opera, tom. iii. p. 858.

[282:3] "Life of Alexander Severus," by Lampridius.

[282:4] Euseb. viii. 1.

[284:1] Cyprian, "De Laude Martyrii," Opera, pp. 620, 621. See also Tertullian, "Ad Scapulam," c. 5. ad finem.

[285:1] Tertullian, "Apol." 50.

[287:1] Tertullian, "De Idololatria," c. 17.

[287:2] Matt. x. 35, 36.

[287:3] Tertullian, "Apol." c. 3, and "Ad Nationes," i. § 4.

[287:4] 1 Cor. xv. 19.

[288:1] The Christians long gloried in the fact that Nero was their first persecutor. See Tertullian, "Apol." c. 5.

[289:1] Plinii, "Epist." lib. x. epist. 97.

[290:1] Matt. xiii. 55; Mark vi. 3. That Simon and Simeon are the same, see Acts xv. 7, 14.

[290:2] Trajan died A.D. 117, and if Simeon was born a year after Jesus, he entered upon the 120th year of his age about the close of this Emperor's reign. See Greswell's "Dissertations," vol. ii. pp. 127, 128. It was the opinion of

Tertullian that Mary had other sons after she gave birth to our Lord. See Neander's "Antignostikus," and Tertullian "De Monogamia," c. 8.

[293:1] The account of the trial of himself and his companions, as given in the "Acta Sincera Martyrum" by Ruinart, bears all the marks of truth.

[293:2] An account of his martyrdom is given in a circular letter of the Church of Smyrna. See Jacobson's "Patres Apostolici," tom. ii. p. 542. Euseb. iv. 15.

[294:1] These places are distant from each other about seventeen miles.

[296:1] Euseb. v. 1.

[296:2] Among the Romans a concubine held a certain legal position, and was in fact a wife with inferior privileges. Converted concubines were admitted to the communion of the ancient Church. See Bunsen's "Hippolytus," iii. 7.

[296:3] Mosheim ("Commentaries" by Vidal. ii. 52, note) and many others, refer the transaction recorded in the text to the reign of Hadrian, but without any good cause. Tertullian, who tells the story ("Ad Scapulani," c. 5), evidently alludes to a transaction which had recently occurred. In the reign of Commodus there was a proconsul named Arrius Antoninus who was put to death. See Lamprid, "Vita Commodi," c. 6, 7. See also Kaye's "Tertullian," p. 146, note; and "Neander's General History" by Torrey, i. 162, note.

[296:4] Clemens Alexandrinus apparently refers to the times immediately following the death of Commodus when he says—"Many martyrs are daily burned, crucified, and decapitated before our eyes." Strom, lib. ii. p. 414.

[297:1] Tertullian, "Ad Scapulam," c. 4.

[297:2] Compare Justin Martyr, "Apol." ii. pp. 70, 71, and "Dial, cum Tryphone," p. 227, with Tertullian, "Apol." c. 7.

[297:3] Called libellos.

[297:4] These parties sometimes appealed to Acts xvii. 9, in justification of their conduct.

[298:1] The sacrificati, or those who had sacrificed, as well as offered incense, were considered still more guilty.

[298:2] "Acta Perpetuae et Felicitatis." The martyrs appear to have been Montanists. See Gieseler, by Cunningham, i. 125, note. Tertullian mentions Perpetua, and his language countenances the supposition that she was a Montanist. "De Anima," c. 55.

[300:1] See the "Chronicon" of Eusebius, par. ii., adnot. p. 197. Edit. Venet, 1818.

[301:1] The Roman clergy speak of "the remnants and ruined heaps of the fallen lying on all sides." Cyp. "Epist." xxxi. p. 99. Cyprian complains of "thousands of letters given daily" in behalf of the lapsed by misguided confessors and martyrs. "Epist." xiv. p. 59. The writer here probably speaks somewhat rhetorically, and evidently does not mean, as some have thought, that all these letters were written at Carthage. He speaks of what was done "everywhere," including Italy, as well as the cities of Africa. "Epist." xiv., xxii., xxvi.

[301:2] Dionysius of Alexandria, quoted by Euseb., vi. 41.

[302:1] Euseb. vi. 39.

[302:2] A.D. 249 to A.D. 251.

[302:3] Cyprian, Epist. 82, ad Successum.

[302:4] Cyprian, who seems to have been much respected personally by the high officers of government at Carthage, was, when taken prisoner, granted as great indulgence as his circumstances would permit; but Gibbon, who describes his case with special minuteness, most uncandidly represents it as affording an average specimen of the style in which condemned Christians were treated. As an evidence of the social position of the bishop of Carthage we may refer to the testimony of Pontius his deacon, who states that "numbers of eminent and illustrious persons, men of rank and family and secular distinction, for the sake of their old friendship with him, urged him many times to retire." "Life," § 14.

[303:1] Euseb. vii. 13.

[303:2] See Bingham, ii. p. 451.

[304:1] "De Mortibus Persec." c. 10.

[304:2] Euseb. viii. 2; "De Mort. Persec." c. 13. See also "Neander," by Torrey, i. 202, note.

[305:1] Eusebius, "Martyrs of Palestine," c. 4.

[305:2] Eusebius, "Martyrs of Palestine," c. 9.

[305:3] The Vatican Manuscript, the oldest in existence, was probably written shortly after this persecution. It possesses internal evidences that its date is anterior to the middle of the fourth century. See Horne, iv. 161, 10th edition.

[306:1] Eusebius, viii. 6, 9, 10, 12.

[307:1] Firmilian refers to a noted persecution which "did not extend to the whole world, but was local." Cyprian, "Epist." lxxv. p. 305.

[308:1] The treatise "De Mortibus Persecutorum" is generally attributed to Lactantius who flourished in the early part of the fourth century. The authorship is doubtful.

[308:2] Ps. ix. 16.

[308:3] Herodian, iii. 23. This circumstance, as well as some others here stated, is not mentioned in the work "De Mort. Persec." Tertullian mentions some other remarkable facts, "Ad Scapulam," c. 3.

[308:4] "De Mortib. Persec.," c. 49.

[309:1] Tertullian, "Apol." c. 46.

[310:1] Tertullian, "Apol." 28.

[310:2] Tertullian, "Ad Scapulam," § 2.

[311:1] John xviii. 36.

[312:1] Phil. iii. 18, 19.

[313:1] Cyprian, "De Lapsis," p. 374.

[313:2] Cyprian, "Ad Cornelium," epist. xlix. p. 143. Cyprian also charges one of his deacons with fraud, extortion, and adultery. Epist. xxxviii. p. 116.

[313:3] Cornelius of Rome in Euseb. vi. 43.

[315:1] See Eusebius, v. 3, vi. 9.

[315:2] See Neander's "Antignostikus," part ii. sect. ii. at the end. It appears that the Christian ascetics adopted the dress of the pagan philosophers.

[315:3] Cyprian, "De Habitu Virginum," pp. 354, 361.

[315:4] Still, in the time of Origen, the sons of bishops, presbyters, and deacons valued themselves upon their parentage.—Origen in "Matthaeum" xv. opera, tom. in. p. 690. Even Cyprian bears honourable testimony to certain married presbyters. See "Epist." xxxv. p. 111. See also "Epist." xviii. p. 67. Cyprian himself was indebted for his conversion to an eminent presbyter, named Caecilius, who had a wife and children. "Life of Cyprian," by Pontius the Deacon, § 5.

[315:1] Cyprian, "Epist." lxii. p. 219. Concerning the Subintroductae, see also the letter relating to Paul of Samosata in Euseb. vii. 30.

[316:1] Jerome and Athanasius.

[316:2] See Medhurst's "China," p. 217. The symbol of the cross was engraved on the walls of the temple of Serapis. "When the temple of Serapis was torn down and laid bare," says Socrates, "there were found in it, engraven on stones, certain characters, which they call hieroglyphics, having the forms of crosses. Both the Christians and Pagans on seeing them, thought they had reference to their respective religions." "Ecc. Hist." v. 17.

[316:3] Prescott, "Conquest of Mexico," in. 338-340. See also note, p. 340. Sir Robert Ker Porter mentions a block of stone found among the ruins of Susa, having, on one side, inscriptions in the cuneiform diameter; and, on another, hieroglyphical figures with a cross in the corner. See his "Travels," vol. ii. p. 415. Among the ancient pagans, the cross was the symbol of eternal life, or divinity. On medals and monuments of a date far anterior to Christianity, it is found in the hands of statues of victory and of figures of monarchs. See also Tertullian, "Apol." c. 16.

[317:1] Tertullian, "De Praescrip. Haeret." c. 40. See also Kaye's Tertullian, p. 441. "The ancient world was possessed by a dread of demons, and under an anxious apprehension of the influence of charms, sought for external preservatives against the powers of evil, and accompanied their prayers with external signs and gestures." Bunsen's "Hippolytus," iii. 351.

[317:2] See Justin Martyr, "Dialogue with Trypho," pp. 259, 318, and "Apol." ii. p. 90. Tertullian, "Adv. Judaeos," c. 10. In the "Octavius" of Minucius Felix, the following remarkable passage occurs:—"What are your military ensigns, and banners, and standards, but crosses gilded and ornamented? Your trophies of victory not only imitate the appearance of a cross, but also of a man fixed to it. We discern the sign of a cross in the very form of a ship, whether it is wafted along with swelling sails, or glides with its oars extended. When a military yoke is erected there is a sign of a cross, and, in like manner, when one with hands stretched forth devoutly addresses his God. Thus, there seems to be some reason in nature for it, and some reference to it in your own system of religion." The monogram [symbol: Chi-Rho], composed of the initial Greek capitals [Greek: Chi] and [Greek: Rho] of the name [Greek: christos], was in use among the heathen long before our era. It is to be found on coins of the Ptolemies. Aringhus, "Roma Subterranea," ii. p. 567.

[318:1] Tertullian maintains ("Ad Jud." c. xi.) that the mark mentioned Ezekiel ix. 4 was the letter T, or the sign of the cross. See a Dissertation on this subject by Vitringa, "Observationes Sacrae," lib. ii. c. 15. See also Origen. "In Ezechielem," Opera, tom. iii. p. 424, and Cyprian to Demetrianus, § 12. It would appear that the worshippers of Apollo used to mark themselves on the forehead with the letters [Greek: CHI ETA]. See Kitto's "Cyclopaedia of Bib. Lit." art. FOREHEAD.

[318:2] Tertullian, "De Corona." c. 3. By the Romans, crosses were erected in conspicuous places to intimidate offenders, just in the same way as the drop is now exhibited in the front of a jail. It is not improbable that some of these crosses were afterwards worshipped by the Christians! Aringhi mentions a stone, to be seen in his own time in the Vatican, which was treated with the same absurd reverence. On this stone many of the early Christians were said to have suffered martyrdom, probably by decapitation; but it was afterwards held "in very great honour" at Rome, and regarded as "a sacred thing!" "Roma Subterranea,'" i. 219.

[319:1] Minucius Felix, "Octavius," c. 24. There is a similar passage in Tertullian, "Apol." c. 12.

[319:2] Clemens Alexandrinus, "Paedagog." iii. Opera, pp. 246, 247.

[319:3] Clemens Alexandrinus, "Stromat." v. Opera, p. 559.

[320:1] Canon 30. The comment of the Roman Catholic Dupin upon this canon is worthy of note. "To me," says he, "it seems better to understand it in the plainest sense, and to confess that the Fathers of this Council did not approve the use of images, no more than that of wax candles lighted in full daylight."—History of Ecclesiastical Writers, Fourth Century.

[320:2] Tertullian, "De Pudicitia," c. 7. But all were not so scrupulous, for Tertullian elsewhere complains that the image-makers were chosen to church offices. "De Idololatria," c. 7.

[320:3] Tertullian, "De Idololatria," c. 6.

[321:1] Cyprian, "Ad Donatum," Opera, p. 5.

[321:2] Tertullian, "De Spectaculis," c. 4. According to the English Liturgy the person baptized "renounces the devil and all his works, the vain pomp and glory of the world." This was originally intended to apply to such exhibitions as those mentioned in the text.

[322:1] Tertullian, "De Pudicitia," c. 7. Theophilus to Autolycus, book iii.

[322:2] Tertullian "Apol." c. 44. Minucius Felix, in his "Octavius," makes a similar statement:—"The prisons are crowded with criminals of your religion, but no Christian is there, unless he is either accused on account of his faith, or is a deserter from his faith."

[322:3] Justin Martyr, in his Dialogue with Trypho the Jew, says to him—"Your blind and foolish teachers even to this day permit every one of you to have four or five wives."—Opera, p. 363.

[323:1] 1 Tim. iii. 2, 12.

[323:2] Rom. vii. 1-3; 1 Cor. vii. 2.

[323:3] The Montanists, in their extravagance, insisted that any one who contracted a second marriage after the death of his first wife should be excommunicated.

[323:4] 2 Cor. vi. 14.

[324:1] Tertullian, "Ad Uxorem," ii. 4.

[324:2] Gibbon, "Decline and Fall," chap. ii. Some writers, such as Zumpt and Merivale, consider this estimate quite extravagant. Others again think it quite too low. See Schaff's "History of the Christian Church," p. 316. New York, 1859.

[324:3] Gal. iii. 28.

[325:1] Onesimus, the slave mentioned Philem. 10, 16, probably became a Christian minister.

[325:2] 1 Cor. vii. 21.

[325:3] 1 Cor. vii. 20-22.

[325:4] 1 Tim. vi. 1, 2.

[325:5] Kindness to slaves was particularly enjoined by the early Church teachers. See Cyprian, "Lib. Tres. Test. adv. Judaeos," lib. iii. § 72, 73.

[325:6] It is stated in the "Octavius" of Minucius Felix that, in the estimation of the heathen, "for a slave to be partaker in certain religious ceremonies is deemed abominable impiety." (c. 25.)

[326:1] One of the laws made by Constantine shortly after his conversion sanctioned the manumission of slaves on the Lord's day.

340

[326:2] Thus, on one occasion, Cyprian raised a contribution of about £900 in Carthage to purchase the release of some Christians of Numidia. Cyprian, Epist. lx. p. 216. Tertullian said to the heathen, "Our charity dispenses more in every street, than your religion in each temple."—Apol. c. 42.

[327:1] About A.D. 252.

[327:2] Cyprian, "Ad Demetrianum," and "De Mortalitate." "Vita Cypriani per Pontium," c. 9.

[327:3] Euseb. vii. 22.

[328:1] Athanasius, "Hist. Arian. ad Monachos," § 64.

[329:1] Luke xxii. 24-26.

[329:2] Rom. i. 8, 13.

[330:1] Gal. ii. 7-9.

[330:2] Rom. xvi. 3-15.

[330:3] Acts ii. 10.

[330:4] Euseb. ii. 22.

[330:5] Period 1. sec. i. chap. x.

[331:1] Hegesippus seems to have been the first who attempted to draw up a list of the bishops, or presiding presbyters of Rome. See Pearson's Criticism on Euseb. iv. 22, in his "Minor Works," vol. ii. p. 319, Oxford, 1844; and Routh's "Reliquiae," i. pp. 270, 271.

[331:2] Thus, Irenaeus (i. 27) speaks of Hyginus as the ninth, and again (iii. 3), as the eighth in succession from the apostles.

[331:3] Thus, Irenaeus affirms (iii. 3) that Linus was the immediate successor of the apostles, whilst Tertullian, who was his contemporary, and who possessed equally good means of information, assigns that position to Clement. "De Praescrip. Haeret." c. 32.

[331:4] Euseb. iii. 4.

[332:1] Irenaeus, "Contra Om. Haer." iii. 3, § 3. Bunsen has justly remarked that, "with Telesphorus the most obscure period of the Roman Church terminates."—Hippolytus, iv. pp. 209, 210.

[332:2] Irenaeus, iii. 4, § 3.

[332:3] This name continued to be given to the Roman bishop until at least the close of the second century. See Irenaeus quoted in Euseb. v. 24.

[332:4] [Greek: katholikos]. See this subject more fully illustrated in Period II. sec. iii. chap. viii.

[333:1] "Qui absistunt a principali successione, et quocunque loco colligunt, suspectos habere (oportet) vel quasi haereticos et malae sententiae; vel quasi scindentes et elatos et sibi placentes; aut rursus ut hypocritas, quaestus gratia et vanae gloriae hoc operantes." Irenaeus, iv. 26, § 2.

[333:2] See Period II. sec. iii. chap. vii.

[333:3] Blondel's "Apologia pro sententia Hieronymi," p. 18. Under ordinary circumstances the new president, or bishop, was often elected before his predecessor was buried. See Bingham, book ii. c. xi. § 2.

[333:4] See Pearson's "Minor Works," ii. 520.

[333:5] This method of appointment continued to be observed long afterwards in some parts of the Church. See Bingham, book iv. chap. i. sec. i. At Alexandria in the beginning of the fourth century the presbyters selected three of their senior members, of whom the people chose one. Cotelerius, ii., app. p. 180.

[334:1] [Greek: Ton tês episkopês klêron]. "Irenaeus," ed. Stieren, i. p. 433.

[334:2] The Paschal feast. Irenaeus admits that this point formed only a subordinate topic of discussion. See Stieren's "Irenaeus," i. p. 826, note 6.

[334:3] See Period II. sec. iii. chap. vii.

[334:4] Euseb. iv. 14.

[335:1] Cyprian speaks of sending messengers to Rome "to ascertain and report as to any rescript published respecting" the Christians. "Epist. ad Successum." The Roman clergy could at once supply the information.

[336:1] Extract of a letter from Dionysius of Corinth, preserved in Eusebius, iv. 23.

[336:2] The testimonies to this fact may be found discussed in Minter's "Primordia Eccelesiae Africanae," p. 10. Herodian, who flourished in the third century, speaks of Carthage as the next city after Rome in size and wealth. Lib. vii. 6.

[336:3] In this way we may readily account for various statements in Tertullian and Cyprian.

[337:1] We here see how a father who wrote so soon after the apostolic age, blunders egregiously respecting the history of the Apostolic Church.

[337:2] So I understand "his qui sunt undique." See Wordsworth's "Hippolytus," p. 200. We have thus a remarkable proof that the word catholic was not in use when Irenaeus wrote, for he here expresses the idea by a circumlocution.

[337:3] "Propter potentiorem principalitatem."

[337:4] Irenaeus iii. 3. See on this passage Gieseler, by Cunningham, i. 97, note. See also Period II. sec. iii. chap. viii.

[337:5] The circular letter relating to the martyrdom of Polycarp quoted in Euseb. iv. 15. It was probably written a considerable time after the death of the martyr, as it speaks of the way in which his memory was cherished when it was drawn up. § 19. As it uses the word catholic it must have been written after the appearance of the work of Irenaeus.

[337:6] Irenaeus quoted in Euseb. v. 24. See Period II. sec. iii. chap. viii.

[339:1] We have an extract from them in Euseb. v. 4.

[339:2] Period II. sec. i. chap. ii. p. 296.

[339:3] Hippolytus, "Refut. Om. Haeres." book ix.

[340:1] This probably occurred early in the reign of Septimius Severus, who at first is said to have been very favourable to the Church. Shortly before, many in Rome of great wealth and eminent station had become Christians.—Euseb. v. c. 21.

[340:2] See a more minute account of this controversy in Period II. sec. iii. chap. xii.

[340:3] This is evident from the fact that Hippolytus is scarcely willing to recognise some of the Roman bishops, his contemporaries. But meanwhile both parties probably belonged to the same synod. Hippolytus seems to have been the leader of a formidable opposition.

[341:1] Matt. xvi. 18.

[341:2] See the Muratorian fragment in Bunsen's "Analecta Ante-Nicaena," i. 154, 155. This, according to Bunsen, is a fragment of a work of Hegesippus, and written about A.D. 165. Hippolytus, i. 314.

[341:3] "Hermae Pastor," lib. iii. simil. ix. § 12-14. "Petra haec.... Filius Dei est.... Quid est deinde haec turris? Haec, inquit, ecclesia est.... Demonstra mihi quare non in terra aedificatur haec turris, sed supra petram."

[341:4] Tertullian, "De Praescrip." xxii. "Latuit aliquid Petrum aedificandae ecclesiae petram dictum?" Tertullian here speaks of the doctrine as already current. Even after he became a Montanist, he still adhered to the same interpretation—"Petrum solum invenio maritum, per socrum; monogamum praesumo per ecclesiam, quae super illum, aedificata omnem gradum ordinis sui de monogamis erat collocatura."—De Monogamia, c. viii. Again, in another Montanist tract, he says—"Qualis es, evertens atque commutans manifestam domini intentionem personaliter hoc Petro conferentem? Super te, inquit, aedificabo ecclesiam meam."—De Pudicitia, c. xxi. See also "De Praescrip." c. xxii. According to Origen every believer, as well as Peter, is the foundation of the Church. "Contra Celsum," vi. 77. See also "Comment in Matthaeum xii.," Opera, tom. iii. p. 524, 526.

[342:1] See this subject more fully explained in Period II. sec. iii. ch. viii.

[343:1] Even the letters of Victor, which created such a sensation throughout the Church, are not forthcoming. See Pearson's "Vindiciae Ignatianae," pars 2, cap. 13, as to the spuriousness of those imputed to him.

[343:2] They extend from Clement, who, according to some lists, was the first Pope, to Syricius, who was made Bishop of Rome A.D. 384. All candid writers, whether Romanists or Protestants, now acknowledge them to be forgeries. They may be found in "Binii Concilia." They made their appearance, for the first time, about the eighth century.

[344:1] This is the date assigned to its erection by Bunsen, but Dr Wordsworth argues that it was erected earlier.

[344:2] 22d August.

[345:1] The first edition appeared at Oxford in 1851, exactly three hundred years after the discovery of the statue.

[345:2] This point has been fully established by Bunsen and Wordsworth.

[345:3] This is expressly stated by Tertullian, "Adversus Praxeam," c. i.

[345:4] See Bower's "History of the Popes." Victor, 13th Bishop.

[345:5] According to the commonly received chronology, Victor occupied the papal chair from A.D. 192 to A.D. 201; Zephyrinus from A.D. 201 to A.D. 219; and Callistus from A.D. 219 to A.D. 223.

[346:1] [Greek: andros idiôtu kai aischrokerdous].

[346:2] [Greek: apeiron tôn ekklêsiakôn horôn].

[346:3] "Philosophumena," book ix.

[348:1] "Philosophumena," book ix.

[348:2] 14th October.

[348:3] "Philosophumena," book i., prooemium.

[348:4] [Greek: dedoikôs eme].

[348:5] Bunsen describes Hippolytus as "a member of the Roman presbytery" ("Hippolytus," i. 313), but he is here evidently mistaken. Hippolytus was at the head of a presbytery of his own, the presbytery of Portus. The presbytery of Rome was confined to the elders or presbyters of that city. The presbyter Hippolytus mentioned by some ancient writers seems to have been a quite different person from the bishop of Portus.

[348:6] "Philosophumena," book ix.

[349:1] It is probable that the bishop was at first chosen by lot out of a leet of three selected by the presbytery from among its members. (See preceding chapter, p. 333, note.) An appointment was now made out of this leet of three, not by lot, but by popular suffrage.

[349:2] Euseb. vi. 29.

[350:1] Evidently from [Greek: kata], down, and [Greek: kumbos], a cavity. Mr Northcote, in his work on the "Roman Catacombs," published in 1857, calculates that the streets in all, taken together, are 900 miles long!

[350:2] See "Three Introductory Lectures on Ecclesiastical History," by William Lee, D.D., of Trinity College, Dublin, p. 27.

[350:3] It is probable that many were condemned to labour in these mines as a punishment for having embraced Christianity. See Lee's "Three Lectures," p. 28.

[350:4] Maitland's "Church in the Catacombs," p. 24. Dr Maitland visited Rome in 1841, but his inspection of the Lapidarian Gallery seems to have been regarded with extreme jealousy by the authorities there. After having obtained a licence "to make some memoranda in drawing in that part of the Museum," he was officially informed that "his permission did not extend to the inscriptions", and the communication was accompanied by a demand that "the copies already made should be given up." To his refusal to yield to this mandate we are indebted for many important memorials to be found in his interesting volume.

[351:1] See Maitland, pp. 27-29.

[352:1] Maitland, p. 14.

[352:2] Maitland, pp. 33, 41, 43, 170.

[352:3] "Philosophumena," book ix.

[352:4] As Carthage now furnished Rome with marble and granite, it is probable that the quarrymen and sand-diggers of the catacombs came frequently into contact with the Carthaginian sailors; and we may thus see how, in the time of Cyprian, there were such facilities for epistolary intercourse between the Churches of Rome and Carthage. Under favourable circumstances, the mariner could accomplish the voyage between the two ports in two or three days.

[353:1] "Philosophumena," book ix. Tertullian corroborates the charges of Hippolytus. See "De Pudicitia," cap. i.

[353:2] We know, however, that, long after this period, married bishops were to be found almost everywhere. One of the most eminent martyrs in the Diocletian persecution was a bishop who had a wife and children. See Eusebius, viii. c.9. Clemens Romanus, reputed one of the early bishops of the Western capital, speaks as a married man. See his "Epistle to the Corinthians," § 21.

[353:3] Maitland, pp. 191-193. These inscriptions may be found also in Aringhi, i. 421, 419.

[353:4] Aringhi, ii. pp. 228; Rome, 1651.

[354:1] Cyprian to Antonianus, Epist. lii, p. 151.

[355:1] Cyprian speaks of "the blessed martyrs, Cornelius and Lucius." Epist. lxvii. p. 250.

[355:2] See Cyprian's "Epistle to Successus," where it is stated that "Xystus was martyred in the cemetery [the catacombs] on the eighth of the Ides of August, and with him four deacons."

[355:3] This fragment may be found in Euseb. vi. 43.

[355:4] For an account of their duties see Period II. sec. iii. chap. x.

[355:5] According to some manuscripts, there were, not forty-six, but forty-two presbyters, seven deacons, seven sub-deacons, and forty-two acolyths. At a later period, we find three presbyters connected with each Roman church. There were fourteen regions in the city, and supposing a congregation in each, there would now be three presbyters, one deacon or sub-deacon, and three acolyths belonging to each church. See Blondel's "Apologia," p. 224.

[356:1] Cornelius (Euseb. vi. 43) calls him "a malicious beast," but he evidently writes under a feeling of deep mortification.

[357:1] Firmilian, "Cypriani Epistolae," lxxv.

[357:2] Matt. xvi. 16-18.

[357:3] John i. 42.

[357:4] See 1 Pet. ii. 5. Peter adds, as if to illustrate Matt. xvi. 18—"Wherefore also it is contained in the Scripture—Behold I lay in Zion a chief corner stone, elect, precious; and he that believeth on him shall not be confounded." 1 Pet. ii. 6.

[358:1] Matt. vii. 24, 25.

[358:2] See Tertullian, "De Praescrip." xxii.; and Cyprian to Cornelius, Epist. lv. p. 178, where he says—"Petrus, tamen, super quem aedificuta ab eodem Domino fuerat ecclesia." See also the same epistle, pp. 182, 183, and many other passages.

[358:3] Thus, Cyprian in his letter to Quintus (Epist. lxxi. p. 273) makes the following awkward attempt to get over the difficulty:—"Nam nec Petrus, quem primum Dominus elegit, et super quem aedificavit ecclesiam suam, cum secum Paulus de circumcisione postmodum disceptaret, vindicavit sibi aliquid insolenter aut arroganter assumpsit, ut diceret se primatum tenere et obtemperari a novellis et posteris sibi potius oportere."

[359:1] A.D. 325.

[359:2] The Suburbicarian Provinces comprehended the three islands of Sicily, Corsica, and Sardinia, and the whole of the southern part of Italy, including Naples and nearly all the territory now belonging to Tuscany and the States of the Church. See Bingham, iii. p. 20.

[359:3] Basil, Ep. 220.

[360:1] Euseb. vii. 50.

[360:2] Thus we read of "the blessed Pope Cyprian," bishop of Carthage. Cyprian, Epist. ii. p. 25. The name was sometimes given to the head of a monastery. In the catacombs there was found an inscription probably to the memory of a Pope of this description. See Maitland, p. 185. See also Routh's "Reliquiae," iii. pp. 256, 265.

[360:3] See Bower, "Marcellus," 29th Bishop.

[360:4] That is, from the autumn of A.D. 304 to the spring of A.D. 308. See Burton's "Lectures on the Ecc. Hist, of the First Three Cent." ii. p. 433.

[361:1] In the life of Marcellus we read of so many places of worship in Rome. See "Hist. Platinae De Vitis Pontif. Roman," p. 40, Coloniae, 1593. Optatus speaks of forty churches in Rome at this time; but he is probably mistaken as to the date. There may have been so many after the establishment of Christianity by Constantine. There were only fifty churches in the Western capital in the beginning of the fifth century. See Neander, i. 276; Edit. Edinburgh, 1847.

[362:1] In Matt. xvi. 18. Opera, tom. ii. p. 344; Edit. Eton, 1612.

[362:2] In Joh. i. 50. Opera, tom. ii. p. 637; Edit. Eton, 1612.

[362:3] "In Johann. Evang. Tractat." 124, § 5. Opera, tom. ix. c. 572. Augustine had before held the more fashionable view. See "Barrow on the Pope's Supremacy," by Dr M'Crie, p. 78.

[365:1] The references in this work to the Apostolic Fathers by Cotelerius are to the Amsterdam Edition, folio, 1724.

[365:2] This is the date assigned to it by Bunsen. "Hippolytus," i. 309. It is not probable that Polycarp was at the head of the eldership of Smyrna much earlier. See Period II. sec. iii. chap, v., note.

[365:3] According to Ussher in A.D. 169.

[365:4] See Pearson's "Minor Works," ii. 531.

[366:1] The original narrative may be found in the Dialogue with Trypho.

[366:2] The references to Justin in this work are to the Paris folio edition of 1615.

[367:1] He afterwards became the founder of a sect noted for its austere discipline. His followers used water, instead of wine, at the celebration of the Lord's Supper. They lived in celibacy, and observed rigorous fasts.

[367:2] The writer says of the temple (chap. xvi.)—"It is now destroyed by their (the Jews) enemies, and the servants of their enemies are building it up." Jerusalem was rebuilt by Hadrian about A.D. 135, and the name Aelia given to it.

[368:1] Two short letters ascribed to Pius are mentioned Period II. sec. iii. chap. vii. For a long time Barnabas, the author of the epistle, was absurdly confounded with the companion of Paul mentioned Acts xiii. 1, and elsewhere; and Hermas was supposed to be the individual saluted in Rom. xvi. 14. Hence these two writers have been called, like Polycarp and others, Apostolic Fathers.

[368:2] Eusebius, who has preserved a few fragments of this author, describes him as a very credulous person. See his "Hist." iii. 39.

[368:3] In the text it has not been considered necessary to mention all the writers, however small their contributions to our ecclesiastical literature, who appeared during the second and third centuries. Hence, Melito of Sardis, Caius of Rome, and many others are unnoticed. The remaining fragments of these early ecclesiastical writers may be found in Routh's "Reliquiae," and elsewhere.

[368:4] [Greek: haemôn, tôn en Keltois diatribontôn kai peri barbaron dialekton to pleiston ascholoumenôn].—Contra Haereses, lib. i. Praef.

[369:1] The references to Irenaeus in this work are to Stieren's edition of 1853.

[369:2] Wordsworth has remarked that in the "Philosophumena" of Hippolytus we have some of the lost text of Irenaeus. St Hippolytus, p. 15.

[369:3] Such is the testimony of Jerome. See Cave's "Life of Irenaeus."

[369:4] Euseb. "Hist." iii. 39.

[369:5] Irenaeus adopted the millenarianism of Papias.

[370:1] This is evident from his own statements. See his "Apology," c. 18, and "De Spectaculis," c. 19. The references to Tertullian in this work are either to the edition of Oehler of 1853, or to that of Rigaltius of 1675.

[370:2] According to some the population of Carthage at this time amounted to hundreds of thousands. "The intercourse between Carthage and Rome, on account of the corn trade alone, was probably more regular and rapid than with any other part of the Empire."—Milman's Latin Christianity, i. p. 47.

[370:3] See Euseb. ii. 2, 25.

[370:4] Such is the testimony of Jerome, who asserts farther that the treatment he received from the clergy of Rome induced him to leave that city.

[370:5] Such as the tracts "De Pallio" and "De Jejuniis."

[371:1] As a choice specimen of his vituperative ability his denunciation of Marcion may be quoted—"Sed nihil tam barbarum ac triste apud Pontum quam quod illic Marcion natus est, Scythia tetrior, Hamaxobio instabilior, Massageta inhumanior, Amazona audacior, nubilo obscurior, hieme frigidior, gelu fragilior, Istro fallacior, Caucaso abruptior."—Adversus Marcionem, lib. i. c. 1.

[371:2] Victor of Rome, who was contemporary with Tertullian, is said to have written in Latin, but the extant letters ascribed to him are considered spurious.

[372:1] Such, according to Jerome, was the practice of Cyprian.

[372:2] He is supposed to have died at an advanced age, but the date of his demise cannot be accurately determined. Most of his works were written between A.D. 194 and A.D. 217.

[372:3] The part of the work "Adversus Judaeos," from the beginning of the ninth chapter, is taken chiefly from the third book of the Treatise against Marcion, and has apparently been added by another hand.

[374:1] "Admonitio ad Gentes," Opera, p. 69. Edit. Coloniae, 1688.

[374:2] "Stromata," book v.

[374:3] See Kaye's "Clement of Alexandria," p. 378.

[374:4] Period II. sec. i. chap. v. p. 344.

[375:1] Prudentius. See Wordsworth's "Hippolytus," p. 106-112.

[377:1] He had acted literally as described, Matt, xix. 12.

[377:2] Euseb. vi. 3.

[377:3] Euseb. vi. 21.

[378:1] He says Celsus lived in the reign of Hadrian and afterwards. "Contra Celsum," i. § 8; Opera, tom. i. p. 327. The references to Origen in this work are to the edition of the Benedictine Delarue, 4 vols. folio. Paris, 1733-59.

[379:1] The three other Greek versions were those of Aquila, of Symmachus, and of Theodotion.

[379:2] Origen, in his writings, repeatedly refers to Philo by name. See Opera, i. 543.

[379:3] See Euseb. ii. c. 17.

[380:1] Thus he declares-"The prophets indicating what is wise concerning the circumstances of our generation, say that sacrifice is offered for sin, even the sin of those newly born as not free from sin, for it is written—'I was shapen in wickedness, and in sin did my mother conceive me.'"—Contra Celsum, vii. § 50.

[380:2] He held, however, that Satan is to be excepted from the general salvation. See "Epist. ad Amicos Alexandrinos," Opera, i. p. 5.

[381:1] See Sage's "Vindication of the Principles of the Cyprianic Age," p. 348. London, 1701.

[382:1] In the case of these epistles, much confusion arises, in the way of reference, from their various arrangement by different editors. The references in this work to Cyprian are to the edition of Baluzius, folio, Venice, 1728. Baluzius, in the arrangement of the letters, adopts the same order as Pamelius, but Epistle II. of the latter is Epistle I. of the former, and so on to Epistle XXIII. of Pamelius, which is Epistle XXII. of the other. Baluzius here conforms exactly to the numeration of the preceding editor by making Epistle XXIV. immediately follow Epistle XXII., so that from this to the end of the series the same references apply equally well to the work of either. The numeration of the Oxford edition of Bishop Fell is, with a few exceptions, quite different.

[382:2] Mr Shepherd has completely failed in his attempt to disprove the genuineness of these writings. They are as well attested as any other documents of antiquity.

[383:1] See Period II. sec. i. chap. ii. p. 302, note.

[383:2] It has not been thought necessary in this chapter to notice either Arnobius, an African rhetorician, who wrote seven Books against the Gentiles; or the Christian Cicero, Lactantius, who is said to have been his pupil. Both these authors appeared about the end of the period embraced in this history, and consequently exerted little or no influence during the time of which it treats.

[384:1] His life was written by Gregory Nyssen about a century after his death.

[385:1] See a preceding note in this chapter, p. 367.

[385:2] Matt. x. 29.

[385:3] Scorpiace, c. ix.

[385:4] Stromata, book iii.

[385:5] Matt, xviii. 20.

[385:6] "For," says he, "from the first hour to the third, a trinity of number is manifested; from the fourth on to the sixth, is another trinity; and in the seventh closing with the ninth, a perfect trinity is numbered, in spaces of three hours."-On the Lord's Prayer, p. 426.

[386:1] "Contra Celsum," v. § 11.

[386:2] Theophilus to Autolycus, lib. ii. § 24.

[386:3] In proof of this see his treatise "Contra Celsum," i. 25, also "Opera," iii. p. 616, and iv. p. 86.

[386:4] "Contra Haereses," ii. c. xxiv. § 2. See Matt. i. 21.

[386:5] "Contra Haereses," ii. c. xxxv. 3. He seems to have confounded Adonai and Yehovah. The latter word was regarded by the Jews as the "unutterable" name. Hence it has been thought that in the Latin version of Irenaeus we should read "innominabile" for "nominabile." See Stieren's "Irenaeus," i. 418.

[386:6] "Paedagogue," book i. See Gen. xxxii. 28.

[386:7] "Stromata," book v. Sec Gen. xvii. 5. Not a few of these mistakes may be traced to Philo Judaeus. Thus, this interpretation of Abraham may be found in his "Questions and Solutions on Genesis," book iii. 43.

[386:8] "Apol." ii. p. 88.

[386:9] "Dialogue with Trypho," Opera, p. 268.

[386:10] "Apol." ii. p. 76.

[386:11] "Apol." ii. p. 86.

[387:1] "Contra Haereses," ii. c. xxii. § 5.

[387:2] He thus makes His ministry about a year in length. "Adversus Judaeos," c. viii.

[387:3] "De Cultu Feminarum," lib. i. c. 2, and lib. ii. c. 10.

[387:4] See Kaye's "Tertullian," p. 196. See also Warburton's "Divine Legation of Moses," i. 510. Edit. London, 1837.

[387:5] "Adversus Hermogenem," c. 35, and "Adversus Praxeam," c. 7.

[389:1] In 1842, Archdeacon Tattam, who had returned only about three years before from Egypt, where he had been searching for ancient manuscripts, set out a second time to that country, under the auspices of the Trustees of the British Museum, chiefly for the purpose of endeavouring to procure copies of the Ignatian epistles. On this occasion he succeeded in obtaining possession of the Syriac copy of the three letters published by Dr. Cureton in 1845. Shortly before the Revolution of 1688, Robert Huntingdon, afterwards Bishop of Raphoe, and then chaplain to the British merchants at Aleppo, twice undertook a voyage to Egypt in quest of copies of the Ignatian epistles. On one of these occasions he visited the monastery in the Nitrian desert in which the letters were recently found.

[390:1] Of the writers who have taken a prominent part in the Ignatian controversy we may particularly mention Ussher, Vossius, Hammond, Daillé, Pearson, Larroque, Rothe, Baur, Cureton, Hefele, and Bunsen.

[390:2] Matt, xviii. 2-4; Mark ix. 36.

[390:3] There has been a keen controversy respecting the accentuation of [Greek: Theophoros]. Those who place the accent on the antepenult ([Greek: Theó'phoros]) give it the meaning mentioned in the test; whilst others, placing the accent on the penult ([Greek: Theophó'ros]), understand by it God-bearing, the explanation given in the "Acts of the Martyrdom of Ignatius." See Daillé, "De Scriptis quae sub Dionysii Areop. et Ignatii Antioch. nom. circumferuntur," lib. ii. c. 25; and Pearson's "Vindiciae Ignatianae," pars. sec. cap. xii.

[391:1] Cave reckons that at the time of his martyrdom he was probably "above fourscore years old." See his "Life of Ignatius."

[391:2] See Period II. sec. in. chap. v. Evodius is commonly represented as the first bishop of Antioch.

[392:1] "Fuerunt alii similis amentiae: quos, quia cives Romani erant, annotavi in Urbem remittendos."—Plinii, Epist. lib. x. epist. 96.

[392:2] The Greek says the ninth, and the Latin the fourth year. According to both, the condemnation took place early in the reign of Trajan. See also the first sentence of the "Acts." In his translation of these "Acts," Wake, regardless of this statement, and in opposition to all manuscript authority, represents the sentence as pronounced "in the nineteenth year" of Trajan.

[392:3] See Jacobson's "Patres Apostolici," ii. p. 504. See also Greswell's "Dissertations," vol. iv. p. 422. It is evident that the date in the "Acts" cannot be the mistake of a transcriber, for in the same document the martyrdom is said to have occurred when Sura and Synecius were consuls. These, as Greswell observes, were actually consuls "in the ninth of Trajan." Greswell's "Dissertations," iv. p. 416. Hefele, however, has attempted to show that Trajan was really in Antioch about this time. See his "Pat. Apost. Opera Prolegomena," p. 35. Edit. Tubingen, 1842.

[393:1] "Acts of his Martyrdom," § 8.

[393:2] He is said, when at Smyrna, to have been visited by a deputation from the Magnesians. But had notice been sent to them as soon as he arrived at Smyrna, the messenger would have required three days to perform the journey; and had the Magnesians set out instantaneously, they must have occupied three days more in travelling to him. Thus, notwithstanding all the precipitation with which he was hurried along, he could scarcely have been less than a week in Smyrna. See "Corpus Ignatianum," pp. 326, 327.

[394:1] "He was pressed by the soldiers to hasten to the public spectacles at great Rome." "And the wind continuing favourable to us, in one day and night we were hurried on."—Acts of his Martyrdom, § 10, 11.

[394:2] Philadelphia is distant from Troas about two hundred miles. "Corpus Ignatianum," pp. 331, 332. Here, then, is another difficulty connected with this hasty journey. How could a deputation from Philadelphia meet Ignatius in Troas, as some allege they did, if he did not stop a considerable time there? See other difficulties suggested by Dr Cureton. "Cor. Ignat." p. 332.

[395:1] Such is the opinion maintained by the celebrated Whiston in his "Primitive Christianity." More recently Meier took up nearly the same position.

[395:2] See Preface to the "Corpus Ignatianum," p. 4.

[395:3] Published in 1849. In 1846 he published his "Vindiciae Ignatianae; or the Genuine Writings of St Ignatius, as exhibited in the ancient Syriac version, vindicated from the charge of heresy."

[396:1] In 1847 another copy of the Syriac version of the three epistles was deposited in the British Museum, and since, Sir Henry Rawlinson is said to have obtained a third copy at Bagdad. See "British Quarterly" for October 1855, p. 452.

[396:2] Dr Lee, late Regius Professor of Hebrew in Cambridge, Chevalier Bunsen, and other scholars of great eminence, have espoused the views of Dr Cureton.

[396:3] By Archbishop Ussher in 1644, and by Vossius in 1646.

[396:4] Such was the opinion of Ussher himself. "Concludimus ... nullas omni ex parte sinceras esse habendas et genuinas." Dissertation prefixed to his edition of "Polycarp and Ignatius," chap. 18.

[397:1] Pearson was occupied six years in the preparation of this work. The publication of Daillé, to which it was a reply, appeared in 1666. Daillé died in 1670, at the advanced age of seventy-six. The work of Pearson did not appear until two years afterwards, or in 1672. The year following he received the bishopric of Chester as his reward.

[397:2] "In the whole course of my inquiry respecting the Ignatian Epistles," says Dr Cureton, "I have never met with one person who professes to have read Bishop Pearson's celebrated book; but I was informed by one of the most learned and eminent of the present bench of bishops, that Porson, after having perused the 'Vindiciae,' had expressed to him his opinion that it was a 'very unsatisfactory work.'"—Corpus Ignat., Preface, pp. 14, 15, note. Bishop Pearson's work is written in Latin.

[397:3] The "Three Epistles" edited by Dr Cureton contain only about the one-fourth of the matter of the seven shorter letters edited by Ussher.

[398:1] Dr Cureton has shewn that even the learned Jerome must have known very little of these letters. "Corpus Ignat.", Introd. p. 67.

[398:2] Euseb. iii. c. 36.

[399:1] Euseb. i. c. 13.

[399:2] "Corpus Ignatianum," Introd. p. 71.

[399:3] Proleg. in "Cantic. Canticorum," and Homil. vi. in "Lucam."

[399:4] In the Epistle to the Romans, and the Epistle to the Ephesians.

[399:5] He quotes the words—"I am not an incorporeal demon," from the "Doctrine of Peter;" but they are found in the shorter recension of the seven letters in the "Epistle to the Smyrnaeans," § 3. Had this epistle been known to him, he would certainly have quoted from an apostolic father rather than from a work which he knew to be spurious. See Origen, "Opera," i. p. 49, note.

[400:1] "Opera," ii. 20, 21; iii. 271.

[400:2] See Period II. sec. ii. chap. i. p. 367. Origen, "Opera," iv. 473.

[400:3] Ibid. p. 368.

[400:4] "Opera," i. 79; iv. 683.

[400:5] "Contra Haereses," lib. v. c. 28, § 4. "Quidam de nostris dixit, propter martyrium in Deum adjudicatus ad bestias: Quoniam frumentum sum Christi, et per dentes bestiarum molor, ut mundus panis Dei inveniar."

[401:1] Thus he speaks of "Saturninus, who was from Antioch." "Contra Haereses," lib. i. c. 24, § 1.

[401:2] It seems to have been soon translated into Syriac. See Bunsen's "Hippolytus," iv. Preface, p. 8.

[401:3] See large extracts from this letter in Euseb. v. c. i. Also Routh's "Reliquiae," i. 329.

[402:1] Irenaeus, "Contra Haereses," lib. iii. c. 2, § 1, 2.

[402:2] Lib. iii. c. 3, § 3.

[402:3] Lib. iii. c. iii. § 4.

[402:4] Lib. v. c. xxxiii. § 3, 4.

[402:5] Lib. iv. c. vi. § 2.

[402:6] In his "Vindiciae," (Pars. i. cap. 6,) Pearson attempts to parry this argument by urging that Irenaeus does not mention other writers, such as Barnabas, Quadratus, Aristidus, Athenagoras, and Theophilus. But the reply is obvious—1. These writers were occupied chiefly in defending Christianity against the attacks of paganism, so that testimonies against heresy could not be expected in their works. 2. None of them were so early as Ignatius, so that their testimony, even could it have been obtained, would have been of less value. Some of them, such as Theophilus, were the contemporaries of Irenaeus. 3. None of them held such an important position in the Church as Ignatius.

[403:1] He was martyred A.D. 167, at the age of eighty-six. According to the Acts of his Martyrdom, Ignatius was martyred sixty years before, or A.D. 107. Polycarp must, therefore, have been now about twenty-six. See more particularly Period II. sec. ii. chap. v. note.

[403:2] Sec. 4.

[403:3] Secs. 5, 6.

[403:4] Sec. 11.

[403:5] Sec. 3.

[404:1] [Greek: ou monon en tois makariois Ignatiô, kai Zôsimô, kai Rouphô, alla kai en allois tois ex humôn].—§ 9.

[404:2] See Baronius, "Annal. ad Annum." 109, tom. ii. c. 48, and Jacobson's "Pat. Apost." ii. 482, note 6. Edit. Oxon., 1838.

[405:1] Epist. xxxiv. p. 109.

[405:2] "Scripsistis mihi, et vos et Ignatius, ut si quis vadit ad Syriam, deferat literas meas quas fecero ad vos." The Greek of Eusebius is somewhat different, but may express the same sense. See Euseb. iii. 36. There is an important variation even in the readings of Eusebius. See Cotelerius, vol. ii. p. 191, note 3.

[405:3] Thus Bunsen, in his "Ignatius von Antiochen und seine Zeit," says—"At the present stand-point of the criticism of Ignatius, this passage can only be a witness against itself." And, again—"The forger of Ignatius has interpolated this passage." And, again—"The connexion is entirely broken by that interpolation." (Pp. 108, 109.) Viewed as a postscript, it is not remarkable that the transition should be somewhat abrupt.

[405:4] "Et de ipso Ignatio, et de his qui cum eo sunt, quod certius agnoveritis, significate."

[406:1] See the "Acts of his Martyrdom," § 10, 12.

[406:2] See this "Epistle," § 1, 9.

[406:3] "Epistolas sane Ignatii, quae transmissae sunt vobis ab eo, et alias, quantascunque apud nos habuimus, transmisimus vobis." According to the Greek of Eusebius we should read "The letters of Ignatius which were sent to us ([Greek: hêmin]) by him." Either reading is alike perplexing to the advocates of the Syriac version of the Ignatian epistles. See Jacobson, ii. 489, not. 5.

[406:4] See a preceding note, p. 405.

[407:1] It would seem that only two Greek copies are known to exist, both wanting the concluding part. See Cotelerius, vol. ii. p. 186, note 1.

[407:2] It is not easy to understand the meaning of the passage—"Si habuerimus tempus opportunum, sive ego, seu legatus quem misero pro vobis." Some words seem to be wanting to complete the sense.

[407:3] [Greek: Smurnan] for [Greek: Surian]. In the beginning of the Epistle from Smyrna concerning Polycarp's martyrdom, the Church is said to be— [Greek: hê paroikousa Smurnan.] The very same mistake has been made in another case. Thus, in an extract published by Dr Cureton from a Syriac work, Polycarp is called Bishop in Syria, instead of in Smyrna. See "Corpus Ignatianum," p. 220, line 5 from the foot. Such mistakes in manuscripts are of very frequent occurrence. See "Corpus Ignatianum," pp. 278, 300. A more extraordinary blunder, which long confounded the critics, has been recently corrected by Dr Wordsworth. See his "St. Hippolytus," pp. 318, 319, Appendix.

[409:1] Pearson alleges that the reason why Tertullian does not quote Ignatius against the heretics was because he did not require his testimony! He had, forsooth, apostolic evidence. "Quasi vero Ignatii testimonio opus esset ad eam rem, cujus testem Apostolum habuit." "Vindiciae," Pars. prima, caput. xi. He finds it convenient, however, to mention Hermas, Clement of Rome, Justin Martyr, and many others.

[409:2] See also in Euseb. v. 28, a long extract from a work against the heresy of Artemon in which various early writers, who asserted that "Christ is God and man," are named, and Ignatius omitted.

[409:3] See Neander's "General History," by Torrey, i. 455. Octavo Edition Edinburgh, 1847. See also Kaye's "Tertullian," p. 415.

[409:4] The number of spurious writings which appeared in the early ages was very great. Shortly after the date mentioned in the text it is well known that an individual named Leucius forged the Acts of John, Andrew, Peter, and others. See Jones on the "Canon," p. 210, and ii. p. 289.

[410:1] This is a literal translation of part of the superscription of the letter as given by Dr Cureton himself in his "Epistles of Saint Ignatius," p. 17. In the "Corpus Ignatianum" he has somewhat weakened the strength of the expression by a more free translation—"To her who presideth in the place of the country of the Romans." "Corp. Ignat." p. 230. Tertullian speaks ("De Praescrip." c. 36) of the "Apostolic sees presiding over their own places"—referring to an arrangement then recently made which recognised the precedence of Churches to which Apostles had ministered. This arrangement, which was unknown in the time of Ignatius, was suggested by the disturbances and divisions created by the heretics. Though the words in the text may be quoted in support of the claims of the bishop of Rome, they do not necessarily imply his presidency over all Churches, but they plainly acknowledge his position as at the head of the Churches of Italy.

[411:1] See Euseb. iii. 36.

[411:2] See preceding note, p. 406.

[411:3] "Corpus Ignatianum," Intro, p. 86, note.

[412:1] See "Corpus Ignatianum," pp. 265, 267, 269, 271, 286.

[412:2] See Blunt's "Right Use of the Early Fathers." First Series. Lectures v. and vi.

[414:1] It would be very unfair to follow up this comparison by speaking of the Trustees of the British Museum, as the representatives of hierarchical pride and

352

power, proceeding, like Tarquin at the instigation of his augurs, to give a high price for the manuscripts. We believe that these gentlemen have rendered good service to the cause of truth and literature by the purchase.

[414:2] Bunsen rather reluctantly admits that the highest literary authority of the present century, the late Dr Neander, declined to recognise even the Syriac version of the Ignatian Epistles. See "Hippolytus and his Age," iv. Preface, p. 26.

[415:1] See "Corpus Ignat." Introd. p. 51.

[416:1] Thus, in his "Epistle to the Corinthians," Clemens Romanus, on one occasion, (§ 16,) quotes the whole of the 53d chapter of Isaiah; and, on another, (§ 18,) the whole of the 51st Psalm, with the exception of the last two verses.

[416:2] How different from the course pursued by Clement of Rome and by Polycarp! Thus, Clement says to the Corinthians—"Let us do as it is written," and then goes on to quote several passages of Scripture. § 13. Polycarp says—"I trust that ye are well exercised in the Holy Scriptures" and then proceeds, like Clement, to make some quotations. § 12.

[416:3] Phil. iii. 3.

[416:4] Eph. vi. 17.

[416:5] Heb. xii. 1, 2.

[416:6] "Epistle to Polycarp." Lest the plain English reader should believe that the folly of the original is exaggerated in the translation, I beg to say that, here and elsewhere, the English version of Dr Cureton is given word for word.

[417:1] Sec. 8.

[417:2] See Period II. sec. ii. chap. ii. p. 403.

[417:3] Epistle to Philemon, 10.

[418:1] See Daillé, lib. ii. c. 13. p. 316.

[418:2] According to some accounts, Timothy presided over the Church of Ephesus until nearly the close of the first century, when he was succeeded by Gaius. See Daillé, ii. c. 13. Some attempt to get over the difficulty by alleging that there was a second Onesimus in Ephesus, who succeeded Gaius, but of this there is no evidence whatever. The writer who thought that Ignatius had been at school with Polycarp, also believed, and with greater reason, that he was contemporary with the Onesimus of the New Testament.

[418:3] "Epistle to the Romans."

[419:1] Euseb. v. 21.

[419:2] See Period II. sec. i. chap. v. p. 354.

[419:3] Paul was certainly at Rome before Peter, and according to the reading of some copies of Irenaeus, in the celebrated passage, lib. iii. c. 3. § 2, the Church of Rome is said to have been founded by "Paul and Peter" (see Stieren's "Irenaeus," i. 428); but Ignatius here uses the style of expression current in the third century, and speaks of "Peter and Paul."

[419:4] In the Epistle to Polycarp, Ignatius says, "If a man be able in strength to continue in chastity, (i.e. celibacy,) for the honour of the body of our Lord, let him continue without boasting." Here the word in the Greek is [Greek: hagneia]. But this word is applied in the New Testament to Timothy, who may have been "the husband of one wife." See 1 Tim. iv, 12, and v. 2. It is also applied by Polycarp, in his Epistle, to married women. "Let us teach your (or our) wives to walk in the faith that is given to them, both in love and purity" ([Greek: agapê kai hagneia]).—Epistle to the Philippians, § 4. See also "The Shepherd of Hermas," book ii. command. 4; Cotelerius, i. 87.

[420:1] This is very evident from the recently discovered work of Hippolytus, as well as from other writers of the same period. See Bunsen's "Hippolytus," i. p. 312.

[420:2] Euseb. vii. 30.

[420:3] Some have supposed that this was the church of Antioch, but it is not likely that Paul would have cared to retain the church when deserted by the people. Besides, the building is called, not the church, but "the house of the Church" ([Greek: tês ekklêsias oikos]).

[420:4] If the reading adopted by Junius, and others, of a passage in the 4th chapter of his Epistle be correct, Polycarp must have been a married man, and probably had a family. "Let us teach our wives to walk in the faith that is given to them, both in love and purity,.... and to bring up their children in the instruction and fear of the Lord." See Jacobson's "Pat. Apost." ii. 472, note.

[421:1] Period II. sec. iii. chap. vii.

[421:2] See his "Epistle to the Corinthians," c. 42, 44, 47, 54.

[421:3] See Westcott on the "Canon," pp. 262, 264, 265.

[421:4] "In the estimation of those able and apostolical men who, in the second century, prepared the Syriac version of the New Testament for the use of some of the Oriental Churches, the bishop and presbyter of the apostolic ordination were titles of the same individual. Hence in texts wherein the Greek word episcopos, 'bishop,' occurs, it is rendered in their version by the Syriac word 'Kashisha,' presbyter."—Etheridge's Syrian Churches and Gospels, pp. 102, 103.

[421:5] The use of the word catholic in the "Seven Epistles," edited by Ussher, is sufficient to discredit them. See "Epist. to Smyrnaeans," § 8. The word did not come into use until towards the close of the second century. See Period II. sec. iii, chap. viii., and p. 337, note.

[422:1] "Epistle to the Ephesians."

[422:2] Daillé has well observed—"Funi Dei quidem verbum, ministerium, beneficia non inepte comparaveris; Spiritum vero, qui his, ut sic dicam, divinae benignitatis funiculis, ad nos movendos et attrahendos utitur, ipsi illi quo utitur, funi comparare, ab omni ratione alienum est."—Lib. ii. c. 27, pp. 409, 410.

[422:3] Col. ii. 18.

[423:1] "Epistle to the Ephesians."

[423:2] Matt. xxvi. 39.

[423:3] John xxi. 18.

[423:4] 2 Tim. iv. 17.

[424:1] We have here an additional and very clear proof that Polycarp, in his Epistle, is not referring to Ignatius of Antioch. Instead of pronouncing the letters now current as treating "of faith and patience, and of all things that pertain to edification," he would have condemned them as specimens of folly, impatience, and presumption. Dr Cureton seems to think that, because Ignatius was an old man, he was at liberty to throw away his life ("Corp. Ignat." p. 321); but Polycarp was still older, and he thought differently.

[424:2] Sec. 4.

[424:3] See "Corpus Ignatianum," p. 253.

[424:4] The reader is to understand that all the extracts given in the text are from the Syriac version of the "Three Epistles."

[425:1] "Epistle to the Ephesians."

[425:2] "Epistle to the Romans." Pearson can see nothing but the perfection of piety in all this. "In quibus nihil putidum, nihil odiosum, nihil inscitè aut imprudenter scriptum est." ... "Omnia cum pia, legitima, praeclara."—Vindiciae, pars secunda, c. ix.

[425:3] From A.D. 208 to A.D. 258.

[425:4] Thus in the "Acts of Paul and Thecla," fabricated about the beginning of the third century, Thecla says—"Give me the seal of Christ, (i.e. baptism,) and no temptation shall touch me," (c. 18.) See Jones on the "Canon of the New Testament," ii. p. 312.

[426:1] "Epistle to Polycarp."

[426:2] 1 Cor. xiii. 3.

[426:3] See Blunt's "Early Fathers," p. 237. See also Origen's "Exhortation to Martyrdom," § 27, 30, 50.

[426:4] According to Dr Lee, a strenuous advocate for the Syriac version of the "Three Epistles," this translation, as he supposes it to be, was made "not later perhaps than the close of the second, or beginning of the third century." "Corpus Ignat." Introd. p. 86, note. Dr Cureton occasionally supplies strong presumptive evidence that the translation has been made, not from Greek into Syriac, but from Syriac into Greek. "Cor. Ignat." p. 278.

[426:5] Though Milner, in his "History of the Church of Christ," quotes these letters so freely, he seems to have scarcely turned his attention to the controversy respecting them. Hence he intimates that Ussher reckoned seven of them genuine, though it is notorious that the Primate of Armagh rejected the Epistle to Polycarp. (See Milner, cent. ii. chap, i.) Others, as well as Milner, who have written respecting these Epistles, have committed similar mistakes. Thus, Dr Elrington, Regius Professor of Divinity in Trinity College, Dublin, the recent editor of "Ussher's Works," when referring to the Primate's share in this controversy, speaks of "the recent discovery of a Syriac version of four Epistles by Mr Cureton!" "Life of Ussher," p. 235, note.

[428:1] "Instit." lib. i. c. xiii. § 29.

[429:1] See Bunsen's "Hippolytus," i. p. 27.

[430:1] Period I. sec. ii. chap, iii. pp. 202, 203.

[430:2] See Tertullian, "Adversus Hermogenem," c. x. and iv.

[430:3] [Greek: gnôsis].

[431:1] Ps. cxiii. 6.

[431:2] See Tertullian, "Adversus Marcionem," lib. i. c. 2. About this time many works were written on the subject. Eusebius mentions a publication by Irenaeus, "On Sovereignty, or on the Truth that God is not the Author of Evil," and another by Maximus on "The Origin of Evil." Euseb. v. 20, 27.

[431:3] Irenaeus, "Contra Haeres." lib. i. c. 24, § 7.

[433:1] Irenaeus, lib. i. c. 24. According to Clemens Alexandrinus, Basilides flourished in the reigns of Hadrian and Antoninus Pius. "Stromata," lib. vii. Opera, p. 764.

[433:2] [Greek: Buthos kai ennoia, nous kai alêtheia, logos kai zôê].

[433:3] According to some, Valentine was the disciple of Marcion. Clemens Alexandrinus states that Marcion was his senior. "Strom." lib. viii. Tertullian says expressly that Valentine was at one time the disciple of Marcion. "De Carne Christi," c. 1.

[434:1] See Neander's "General History," by Torrey, ii. pp. 171, 174, notes.

[434:2] See Kaye's "Clement of Alexandria," pp. 316, 317.

[435:1] The Ophites carried this feeling so far as to maintain that the serpent which deceived Eve was no other than the divine Aeon Sophia, or Wisdom, who thus weakened the power of Ialdabaoth, or the Demiurge.

[435:2] See Mosheim, "De Caussis Suppositorum Librorum inter Christianos Saeculi Primi et Secundi." "Dissert, ad Hist. Eccl. Pertin." vol. i. 221.

[437:1] His great text was Rev. xx. 6, 7. Hence some now began to dispute the authority of the Apocalypse.

[437:2] Others, who do not appear to have been connected with Montanus, but who lived about the same time, held the same views on the subject of marriage. Thus, Athenagoras says—"A second marriage is by us esteemed a specious adultery."—Apology, § 33.

[437:3] "Nam idem (Praxeas) tunc Episcopum Romanum, agnoscentem jam prophetias Montani, Priseae, Maximillae, et ex ea agnitione pacem ecclesiis Asiae et Phrygiae inferentem, falsa de ipsis prophetis et ecclesiis eorum adseverando et praecessorum ejus auctoritates defendendo coegit et litteras pacis revocare jam emissas et a proposito recipiendorum charismatum concessare."—Tertullian, Adv. Praxean., c. i.

[438:1] Euseb. v. 16.

[438:2] It would appear, however, that it maintained a lingering existence for several centuries. Even Justinian, about A.D. 530, enacts laws against the Montanists or Tertullianists.

[438:3] Isaiah xlv. 5, 7.

[439:1] Augustin, "Contra Epist. Fundamenti," c. 13.

[439:2] On the ground that their oil is the food of light! Schaff's "History of the Christian Church," p. 249.

[441:1] We find Tertullian, after he became a Montanist, dwelling on the distinction of venial and mortal sins. See Kaye's "Tertullian," pp. 255, 339.

[441:2] Rom. vi. 23.

[442:1] 1 Thess. v. 22.

[442:2] James i. 15.

[442:3] See Cudworth's "Intellectual System," with Notes by Mosheim, iii. p. 297. Edition, London, 1845.

[442:4] See Hagenbach's "History of Doctrines," i. p. 218.

[442:5] See Kaye's "Tertullian," p. 348.

[442:6] The doctrine of Purgatory, as now held, was not, however, fully recognised until the time of Gregory the Great, or the beginning of the seventh century.

[443:1] See Mosheim's "Institutes," by Soames, i. 166.

[443:2] Marcion, it appears, declined to baptize those who were married. "Non tinguitur apud illum caro, nisi virgo, nisi vidua, nisi caelebs, nisi divortio baptisma mercata."—Tertullian, Adver. Marcionem, lib. i. c. 29.

[443:3] See Neander's "General History," ii. 253.

[443:4] In the "Westminster Review" for October 1856, there is an article on Buddhism, written, indeed, in the anti-evangelical spirit of that periodical, but containing withal much curious and important information.

[444:1] Col. ii. 23.

[446:1] The most remarkable instance of this is the condemnation of the word [Greek: homoousios], as applied to our Lord, by the Synod of Antioch in A.D. 269. It is well known that the very same word was adopted in A.D. 325, by the

Council of Nice as the symbol of orthodoxy; and yet these two ecclesiastical assemblies held the same views. See also, as to the application of the word [Greek: hupostauis], Burton's "Ante-Nicene Testimonies," p. 129.

[446:2] "The inference to be drawn from a comparison of different passages scattered through Tertullian's writings is, that the Apostle's Creed in its present form was not known to him as a summary of faith; but that the various clauses of which it is composed were generally received as articles of faith by orthodox Christians."—Kaye's Tertullian, p. 324.

[446:3] These may be found in Routh's "Reliquiae." Eusebius has preserved many of them.

[447:1] "Si quis legat Scripturas.....et erit consummatus discipulus, et similis patrifamilias, qui de thesauro suo profert nova et vetera."—Irenaeus, iv. c. 26, § i.

[447:2] "Ubi fomenta fidei de scripturarum interjectione?"—Tertullian, Ad Uxorem, lib. ii. c. 6.

[447:3] As in the case of Origen. In the Didascalia we meet with the following directions—"Teach then your children the word of the Lord..... Teach them to write, and to read the Holy Scriptures." —Ethiopic Didascalia, by Platt, p. 130.

[447:4] Euseb. viii. c. 13.

[448:1] Clemens Alexandrinus, "Stromata," lib. vii.

[448:2] Homil. xxxix. on Jer. xliv. 22.

[448:3] Period I. sec. ii. chap. i. p. 184.

[448:4] The fathers traced analogies between the four Gospels and the four cardinal points, the living creatures with four faces, and the four rivers of Paradise. See Irenaeus, lib. iii. c. xi. § 8; and Cyprian, Epist. lxxiii., Opera, p. 281.

[449:1] Such as the Epistle of Barnabas and the Shepherd of Hermas.

[449:2] See Westcott on the Canon, pp. 452, 453.

[449:3] "The opinion that falsehood, was allowable, and might even be necessary to guide the multitude, was," says Neander, "a principle inbred into the aristocratic spirit of the old world."—General History, ii. p. 72.

[449:4] Such as the numerous works ascribed to Clemens Romanus, and the Ignatian Epistles.

[450:1] Cyprian, Epist. lxxiv. p. 294.

[450:2] Cyprian, Epist. lxxiv. p. 296.

[450:3] Cyprian, Epist. lxxiv. p. 294.

[450:4] The conflicting traditions relative to the time of keeping the Paschal feast afford a striking illustration of this fact.

[450:5] See Kaye's "Justin Martyr," p. 75.

[450:6] "Originis vitium." "Malum igitur animae.... ex originis vitio antecedit."—De Anima, c. 41. Cyprian calls it "contagio antiqua." "Innovati Spiritu Sancto a sordibus contagionis antiquae."—De Habitu Virginum, cap iv.

[450:7] "Per quem (Satanan) homo a primordio circumventus, ut praeceptum Dei excederet, et propterea in mortem datus exinde totum genus de suo semine infectum suae etiam damnationis traducem fecit."—De Testimonio Animae, c. iii.

[451:1] "Nothing can be less systematic or less organized than their notions on this subject; I might say, often even contradictory; such inconsistency partly, perhaps, arising from the point never having been canvassed by men with any care, as it eventually was by controversialists of a later day,... and partly from the embarrassment of their position; for whilst Scripture and self-experience compelled them to admit the grievous corruption of our nature, they had perpetually to contend against a powerful body of heretics, who made such corruption the ground for affirming that a world so evil could not have been created by a good God, but was the work of a Demiurgus" —Blunt's Early Fathers, pp. 585, 586.

[451:2] "Paedagogue," lib. i.

[451:3] See Kaye's "Clement," p. 432. See also the comments of Neander, "General History," ii. 388.

[451:4] Pliny's Epistle to Trajan.

[451:5] See various passages in Justin's Dialogue with Trypho, and in Origen against Celsus.

[452:1] Thus Origen says—"We do not pay the highest worship to Him who appeared so lately, as to a person who had no previous existence, for we believe Him when He says himself—'Before Abraham was, I am.'"—Contra Celsum, viii. § 12.

[452:1] The origin of this name has been much controverted. It is probable that it was derived from Ebion, the founder of the sect. See Period I. sect. ii. chap. iii. p. 206. Among other things the party seem to have inculcated voluntary poverty.

[452:3] This passage, which is somewhat obscure as it stands in the original, has been misinterpreted by Unitarian writers from generation to generation. The rendering which they commonly give of it makes it quite inconsistent with the context, and with the statements of Justin elsewhere. See Kaye's "Justin," p. 51.

[453:1] Thus Tertullian says, "The only man without sin is Christ, because Christ is also God."—De Anima, cap. xli. Justin Martyr complains that the Jews had expunged from the Septuagint many passages "wherein it might be clearly shewn that He who was crucified was both God and man."—Dialogue with Trypho, § 71.

[453:2] Euseb. v. 28.

[454:1] Euseb. v. 27, 30. Epiphanius, "Haer." 65, 1.

[454:2] The superscription of this epistle is a sufficient refutation of much of the reasoning of Mr Shepherd against the genuineness of the Cyprianic correspondence, as here the names of a crowd of bishops are given without any mention whatever of their sees.

[454:3] Euseb. vii. 30.

[454:4] [Greek: trias] or trinitas.

[454:5] This is, however, by no means clear, as there is nothing in his works to indicate that he held such a position.

[454:6] "Ad Autolycum," ii. c. 15. [Greek: tupoi eisin tes Triados].

[455:1] Thus Irenaeus says—"There is ever present with Him (the Father) the Word and Wisdom, the Son and Spirit."—Contra Haereses, iv. 20, § 1. It may here be proper to add that the early Christians worshipped the third Person of the Trinity. Thus, Hippolytus says—"Through Him (the Incarnate Word) we form a conception of the Father; we believe in the Son; we worship the Holy Ghost."—Contra Noetum, c. 12.

[455:2] "Legat. pro. Christianis," c. 10.

[455:3] "Legat. pro. Christ." c. 12.

[456:1] "Monarchiam, inquiunt, tenemus."—Tertullian, Adv. Praxean, c. 3.

[456:2] "Athanas de Synodis," c. 7.

[456:3] Hippolytus, "Philosophumena," book ix.

[456:4] He flourished about A.D. 220, and was contemporary with Hippolytus. See Bunsen, i. 131.

[457:1] Hermias speaks of the Trinity of Plato as "God, and matter, and example."—Sec. 5.

[457:2] "Doleo bona fide Platonem omnium haereticorum condimentarium factum. ... Cum igitur hujusmodi argumento illa insinuentur a Platone quae haeretici mutuantur, satis haereticos repercutiam, si argumentum Platonis elidam."—De Anima, c. 23.

[457:3] "Adversus Praxeam," c. 2, 3.

[458:1] "Paedagogue," book i. c. 5, 6, 11.

[458:2] Opera, p. 74.

[458:3] "Paedagogue," book i. c. 1.

[458:4] "Stromata," book ii.

[458:5] Justin, Opera, p. 500.

[459:1] See Kaye's "Clement," pp. 431, 435.

[459:2] Epist. i. ad Donatum, Opera, p. 3.

[459:3] The philosophers, according to Justin, maintained a general, but denied a particular providence. Dial, with Trypho, Opera, p. 218. Some who call themselves Christians adopt this portion of the pagan theology.

[460:1] "Non facti solum, verum et voluntatis delicta vitanda, et poenitentia purganda esse."—Tertullian, De Paenitentia, c. iii.

[460:2] "Hoc enim pretio Dominus veniam addicere instituit."—Tert. De Paenit. c. vi.

[460:3] Clemens Alexandrinus, "Strom." book vi.

[460:4] "Sufficiat martyri propria delicta purgasse."—Tertullian, De Pudicitia, c. 22.

[460:5] See Kaye's "Tertullian," p. 431. Origen speaks of the baptism of blood (martyrdom) rendering us purer than the baptism of water. Opera, ii. p. 473.

[460:6] Epist. lxxvi. Opera, p. 322.

[460:7] Epist. lv. p. 181.

[461:1] Ps. cxix 18, 19.

[463:1] See the Apology of Athenagoras, secs. 3, 10; and Minucius Felix, c. 10.

[463:2] "Nostrae columbae etiam domus simplex, in editis semper et apertis, et ad lucem."—Tertullian, Advers. Valent. c. 3.

[463:3] Life of Alexander Severus, by Lampridius, c. 49.

[464:1] See Kennett's "Antiquities of Rome," p. 41.

[464:2] Bingham has proved, by a variety of testimonies, that such was the order of the ancient service. See his "Origines," iv. 383, 400, 417. The early Christians thus literally obeyed the commandment—"Come before his presence with singing;" "Enter into his gates with thanksgiving, and into his courts with praise."—(Ps. c. 2, 4.).

[464:3] See 1 Cor. xiv. 26. See also Euseb. v. 28.

[464:4] At the end of his "Paedagogue." This hymn to the Saviour was composed by Clement himself.

[465:1] Euseb. vii. 30.

[465:2] See Bingham, i. p. 383. Edit. London, 1840.

[465:3] Chrysostom in Psalm cxlix. See Bingham, ii. 485.

[466:1] [Greek: hosê dunamis.] See Origen, "Contra Celsum," iii. 1 and 57; Opera, i. 447, 485.

[466:2] "Apol." ii. p. 98.

[466:3] "Suspicientes Christiani manibus expansis denique sine monitore, quia de pectore oramus."—Apol. c. 30. The omission of a single word, when repeating the heathen liturgy, was considered a great misfortune. Chevallier says, speaking of this expression sine monitore—"There is probably an allusion to the persons who were appointed, at the sacrifices of the Romans, to prompt the magistrates, lest they should incidentally omit a single word in the appropriate formulae, which would have vitiated the whole proceedings."—Translation of the Epistles of Clement, &c., p. 411, note.

[466:4] Opera, i. 267.

[466:5] See Minucius Felix.

[466:6] Tertullian, "De Oratione," c. 14.

[466:7] See Bingham, iv. 324. In prayer the Christians soon began to turn the face to the east. See Tertullian, "Apol." c. 16. This custom appears to have been borrowed from the Eastern nations who worshipped the sun. See Kaye's "Tertullian," p. 408.

[467:1] Thus Prideaux mentions how the Persian priests, long before the commencement of our era, approached the sacred fire "to read the daily offices of their Liturgy before it."—Connections, part i., book iv., vol. i. p. 218. This liturgy was composed by Zoroaster nearly five hundred years before Christ's birth.

[467:2] See Clarkson on "Liturgies," and Hartung, "Religion der Romer." It is remarkable that the old pagan Roman liturgy, in consequence of the change in the language from the time of its original establishment, began at length to be almost unintelligible to the people. It thus resembles the present Romish Liturgy. The pagans believed that their prayers were more successful when offered up in a barbarous and unknown language. See Potter's "Antiquities of Greece," i. 288. Edit. Edinburgh, 1818. The Lacedaemonians had a form of prayer from which they never varied either in public or private. Potter i. 281.

[467:3] "In the persecutions under Diocletian and his associates, though a strict inquiry was made after the books of Scripture, and other things belonging to the Church, which were often delivered up by the Traditores to be burnt, yet we never read of any ritual books, or books of divine service, delivered up among them."—Bingham, iv. 187.

[467:4] It is worthy of note that, in modern times, when there is any great revival of religion, forms of prayer fall into comparative desuetude even among those by whom they were formerly used.

[468:1] See Tertullian, "De Oratione," c. 9; and Origen, "De Oratione."

[468:2] 1 Tim. ii. 2.

[468:3] Tertullian, "Apol." c. 39.

[468:4] See Tertullian, "De Praescrip." c. 41.

[468:5] See Guerike's "Manual of the Antiquities of the Church," by Morrison, p. 214.

[468:6] Guerike's "Manual," p. 213.

[469:1] There is reference to this in the "Apostolic Constitutions," lib. ii. c. 57. Cotelerius, i. 266.

[469:2] Euseb. vii. 30.

[470:1] See Bingham, ii. 212.

[470:2] Letter from Pius of Rome to Justus of Vienne.

[470:3] Bingham, ii. 451.

[470:4] See Period II. sec. i. chap. iii. p. 320.

[472:1] See the "Epistle of the Church of Smyrna," giving an account of his martyrdom, § 9.

[472:2] The Latin version of his words, as given by Jacobson, is— "Octogesimum jam et sextum annum aetatis ingredior."—Pat. Apost. ii. 565. See also the "Chronicum Alexandrinum" as quoted by Cotelerius, ii. 194; and Gregory of Tours, "Hist." i. 28.

[472:3] He is represented as standing, when offering up a prayer of about two hours' length (§ 7), and as running with great speed (§ 8). Such strength at such an age was extraordinary. The Apostle John is said to have lived to the age of one hundred; but, towards the close of his life, he appears to have lost his wonted energy.

[472:4] "Apol." ii. Opera, p. 62. See Dr Wilson's observations on this passage in his "Infant Baptism," pp. 447, 448.

[473:1] Dialogue with Trypho. Opera, p. 261.

[473:2] There may here be a reference to 1 Cor. vii. 14.

[473:3] Book ii. c. xxii. § 4.

[473:4] Thus he says—"Giving to His disciples the power of regeneration unto God, He said to them—Go and teach all nations, baptizing them in the name of the Father, and of the Son, and of the Holy Ghost."—Book iii. c. xvii. § 1. Thus, too, he speaks of the heretics using certain rites "to the rejection of baptism, which is regeneration unto God."—Book i. c. xxi. § 1. Irenaeus here apparently means that baptism typically is regeneration, in the same way as the bread and wine in the Eucharist are typically the body and blood of Christ.

[474:1] That infant baptism was now practised at Alexandria is apparent also from the testimony of Clemens Alexandrinus, who, in allusion to this rite, speaks of "the children that are drawn up out of the water."—Paedag. iii. c. 11.

[474:2] Hom. xiv. in "Lucam." Opera, iii. 948. See also Opera, ii. 230. Hom. viii. in "Leviticum."

[474:3] Comment. in "Epist. ad Roman," lib. v. Opera, iv. 565.

[475:1] "De Baptismo," c. 18.

[475:2] Acts ii. 41.

[475:3] Acts viii. 37, 38; xvi. 31-33.

[476:1] "Parents were commonly sponsors for their own children ... and the extraordinary cases in which they were presented by others, were commonly such cases, where the parent could not, or would not, do that kind office for them; as when slaves were presented to baptism by their masters, or children whose parents were dead, were brought, by the charity of any who would shew mercy on them; or children exposed by their parents, which were sometimes taken up by the holy virgins of the Church, and by them presented unto baptism. These are the only cases mentioned by St Austin in which children seem to have had other sponsors."—Bingham, iii. 552.

[476:2] Mark x. 14.

[476:3] Compare Mark x. 13-16 with Luke xviii. 15, 16.

[477:1] See Acts xvi. 15.

[477:2] "De Baptismo," c. viii. xvi.

[477:3] "It would be thought by many a cruelty to place a person without his own consent, and in unconscious infancy, in a situation, so far, much more disadvantageous than that of those brought up pagans, that if he did ever—

suppose at the age of fifteen or twenty—fall into any sin, he must remain for the rest of his life—perhaps for above half a century—deprived of all hope, or at least of all confident hope, of restoration to the divine favour; shut out from all that cheering prospect which, if his baptism in infancy had been omitted, might have lain before him."—Archbishop Whately's Scripture Doctrine concerning the Sacraments, p. 11, note.

[478:1] Acts ii. 38, 39.

[478:2] Gen. xvii. 12; Lev. xii. 3.

[479:1] Epist. lix. pp. 211, 212.

[479:2] Laurentius, a Roman deacon, who flourished about the middle of the third century, is represented as baptizing one Romanus, a soldier, in a pitcher of water, and another individual, named Lucillus, by pouring water upon his head. See Bingham, iii. 599.

[480:1] Here the validity of the ordinance is made to depend upon the personal character of the administrator.

[480:2] Epist. lxxvi. p. 321.

[480:3] Epist. lxxiv. p. 295.

[480:4] Epist. lxxvi. p. 317. In like manner Clement of Alexandria says—"Our transgressions are remitted by one sovereign medicine, the baptism according to the Word." See Kaye's "Clement," p. 437.

[480:5] Epist. lxx. p. 269.

[480:6] Tertullian, "De Baptismo," c. 1.

[480:7] Cyprian, "Con. Carthag." pp. 600, 602.

[480:8] See Kaye's "Clement of Alexandria," p. 441, and Tertullian, "De Corona," c. 3.

[480:9] Tertullian, "De Baptismo," c. 7.

[480:10] Tertullian, "De Baptismo," c. 8.

[481:1] "De Resurrectione Carnis," c. 8.

[481:2] "In the name of the Father, and of the Son, and of the Holy Ghost."—Matt, xxviii. 19.

[481:3] Bingham, iii. 377.

[483:1] Rev. xxii. 18, 19.

[484:1] "Apol." ii. Opera, pp. 97, 98.

[485:1] In an article on the Roman Catacombs, in the "Edinburgh Review" for January 1859, the writer observes—"It is apparent from all the paintings of Christian feasts, whether of the Agapae, or the burial feasts of the dead, or the Communion of the Holy Sacrament, that they were celebrated by the early Christians sitting round a table."

[485:2] This calumny created much prejudice against them in the second century. See Justin Martyr's "Dialogue with Trypho," § 10; and the "Apology of Athenagoras," § 3. If Pliny refers to the Eucharist when he speaks of the early Christians as partaking of food together, it is obvious that they must then have communicated sitting, or in the posture in which they partook of their ordinary meals.

[485:3] Tertullian, "De Oratione," c. 14.

[485:4] See Euseb. vii. 9.

[485:5] Justin Martyr, "Apol." ii. 98; and Tertullian's "Apol." c. 39.

[486:1] Epist. lxiii. "To Caecilius," Opera, p. 229.

[486:2] Larroque's "History of the Eucharist," p. 35. London, 1684.

[486:3] Cyprian, "De Lapsis," Opera, pp. 375, 381. This was probably the result of carrying to excess a protest against the Montanist opposition to infant baptism. Such a reaction often occurs. It was now maintained that the Lord's Supper, as well as Baptism, should be administered to infants.

[486:4] At an earlier period it was dispensed in presence of the catechumens. See Bingham, iii. p. 380.

[486:5] "De Oratione Dominica," Opera, p. 421.

[487:1] See Kaye's "Tertullian," p. 357.

[487:2] See Gieseler's "Text Book of Ecclesiastical History," by Cunningham ii. 331, note 3.

[487:3] "Dialogue with Trypho," Opera, pp. 296, 297.

[487:4] See Kaye's "Clement of Alexandria," p. 445.

[487:5] [Greek: akeraioterôn], Opera, in. p. 498.

[488:1] In Mat. tom. xi. Opera, iii. 499, 500.

[488:2] Epist. lxiii. "To Caecilius," Opera, p. 225.

[488:3] Epist. lxiii. Opera, 228.

[488:4] Matt, xviii. 20.

[489:1] Irenaeus, "Contra Haereses," v. c. 2, § 3. Clement of Alexandria says that "to drink the blood of Jesus is to partake of the incorruption of the Lord."—Paedagogue, book ii.

[489:2] "Contra Haereses," iv. c. 18, § 5.

[489:3] This feeling prevailed in the time of Tertullian. "Calicis aut panis etiam nostri aliquid decuti in terram auxie patimur."—De Corona, c. 3.

[489:4] Hom. xiii. in "Exod." Opera, ii. 176.

[489:5] Ps. xii. 6.

[490:1] See Kaye's "Justin Martyr," p. 94. Irenaeus, iv. o. 17, § 5. Tertullian, "De Oratione," c. 14.

[490:2] "Nonne solemnior erit statio tua, si et ad aram Dei steteris?" Tertullian, "De Oratione," c. 14, or, according to Oehler, c. 19.

[491:1] Matt. iii. 5, 6.

[491:2] Acts xix. 17, 18.

[493:1] Acts xvi. 33.

[493:2] "Apol." ii. Opera, p. 93, 94.

[493:1] "De Paenitentia," c. ix.

[493:2] Joshua vii. 6; Esther iv. 1; Isaiah lviii. 5; Ezek. xxvii. 30.

[494:1] See a "Memorial concerning Personal and Family Fasting," by the pious Thomas Boston. Edinburgh, 1849.

[494:2] Matt. ix. 15.

[494:3] Lev. xxiii. 27.

[494:4] The text Matt. ix. 15 was urged in support of this observance. See Tertullian, "De Jejun." c. ii.

[494:5] "Wednesday being selected because on that day the Jews took counsel to destroy Christ, and Friday because that was the day of His crucifixion."—Kaye's Tertullian, p. 418. As Wednesday was dedicated to Mercury and Friday to Venus, this fasting, according to Clement, signified to the more advanced disciple, that he was to renounce the love of gain and the love of pleasure. Kaye's "Clement," p. 454.

[495:1] These Xerophagiae, or Dry Food Days, were even now objected to by some of the more enlightened Christians on the ground that they were an import from heathenism. Tertullian, "De Jejun." c. ii.

[495:2] Col. ii. 23.

[495:3] Thus Cyprian, Epist. liii. p. 169, speaks of a penance of three years' duration.

[496:1] Socrates, v. c. 19.

[497:1] See canon xi. of the Council of Nice.

[497:2] See Cyprian, Epist. xl., p. 53, and "ad Demetrianum," p. 442.

[497:3] See p. 419, note §.

[497:4] See p. 460.

[498:1] Rom. iii. 28.

[498:2] Matt. iii. 8.

[498:3] Isa. lviii. 6-8.

[499:1] Period II. sec. iii. chap. i. pp. 465, 466.

[499:2] 1 Tim. v. 17.

[500:1] Apost. Constit. ii. c. 17.

[500:2] Phil. iv. 3.

[500:3] No less than five persons are mentioned as having preceded Polycarp in the see of Smyrna, viz., Aristo, Strataeas, another Aristo, Apelles, and Bucolus. See Jacobson's "Patres Apostolici," ii. 564, 565, note. It is not at all probable that he became the senior presbyter long before the middle of the second century. Irenaeus, indeed, tells us that he was constituted bishop of Smyrna by the apostles (lib. iii. c. 3, § 4)—a statement which implies that at least two of the inspired heralds of the gospel were concerned in his designation to the ministry; but as he was still only a boy of nineteen when the last survivor of the twelve died in extreme old age, the words cannot mean that he was actually ordained by those to whom our Lord originally entrusted the organization of the Church. The language was probably designed simply to import that John and perhaps Philip had announced his future eminence when he was yet a child, and that thus, like Timothy, he was invested with the pastoral commission "according to the prophecies" which they had previously delivered. See 1 Tim. i. 18; iv. 14.

[501:1] Sec. 74.

[502:1] Sec. 54.

[502:2] Sec. 44.

[502:3] Sec. 44. All these quotations attest the late date of the Epistle. Tillemont places it in A.D. 97. Eusebius had evidently no doubt as to its late date. See his "History," iii. 16.

[502:4] Sec. 57.

[502:5] For many centuries it was considered lost. At length in the reign of Charles I. a copy of it was discovered appended to a very ancient manuscript containing the Septuagint and Greek Testament—the manuscript now known as the Codex Alexandrinus.

[502:6] Euseb. iii. 16; iv. 23.

[503:1] See the Romish Breviary under the 23d of November, where a number of absurd stories are told concerning him.

[503:2] Sec. 42.

[503:3] They continued to be so used when the Peshito version of the New Testament was made. That version is assigned by the best authorities to the former half of the second century. See p. 421, note.

[503:4] It is probably of nearly the same date as the first Apology of Justin Martyr.

364

[504:1] [Greek: hoi sun autoi presbuteroi]—evidently equivalent to [Greek: sumpresbuteroi]. See 1 Pet. v. i.

[504:2] Phil. i. 1.

[504:3] Sec. 5.

[504:4] Sec. 6.

[504:5] Jerome, "Comment. in Tit."

[504:6] 1 Cor. xiv. 40.

[505:1] As in Acts xiv. 23.

[505:2] I make no apology for employing a word which, even the Benedictine Editor of Origen has adopted. Thus he speaks of the "senatores et moderatores ecclesiae Dei."—Contra Celsum. iii. 30, Opera, i. 466.

[505:3] Such as Acts xxi. 18; Gal. ii. 12.

[506:1] "At Antioch some, as Origen and Eusebius, make Ignatius to succeed Peter. Jerome makes him the third bishop, and placeth Evodius before him. Others, therefore, to solve that, make them contemporary bishops; the one, of the Church of the Jews; the other, of the Gentiles.... Come we to Rome, and here the succession is as muddy as the Tiber itself; for here Tertullian, Rufinus, and several others, place Clement next to Peter. Irenaeus and Eusebius set Anacletus before him; Epiphanius and Optatus both Anacletus and Cletus; Augustinus and Damasus, with others, make Anacletus, Cletus, and Linus all to precede him. What way shall we find to extricate ourselves out of this labyrinth?"—Stillingfleet's Irenicum, part ii. ch. 7. p. 321.

[506:2] "Polycarp, and the elders who are with him, to the Church of God which is at Philippi."

[506:3] A Roman deacon of the fourth century. His works are commonly appended to those of Ambrose.

[507:1] "Primum presbyteri episcopi appellabantur, ut, recedente uno, sequens ei succederet."—Comment. in Eph. iv.

[507:2] "Ut omnis episcopus presbyter sit, non omnis presbyter episcopus; hic enim episcopus est, qui inter presbyteros primus est."—Comment. in 1 Tim. iii. According to a learned writer this arrangement extended farther. "Ita, uti videtur, comparatum fuit, ut defuncto presbytero, primus ordine diaconus locum occuparet ultimum presbyterorum, novusque in locum novissimum substitueretur diaconus; decedente vero episcopo, primus ordine presbyter in ejus locum sufficeretur, et primus in ordine diaconorum novissimam presbyterii sedem capesseret."—Thomae Brunonis Judicium de auctore Can. et Const. quae apost. dicuntur. Cotelerius, ii. Ap. p. 179.

[507:3] 1 Pet. v. 5. It is a curious and striking fact, arguing strongly in favour of the antiquity of their Church polity, that among the Vaudois Barbs of old the claims of seniority were distinctly acknowledged. The following rule of discipline is taken from one of their ancient MSS. "He that is received the last (into the ministry by imposition of hands) ought to do nothing without the permission of him that was received before him."—Moreland, History of the Evang. Ch. of the Valleys of Piedmont, p. 74.

[507:4] He is speaking immediately before of presbyters. See 1 Pet. v. 1-4.

[507:5] Matt. x. 2, "The first, Simon, who is called Peter." Mark iii. 16; Luke vi. 14; Acts i. 13.

[507:6] Jerome in "Jovin," i. 14.

[508:1] Savigny's "History of the Roman Law," by Cathcart, i. pp. 62, 63, 75.

[508:2] Euseb. iii. 23. [Greek: ho presbutês].

[508:3] In Africa the senior bishop or metropolitan was called father. See Bingham, i. 200. In the second century we find the name given to the Roman bishop. See Routh's "Reliquiae," i. 287. According to Eutychius, his predecessor in the see of Alexandria in the early part of the third century was called "Baba (Papa), that is, grandfather."

[509:1] Euseb. v. 1.

[509:2] He was one hundred and sixteen years of age in A.D. 212 (Euseb. vi. 11), so that in A.D. 196, or about the time of the Palestinian Synod at which he presided (Euseb. v. 23), he was a century old.

[509:3] Etheridge's "Syrian Churches," pp. 9, 10.

[509:4] See 1 Tim. iv. 12.

[509:5] That is, Anacletus, Evaristus, Alexander, Sixtus, Telesphorus, and Hyginus; but some consider Anacletus the same as Cletus, who is supposed to have died before Clement.

[510:1] Pearson has noticed this fact, and has endeavoured to erect upon it an argument against the current chronology. See his "Minor Works," ii. 527. It would appear that the names of the three bishops of Smyrna next after Polycarp were Thraseas, Papirius, and Camerius. At least two of these had passed away a considerable time before the Paschal controversy. See Greswell's "Dissertations," iv. part ii. p. 600, note.

[510:2] Hist. iv. 5.

[510:3] According to Eusebius his appointment took place after the destruction of Jerusalem, or about A.D. 71. He was, therefore, at the head of the Church forty-five years, as his martyrdom occurred in A.D. 116. According to this reckoning he was in his seventy-fifth year when made president.

[510:4] This explanation of the matter approximates to that given by Tillemont. "Cela peut etre venu de ce qu'on les choisissoit entre les plus agez du Clergé pour les faire Evesques: car on ne voit pas qu'ils ayent esté plus persecutez que d'autres."—Mém. pour servir à l'Histoire Ecclesiastique, tom. ii. part ii. p. 40. It would appear from Eusebius (iii. 32), that at the time of the death of Simeon there were still living a number of very old persons who were relatives of our Lord. Some of these were, probably, elders in the Church of Jerusalem.

[511:1] He is said in the "Chronicon" of Eusebius to have presided sixteen years.

[511:2] Euseb. v. 12.

[512:1] In the tenth century, the darkest and most revolting period in the history of the Popedom, there were twenty-four bishops of Rome. Some of these reigned only a few days; at least one of them was strangled; several of them died in prison; and several others were driven from the see or deposed. There have been only twenty-four Popes in the last two hundred and fifty years.

[512:2] There have been only twenty-eight Archbishops of Canterbury since 1454.

[512:3] In the middle of the third century we find Firmilian appealing to it as a witness against the Church of Home. Cyprian, Epist. lxxv. Opera, p. 303.

[512:4] "Hist." vi. 20.

[513:1] "Hist." iv. 5; v. 12.

[513:2] Such as, after the death of the aged Simeon, when Justus, at the age of fivescore and ten, was advanced to the presidential chair.

[514:1] Irenaeus, iii. 2. Tertullian, "De Praescrip. Haeret." § 25.

[514:2] "Ad eam iterum traditionem, quae est ab apostolis, quae per successiones presbyterorum in ecclesiis custoditur, provocamus eos."—Irenaeus, iii. 2.

[514:3] Irenaeus here speaks in the language of his own times, and refers to the presidents, or senior ministers, of the presbyteries. In like manner Hilary says that the change in the mode of appointing the president of the presbytery was made by the decision of many priests (multorum sacerdotum judicio), though the title priest was not given to a Christian minister when the alteration was originally proposed.

[514:4] Irenaeus, iii. 3.

[515:1] Period II. sec. i. chap. iv.; and Period II. sect. iii. chap. vii.

[515:2] According to a very ancient canon, no one under fifty years of age could be made a bishop. See Bunsen's "Hippolytus," iii. 56. Even in the time of Cyprian much stress was still laid upon age. See Cyprian, Epist. lii. p. 156.

[515:3] Sec Period II. sect. iii. chap. xi. See also Bingham, i. 198.

[515:4] Münter's "Primordia Ecclesiae Africanae," p. 49. See also Bingham, vi. 377-379.

[516:1] Bingham, i. 201.

[516:2] Binius, i. 5. Fourth Council of Toledo, canon 4.

[516:3] Bingham, i. 204.

[517:1] Bunsen dates it about A.D. 200. "Hippolytus and his Age," p. 114. The recently discovered treatise of Hippolytus against all heresies shews that Noetus must have appeared much earlier than most modern ecclesiastical historians have reckoned.

[517:2] Routh, "Scriptorum Ecclesiasticorum Opuscula," tom. i. pp. 49, 50. Oxon, 1858. This extract proves that the Church of Smyrna continued under presbyterial government long after the time of Polycarp. Other Churches about this time were in the same position. See Eusebius, v. 16.

[518:1] During the Paschal controversy the Churches of Jerusalem, Caesarea, and others sided with Rome, and then probably adopted her ecclesiastical regimen. It had, perhaps, been generally adopted in Asia Minor during the Montanist agitation.

[518:2] Chapter vii. of this section.

[519:1] The word catholic came now into use. The minister of the Word was called a priest, and the communion table, an altar.

[519:2] Euseb. v. 12.

[519:3] Euseb. vi. 10. The word [Greek: cheirotonian] here employed is indicative of a popular choice. See also the "Chronicon" of Eusebius.

[519:4] Münter's "Primordia Eccles. Afric.," pp. 25, 26.

[520:1] Acts x. 1, 45-48; xxi. 8.

[520:2] "Hist." v. 22.

[520:3] "Hist." v. 23; v. 25; vi. 19; vi. 23; vi. 46; vii. 14, &c, &c.

[520:4] "Annal." p. 332.

[520:5] See Lardner's Works, vii. 99. Edit. London, 1838.

[521:1] Eusebius, vi. 26. Towards the close of his episcopate Demetrius held several synods in Alexandria, at which a considerable number of bishops were present.

[523:1] It would appear that the "Ecclesiastical History" of Eusebius was published shortly after Constantine first publicly recognized Christianity. That event took place in A.D. 324, and with that year the history terminates.

[523:2] "Vita Malchi," Opera, iv. pp. 90, 91. Edit. Paris, 1706.

[524:1] "Antequam Diaboli instinctu, studia in religione fierent, et diceretur in populis, Ego sum Pauli, ego Apollo, ego autem Cephae, communi presbyterorum consilio ecclesiae gubernabantur. Postquam vero unusquisque eos quos baptizaverat suos putabat esse, non Christi, in toto orbe decretum est, ut unus de presbyteris, electus superponeretur caeteris, ad quem omnis ecclesiae cura pertineret, et schismatum semina tollerentur."—Comment. in Titum. The language here used bears a strong resemblance to that employed by Lactantius long before when treating of the same subject—"Multae haereses extiterunt, et instinctibus daemonum populus Dei scissus est."—Instit. Divin., lib. iv. c. 30.

[525:1] 1 Cor. i. 12.

[525:2] "Hic locus vel maxime adversum Haereticos facit qui pacis vinculo dissipato atque corrupto, putant se tenere Spiritus unitatem; quum unitas Spiritus in pacis vinculo conservetur. Quando enim non idipsum omnes loquimur, et alius dicit Ego sum Pauli, Ego Apollo, Ego Cephae, dividimus Spiritus unitatem, et eam in partes ac membra discerpimus."-Comment, in Ephes., lib. ii. cap. 4. Again, we find him saying-"Neonon et dissensiones opera carnis sunt, quum quis nequaquam perfectus, eodem sensu, et eadem sententia dicit. Ego sum Pauli, et ego Apollo, et ego Cephae, et ego Christi. ...Nonnumquam evenit, ut et in expositionibus Scripturarum oriatur dissensio, e quibus haereses quoque quae nunc in carnis opere ponuntur, ebulliunt."—Comment, in Epist. ad Galat., cap. 5.

[525:3] Philip, i. 1, 2.

[526:1] Acts xx. 17, 28.

[526:2] Our translators, as it would appear acting under instructions from James I., here render the word "overseers."

[526:3] The Church of Rome, of which Jerome was a presbyter, long hesitated to receive the Epistle to the Hebrews. Its opposition to ritualism seems, in the third and fourth centuries, to have been offensive to the ecclesiastical leaders in the Western metropolis. In the first century no such doubts respecting it existed among the Roman Christians. See Period I. sec. ii. chap. i. p. 183.

[526:4] Heb. xiii. 17. The reading of Jerome, here, as well as in the case of other texts quoted, differs somewhat from that of our authorized version. He seems to have often quoted from memory.

[527:1] 1 Pet. v. l, 2.

[527:2] It may suffice to give in the original only the conclusion of this long quotation. "Paulatim vero, ut dissensionum plantaria evellerentur, ad unum omnem solicitudinem esse delatam. Sicut ergo presbyteri sciunt se ex ecclesiae consuetudine ei qui sibi praepositus fuerit esse subjectos; ita episcopi noverint se magis consuetudine quam dispositionis dominicae veritate presbyteris esse majores."—Comment, in Titum.

[527:3] See Period I. sec. i. chap. 10. p. 157.

[527:4] Thus Dr Burton says that "the Epistles of St John were composed in the latter part of Domitian's reign."—Lectures, i. 382. Jerome was evidently of this opinion, for he says that, in his First Epistle, he refers to Cerinthus and Ebion, who appeared towards the close of the first century. "Jam tunc haereticorum semina pullularent Cerinthi, Ebionis, et caeterorum qui negant

368

Christum in carne venisse, quos et ipse in Epistola sua Antichristos vocat."—
Proleg. in Comment, super Matthaeum.

[528:1] 2 John 1.

[528:2] 3 John 1.

[528:3] Epist. ci. "Ad Evangelum."

[528:4] Period II. sec. iii. chap. 5. p. 500.

[528:5] Sec. 1.

[528:6] The reader may find the quotations in the preceding chapter, pp. 501, 502.

[528:7] Thus Milner says that "so far as one may judge by Clement's Epistle," the Church of Corinth, when the letter was written, had Church governors "only of two ranks," presbyters and deacons.—Hist. of the Church, cent. ii. chap. 1.

[528:8] As the letter supplies no trace whatever of the existence of a bishop in the Church to which it is addressed, Pearson is sadly puzzled by its testimony, and gravely advances the supposition that the bishop of Philippi must have been dead when Polycarp wrote! "Vindiciae Ignatianae," pars ii. cap. 13. Rothe is equally perplexed by the Epistle of Clement. He says that "in the whole Epistle there is never any reference to a bishop of the Corinthian community," and he admits that, when the letter was written, "the Corinthian community had no bishop at all;" but, to support his favourite theory, he contends, like Pearson, that the bishop of Corinth must also have been dead! "Die Anfange der Christlichen Kirche," pp. 403, 404. Strange that the bishop of Corinth and the bishop of Philippi both happened to be dead at the only time that their existence would have been of any historical value, and that no reference is made either to them or their successors!

[529:1] See Euseb. iv. c. 11.

[529:2] Euseb. in. 32, and iv. 22.

[529:3] Euseb. iii. 32. It was probably immediately after the election of Marcus, as bishop of Jerusalem, that Thebuthis became a heretic. See Euseb. iv. 22. About that time the sect of the Nazarenes originated.

[530:1] Origen, "Contra Celsum," iii. § 10, Opera, i. 453, 454.

[530:2] "Dialogue with Trypho," Opera, p. 253.

[530:3] "Contra Haeres." i. 27, § 1.

[530:4] "Strom." p. 764.

[530:5] Epist. lxxiv. Opera, p. 293. The ancient writers speak of all the early schismatics as heretics. Thus Novatian, though sound in the faith, is so described. Cyprian, Epist. lxxvi. p. 315. When, therefore, Jerome speaks of the early schismatics he obviously refers to the heretics. Irenaeus says of them—"Scindunt et separant unitatem ecclesiae."—Lib. iv. c. xxvi. § 2. In like manner Cyprian represents "heresies and schisms" as making their appearance after the apostolic age, and as inseparably connected. "Cum haereses et schismata postmodum nata sint, dum conventicula sibi diversa constituunt."—De Unitate Eccles., Opera, p. 400.

[531:1] The existence of heresy in Gaul in the second century is established by the fact that Irenaeus spent so much time in its refutation. Had he not been annoyed by it, he never would have thought of writing his treatise "Contra Haereses."

[531:2] Valentine himself seems to have been a presbyter. He at one time expected to be made bishop.

[532:1] Such is the statement of Hilary—"Immutata est ratio, prospiciente concilio, ut non ordo sed meritum crearet episcopum, multorum sacerdotum judicio constitutum, ne indignus temere usurparet, et esset multis scandalum."— Comment. in Eph. iv.

[532:2] See Period II. sec. i. chap. iv. pp. 333, 334, 349.

[533:1] At an early period, out of three elders nominated by the presbytery, one was chosen by lot; subsequently, out of three elders chosen by lot, one was elected by the people. See pp. 333, 349.

[533:2] "Collocatum."

[533:3] Epist. ci. "Ad Evangelum."

[534:1] A few passages of the letter may here be given in the original. "Manifestissime comprobatur eundem esse episcopum atque presbyterum.... Quod autem postea unus electus est, qui cicteris praeponeretur, in schismatic remedium factum est, ne unusquisque ad se trahens Christi ecclesiam rumperet. Nam et Alexandriae à Marco Evangelista usque ad Heraclam et Dionysium Episcopos, presbyteri semper unum ex se electum in excelsiori gradu collocatum episcopum nominabant."-Epist. ci. ad Evangelum.

[535:1] Matt. xx. 26, 27.

[535:2] The view here taken is sustained by the verdict of learned and candid episcopalians. "When elders were ordained by the apostles in every Church, through every city, to feed the flock of Christ, whereof the Holy Ghost had made them overseers: they, to the intent that they might the better do it by common counsel and consent, did use to assemble themselves and meet together. In the which meetings, for the more orderly handling and concluding of things pertaining to their charge, they chose one amongst them to be the president of their company and moderator of their actions."—The Judgment of Doctor Rainoldes touching the Original of Episcopacy more largely confirmed out of Antiquity, by James Ussher, Archbishop of Armagh. Ussher's Works, vii. p. 75.

[537:1] Pearson has endeavoured to destroy the credit of this chronology, and has urged against it the authority of the "Annals of Eutychius!" "De Successione prim. Rom. Episc." He had before laboured to prove that the testimony of these "Annals" is worthless. "Vindic. Ignat." pars i. c. xi.

[537:2] The chronology of Eusebius, as arranged by Bower in his "Lives of the Popes," stands thus:—

Evaristus, A.D. 100 to A.D. 109.
Alexander, A.D. 109 to A.D. 119.
Sixtus (or Xystus), A.D. 119 to A.D. 128.
Telesphorus, A.D. 128 to A.D. 139.
Hyginus, A.D. 139 to A.D. 142.
Pius, A.D. 142 to A.D. 157.
Anicetus, A.D. 157 to A.D. 168.
Soter, A.D. 168 to A.D. 176.
Eleutherius, A.D. 176 to A.D. 192.
Victor, A.D. 192 to A.D. 201.

[538:1] The following is the chronology of Pearson:—

Clement died A.D. 83.
Evaristus, A.D. 83 to A.D. 91.

370

Alexander, A.D. 91 to A.D. 101.
Xystus, A.D. 101 to A.D. 111.
Telesphorus, A.D. 111 to A.D. 122.
Hyginus, A.D. 122 to A.D. 126.
Pius, A.D. 127 to A.D. 142.
Anicetus, A.D. 142 to A.D. 161.
Soter, A.D. 161 to A.D. 170.
Eleutherius, A.D. 170 to A.D. 185.
Victor, A.D. 185 to A.D. 197.
—"Minor Works," ii. pp. 570; 571.

[539:1] I have endeavoured, from the records of the late Synod of Ulster, to estimate the medium length of the incumbency of a moderator for life, being the senior minister of a presbytery of from ten to fifteen members, and have found that the average of thirty-six successions amounted to between eight and nine years. In these presbyteries young ministers generally constituted a considerable portion of the members. Had they all been persons advanced in life, the average must have been greatly reduced.

[539:2] During that part of the second century which terminated with the death of Hyginus, the average duration of the life of a Roman bishop very little exceeded eight years; whereas, during the remainder of the century, it amounted to nearly twelve years. According to the chronology of Pearson the disproportion is still greater, being as eight years and a fraction to fourteen years. If we insert the episcopate of Anacletus, it will be nearly as seven to fourteen.

[539:3] In the verses erroneously attributed to Tertullian, the Church of Rome is represented as in a flourishing state when visited by Cerdo.

"Advenit Romam Cerdo, nova vulnera gestans
Detectus, quoniam voces et verba veneni
Spargebat furtim; quapropter ab agmine pulsus,
Sacrilegum genus hoc genuit spirante dracone.
Constabat pietate vigens Ecclesia Romae
Composita a Petro, cujus successor et ipse
Jamque loco nono cathedram suscepit Hyginus."

[540:1] Euseb. iv. 11. Irenaeus says that Valentine, the most famous and formidable of the Gnostic teachers, "came to Rome under Hyginus, was in his prime under Pius, and lived until the time of Anicetus."—Contra Haeres., iii. 4. § 3. Cyprian speaks of "the more grievous pestilences of heresy breaking forth when Marcion the Pontian emerged from Pontus, whose master Cerdo came to Rome during the episcopate of Hyginus."—Epist. lxxiv. He adds—"But it is acknowledged that heresies afterwards became more numerous and worse."— Epist. lxxiv. Opera, pp. 293, 294.

[540:2] Euseb. iv. 11. See also a fragment attributed to Irenaeus in Stieren's edition, i. 938.

[540:3] See Mosheim, "Commentaries," by Vidal, ii. 266.

[541:1] Hieronymus, "Comment, in Titum."

[541:2] Ibid.

[541:3] "Tamen postquam in omnibus locis ecclesiae sunt constitutae, et officia ordinata, aliter composita res est, quam coeperat."—Comment. in Epist. ad Ephes. cap. 4.

[541:4] "Ideo non per omnia conveniunt scripta apostoli ordinationi, quae nunc in ecclesia est; quia haec inter ipsa primordia sunt scripta."—Ibid.

[541:5] "Ut non ordo, sed meritum crearet episcopum."—Ibid. Hilary appears to have believed with Jerome that the Church was originally governed "by the common council of the presbyters," but that, meanwhile, with their sanction, or under peculiar circumstances, deacons might preach and even laymen baptize. Such, too, seems to have been the opinion of Tertullian. See Kaye's "Tertullian," pp. 226, 448. Hilary, however, maintained that this arrangement was soon abrogated. "Coepit alio ordine et providentia gubernari ecclesia; quia si omnes eadem possent, irrationabile esset, et vulgaris res, et vilissima videretur."

[543:1] Irenaeus, iii. 3, § 3.

[544:1] See Period II. sec. 1. chap. iv. pp. 334-336.

[544:2] Irenaeus, i. 24, § 1; i. 28, § 1.

[544:3] Thus, Valentine travelled from Alexandria to Rome, and afterwards settled in Cyprus. Marcion, who was originally connected with Pontus, and who taught in Rome, is said to have also travelled in Egypt and the East.

[545:1] "Blondelli Apologia pro Sententia Hieronymi," p. 18. Blondel makes the vacancy of four years' continuance.

[545:2] Pearson's "Minor Works," ii. p. 571.

[546:1] Epiphanius, "Haeres." 42, Opera, tom. i. p. 302.

[546:2] See Burton's "Lectures," ii. 98.

[546:3] "Speraverat episcopatum Valentinus, quia et ingenio poterat et eloquio. Sed alium ex martyrii praerogativa loci potitum indignatus de ecclesia authenticae regulae abrupit."—Adv. Valent. c. iv.

[546:4] Tertullian states that Valentine at first believed the doctrine of the Catholics in the Church of Rome. "Be Praescrip." c. 30. When he came to the city he was admitted to communion. He set up a distinct sect after Pius was made bishop. It is impossible, therefore, to avoid the inference that he was mortified because he was not himself chosen. Tertullian here confounds Eleutherius and Hyginus.

[547:1] The unwillingness even of Tertullian to say anything to its prejudice has been often remarked. See Neander on a passage in the tract "De Virg. Veland." in his "Antignostikos," appended to his "History of the Planting and Training of the Christian Church," in Bohn's edition, ii. 420. See also the same, p. 429. See also "De Pudicitia," c. 1.

[547:2] They are quoted as genuine by Binius, Baronius, Bona, Thorndike, Bingham, Salmasius, and many others. Bishop Beveridge speaks of one of them as of undoubted authority. "In indubitata illius epistola."—Annot. in Can. Ap. See Cotelerius, i. 459. Pearson rejects them as spurious, whilst contending so valiantly for the Ignatian Epistles.

[547:3] Such as Missa and Titulus. But that Pastor really did erect a place in which the Christians assembled for worship, as stated in one of these letters, is not improbable. See Routh's "Reliquiae," i. 430. Pearson objects to them on the ground that Eleutherius is spoken of in one of them as a presbyter, whereas Hegesippus describes him as deacon afterwards in the time of Anicetus. See Euseb. iv. 22. But it is not clear that Hegesippus here uses the word deacon in its strictly technical sense. He may mean by it minister or manager, and may design to indicate that Eleutherius was the most prominent official personage under Anicetus, occupying the position afterwards held by the archdeacon.

[548:1] "Presbyteri et Diaconi, non ut majorem, sed ut ministrum Christi te observent."

[549:1] That, in the time of Marcion, there were Roman presbyters who had been disciples of the apostles, see Tillemont, "Mémoires," tom. ii. sec. par. p. 215. Edit. Brussels, 1695.

[550:1] "Presbyteri illi qui ab apostolis educati usque ad nos pervenerunt, cum quibus simul verbum fidei partiti sumus, a Domino vocati in cubilibus aeternis clausi tenentur."

[550:2] Pearson ("Vindiciae," par. ii. c. 13) has appealed to a letter from the Emperor Hadrian to the Consul Servianus as a proof that the terms bishop and presbyter had distinctive meanings as early as A.D. 134. The passage is as follows:—"Illi qui Serapim colunt, Christiani sunt; et devoti sunt Serapi, qui se Christi episcopos dicunt. Nemo illic Archisynagogus Judaeorum, nemo Samarites, nemo Christianorum Presbyter.... Ipse ille Patriarcha, quum Aegyptum venerit, ab aliis Serapidem adorare, ab aliis cogitur Christum." Such a testimony only shews that Pearson was sadly in want of evidence. This same letter has in fact often been adduced to prove that the terms bishop and presbyter were still used interchangeably, and such is certainly the more legitimate inference. See Lardner's remarks on this letter, Works, vol. vii. p. 99. Edit. London, 1838.

[550:3] "The Philippians appear to have continued to live under the same aristocratic constitution (of venerable elders) about the middle of the second century, when Polycarp addressed his Epistle to them."—Bunsen's Hippolytus, i. 369.

[551:1] [Greek: proestôs], Opera, pp. 97-99.

[551:2] "Episcopi, id est, praesides ecclesiarum."—Lib. iii. simil. ix. c. 27. There is a parallel passage to this in Tertullian, "De Baptismo," c. 17—"Summus sacerdos, qui est episcopus." This is, perhaps, the first instance on record in which a bishop is called the chief priest. Hence the necessity of the interpretation—"qui est episcopus." Pastor considered an explanation of the title "episcopus" equally necessary.

[551:3] Neander supposes this work to have been written A.D. 156. "General History," ii. 443.

[551:4] See Period II. sec. ii. chap. i. p. 368.

[552:1] So high indeed is its authority that many facts taken from it are recorded in the "Breviary." Even Bunsen appeals to it. See "Analecta Antenicaena," iii. 52, 53.

[552:2] Binius makes the following abortive attempt to explain the statement- "Quòd hierarchicus catholicae ecclesiaeae ordo, quo presbyteri episcopis, diaconi presbyteris, populus presbyteris et diaconis subditus est, ab Hygino compositus esse hic dicitur, non aliter intelligi potest, quàm quod Hyginus hierarchiae ecclesiasticae jam tempore apostolorum a Christo Domino constitutae, et a sanctis Patribus ipso antiquioribus comprobatae, quaedam duntaxat injuria temporum et scriptorum deperdita addiderit, vel eadem quae Divino jure instituta, et a patribus comprobata sunt, hac constitutione sua illustraverit." — Concilia, i. 65, 66.

[552:3] "Hic clerum composuit, et distribuit gradus."—Binii Concil. i. 65. Baronius, ad annum, 158.

[553:1] When referring to this statement Baronius says—"Porrò quod ad gradus cujusque ordinis in Ecclesia, quo ecclesiastica habetur composita hierarchia, jam a temporibus apostolorum haec facta esse, Ignatio auctore et aliis, tomo primo Annalium demonstravimus; verum aliqua antiquae formae ab Hyginio fuisse addita, vel eadem illustrata, aequum est aestimare."

[554:1] See Kaye's "Tertullian," p. 414.

[555:1] 1 Tim. v. 17.

[555:2] Euseb. iv. 11; iv. 19. Dr Burton has well observed that Alexandria and Antioch were "the hotbeds from which nearly all the mischief arose, which, under the name of philosophy, inundated the Church in the second century."—Lectures, vol. ii. p. 103.

[556:1] Period II. sec. iii. chap. v. pp. 516, 517.

[556:2] "Quanquam sunt inter scriptores ecclesiasticos qui putaverint Polycarpum Romam venissè, ut quaereret de festo paschatis: ex his Irenaei verbis luco clarius elucet, ob alias causas Ioannis apostoli discipulum Romam profectum esse."—Stieren's Irenaeus, i. p. 826, note.

[557:1] Euseb. v. 24.

[557:2] Stieren's "Irenaeus," i. 827.

[557:3] First, as his senior; and secondly, as a disciple of the apostles.

[557:4] It was a standing rule of the Church that a strange bishop should be thus treated. See "Didascalia," by Platt, p. 97.

[559:1] "Paulatim vero, ut dissensionum plantaria evellerentur, ad unum omnem solicitudinem esse delatam."—Comment. in Tit.

[560:1] Period II. sec. iii. chap. 5, pp. 510, 512, 516, 520.

[560:2] But the presiding elders now began generally to be called bishops.

[560:3] Thus, though, as we may infer from the testimony of Tertullian, Christianity was planted in North Britain in the second century, the universal tradition is that originally there were no bishops in that country. According to an ancient MS. belonging to the former bishops of St Andrews, and to be found in the "Life of William Wishart," one of their number who lived in the thirteenth century, the first bishop created in Scotland was elected in A.D. 270. See Jamieson's "Culdees," pp. 101, 101.

[561:1] Song of Solomon, vi. 9; Ps. xlv. 9. "Sub Apostolis nemo Catholicus vocabatur.....Cum post Apostolos haereses extitissent, diversisque nominibus columbam Dei atque reginam lacerare per partes et scindere niterentur; nonno cognomen suum ecclesia postulabat, quae incorrupti populi distingueret unitatem?"

[562:1] Pacian, "Epist. to Sympronian," secs. 5 and 8. Pacian is said to have been bishop of Barcelona. He died A.D. 392.

[562:2] Epist. lxix. 265, 266.

[563:1] Justin Martyr, Opera, p. 99.

[563:2] According to the "Apostolic Constitutions" the deacons were not at liberty to baptize. Lib. viii. c. 28.

[563:3] "De Baptismo," c. 17.

[563:4] Tertullian thus corroborates the testimony of Jerome.

[563:5] "In the sixth century the clergy of Italy complained to Justinian that, owing to the vacancy of sees, 'an immense multitude of people died without baptism.' Even so late as the time of Hinemar (the ninth century) baptisms were still performed by the bishop, and they alone were considered canonical."—Palmer's Episcopacy Vindicated, p. 35, note.

[564:1] "It appears to have been the custom at Rome and other places to send from the cathedral church the bread consecrated to the several parish churches."—Stillingfleet's Irenicum, pp. 369, 370. "Thomassinus shown that in the fifth century the presbyters of Rome did not consecrate the Eucharist in their respective churches, but it was sent to them from the principal church."—Palmer, p. 35, note.

[564:2] Thus Rome is called the "principal Church" in regard to Carthage. Cyprian, Epist. lv. p. 183.

[564:3] Tertullian apparently refers to this when he says—"Una omnes probant unitate communicatio pacis et appellatio fraternitatis, et contesseratio hospitalitatis."—De Praescrip. c. 20.

[564:4] "Ecclesiis apostolicis matricibus et originalibus fidei."

[565:1] "Cathedrae apostolorum suis locis praesident." These words clearly indicate that the Churches founded by the apostles were now recognized as centres of unity for the surrounding Christian communities.

[565:2] It is worthy of note that, in the second canonical epistle ever written by Paul, he warns this Church of the coming of the Man of Sin. (2 Thess. ii. 3.) It appears from the text that thus early it was identified with the system which resulted in the establishment of the Papacy. It is equally remarkable that the bishop of Thessalonica was the first Papal Vicar ever appointed. See Bower's "History of the Popes," Damasus, thirty-sixth bishop; and Gieseler, i. 264.

[565:3] "De Praescrip." xxi., xxxvi.

[565:4] The tendency of "Church principles" to terminate in the recognition of a universal bishop has appeared in modern as well as in ancient times. "What other step," says a noble author, "remains to stand between those who held those principles and Rome? Only one: that the priesthood so constituted, invested with such powers, is organized under one head—a Pope....The space to be traversed in arriving at it is so narrow, and so unimpeded by any positive barrier, either of logic or of feeling, that the slightest influence of sentiment or imagination, of weakness or of superstition, is sufficient to draw men across."—Letter from the Duke of Argyll to the Bishop of Oxford, p. 23. London, Moxon, 1851.

[566:1] Tertullian says that John, as well as Peter and Paul, had been in Rome. "De Praescrip." xxxvi.

[567:1] "Contra Haeres." iii. c. iii. § 2.

[567:2] "Maximae et antiquissimae et omnibus cognitae, a gloriosissimis duobus apostolis Petro et Paulo Romae fundatae et constitutae ecclesiae."—Irenaeus, iii. c. iii. § 2.

[567:3] We find this designation in some of the early canons. See Bunsen's "Hippolytus," iii. 50.

[567:4] Euseb. v. 24.

[568:1] See the statement of Cyprian in the Council of Carthage, "Opera," p. 597; and Jerome, in his Epistle to Evangelus, "Opera," iv. secund. pars. p. 803.

[568:2] "Pontifex scilicet Maximus, quod est episcopus episcoporum, edicit: Ego et moechiae et fornicationis delicta poenitentia functis dimitto."—Tertullian, De Pudicitia, c. 1. "Neque enim quisquam nostrum episcopum se esse episcoporum constituit."—Cyprian, Con. Car., Opera, 597.

[569:1] "Ecclesiae catholicae radicem et matricem."—Epist. xlv. p. 133.

[569:2] "Navigare audent et ad Petri cathedram atque ad ecclesiam principalem unde unitas sacerdotalis exorta est."—Epist. lv. p. 183. "Nam Petro primum Dominus, super quem aedificavit ecclesiam, et unde unitatis originem instituit et ostendit, potestatem istam dedit."—Epist. lxxiii. p. 280. See also Epist. lxx.-"Una ecclesia a Christo Domino super Petrum origine unitatis et ratione fundata."

[570:1] The word catholic first occurs in the Epistle of the Church of Smyrna giving an account of the martyrdom of Polycarp, but that letter was probably not written until at least twenty years after the event which it records. See Period II. sec. i. chap. iv. p. 337. It is remarkable that the word is not found in Irenaeus, or used by his Latin interpreter. The pastor of Lyons, however, recognizes the distinction indicated by the word catholic, for he speaks of the ecclesiastici or churchmen, and of those "qui sunt undique." Stieren's "Irenaeus," i. 430, 502, note. The word catholic was obviously quite current in the time of Tertullian.

[570:2] Particularly Matt. xvi. 18. Clemens Alexandrinus says that our Lord baptized Peter only, and that Peter then baptized other apostles. See Kaye's "Clement," p. 442; and Bunsen's "Analecta Antenic." i. p. 317. See also Origen, "Opera," ii. 245; and Firmilian's "Epistle."

[571:1] Even Polycrates of Ephesus admits that he had been requested by Victor to convene a synod. Euseb. v. 24. About sixty years afterwards Cyprian writes to Stephen of Rome requesting him to send letters into Gaul that Marcianus the bishop, who had sided with Novatian, "being excommunicated, another may be substituted in his room."—Cyprian, Epist. lxvii. pp. 248, 249.

[572:1] Thus he says—"For neither did Peter, whom the Lord chose first, and on whom He built His Church, when Paul afterwards disputed with him about circumcision, claim or assume anything insolently and arrogantly to himself, so as to say that he held the primacy."—Epist. lxxi. p. 273.

[573:1] Gen. xi. 4.

[573:2] Book I. vision iii. § 3, &c.

[574:1] Rev. xiv. 6-8.

[575:1] 1 Tim. v. 17.

[576:1] See Bunsen's "Hippolytus," ii. 305, and iii. 35, 36.

[576:2] Bunsen's "Hippolytus," iii. 36.

[576:3] "Apost. Constit." ii. 57.

[576:4] [Greek: kai oute ho panu dunatos en logô tôn en tais ekklêsiais proestôtôn, hetera toutôn erei (oudeis gar huper ton didaskalon) oute ho asthenês en tô logo elattôsei tên paradosin].—Contra Haereses, i. c. 10. § 2.

[576:5] "Optatus adv. Donat." vii. 6.

[576:6] 1 Cor. xiv. 5, 24, 26, 31.

[577:1] Euseb. vi. 19. It is to be observed that these laymen, having the sanction of the ecclesiastical authorities, were thus virtually licensed to preach.

[577:2] "Apost. Constit." vii. 46. There was a Church at Cenchrea in the time of the apostles. Rom. xvi. 1. Strabo calls Cenchrea a village, lib. viii.

[577:3] See Bingham, iii. 129.

[577:4] Cyprian, "Council of Carthage." Girba, Mileum, Badias, and Carpi, the sees of these bishops, were all small places with, no doubt, a still smaller Christian population.

[578:1] Cyprian, "Council of Carthage."

[578:2] Euseb. vii. 30.

[578:3] See Sage's "Vindication of the Principles of the Cyprianic Age," p. 348. Edit., London, 1701.

[578:4] See Period II. sec. i. chap. v. pp. 355, 356.

[578:5] See Bingham, i. 41, 43.

[579:1] Bunsen's "Hippolytus," i. 129; and Wordsworth, p. 257. It would appear from Celsus that not a few of the Church teachers in the second century supported themselves by manual labour. See Origen, Opera, i. 484.

[579:2] "Adleguntur in ordinem ecclesiasticum artifices idolorum."—De Idololatria, c. vii. Malchion, one of the presbyters of Antioch in the time of Paul of Samosata, was the head-master of one of the principal schools in the place. Euseb. vii. 29.

[579:3] Cyprian, Epist. lxvi. p. 246. In after times the bishop himself was the grand-executor, having the charge of all the wills of his diocese!

[581:1] Council of Elvira, A.D. 305, 18th canon.

[581:2] Period II. sec. iii. chap. vi. p. 533.

[581:3] "Nam et Alexandria à Marco Evangelista usque ad Heraclam et Dionysium Episcopos, presbyteri semper unum ex se electum, in excelsiori gradu collocatum Episcopum nominabant; quomodo si exercitus Imperatorem faciat; aut Diaconi eligant de se quem industrium noverint, et Archidiaconum vocent."— Epist. ad Evangelum.

[581:1] Heraclas now succeeded him. The immediate successor of Heraclas was Dionysius.

[581:2] "Apud nos quoque et fere per provincias universas tenetur."—Cyprian, Epist. lxviii. p. 256. The arrangement of which Cyprian speaks was now, perhaps, pretty generally established in the West, but he may have understood, through his intercourse with Firmilian, that in some parts of the East a different usage still prevailed.

[581:3] "Nam et Alexandriae."

[582:1] Eutychius, the celebrated patriarch of Alexandria who flourished in the beginning of the tenth century, makes this assertion. According to this writer there were originally twelve presbyters connected with the Alexandrian Church; and, when the patriarchate became vacant, they elected "one of the twelve presbyters, on whose head the remaining eleven laid hands, and blessed him and created him patriarch."—See the original passage in Selden's Works, ii. c. 421, 422; London, 1726. This passage furnishes a remarkable confirmation of the testimony of Jerome as to the fact that the Alexandrian presbyters originally made their bishops, but it is probably not very accurate as to the details. As to the laying on of hands it is not supported by Jerome.

[582:2] The case is different with the modern English archdeacon who is a presbyter.

[583:1] "A fratribus constitutus et colobio episcoporum vestitus."

[583:2] "Saluta omne collegium fratrum, qui tecum sunt in Domino."

[583:3] The practice seems to have continued longer at Alexandria than at Rome and various other places.

[583:4] The statement of Jerome is not inconsistent with the fact that the senior elder was originally the president or bishop, for he was recognized as such by mutual agreement. Neither is it at variance with the idea that the elders sometimes made a selection by lot out of three of their number previously put in nomination. There are good grounds for believing that even after bishops begun to be elected by general suffrage, the people were in some places restricted to certain candidates chosen from among the elders by lot. Cyprian apparently refers to this circumstance when he says that he was chosen by "the judgment of God" as well as by the vote of the people. Epist. xl. p. 119. The people of Alexandria, towards the close of the third and beginning of the fourth century, are said to have been restricted to certain candidates. See p. 333, Period II. sec. i. chap. iv. Cornelius of Rome is said to have been made bishop by "the judgment of God and of his Christ" and by the votes of the people. Cyprian, Epist. lii. pp. 150, 151.

[584:1] Euseb. v. 24.

[585:1] "Contra Haereses," iv. c. 26, secs. 2, 4. "Quapropter eis qui in ecclesia sunt, presbyteris obaudire oportet, his qui successionem habent ab apostolis, sicut ostendimus; qui cum episcopatus successione charisma veritatis certum secundum placitum Patris acceperunt; reliquos vero, qui absistunt a principali successione, et quocunque loco colligunt, suspectos habere vel quasi haereticos et malae sententiae.... Ab omnibus igitur talibus absistere oportet; adhaerere vero his qui et apostolorum, sicut praediximus, doctrinam custodiunt, et cum presbyterii ordine sermonem sanum et conversationem sine offensa praestant."

[585:2] This was long the received doctrine. Thus, the author of the "Questions on the Old and New Testament" says—"Quid est episcopus nisi primus presbyter?"—Aug. Quaest. c. 101.

[585:3] "Onmis potestas et gratia in ecclesia constituta sit, ubi praesident majores natu, qui et baptizandi et manum imponendi et ordinandi possident potestatem."—Firmilian, Epist. Cyprian, Opera, p. 304.

[586:1] See Bunsen's "Hippolytus," ii. 351-357. See also Fabricius, "Biblioth. Graecae," liber v. p. 208. Hamburg, 1723.

[586:2] The earliest of these canons was probably framed only a few years before the middle of the third century. They were called apostolical perhaps because concocted by some of the bishops of the so-called apostolic Churches.

[586:3] The collection to which it belongs bears the designation of the "Canons of Abulides,"—the name of Hippolytus in Abyssinian, as their calendar shews. Bunsen, ii. 352. The canons edited by Hippolytus were, no doubt, at one time acknowledged by the Western Church.

[586:4] Bunsen's "Hippolytus," iii. 43, and "Analecta Antenicaena," iii. 415.

[587:1] Eutychius intimates that the Alexandrian presbyters continued to ordain their own bishop until the time of the Council of Nice. It is not improbable that, until then, some of them may have continued to take part in the ordination, and the statement of the Alexandrian patriarch may be so far correct.

[587:2] See Bunsen, iii. 45.

[587:3] Where the bishop, as in the case contemplated in a canon quoted in the text, had to depend for his official income on the contributions of twelve families, it is plain that the elders could expect no remuneration for their services. As the hierarchy advanced these ruling elders disappeared. Hence Hilary says—"The synagogue, and afterwards the Church, had elders, without whose counsel nothing was done in the Church, which, by what negligence it grew into disuse I know not; unless, perhaps, by the sloth, or rather by the pride of the teachers, while they alone wished to appear something."—Comment on 1 Tim. v. 1. Some late writers have contended that these elders (seniores) were not ecclesiastical officers at all, but civil magistrates of municipal corporations peculiar to Africa. It must, however, be recollected that Hilary was a Roman deacon of the fourth century, and that he speaks of them as belonging to the Church before the civil establishment of Christianity.

[590:1] Thus, Firmilian speaks of "seniores et praepositi," and of the Church "ubi praesident majores natu."—Cyprian, Opera, p. 302 and 304.

[590:2] Justin Martyr, Opera, p. 99.

[590:3] In the days of Origen the episcopal office was not unfrequently coveted for its wealth. Origen, Opera, iii. p. 501. See also Cyprian, Epist. lxiv. p. 240.

[591:1] Comment, in Matt., Opera, iii. p. 723.

[591:2] See Period II. sec. i. chap. v. p. 354.

[592:1] Euseb. vi. 43.

[592:2] Tertullian, "Praescrip. Haeret." c. 41. This office, even in the fourth century, was often committed to mere children—a sad proof that the importance of reading the Word effectively was not duly appreciated.

[592:3] Origen makes mention of them, Opera, ii. p. 453; and Firmilian, Cyprian, Epist. lxxv. p. 306.

[592:4] Cyprian, Epist. lii. p. 150.

[592:5] As in the case of Fabian of Rome. Euseb. vi. 29.

[593:1] Bingham, i. 356, 359.

[593:2] Cyprian, Epist. lv. pp. 177, 178; xl. pp. 119, 120.

[593:3] Epist. xxxiii. p. 105.

[594:1] Epist. xxiv. pp. 79, 80.

[594:2] Epist. xxxiv. pp. 107, 108.

[594:3] Epist. xxxv. p. 111.

[595:1] Bishops and presbyters appear to have continued to ordain bishops in the time of Origen. His "Commentaries on Matthew," written according to his Benedictine editor in A.D. 245 (see Delarue's "Origen," iii. Praef.), speak of bishops and presbyters "committing whole churches to unfit persons and constituting incompetent governors."—Opera, iii. p. 753.

[595:2] It would appear that the five presbyters who opposed Cyprian constituted the majority of the presbytery. Cyprian, Epist. xl. pp. 119, 120. See also Sage's "Vindication of the Principles of the Cyprianic Age," p. 348.

[595:3] Euseb. vi. 29.

[596:1] Cyprian, Epist. xxxi. pp. 99, 100.

[596:2] Cyprian, Epist. iv. p. 31.

[596:3] Cyprian, Epist. xxxiii. p. 106, xxxiv. p. 107, lviii. p. 207, lxxi. p. 271, lxxvii. p. 327. Euseb. vii. 5.

[596:4] Thus we find him going so far as to complain that his presbyters "with contempt and dishonour of the bishop arrogate sole authority to themselves."—Epist. ix. p. 48.

[596:5] Epist. xlix. p. 143. See Neander's "General History," i. 307, and Burton's "Lectures on the Ecc. Hist, of the First Three Centuries," ii. 331. Burton repudiates the attempts of Bingham and others to explain away this proceeding.

[597:1] They are called so for the first time in the Council of Ancyra. They had before always been called simply bishops. It has been remarked that we never find any chorepiscopi among the African bishops, though many of them occupied as humble a position as those so designated elsewhere.

[597:2] Canon xiii., "Canones Apost. et Concil. Berolini," 1839.

[598:1] In the case of Novatian. Euseb. vi. 43.

[599:1] These presbyters were called Doctores. Cyprian, Epist. xxxiv. p. 80.

[599:2] It would appear that, even at the time of the Council of Carthage held

A.D. 397, a bishop had sometimes only one presbyter under his care. See Dupin's account of the Council.

[599:3] Bingham, i. 198; and Beveridge, "Cotelerius," tom. ii. App. p. 17.

[600:1] See Period II. sec. i. chap. ii. p. 302, and p. 355.

[601:1] Euseb. vi. 43.

[601:2] Bunsen's "Hippolytus," iii. 50. Another canon says—"He who is worthy out of the bishops ... putteth his hand upon him whom they have made bishop, praying over him."—Bunsen, iii. 42.

[601:3] See chapter viii. of this section, pp. 565, 567.

[602:1] Bunsen, iii. 111.

[602:2] Euseb. viii. 1.

[603:1] The following observation of a distinguished writer of the Church of England is well worthy of consideration. "The remains of ancient ecclesiastical literature, especially those of the Latin Church, teach us that the corruption of Christianity of which Romanism is the full development, manifested itself, in the first instance, not in the doctrines which relate to the spiriting life of the individual, but in those connected with the constitution and authority of the Christian society."—Litton's Church of Christ, p. 12.

[604:1] "Can. Apost." xiv. "Concil. Nic." xv.

[604:2] Euseb. "Martyrs of Palestine," c. 12.

[604:3] Euseb. viii. i.

[605:1] Acts xxvi. 16-18.

[605:2] Such was the case with the churches mentioned Acts xiv. 23, and Titus i. 5.

[606:1] Trajan regarded with great suspicion all associations, even fire brigades and charitable societies. See Pliny's "Letters," book x., letters 43 and 94.

[607:1] Such as Mosheim, "Instit." i. 149, 150; Neander, "General History," i. 281.

[607:2] During the first forty years of the second century Gnosticism did not excite much notice, and as the Church courts must have been occupied chiefly with matters of mere routine, it is not remarkable that their proceedings have not been recorded.

[607:3] We have no contemporary evidence to prove that ordinations took place in the former half of the second century, and yet we cannot doubt their occurrence.

[608:1] Acts xx. 17.

[608:2] "In Mileto enim convocatis episcopis et presbyteris, qui erant ab Epheso et a reliquis proximis civitatibus."—Contra Haeres, iii. c. 14. § 2.

[608:3] Cyprian, Epist. lxviii. § 256.

[608:4] The new bishop was often chosen before the interment of his predecessor; and even when the senior elder was the president, it is probable that the neighbouring pastors assembled to attend the funeral of the deceased pastor, and to be present at the inauguration of his successor.

[609:1] See Chapter vi. of this Section, p. 524.

[609:2] The old writer called Praedestinatus speaks of several synods held in reference to the Gnostics before the middle of the second century. He may have had access to some documents now lost, but the testimony of a witness who lived in the fifth or sixth century is not of much value.

[610:1] "In toto orbe decretum est ut unus de presbyteris electus superponeretur caeteris."—Com. in Titum.

[610:2] Euseb. v. 16.

[610:3] See Routh's "Reliquiae," ii. 183, 195.

[611:1] Mosheim ("Commentaries" by Vidal, ii. 105) has made a vain attempt to set aside the Latin translation of this passage by Valesius, as he saw that it completely upsets his favourite theory. But any one who carefully examines the Greek of Eusebius may see that the rendering complained of is quite correct. It cannot be necessary to point out to the intelligent reader the transparent sophistry of nearly all that Mosheim has written on this subject.

[611:2] Euseb. v. 23.

[612:1] See Period II. sec. iii. chap. v. p. 509.

[612:2] Tertullian, "De Jejun," c. xiii.

[613:1] "Aguntur praeterea per Graecias illa certis in locis concilia ex universis ecclesiis."

[613:2] "Ipsa repraesentatio totius nominis Christiani magna veneratione celebratur." Mosheim argues from these words that the bishops attended these assemblies, not by right of office, but as representatives of the people! He might, with more plausibility, have contended that they were held only once a year. "Ista sollemnia quibus tunc praesens patrocinatus est sermo."

[614:1] Euseb. v. 24. Hippolytus complains of a bishop of Rome that he was "ignorant of the ecclesiastical rules,"—a plain proof, not only that synods were in existence in the West, but also that a knowledge of canon law was considered an important accomplishment. See Bunsen, ii. 223.

[614:2] Cyprian (Epist. lxxiii.) speaks of a large council held "many years" before his time "under Agrippinus," one of his predecessors. This bishop appears to have been contemporary with Tertullian.

[614:3] In his book "De Pudicitia," c. 10, he speaks of the "Pastor" of Hermas as classed among apocryphal productions "ab omni concilio ecclesiarum"— implying that it had been condemned by African councils, as well as others.

[614:4] The prevalence of the Montanistic spirit in Asia Minor may account for this.

[615:1] See Potter's "Antiquities of Greece," i. 106.

[615:2] See Mosheim's "Commentaries," cent. ii. sect. 22.

[616:1] "Per singulos annos seniores et praepositi in unum conveniamus."

[616:2] Cyprian, Epist. lxxv. pp. 302, 303.

[616:3] In Africa, however, this arrangement was not established even in the fifth century. There, the senior bishop still continued president.

[617:1] This canon somewhat differs from the fifth of the Council of Nice, as the latter requires the first meeting to be held "before Lent." It is somewhat doubtful which canon is of higher antiquity.

[619:1] "Seniores et praepositi."—Epist. Cypriani, Opera, p. 302.

[619:2] "The Councils of the Church," by Rev. E.B. Pusey, D.D., p. 34 Oxford, 1857.

[619:3] Pusey, p. 58.

[619:4] Ibid. p. 66.

[619:5] Ibid. p. 95.

[619:6] As in the case of Athanasius at the Council of Nice.

[619:7] As witnesses and commissioners may still be heard by Church courts.

[619:8] "Graviter commoti sumus ego et collegae mei qui praesentes aderant et compresbyteri nostri qui nobis assidebant"—Cyprian, Epist. lxvi. p. 245.

"Residentibus etiam viginti et sex presbyteris, adstantibus diaconibus et omni plebe."—Concil. Illiberit.

[620:1] Euseb. vii. 30.

[621:1] Prov. xi. 14.

[621:2] Mosheim's "Institutes," by Soames, i. 150.

[624:1] See Mosheim's "Commentaries," cent. ii. sec. 39; American edition by Murdock.

[624:2] Acts xxiv. 5.

[624:3] Euseb. iv. 5.

[625:1] The English name Easter is derived from that of a Teutonic goddess whose festival was celebrated by the ancient Saxons in the month of April, and for which the Paschal feast was substituted.

[626:1] Pentecost, called Whitsunday or White-Sunday, on account of the white garments worn by those who then received baptism, was observed as early as the beginning of the third century. Origen, "Contra Celsum," book viii. Tertullian, "De Idololatria," c. 14. We have then no trace of the observation of Christmas. See Kaye's "Tertullian," p. 413.

[626:2] See Mosheim's "Commentaries," by Murdock, cent. ii. sec. 71. Dr Schaff seems disposed to deny this, but he assigns no reasons. See his "Hist. of the Christ. Church," p. 374.

[626:3] Even as to this point there is not unanimity—some alleging that our Lord partook of the Paschal lamb on the night preceding that on which it was eaten by the Jews.

[627:1] This is distinctly asserted by Irenaeus. "Anicetus and Pius, Hyginus with Telesphorus and Xystus, neither did themselves observe, nor did they permit those after them to observe it. And yet though they themselves did not keep it, they were not the less at peace with those from churches where it was kept, whenever they came to them, although to keep it then was so much the more in opposition to those who did not."—Euseb. v. 24.

[629:1] It would appear that the Armenians, the Copts, and others, still observe this rite. Mosheim's "Comment." cent. ii. sec. 71. As to the continuance of this custom at Rome, see Bingham, v. 36, 37.

[629:2] Socrates, an ecclesiastical historian of the fifth century, has expressed himself with remarkable candour on this subject. "It appears to me," says he, "that neither the ancients nor moderns who have affected to follow the Jews have had any rational foundation for contending so obstinately about it (Easter). For they have altogether lost sight of the fact that when our religion superseded the Jewish economy, the obligation to observe the Mosaic law and the ceremonial types ceased.... The Saviour and His apostles have enjoined us by no law to keep this feast: nor in the New Testament are we threatened with any penalty, punishment, or curse for the neglect of it, as the Mosaic law does the Jews."—Ecc. Hist. v. c. 22.

[629:3] This system seems to have been in existence in the time of Tertullian. See Tertullian, "Ad. Martyr." c. 1., and "De Pudicitia," c. 22.

[630:1] Cyprian speaks of a confessor spending his time "in drunkenness and revelling," (Epist. vi. p. 37,) and of some guilty of "fraud, fornication, and adultery." (De Unit. Ecc. p. 404.)

[630:2] Thus Cyprian says—"Lucianus, not only while Paulus was still in prison, gave letters in his name indiscriminately written with his own hand, but

382

even after his decease continued to do the same in his name, saying that he had been ordered to do so by Paulus."—Epist. xxii. p. 77.

[630:3] Cyprian, Epist. x. p. 52.

[631:1] Apostasy in time of persecution was considered a mortal sin. Adultery was placed in the same category. Cyprian, Epist. lii. p. 155. At one time Cyprian himself held the sentiments of the stricter party. See his "Scripture Testimonies against the Jews," book iii. § 28, p. 563.

[633:1] Cyprian, Epist. lxxiii. p. 279, and lxxiv. p. 295.

[633:2] Cyprian, Epist. lxxiii. p. 277, 278.

[634:1] In Stieren's "Irenaeus," i. 824, there is a different reading of this passage, according to which some continued the fast forty days.

[634:2] Euseb. v. 24.

[636:1] John x. 11, 27, 28.

[636:2] Eph. v. 25-27.

[636:3] Matt, xxviii. 20.

[636:4] 1 Pet. i. 5.

[636:5] Matt. xvi. 18.

[637:1] Eph. iv. 3.

[637:2] Eph. iv. 13.

[637:3] Eph. iv. 13.

[637:4] No writer since the Reformation has discussed the subject of the Church with more learning and ability than the Rev. Dr Hodge of Princeton. Those who wish to be thoroughly acquainted with all the bearings of the question should consult his "Essays and Reviews," New York, 1857. Also the "Princeton Review." See also an article of his taken from the "Princeton Review" in the "British and Foreign Evangelical Review" for Sept. 1854.

[637:5] Matt. xiii. 47-50.

[638:1] 1 Cor. i. 11, 12.

[638:2] Gal. i. 6, iii. 1.

[638:3] Rev. iii. 1.

[639:1] Thus, Melito of Sardis is said to have written a work "On the Church." Euseb. iv. 26.

[639:2] Apostles' Creed. For another form see Bunsen's "Hippolytus," iii. 25, 27.

[640:1] 3 John 9, 10.

[640:2] He appears, for certain reasons now unknown, to have been dissatisfied with some disciples who had been engaged in missionary work; and he had influence sufficient to procure the excommunication of the brethren who entertained them.

[640:3] He would be a bold man who would assert that all the pious members of the Society of Friends are in a hopeless condition.

[641:1] Heb. xii. 23.

[641:2] See Rothe's "Anfange der Christlichen Kirche," p. 575.

[641:3] Cyprian, Epist. lxxvi. p. 316.

[641:4] Epist. lxix. p. 265.

[641:5] Epist. lxii. p. 221.

[642:1] "De Unit. Ecc." p. 397. See also Lactantius, "De Vera Sapientia," lib. iv. p. 282.

[642:2] Eph. iv. 12.

[642:3] Acts xx. 32.

[643:1] Rev. i. 6.

[644:1] If our authorized version of the English Bible is to be regarded as a standard of correct usage, the word priest cannot be properly employed to designate a Christian minister. In the New Testament, as stated in the text, a minister of the word is never called a priest ([Greek: hiereus]), and the latter term, when used in reference to an official personage in our English Bible, always denotes an individual who offers sacrifice. To call a gospel minister a priest is, therefore, at once to adopt an incorrect expression and to insinuate a false doctrine. The English word priest is derived, not as some say, from the Greek [Greek: presbuteros] through the French prêtre, but from the Greek [Greek: proestôs], in Latin praestes, and in Saxon preost. See Webster's "Dictionary of the English Language."

[644:2] Epist. lxix. p. 264.

[644:3] Thus, Tertullian speaks of the "ordo sacerdotalis." "De Exhor. Cast." c. vii.

[645:1] Cyprian, Epist. lxiii. p. 230; lxiv. p. 239.

[645:2] Cyprian, Epist. lxix. p. 264. Cotelerius, i. 442. The Eucharist is called a sacrifice by Justin Martyr (see his Dialogue with Trypho., "Opera," p. 260) apparently in a figurative sense, but when dispensed by a minister called a priest, such language became exceedingly liable to misconception.

[645:3] In proof of this see Cyprian, Epist. lvi. p. 200, and lxiii. p. 231. In the former place Cyprian says—"Mindful of the Eucharist, the hand which has received the Lord's body may embrace the Lord himself."

[645:4] Heb. v. 4; Acts xx. 28, xxvi. 16.

[646:1] Cyprian, Epist. xlvi. p. 136.

[646:2] Epist. lxix. p. 262. See also Epist. lv. p. 177. "If any amount of difference of opinion as to the truth or untruth of the teaching of a geographical priesthood, will justify separation under another Christian ministry, then it at once ceases to be true that there can be but one bishop, or one priest, over any given area in which such differences exist; there then may obviously be as many bishops, or as many priests, as there may be different bodies of men differing from each other's teaching in what they deem sufficiently essential points to justify separation."—Letter from the Duke of Argyll to the Bishop of Oxford, p. 8.

[647:1] Epist. lxix. p. 264.

[647:2] Acts x. 48.

[648:1] Jerome, "Catalogue of Ecclesiastical Writers."

[648:2] Some of those called heretics had many martyrs. Euseb. v. 16.

[648:3] "De Unit. Ecc." Opera, p. 399.

[648:4] "De Unit. Ecc." p. 401.

[648:5] "De Unit. Ecc." p. 401.

[649:1] Jeremiah xxiii. 21, 22.

[649:2] Phil. i. 15, 18. See also Mark ix. 38, 39.

[649:3] Cyprian himself makes this admission. Epist. lxxvi. p. 319.

[649:4] Epist. lii. p. 156.

[649:5] Epist. lxxvi. p. 319.

[650:1] Rom. x. 13,17.

[650:2] Tertullian did not hold the doctrine of her perpetual virginity. See "De

384

Monog." c. 8, and "De Carne Christi," c. 23. Neither did he believe in her immaculate conception. See Kaye's "Tertullian," p. 338.

[652:1] One of the most distinguished and sagacious of modern missionaries has called attention to this fact. See Livingstone's "Missionary Travels in South Africa," p. 107.

[654:1] Maximian, in his famous edict of toleration, lays great stress on this circumstance. "De Mortibus Persecutorum," c. 34.

[654:2] Cornelius to Cyprian, Epist. xlvi. p. 136.

[654:3] "De Unit. Eccles." p. 397.

[654:4] Epist. lii. p. 156.

[654:5] Matt. xvi. 18.

[654:6] Cyprian, Epist. xl. pp. 120, 121.

[656:1] 2 Cor. iii. 17.

[656:2] Isa. xl. 4, 5.

[656:3] Isa. lii. 8.

[656:4] Zech. xiv. 9.